McLuhan in Space
A Cultural Geography

Richard Cavell

The first book to propose that Marshall McLuhan be read as a spatial theorist, *McLuhan in Space* argues that *space* is the single most consistent concept in McLuhan's vast and eclectic body of work. Richard Cavell demonstrates how McLuhan extended insights derived from advances in physics and artistic experimentation into a theory of acoustic space, which he then used to challenge the assumptions of visual space that had been produced through five hundred years of print culture.

The notion of acoustic space provided McLuhan with a heuristic probe of prodigious range, allowing him to examine critically the many social and cultural forms of contemporary media production. It also enabled him to cross over intellectually from the purely theoretical realm into that of artistic production, where his interests in radical notions of spatial production were shared by a range of avant-garde artists from bpNichol to Glenn Gould, from John Cage to R. Murray Schafer, from Iain Baxter to the Fluxus artists – an artistic milieu in which McLuhan increasingly came to situate his work. Cavell's book is the first to examine McLuhan's work in light of this artistic backdrop, and the first to examine his contribution to Canadian studies.

RICHARD CAVELL is Professor of English and Director of the International Canadian Studies Centre, University of British Columbia.

RICHARD CAVELL

McLUHAN IN SPACE

A Cultural Geography

UNIVERSITY OF TORONTO PRESS
Toronto Buffalo London

© University of Toronto Press Incorporated 2002
Toronto Buffalo London
Printed in Canada

Reprinted in paperback with corrections 2003

ISBN 0-8020-3610-4 (cloth)
ISBN 0-8020-8658-6 (paper)

Printed on acid-free paper

National Library of Canada Cataloguing in Publication

Cavell, Richard, 1949–
  McLuhan in space : a cultural geography / Richard Cavell.

  Includes bibliographical references and index.
  ISBN 0-8020-3610-4 (bound). – ISBN 0-8020-8658-6 (pbk.)

  1. McLuhan, Marshall, 1911–1980 – Contributions in space and time.
  2. Space and time.   3. Space and time in art.   I. Title.
  P92.5.M24C39 2002   114′.092   C2001-904010-5

This book has been published with the help of a grant from the Humanities and Social
Sciences Federation of Canada, using funds provided by the Social Sciences and
Humanities Research Council of Canada, and with the financial support of the Office
of the Dean, Faculty of Arts, University of British Columbia.

University of Toronto Press acknowledges the financial assistance to its publishing
program of the Canada Council for the Arts and the Ontario Arts Council.

University of Toronto Press acknowledges the financial support for its publishing
activities of the Government of Canada through the Book Publishing Industry
Development Program (BPIDP).

For Peter

Contents

Sigla

Abbreviations are used to refer to the following works. Publication details for these works appear in 'Details of Sigla,' following the Notes.

Works by Marshall McLuhan

CA	*From Cliché to Archetype*
COB	*Culture Is Our Business*
CC	*The City as Classroom*
Ctb	*Counterblast* (1969)
Cwl	'Culture without Literacy' *Explorations 1*
ExC	*Explorations in Communication*
EM	*Essential McLuhan*
Exp	*Explorations*
GG	*The Gutenberg Galaxy*
GV	*The Global Village*
IL	*The Interior Landscape*
L	*The Letters of Marshall McLuhan*
LI	'The Later Innis'
LM	*Laws of Media*
MB	*The Mechanical Bride*
ML	*The Medium and the Light*
MM	*The Medium Is the Massage*
RPM	*Report on Project in Understanding New Media*
TT	*Take Today: The Executive as Dropout*
TVP	*Through the Vanishing Point*
UM	*Understanding Media*
VVV	*Verbi-Voco-Visual Explorations*
WPGV	*War and Peace in the Global Village*

Other Works

BC	*The Bias of Communication* (Innis)
C&D	*Civilization and Its Discontents* (Freud)
CTS	*The Culture of Time and Space* (Kern)
EmC	*Empire and Communications* (Innis)
EFS	*Empathy, Form and Space* (Mallgrave and Ikonomou)
EU	*Marshall McLuhan: Escape into Understanding* (Gordon)
4D	*The Fourth Dimension and Non-Euclidean Geometry in Modern Art* (Henderson)
FW	*Finnegans Wake* (Joyce)
GGR	*The Glenn Gould Reader* (Gould)
HC	*History and Communications* (Patterson)
MHC	*McLuhan: Hot and Cool* (Stearn)
M&M	*Marshall McLuhan: The Medium and the Messenger* (Marchand)
MMR	*McLuhan, or Modernism in Reverse* (Willmott)
MTC	*Mechanization Takes Command* (Giedion)
OSI	*Our Sense of Identity* (Ross)
Pr	*Prosthesis* (Wills)
PS	*The Production of Space* (Lefebvre)
RVM	*The Medium Is the Rear-View Mirror* (Theall)
TCM	*Technology and the Canadian Mind* (Kroker)
TIF	*Teoria e invenzione futurista* (Marinetti)
TWM	*Time and Western Man* (Lewis)
Unth	*Unthinking Modernity: Innis, McLuhan, and the Frankfurt School* (Stamps)
VM	*The Virtual Marshall McLuhan* (Theall)
WWMM	*Who Was Marshall McLuhan?* (Nevitt and McLuhan)

PREFACE

'Space' in McLuhan

This book argues that *space* constitutes the single most consistent conceptual category in the work of Marshall McLuhan. Put another way, space is the notion that connects a multiplicity of elements in McLuhan's large and diverse *œuvre*. McLuhan made constant reference to space throughout his career, and the various dimensions of his thought are articulated through notions of spatial biases, sensations, and modes of production. It was space, furthermore, which anchored the system of ideas that connected McLuhan to artists and theorists with whose work his own is most productively situated.[1]

This may strike some readers as a broad characterization of a thinker who is most often thought of as skimming along the surfaces of the phenomena to which he addressed himself rather than treating them in depth. One of the goals my study has set for itself, thus, is to demonstrate the consistency within McLuhan's thought, and the way in which, after a crucial turning point in his intellectual career, he developed his notions of spatial production. Other readers may ask where the traditional paradigms of McLuhanesque inquiry – communications, media, and so on – are in this analysis. They are certainly present, but as subsets of the larger, spatial categories to which McLuhan returned again and again. Yet other readers may question the importance of space as a category of analytical inquiry; for this reason, much of the first chapter of this book is devoted to setting up the context of spatial inquiry in which McLuhan saw himself working.

That context includes McLuhan's early reading of Wyndham Lewis's *Time and Western Man*, one of the great texts of spatial philosophy of the early twentieth century. It also includes McLuhan's encounter with changing norms of spatial analysis at Cambridge University, where post-Einsteinian advances in the physical understanding of space were very much in the air when McLuhan arrived there to do his graduate studies. McLuhan also mined the architectural theory of Siegfried Giedion for its insights about the enclosure of space. His understanding of space was further broadened by his encounter in the work of Harold Innis with the notion of spatial and temporal biases within systems of communication, and through the work of McLuhan's collaborator Edmund Carpenter on cultural constructions of space within the 'Eskimo' communities studied by Carpenter, as well as in the work of Helmholtz on spatial sensation and the related work of Thomas Lipps and others on sensory empathy. And McLuhan was profoundly influenced by the notion of acoustic space first broached to him by Carleton Williams.

The tracing of this critical, theoretical, and methodological context and the placing in it of McLuhan's works, from his early essays through *The Mechanical Bride* to *Understanding Media*, occupies the first half of this book, which is primarily concerned with McLuhan's analysis of visual space in terms of print technology, his rejection of that space, and his critical formulation of acoustic spacetime. Because McLuhan situated his work between critical and artistic discursive systems, the second half of this book reads McLuhan within the discursive system of artistic production, especially as it intersects with notions of spatiality. In these chapters, McLuhan constitutes the *ground* rather than the figure. This approach is consistent with McLuhan's own tendency to address himself to artists and to do so as a practising artist in his own right. It accords as well with the insight McLuhan derived from Innis that spatial and temporal biases were artistic indices as much as they were historical ones. This part of the book argues for the importance of understanding acoustic space as a *hybrid* of oral and literate modalities. It further argues for a materialist reading of McLuhan's spatial theories; that is, it argues that McLuhan developed his spatial theories as a mode of social critique and that McLuhan understood the category of space – and particularly *acoustic* space – as material rather than 'abstract.' This position represents a significant departure from the current critical consensus on McLuhan; however, it is a conclusion towards which McLuhan's thoughts about space consistently point. This materialist approach to space is a legacy from Innis, though I also argue that the single most important moment in McLuhan's intellectual career was his *break* from Innis's notions of time and space. I discuss this break in detail in the first chapter, and return to it in the last, which examines the Canadian context of McLuhan's thought and the ways in which his thought manifested itself in his writings on Canada.

Part one of this book, 'Spaced,' follows a historical trajectory, from McLuhan's early forays into spatial theory, through *The Mechanical Bride*, where McLuhan's approach to space and time becomes a major methodological issue, to the seminal 1953 essay 'The Later Innis,' in which he arrives – *contra* Innis – at the position *vis-à-vis* space and time that he would hold to for the remainder of his career. The first section continues with the examination of two of McLuhan's major works, *The Gutenberg Galaxy* and *Understanding Media*, which constitute a spatial trilogy with *Through the Vanishing Point*, discussed in part two. Part two is configurational, rather than linearly historical, examining McLuhan within the context of artistic practice (specifically the book arts, concrete poetry, soundscape, and music) and specific artistic movements, from Futurism to the Bauhaus and from Situationism to Fluxus. The last of these configurations is psychogeographical, and places McLuhan's spatial practices within their Canadian context.

The first chapter of part one, 'A Short History of Space,' provides both an overview of the book and of the topic of spatial production. It argues that McLuhan is foundational within the theory of spatial production and that the concept of space is the prime category of his thought. The second chapter, 'Mechanization and Its Discontents,' focuses on *The Mechanical Bride*, on the linkages between perspectival space and mechanization, and on the importance of the work of Siegfried Giedion and Sigmund Freud for McLuhan; Giedion's *Mechanization Takes Command* and Freud's *Civilization and Its Discontents* remain points of reference in this and the following two chapters. 'The Physics of

Flatland' reads *The Gutenberg Galaxy* as the first instalment of McLuhan's grand history of the production of space, to which *Understanding Media* is the synchronic counter-part – a rhetoric of uttering as outering or prosthetic aesthetics (chapter 4). Interfacing the first and second parts is a short section, 'The Intellectual as *Vates*,' which argues that McLuhan's work entered a profoundly recursive phase with the writing of *Understanding Media* (a reworking of the *Report on Project in Understanding New Media*), after which he sought to be read as an artist/critic. Part two, 'Scaped,' thus reverses figure and ground, reading McLuhan as an artist among critics and as a critic among artists. Chapter 5 places the works of this phase of McLuhan's career – primarily *Through the Vanishing Point* – within the tradition of artistic production that McLuhan understood himself to be working in (pre-eminently the *livre d'artiste*), and reads his work through that of other artists working in this tradition, such as Joyce Wieland and Michael Snow. Chapter 6, 'Visible Speech,' examines how the orality/literacy dynamic affected the work of artists such as Glenn Gould, R. Murray Schafer, and bpNichol; in doing so it seeks to place McLuhan in a critical context which argues that he did not theorize 'orality' so much as an interface of oral and literate elements of social and cultural production. Chapter 7, 'Art without Walls,' focuses on the conceptualist art movement and ways in which it addressed the materiality of artistic communication. Canadian conceptualists such as Iain Baxter saw themselves working within a McLuhanesque milieu that extended internationally to include – often agonistically – the Situationists and the Fluxus movement. The final chapter, 'Borderlines,' examines McLuhan the artist-as-theorist in his relationship with Northrop Frye (that other Canadian critic with whom, like Innis, McLuhan engaged critically throughout his career) and within a specifically Canadian context, reading Frye and McLuhan in dialogue. The postface determines McLuhan's place within contemporary spatial theory.

In a 1988 review of McLuhan's *Letters* published in *Saturday Night* under the title 'False Prophet,'[2] Michael Bliss writes that '[t]he young wonder who Marshall McLuhan was. Maybe some kind of TV commentator in the sixties? The rest of us remember "the medium is the message," and "a global village," and that McLuhan was otherwise unintelligible. He was famous for a while, and then sort of disappeared. You may have read the obituaries in 1980. Does anyone take seriously today this Canadian academic who was once billed as "the most important thinker since Newton, Darwin, Freud, Einstein, and Pavlov"?' (59). In fact, McLuhan has been read with increasing interest in the period since Philip Marchand published his superb biography of McLuhan, *Marshall McLuhan: The Medium and the Messenger* (preceded by the illuminating *Letters* edited by William Toye et al.). My debts to these two sources are evident throughout. I have likewise learned much from the way in which Judith Stamps, in *Unthinking Modernity*, and Glenn Willmott in *McLuhan: Modernism in Reverse*, positioned McLuhan *vis-à-vis* Modernism, and was impressed, in addition, by Willmott's insistence on McLuhan's consistency as a thinker. *Who Was Marshall McLuhan?* proved to be a goldmine of information not retrievable elsewhere. Many of the insights in Donald Theall's groundbreaking study, *The Medium Is the Rear-View Mirror*, are as fresh now as they were in 1971. Paul Levinson's insistence (in a review and in one chapter of *Digital McLuhan*) on the importance of the category of space in McLuhan's thought has been an inspiration for my own work. Terence Gordon's recent study of McLuhan, *Escape into Understanding*, provided further pieces of a biographical puzzle that is still not complete. Other studies that I have found particularly useful include Arthur Kroker's *Technology and the Canadian Mind*; Graeme Patterson's *History and Communications*; the CD-ROM *Understanding McLuhan*, and the related book *Forward through the Rearview Mirror;*[3] Paul Grosswiler's *Method Is the Message*; Gary Genosko's *McLuhan and Baudrillard*; Donald Theall's *The Virtual Marshall McLuhan*; and Christopher Horrocks's *Marshall McLuhan and Virtuality*.

But the interest in McLuhan has proceeded along other channels as well, channels that, when examined closely – and this is the focus in the second half of my study – reveal not so much a revival as a *continuation* of interest. For if McLuhan's critical reputation declined severely during the 1970s (though this decline was largely limited to North America, where he was almost exclusively read as a communications critic; scholars such as Eco, Lefebvre, Baudrillard, Kittler, Deleuze and Guattari, Barthes, and Derrida were enough under his influence either to follow in his footsteps, ask to collaborate with him, or seek to refute him), what I can only call his *artistic* reputation has continued to grow. By artistic I mean both his recuperation by a wide range of artists and by media production in general. However, it is important to note that, for McLuhan, 'artist' had a much wider meaning than it is conventionally given. If McLuhan sought to be read as an artist, he did so by way of expanding the definition of artist (or foregrounding an aspect of artistic production) to embrace the *critical* response to social context. In a sense, then, all persons were artists in their potential to respond to phenomena – including technologized phenomena – critically.

Evidence of McLuhan's staying power within this expanded field of artistic production is provided by comments such as those of S.L. Simpson, who has said about the work shown in her Toronto gallery during the 1980–1990 decade that the 'issues that permeate the gallery are cultural factors I've grown up with, like Andy Warhol and Marshall McLuhan.'[4] The comment is telling, for it also reminds us of McLuhan's international influence on precisely such artists as Warhol, who 'appointed him to the office of honorary muse,' in the words of Lewis Lapham, author of the introduction to the reissue of *Understanding Media.*[5] The magazine *Wired,* which focuses on cyberculture (first issue 1993), has likewise proclaimed McLuhan its 'Patron Saint.'[6] The *Utne Reader* of January–February 1995 contains an article on the 'Marshall McLuhan Revival' (30–1) in an issue devoted to 'visionaries.' In May of 1994 the New York Theatre Workshop, an experimental company, produced *The Medium*, conceived and directed by Anne Bogart, who writes that the play 'uses [McLuhan's] insights to create a theater piece about who we are becoming vis à vis the radical developments in technology that surround us' (brochure given out at performance); more recently (April 2000), Baffin Island Productions premiered a rock opera, *The Illumination of Marshall McLuhan*, in his birthplace, Edmonton. Ellen Lupton curated an exhibition at the Cooper-Hewitt Museum (New York) in 1993 called *Mechanical Brides: Women and Machines from Home to Office,*[7] which acknowledges that '[b]y looking seriously at popular media, Betty Friedan and Marshall McLuhan studied their own society in the way anthropologists examine foreign cultures. They set precedents for the field now called cultural studies' (10). A.S. Byatt makes a telling reference to McLuhan at the beginning of her 1996 novel, *Babel Tower*. A book on contemporary science-fiction writing, *Storming the Reality Studio*,[8] acknowledges McLuhan as a significant predecessor within the field of cyberpunk, as he is of cyberspace (in the volume of that name edited by Michael Benedikt).[9] And, in a gesture that tellingly responds to the question posed at the end of Bliss's review of McLuhan's *Letters*, the *Globe and Mail* of 22 July 1995 treated the McLuhan revival as front-page news (with a two-page follow-up in the Arts section [C1 and C2]).

Significantly, McLuhan's works are given contemporary pertinence, even though they had been published up to half a century before. Yet it would do McLuhan's thought a disservice to call him (as many do) a prophet, for this would actually limit his significance to having somehow predicted the present moment. Thus, while Paul Levinson, in *Digital McLuhan*, can cite McLuhan as the prophet of the Internet, so can Nicholas Shakespeare make Bruce Chatwin a prophet of precisely the same phenomenon, at which point the usefulness of the 'prediction' breaks down.[10] As *Laws of Media* (written with Eric McLuhan) reveals, however, McLuhan's concerns were much more fluid and sought to articulate the dynamics of technological change rather than simply guess what was next. Books such as Derrick de Kerckhove's *The Skin of Culture: Investigating the New Electronic Reality*[11] incorporate this aspect of McLuhan's thought, the paradoxes of which are neatly summarized by Leon Surrette: 'Although we should not be overly impressed at McLuhan's prescience in forecasting a future which he helped to formulate, there is enough similarity between his cultural forecasts and the events to give pause to those who have rejected him as a clown, faker, or opportunist.'[12] For McLuhan, the future was what had *already* happened: 'there is no future. It is already here.'[13]

What follows is both a re-evaluation and a repositioning of McLuhan. My book does not seek to discuss McLuhan primarily in the context in which he has usually been evaluated – communications theory, media studies, Modernism. It seems to me that McLuhan is far too problematically a communications or media theorist for scholars to continue to read his work squarely within such paradigms.[14] Likewise, his work treats Modernism as a particular moment in the history of the West (and he was very much aware of other histories, as his Canadian stance would demand of him), and I therefore consider him to be writing from within a postmodernist (and poststructuralist) sensibility, as well as from within the Canadian 'counter-environment.' I feel that my position here has been more than confirmed by the recent studies of Stamps, Vermillac, and Wilmott, all of whom represent McLuhan as 'unthinking Modernity' (to use Stamps's locution). My re-evaluation of McLuhan treats him as one of the major founders of a particular discourse on spatiality. In this aspect of my research, I found myself gravitating towards spatial theory as articulated within geography, since it is in that discipline that space (and place) are being most actively theorized; I acknowledge this aspect of the book in the subtitle, though in a way that also challenges geography to examine the heuristics of McLuhan's concept of acoustic space.[15] My study thus presents a new critical context for the work of McLuhan, in which that work can be newly evaluated. Jean Baudrillard, whose own work has been massively influenced by McLuhan's, puts it succinctly: 'We are witnessing the end of perspective and panoptic space ... The medium is no longer identifiable as such, and the merging of the medium and the message (McLuhan) is the first great formula of this new age.'[16]

Throughout this book I have sought to draw on McLuhan's full body of work, and especially so from those articles (and books) that are little known, hard to find, or out of print.[17] I have done this largely to correct an imbalance I have observed in McLuhan criticism, which in many cases has tended to rely on two or three works as representative of the whole, perhaps with the assumption that McLuhan repeated himself so often that to read these works is sufficient. McLuhan did repeat himself – for highly strategic reasons, I argue – but that repetition was akin to the replaying of the aria after the thirtieth Goldberg variation, at once the same and utterly different. The intellectual archaeology involved in sourcing McLuhan's texts has been one of the most rewarding aspects of my research, and I want very much to share the results of that research with my reader, in the hope of providing a wider context for our understanding of a thinker whose resonances will continue to flow through the many spaces his interdisciplinary research opened for us.

I have drawn on aspects of chapter 1 of this book in 'McLuhan and Spatial Communication,' *Western Journal of Communication* 63.3 (1999): 348–63, and on aspects of chapter 8 in 'Material *Querelle*: The Case of Frye and McLuhan,' *Essays in Canadian Writing* 68 (2000): 238–61. As well, I have provided an overview of the findings of part one of my study in the contribution I have made to *The McLuhan Symposium*, published by the University of Ottawa Press as the record of a conference held there in May of 2000.

I have incurred many debts in the writing of this book, and one of the great pleasures of bringing a large project such as this to an end is to have the opportunity to thank the many friends and colleagues who have helped and encouraged me along the way. At the University of British Columbia, where I teach in the English Department and chair Canadian Studies, Sherrill Grace (English) and Derek Gregory (Geography) were both encouraging personally and through the examples of their own research; and my years of friendship with Margery Fee were a resource on which I frequently called. My thanks as well to Sherry McKay, Patricia Vertinsky, Becki Ross, John O'Brian, and Dianne Newell, all of the University of British Columbia (UBC), as well as to the exemplary staff of Shared Resources in the UBC Library. Richard Pollay, of the Faculty of Commerce, generously gave me his collection of McLuhaniana; Doreen Oke of the School of Music introduced me to the intricacies of the baroque keyboard. Scott Watson, director and curator of UBC's Morris and Helen Belkin Gallery, generously made available the gallery's archival material on the arts festivals with which McLuhan was associated. Iain Baxter (University Professor, University of Windsor) kindly made available a number of his artworks, from which I was able to select the cover image; I am grateful to Catriona Jeffries, of the Catriona Jeffries Gallery (Vancouver) for putting me in touch with Iain Baxter. The directed reading course I did on McLuhan with Matt Thompson during the last stages of writing this book provided a critical and creative context for testing the notions developed in the following pages.

The writing of this book was also helped by the late Marjorie Ferguson (University of Maryland); McLuhan's first biographer, Philip Marchand (*The Toronto Star*); Edward Said (Columbia University); Eric McLuhan (Toronto); Elizabeth Leedham-Green (the Library of Cambridge University); the late Claude Bissell (Massey College, Toronto); Anthony Parel (University of Calgary); Robin Fisher (National Archives of Canada); the late Dick Higgins (Barrytown, N.Y.); Nicky Drumbolis (Letters Books, Toronto); R. Murray Schafer (Bancroft, Ontario); Lorne Tulk (CBC, Toronto); Stephen Willis (Music Division, National Library of Canada); Garry Neill Kennedy (Nova Scotia College of Art and Design); Gary Genosko (McLuhan Program, Toronto); Shirley Neuman (University of Michigan, Ann Arbor); Robert McKaskell (Windsor University Art Gallery); Graham Whitham (senior examiner in art history, Associated Examination Board, London); W. Terence Gordon (Dalhousie University); the late Wilfred Watson (University of Alberta); Gilian Cucchini (formerly of the Istituto di Anglistica, Università degli studi di Padova); and Stephen Daniels (Nottingham University); specific thanks are given in the notes. My thanks also to the staff of the Video In (Vancouver), to the librarians in the Special Collections division of the University of Alberta Library, and to the Archives and Rare Books division of the University of Cincinnati Library.

I am grateful to the Estate of Herbert Marshall McLuhan, and to Gingko Press, for permission to quote from archival and other material, and to Harvard University Press for permission to reprint the material from Walter Ong's *Ramus*.

Chris Bucci, my editor at the Press, was a delight to work with, as was Margaret Allen, who copyedited the manuscript scrupulously.

The research and writing of this book were supported by an Izaak Walton Killam Research Fellowship, for which I am deeply grateful, as well as by two grants from the Humanities and Social Sciences Federation of Canada. The publication of the book was subvented by the Aid to Scholarly Publications Program, as well as by the Faculty of Arts, University of British Columba; it is a pleasure to thank Dean Alan Tully for his support.

It was from Marshall McLuhan himself that I first heard of acoustic space; this book is a footnote to that conversation.

Finally, I must thank Susan Kent Davidson and R.I.K. Davidson for their friendship over many years: R.I.K. enjoys reminding me that *The Gutenberg Galaxy* was only *one* of the books he edited in 1962; Susan remains the most loyal and constant of friends, her integrity my inspiration ever since the glory days of graduate school, when, indeed, 'there were no walls on the street.'

This book is dedicated to Peter Dickinson in love and admiration.

PART ONE

SPACED

CHAPTER ONE

A Short History of Space

The culture of print has rendered people extremely insensitive to the language and meaning of spatial forms.

Marshall McLuhan, Explorations 1

Picnic in Space

In 1973, Marshall McLuhan made a film for the *Great Minds of Our Times* series called *Picnic in Space*.[1] The film begins with static and McLuhan's voice-over speaking about several kinds of space – visual, acoustic, Greek, Roman, enclosed, open, and so on. Then we see the title, against a blue background, cutting to McLuhan walking on a parking lot set against a backdrop of buildings in the Gothic academic style. McLuhan enters into an automobile and is filmed as reflected in its rear-view mirror. He speaks of how the Greeks never thought of the world as 'coming in'[2] and expatiates on the meaning of the phrase 'Keep me in the apple of thine eye' (which meant, he says, 'keep me in existence'). Throughout this sequence there are cuts to the film's leitmotif, a close-up shot of Mondrian's *Broadway Boogie-Woogie* (complete with boogie-woogie piano music on the sound track).[3] McLuhan takes this as a representation of acoustic (boogie-woogie) space (Broadway) in its allusion to a discontinuous musical form that is analogous to the discontinuities of the post-Euclidean space embodied in Mondrian's painting. The painting's musical interface is a further reminder that three-dimensional space is only one kind of space and that acoustic, or non-linear, space exists in the realm of sight as well as of hearing and tactility generally. These insights are conveyed variously, through references to Muybridge's photos of horses as proto-cinematography, to Warhol's Brillo pad paintings and Marilyn Monroe silkscreens, to cartoons and the related work of Roy Lichtenstein, and to the spatio-cultural significance of Japanese flower arranging. Most of the dialogue in the film takes place in a country field under a couple of apple trees where McLuhan and his longtime collaborator Harley Parker (co-producer of *Through the Vanishing Point: Space in Poetry and Painting* [1968] and *Counterblast* [1969]), sit down to a picnic. (Parker is reminded of the Qu'Appelle Valley and of Fort William, where he was brought up; McLuhan of the Assiniboine and the Red

River Valley.) They are accompanied by a woman who, in a separate sequence, is figured as an aviatrix (there is a reference to Amelia Earhart) piloting a yellow biplane; there are also visual references to the Wright Brothers, to Lindbergh, to a rocket launch,[4] and to the rock group Jefferson Airplane[5] (another allusion to acoustic space). At one point, McLuhan turns on a flashlight in the middle of this field and remarks that light does not have a point of view; it radiates in all directions at once, giving it a spherical, auditory character. McLuhan then repeats (at the 17-minute, 19-second mark in the documentary) the film's opening spiel: 'We ought to have a few words about why space has never been studied. Why not mention the Greek discovery of visual space, the Roman discovery of enclosed space and then also their discovery of the straight road. Bosch, Munch, Cubism, Joyce, hardware, software.' McLuhan notes the dependence of scientific truth on the notion of repetition as produced through the post-Gutenberg experience of visual space; as he does so, that sequence of film is replayed. McLuhan goes on to state that scientific inquiry, as it becomes more sophisticated, has begun to notice that all experiments contain subtle differences and for this reason science is starting to abandon representation through visual space. In the same way, 'upside down' is culturally defined (at which point the film's images turn upside down) and not natural. There are, in fact, throughout the film, ironic and self-conscious references to the film's chaos, its lack of a script, and the fact that it never seems to arrive at its beginning ('By the way, Bruce, have you run out of film yet?').[6]

Picnic in Space powerfully encapsulates the central nodes of McLuhan's cultural theories, and it does so with consistent reference to space: visual, acoustic, audile/tactile, figure/ground, environment/counter-environment, global/village, and so on. His re-emergence as an important cultural theorist has likewise taken place as part of the spatial turn of contemporary theorizing and artistic production. Yet to discuss McLuhan as a 'theorist of space' constitutes an unaccustomed vantage on a figure who is almost exclusively known as a theorist of media and communications.[7] Given McLuhan's early interest in the way the alphabet spatialized orality, however, and the profound influence on him of the concept of acoustic space and of Harold Adams Innis's notion of spatial and temporal biases, the development of these interests into a broader concern with spatialization is coherent with the overall trajectory of his intellectual career, as it is with the broader cultural currents of his time (as formulated, for example, by Stephen Kern in *The Culture of Time and Space*). This study does not seek to lessen McLuhan's importance in the field of communications and media; rather, its goal is to add another dimension to McLuhan's concern with communications and media by placing it within his broader interest in the production of space. What this study *does* argue is that space is the single most consistent conceptual category within McLuhan's highly eclectic body of work, and it discusses McLuhan's work in the context of spatial histories and contemporary practice within 'spatial science' and in the context of the 'spatial arts.'

McLuhan's writings on communications bear little resemblance to classic theories, either in terms of what gets communicated or of who (or what) does the communicating. In 1952, in 'Technology and Political Change,' McLuhan stated that

It is perhaps useful to consider that any form of communication written, spoken, or gestured has its own aesthetic mode, and that this mode is part of what is said. Any kind of communication has a great effect on what you decide to say if only because it selects the audience to whom you can say it. The unassisted human voice which can reach at most a few dozen yards, imposes various conditions on a speaker. However, with the invention of the alphabet the voice was translated to a visual medium with the consequent loss of most of its qualities and effects. But its range in time and space was thus given enormous extension. At the same time that the distance from the sender of the recipient of a message was extended, the number of those able to decipher the message was decreased. Writing, in other words, was a political revolution. It changed the nature of social communication and control.[8]

In the same vein, McLuhan stated in a dialogue with G.E. Stearn that

Communication, in the conventional sense, is difficult under any conditions. People prefer *rapport* through smoking or drinking together. There is more communication there than there ever is by verbal means. We can share environments, we can share weather, we can share all sorts of cultural factors together but communication takes place only inadequately and is very seldom understood ... There is a kind of illusion in the world we live in that communication is something that happens all the time, that it's normal ... Actually, communication is an exceedingly difficult activity. In the sense of a mere point-to-point correspondence between what is said, done, and thought and felt between people – this is the rarest thing in the world. If there is the slightest tangential area of touch, agreement, and so on among people, *that* is communication in a big way. The idea of complete identity is unthinkable. Most people have the idea of communication as something matching between what is said and what is understood. In actual fact, communication is *making*. The person who sees or heeds or hears is engaged in making a response to a situation which is mostly of his own fictional invention.[9]

What McLuhan is suggesting here is that dialogue is the fundamental mode of communication, in that it acknowledges communication as a process (making) rather than as a matching up of ideas and words.[10] He also suggests that 'communication' is a much broader concept than the term is normally used to convey. If communication is multirelational, then a linear sender–receiver model is inadequate to describe it: 'when I sit down to write about complicated problems,' states McLuhan in the same interview, 'moving on several planes, I deliberately move into multi-level prose. This is an art form' (294). As Derrick de Kerckhove has noted, '[c]ontrary to the Shannon-Weaver model of communication devised in the late forties for application to information theory and machines, McLuhan's interpretation was that in communication there is no transportation of information (concepts or 'content') from a source to a target, but a transformation of the source and target simultaneously.'[11] McLuhan particularly objected to the exclusion of 'noise' by the Shannon-Weaver model; as he wrote in 1976, '[w]hat they call "NOISE," I call the *medium* – that is, all the side-effects, all the unintended patterns and changes. Their model is from the telegraph which they see merely as a kind of pipeline for transportation. Recently, while debating the Alaska oil pipeline here in Canada, it was brought out vividly that it would destroy the indigenous peoples, in all directions. The Shannon/Weaver model of communication is merely a transportation model which has no place for the side-effects of the service environments.'[12] Thus, if '[a]ll communications models account for the transmission of a signal or message between a sender and a receiver in some mutually decipherable code,'[13] then McLuhan's communications work is decidedly anomalous. Yet, as David Crowley and David Mitchell have written, 'it will make little sense going forward to insist upon ... dualisms associated with our communicational modalities: sender-receiver, encoding-decoding, production-consumption. We are all senders and receivers, encoders and decoders, producers and consumers now.'[14] This position reflects McLuhan's concerns with the possibilities and conditions of communication – communication as figure and ground, rather than as figure alone, a concern given its most telling embodiment in his (now classic) observation that 'the medium is the message.'[15]

McLuhan's notion of communication combines a spatial model with a sensory one, McLuhan insisting that media were extensions of our senses. Thus, while communication remained a constant concern, the larger conceptual categories to which he returned again and again were those of spatial production. As he writes in *The Gutenberg Galaxy*, the 'invention of the alphabet, like the invention of the wheel, was the translation or reduction of a complex, organic interplay of spaces into a single space ... Today, such translation can be effected back and forth through a variety of spatial forms which we call the "media of communication." But each of these spaces has unique properties and impinges upon our other senses or spaces in unique ways' (45). A quarter of a century later (and with a consistency that belies the division of his career into 'early' and 'late' phases) McLuhan (with Eric McLuhan) was writing of the transition from 'visual space' to 'post-Euclidean Acoustic Space' (*Laws of Media*).[16] If McLuhan's basic question was (in the words of his longtime collaborator Barrington Nevitt) '"What effects does any medium, as such, have upon our sensory lives?"' (*WWMM* 143), his basic answer had to do with changes in the perception of space, in that space was the medium of communication: uttering as outering.

Even from this brief summary of McLuhan's notion of communication, it should be clear that the general significance of his departure from the Shannon-Weaver model has to do with McLuhan's interest in context (as opposed to content), with making as opposed to matching; that is, his work sought to enlarge communications models to embrace the contexts of communication and, in doing so, to address larger sociopolitical and cultural questions than content-focused communications theories would allow him to do. This shift from content to context, from message to medium, also represented – in terms of the historical development of communications theory – a shift from time to space, though in McLuhan's formulations these terms were interwoven dynamically and were present relationally.

McLuhan productively situated his work within the increasing spatialization of contemporary social and critical (in which I include literary) theory in the half-century since the end of the Second World War, a spatialization out of whose Modernist context McLuhan's own work emerged and to which it subsequently made a significant postmodernist contribution. As Henri Lefebvre writes in *The Production of Space*,

The fact is that around 1910 a certain space was shattered. It was the space of common sense, of knowledge (*savoir*), of social practice, of political power, a space thitherto enshrined in everyday discourse, just as in abstract thought, as the environment of and

channel for communications; the space, too, of classical perspective and geometry, developed from the Renaissance onwards on the basis of the Greek tradition (Euclid, logic) and
bodied forth in Western art and philosophy, as in the form of the city and town. Such were
the shocks and onslaughts suffered by this space that today it retains but a feeble pedagogical reality, and then only with great difficulty, within a conservative educational system.
Euclidean and perspectivist space have disappeared as systems of reference, along with
other former 'commonplaces' such as the town, history, paternity, the tonal system in music,
traditional morality, and so on.[17]

The immediate context of this spatialization, for McLuhan, was Modernist literature,
which had, for him, many parallels to what he saw as that *other* transitional moment in
the history of media – and thus of space – the European Renaissance. As he writes in
'Joyce, Mallarmé, and the Press' (1953), '[i]f the Jacobeans were receding from a
pictographic culture toward the printed page, may we not meet them at the point where
we are receding from the printed word under the impetus of pictorial technology?' (*IL* 6).
It must be emphasized here that McLuhan saw Modernism as representing the transition
from a print oriented and visual culture to an electronically oriented and 'acoustic'
culture, just as the Renaissance was the interface between a dying orality and the birth of
a culture in which the eye would come to dominate. Yet, as Judith Stamps, Glenn
Wilmott, and M. Michel Vermillac have separately argued, McLuhan's project was one
of '*unthinking* modernity' (to use Stamps's locution), and especially its progressivist
assumptions (as the preceding quotation makes clear); indeed, his project is more
productively assessed within the context of postmodernism, the historical moment that is
paradigmatically 'about' spatiality (as opposed to a rigidly linear temporality), as a host
of theorists (Innis, Jameson, Giddens, Harvey, Lefebvre, Baudrillard, Soja, Foucault,
Gregory, and others) have argued.

Spatial Form

The terms in which the spatializing tendencies of literary Modernism have tended to be
understood were set out by Joseph Frank in what has become the *locus classicus* of
spatial theory in literature, his 1945 essay 'Spatial Form in Modern Literature.'[18] Frank
argues that in literary Modernism there is a tendency to affirm simultaneity over
sequentiality; as Frank puts it, Modernist writers 'ideally intend the reader to apprehend
their work spatially, in a moment of time, rather than as a sequence.'[19] Frank sets his
essentially formalist argument in the context of G.E. Lessing's 1766 *Laocoön*, which
argues for a generic distinction between the spatial arts of painting (and the plastic arts in
general) and the temporal arts of poetry (and literature generally). Frank argues that
Lessing's distinction between space and time is important less as a generic marker than
as 'a new approach to aesthetic form' (45); Frank seeks thus to liberate space and time
from their generic specificities and to redeploy these terms as indices of perception. For
Lessing, 'aesthetic form is not an external arrangement provided by a set of traditional
rules. Rather, it is the relation between the sensuous nature of the art medium and the
conditions of human perception' (46). Among Frank's Modernist exemplars of spatial
form in literature are two – Mallarmé and Joyce – who had a special significance for

McLuhan. It is to Mallarmé that Frank traces the 'space-logic' (49) that had come to dominate Modern poetry: '[t]he meaning-relationship is completed only by the simultaneous perception in space of word-groups that have no comprehensible relation to each other when read consecutively in time' (49). It was Mallarmé who 'dislocated the temporality of language far more radically than either Eliot or Pound has ever done' (49). The prose equivalent of this dislocation is to be found in Joyce's *Ulysses*, which is 'composed ... of a vast number of references and cross references that relate to each other independently of the time sequence of the narrative' (51), Joyce's object being to present 'a picture of Dublin seen as a whole' (51).

Frank places his comments about spatialization in the service of an argument that Modernist literature is increasingly self-reflexive, that only a formal poetics can respond to this self-reflexivity, and that myth is the inevitable product of the collapse of (historical) time into space. McLuhan did not follow Frank in this direction, however – his literary criticism is neither formalist nor 'myth criticism,' though he consistently gave attention to aspects of form and of myth in his writing. Rather, what distinguishes McLuhan's notion of spatialization from Frank's is McLuhan's insistence on the interrelationship of space with time and his rejection of abstract categories of analysis; in addition, McLuhan's critical works themselves exhibit the artistic qualities about which Frank is writing here, thus making problematical the critical distancing effect that is the concomitant of spatialization in Frank's formulation. These differences in McLuhan's approach to literary spatialization are evident in his 1953 article 'Joyce, Mallarmé, and the Press.' McLuhan's central concern with spatial qualities in the works of these two writers gives place to a discussion of the popular press. McLuhan connects the two through a historical juxtaposition of Renaissance and Modernist sensibilities, which are allied because both represent transitional moments from orality to print and vice versa (and thus from acoustic to visual space and back again), the popular press being an 'orally empathic'[20] medium through its non-linear, anti-hierarchical, and 'mixed' (as opposed to 'equitone') qualities (the opposite qualities to those supported by print), all of which largely derive from the tendency of the popular press to record the spoken word. McLuhan relates this oral/literate dynamic to Plato's 'alarm in the *Phaedrus*' (*IL* 6) at the destruction of orality by literacy, a destruction that threatened a profound forgetting – what Joyce calls in *Finnegans Wake* an 'abcedmindedness' (1.1.18 in the Viking edition) – precisely through the massive ability of print to store information, thereby sundering memory from mind. As McLuhan remarks, '[e]xact verbal recall is scarcely a problem for pre-literate cultures' (*IL* 7). In the same essay, McLuhan is concerned with the way in which print fostered nationalism (8) and contributed to 'psychic withdrawal' (7); with the moral versus the cognitive view of art; and with the possibility that the popular press constitutes a 'radically democratic aesthetic' (14).

What this comparison between Frank's and McLuhan's methodologies reveals is McLuhan's far greater sensitivity to context: social, political, and historical.[21] It was Frank's formalism, in fact, that garnered the greatest amount of resistance from critics; much of this criticism was based on the assumption that the focus on space meant a concomitant denial or refusal of the temporal, of history. In 1977, thirty-two years after the publication of his 'spatial form' essay, Frank addressed himself to his critics.[22] As he notes, 'most of the discussion has turned on the larger cultural implications of the artistic tendency represented by my examples' ('Answer' 234). That discussion framed itself in terms of '"the turn from history toward myth"' (238), with Frank being seen as encouraging 'forms that negate history and time' (239), the implication being that, in so doing, such works deny the dimension in which political change takes place. Frank's reply to such critiques are noteworthy: 'One would have to be a fool ... or a fanatic,' Frank writes, 'to claim that, after the experiences of the first three-quarters of the twentieth century, there are no good grounds for refusing to worship before the Moloch of "history" in the old starry-eyed nineteenth-century fashion, with its built-in theological postulates. Lévi-Strauss has neatly exposed the intellectual naiveté of such a blind faith in history in his polemic with Sartre (*La Pensée Sauvage*); and we now see such faith as part of the same Western ethnocentrism that Worringer discarded long ago as a criterion for the plastic arts' (239). As Frank acknowledges, the most powerful critic of 'spatial form' was Frank Kermode;[23] what disturbs Frank most about Kermode's criticism is its implication that '"spatial form" invariably [is] equated ... with the myth of fascist totalitarianism' (248). Frank notes that 'such facile *identifications* between Fascism and *avant-garde* art' (248, n14) are not supported historically, and Kermode, in his reply to Frank, agreed.[24] The real bone of contention, according to Frank, is Kermode's antipathy to the work of Wyndham Lewis, who, Frank recalls, 'was the most vigorous and loquacious English champion of "space" and "spatiality" against the time-flux of Bergsonism' (248).

Time (and Space) and Western Man

Wyndham Lewis's spatial theories had a significant influence on McLuhan. Having read Lewis's *Time and Western Man* (1927) while he was at Cambridge (*M&M* 70), McLuhan subsequently came to know Lewis in Windsor, Ontario, where Lewis was spending the war years and McLuhan was teaching at Assumption College. Writing about Lewis in 1954, McLuhan focuses on Lewis's quest to 'arrest the flux of existence in order that the mind may be united with that which is permanent in existence.'[25] In terms reminiscent of the debate between Frank and his critics, McLuhan states that 'there is no need to immerse ourselves again in the destructive element of the Time flux; ... We have ... the means to awaken permanently from the repetitive nightmare of history' (84). It was in the service of such an argument that Lewis had attacked Oswald Spengler, author of *The Decline of the West*, who retailed the time flux in terms of 'progress'; to this sense of continuity, Lewis opposed the discontinuities of patterns juxtaposed in space (as he did in his Vorticist artworks). This 'world of Space as opposed to the world of memory and history' (85), as McLuhan put it, was evident pre-eminently to the artist, who was able to perceive patterns. 'By comparison with the intensity that is revealed in the contemplation of this spatial reality,' continues McLuhan, 'the vision of the Time mind ... is that of the sentimental tourist' (85–6). With Lewis, it is 'the contemplation of ... spatial reality' that matters (86).[26] The symbol for Lewis of the artist's ability to perceive the still moment of art within the flux of existence was the vortex, a symbol that for McLuhan was resonant as well of Poe's 'maelstrom.' Lewis had written, in the 'Author's Preface' to *Time and Western Man*, that when

everything is in question, and where all traditional values are repudiated, the everyday problems have become, necessarily, identical with the abstractions from which all concrete things in the first place come. And the everyday life is too much affected by the speculative activities that are renewing and transvaluing our world, for it to be able to survive in ignorance of those speculations. So everyone ... has this alternative. Either he must be prepared to sink to the level of chronic tutelage and slavery, dependent for all he is to live by upon a world of ideas, and its manipulators, about which he knows nothing: or he must get hold as best he can of the abstract *principles* involved in the very 'intellectual' machinery set up to control him.[27]

This position is remarkably close to the one McLuhan espouses in *The Mechanical Bride*: it is the ability to discern the pattern within the whirling vortex that distinguishes the artist. The image of the vortex neatly embodies the space/time opposition with which Lewis concerns himself in *Time and Western Man*. To give oneself up to the flux of time is to accede to passivity; to distance oneself from it through stasis is to gain a critical vantage. (This point represented one of Lewis's major disagreements with Henri Bergson, against whom he polemicizes most fiercely; for Bergson, 'the intellect "spatialized" things' [160], thus removing them from the reality of flux.) This distancing effect characterizes the stance of the artist, for whom art is 'the purest human consciousness' (*TWM* 23), where 'consciousness' must be taken to mean awareness. Media such as advertising dim this awareness, hypnotizing the masses 'into a sort of hysterical imbecility by [their] mesmeric methods' (*TWM* 25). Lewis is negotiating paradoxical territory here, in that the instruments of enslavement are also those of liberation (cf *TWM* 217); he never quite confronts the paradox, except by taking the moral high-road. McLuhan's approach was to *employ* the very techniques he was critiquing (especially in the works published after *The Mechanical Bride*). This represented a shift from Lewis's static, binaristic model of spatial arrest and temporal flux to a more dynamic model of space–time that McLuhan derived from contemporary physics and that allowed him to theorize a critical position that emerged from *within* the phenomena he was examining.[28]

Lewis's critique of time extended to a critique of progressivism: 'what today,' he asks, 'in Europe or America is there to give our representatives this insolent confidence in the superiority of our time?' (214) This critique leaves itself open to charges of ahistoricism (and fascism) similar to those levelled against Frank (and the charge of ahistoricism was also made about McLuhan). Lewis, however, argued that the historicist position was itself fascistic: 'the Fascist Revolution ... is an imitation of antiquity' (34). In addition, he argued, it was fatalistic: 'It is not our place – what next! – *to make History*: it is History that makes us' is his summary of the time position; 'A truly chronological or time-minded person knows better than to alter or criticize anything' (216). He continues, sarcastically: '[t]he historical writer ... is distracting people from a living Present (which becomes dead as the mind withdraws) into a Past into which they have gone to live. It is a hypnotism that is exercised by the time-vista, or by those time-forms or exemplars that are relied upon for the mesmeric effect. The intelligence to which this method is natural is the opposite of the creative, clearly' (249). To this time-world Lewis opposes 'the direct, spatial *sensation*' (218). This insistence upon the sensory is important, as Sheila Watson has noted; Lewis 'was not speaking about visual sensation, or the "isolated eye." ... It is against "the subjective disunity caused by the separation or separate treatment of the senses principally of sight or touch" that the argument of this work

[*TWM*] is directed.'[29] What particularly concerned Lewis, suggests Watson, was the '"disintegration finally of any public thing at all"' (9), a concern which implies that the *sensus communis* (the senses acting together) should also be understood as promoting a sense of community (as the multisensory phenomenon of orality had), all of which were themes that McLuhan would take up. Another link between McLuhan and Lewis is the insistent focus on the present as worthy of critical examination. 'The world of Space,' Lewis writes, 'is the world of a "pure Present." For the past of that space-world is dead and gone; all its elements are regrouped ... For the world of Space ... yesterday no longer exists' (218). The critical consciousness informed by a spatializing sensibility, then, is placed in the paradoxical position of having to create a history of the present. 'We have indeed *lost our Present*' writes Lewis; 'in a bergsonian attempt to crush all the Past into it, and too much of the Future at a time, as well' (224).

While Lewis's direct target in *Time and Western Man* is Bergson and his 'Time-doctrine,' which Lewis judged to be 'anti-physical and pro-mental' (412), he also directed a good deal of criticism against James Joyce. Lewis critiques *Ulysses* as 'a *time-book*' (81). The effect of this time quality is to produce the image of a 'very mechanical' and 'very dead' universe (91). Joyce's response to this critique was parody, writing, in part 2 of *Finnegans Wake*, of 'that most improving of roundshows, *Spice and Westend Woman* (utterly exhausted before publication, indiapepper edition shortly)' (*FW* 2.2.292). Lewis's criticisms of Joyce appear initially to have influenced McLuhan; Marchand records Hugh Kenner's comment that '"McLuhan despised [Joyce] as merely 'mechanical,' a "contriver"'" (*M&M* 94), precisely the terms Lewis used against Joyce. Yet Joyce was one of the authors McLuhan had read in his very formative Cambridge years, and he began to read *Finnegans Wake* obsessively in the 1950s (*M&M* 94). McLuhan was thus presented with the problem of reconciling Joyce within the overall theory of space that he (McLuhan) was developing, since, clearly, Joyce had by this point become too important to McLuhan to be simply rejected. Donald Theall remarks that 'Lewis and Joyce, who had deep suspicions of one another, do not reconcile themselves at any level to provide a co-ordinated aesthetic' (*RVM* 176). Indeed, Theall continues, 'Lewis' aesthetic is more satisfying than McLuhan's for the simple reason that McLuhan does not take the very specific stance with respect to the so-called time philosophy' (176). Yet McLuhan did take such a stance in his formulation of the concept of acoustic space, a space that was empathically aural (and thus non-linear), and a space that was conflated with time – the space you hear, rather than the space you see. McLuhan thus adopted with Joyce the strategy that, at about the same time, he adopted with the work of Innis and his 'plea for time': McLuhan spatialized the time concept through the metaphor of the auditory (a metaphor that had resonances with T.S. Eliot's 'auditory imagination' as well as with the work of the audiologist Georg von Békésy). The spatialized word, returned to the auditory realm by the (Joycean) pun (which signifies through a simultaneity of effects, rather than sequentially and linearly), thus becomes the orally empathic sign of dialogue.

But McLuhan was left with a further problem to solve, since the pun was still within the visual mode of linear typography. McLuhan found the solution to this problem in the very place where Joyce had parodied Lewis; what we find there is a text made up of diagrams (2.2.293), footnotes, marginal glosses, and drawings (2.2.308). This interaction of the verbal, the vocal, and the visual – 'verbivocovisual,' in the words of *Finnegans Wake* (2.2.341, line 18) – represented for McLuhan the chief mode of resistance to the linearity of print and all the negativities with which he would come to associate it in *The Gutenberg Galaxy*.

Space and Time and Architecture

One of Joyce's friends in Zurich was Siegfried Giedion, whose *Space, Time and Architecture*[30] was, McLuhan claimed, 'one of the great events of my lifetime' (interview with Stearn, *MHC* 269): 'Giedion began to study the environment as a structural, artistic work – he saw language in streets, buildings, the very texture of form' (270). Lefebvre, in *The Production of Space*, has credited Giedion with 'the first initiative taken towards the development of a history of space' (126). McLuhan was influenced by Giedion's insistence on organic interconnections among cultural phenomena, upon the need for an interdisciplinary approach to such phenomena, and by the sense that history (as McLuhan puts it in *The Gutenberg Galaxy*) comprises 'configurations rather than sequences' (216) of events – that history is dynamic rather than static. Giedion's non-hierarchical interest in cultural production led him to the notion of anonymous (unnamed) artistic expression, a notion that McLuhan related to the return to tribalism (for Giedion, the 'primitive' [818]). As McLuhan wrote in 'Culture without Literacy' with reference to this notion of anonymous creation, it is necessary, from such a point of view, 'to regard not only words and metaphors as mass media but buildings and cities as well' (*Exp* 1: 125).

Giedion insists in his book (and especially in Part VI, 'Space-Time in Art, Architecture, and Construction') on the importance of artists to an organically functioning society: 'The artist ... functions a great deal like an inventor or a scientific discoverer: all three seek new relations between man and his world' (432). The artist was particularly important in conceptualizing, at the beginning of the twentieth century, the new space orientation of Cubism, in which spaces are 'juxtaposed and interrelated' (497). This space figured the end of Euclidean geometry: '[l]ike the scientist, the artist has come to recognize that classic conceptions of space and volumes are limited and one-sided ... The essence of space as it is conceived today is its many-sidedness, the infinite potentiality for relations within it. Exhaustive description of an area from one point of reference is, accordingly, impossible; its character changes with the point from which it is viewed. In order to grasp the true nature of space the observer must project himself through it' (435–6). McLuhan developed this notion in terms of an acoustic space that was not constructed according to the 'laws' of perspective but went 'through the vanishing point,' as he put it in the title of his 1968 book. Giedion goes on to note that it was Apollinaire who was the first to signal the end of Renaissance space through a 'calligrammatology' that undermines the sequentiality and fragmentation of alphabetical space. This verbal/visual crossing over is another key point for Giedion, and one to which McLuhan returned often – the notion that time, as the 'fourth dimension,' added the element of simultaneity to the formerly static planes of Renaissance vision. For Giedion, this shift was marked paradigmatically by the dynamic sculpture of such Futurists as Boccioni (445), whom McLuhan invokes in this connection in *The Mechanical Bride*. Associated with this artistic sensibility was the return to the irrational (or non-rational): 'We again realize that the principles of form are based on more profound and significant elements than rigid logic' (872). As Judith Stamps has noted, 'McLuhan, too, came to call for an end to logic's dominance' (*Unth* 109). This non-rational approach to phenomena coincided with the symbolizing, conceptualizing ability of the artist, who proceeded ana-logically, as opposed to the 'specialist' (*Space, Time and Architecture* 708), who lacked (in Giedeon's formulation) the overarching, universal, 'cosmic' vision (549) of the artist: 'Armies of specialists are no help when what is missing is a universal attitude covering the whole of life' (708). Thus, the history of spaces that Giedion provides in *Space, Time and Architecture* is not categorical but a history of the *orientation* of spaces and of spatial effects. He posited three of these orientations: first, the interplay of volumes, characterizing the cultures of Egypt, Sumer, and Greece; then, the vaulted interior space of the Renaissance into the eighteenth century; in the third orientation, coinciding with the twentieth century, architecture seeks to effect 'a hitherto unknown interpenetration of inner and outer space' (lvi).

Canadian Spaces

McLuhan has traditionally been understood in the context of the European Modernism whose spatial (and temporal) history Giedion delineates in *Space, Time and Architecture*, and that context is inarguably part of McLuhan's formative intellectual context. Yet McLuhan saw Modernism as a transitional phase leading to acoustic, non-Euclidean space; his sensibilities were thus more closely allied to what has come to be called postmodernism, and they were so in large measure by virtue of his Canadian, 'counter-environmental' positioning. As David Cook has argued, 'the effect of the landscape [in Canada] has displaced what has traditionally been the role of the "Giants in Time" with the new spectre of the "Giants" who will conquer space.'[31] This is so, as well, in the sense that the Canadian artist/theorist confronts cultural history not as a succession of moments/periods/epochs but all at once, in spatial deployment. Thus Canada produces an Earle Birney, who uses Anglo-Saxon forms to write of contemporary issues; a Northrop Frye, who sees all of literary production spread out in a timeless pattern of recurring structures; a Harold Innis, who juxtaposes vast historical periods within the range of a pair of sentences. It was out of this spatializing sensibility that McLuhan likewise emerged.[32]

The earliest of these Canadian thinkers about space was Richard Maurice Bucke, best known as the author of *Cosmic Consciousness*, published in 1901.[33] Bucke was medical superintendent of the London, Ontario, insane asylum in the late nineteenth century, where he made a number of significant and far-reaching reforms. He also befriended and became the first biographer of Walt Whitman. Out of these strands, Bucke wove a thesis about 'the evolution of the human mind' (as his subtitle puts it) towards an ever greater sensory awareness, which Bucke called 'cosmic consciousness.' Bucke proposes, in effect, a form of secular transcendence that he associates in particular with the technology of 'aerial navigation' (4), before which 'national boundaries, tariffs, and perhaps distinctions of language will fade out. Great cities will no longer have reason for being and will melt away ... Space will be practically annihilated' (4–5).[34] McLuhan makes reference to Bucke in an essay on John Dos Passos (*IL* 57), and the phrase 'cosmic consciousness' appears in *Understanding Media* (84) in the context of the communicational potential of computers.[35] The thought of Bucke and McLuhan is closest in its translation of modes of transportation into modes of communication (Bucke predating, here, the Innis of the fur-trade study) and positing, based on this relationship, a form of global awareness.[36] An additional link between McLuhan and Bucke is their interest in brain activity as a sign of altered states of perception. Bucke cited insanity as a sign of the rapid shift into cosmic consciousness, and McLuhan spent much of his later career meditating on the significance of the predominance between left and right hemispheres of the brain.[37]

Another Canadian thinker within the milieu from which McLuhan would emerge was Reginald Aubrey Fessenden, a pioneer in the invention of electronic modes of communication, and whom some credit with the invention of the television. Fessenden was engineering commissioner of the Ontario Power Commission in 1923 when he published the first volume of *The Deluged Civilization of the Caucasus Isthmus*.[38] Like Bucke, Fessenden is concerned with consciousness, though his interest is more in its origin than its development, Fessenden ascribing the origin of speech to the Caucasus isthmus. The most astounding part of Fessenden's study, however, is the last, where he relates advances in technology to his overall theme, which is the re-establishment of the oneness lost with the deluge: 'This incentive to progress is best provided by creating improved means of communication' (96). Fessenden also suggests that media of communication develop discontinuously – that the telephone, for instance, is not an outgrowth of the telegraph. Of particular note is Fessenden's patent on a 'sound writing language,' which would 'eliminate the necessity of writing by hand or typewriter and serve as a universal language' (134). McLuhan refers to Fessenden in *Take Today* as 'the Forgotten Father of "Wireless Telephony"' (249).

A Canadian writer who, like Fessenden, grasped some of the implications of electronic media for artistic representations was John Murray Gibbon, a highly prolific author who was also public-relations officer for the Canadian Pacific Railway. Gibbon is of indirect significance to McLuhan in that he was the first to make major use of the mosaic concept to describe Canada, in *Canadian Mosaic: The Making of a Northern Nation* (1938); the concept was to be taken up by McLuhan as a metaphor of acoustic space (following from Georg von Békésy's use of the metaphor), and afterwards by John Porter in *The Vertical Mosaic* (1965). Of greater interest, however, are Gibbon's studies of song. The first of these was *Canadian Folk Songs* (1927; rev. 1949), in which Gibbon collected and translated thirty-two Québécois songs. Of a more theoretical bent is his 1930 work, *Melody and the Lyric: From Chaucer to the Cavaliers*.[39] In this book, Gibbon details the relationship between poetry and song in England up to the time of Herrick, when poetry ceased for all intents and purposes to be a sung form – 'printed books were comparatively rare before Elizabeth's reign' (viii). However, he also sees a return to this tradition in the modern poet – specifically, Ezra Pound (196) – and allies this recovery of orality to the 'invention of the photostat' (ix), which makes it 'possible nowadays for those who live even in so new a country as Canada to peruse in facsimile medieval scripts' (ix).

More akin to McLuhan[40] (and to Wyndham Lewis) through his interest in advertising, and directly influenced by Bucke's *Cosmic Consciousness*, was Bertram Brooker, who was also an artist, poet, novelist (*Think of the Earth* won the first Governor General's award for fiction), musician, and essayist – like McLuhan, Brooker published essays in the *Sewanee Review*. What specifically links Brooker to Bucke is Brooker's belief in a state of transcendent unity, which he termed 'unitude.'[41] Brooker was also an early participant in cinematic culture, having sold 'two dozen or more scenarios to Vitagraph' (*Sounds Assembling* 11), a major silent film company. Brooker's poetry is remarkable for its sensitivity to spacing (as among the Imagists, but more diffusely), a quality he identifies as important to him in a review he wrote about e.e. cummings in *The Canadian Forum* of July 1930:

> To say that there is a fourth-dimensional quality in Cummings' work is not to suggest that it is simply a jumble of hazy images going off in all directions ... but rather to hint at the removal of phenomena from ordinary space-time dimensions into a realm which, like the fourth dimension, demands the transcendence of ordinary mathematics to become intelligible.
>
> In this respect, his [Cummings's] poetry relates to that type of abstract painting which cannot be called two-dimensional, and yet possesses, instead of the usual space-perspective that makes a painting three-dimensional, a new and puzzling illusion of space that is foreign to normal visual experience. (quoted in *Sounds Assembling* 69–70)

Here the comparison with abstract art is significant, given Brooker's own work in this area. His painting *Sounds Assembling* is significant in its spatialization of the sonic, akin to McLuhan's notion of acoustic space. In addition to his artistic work, Brooker also published, under the pseudonym 'Richard Surrey,' two books on advertising: *Layout Technique in Advertising* (1929), and *Copy Technique in Advertising* (1930). What makes these books of interest to the contemporary reader is that they comprise, in effect, an artistic credo, not only through their range of allusions to works of art, but in the constant extension of commentary from the realm of advertising to that of artistic production in general: 'It may be interesting to those who are little acquainted with any sort of art technique to know that "division of space" is not merely a law of Layout, but a fundamental of all art.'[42] It is this 'ancient emphasis on design and pattern' (12) that 'modern' artists have rediscovered. 'This,' continues Brooker, 'is the whole aim of Cezanne, ... who "fathered" the modern movement. His attempt was not to paint nature faithfully, but to *organize* the space in his picture so that the pattern of his "divisions" became not merely a surface design, but a "cutting up" of three dimensions' (14). What is implicit here is the continuity between advertising techniques and those of art; thus, in *Copy Technique in Advertising*, we find Brooker making reference to such writers as Balzac, Butler, Cocteau, Coleridge, Conrad, Dickens, Flaubert, Ford Madox Ford, Ibsen, Kipling, Lawrence, Shakespeare, Shaw, Tolstoy, and Verga, among others, and it was this sense of the confluence of advertising and artistic technique that characterized works of McLuhan as well – particularly *The Mechanical Bride* (1951).

Brooker's insistence on the spatialization of words in poetry (as in his review of cummings) is a key element in the linguistic theories of the last of the Canadian spatial thinkers to be considered here, R.A. Wilson, in whose work W. Terence Gordon has documented McLuhan's interest (*EU* 324). In 1937, Wilson published *The Birth of*

Language: Its Place in World Evolution and Its Structure in Relation to Space and Time, which went on to achieve fame when Bernard Shaw championed the book in England, writing a preface for the second edition. Wilson, who was professor of English at Saskatchewan, is concerned in his book – as were Bucke and Brooker and Fessenden – with a history of the evolution of consciousness, one aspect of which, he argued, is language. Wilson takes as his point of departure Kant's insistence that space and time constitute the fundamental bases of knowledge. His book thus constitutes an attempt 'to explore the nature of language in relation to space and time.'[43] Wilson surveys accounts of the origin of language in the Bible, Plato, and Rousseau, designating the latter as transitional from supernatural to natural (or 'scientific') theories of language origin, with the natural approach emerging fully fledged in Herder's 1772 treatise on the *Origin of Language*. Herder is important not only for his scientific approach to language, but also because he points towards Charles Darwin, whose evolutionary theory Wilson considers to be of prime importance for the study of language. However, unlike Darwin, who believed human and non-human languages to be different in degree and not kind, Wilson posits a difference between them based on natural versus conventional sounds. For Wilson, this difference betokens the divergence of mental powers in humans and non-humans: 'time-and-space holds the animal's mind; man's mind holds time-and-space' (137). Language evolves from the need to mediate between the natural (or phenomenal) world and the mental world produced by consciousness. It was significant that the form of this language was oral rather than gestural because oral speech could easily be broken down into letters indicating tonalities: 'The enormous advantage of this analysis into elements for the purpose of converting sound-speech into visual speech is apparent at once, since the whole thing can be done by twenty-six spatial symbols' (161). It is Wilson's insistence on written language as the spatial extension of verbal sounds that links him with McLuhan, who writes in 'Culture without Literacy' (*Exp* 1) that 'writing is the spatializing and arrest of oral speech' (119).

'The Problem of Space'

Many of the spatial notions that characterize McLuhan's thought were thus available to him in Canada before he embarked on his graduate studies at Cambridge. Two of the most significant of these notions, however, he encountered upon his return from Cambridge: Innis's notion of temporal and spatial biases, and the concept of acoustic space introduced to him by Carleton Williams.

The influence of Innis on McLuhan was neither simple nor direct.[44] McLuhan was an eclectic thinker who rarely failed to transform any idea he encountered. While Innis's paradigm of spatial and temporal biases within cultures of communication had a profound effect on McLuhan, McLuhan departed radically from Innis's formulation of the ways in which these biases interacted to produce social and cultural phenomena.[45]

Although Innis began his career as an economic historian, with studies of Canadian staples such as fur and cod, what interested McLuhan most was 'the later Innis,' as he put it in his seminal 1953 article of that title. The 'later Innis' was contained in two books written at the end of Innis's career: *Empire and Communications* and *The Bias of Communication*. *Empire and Communications* (1950) traces the history of communication from Egypt to the era of movable type and is organized around the concepts of the oral and written traditions and their effects on time and space.[46] In seeking to trace these effects, Innis confesses to a Canadian bias: his study of Canadian staples had taught him that 'each staple in turn left its stamp, and the shift to new staples invariably produced periods of crises in which adjustments in the old structure were painfully made and a new pattern created in relation to a new staple.'[47] If this were so with reference to the staple industries, could this insight be extended to the communications 'industries'? Innis believed it could, and that, indeed, these studies were linked, because, as McLuhan put it, 'the trade-routes of the mind' were extensions of 'the trade-routes of the external world' (LI 385).[48] Innis's thesis was that communications media developed space and time biases: 'Media that emphasize time are those that are durable in character, such as parchment, clay, and stone. Media that emphasize space are apt to be less durable and light in character, such as papyrus and paper' (7). While Innis remained with this insight in his second study, *The Bias of Communication* (1951) he introduced into it a moralistic element, as is evident in the essays 'The Problem of Space' and 'A Plea for Time.' McLuhan's rejection of moralization subsequent to *The Mechanical Bride* (1951), rendered him unsympathetic to this approach, and it was at this point that McLuhan made his most significant intellectual departure from Innis, a departure that had a profound significance for McLuhan's theory of space.[49]

The biases of *The Bias of Communication* are already evident in *Empire and Communications*, where Innis favours 'the oral tradition and Greek civilization' (the title of the fourth chapter) over 'the written tradition and the Roman empire' (the title of the fifth). 'The spread of writing,' Innis argues, 'destroyed a civilization based on the oral tradition, but the power of the oral tradition as reflected in the culture of Greece has continued throughout the history of the West, particularly at periods when the dead hand of the written tradition threatened to destroy the spirit of Western man' (57). It is clear that for Innis one of the major negative qualities of space was stasis. As he writes, 'science found its ideal in geometry, the science of space measurement, and was concerned with the static aspect of structure, arrangement, and order' (65). In Rome, it was 'the spread of writing [that] contributed to the downfall of the Republic and the emergence of the empire' (100). Paper 'hastened the development of political bureaucracy with its emphasis on the concept of space' (140). Innis concludes his book by arguing that 'Mass production and standardization are the enemies of the West. The limitations of mechanization of the printed and the spoken word must be emphasized and determined efforts to recapture the vitality of the oral tradition must be made' (169–70). The antipathy that emerges here against writing (the space bias), and the approbation of speech (the time bias), become overt in *The Bias of Communication*, where Innis writes in his last essay, 'My bias is with the oral tradition, particularly as reflected in Greek civilization, and with the necessity of recapturing something of its spirit' (190).[50] What urges him to express such a bias is both a distaste for contemporary society[51] and the formulation of a 'cyclical theory' of social development, accompanied by a notion of history as 'not a seamless web but rather a web of which the warp and the woof are space and time woven in a very uneven fashion and producing distorted patterns' ('Preface' vii). Yet Innis's first essay, 'Minerva's Owl,' belies such a view of history, and tends to present, rather, the history of communications as a single fabric (if not a seamless one), in its movement from 'clay, the stylus, and cuneiform script' to 'radio in the second quarter of the present century' (*BC* 3).

For McLuhan, the two most important essays in *The Bias of Communication* were 'A Plea for Time' and 'The Problem of Space.' In the first of these, Innis expresses his 'concern about the disappearance of an interest in time,' which leads to 'an undue obsession with the immediate' (61);[52] this space bias characterizes the period in which Innis himself is writing and links him with Lewis (whose *Time and Western Man* Innis cites). The plea Innis makes is for 'a stable society [that] is dependent on an appreciation of a proper balance between the concepts of space and time' (64). In 'The Problem of Space' Innis draws on two texts that became of particular importance to McLuhan, F.M. Cornford's 'The Invention of Space,' and Giedion's *Space, Time and Architecture*. Innis associates the space bias with militarism and the expansion of empires, as well as with certain shifts in artistic sensibility: 'A decline of the oral tradition meant an emphasis on writing (and hence on the eye rather than the ear) and on visual arts, architecture, sculpture, and painting (and hence on space rather than time)' (130–1; Innis cites Lessing in this regard on 102).

McLuhan's work has often been explicated and assessed in the context of Innis's, such explications taking as their point of departure McLuhan's comment in *The Gutenberg Galaxy* that this work was but a 'footnote' to Innis's (*GG* 50; McLuhan cites Innis himself here; see 'The Bias of Communication,' *BC* 33). While it is true that Innis's work occasioned the single most profound shift in McLuhan's intellectual career (notable, otherwise, for its consistency), that shift represented a fundamental *distancing* from Innis in terms of the latter's configurations of the concepts of time and, especially, space, in terms of Innis's strict adherence to Lessing's distinction between spatial arts and temporal arts, and in terms of Innis's assertion that the confluence of space and time would ideally issue in a form of balance. At the same time, McLuhan throughout his career acknowledged Innis's brilliant realization that the central concern of contemporary culture would be precisely the 'problem of space.'

McLuhan's essay 'The Later Innis,' published in 1953, is about 'the basic change which occurred in the thought of Innis in his last decade,' and thus mirrors the change in McLuhan's own thinking occasioned by his encounter with Innis. The change McLuhan sees in the work of Innis is the shift in attention 'from the trade-routes of the external world to the trade-routes of the mind' (LI 385), a process of internalization that had dominated McLuhan's interests in his literary essays (such as 'Tennyson and Picturesque Poetry' and 'The Aesthetic Moment in Landscape Poetry') edited under the title *The Interior Landscape*. McLuhan credits Innis with observing that the era of mechanical production had come to an end and had been replaced by 'the packaging of information' (LI 385), a change that gave a compelling urgency to the theses of *Empire and Communications* and *The Bias of Communication*. However, McLuhan argues that Innis's lack of training 'in the use of the tools of artistic analysis' (387) caused him both to ignore a number of the finer points raised by the material uncovered by his own research and to neglect language completely as 'the greatest mass medium of communication' (390); Innis achieves in compensation, 'a panoramic survey' (388–9). That panorama is presented in 'an ideogramic prose' (389), which, however, 'was perhaps an effort to hide even from [Innis] himself the growing pessimism about the trends *which were anything but obscure to him*' (389; emphasis added). Clearly, as McLuhan's subsequent work would reveal, what concerned him was the powerful awareness within twentieth-century art (and here Duchamp was his prime example) that space and time were relational and in precisely the same way that electric 'speed-up' had encapsulated geography and time (as McLuhan puts it in *Explorations*). Hence McLuhan's comment in the 1953 review of Innis's *Changing Concepts of Time*[53] that 'Professor Innis experienced a serious conflict between his loyalties to certain nineteenth century concepts and the realities he perceived in this century' ('Review' 46). The suggestion is inescapable: Innis refused to acknowledge conclusions (i.e., about space and time) that were nevertheless obvious to him. To put it another way, McLuhan was suggesting that Innis failed to see that his insights were produced spatially, through juxtaposition (though these juxtapositions are much more sequential than they were in McLuhan's practice; in this sense, Innis's work was truly time-biased, as he himself admitted).

Eric Havelock (a classicist who influenced both Innis and McLuhan) writes in his 1982 memoir of Innis that 'at times Innis shows signs of going so far as to treat economic science as a branch of moral science, of morality.'[54] Innis's moralistic bias prevents him from inquiring into 'whether there exists any support for time outside the realm of orality and religion' (31). Havelock further notes that, 'despite his theoretic adherence to the concept of equilibrium, Innis' later writings betray an increasing concern to make what he calls in one paper, a Plea for Time. (*He does not plead for space*)' (31; emphasis added). This observation is important, since it has direct bearing on the most highly charged aspect of Innis's moralizing, namely his projection of (or plea for) a return to the orality (and temporality) of the ancient Greeks. (Ironically, it is a similar thesis that is commonly – though incorrectly – ascribed to McLuhan.) Nowhere does Innis convey the sense of the modern 'speed-up' of time that had so deeply impressed McLuhan, the sense of time as formulated by the Futurists – time as an assault, as a form of battery, as a violent affront to tradition and stability. Nor do we derive from Innis the sense of time as colonizer, valorizing an authentic past (that of the colonizer) over a present (that of the colonized) deemed to be inauthentic, as Johannes Fabian has argued in *Time and the Other*.[55] The solution is not simply to spatialize time, Fabian argues, for 'anthropology's efforts to construct relations with its Other by means of temporal devices implied affirmation of difference as *distance*' (16). McLuhan's response to this problem was to formulate a spacetime that dynamized distance in the model of a global village, a model which significantly avoids the '*denial of coevalness*' (30) that stands at the heart of Fabian's critique of temporal colonization.[56] As Fabian writes, '[o]nce Time is recognized as a dimension, not just a measure, of human activity, any attempt to eliminate it from interpretive discourse can only result in distorted and largely meaningless representations' (24).

Had Innis 'read' history with an artist's rather than an economist's sensibility, he would have been acutely sensitive to the paradox in which he found himself, a paradox that McLuhan states as follows: 'Again and again Innis was faced in his own plea for time by the paradox that bureaucratic structures were the principal means of social continuity. *Yet these structures, whether in religion, empire, or commerce, were the result of a mastery of space*' (LI 391; my emphasis). In terms of McLuhan's development of a theory of space that would address the history of social and cultural forms, this is his single most important observation. The continuity that Innis again and again ascribes to the time bias is here reinscribed by McLuhan in terms of spatial production. In effect, what McLuhan is saying is that all the evidence Innis has collected testifies against him. '[I]n an involuntarily contradictory way, Innis was fighting for the return of the oral tradition with the weapons of the written tradition' (392). What Innis had failed to do was to incorporate the *dynamism* of space and time into his working model and thus to confront the implications of his own observations. If McLuhan were to follow from Innis – as indeed he was – then he himself must confront this paradox: how to accommodate what was clearly a spatial bias in contemporary cultural production – 'by pushing spatial communication to its limits we have today created a global melting pot of peoples and cultures which can only end by making of the world a single city' (391) – while at the same time incorporating the dynamism McLuhan saw as fuelling the paradoxes of the age – 'as the nineteenth century extended its lines of communication in space, it became nostalgic about the human past[;] ... the murder of time in the name of power and money produced modern archaeology and anthropology, and an historical consciousness of the unity of the human family possessed by no other age' (391). McLuhan's response to this paradox was thus not simply to prescribe more spatial control as a remedy for 'the excesses of spatial monopoly of knowledge and communication' (392), achieving in this way a form of 'balance'; as McLuhan stated in a dialogue with Pierre Babin, '[e]quilibrium is a principle inherited from Newton[;] ... [it] is not possible at the speed of light.'[57] Rather, McLuhan's response was to identify space as a site of resistance, as a dynamic: *'the trick is in finding the principle of intelligibility not in concepts of underlying essences or forms but in active relationships in existing dynamic situations'* (LI 393; emphasis added). The care with which McLuhan articulated these differences with Innis thus belies James W. Carey's contention that 'McLuhan has neglected or ignored the principal argument developed by Innis,' which, as Carey puts it, proposed that 'time meant the sacred, the moral, the historical; space the present and the future, the technical and the secular.'[58] McLuhan was fully aware of this argument and rejected it. Carey's argument that 'the most visible effects of communications technology are on social organization and not on sensory organization' (293) is likewise called into question by McLuhan's contention that the *sensus communis* is at once sensory and social, in that media of communication are extensions of the body.

McLuhan maintained the position outlined in 'The Later Innis' (1953) in his 1964 introduction to Innis's *The Bias of Communication*, which is to say, through the period when he produced two of his most significant works, *The Gutenberg Galaxy* and *Understanding Media*. A decade before *Understanding Media*, however, McLuhan encountered the concept that was to supply him with the paradigm for extending Innis's notion of the space/time bias while not abandoning the insight – the insight that McLuhan derived from Innis himself – that contemporary culture was biased spatially.[59] What McLuhan needed was a concept of space that was not static and not limited to the visual. He found this dynamic in the concept of acoustic space, a concept with the utterly poetic ability of uniting the qualities (so admired by Innis) of the oral and aural while maintaining the notion of a space bias.

In 1954 (the year after the publication of 'The Later Innis'), Carleton Williams, a member of McLuhan's seminar, presented a paper on 'Acoustic Space' (*M&M* 123);

McLuhan recounted the event as follows:

> I vividly recall an occasion when I made my first encounter with acoustic space as a concept. Professor Jacqueline Tyrwhitt ... was a member of our Toronto seminar on Culture and Communications. She had been explaining some of Siegfried Giedion's recent findings in which he discriminated between enclosed and unenclosed spaces. Since that time his study of *The Beginnings of Architecture* has brought these matters into a luminous focus. As Professor Tyrwhitt followed his exploration of Egyptian as contrasted with Roman space, she stressed the point that a pyramid did not enclose any space since darkness is to space what silence is to sound. In the same way, an Egyptian temple does not enclose space since it, too, is dark. Even the Greeks never achieved true closure of space. At this point psychologist Carl Williams ... intervened. He observed that unenclosed space could best be considered as acoustic or auditory space. Williams had long been associated with E.A. Bott, who has spent his life studying auditory space. Bott's formula for auditory space is simply that it has no centre and no margins since we hear from all directions simultaneously.[60]

According to Williams, Giedion's enumeration of space concepts such as the cave, the stadium, and the heavens had reminded him of Herman von Helmholtz's use of the concept of '"auditory space" to describe the notion of space experienced by a blind person' (*WWMM* 144). This concept 'struck Marshall with great force,' Williams maintained, and its importance in McLuhan's subsequent career is inestimable.[61]

McLuhan no doubt immediately remarked on Williams's example of a blind person, an example that would have highlighted for McLuhan that *space had an existence outside the realm of the visual*. In other words, visual space was only one kind of space.[62] This insight was confirmed when McLuhan read Jacques Lusseyran's *And There Was Light* (1963), which details the author's encounter with blindness at the age of eight in terms of his rediscovery of space: 'I threw myself forward into the substance which was space, but which I did not recognize because it no longer held anything familiar to me,' he writes of his first experience in the new space that blindness brings him.[63] Out of this experience he learns that 'everything in the world has a voice and speaks' (21): '[s]ounds had the same individuality as light. They were neither inside nor outside, they were passing through me. They gave me my bearings in space and put me in touch with things. It was not like signals that they functioned, but like replies ... [M]ost surprising of all was the discovery that sounds never came from one point in space and never retreated into themselves. There was the sound, its echo, and another sound into which the first sound melted and to which it had given birth, altogether an endless procession of sounds' (23–4). Not even Francis Cornford's brilliant essay 'The Invention of Space' had told McLuhan that the visual was only one kind of space; it had merely told him that there were changing concepts of *visual* space.[64] But here was another space: dynamic, linked to orality, and independent of the negative qualities associated with the visual. It was at this moment that time ceased to be an absolute within McLuhan's intellectual terrain. He had found a way of incorporating time *relationally* into a spatial configuration through the dynamic of the acoustic. As Marchand puts it, 'if space is regarded as the world created by sound ... its characteristics are completely different from those of visual space. It has no fixed boundaries, no center, and very little sense of direction ... It is more immediately connected to the nervous system than anything visual' (*M&M* 123–4). This latter point, furthermore, had the effect of confirming Lewis's insight about the sensuous nature of space ('The *image* is not as strong a thing as the direct, spatial *sensation*,' *TWM* 218), a point that would be of crucial importance when McLuhan came to expand the notion of acoustic space in the direction of the 'audile-tactile.'

It was acoustic space, then, that McLuhan had intuited in his reading of Innis, but that he had been unable at the time of his 1953 essay to formulate. In a sense, it was Innis himself who had directed McLuhan in this way, what with Innis's insistence upon the need for a return to the values he associated with orality. That insistence, however, was recidivist, prompted by a moralistic yearning for the oral culture of ancient Greece. Yet, as Havelock has pointed out, Innis's 'moral preference for the oral word is colored by a certain romanticism which history fails to justify ... [A]fter all, it was mainly the alphabet which released the energies of this culture into history' (42),[65] and, as McLuhan had learned from R.A. Wilson, the alphabet was a spatializing phenomenon. Thus, having taken as his project the exploration of what Innis had called 'the problem of space,' and having become convinced that electronic media were returning society to a condition analogous to that of the orality Innis revered, McLuhan found in the concept of acoustic space the paradoxical interface of these two crucial concepts. Accordingly, in his 1964 essay on Innis (the introduction to *The Bias of Communication*), the notion of the acoustic appears prominently. Noting that Innis 'is quite capable of inaccurate observation during the running of his tests of the interactions of social forms' ('Introduction' to *BC* x), McLuhan cites the specific case of Innis's failure to note the transitional nature of the present historical moment, suspended between literate culture and the orally empathic culture of electronic media. Innis's 'technological blindness' (xii) also leads him to misread Lewis's *Time and Western Man* as asserting that 'the fashionable mind is the time-denying mind' (Innis *BC* 89). For Lewis, as we have seen, it was just the opposite. As McLuhan remarks, 'Because of his own deep concern with the values of tradition and temporal continuity, Innis has managed to misread Wyndham Lewis radically' (xiii). These misreadings, argues McLuhan, derive from a failure to distinguish between 'the modalities of the visual *and the audible*' (xiii; emphasis added): 'He is merely assuming that an extension of information in space has a centralizing power regardless of the human faculty that is amplified and extended. But whereas the visual power extended by print does indeed extend the means to organize a spatial continuum, the auditory power extended electrically *does in effect abolish space and time alike*' (xiii; emphasis added). When McLuhan writes here that the auditory power 'abolishes' space, he refers to the abolition of *visual* space and asserts the viability of the post-Einsteinian concept of spacetime (wherein space and time are collapsed) in speaking of electronic media.[66] As McLuhan succinctly states in *Understanding Media*, '[b]oth time (as measured visually and segmentally) and space (as uniform, pictorial, and enclosed) disappear in the electronic age of instant information' (*UM* 138). Acoustic space encapsulates time as a dynamic of constant flux. Thus, rather than ignoring Innis's theses, as Carey suggested, 'McLuhan has neglected or ignored the principal argument developed by Innis.'[67] McLuhan arrived at his position carefully, largely by working out the implications of Innis's notion (as Carey puts it) that 'Western history ... [was] ending with spatial organization' (280). Carey's misreading derives from his assumptions that the only alternative to time is (visual) space, and that McLuhan's concept of space is static and continuous. In fact, it was dynamic and discontinuous, and it was not visual but acoustic.

What solidified McLuhan's notion of acoustic space was his reading (before 1960) of Georg von Békésy's *Experiments in Hearing*. Von Békésy introduces his work with two visual images, a Persian mosaic and a Renaissance woodcut, in order to illustrate his choice of methodology: 'When in a field of science a great deal of progress has been made and most of the variables are known, a new problem may more readily be handled by trying to fit it into the existing framework. When, however, the framework is uncertain and the number of variables large the mosaic approach is much the easier.'[68] Von Békésy thus allies auditory research with the mosaic approach; as McLuhan puts it in 'Cybernation and Culture,' 'the world of the flat iconic image, [von Békésy] points out, is a much better guide to the world of sound than three-dimensional and pictorial art. The flat iconic forms of art have much in common with acoustic or resonating space. Pictorial three-dimensional art has little in common with acoustic space because it selects a single moment in the life of a form, whereas the flat iconic image gives an integral bounding line or contour that represents not one moment or one aspect of a form, but offers instead an inclusive integral pattern.'[69] The spatialization of the aural is specifically examined in the eighth chapter of von Békésy's book, 'The Spatial Attributes of Sound' (originally published in 1930). 'In no other field of science,' writes von Békésy, 'does a stimulus produce so many different sensations as in the area of directional hearing' (272). His experiments showed that 'perception of the distance of a sound ... was determined simply by the loudness' (280), and goes on to make a significant visual analogy with this way of perceiving acoustic space: 'The less the loudness, the farther away from the head the sound image seemed to be, and when the loudness remained constant this distance was always the same. However, the conditions were indeterminate as to front-back location. It was possible for a subject voluntarily to shift the image from front to back or vice-versa. *These conditions have an analogy in vision in the perception of reversible perspective figures ... where the shaded surface can be seen as in front of, or behind, or on the same plane with the other surfaces*' (280–1; emphasis added). Von Békésy's analogy suggests the confluence of the acoustic dynamic with that of the figure/ground gestalt, the two-dimensional planar relationship that McLuhan theorized as more involving because it was not tied to the fixed positionality (point of view) characteristic of Renaissance art – it was, in fact, characteristic of the mosaic. What animated the acoustic dynamic was the concept of resonance (or interval), and this was the other major concept McLuhan found in von Békésy (who adapted it from Helmholtz). 'Resonance' conceptualizes the break in the uniformity and continuity of space *as visualized*; it is a sign, in other words, of the discontinuity of acoustic space, of the fact that it produces meaning through gaps (including the gaps between elements of a dialogue). In his one surviving letter to Innis (14 March 1951), McLuhan refers to this concept as 'the discontinuous juxtaposition of unrelated items' (*L* 221); at the end of his career, he simply referred to it as 'the fecund interval.'[70]

Getting Spaced

McLuhan has been consistently (though not exclusively) devalorized in comparisons with Innis. John O'Neill, writing in *Canadian Forum*'s May 1981 homage to McLuhan, refers to 'McLuhan's wilful loss of Innis-sense.'[71] Arthur Kroker writes, in *Technology and the Canadian Mind*, that 'in contrast to McLuhan's almost giddy celebration of "space" as the locus of modern experience (*The Medium is the Massage*), Innis appealed in *Empire and Communications* as well as *The Bias of Communication* for a reintegration of "time and space" in western experience.'[72] Donald Theall states, in a 1981 paper on 'Exploration in Communications since Innis,' that 'some of Innis' major challenges for future communication studies may be overlooked in the process of separating his later work from the ways in which McLuhan discussed it.'[73] This point of view persists; as Elspeth Probyn has written recently, 'I remember well when I first read Innis' work. It was, thankfully, before I read his vulgarizer Marshall McLuhan.'[74] These arguments (and others like them) are unified by their insistence that McLuhan failed to produce a material model of communication; that his model, rather, was abstract, and, being abstract, was utopian. Critiques such as these were most often made from a Marxist position, a position McLuhan was said to have ignored in his approach to media.[75] For example, Theall remarks, in *The Medium Is the Rear-View Mirror*, that 'as far as Marx is concerned, [McLuhan] shows in none of his works any awareness either of the content of Marxism or its relevance to his particular kind of determinism' (204).[76] It is certainly the case that McLuhan was not sympathetic to Marxist critique. As he wrote in 1970, 'the Marxist hangup has always resulted from accepting the products of human toil and knowledge as products that do not alter the total environment. Marxists have chosen to ignore the "invisible" or *total* information environment created by industrial hardware' (*L* 402).[77] Marx's insights (according to McLuhan) derived from his observations of a mechanical culture,[78] but this culture had already been superseded by the electric age at the time Marx was writing. As Jean Baudrillard summarizes, 'MacLuhan [*sic*] reproche à Marx d'avoir axé toute son analyse sur un medium – la machine – déjà dépassé à son époque par le télégraphe, et autres formes "implosives." Déjà la dynamique "mécanique" s'inversait devant une problématique nouvelle, que Marx n'a pas vu, et qui rendait caduque toute son analyse.'[79] For McLuhan, the invisibilia of electronic communications – what he called 'the environment' – constituted the fundamental materiality of contemporary social and cultural production.[80]

The globality of terms such as 'environment' emphasized McLuhan's position that space was the cultural dominant of contemporary society, and the Marxist critique[81] of McLuhan was largely based on this insistence (as Kroker's comment makes clear): in focusing on space, McLuhan appeared to be ignoring time, and, in doing so, rejecting the dimension of social change.[82] Judith Stamps quotes appositely from Marx's *Capital* (vol. 1): ' "The subordination of man to the machine situation arises in which men are effaced by their labour; in which the pendulum of the clock has become as accurate a measure of the relative activity of two workers as it is of the speed of two locomotives ... time is everything, man is nothing ... Time sheds its qualitative, variable, flowing nature; it freezes into an exactly delimited, quantifiable continuum filled with quantifiable things ... in short, it becomes space" ' (*Unth* 6).[83] As McLuhan suggested, this view of space (and time) is a mechanical one (as Marx's examples make clear), and assumes that space is static and ahistorical.[84] The concept of acoustic space had taught McLuhan differently, however; this space was dynamic by virtue of the fact that temporality was one of its dimensions – indeed, this space was the domain of social production itself (rather than a neutral container of the social realm).[85]

It is precisely this notion of the *production* of space (to use Lefebvre's locution) that has come to characterize contemporary criticism, including (post)Marxist criticism; as such, it may be said that the critiques made of McLuhan were much more representative of their historical moment than McLuhan's insights were of his. As Patricia Marchak has written, 'the focus on class and nation inhibited appreciation of the role of technology. Technology is always a social construction, but it does not follow that any generation can change it if it so wishes. The industrial revolution did not have to take the form it did, but once it was underway the momentum carried it through three centuries despite plenty of opposition. The current technological revolution, anchored in integrated circuits and biotechnology, has the same momentum. I think the nature of such momentum, and the impacts and context of technological innovation, are not well examined in any social science paradigm, from neoclassical through to neo-Marxist.'[86] Marchak goes on to state that 'the "old" industrial societies are losing much that was characteristic of "modernism." The "newly industrializing countries" ... are gaining industrial capacities, not all of this in dependent form, and thus the spatial dimension of the global economy has become a paramount feature of the theoretical debate in the 1990s' (262).[87] From this stance, Innis's insistence on an equilibrium of space and time was deeply ahistorical.[88] As for the criticism that McLuhan ignored the institutional matrix of the phenomena he wrote about (especially as compared to Innis), Graeme Patterson has noted that the second part of *Understanding Media* is concerned with institutions, as is *Take Today*; Patterson also points out that McLuhan devoted much of his writing to language, which is 'perhaps the most basic of the institutions of mankind.'[89]

Assessing McLuhan in the context not only of Innis but also of Walter Benjamin and the Frankfurt School, Judith Stamps has written that 'Innis and McLuhan were critics of modernity ... [and] they invented a uniquely Canadian version of critical theory – a fusion of critical political economy and of the critical rationality associated with the early Frankfurt School and its followers' (*Unth* xv). Stamps posits an early and a late McLuhan, with the late McLuhan being much less a critic of and much more an apologist for technology. However, if McLuhan's career has a turning point, it occurs much earlier, in 1951–1953, after the publication of *The Mechanical Bride* and the *Queen's Quarterly* article on Innis; for the rest of his career, McLuhan was remarkably consistent.[90] This point is important, because to posit the dividing point in McLuhan's career as having its origin with McLuhan's departure from Innis's methodology is to make a claim about McLuhan's attitude towards space and time and the related phenomena of literacy and orality. McLuhan was not arguing for a return to the values of orality/temporality, as Innis was. Rather, he was extending Innis's insight that the bias of contemporary culture was spatial, while reconfiguring the (visually) spatial in terms of the *acoustic*, since this was the effect that electronic media were having on visual culture. In fact, far from positing a return to orality, McLuhan writes, in *Understanding Media*, that the effect of contemporary media technology was to bring us to 'speechlessness' (*UM* 84). Stamps's argument that the critiques of contemporary culture made by Innis and McLuhan are 'part of a broad scholarly convergence on the belief that the West is caught up in a static and dichotomous paradigm' and that they share 'in a general attempt to transcend the old paradigm by developing a dynamic, non-dichotomous one based on the special qualities of sound' thus tends to describe McLuhan's work more than Innis's. The 'dialogue' that, Stamps argues, is the goal towards which McLuhan was working is a notion that likewise requires clarification; dialogue, in McLuhan's work, has much more in common with Bakhtinian dialogism than with a literal dialogue.[91] However, Stamps's point is well taken when she notes that McLuhan often constructed his written works 'to *resemble* or *mimic* an open dialogue' (*Unth* 135; emphasis added). To this formulation I would add that such a written dialogue is a spatial form in which meaning is produced through juxtaposition (what McLuhan referred to as a 'spatial dialogue' in *Through the Vanishing Point*). McLuhan insisted that the importance of dialogue was that it belonged to a humanistic tradition,[92] and McLuhan's humanism flowed directly from his notion that our total environment – including its technologies – was a human construct; as James Carey has succinctly noted, McLuhan's work 'celebrates not the evils of technology ... not its inhumanity but its terrible humanity.'[93]

Stamps characterizes McLuhan and Innis as seeing 'modernity as a pathological kind of present-mindedness or, since present-mindedness negates time, a kind of spatial bias' (6). That McLuhan saw contemporary culture as subject to a spatial bias is inarguable; however, he did not treat this bias as, by definition, negative. Stamps goes on to argue that 'the theorists enhanced their understanding of modernity by demonstrating that the spatial bias is also a visual bias, a mentality that favours vision or seeing over hearing or listening' (7). McLuhan, however, insisted (post 1953) on a space whose properties were *acoustic*, and thus radically different from the properties of visual space. The 'spatial' and the 'visual' were not coterminous for McLuhan; the spatial also extended into the 'oral' through the concept of acoustic space. It was *visual* space, thus, that McLuhan critiqued. It was *visual* space that was static, not the spatial *per se*. Indeed, *acoustic* space was fundamentally dynamic. Stamps states, appositely, that McLuhan's work is characterized by tensions 'that derive from his attempt to combine static and historical viewpoints' (109). He did this through the concept of acoustic *space*. Thus, McLuhan did *not* see himself as working 'against the spatial bias'; he saw himself working *within* the spatial bias, but *against* visual space. He did *not* point the way to 'a new, non-spatial epistemology' (119); on the contrary, his work is deeply characterized by the attempt to theorize space, and includes a major work in this regard, *Through the Vanishing Point: Space in Poetry and Painting*. Stamps, in fact, notes that McLuhan 'counter[ed] the visual approach ... with a concept that he called acoustic space' (133) and that his work 'is best seen as a part of a larger Western project of rethinking the cultural dimensions of space-time relations by employing models built around the temporal qualities of sound' (151). This, however, does not capture fully the radical nature of his project: McLuhan built his critique around the *spatial* qualities of sound, a space that incorporated the temporal as one of its dimensions.

Acoustic Spaces

When McLuhan wrote in 'The Later Innis' that Innis, in his last works, had moved from the trade routes of the world to the trade routes of the mind, he employed a geographical metaphor that was to have profound implications for his subsequent work, perhaps the foremost of which was that space would remain for him both metaphor and materiality, a fundamentally dynamic site of dialogue, translation, and exchange.[94] McLuhan never abandoned this metaphor, to the extent that he worked with the notion of a counter-environment that could be emplotted both culturally and geographically (and that was paradigmatically Canadian).[95] 'Counter-environment' represented McLuhan's reconfiguration of the centre–margin duality he inherited from Innis and that he dislocated, retaining, however, its imbrication within the imperial theme. If McLuhan is read in the context of Innis (and he asks to be) he would then perforce be read as concerned with writing a 'spatial history,' to use Paul Carter's term, a concern that at once reflected McLuhan's interest in colonization while elaborating Innis's history of empires as histories of communications. Carter makes the connection clearly: 'Imperial space ... with its ideal, neutral observer and its unified, placeless Euclidean passivity, was a means of foundation, a metaphorical way of transforming the present into a future enclosure, a visible stage, an orderly cause-and-effect pageant.'[96] McLuhan's critique of the visual regime imposed by print has a similar context,[97] and his production of non-linear texts with no point of view has a decolonizing agenda, as in this passage from the 1954 pamphlet 'Counterblast':

B L A S T

england ancient GHOST of culture
POACHING the EYES of the
canadian HAMLETS

U S A
COLOSSUS of the South, horizontal
HEAVYWEIGHT flattening the
canadian imagination

CBC   BBC   NBC   CBS
nets of the BIG GAME hunters, lairs of
the NEW BABBITTS

Cast in these terms, McLuhan's 'break' with Innis over the issue of space can be seen not as an attempt to establish an ahistorical, apolitical site of spatial superfoetation but rather for what it was: a collapsing of Innis's space and time binary into the concept of a historicized (because produced in history) spatiality. As Kristin Ross has suggested in *The Emergence of Social Space*, arguing from the example of Rimbaud, space pluralizes history by extracting it from rigid and univocal temporality.[98] McLuhan had made a similar argument in *Counterblast* (the 1969 book of that title), where he writes that 'instead of using a single external space to evoke and control mental states, it was suddenly discovered [by Rimbaud et al.] that many spaces and many times could be included in a single poem or picture' (*Ctb* 83). This observation provides yet another motive for McLuhan's suggestion that the Modernist art he is usually taken as celebrating as a *terminus ad quem* was in fact only an intermediate stage of the phenomena he was describing: to go beyond the Modernist statement was to displace Europe as centre, as environment. To put this another way: for McLuhan, the global (environmental) was *situated*, and hence his paradoxical formulation of the global *village*, by which he sought to embody spatial location as a dynamic. What this implies is that McLuhan's concept of space was not totalized but materialized and localized, and it was so in terms of a dynamic process. Where Modernist space was synchronic, McLuhan theorized a postmodernist diachronics of space – indeed, it may be the spatial juxtaposition of histories that is the most powerful sign of postmodernism. This space has much in common with Foucault's notion of 'heterotopian' space, 'the space in which we live, which draws us out of ourselves, in which the erosion of our lives, our time and our history occurs, the space that claws and [gnaws] at us.'[99]

Yet McLuhan was not proposing a cultural geography in the generally accepted sense. Indeed, having deconstructed the nature/culture binary to the extent that he proposed that nature had imploded into culture, what he was proposing was more like a 'virtual geography,'[100] to use McKenzie Wark's formulation.[101] Wark proposes that the everyday world comprising our 'geography of experience' (vi) is paralleled by another made of 'the terrain created by the television, the telephone, the telecommunications networks crisscrossing the globe,' terrain that 'generally permeates our experience of the space we experience firsthand' (vi). This is the dynamic of the global village;[102] it also recalls McLuhan's suggestion that we had gone through the vanishing point of postclassical visual representation such that our bodies were now themselves the mediators of space through the technological extensions of our perceptual abilities, and it is this observation which has made McLuhan's thought so amenable to those who theorize virtual reality and cyberspace.[103] It is precisely this amenability, however, that has caused McLuhan's work in the area of spatial theory to be undervalued. It is only relatively recently that the disciplinary practice of geography has opened itself up to the sort of theoretical dislocation McLuhan was practising early in his career and that is summarized by the title of a collection of his essays, *The Interior Landscape*. It was the making of such (virtual) geographies that was, for McLuhan, one of the primary activities of a culture.

If McLuhan can be called a 'founding father' of postmodernism, as Marjorie Ferguson has suggested,[104] it is precisely in having established the spatial as the most significant dimension of postmodernist inquiry, be it in geography or media theory. Ferguson seeks to re-evaluate McLuhan in the light of the postmodernist condition, writing that, 'however monocausal, mediacentric and psychologistic, he did relate technology and cultural artifacts to the historical era in which they are embedded. Admittedly he did this more by *a*historical exaggeration of the order of the invention of printing bringing about the Renaissance, than by scholarly canons of temporality' (82). Ferguson does not make allowance for the possibility, however, that instead of the scholarly canons of temporality, McLuhan invoked the non-canonical realm (at least in theoretical terms) of the spatial. Indeed, many of the postmodernist theorists she cites in the course of her discussion of McLuhan are theorists who have sought to investigate the implications of spatialization, such as Bell, Harvey, Jameson, and Baudrillard. Noting that 'McLuhanism penetrated the Francophone intellectual zeitgeist of the 1960s' (84), Ferguson goes on to record 'an encounter between French Marxists and structuralists where Lefebvre, arguing for the development of a theory of the text, requests that some attention be paid to McLuhan even if he was "un peu charlatanesque"' (84). Lefebvre duly acknowledged his debt to McLuhan in *The Production of Space* (1991; French edition 1974). This monumental work seeks to present a (post)Marxist critique of social space. Poststructuralist in its orientation, it historicizes the concept of space through an insistence that it is a product of the socius. Thus, space is dynamic, in history, and a site of resistance. Lefebvre analyses concepts of absolute, abstract, contradictory, and differential space. Abstract space is the invention of Euclidean geometry; it is infinite and empty (*PS* 1). What has been inherited from this notion of abstract space is space as a '"mental place"' (3), and this notion has come to have a wide application: 'We are forever hearing about the space of this and/or the space of that: about literary space, ideological spaces, the space of the dream, psychoanalytic topologies, and so on and so forth' (3). What is lacking in such formulations, as Lefebvre notes, is an account of the social production of space itself (that which mediates between the social and the mental) (6). Put in other terms, space is active and not passive (cf Lewis). It is precisely this activity – space as process – that Lefebvre wishes to theorize as the 'universal' and the 'abstract' of social space (15). To it he counterposes the static space that is the product of the state (23; cf Innis) and to which Marx reacted with a 'vigorous reinstatement of historical time as revolutionary time' (21). Since Hegel, it has been 'only Nietzsche ... [who] has maintained the primordiality of space and concerned himself with the spatial problematic – with the repetitiveness, the circularity, the simultaneity of that which seems diverse in the temporal context and which arises at different times' (22).

Lefebvre suggests that one of the reasons why space has been undertheorized is the dominance of writing: 'to underestimate, ignore and diminish space amounts to the overestimation of texts, written matter, and writing systems, along with the readable and the visible, to the point of assigning to these a monopoly on intelligibility' (62). McLuhan would have more precisely argued that the underestimation of *acoustic* space arises from the overestimation of *visual* space and those modes of thought, those ideologies, produced along with it by alphabet technologies and further extended by print. It is here, in fact, that Lefebvre locates McLuhan's contribution to the theorization of space – in his delineation of how a particular space (visual) was produced through writing (261, n26, and again 286, citing *The Gutenberg Galaxy*).[105] This 'abstract space' is 'a product of violence and war, [and thus] it is political; instituted by a state, it is institutional' (285). As a '"counter-space"' (383) to this abstract space, Lefebvre proposes '"differential"' space, which is analogous to McLuhan's 'acoustic' space (and Foucault's heterotopic space).[106] As Mark Gottdiener remarks in *The Social Production of Urban Space*, this concept is Lefebvre's most significant contribution to the theory of space: 'the most important theoretical aspect of space is its multifaceted nature. Space cannot be reduced merely to a location or to the social relations of property ownership – it represents a multiplicity of sociomaterial concerns. Space is a physical location, a piece of real estate, and simultaneously an existential freedom and a mental expression.

Space is both the geographical site of action and the social possibility for engaging in action ... This idea is fundamental to Lefebvre's notion of praxis, which stands at odds with other Marxian attitudes toward political struggle.'[107] This is not to suggest, by analogy, that McLuhan was making a Marxist analysis of space; rather, it is to demonstrate how the Marxism used to critique McLuhan in the 1970s and 1980s has itself moved towards a position very much congruent with McLuhan's. As Doreen Massey has remarked, the 'broad position – that the social and the spatial are inseparable and that the spatial form of the social has causal effectivity – is now accepted increasingly widely, especially in geography and sociology.'[108] This suggests that a consideration of McLuhan's formulation of a theory of space can provide the basis for a revaluation of his work.[109]

To combine a notion of space as socially produced with an inquiry into the technologies of spatial production is to work towards a social theory of the production of space. McLuhan sought to examine not only how society produces space but also how technologies of space produce society. Because his concerns were 'environmental,' he sought to understand artistic production within these broader spatial contexts; as Innis had suggested, spatial and temporal biases were indices as much of artistic production as they were of social, political, and economic structures (BC 102–3; 130–1).[110] 'The anxiety of our era has to do fundamentally with space, no doubt a great deal more than with time' wrote Foucault in 1967 ('Of Other Spaces' 23). What the following chapters seek to do is locate McLuhan within that discourse which continues to pursue what Innis so tellingly referred to as the 'problem of space.'

CHAPTER TWO

Mechanization and Its Discontents

Whereas in external landscape diverse things lie side by side, so in psychological landscape the juxtaposition of various things and experiences becomes a precise musical means of orchestrating that which could never be rendered by systematic discourse.

Marshall McLuhan, 'Tennyson and Picturesque Poetry'

The Mechanical Bride

The extent to which McLuhan's encounter with Innis focused his thoughts on 'the problem of space' can be determined by examining McLuhan's first extended work, *The Mechanical Bride* (1951), written in the period leading up to McLuhan's decisive 1953 essay, 'The Later Innis.' In that essay, McLuhan adopts the historical focus of Innis's space and time articulation, while distancing himself from Innis's static characterization of these modalities. In *The Mechanical Bride*, however, McLuhan, deeply influenced by Wyndham Lewis and Siegfried Giedion, figured space and time in binary opposition, while exhibiting an awareness of the inadequacy of this formulation. Thus we find McLuhan arguing both that time is the bias of mechanical societies as space is of 'primitive' ones (*MB* 85), and that space and time have collapsed into the simultaneity of spacetime (80). The unresolved tension between the two positions characterizes the book as a whole. This tension has methodological implications as well: was McLuhan to adopt the position of 'arrest' advocated by Lewis (and associated with spatialization), or was he to heed Giedion's critique that this 'specialist' approach lacked organic insight and thus immerse himself in the material that he was critiquing (a position associated with the flux of temporality)?

  The Mechanical Bride is composed of fifty-nine short (two to three pages, on average) analyses, mostly of advertisements published during the 1940s in the United States. The ads range widely, from puffs for *Time* magazine and *Modern Screen* to blurbs for waterproof caskets, automobiles,[1] light bulbs, clothing, the Great Books, and drugstore romances. There are also analyses of newspaper layout, comic books (*Blondie, Tarzan, Superman, Li'l Abner*), market research, John Wayne movies, and detective fiction. Taken as a whole, these elements constitute (as the subtitle puts it) *The Folklore of*

Industrial Man. While the range of the material analysed is large, the thematic focus remains constant: advertisements figure the mechanization and fragmentation of all aspects of intellectual and emotional life, including the libidinal. 'Ads,' writes McLuhan, 'not only express but also encourage that strange dissociation of sex not only from the human person but even from the unity of the body' (99; 'dissociation' has the flavour, here, of T.S. Eliot's 'dissociation of sensibility').[2] McLuhan's style parodies this dissociation in a compositional montage where each sentence strains towards the foreground – the paragraph in which McLuhan observes how advertisements displace sexuality ends abruptly with the observation that 'the Hiroshima bomb was named "Gilda" in honor of Rita Hayworth' (99).[3]

It is comments such as this one which have caused *The Mechanical Bride* to be read as McLuhan's most moralistic work, the one in which he most forcefully distances himself from the material that he is critiquing. As Dennis Duffy argued in his 1969 study of McLuhan, '*The Mechanical Bride* takes an explicit moral stance which the author with minor exceptions was never to take again.'[4] McLuhan, however, stated in his 1969 interview with Eric Norden that '*until* I wrote my first book, *The Mechanical Bride*, I adopted an extremely moralistic approach to all environmental technology';[5] and he writes in the 'Preface' to *The Mechanical Bride* that 'Many who are accustomed to the note of moral indignation will mistake [his] amusement for mere indifference' (v).[6] McLuhan's stance towards morality in *The Mechanical Bride*, in fact, resembles that of Wyndham Lewis in *Time and Western Man*: 'We shall aim to get behind morals, which is the same order of enterprise as getting behind Romance' (16), writes Lewis, using a formulation in which 'Romance' is to be read as synonymous with advertising: 'Advertisement (in a grotesque and inflated form) is a pure expression of the romantic mind' (11). For McLuhan, the advertising milieu was likewise characterized by 'mushy sensual content' and 'pulsating, romantic glamour' (*MB* 4), and it was the advertisement itself which placed the 'moral' in question by conflating it with technique and producing a mechanical substitute for it. In analysing 'Know-How' McLuhan describes it as 'at once a technical and a moral sphere. It is a duty for a woman to love her husband and also to love that soap that will make her husband love her. It is a duty to be glamorous, cheerful, efficient, and, so far as possible, to run the home like an automatic factory' (32). Elsewhere in the book McLuhan states that 'we no longer have a rational basis for defining virtue or vice. And the slogan "Crime Does Not Pay" is the expression of moral bankruptcy in more senses than one. It implies that if crime could pay, then the dividing line between virtue and vice would disappear' (31). '"High moral tone"' is here placed on the same level as 'high production, high profits, high frequency of gadgets, perhaps high employment' (140), which is to say on the level of mechanical production.

But it is by precisely the same token that the moral is made to coincide with the formal in *The Mechanical Bride*. Duffy's remark that in McLuhan's subsequent works 'the interest lies no longer in the degree of intelligence and sensitivity exhibited in the *content* of the [work] (as was the case in *The Mechanical Bride*), but rather the cultural implication of the ... form and appearance' (13) is belied by virtually every page in the book, which appropriates the form and appearance of magazine and newspaper copy (and the glibness of advertising text). If there is a 'problem of space' in this book, then, it has most immediately to do with the formal (and methodological) implications of the advertisements themselves, as mirrored in the techniques McLuhan uses to critique them. He would have found a model for such techniques in the work of Lewis, whose two *Blast* volumes (1914; 1915) play with typefaces and page formats in a way that derives from advertising,[7] and directly influenced McLuhan's 1954 pamphlet and 1969 book, both entitled *Counterblast*.[8] By comparison with these works (especially the later one), *The Mechanical Bride* is visually quite tame, yet it points towards these works both stylistically and philosophically. As McLuhan put it in the 1969 interview with Norden, 'I perceived [while writing *MB*] how sterile and useless [Rousseauvian utopianism] was, and I began to realize that the greatest artists of the 20th Century – Yeats, Pound, Joyce, Eliot – had discovered a totally different approach, based on *the identity of the processes of cognition and creation* ... I began to study the new environment ... and I soon realized that [it] could not be dismissed by moral outrage or pious indignation ... I adapted *some* of this new approach in *The Mechanical Bride* by attempting to *immerse* myself in the advertising media in order to apprehend their impact on man' (265–6; emphases added). *The Mechanical Bride* has appeared to so many readers to be a 'moral' book because McLuhan parodies throughout the moralistic tone of advertising, as he does its techniques, by writing from within them, actualizing rhetorically the vortex metaphor of Poe's maelstrom story, which McLuhan repeatedly invokes. 'Poe's sailor in "The Maelstrom,"' he writes, 'saved himself by co-operating with the action of the "strom" itself' (75). Writing five years before the publication of *The Mechanical Bride*, McLuhan was interpreting Poe's story much more along the lines of Lewis's notion of arrest: 'The sailor in [Poe's] story *The Maelstrom* [*sic*] is at first paralysed with horror. But in his very paralysis there is another fascination which emerges, a power of detached observation which becomes a "scientific" interest in the action of the strom [*sic*].'[9] It is this position of detachment that McLuhan was in the process of retheorizing in *The Mechanical Bride*, though not completely with success, and hence the book's 'space/time' tension.

McLuhan proceeds in *The Mechanical Bride* 'by providing typical visual imagery of our environment and dislocating it into meaning' (vi), interrupting the continuity of ad and 'copy' by juxtaposing them with his own analyses. The book thereby 'reverses that process' through which the ads are constructed, substituting disjunction for continuity: 'A whirling phantasmagoria can be grasped only when arrested for contemplation' (v). This was precisely the response Lewis had advocated with regard to Bergson and 'The Time School' (*TWM* 2.1), and it had in addition, for McLuhan, a Joycean resonance of 'the creative process as the natural process of apprehension arrested and retraced.'[10] McLuhan achieves the effect of verbal arrest through the 'omission of syntactical connections' (85), which is at once the technique of syncopation and of symbolization – 'the abrupt apposition of images, sounds, rhythms, facts [that] is omnipresent in the modern poem, symphony, dance, and newspaper' (85–6). In this way McLuhan seeks to demonstrate a dimension of unity within the fragmentation of an increasingly mechanistic society: 'there can be symbolic unity among the most diverse and externally unconnected facts or situations' (80). In support of this contention, McLuhan cites Margaret Mead, who, 'as an anthropologist ... works on the postulate of the organic unity or "cultural regularity" of societies' (65). Similarly, Siegfried Giedion, in *Mechanization Takes Command*, shows the need for 'orchestrating the arts and sciences in the fullest interest of individual and social life' (50).

This is not, McLuhan contends, to posit the organic as the alternative to the mechanical: 'since all organic characteristics can now be mechanically produced, the old rivalry
between mechanism and vitalism is finished' (34). Rather, it is to embrace 'the symbolist
esthetic theory of the late nineteenth century ... [that] leads to a conception of orchestrating human arts, interests, and pursuits rather than fusing them in a functional biological
unit ... Orchestration permits discontinuity and endless variety without the universal
imposition of any one social or economic system. It is a conception inherent not only in
symbolist art but in quantum and relativity physics. Unlike Newtonian physics, it can
entertain a harmony that is not unilateral, monistic, or tyrannical. It is neither progressive
nor reactionary but embraces all previous actualizations of human excellence while
welcoming the new in a simultaneous present' (34). This would be an 'organicism' based
on difference rather than identity, and as such would fly in the face of mechanistic
culture, founded as that culture is on the endless production of interchangeable parts.
Because industrial technique was born in the Newtonian age, its 'passionate dream of
unlimited monopolistic power still carries over into the new age of relativity physics.
But the dream of relativity physics is not of centralism but of pluralism. It is not
centralist but distributist in the matter of power and control. And to see this new vision at
work side by side with the old one is to permit the reformer a sure method of diagnosis
and therapeutic suggestion. *It permits the reformer to co-operate with the same forces
that have produced the disease, in order to point the way to health*' (22; my emphasis).
This 'classically medical approach to understanding technology,'[11] as Arthur Kroker
puts it, identifies McLuhan's concern with 'the *interface* of biology and technology'
(*TCM* 71; my emphasis), a concern that remained of key importance to McLuhan's
critique of technology. Here that interface is configured in terms of content and form:
while the content is debased, the form points towards the possibility of a heightened
critical awareness. There is an unresolved tension, however, between the need to arrest
the temporal flux of advertising in order to achieve this heightened awareness and the
larger philosophical implications (as McLuhan sees them) of the space/time binary. 'For
tribal man,' McLuhan writes, 'space was the uncontrollable mystery. For technological
man it is time that occupies the same role. Time is still loaded with a thousand decisions
and indecisions which terrify a society that has yielded so much of its autonomy to
merely automatic processes and routines' (*MB* 85). Time is clearly associated here with
mechanical processes, space with organic (or premechanical) ones, but McLuhan's logic
leads to an identification of the 'primitive' and the 'arrested' that is not followed through
in the book.

As he was to do in other works, such as *The Gutenberg Galaxy* and *From Cliché to
Archetype*, McLuhan produces in *The Mechanical Bride* a discontinuous narrative with
'a circulating point of view' that thus forgoes the 'need for it to be read in any special
order' (*MB* vi). Following Giedion in *Mechanization Takes Command*, McLuhan invokes, at the outset of his book, the historian Jacob Burckhardt,[12] whose *Civilization of
the Renaissance in Italy* (1860) advanced the notion 'that the meaning of Machiavelli's
method was to turn the state into a work of art by the rational manipulation of power'
(*MB* vi). This implies, for McLuhan, that 'it has been an open possibility to apply the
method of art analysis to the critical evaluation of society' (vi), a notion of crucial
importance to McLuhan's career. 'Today,' McLuhan goes on to note, 'we are in a

position to criticize the state as work of art and the arts can often provide us with the tools of analysis for that job. The arts both as storehouse of achieved values and as the antennae of new awareness and discovery make possible both a unified and an inclusive human consciousness in which there is easy commerce between old and new, between assured success and tentative inquiry and experiment' (87). It is in this context that the opening exhibit on the 'Front Page' (fig. 2.1) is of crucial significance to the book as a whole. Like a newspaper or magazine page, *The Mechanical Bride* is formally structured as columnar text (or 'copy'), with pictorial ads, interspersed with bold-faced riders that ask the sort of *faux-naif* question analysed by McLuhan in a number of the ads. In adopting the newspaper page as an artistic (and critical) manifesto, McLuhan invokes as his predecessors 'the French symbolists, followed by James Joyce in *Ulysses*, [who] saw that there was a new art form of universal scope present in the technical layout of the modern newspaper. Here is a major instance of how a by-product of industrial imagination, a genuine agency of contemporary folklore, led to radical artistic developments' (4), the front page of the *New York Times* comprising 'the visual technique of a Picasso, the literary technique of James Joyce' (3).[13] McLuhan effectively parallels his own technique with that of Joyce when he states that 'To write his epic of the modern Ulysses [Joyce] studied all his life the ads, the comics, the pulps, and popular speech' (58). Similarly, McLuhan concentrates not on the icons of high culture, but on comic strips and underwear ads. '[T]he student of popular culture,' he writes, 'develops the same sort of eye for morphological conformities as the folklorist and anthropologist do for the migration of symbols and situations. When the same patterns recur, these observers are alerted to the possibilities of similar underlying dynamics' (96). The implications of the collaged/montaged elements in the front-page presentation of news are both political and historical: politically, they imply that 'henceforth this planet is a single city' (3); historically (as in Arnold Toynbee's *A Study of History*), 'all civilizations [become] contemporary with our own' (3). McLuhan argues that it is the formal or structural implications of the newspaper that are significant, not the content, in the same way that modern art 'lack[s] ... a message' (4), and that this form inevitably points towards unity. Thus, if Giedion saw the presence of a scrap of newspaper in a Bracque collage as a sign of the 'everyday' or the 'common,' McLuhan sees it as asserting a structural kinship that vaults over such hierarchical distinctions. 'Mallarmé and Joyce refused to be distracted by the fashion-conscious sirens of content and subject-matter and proceeded straight to the utilization of the universal forms of the artistic process itself' (75).

There are interesting comparisons to be made concerning McLuhan's formulation of space and time in the periods immediately before and after his decisive 1953 essay, 'The Later Innis.' Writing in 'James Joyce: Trivial and Quadrivial' (1953), McLuhan argues that Newtonian science devalued rhetoric by advancing a spatial and pictorial model of the universe. Poetry thus sought to convey states of mind in terms of landscape, and psychology in terms of space. As a result, 'time, tradition, and language' (*IL* 25) are devalorized. McLuhan here counterpoints 'the spatial power and emptiness of the press' (*IL* 31), as figured in the Aeolus chapter of *Ulysses,* to 'reminiscences of great orations (communications in time).' Yet, in an essay published the following year (1954), 'Joyce, Mallarmé, and the Press,' McLuhan is much more concerned with making his points in the context of a spacetime dynamic, writing that *Ulysses* is structured as 'a newspaper

Front Page.

THESE are only a very few of the questions raised even by the quiet front page of *The New York Times*. Many further questions are raised by the more sensational newspapers. But any paper today is a collective work of art, a daily "book" of industrial man, an Arabian Night's entertainment in which a thousand and one astonishing tales are being told by an anonymous narrator to an equally anonymous audience.

It is on its technical and mechanical side that the front page is linked to the techniques of modern science and art. Discontinuity is in different ways a basic concept both of quantum and relativity physics. It is the way in which a Toynbee looks at civilizations, or a Margaret Mead at human cultures. Notoriously, it is the visual technique of a Picasso, the literary technique of James Joyce.

But it would be a mistake to join the chorus of voices which wails without intermission that "Discontinuity is chaos come again. It is irrationalism. It is the end." Quantum and relativity physics are not a fad. They have provided new facts about the world, new intelligibility, new insights into the universal fabric. Practically speaking, they mean that henceforth this planet is a single city. Far from making for irrationalism, these discoveries make irrationalism intolerable for the intelligent person. They demand much greater exertions of intelligence and a much higher level of personal and social integrity than have existed previously.

In the same way, the technique of Toynbee makes all civilizations contemporary with our own. The past is made immediately available as a working model for present political experiment. Margaret Mead's *Male and Female* illustrates a similar method. The cultural patterns of several societies, quite unrelated to one another, or to our own, are abruptly overlayered in cubist or Picasso style to provide a greatly enriched image of human potentialities. By this method the greatest possible detachment from our own immediate problems is achieved. The voice of reason is audible only to the detached observer.

And it is equally so with the popular modern press, despite all its faults. That huge landscape of the human family which is achieved by simply setting side by side disconnected items from China to Peru presents a daily image both of the complexity and similarity of human affairs which, in its total effect, is tending to abolish any provincial outlook.

Quite independently of good or bad editorial policies, the ordinary man is now accustomed to human-interest stories from every part of the globe. The sheer technique of world-wide newsgathering has created a new state of mind which has little to do with local or national

What's the score here? Why is a page of news a problem in orchestration?

How does the jazzy, ragtime discontinuity of press items link up with other modern art forms?

To achieve coverage from China to Peru, and also simultaneity of focus, can you imagine anything more effective than this front page cubism?

You never thought of a page of news as a symbolist landscape?

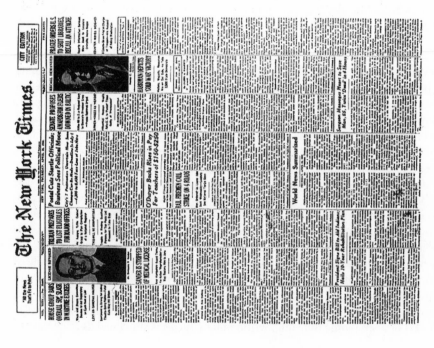

Figure 2.1. 'Front Page,' from McLuhan, *The Mechanical Bride*: the newspaper remained the classic example for McLuhan of orally empathic (acoustic) space, in that it fused the spatial, in its distribution of news items across the page, with the temporal – the date line.

landscape' (16); just as that novel is 'an abridgement of all space in a brief segment of time, [so] the *Wake* is a condensation of all time in the brief space of "Howth castle and environs"' (16). From a position characterizing space and time as oppositional (as Lewis and Innis had done, in their own ways), McLuhan, in the later essay, reconfigures these notions dynamically and relationally.

Mechanization Takes Command

The work cited most often in *The Mechanical Bride* is Margaret Mead's *Male and Female*.[14] Subtitled *A Study of the Sexes in a Changing World*, Mead's book seeks to account for changing gender roles in American culture by drawing major analogies with her anthropological studies of South Sea cultures; as such, her book is relevant to McLuhan's analyses in *The Mechanical Bride* of gender roles as manifested in comic strips such as *Blondie* (*MB* 68–9). Mead's book is congruent with others McLuhan cites in *The Mechanical Bride* to the extent that it seeks to critique normative notions (in this case of gender roles) that McLuhan saw as being in a state of flux occasioned by the end of the mechanical era. 'Since current art and science alike,' he writes, 'show that we have entered a new era, it is now especially important to recognize the intellectual limitations of the past era of mechanization. Market research today is a useful instance of new methods being employed in the old mechanical spirit. Dr. Margaret Mead, on the other hand, is using the same methods with that full sense of responsibility and respect for the vital interests and the harmonic relations of an entire society. Market research and opinion polls are not carried on in this spirit but rather with an eye to local and particular interests' (*MB* 50). This is especially interesting coming from the author who would theorize the global village, thereby demonstrating the interfusion of the local with the global, but that insight would come only at the end of the decade, when McLuhan had fully worked out the space/time interface.

The citations from Mead point, once again, to the tension between arrest and immersion that characterizes *The Mechanical Bride* as a whole. As Ellen Lupton states in her catalogue to the 1993 exhibition *Mechanical Brides: Women and Machines from Home to Office*,[15] McLuhan, along with Betty Friedan, was among the first to have 'look[ed] seriously at popular media ... [and] studied their own society in the way anthropologists examine foreign cultures' (10).[16] This anthropological aspect of McLuhan's study (evoked explicitly through his citations from Mead) implies a distancing from the cultural values he is critiquing. At the same time, he elsewhere espouses a methodology that allows him to use the very techniques he is critiquing. This tension is likewise evident in the work that stands most fully behind *The Mechanical Bride*, Siegfried Giedion's *Mechanization Takes Command: A Contribution to Anonymous History* (1948).[17]

Giedion's book provides an overview of mechanical invention, from the classical era to the present, with the emphasis very much on the period from *circa* 1800 to the achievement of 'full mechanization' (ix) in the period 1918 to 1939. The mechanization of agriculture, food preparation, the home (especially the kitchen and bath), and transportation all come under Giedion's scrutiny. An important feature of Giedion's book is its insistent paralleling of mechanical with artistic production, to suggest both 'how deeply mechanization penetrated man's inner existence' (44) and how 'machines, these marvels of efficiency, are transformed into irrational objects, laden with irony, while introducing a new aesthetic language' (44). *Mechanization Takes Command*, like *Space, Time and Architecture* (1941), is concerned with the history of space. Although Giedion's major focus is on the nineteenth and early-twentieth centuries, he traces the thread of his subject historically, from the European Middle Ages to early-twentieth-century America. As McLuhan wrote in a 1949 review of *Mechanization*, '[i]t is this intense preoccupation with contemporary problems of thought and feeling, and with the occasional triumphs of a unified sensibility, that has led Giedion to a study of American life which has been rivaled, and at a different level, only by De Tocqueville.'[18] Giedion assigns to the European Middle Ages the original moment of what he calls 'the dignity of space ... [which] lasted until nineteenth-century industrialism blurred the feelings' (301). A particular characteristic of medieval space is the fact that 'a medieval room seems finished [*sic*] even when it contains no furniture. It is never bare' (301), a concept McLuhan repeated almost verbatim in a 1974 letter: 'Siegfried Giedion in *Mechanization Takes Command* has a section on medieval comfort, in which he explains that a medieval space was furnished [*sic*] even when empty, because of its acoustic properties' (letter to R. Murray Schafer, 16 December 1974, *L* 508).[19] The notion that such space is acoustic was McLuhan's, and it goes some way towards explaining Giedion's comment: within an oral (or scribal) culture, social life is organized around oral/acoustic properties and values that are organic and holistic, and this is reflected in spatial constructions – the medieval room is 'of a piece' with its furnishings, in other words. McLuhan's 1974 interpretation of Giedion's comment, however, indicates the extent to which Giedion's 'spatial history' lacks nuance; where McLuhan posits different constructions of space, from the invention of the alphabet through manuscript culture to Gutenberg and then the electronic era, Giedion's view of space is much more homogeneous (and nostalgic). It is mechanization, for Giedion, that breaks down the organic values of space, leading to what Giedion calls 'spatial disintegration' in which 'furniture loses its relatedness to the surrounding space' (*MTC* 342; cf his reference to the 'devaluation of space' in the comment to fig. 193, p. 336).

The thesis of Giedion's book, however, is much more productive than his notion of space would imply; he argues that the unifying element in the history of mechanization is the attempt to capture movement. Giedion sees these attempts as culminating in E.-J. Marey's 1885 invention of a photogun designed to 'register phases of a bird's flight' (*MTC* 21, fig. 6) through its capability of producing sixteen exposures a minute. With this device, Marey sought to render 'the true form of a movement as it is described in space' (21), but which nevertheless '"escapes the eye"' (Giedion quoting Marey, 21).This latter point is highly significant and serves to pinpoint the paradoxical enterprise on which Marey was engaged: what he sought was to express visually elements of movement, dynamism, and flux, which, by their nature, exist outside the realm of the visual as constructed by perspectival space, which is to say outside the realm of the mechanical. As Marta Braun puts it in her study of Marey, his 'photographs shattered ... [Renaissance temporal and spatial] unity; viewers now had to unravel the successive parts of the work in order to understand that they were looking not at several men moving in single file, but at a single figure successively occupying a series of positions in space.'[20] Marey's experiments demonstrated, in effect, that the dimension of movement in time was inseparable from the dimension of space. Indeed, as Mary Ann Doane points out, Marey 'viewed the antagonistic relationship between space and time as a potential obstruction to his project, which, because it was explicitly concerned with movement, required references to *both* spatial and temporal coordinates.'[21] Significantly, Marey saw space *and* time as '"the two elements of *movement*"' (quoted by Braun 83; my emphasis), thereby indicating his awareness that space, like time, was a dynamic concept. The implications of Marey's experiments for Giedion's history of the mechanical era were thus profound: the experiments highlighted the tendency of mechanistic culture to produce space and time as separate categories (the problem that space–time managers such as F.W. Taylor and Frank Gilbreth sought to analyse), and yet they called this separation into question by requiring the interfusion of space and time if the experiments were to succeed. The fact that Giedion saw Marey's experiments as the ultimate *fulfilment* (rather than dissolution) of the mechanical era indicates the extent to which Giedion's thought was bound up with the mechanistic paradigm, even though he deeply critiqued it. Similarly, McLuhan's indebtedness to Giedion in *The Mechanical Bride* is such that, although McLuhan critiques mechanistic culture there, he does not fully extend this critique into a reconfiguration of his binaristic notions of space and time underpinning that critique; this would occur only as a result of his reading Innis.

Works of Art in the Age of Mechanical Reproduction

Mary Anne Doane has suggested that Marey's use of multiple photographic images to capture movement is symptomatic of 'a discursive thematic of excess and oversaturation' inaugurated by 'the advent of mechanical reproduction' (Doane 313), an advent McLuhan tied to the invention of the printing press.[22] What this excess sought to represent was 'a spatial continuum without the gaps or lacks conducive to the production of historical significance' (Doane 313). The fact that this excess was devoted to the capture of *movement* indicated that time was 'no longer the benign phenomenon most easily grasped by the notion of flow but a troublesome and anxiety-producing entity that must be thought in relation to management, regulation, storage, and representation ... [within] the philosophical, psychoanalytic, and scientific realms' (Doane 314–15).[23] In artistic terms, these changes in the perception of time and space were among the major factors opening up possibilities for modes of representation in other than perspectival configuration. One such mode was montage, which rendered the spatial continuum as a series of discontinuities and was a significant response to the dehistoricization attendant upon the (photographic) work of art in the age of mechanical reproduction. This is the *procédé* that Giedion suggests he is employing in *Mechanization Takes Command*: 'The meaning of history arises in the uncovering of relationships ... These relations will vary with the shifting point of view, for, like constellations of stars, they are ceaselessly in change ... History writing is ever tied to the fragment. The known facts are often scattered broadcast, like stars across the firmament' (*MTC* 2–3).[24] Given that the 'spatial continuum' was a product of perspective, to render it discontinuous one would have to interrupt the space it produced, juxtapose its parts, open up gaps in it, and make it subject to difference. This disruption of visual space became McLuhan's methodology in *The Mechanical Bride* (and more radically in works such as *Verbi-Voco-Visual Explorations*,

The Medium Is the Massage, War and Peace in the Global Village, Counterblast, Through the Vanishing Point, and *Culture Is Our Business*).[25] McLuhan cites (in *MB*) Sergei Eisenstein's *Film Sense*, which quotes René Guilleré's comment that in jazz '"Rhythm is stated by angle"' whereas '"Classical music was based on planes ... In jazz all elements are brought to the foreground. This is an important law which can be found in painting, in stage design, in films, and in the poetry of this period"' (87). This foregrounding – the musical equivalent of montage – describes an annihilation of the Renaissance norms of perspective: instead of a single point of view, there are many, competing points of view (though the term is rendered meaningless by this multiplicity). McLuhan had encountered such a technique in the later Innis; as he writes in his 1953 article of that title, 'in his later prose the linear development of paragraph perspectives is abandoned almost entirely in favour of the rapid montage of single shots. He juxtaposes one condensed observation with another, mounts one insight or image on another in quick succession to create a sense of the multiple relationships in process of undergoing rapid development from the impact of specific technological changes' (LI 389).[26]

In considering montage as especially tailored to critiquing visual space, McLuhan can be productively compared with Walter Benjamin,[27] to whom he is linked by a mutual interest in the work of Giedion.[28] Benjamin was particularly influenced by Giedion's insistence on the dreamlike quality of late-nineteenth-century architecture (Buck-Morss 85), a quality Benjamin related to the work being produced then by engineers, especially in the area of ironwork scaffolding as used for the structure of arcades (Buck-Morss 39): 'Benjamin noted that these buildings were connected with transitoriness in both the spatial sense (as railroad stations, places of transit) and the temporal one (as galleries for world expositions, typically torn down after they closed). Spared the self-conscious mediation of "art," such structures settled into the collective imagination in an unconscious form, as buildings for use rather than contemplation – at least for a time' (Buck-Morss 129–30). It was this embodiment of a collective unconscious that Giedion had seen in these arcades, an insight he repeated in *Mechanization Takes Command* through the notion of 'anonymous history.' For Benjamin, as Buck-Morss points out, this notion of the 'unconscious' was double-pronged, 'on the one hand, because of its distracted dreaming state, and on the other, because it was unconscious of itself, composed of atomized individuals, consumers who imagined their commodity dreamworld to be uniquely personal ... and who experienced their membership in the collectivity only in an isolated, alienating sense, as an anonymous component of the crowd' (Buck-Morss 260). Benjamin's political project, then, was to awaken these sleepers, and he sought to do this especially in his vast *Arcades* project, which was to take the form of juxtaposed texts and images,[29] what Benjamin called dialectical images: '"In the dialectical image, the past of a particular epoch [...] appears before the eyes of [... a particular, present epoch] in which humanity, rubbing its eyes, recognizes precisely this dream *as* a dream. It is in this moment that the historian takes upon himself the task of dream interpretation."'[30] The *Arcades* project is thus '"concerned with dissolving mythology into the space of history,"'[31] resulting, according to Michael Jennings, in 'the construction of a new, alternative "image-space" (*Bildraum*) which might have a revolutionary effect on human understanding.'[32] It was in conceiving this project that Benjamin turned to montage.

The most telling aspect of montage, for Benjamin, was the fact that 'the image's ideational elements remain unreconciled, rather than fusing into one "harmonizing perspective,"' as Buck-Morss puts it (67, quoting from a letter of Benjamin to Adorno). McLuhan utilized this aspect of montage, as well as its tendency (as Buck-Morss expresses it) to '[make] visible the gap between sign and referent' (68). He accomplished this in *The Mechanical Bride* by the use of boldface text, designed to undermine the seamless relationship between text and image in the ads to which it was juxtaposed, drawing attention to itself and the ironic questions it framed. McLuhan's procedure involved the use of appropriation, decontextualization, and recontextualization to produce irony and parody, and the elimination of connectives, such that each sentence appears to be foregrounded. What is significant in the montage practices of both Benjamin and McLuhan is that montage becomes an agent for the historicization of space. As Judith Stamps has noted, 'Benjamin accepted Lukács's critical analysis of the spatial bias of modernity. But he liked to juxtapose that analysis with a mystical outlook which viewed the same bias as a possible source of liberatory inspiration ... Benjamin argued that the present-mindedness of the visual society was already a kind of living montage or quasi-constellation. It had a chaotic, discontinuous quality that was one of the sources from which the new sound-oriented paradigms drew their inspiration' (*Unth* 38). Montage (as a non-linear practice) is thus another of the ways in which the historicization of space becomes linked with orality (the acoustic being the realm of non-linear signification) in McLuhan's work, as his citation from Eisenstein of the passage about jazz (*MB* 87) suggests.

As Benjamin puts it in his well-known essay, the mechanically reproduced work of art has a significant effect on perception: 'With the close-up, space expands; with slow motion, movement is extended ... Evidently a different nature opens itself to the camera than opens to the naked eye – if only because an unconsciously penetrated space is substituted for a space consciously explored by man ... The camera introduces us to unconscious optics as does psychoanalysis to unconscious impulses' ('Work of Art' 236–7). Benjamin does not see these changes as necessarily negative – 'the fact that the new mode of participation first appeared in a disreputable form must not confuse the spectator' (239). Similarly, McLuhan writes in *The Mechanical Bride* that because an ad employs 'the same technique as Picasso' (80), the technique is not thereby debased; rather, the technique is debased by the service in which it is placed. This is to posit a redemptive quality in technology, but only by virtue of splitting form off from content, a separation that tends to belie McLuhan's insistence on the importance of his subject matter, an inconsistency he would overcome only by aligning medium with message and by insisting on the coterminous nature of criticism and art.[33]

A prime example of this blurring of the critical and artistic genres, for McLuhan and Giedion alike, was the work of Marcel Duchamp. 'Marcel Duchamp and others,' Giedion writes, 'resort to elements such as machines, mechanisms, and ready-made articles as some of the few true products of the period, to liberate themselves from the rotten art of the ruling taste' (*MTC* 44). To illustrate this suggestion, Giedion juxtaposes photographs by Marey and by Eadweard Muybridge[34] with Duchamp's *Nude Descending the* [*sic*] *Staircase* (*MTC* 27), a work that, like Marey's photographs, alludes to the collapsing of space and time into a single spacetime. McLuhan refers to this work in *The Mechanical Bride* as 'an artichoke doing a striptease' (100),[35] and, in an unpublished, undated note on Duchamp,[36] he describes it in terms of a critique of the mechanical age: 'Duchamp's nude reveals the fragmented, analytic abstractions of the industrial process as a skeletal charade, a retrieval of the ancient rituals of *le danse macabre*. Far beyond any process known to the medieval world, the dance of the machines during the past two centuries represents the most violent and lethal expression of human somnambulism and self-hypnotism. Duchamp's nude is a comic mime of the descent of a somnambulist robot world, via the stages of a precisely etiolated rational pattern of relentless progress' (a–b). The breaking up of visual continuity in the *Nude* enables other 'tactile-kinesthetic' (b) values to be asserted, and in this way the painting 'is enormously more rich and involving than photographic representation' (b). Duchamp's work thus figures at once the death of the mechanical age and the birth of the new 'electric age of *quanta* and quantum mechanics [which] returns to the unvisualisable universe of instant speeds and sub-visual resonance ... Duchamp's nude is the ghost of the old mechanical world stripped to its iconic pattern' (c).

It was another of Duchamp's 'erotic apparatuses' that, as Harold Rosenberg noted, 'unmistakably inspired' *The Mechanical Bride*,[37] namely *The Bride Stripped Bare by Her Bachelors, Even* (commonly known as *The Large Glass*). According to Rosalind Krauss, it is 'the physics of vision [Duchamp] wants to stress' in this work,[38] but from an '"antiretinal"' and thus '"conceptual"' position[39] (Krauss quoting Duchamp 108). This amounts to an 'attack on the whole system of the visual as that is put into place by mainstream modernism' (Krauss 123). Duchamp achieves this effect through highly economical means: two large pieces of glass (recalling those behind which reposed the commodities in Benjamin's arcades) are framed in and bisected by metal sheathing, figuring non-human, mechanical forms, together with those that are vaguely organic in appearance.[40] In Linda Dalrymple Henderson's description, 'the sense of the artist's hand has been replaced, as Duchamp wished, by the look of machine fabrication in a variety of materials on glass. Not only is the style of the *Large Glass* machine-oriented; the subject matter of this work is set forth in creaturely machine images.'[41] Henderson goes on to describe Duchamp's apparatus as 'a lovemaking machine made up of a "Bride" above and a complex "Bachelor Apparatus" below' (130). The fact that the two sections are separated by a metal strip implies, however, the 'split that exists in our period between thought and feeling' as Giedion expressed it (*MTC* [v]), and echoes as well McLuhan's comment about 'our highly cerebral Sex life and the visual stimulants provided by ads and entertainment' (*MB* 79).[42] Here, private space has disappeared at the same time as art has been removed from its traditional space of valorization; Duchamp embodies both of these elements in an image of the mechanization of sexuality, his Bride being, in Henderson's terms, 'automobilelike' (*4D* 119).[43] McLuhan argues that one of the prime ways in which sex has been mechanized is through the statistical survey. In the exhibit titled 'Eye Appeal' (where 'eye' displaces 'sex'), he suggests that the extension of statistical market surveys to sexual attitudes (via such studies as William Kinsey's *Sexual Behavior of the Human Male*) is likewise an extension of the mechanical into the sexual (a concept to which he would return both in the interview with Norden and in *Understanding Media*, where he writes that 'man becomes ... the sex organs of the machine world' [*UM* 46]). McLuhan's argumentation in 'Eye Appeal' merits attention. He begins by reminding us that 'numbers, in statistical science, appear as curves' (*MB*

79) – this in juxtaposition to an ad for Mennen Skin Bracer that features a woman dressed in a bikini. Thus, 'the relation between these facts and the present ad ... is not so whimsical as a mere glance might lead one to suppose' (*MB* 79). Through the repetition of the concept of the 'curve' (together with the agency of a pun) McLuhan is able to extend the concept of the mechanical into the organic – 'the interfusion of sex and technology' (*MB* 94) – while at the same time alluding to the 'curved' space of non-Euclidean geometry that promises a renewed access to the organic insofar as it is non-uniform and defined by experience in depth.

Duchamp's *Large Glass* provides a productive gloss on McLuhan's argument. According to Henderson, Duchamp was concerned with expressing a 'new physics' of 'non-Euclidean geometry' (*4D* 132). While in works such as the *Nude Descending a Staircase* this took the form of rejecting 'Euclid's assumption of the indeformability of figures in movement' (132), in *The Large Glass* Duchamp was interested in contrasting the 'four-dimensional Bride' with 'the three-dimensionality of the Bachelors [which] would be emphasized by a strict application of the canons of Renaissance perspective' (132), creating thus a '"fractured space."'[44] The immediate effect of this conflict of spaces in the *Glass* is the demonstration that Euclidean space was not natural but a construct, and specifically a construct of mechanical culture (or, more generally, of a mechanistic concept of the universe). Duchamp had arrived at this position through his reading of Henri Poincaré's theories of perceptual space, which were subdivided into visual, tactile, and motor, the last of these being a space of pure sensation (cf *4D* 82). It is this space that is identified with the Bride and that remains inaccessible. Like the *Nude*, the *Bride* paradoxically reveals how the eye diminishes the sensual, how 'eye appeal' (in McLuhan's formulation) comes to replace sex (or sensory) appeal. To escape from the world dominated by the eye was to escape from the de-eroticized mechanical world into a resensualized world promising (like Bucke's cosmic consciousness) greater sensory awareness.

Psychopathologies

If Giedion's *Mechanization Takes Command* is *The Mechanical Bride*'s most immediate intertext, Freud's *Civilization and Its Discontents* glosses the wider concerns of McLuhan's book, which, according to its jacket, 'might well be termed a psychological *100,000,000 Guinea Pigs.*' The sense that mechanical civilization comprises a mass dreamwork within 'the collective public mind' (v) pervades *The Mechanical Bride*[45] (as it pervades Benjamin's *Arcades* project). 'Industrial man,' writes McLuhan in the first exhibit, 'lives amid a great flowering of technical and mechanical imagery of whose rich human symbolism he is mainly unconscious' (*MB* 4), given his 'dream state' (10). McLuhan states that 'the folklore of ... industrial society' resulted from the Cartesian 'wish for a universal mathematical unity in thought and society' (50), and that in mechanical culture 'we are justified in seeing a wish-fulfillment on a huge scale as surely as the psychologist is justified in deciphering wishes in the dream symbols of his patients' (50).[46] The implications of this insight are profound; as McLuhan puts it in his article 'Inside Blake and Hollywood,' 'all the conscious intellectual activity of an industrial society is directed to non-human ends.'[47] It is precisely because of this displacement that the 'extensions of man' must be studied, for in them now lies the essence of humanity. Through this formulation, McLuhan places himself as cultural critic in the position of the psychoanalyst, trying to 'find the clue to understanding and guiding our world in more reasonable courses' (*MB* 50), such that '[c]onsciousness will come as a relief' (*MB* 128).[48] Notably, McLuhan writes in the *The Gutenberg Galaxy* that 'it is not helpful to talk about the unconscious as the domain of the unknown, or as an area more profound than ordinary consciousness' (*GG* 245); in fact, the unconscious was for McLuhan 'the ever-mounting slag-heap of rejected awareness' (*GG* 245), as if the unconscious had become extruded into the technological environment (as Benjamin suggested it had). McLuhan's task was thus the opposite of Freud's: to restore to us our *conscious* selves by a sharpening of critical awareness. And because it was a mass dream from which we must awake, this heightened awareness promised nothing less than a cosmic consciousness.

McLuhan cast himself as a Freudian from the beginning of his career, subtitling one of his unachieved works 'A Study in the Psychology of Culture' (*M&M* 70); as Jonathan Miller remarked, McLuhan sought to do ' "for the fact of visual space what Freud did for sex, namely to reveal its pervasiveness in the structuring of human affairs." '[49] He had been introduced by his St Louis friend Felix Giovanelli to the work of the Freudian Gershon Legman, whose journal *Neurotica* had published parts of *The Mechanical Bride* (*M&M* 120), as well as McLuhan's 'The Psychopathology of *Time* and *Life*' (1949). This essay is directly related to the general thematic of *The Mechanical Bride* through its argument that these magazines contain 'all the senescent and servile appeal of the brittle and lifeless perfection of machined thoughts and feelings. Mr. Luce wants the best imitation of thought and feeling that the machine can produce.'[50] In this article (as in the book), McLuhan focuses, thus, not on the thought processes of human subjects, as Freud did in *The Psychopathology of Everyday Life* (1901), but on the 'capsulated thoughts' ('Psychopathology of *Time*' 159) and emotions of magazines and their advertisements. Whereas Freud deals with a number of case histories in his chapter on 'Slips of the Tongue,' for McLuhan it is the ad itself that 'is like a slip of the tongue that reveals a hidden attitude' (*MB* 137). The subject has become displaced in an 'annihilation of the human ego' (*MB* 33) that has taken place through the identification of humans with their machines. This process McLuhan eventually formulated in terms of extension and amputation, a dynamic he metaphorized through the myth of Narcissus, which became to his work what the Oedipus myth was to Freud's.

Despite any intellectual affinities that McLuhan might have felt with Gershon Legman, when he came to write *The Mechanical Bride* it resembled not at all Legman's *Love and Death*[51] (even though he refers to Legman a number of times, as Legman does McLuhan once). *Love and Death*, a study of comic books, is primarily concerned with the fact that descriptions of murder are acceptable in literature whereas those of sexuality are not – hence the subtitle, *A Study in Censorship*. Marchand records that Legman was 'too Freudian' for McLuhan's taste (*M&M* 120). McLuhan, it is true, tended to be unorthodox in his reading of Freud – 'Freud on the causes of homosexuality is just a bloody comic,' he wrote to Giovanelli in a letter of 30 April 1949: 'Penis envy for girls, castration terror for men' (*L* 213). He preferred the later, more socially engaged works of Freud (and his 'culturalist' followers such as Karen Horney),[52] writing, for example (in a letter to Rollo

May dated 14 December 1972), that 'Freud paid no attention to the *ground* of psychic conditioning, except tangentially, in *Civilization and Its Discontents*' (*L* 458).[53] It was the 'merely individualist psychology of Freud [that had] flunked out in the new age of tribal and corporate identities' (*L* 393). He was thus better disposed towards Horney, who critiqued 'Freud's disregard of cultural factors' and his tendency 'to attribute social phenomena primarily to psychic factors and these primarily to biological factors.'[54] Another major difference between the cultural theories of Freud and of McLuhan concerns the status of 'civilization.' Whereas Freud sought to present civilization as natural, in that it grew out of certain basic desires, civilization was for McLuhan the product of a specific set of technologies. Writing in 'What T.V. Is Really Doing to Your Children' (1967), he states that '[o]ver a long period of time the Western world has built a society based upon the kinds of experience and order derived from the written and printed word – a literate society. We call it civilization, in contrast to the patterns of experience and action that prevail in nonliterate, or primitive, societies.'[55] Nor was our perceptual life a given; rather, it was the product of certain ratios among the senses, and thus subject to change. To Freud's comment that 'what we call our civilization is largely responsible for our misery, and ... we should be much happier if we gave it up and returned to primitive conditions' (*C&D* 38), McLuhan replied that such a return was imminent (though with a different emphasis on 'primitive'). 'Our man-made visual environment,' he writes in *War and Peace in the Global Village*, 'which has persisted with various modulations of stress since the fifth century B.C., constitutes what we call the Western world. It's our own ingenuity and inventiveness that guarantee that this environment must now be superseded' (13). As Milton Klonsky has asserted, 'Freud's Olympian pronunciamento: "Where id was, there ego shall be," has [in McLuhan] been strangely reversed.'[56] McLuhan did not share Freud's linearly Darwinian model of civilization and his Faustian notion of *streben* – 'a striving towards the two confluent goals of utility and a yield of pleasure' (*C&D* 48). And if, for McLuhan, civilization was mutable, so was the sexuality that Freud placed at the origin of civilization. Writing on 'The Future of Sex,' McLuhan states that 'the members of the younger generation show in their clothes and their music, their activities and their language, that they reject unequivocally the sexual world of their elders.'[57] He goes on: 'men and women are differentiated in ways that go far beyond biological imperatives' (12). Indeed, McLuhan saw that Freud's notion of 'man [having] ... become a kind of prosthetic God' through the 'auxiliary organs' provided him 'by his science and technology' (*C&D* 43–4) had profoundly displaced the biological realm of being.

   As McLuhan sensed, Freud's predominantly linear, temporal model of civilization also underpinned his notion of the psyche. '[I]n mental life nothing which has once been formed can perish ... everything is somehow preserved' Freud writes in *Civilization and Its Discontents* (16). In explaining this, Freud makes an analogy with the history of the city of Rome, where the past is preserved only haphazardly, and often only in ruins. In the psyche, however, 'nothing that has once come into existence will have passed away and all the earlier phases of development continue to exist alongside the latest one' (18). Represented as the history of Rome, the psyche would have to be figured in such a manner that 'on the Piazza of the Pantheon we should find not only the Pantheon of to-day, as it was bequeathed to us by Hadrian, but, on the same site, the original edifice erected by Agrippa; indeed, the same piece of ground would be supporting the church of Santa Maria sopra Minerva and the ancient temple over which it was built' (18). Clearly, Freud concludes, '[i]f we want to represent historical sequence in spatial terms we can only do it by juxtaposition in space: the same space cannot have two different contents ... It shows us how far we are from mastering the characteristics of mental life by representing them in pictorial terms' (19). *Civilization and Its Discontents* thus confronts the problem of representing the temporal processes of the mind spatially.[58] Freud addresses this problem through the famous analogy with Rome, suggesting that the spacetime of the mind can only be represented outside the realm of the perspectival, or 'pictorial,' as Freud puts it (19).[59] The problem encountered here by Freud is similar to the one faced by Marey and Duchamp: how to represent a temporal experience in spatial terms, or through a spatial medium. Giedion indirectly throws the problem into relief by positing a connection between Freud and F.W. Taylor (*MTC* 100), the founder of space/time management studies, which combined 'scientific management and experimental psychology' (100).[60] What linked Freud and Taylor was not simply their interest in 'revealing the inside of processes' (100), as Giedion states, but their desire to *represent* these processes *spatially.*[61] McLuhan likewise saw Taylor's study of processes as posing a problem of representation. Writing in *Take Today* (1972), he stated that 'Taylor, by pushing this arrested fragmented montage of actions to an extreme point of analysis, was in fact moving from the factory to the film form of organization. As soon as the film form is speeded up, it loses all its jerky still-shot character and becomes an involving experience ... With speed-up, the pattern of the process manifests itself again abundantly' (*TT* 257).

Like Freud, for whom modernity had become 'a pathology of temporality' (Doane 315),[62] McLuhan located the terror of modern culture in the temporality of 'automatic processes and routines' (*MB* 85). Both theorists faced a similar impasse in the attempt to represent this space/time conflict historically. 'The impasse of [Freud's] spatial model of memory forces him to produce a theory of temporality as the discontinuous mode of operation of the pysche itself,' writes Doane (315); 'time is therefore conceptualized within the problematic of determining what is storable, what is representable' (323). In *The Mechanical Bride*, McLuhan left unresolved the historical distinction he had made between space and time (the attribution of a spatial orientation to primitive cultures and a temporal one to technologized cultures), on the one hand, and, on the other, his refusal of such a distinction through notions of cultural simultaneity and of space/time collapse. Like Marey and Giedion, Freud and the McLuhan of *The Mechanical Bride* had conceptualized space and time as comprising separate realms, while the thrust of the arguments they made through these categories problematized such exclusivity. Thus, Freud sought to supplant the topographical model of the psyche with a dynamic one; Marey sought to represent movement through a spatial medium; Giedion looked for 'the power to integrate' (*MTC* 719) space and time within mechanization itself.

Duchamp's formulation of the problematic was telling: he connected the perspectival construction of space to the mechanical era, within which the spacetime problem would remain forever frustrating, because perspectival space excluded the temporal dimension. He represented this problematic in his *Rotoreliefs* (1935), discs with spiral designs that were then mechanically rotated (forerunners of kinetic art), thus undermining what Rosalind Krauss has called 'the modernist campaign for visual mastery.'[63] Krauss

continues: 'For the throb of his revolving discs, pulsing as they do with erotic sugges-
tiveness, opens the very concept of visual autonomy – of a form of experience that is
wholly and purely optical, owing nothing to time – to the invasion of a sense of dense,
corporeal pressure. Not simply because as the spirals swell and deflate they suggest a
succession of organs, breast turning into eye turning into belly turning into womb, or
even the pulse of erotic friction. But because the pulse itself, in its diastolic repetitiveness, associates itself with the density of nervous tissue, with its temporality of feedback,
of response time, of retention and protension, of the fact that, without this temporal
wave, no experience at all, visual or otherwise, could happen' (135). This critique of the
visual as a denial of the senses-in-ratio (or *sensus communis*) was crucial to McLuhan's
own work; it was precisely the mechanization of the sensory that had led to the
displacement emblematized by McLuhan in his title *The Mechanical Bride*. This displacement was directly tied to the displacement of the sensory ratio by the predominance
of the visual that had been achieved in the era of print, the printing press being the great
original of mechanical culture. A similar critique of visual space is made in Duchamp's
The Large Glass, which represents an eternal case of auto(-)eroticism generated by a
concept of space – visual space – defined by fixed positions and bounded linearities, all
of which Duchamp subverts by the use of a transparent medium, glass – the 'light
through' of stained glass (and television, as McLuhan would have it) as opposed to the
'light on' technology of the printed page and the cinema.[64] McLuhan might have been
referring to *The Large Glass* when he wrote in 'Joyce, Mallarmé, and the Press': 'for that
school of thought for which the external world is an opaque prison, art can never be
regarded as a source of knowledge but only as a moral discipline' (*IL* 12). This is
likewise one of the major themes in *The Mechanical Bride*.

   The Mechanical Bride reflects the prime lesson that McLuhan had learned about
space and time from Innis: that they were relational. In the works McLuhan wrote after
The Mechanical Bride, he followed this model through to its logical endpoint, dynamizing
the relationship itself such that it issued in a dynamic theory of spacetime. In *The
Mechanical Bride*, however, McLuhan had yet to formulate these insights, and the work
remains conflicted in its conceptions of space and time. That McLuhan clearly perceived
this spacetime problematic in *The Mechanical Bride* is evident in his commentary on the
ad for Berkshire stockings, which he likens to a painting by Picasso, the connection
being the fact that both use 'juxtaposition and contrast' and a 'withholding [of] the
syntactical connection' to achieve 'a single image of great intensity' (80). Such techniques, he goes on to note, are also part of the methodology of physics, as A.N.
Whitehead states in *Science and the Modern World*: '"my theory involves the entire
abandonment of the notion that simple location is the primary way in which things are
involved in space-time"' (80).[65] McLuhan referred to this spacetime as 'acoustic space';
it was his 'talking cure'[66] for a civilization beset by the discontents of mechanization.

   While never a Freudian, McLuhan nevertheless maintained in his works subsequent to
The Mechanical Bride a residue of ideas from his encounter with Freud. The importance
of jokes as elaborated by Freud in *Jokes and Their Relation to the Unconscious*, the
references to the Narcissus myth, the significance of sensory apprehension,[67] and the
concept of prosthetic extension[68] were all issues McLuhan addressed throughout his
career. McLuhan's subsequent distancing of himself from *The Mechanical Bride* had
less to do with his position *vis-à-vis* Freud, however, than with his realization that to

critique mechanization was to critique an era that had already been superseded by the electric age. As he said of *The Mechanical Bride* in his 1959 article 'Myth and Mass Media,' 'Turning literary guns on the new iconology of the Madison Avenue world is easy. It is easy to reveal mechanism in a postmechanical era. But I failed at that time to see that we had already passed out of the mechanistic age into the electronic, and that it was this fact that made mechanism both obtrusive and repugnant.'[69] It is clear that McLuhan perceived this problem while writing the book; what he lacked, however, was a way of formulating it. As Donald Theall has suggested, 'McLuhan could well have turned from *The Mechanical Bride*, because he did not know how to encompass at that early stage the complexities of the social, aesthetic and neurocultural components of the texts which he felt had to be simultaneously held in perspective to meet the demands of his multidisciplinary program for a new humanism.'[70] He required an aetiology of the mechanical that would effectively allow him to encapsulate the differences between the mechanical and the electronic such that they would provide him with the basis for a grand cultural theory along the lines of *Civilization and Its Discontents*, which remained an important model. This panoramic element was provided by Innis's notion that all technological media manifest themselves through biases of space or time. The element linking the psychical to the mechanical McLuhan derived from an analysis by J.C. Carothers of how print technology influenced psychic response to phenomena.

Carothers's 'Culture, Psychiatry, and Written Word' (1959) was, McLuhan acknowledged, the direct stimulus for *The Gutenberg Galaxy* (*M&M* 153). The theme of Carothers's article is that 'literacy in a society, or the lack of it, plays an important part in shaping the minds of men and the patterns of their mental breakdown.'[71] Comparing these patterns in sample groups of Africans and western Europeans, Carothers notes the coincidence of literacy with such psychopathologies as schizophrenia (307), leading him to the conclusion that 'whereas the Western child is early introduced to ... a multiplicity of items and events which constrain him to think in terms of spatiotemporal relations and mechanical causation, the African child receives instead an education which depends much more exclusively on the spoken word and which is relatively highly charged with drama and emotion' (308). The implications, suggest Carothers, are that 'rural Africans live largely in a world of sound ... whereas the western European lives much more in a visual world which is on the whole indifferent to him, and that this difference is of fundamental importance for the development of thought' (308). It is significant that Carothers arrives at this thesis without invoking Freud, for the implications of Carothers's piece is the destabilization of the Eurocentric (as well as patriarchal, visual, mechanistic) model of the psyche that Freud developed. Carothers's argument was important to McLuhan for the synthesis it achieved among a number of diverse elements with which McLuhan had been grappling for at least a decade: psychic response, orality[72] and literacy, spatiotemporal relations, the visual and the acoustic, and cultural relativity. To these elements, McLuhan's encounter with Innis added a vast historical scaffolding that McLuhan brought to bear on the writing of his next major work, *The Gutenberg Galaxy*. While McLuhan invokes a Freudian *locus classicus* at the beginning of *The Gutenberg Galaxy* – the opening scene of King Lear (analysed by Freud in 'The Theme of the Three Caskets' [1913]) – he expands Freud's psychodrama of 'dumbness' and 'death'[73] into a history of print culture and its coming demise in the era of electronic media.

CHAPTER THREE

The Physics of Flatland

*[L]andscape plays an indispensable role in every stage of both fission and fusion.
In art as in physics fission preceded fusion.*

Marshall McLuhan, 'The Aesthetic Moment in Landscape Poetry'

Explorations in Space

In the work he produced after *The Mechanical Bride*, McLuhan developed a broad
historical framework in which he situated mechanical culture in relation to the invention
of printing, the oral culture that preceded print, and the emerging electronic culture. At
the same time, he developed a dynamic methodology with which to analyse such
changes – a dynamic of 'immersion' rather than 'arrest.' Giedion's *Mechanization Takes
Command* and Freud's *Civilization and Its Discontents* demonstrated to McLuhan
(though in different ways) that the notion of arrest was inadequate, both metaphorically
and methodologically, to the dynamic of electronic 'speed-up.' This methodological
insufficiency was figured as a spatial problematic: Giedion's *Mechanization* had suggested that Marey's experiments to capture movement through photography pointed
towards the end of mechanical space; Freud's Roman metaphor showed the inadequacy
of three dimensions to represent psychic history. These problems, furthermore, were
interrelated: Giedion suggested that the mechanical world was a vast *traumspiel*, a
phantasmagoria – Locke's swoon (*GG* 17); Freud's work had convinced McLuhan that
what he wanted to produce was a psychopathology of our waking rather than our
unconscious lives – if 'a culture can be locked in the sleep of any one sense' (*GG* 73),
what McLuhan wanted to do was wake it up. In this way, McLuhan's historical concerns
(as developed in *The Gutenberg Galaxy*) extended to a concern in *Understanding Media*
with the psychology of perception and how perceptions conditioned – indeed, constructed – social space. McLuhan increasingly addressed these psychodynamical issues
through an analogy with spacetime as it was formulated in contemporary physics.[1]

   McLuhan succinctly states the problematic raised by both Giedion and Freud within
the first fifty pages or so of *The Gutenberg Galaxy*. Citing Giedion's discussion in
Mechanization Takes Command of Eadwaerd Muybridge's stop-action photographs, and

Marey's use of the 'myograph' (*GG* 44; the name appears as 'Etienne Jules Morey'), McLuhan comments that in these photographs 'the object is translated out of organic or simultaneous form into a static or pictorial mode. By revolving a sequence of such static or pictorial spaces at a sufficient speed, *the illusion of organic wholeness, or interplay of spaces* [emphasis added], is created. Thus, the wheel finally becomes the means of moving our culture away from the machine' (44; cf 242).[2] Cinematic movement, in other words, belonged not to electronic but to mechanical culture.[3] '[T]ranslating motion into visual terms' was the ultimate expression of the 'medieval world of measurable quantities' that had been facilitated by the formal implications of 'uniform repeatable and movable types' (80). And just as mechanization points the way to understanding the terms of its own dissolution, so with psychoanalysis: to 'follow the contours of process as in psychoanalysis provides the only means of avoiding the product of process, namely neurosis or psychosis' (45). Both mechanization and psychoanalysis were related to the history of typography, mechanization having its roots within the uniformity and repeatability of movable type, as psychoanalysis bears the bias of literacy: 'the work of Jung and Freud is a laborious translation of non-literate awareness into literary terms and like any translation distorts and omits' (72).

It was this realization that the psychodynamics he analysed in *The Mechanical Bride* were part of a much larger phenomenon – the way in which writing transforms speech into visual space – that constituted McLuhan's major insight in the passage from *The Mechanical Bride* to *The Gutenberg Galaxy*.[4] Mechanization, in other words, was not simply a mode of production, but comprised a world view. From this position the history of spatialization became integral to a study of social forms (of which language was the prime exemplar), as Innis had suggested, and to understand the nature of that history would be tantamount to understanding media, both pre- and post-Gutenberg. *The Gutenberg Galaxy* represented the first part of that study, and *Understanding Media* the second. If the 'problem of space' was (for Innis) its dominance in contemporary society, implying a failure to achieve a 'relative equilibrium between religious organization with its emphasis on time and political organization with its emphasis on space' (*BC* 103), for McLuhan the problem was to confront that spatial bias historically and methodologically in order to arrive at a formulation of space (in fact, spacetime) that would at once address Innis's observation that space was the dominant bias of contemporary culture while simultaneously providing a way of critiquing that bias from *within*.

McLuhan inititated this inquiry in *Explorations*, a journal he and anthropologist Edmund Carpenter began publishing in 1953.[5] Appearing three times a year (until 1957, with a final number in 1959), the journal published a wide range of articles by McLuhan and Carpenter, H.J. Chaytor, Northrop Frye, Siegfried Giedion, Robert Graves, Jorge Luis Borges, Fernand Léger, and others. The thrust of the journal was interdisciplinary: 'We envisage a series that will cut across the humanities and social sciences by treating them as a continuum. We believe that anthropology and communications are approaches, not bodies of data' (unpaginated; from the first issue). There is an overwhelming emphasis on space in the articles written and commissioned by the editors: D.C. Williams writes on 'Acoustic Space' (4); Walter Ong on 'Space and Intellect in Renaissance Symbolism' (4); Jean Piaget on 'The Development of Time and Space Concepts in the Child' (5); Carpenter on 'Space Concepts of the Aivilik Eskimos' (5); Giedion on

'Space Conception in Prehistoric Art' (6). As Giedion puts it in that article, the 'problem of space conception is everywhere under discussion' (71 of *EC*). This preoccupation derived from a number of sources: synchronic theories of language; formalist theories of literature; Innis's notion of spatial bias;[6] declining belief in theories of progress and linear history; Einsteinian theories of relativity. Most immediately, for McLuhan, this interest was spurred by Carpenter's work on space perception among the Inuit. Carpenter's article 'Space Concepts of the Aivilik Eskimos' (*Exp* 5 [1955] 131–45) makes clear through a number of examples that spatial perceptions are not absolute but are culturally constructed,[7] and McLuhan and Carpenter elsewhere draw specific analogies between acoustic space and that of the 'Eskimo'.[8] Likewise, in *The Gutenberg Galaxy*, McLuhan cites from Carpenter's book *Eskimo* (issue 9 of *Explorations*) to demonstrate the 'Eskimo's' 'non-visual attitude to spatial forms and orientations,' a 'multidirectional space orientation, which is acoustic or auditory' (66). Carpenter thus provided McLuhan with the specific and focused anthropological dimension of his interest in space; Innis provided the grand historical dimension. Out of these elements, McLuhan derived the dynamic between local and global that characterized his thought.[9]

The central insights emerging from *Explorations* are two: the first is that the culture of print had 'rendered people extremely insensitive to the language and meaning of spatial forms' (Cwl, *Exp* 1: 123). This was so because print dissociated our sensibilities such that we are able to perceive only one form of space, the visual, which is a space constructed by the eyes alone. As McLuhan writes in *The Gutenberg Galaxy*, 'It was precisely the habit of being with one kind of space that made all other spaces seem so opaque and intractable' (180). McLuhan's second major insight of this period was occasioned by his observation that the transition from the eye to the ear facilitated by electronic media had caused visual space to give way to acoustic space, which is 'dynamic, always in flux, creating its own dimensions moment by moment' ('Acoustic Space,' *Exp* 4).[10] McLuhan wished to produce a 'psychodynamics of print' (*Exp* 8; *VVV* item 17) in order to illustrate the nature of the transition from print to electronic culture; this account would not express a linear relationship, however, since he understood electronic media to be retrieving values inherent in the oral cultures that preceded print (and that existed uninterruptedly in societies such as China, which lacked a phonetic alphabet). McLuhan thus had to articulate a notion of non-linear, discontinuous history. This 'posthistoric' notion (Cwl 118) is not ahistorical, however; rather, it constitutes a spatial history, that is, a history that seeks (in the words of Paul Carter) to establish 'the historical claims of spatial experience.'[11] 'Every*where* and every *age* have become *here* and *now*. History has been abolished by our new media' (Cwl 118), writes McLuhan, suggesting that the spatial experiences afforded by contemporary culture are happening too rapidly to be understood in terms of a linear model of history.[12] As McLuhan argues in *The Gutenberg Galaxy*, print produced the idea of a past in distant perspective (58); the simultaneity of auditory space translates this linear model into a historical consciousness in which 'we are no longer limited to a perspective of past societies. We recreate them' (*GG* 60).[13] This multiplicity of spaces is analogous to that of the newspaper page, each of whose elements 'lives in its own kind of space totally discontinuous from all other items' (Cwl 125; cf 'Joyce, Mallarmé and the Press'). Such discontinuous space is paradigmatically 'acoustic.' Whereas the visual 'empties out' space by valorizing only figures (the ground being 'empty space'), acoustic space is the realm of a plenitudinous dynamic between figure and ground: 'the essential feature of sound ... is not its location, but that it *be*' ('Acoustic Space,' *ExC* 67). Whereas visual space is bounded and fixed, acoustic (or auditory) space 'has no boundaries in the visual sense ... There is nothing in auditory space corresponding to the vanishing point in visual perspective' (*ExC* 68). And while visual space is linear and successive, 'the character of auditory space is the simultaneous field of relations which is a perfect sphere.'[14] This simultaneity defines the acoustic: *'oral means "total" primarily, "spoken" accidentally'* (*VVV* item 1, emphasis added). Thus the simultaneity of the newspaper page identifies it as 'oral' in nature (cf *VVV* item 5, 'The Journalist's Dilemma'). What is crucial to note here is that the *spoken* word – orality – is for McLuhan a *spatial* concept ('an auditory spatial unit' [*VVV*, item 19]); this constitutes McLuhan's most significant departure from Innis. For Innis, the history of the West moved from orality to literacy, from the temporal to the spatial; for McLuhan, however, this history was not linear but recursive. While McLuhan accepted Innis's powerful notion of spatial and temporal biases, he placed them within a larger history of the production of spaces – the oral, the scribal, the typographical, and the acoustic. This was not, however, a history of uninflected return, from orality back to orality again. Rather, it was a theory of how the past is reshaped by the present, as in Borges's story of Pierre Menard, or in Glenn Gould's performances of the Goldberg variations, or in the *ricorsi* of Vico, for whom 'all history is contemporary or simultaneous' (*GG* 250), thus exchanging the notion of history as linear narrative for history as dynamic configuration.

McLuhan's interest in 'causal operations in history' (*GG*, unpaginated 'preface' to Prologue)[15] reflects his concern with articulating a historical dynamic of spatial production. This history dynamizes the oral and the scribal, the scribal and the literate, the literate and the acoustic; as such, it requires an analogical methodology, which it achieves through a mosaic or field approach. The methodology, like the subject matter, is thus spatial – 'spatial,' however, not in terms of 'fixed relationships in pictorial space' ('preface') but in an acoustical sense. McLuhan sought to express this dynamism through the 'galaxy' metaphor of his title – one of whose sources was Georg von Békésy's study of the aural. McLuhan suggests, however, that 'environment' could have served him equally well ('preface'). Environment, in McLuhan's lexicon, has the force of 'episteme' in Foucauldian theory – the system of knowledge production characteristic of a given era (or medium). To speak of the Gutenberg environment, then, would imply that the printing press and its ramifications produced the epistemological limits of that given era. The press also produced a specific set of spatial possibilities – indeed, the one coincided with the other, and hence the spatial valence of galaxy and environment, such that it is possible to speak of the 'space of knowledge' in the Gutenberg era, with the Foucauldian implication that the only knowledge possible was the knowledge of (a certain kind of) space, which, in this case, was increasingly a *visual* space. Environments thus act like rhetorics, being 'active processes that reshape people and other technologies alike' (*GG*, 'preface').

This notion had been developed by McLuhan's student Walter Ong, in *Ramus: Method and the Decay of Dialogue* (1958),[16] from which McLuhan quotes extensively in *The Gutenberg Galaxy*. The 'method' of Ong's title was that of visualization, and specifically

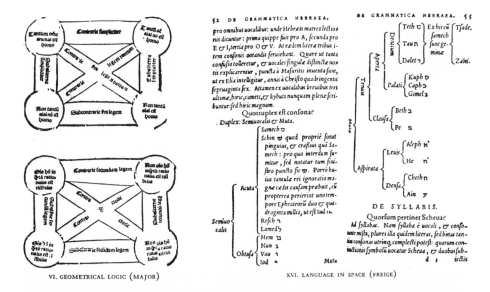

VI. GEOMETRICAL LOGIC (MAJOR)   XVI. LANGUAGE IN SPACE (FREIGE)

Figure 3.1. **Left**: 'Geometrical Logic.' 'The geometrical analysis proved a cul-de-sac for the quantifying drive in logic. This illustration is from a copy of Major's *Libri quos in artibus ... compilavit* (Paris 1506) ... The simple designs here are derived from the squares of opposition common in the manuscript tradition.' Reproduced from Walter Ong, *Ramus: Method and the Decay of Dialogue* (Cambridge, MA: Harvard UP, 1958). **Right**: 'Language in Space.' 'Although he was aware that words are primarily spoken phenomena, the Ramist ... made little of this fact and habitually assigned as the ultimate components of words not phones (sounds) but letters (visual reductions of sounds). Here the Ramist Freige makes a further geometrical reduction of letters themselves, deriving the whole of the Hebrew alphabet out of a ramification of dichotomies – almost, for the dichotomies do not all come out quite evenly. ... The present illustration is from a copy of Freige's *Paedagogus* (Basile, 1582) ...' Reproduced from Ong, ibid.

of diagrammatic representation, which Ong saw as contributing to the 'decay of dialogue.' Here the orality/literacy dynamic (the topic of another of Ong's books)[17] is configured as the decay during the Renaissance of spoken dialogue caused by the increasing use of spatial (visual, actually) modes of communication that were made possible by print technology (fig. 3.1). As Ong puts it, 'at the heart of the Ramist enterprise is the drive to tie down words themselves ... in simple geometrical patterns. Words are believed to be recalcitrant insofar as they derive from a world of sound, voices, cries; the Ramist ambition is to neutralize this connection by processing what is of itself nonspatial in order to reduce it to space in the starkest possible way' (Ong, *Ramus* 89; quoted in *GG* 160). This orality/literacy contest is characteristic more of Innis's work than of McLuhan's, however, in that Ong tends to equate the visual with the spatial. (Hence Ong refers to the acoustic domain as 'nonspatial.') Indeed, immediately after quoting Ong on the Ramist enterprise, McLuhan specifies that '[w]hat is necessary to understand here is that the key to any kind of *applied* knowledge is the translation of a complex of relations into explicit *visual* terms [last emphasis added]' (*GG* 160). Whereas Ong sees Ramus's betrayal of the spoken as residing in the hypervaluation of the spatial, for McLuhan the spatial was also capable of acoustic configuration – indeed, rhetoric was such a useful concept to McLuhan precisely because it represented the dynamics of configured speech. While for Ong the textual and the oral are incompatible (Ong, *Ramus* 273), for McLuhan the textual can be orally empathic, since the spatial and the visual are not codetermined. In these terms, Ong's position is actually closer to that of Ramus than is apparent, since, as Ong tells us, rhetoric was auditory for Ramus whereas dialectic was diagrammatic (280), and these two polarities 'had to be distinct' (280), as they do for Ong. Ramus thus represents the moment when, '[i]deologically, the world of sound has yielded ... to the world of space' (290). While McLuhan would agree with Ong's comment that Ramusian rhetoric is representative of 'a shift toward the visual throughout the whole cognitive field' (281), McLuhan did not understand the reversal of this shift as implying a movement *away* from the spatial (and towards the temporal). For this reason, McLuhan posited the revival of rhetoric, and himself as a *doctus orator* within that tradition. Indeed, it was the ineluctably spatial aspect of rhetoric that argued most tellingly in support of the concept of acoustic space. Ong, however, tended to take orality literally (as it were), arguing that '[a] word is more than a sign of some*thing*, even of an intelligible something such as a concept. It is a cry, a voice, something which comes from the interior of a person, who as a *person* can never be "explained," and which somehow manifests this interior' (110). In *Orality and Literacy: The Technologizing of the Word* (1982), Ong continues to argue for 'the primacy of oral speech' (5) and that '[w]riting [is a] commitment of the word to space' (7) that 'locks [it] into a visual field forever' (192). By contrast, '[t]he spoken word is always an event, a movement in time, completely lacking in the thing-like repose of the written or printed word' (75).

McLuhan's theory of orality and literacy (and the spaces they produce) is more nuanced than Ong's.[18] Had McLuhan not made his decisive 'break' with Innis in 1953, he might have produced books such as *Ramus* or *Orality and Literacy*. However, McLuhan post-1953 was theorizing a non-visual spatiality that he associated analogically with the auditory. Thus, while he argued, like Ong, that spatial models were reductive of oral modes, he did not argue that the oral was exclusively in the realm of the temporal. If Ong's writings are reflective of McLuhan's teachings on these matters, thus, they are so only of the McLuhan who was writing within the ambit of Innis, and not of the McLuhan who had been exposed to the concept of acoustic space.

The Invention of Euclid

The nuances of McLuhan's argument about orality and literacy derive from the central historical analogy of *The Gutenberg Galaxy* that the Renaissance and the Modern are *alike* transitional moments within the shifting vectors of orality and literacy. Just as the Renaissance displayed elements of both the oral and the literate, so did the Modern: 'We are today as far into the electric age as Elizabethans had advanced into the typographical and mechanical age' (*GG* 1). For McLuhan, orality and literacy were in dynamic interrelationship – 'perpetually interacting forms' (*GG*, 'preface') – rather than locked into a historical grid, and this point is of crucial importance for understanding his argument in *The Gutenberg Galaxy*. Rather than suggesting that electronic media were returning us to an oral age, he argues in *The Gutenberg Galaxy* that in 'the electric age ... we encounter new shapes and structures ... which are "oral" in form even when the components of the situation may be non-verbal' (3). This position accords with his notion that electronic culture does not represent a shift from the spatiality of print to the temporality of speech; rather, the electronic era has a spatial bias that is in dynamic flux.

McLuhan's non-linear 'mosaic or field approach' (*GG*, 'preface') to history is comparable to Paul Carter's notion of 'spatial history.' Carter asserts in *The Road to Botany Bay* that the 'kind of history ... which reduces space to a stage, that pays attention to events unfolding in time alone, might be called imperial history' (xvi). Historical chronology 'nullifies time's cultural peculiarities. Chronology is the temporal counterpart of Euclidean space: both are operationally efficient because they deny the historical nature of the realms they manipulate' (xix). To imperial history, Carter counterposes 'spatial history,' whose 'subject is not a physical object, but a cultural one. It is not the geographer's space, although that comes into it. What is evoked here are the spatial forms and fantasies through which a culture declares its presence. It is spatiality as a form of non-linear writing; as a form of history' (xxii). Medium and message coincide within this conceptualization, as McLuhan realized, given that the 'linearity of writing (in contrast with the multidimensionality of experience) and the linearity of the logic it expresses reflects neither the nature of experience nor, for that matter, of history, but rather the limitations of the medium' (*GG* 157). To write spatial history, then, would be to adopt not merely a non-linear methodology, but a non-linear medium as well. In the 'preface' to *The Gutenberg Galaxy*, McLuhan writes that the mosaic or field approach he is employing is 'the only practical means of revealing causal operations in history.' McLuhan counterposes this approach to 'a series of views of fixed relationships in pictorial space,' the equivalent of Carter's stage, which, like pictorial (Euclidean) space, derives from the idea of perspective (and the cognate notion of *historia*), as developed by Alberti in *Della Pittura*.[19] What is noteworthy, here, is that McLuhan counterposes one *spatial* construction – pictorial; Euclidean – with another – mosaic; relational. 'Mosaic,' furthermore, had an auditory resonance for him, in that it was the metaphor employed by von Békésy to describe his own methodology as well as the nature of acoustic space. Similarly, McLuhan's subject matter and methodology are spatial; it is the particularly dynamic quality of his spatial methodology ('perpetually interacting') that allows him to address 'the organization of time and space alike.'

McLuhan's spatial history sounds an imperial theme from the outset. J.C. Carothers's 'Culture, Psychiatry and the Written Word' made the argument that perceptual norms were acculturated and subject to media effects. 'The alphabet,' glosses McLuhan, 'is an aggressive and militant absorber and transformer of cultures, as Harold Innis was the first to show' (*GG* 48), and, as for the alphabet, so for electronic media. An awareness of cultural relativism, however, accompanies the proliferation of electronic media, both because they promote a simultaneous experience of many cultures and because they intensify individual cultural identities (the 'global village' paradox). *The Gutenberg Galaxy*'s opening analysis of *King Lear* is made in this context. Focusing on the dynamic of the play's beginning, McLuhan notes that the map Lear consults embodies a notion of 'space [as] uniform and continuous' (11; cf Carter 204); this embodies the play's principal theme, 'the isolation of the visual sense as a kind of blindness.' In dividing his kingdom, Lear also inaugurates a movement 'from centre to margins' which forecasts a new mode of spatial construction that would deprivilege 'the abstract explicit visual technology of uniform time and uniform continuous space in which "cause" is efficient and sequential, and things move and happen on single planes and in successive order' (*GG* 19).[20] Ironically, writes McLuhan, 'it is still supposed, even by some anthropologists, that Euclidean space and three-dimensional visual perception is a universal datum of mankind' (25). However, the notion of 'civilization' is so closely bound up with the idea of visual, literate space that the term must 'now be used technically to mean detribalized man for whom the visual values have priority' (27).[21] It is thus possible to produce a spatial analysis of the relationship between the phonetic alphabet and printing press, on the one hand, and the values of Western civilization, on the other; this is the major focus of *The Gutenberg Galaxy*, much of which is devoted to a critique of the *visual* space bias within Western culture. This 'polemic against vision,'[22] as John Fekete puts it, argues that the isolation of the sense of sight represents a 'dissociated sensibility of visual-gradient culture' ('Notes toward a Critique' 213). The consequence of this dissociation is the (Euclidean) space that is bounded, static, homogeneous, and continuous. Fekete critiques McLuhan's position by arguing that 'McLuhan's use of his sensory categories is metaphoric, mythic rather than explicative. Thus, he can say that the press mosaic, though it is seen, has an auditory structure, and that television, although seen and heard, is tactile' (215). Yet it is not the visual *per se* but a particular sort of *space* against which McLuhan polemicizes. Indeed, in Fekete's extended quotation from McLuhan's interview with Eric Norden,[23] McLuhan specifically states that it is the visual production of '"linear time and Euclidean space"' (quoted 213; 240–1 of *EM*) that is the object of his critique.

Euclidean (or pictorial) space was the product of a culture that began to valorize sight with the invention of the alphabet. As McLuhan wrote (with Robert Logan) in 'Alphabet, Mother of Invention,' the 'alphabet separated and isolated visual space from the many other kinds of sensory space involved in the senses of smell, touch, kinesthesia, and acoustics. This made possible the awareness of Euclidean space which is lineal, homogeneous, connected, and static.'[24] Euclidean space realized its fullest expression through the codification of vision in the 'laws' of perspective, as in various Renaissance tracts (most famously, Alberti's *Della Pittura*) which sought to institutionalize the regime of the visible by using the rules of geometry as derived from Euclid to produce a system of perspectival representation, the main features of which were the bounded frame (often pictured as an open window), the central and static viewing place, and the use of linear projection to produce a vanishing point (and thereby the effect of a third dimension). It is this Euclidean space (and not vision *per se*) that McLuhan critiques in *The Gutenberg Galaxy*. 'The arbitrary selection of a single static position,' McLuhan writes, 'creates a pictorial space with vanishing point. This space can be filled in bit by bit, and is quite different from non-pictorial space in which *each* thing simply resonates or modulates its own space in visually two-dimensional form' (*GG* 16). The 'visual' and the 'pictorial' do not, thus, completely overlap; rather, the pictorial is a particular construction of the visual effected by the phonetic alphabet and further technologized by the printing press, whereby the printed page and pictorial space acquire similar determinants of fixed position and bounded, linear space.

McLuhan draws on the work of E.H. Gombrich (principally *Art and Illusion*) and William Ivins in support of his polemic against visual space. While McLuhan is in accord with Gombrich's notion that, '[f]ar from being a normal mode of human vision, three-dimensional perspective is a conventionally acquired mode of seeing' (*GG* 16), he takes issue with Gombrich's statement that 'we [should] discard Berkeley's theory of vision, according to which we "see" a flat field but "construct" a tactile space' and thereby 'rid art history of its obsession with space' (quoted in *GG* 52–3). McLuhan counters that 'Berkeley's *New Theory of Vision* (1709) is now favoured by psychologists of our sense lives' (53). More congenial to McLuhan's position, and to the grand theory of spatial production he was articulating in *The Gutenberg Galaxy*, were two books by William Ivins, *Art and Geometry: A Study of Space Intuitions* (1946) and *Prints and Visual Communication* (1953),[25] both of which are cited a number of times in *Gutenberg*. Ivins's theory of spatial production posited that Greek culture was based on metrical geometry and tactile relationships, while the modern derived from perspective and the visual 'space intuition' (*Art and Geometry* ix). Modern space was homogeneous in that 'the eye ... is conscious of no breaks in the continuity of its awarenesses' (1). Tactile awareness, in contrast, 'is not accomplished by a gradual finding in and out of consciousness, but by catastrophic contacts and breakings of contacts' (3). In tactile terms, 'things exist in a series of *here*s in space but where there are not things, space, even though "empty," continues to exist' (5). In a formulation that had enormous resonance for McLuhan, Ivins writes that the hand 'has no point of view and in consequence no vanishing point' (5).

In *Prints and Visual Communication*, Ivins argues that the period 1400 to 1450 represented a breakthrough for technology, in that (1) techniques of repeatability were perfected; (2) perspective was invented, and (3) a theory of the relativity of knowledge was developed (23). The net result of these breakthroughs was to provide 'a tyranny, that, before it was broken up, had subjected large parts of the world to the rule of a blinding and methodically blighting visual common sense' (70).[26] McLuhan developed this theme further in *Gutenberg* with his contention that print had contributed to the rise of nationalism, industrialism, and individualism. With this critique he entered a discourse of visual denigration that has continued unabated, a phenomenon discussed at length by Martin Jay in *Downcast Eyes*.[27] Jay seeks to show that a wide 'antivisual discourse ... is a pervasive but generally ignored phenomenon of twentieth-century thought' (14), although he restricts his remarks to France. This anti-visual discourse encompasses 'Bergson's critique of the spatialization of time ... Sartre's depiction of the sadomasochism of the "look" ... Foucault's strictures against the medical gaze and panoptic surveillance, Debord's critique of the society of the spectacle ... Derrida's double reading of the specular tradition of philosophy and the white mythology, Irigaray's outrage at the privileging of the visual in patriarchy ... and Lyotard's identification of postmodernism with the sublime foreclosure of the visual' (588). The overall import of this anti-ocularcentric debate has been to critique 'the modern project of enlightenment' (589). Jay posits McLuhan (as well as Ivins) as foundational (if hyperbolic in his claims) within this discourse, although Jay does not make McLuhan's crucial distinction between the visual and the spatial.[28] Underlying that distinction was the notion that space was not a given but a construct, and in this regard McLuhan was developing notions articulated in F.M. Cornford's 'The Invention of Space' (1936), which traces the history of space from the pre- to the post-Euclidean.[29] 'When I was taught geometry,' writes Cornford, 'geometry and Euclid were synonomous terms; and it never occurred to me to doubt that I lived and moved in Euclidean space, extending, quite obviously, in all its three dimensions, without limit' (215). This concept of space is now obsolete, states Cornford (quoting the physicist A.S. Eddington). '"Space and time, and also their space-time product, fall into their places as mere mental frameworks of our own construction"' (216).[30] This passage was very significant for the development of McLuhan's notion that the space/time opposition, as formulated by Innis (who also quotes Cornford's citation from Eddington at the head of 'The Problem of Space') was conceptually outmoded. McLuhan's reading of Cornford was far less deterministic than Innis's; in the one reference in *The Gutenberg Galaxy* to 'The Problem of Space' (61, n16), McLuhan superimposes the concept of acoustic space on Innis's notion of orality, thereby deeply problematizing the space/time distinction Innis makes in *The Bias of Communication*.[31]

Flatland Revisited

While Innis concludes 'A Plea for Time' with the biblical injunction '"Without vision the people perish"' (*BC* 91), McLuhan's analysis of *Lear* in *The Gutenberg Galaxy* insists on the fact that vision is itself a form of blindness because it had been (re)constructed through the institution of typography as visual space, with its fixed point of view. The 'anguish of the third dimension' (*GG* 15),[32] McLuhan notes, arises from the separation of the senses through the hegemony of the visual; it is 'the sense of sight in deliberate isolation from the other senses that confers on man the illusion of the third dimension' (16). The third dimension requires a fixed viewing position (point of view) and has a distancing effect on the viewer. In non-pictorial space, by contrast, 'each thing simply resonates or modulates its own space in visually two-dimensional form' (16). As the word 'resonates' indicates, McLuhan associated the two-dimensional with the auditory and with the mosaic, which was von Békésy's metaphor of the auditory. 'The paradox presented by Professor von Békésy is that the two-dimensional mosaic is, in fact, a multidimensional world of interstructural resonance' (*GG* 43), since the space it produces privileges no one point of view or dimension. Whereas in a mosaic, '[c]o-existence and interplay among the figures in the flat field create a multi-levelled and multi-*sensuous* awareness' (*GG* 63; emphasis added), in three-dimensional space, a single, fixed point-of-view predominates. 'It is upon this "fixed point of view" that the triumphs and destructions of the Gutenberg era will be made ... [T]he flat, two-dimensional mosaic form ... is the opposite of inert, as Georg von Békésy discovered in the study of hearing. For dynamic simultaneity is the effect of the two-dimensional, and inert homogeneity the effect of three-dimensionality' (*GG* 127).

McLuhan invokes the term 'flatland' (*GG* 57; 212) in making this critique of visual space, alluding to Edwin Abbott's satirical novel of that title (published 1884).[33] Abbott's novel is part of a large discourse concerning the fourth dimension and non-Euclidean geometry that arose in the late nineteenth century, persisted well into the third decade of the twentieth, and had a significant influence on the cultural production of that period.[34]

Flatland[35] (which Abbott published under the pseudonym 'A Square') concerns a mythical realm of that name: 'Imagine a vast sheet of paper on which straight Lines, Triangles, Squares, Pentagons, Hexagons, and other figures, instead of remaining fixed in their places, move freely about, on or in the surface, but without the power of rising above or sinking below it, very much like shadows – only hard and with luminous edges – and you will then have a pretty correct notion of my country and countrymen' (Abbott 11). The narrator addresses his story to those who inhabit 'Spaceland' (12), the world of three dimensions to which the narrator once journeyed, thereby precipitating his downfall in Flatland. As Linda Dalrymple Henderson has pointed out, Abbott's romance is significant as 'the first example of popular fiction about the fourth dimension. Abbott's tale is based on the premise that the meaning of the third dimension for a two-dimensional being compares to the meaning of the fourth dimension for us' (*4D* 17). McLuhan used precisely the same analogy in a 1958 article, writing that '[a] being equipped with two-dimensional perception would be confounded by an encounter with even a three-dimensional object.'[36] The importance to McLuhan of this analogy concerned his interest in the interpenetration of space and time categories as a way of addressing his dissatisfaction with Innis's static construal of 'the problem of space.'[37] But *Flatland* was also relevant to McLuhan's critique of visual space, since the striking aspect of the fourth dimension was that it could *not* be visualized. Indeed, it is A Square's claim to have *seen* the third dimension that eventually lands him in prison.[38]

Abbott's romance spoke to a general concern with the nature of space that grew up in the mid-nineteenth century; this concern manifested itself particularly in the question of the curvature of space, and the question of the number of dimensions in space (*4D* 10), with the latter being the more popular topic, as the success of Abbott's tale and Lewis Carroll's Alice books (which influenced it) attest (*4D* 21). 'Lewis Carroll took Alice on her trip a century ago,' wrote McLuhan in his 1968 preface to a book on time as the mind's fourth dimension, 'recognizing that we had come to the end of the age of Euclidean space'; consistent with his other writings on the subject, McLuhan phrases his observation in terms of space perception.[39] The influence of fourth-dimensional philosophy was felt very strongly in the visual arts. Apollinaire related the Cubists' interest in space to this philosophy (*4D* 44); pointedly anti-Euclidean, this interest was subsequently associated with relativity theory, especially in the writings of Theo van Doesburg. Van Doesburg's work deeply influenced Siegfried Giedion's *Space, Time and Architecture*, the book McLuhan called a 'revelation' (in the interview with Eric Norden). Giedion was closely associated with Laszlo Moholy-Nagy,[40] whose *Vision in Motion* published the 'ear for an eye' photomontage that McLuhan used as the frontispiece to *Verbi-Voco-Visual Explorations* (and as one of the photos in *The Medium Is the Massage*), and with Moholy-Nagy's disciple Gyorgy Kepes, whose *Language of Vision* (1939) McLuhan quotes in *The Gutenberg Galaxy*. As Dalrymple Henderson remarks, Moholy-Nagy's 'publications, along with those of his disciple Gyorgy Kepes and Giedion's *Space, Time and Architecture*, stand as classic statements of the generalized "space-time philosophy," which was the final product of the interaction of art and relativity in the 1920s' (*4D* 337).[41] Another artist/writer of the period interested in four-dimensional thought was Marcel Duchamp (*4D* 25, 120), who had planned 'a four dimensional Bride' (*4D* 61) at one point in the development of *The Large Glass*; '"I thought of ... an invisible fourth dimension,"' said Duchamp in a 1967 interview, '"something you couldn't see with your eyes"' (quoted *4D* 118). Duchamp connected this work with the chronophotography of E.-J. Marey, which had raised the spectre of a spatial dimension interpenetrated by time, or, more generally, a non-Euclidean mode of representation that would allow for the deformation of bodies in motion, as represented in Duchamp's *Nude* (cf *4D* 132). In his search for the ideal mode through which to represent a four-dimensional bride, Duchamp finally settled on the two-dimensional plane of a mirror (*4D* 151), and here an analogy can be struck with McLuhan's preference for the two-dimensional mosaic instead of the three-dimensional perspectival representation; Duchamp's and McLuhan's spatial configurations likewise constitute a critique of visual space. However, what McLuhan theorized was less a return to plane geometry than a tactile reconfiguration of the planes into a mosaic of interpenetrating surfaces and structures; as he puts it in *From Cliché to Archetype*, '[t]he flat icon has multitudinous layers of significance, whereas the three-dimensional perspective illusion necessarily specializes in one facet at a time' (89).

The quest for four-dimensional modes of representation also had psychologistic overtones, and in this regard Richard M. Bucke's *Cosmic Consciousness* was often invoked as suggesting that 'a moving threshold of consciousness ... can progress to include the fourth dimension of space' (*4D* 197). This movement was characterized by a trajectory from succession to the simultaneity that McLuhan associated with the instantaneity of electricity, and this is the context in which he uses the phrase 'cosmic consciousness' in *Understanding Media* (80; cf *4D* 54). Simultaneity was first used in an artistic context with reference to the Futurists (*4D* 91);[42] philosophically, however, the debate over succession versus simultaneity had a much longer lineage, going back at least as far as Kant, as McLuhan notes in 'Innovation Is Obsolete': 'It is only the visual sense that permits the experience or the concept of continuity and connectedness. The visual sense, enhanced to a position of dominance by the phonetic alphabet, created the basis of Western civilization, which equates rationality with visuality *and space with sight* [emphasis added]. The Kantian categories of space and time with their assumptions of continuity and successiveness are, unconsciously, visual in origin. Preliterate man had no experience or concept of continuity or connectedness, and the non-Euclidean geometries of Lobachevsky and after simply bypass such assumptions' (47; cf *CA* 164). Bergson, also referred to in the 'cosmic consciousness' passage[43] of *Understanding Media*, likewise invoked simultaneity in his spatial theories, although negatively, given that Bergson 'preferred succession to the simultaneity of space and of spatialized time' (*4D* 92). McLuhan's position was indebted to Lewis's *Time and Western Man* (whose vortex was related to fourth-dimensional thought; see *4D* xxii, n11), though by the time of writing *The Gutenberg Galaxy* he was presenting this position not as a binary (space *versus* time) but by collapsing these categories into a spacetime relationship that rendered them both obsolete as absolutes.

McLuhan found an analogue for this spacetime relationship in physics; he was led in this direction by spatial philosophy in general, and in particular by philosophies of hyperspace (the space of four or more dimensions [*4D* 7]) as filtered through such writers as Lewis, Giedion, and Abbott. Hyperspace philosophy is remarkable for having engaged the interest of metaphysics and physics alike. The element that provided the hinge point was a renewed interest in the properties of electricity, occasioned by Einstein's special and general theories of relativity. This interest is evident in books McLuhan drew on for *The Gutenberg Galaxy* such as J.Z. Young's *Doubt and Certainty in Science* (1951),[44] which argued that 'electricity is the condition we observe when there are certain spatial relations between things' (109). The interest in the spatial properties of electricity had a wide vogue among turn-of-the-century disciples of Abbott, such as Charles Howard Hinton (author of a 'sequel' to *Flatland*), whose work *The Fourth Dimension* (1904) specifically associated the fourth dimension with electricity; Hinton is referred to in Lewis's *Time and Western Man*, a book McLuhan knew intimately, and Einstein was by this time very much in the public domain. McLuhan would have encountered intellectually not only these metaphysicians of hyperspace but also physicists of a more academically sanctioned nature during his Cambridge years (October 1934 to September 1936; September 1939 to June 1940).[45] Abbott, the author of *Flatland*, was himself an honorary fellow of St John's College, and his romance makes a number of satirical comments about the university.[46] This indicates that the space/time question was in the air a half-century before McLuhan arrived at Cambridge, and William Garnett's introduction to the 1928 reprint of Abbott's novel suggests that it continued to be so. In that same year, Maurice Maeterlinck published *The Life of Space* (French and English editions),[47] where the fourth dimension is discussed in the context of 'a non-euclidean geometry' (7) as 'the space in which Einstein develops his tremendous problems' (8). It is to Hinton, writes Maeterlinck, that '[a]ll those who have written of the fourth dimension owe something ... even the professional hypergeometricians' (40). Maeterlinck thus does not hesitate to cite Hinton in his bibliography alongside Bergson, Ouspensky, Poincaré, A.S. Eddington, and Whitehead, the latter two being physicists connected to Cambridge.[48] McLuhan's Cambridge experience has been accorded extraordinary significance in his intellectual development – Marchand writes that 'McLuhan's years at Cambridge permanently set the foundations for almost all of his subsequent intellectual work' (*M&M* 41) – although that experience is usually understood in terms of McLuhan's encounter with New Criticism.[49] Yet, as T.E.B. Howarth notes in *Cambridge between Two Wars*, the 'radical changes' in 'Cambridge English' were paralleled by 'the work of the physicists.'[50] The influence on McLuhan of advances in physics was important not only to the development of his spatial theories but also as the avenue along which he was able to undertake most fully the enterprise of critiquing Modernism that critics such as Stamps, Vermillac,[51] and Willmott have ascribed to him. The New Criticism, in contrast, was very much a part of the Modernist sensibility. The autonomous, decontextualized, and dehistoricized model of textuality adhered to by the New Critics was unable to speak to the dynamic issues McLuhan sought to address. He found that model in physics, as enacted through the notion of 'acoustic space'; as he writes in *The Gutenberg Galaxy*, '[t]he new physics is an auditory domain' (27).[52]

From Landscape to Field

Physics is one of the major topoi in *The Gutenberg Galaxy*, providing the key metaphor of the relational, dynamic methodology McLuhan substituted for the concept of 'arrest' that he had employed in *The Mechanical Bride*.[53] In much the same way that Charles

Howard Hinton had argued that the three-dimensionality of the vortex would be represented as a force-field in the fourth,[54] McLuhan sought (analogously with relativity
theory) to establish a relational metaphor that would allow him at once to address what
Innis had termed 'the problem of space' while avoiding the static concept of space that
had underpinned *The Mechanical Bride* and *The Bias of Communication* alike. By
dynamizing the concept of space, McLuhan was likewise heeding Innis's 'plea for time';
as he wrote, 'the dominant mode of time in the Middle Ages was acoustic,' which is to
say spatial, in the sense that the sound of a church bell would have defined a certain
social space.[55] McLuhan specifically links this dynamic model to the historical project
of *The Gutenberg Galaxy* in the first reference he makes in that book to contemporary
physics:[56] 'Hitherto historians of culture have tended to isolate technological events
much in the way that classical physics dealt with physical events. Louis de Broglie,
describing *The Revolution in Physics*, makes much of this limitation of the Cartesian and
Newtonian procedures which are so near those of the historians using an individual
"point of view"' (5). The methodology of the 'single-point-of-view' is thus inadequate to
the mosaic with which electric culture presents the critical intelligence, as McLuhan's
quote from de Broglie makes clear: '"Faithful to the Cartesian ideal, classical physics
showed us the universe as being analogous to an immense mechanism which was
capable of being described with complete precision by the localization of its parts in
space and by their change in the course of time ... But such a conception rested on several
implicit hypotheses which were admitted almost without our being aware of them. One
of these hypotheses was that the framework of space and time in which we seek almost
instinctively to localize all of our sensations is a perfectly rigid and fixed framework
where each physical event can, in principle, be vigorously localized independently of all
the dynamic processes which are going on around it"' (quoted in *GG* 5). McLuhan
argues (as we have seen) that 'not only Cartesian [and Newtonian] but Euclidean
perceptions' (6) are bound up in this static worldview. However, 'the telegraph and ...
radio' (6) are fostering a new perceptual paradigm of 'configuration' (14), which exists
in dramatic opposition to 'continuous, lineal, and uniform sequences for time and space
and personal relationships alike' (14; the context is the discussion of *King Lear*).
McLuhan stresses, however, that this paradigm shift is peculiar to Western and/or literate
cultures. While oral cultures traditionally operate with a configurational dynamics,
'[l]ong-literate cultures have naturally more resistance to the auditory dynamic of the
total electric field culture of our time' (29; cf p 137, where McLuhan writes of 'the
essentially oral character of the electric "field"').

   The dynamic model that McLuhan derived from contemporary physics spoke directly
to his critique of visual space. 'Not only does modern physics abandon the specialized
visual space of Descartes and Newton, it re-enters the subtle auditory space of the non-
literate world' (*GG* 30). McLuhan quotes from Edmund Whittaker's *Space and Spirit*
(1948) in support of the notion that inherent in the visual was the logic of causality,
which 'found its extreme expression in Newtonian physics' (57).[57] The dynamic notions
with which Whittaker opposes this logic are summed up by McLuhan in the term
'galaxy,' and it is in this context that McLuhan states that Whittaker's book 'explains the
title and procedure of the present book' (252). McLuhan focalizes this discussion of the
shift in consciousness heralded by the new physics through an extended discussion of

Mircea Eliade's *The Sacred and the Profane* (trans. 1959), the theme of which is the contest between 'the world of "sacred" or cosmic space and time' and 'the detribalized or "profane" space and time of civilized and pragmatic man' (51). McLuhan argues that Eliade, unaware of the role phonetic literacy played in the desacralization of the 'primitive' world, has in fact misread a mechanical occurrence as a religious one (67). For McLuhan, the 'sacred' should be more accurately characterized as 'auditory space' (68) in order to emphasize that it has '*no inherent religious relevance or importance*' (68; emphasis added).[58] Rather than arguing for a binaristic split between sacred and profane (or acoustic and literate, for that matter), as Eliade does, McLuhan, having adopted from physics the notions of interrelation and simultaneity, argues for their interaction, for 'the relative interplay of the optical and auditory modes in the shaping of human sensibility' (71).[59]

The constantly shifting terminology here, from acoustic to auditory to audile to audile-tactile to tactile to oral to orally empathic, is another way in which McLuhan sought to deconstruct binaristic assumptions about 'orality' and 'literacy,' and to suggest that they are in interplay. As he writes in a crucial passage of *The Gutenberg Galaxy*, '[t]he invention of the alphabet, like the invention of the wheel, was the translation or reduction of a complex, organic interplay of spaces into a single space. The phonetic alphabet reduced the use of all the senses at once, which is oral speech, to a merely visual code. Today, such translation can be effected back and forth through a variety of spatial forms which we call the "media of communication." But each of these spaces has unique properties and impinges upon our other senses or spaces in unique ways' (45). This is to argue analogically with 'the modern physicist,' for whom 'space is not homogeneous, nor is time' (71). Similarly, James Joyce 'discovered the means of living simultaneously in all cultural modes' (75) as in a 'collideorscope,' which 'indicates the interplay in colloidal mixture of all components of human technology' (75). It is through the analogy with physics that the spatial metaphor of 'galaxy' becomes the controlling one of *The Gutenberg Galaxy*: 'Two cultures or technologies can, like astronomical galaxies, pass through one another without collision; but not without change of configuration. In modern physics there is, similarly, the concept of "interface" or the meeting and metamorphosis of two structures' (149). The allusion here to C.P. Snow's *The Two Cultures and the Scientific Revolution* (1959) provides another instance of an outmoded binarism. Returning to Snow's book in *Take Today*, McLuhan writes that 'C.P. Snow is quite innocent of any knowledge about the dynamic origins of literacy, or of science in relation to literacy. Without the long written tradition of the West there would be no science. What Snow calls "two cultures" are the *figure-ground* interface of the components of the same culture. In Plato's time the new *figure* was written, and the old *ground* was oral. In our time the new *figure* of science is acoustic and the old *ground* is visual-written' (*TT* 127). The dynamic model McLuhan proposes here is utterly antithetical to the fixed spaces of the visual culture inaugurated by typography. The 'gutenberg galaxy was officially dissolved' only 'with [the] recognition of curved space in 1905' (*GG* 253). The non-Euclidean, non-lineal world ushered in by relativity theory[60] required a non-teleological methodology through which it could be understood, thus throwing emphasis on process rather than product. In these terms, 'the technique of the suspended judgment [was] the great discovery of the twentieth century in art and physics alike' (278). This technique represented 'a recoil and transformation of the impersonal assembly-line of nineteenth century art and science' (278).

A major methodological implication of the dynamic model that McLuhan develops in *The Gutenberg Galaxy* is that, rather than searching (as he had in *The Mechanical Bride*) for the still point in the midst of flux, as metaphorized by Poe's maelstrom story, in *The Gutenberg Galaxy* and subsequent works McLuhan seeks to immerse himself within that flux. Thus, in *The Gutenberg Galaxy*, arrest is associated with print and with the visual – it is 'the phonetic alphabet' that promotes 'arrested visual analysis' (23). McLuhan quotes from his own article 'Printing and Social Change' (1959) to suggest that print gives only the *appearance* of participation in a process, only the *appearance* of being dynamic: '"The printed word is an arrested moment of mental movement. To read print is to act both as movie projector and audience for a mental movie. The reader attains a strong feeling of participation in the total motions of a mind in the process of thinking. But is it not basically the printed word's 'still shot' that fosters a habit of mind which tackles all problems of movement and change in terms of the unmoved segment or section? Has not print inspired a hundred different mathematical and analytical proce- dures for explaining and controlling change in terms of the unchanging? Have we not tended to apply this very static feature to print itself and talked only of its quantitative effects?"' (*GG* 158; cf 241). Here, *in nuce*, is McLuhan's basis for his 'rejection' of *The Mechanical Bride* – that its methodology was itself mechanical, a product of book culture that electric culture had already rendered outmoded.[61] Once again he revisits the paradox of Marey and others who argue that the 'capture' of movement through chronophotography was the ultimate triumph and illusion – phantasmagoria – of the mechanical culture inaugurated by Gutenberg's invention. McLuhan goes on to write in his 1959 article that '[t]oday we are aware that any pattern of knowledge or of perception is affected by new information and by other co-existing patterns. We are now in the age of the live or dynamic model and of the *field theory* in physics' ('Printing and Social Change' 90). The static model is associated likewise with 'the fixed point of view of the artificially arrested gaze' (96) to which McLuhan counterposes 'cubism, in which the spectator sees at once from inside and outside, from above and below' (103).[62] As he writes in the opening section of *Understanding Media*, 'cubism, by giving the inside and outside, the top, bottom, back, and front and the rest, in two dimensions, drops the illusion of perspective in favor of instant sensory awareness of the whole. Cubism, by seizing on instant total awareness, suddenly announced that *the medium is the message*. Is it not evident that the moment that sequence yields to the simultaneous, one is in the world of the structure and of configuration? Is that not what has happened in physics as in painting, poetry, and in communication? Specialized segments of attention have shifted to total field' (*UM* 13).

Without Perspective

Given that McLuhan's project involved a dynamization of the total field of perception, his own position as critic would necessarily be implicated within this project, as was implied by the concept of acoustic space, which was mosaic in construction, unlike visual space, which was hierarchical (*GG* 139). Chief among the hierarchies that came into being with print were those of inner and outer,[63] public and private, highbrow and lowbrow, author and reader. Print had the effect of 'separating writer and reader, producer and consumer, ruler and ruled, into sharply defined categories. Before printing, these operations were much interfused in the same way as the scribe as producer was involved in reading, and the student was involved in the making of the books he studied' (209). The return to such interfusions was heralded by orally empathic writers such as Joyce, whose comment ' "My consumers are they not my producers? [*sic*]" ' (*GG* 205) McLuhan was fond of quoting. Often read as announcing an era of processual poetics, this comment also pertains to what would come to be known as the 'death of the author,' which, in Roland Barthes's formulation, would coincide with the birth of the reader (which, here, has the force of 'producer'). Authority for McLuhan was the product of print's tendency to individualize subjectivities. To critique visual ideology, then, was to critique the notion of authoritative point of view, with that term having the perspectival pedigree that McLuhan so carefully sketches out in *The Gutenberg Galaxy*.

McLuhan's response to this methodological challenge was to disarticulate his subject position as author/authority. He claimed Innis as his predecessor in this, writing in 'The Humanities in the Electronic Age' (1961) that 'Innis' concern in the *Bias of Communication*, and later, is with the technique of the suspended judgement. That means, not the willingness to admit other points of view, but the technique of how not to have a point of view. This is identical with the problem facing physicists in correcting the bias of the instruments of research' (6). Relatedly, in his 1964 introduction to *The Bias of Communication*, McLuhan cites Chicago school sociologist Robert Ezra Park's 1940 essay 'Physics and Society,' which argues analogically from physics that ' "extensions and improvements which the physical sciences have made to the means of communications are ... vital to the existence of society" ' (*BC* xv). The implicit connection among physics, communications, and the organic workings of society would have been especially appealing to McLuhan, as would Park's comment that 'physics and the application of physical science have entered into the warp and woof of present-day social life.'[64] Not having a point of view would, from this argument, constitute nothing less than a new way of living in society where we all seek to respond critically to social and cultural phenomena. This in fact was necessitated by the unmooring of the knowledge base occasioned by the explosion of information through the agency of electronic media, one effect of which was to promote a shift in notions of authority, as McLuhan writes in 'Inside the Five Sense Sensorium' (1961): 'owing to the new ways of moving and coding information, it has become difficult to exercise delegated authority. Instead, there is growing need for the "authority of knowledge" ' (49). McLuhan accordingly deconstructs his own subject position as author in *The Gutenberg Galaxy* through a process of decentring involving the use of hundreds of quotations from 216 books and articles; by arranging the text as a series of asterisked footnotes; by placing the introduction at the end and thereby displacing the author's 'voice,'[65] as well as by interrupting the lineality and teleology associated with the book.[66] *The Gutenberg Galaxy* was, furthermore, the last book that McLuhan would write 'authoritatively' in that the remainder of his career would be spent re-articulating and reworking earlier material as well as writing collaboratively. This profoundly recursive phase of his career used repetition not merely as a 'sign' or rhetoric of orality[67] but as a way of constantly decentring and de-authorizing his own work, thereby placing it in history, in flux, in dialogue. This was the most daring aspect of McLuhan's intellectual career, and it is thus not surprising that it occasioned the greatest amount of criticism – that his books were repetitive, hackneyed, static. They were, and they were not, with the paradox achieving its force in the contextual mediation to which his works constantly sought to redirect attention, and most profoundly in his insistence that his message was in his medium. Hence McLuhan's insistence on the impossibility of communication in the transparent sense of the the Shannon-Weaver model. Communication was what we lived (which was the idea he developed in *Understanding Media*); communication *was* our social space in that all uttering was outering.[68]

McLuhan's intellectual trajectory, from his critique of 'visual society' to a methodology describable as 'no point of view' (as Judith Stamps puts it), the move from visual to audile, was thus a move from static to dynamic. In the dynamization of his previously arrested methodology, McLuhan sought to *produce tension*, not resolve it (*Unth* 122; 142),[69] and it was his ability to express his observations in dynamic terms that constitutes one of McLuhan's most significant achievements. He metaphorized this dynamic as acoustic (because dialogical) and as spatial (because configurational). The acoustically spatial text, even if visual, would not be so ideologically;[70] rather, it would be orally empathic, largely through its undermining of linear causality. The de-hierarchization of the visual promised by no point of view would liberate tactually/textually the other senses in a trajectory that moved (as Barthes put it) from work to (tactile) text. As McLuhan states, 'An oral manuscript culture had no fear of tactility, the very crux of the interplay of the senses' (*GG* 83). The solution to the problem of space, in other words, was to be found in a reconfiguration of that space as a dynamic process: '[t]he redemption of time occurs ... with space and place' ('Medieval Environment' 12–13).[71]

When McLuhan returned to *The Gutenberg Galaxy* as part of the recursive turn in his career, he did so from a political and economic standpoint (perhaps in reaction to Theall's critique in *The Medium Is the Rear-View Mirror*), focusing once again on Lear, reconfigured as an executive who drops out of his kingdom/corporation.[72] As he writes (with Barrington Nevitt) in *Take Today: The Executive as Dropout* (1972), 'Whereas the medieval monarch had "put on" his subjects as his "corporate mask," the Renaissance prince saw his people contained within visual and geographic boundaries' (20; this passage is followed by a quotation from the discussion of *Lear* in *The Gutenberg Galaxy*). In keeping with the auditory bias according to which this book is constructed, it is written in sound bites (cf 109; 130). *Take Today* defines '[a]uditory imagination' as 'the mind's ear – the complement of visual imagination' (9). This auditory space comprises a posthistorical 'echoland' in that it forms 'an inclusive NOW of all traditions' (*TT* 16). The retrieval of these traditions, however, is not reactionary; rather, it is characteristic of the dynamics of any given society: '*Retrieval is not reaction, but a part of the systole-diastole of a pulsating society*' (65). McLuhan thus critiques Marx's notion of history as a 'plenary category' (67), arguing that '*"There is no such thing as past history, since it is always a fiction fabricated by the preferences of the present"*' (67). Similarly, '[a]n oral resonance erodes the boundaries of the old economics, turning the planet into a single Echoland[:] a word now makes the market. The sequential causality of classical economics is meaningless and fatal' (82).[73] This is so because '[t]here are ... no connections in the material universe. Einstein, Heisenberg, and Linus Pauling have baffled the old mechanical and visual culture of the nineteenth century by reminding scientists in general that the only physical bond in Nature is the resonating interval or "interface." ... It is hard for the conventional and uncritical mind to grasp the fact that *"the meaning of meaning is a relationship"*: a figure-ground process of perpetual change' (86).[74] Metaphorically, the dynamic methodology McLuhan proposes here is analogous to the 'living dialogue' that he affirms in 'The Humanities in the Electronic Age.' Dialogue had gone into decline with the advent of print technology (as Ong had suggested), with its insistence on a sequential, as opposed to relational, mode of thinking. McLuhan writes of Thomas More's awareness that 'the medieval scholastic dialogue, oral and conversational, is quite unsuited to the new problems of large centralist states. A new processing of problems, one thing at a time, "nothing out of due order and fashion," must succeed to the older dialogue. For the scholastic method was a simultaneous mosaic, a dealing with many aspects and levels of meaning in crisp simultaneity' (*GG* 129). With the return to orally inflected modes, however, the necessity of dialogue once again asserts itself, as in the work of Innis, who 'tackled configurations rather than sequences of events in their interplay ... As Innis got more insights he abandoned any mere point of view in his presentation of knowledge' (216–17).

McLuhan also theorized this concept of dialogue as a fundamental principle of social interaction, and, as such, it has much in common with Bakhtin's notion of the dialogical.[75] Writing in 'Culture without Literacy' (*Exp* 1 [1953]), McLuhan states that 'the basic requirement of any system of communication is that it be circular ... That is why presumably the human dialogue is and must ever be the basic form of all civilization. For the dialogue compels each participant to see and recreate his own vision through another sensibility' (Cwl 126–7). This provides the most significant context for McLuhan's comment that linear communication (in the Shannon-Weaver formulation) is rare; communication is not monologically transparent but dialogically inflected, as is the case, paradigmatically, with the pun: 'Discoveries issue from "the resonant interval" of quantum mechanics rather than the visual connection of rational systems. Many people of professional demeanor "shun the punman," having been warned that verbal play is the lowest form of wit. These people have to bite their lips a good deal in order to repress their enjoyment of the most natural feature of all language, namely its inexhaustible richness of incompatible meanings' (*TT* 102).[76] In these terms, language becomes the site where subjective authority is most thoroughly placed in question. The social space of language is thus uncertain, in flux, and comprises a community based on communication that is acoustically decentred and unbounded. The notion of 'the living dialogue,' then, departs significantly from Innis's uninflected 'orality'[77] with its source in an idealized Greece. As McLuhan writes in 'The Humanities in the Electronic Age,' 'what has happened with the electronic advent is not that we move the products of human knowledge or labour to all corners of the earth more quickly. Rather we dilate the very means and *processes* of discourse to make a global envelope of sense and sensibility for the earth. From the moment of the telegraph, extra-sensory perception became a daily factor in shaping the human community and private perception alike. It is not the products of perception and judgement which now reach us by electric media, but involvement in the entire communal process of interfused co-existence' (7). And further: 'We have in the past century moved out of a mechanical into an electric, organic, culture. That is, we have increasingly moved out of a segmental, specialist phase of knowledge into a period of interplay and, as it were, dialogue among all kinds of knowledge' (8). McLuhan suggests that this situation be confronted by '[e]nthron[ing] the living dialogue in centres and between centres, since the entire new technology of our age demands this greatest of all humanist forms of instruction, not as an ideal, but as a daily necessity of action in every area of our communities' (10). If literacy had blinded us to the language and meaning of spatial forms (as McLuhan suggested it had in the first issue of *Explorations*), the imperative of acoustic space, with its multiplity of spaces, was precisely to urge on us a rhetoric of such forms.

CHAPTER FOUR

Prosthetic Aesthetics

The etymology of all human technologies is to be found in the body itself: they are, as it were, prosthetic devices, mutations, metaphors of the body or its parts.
Marshall McLuhan with Bruce Powers, *The Global Village*

Senses of Space

McLuhan developed his theory of space in three major phases. The first of these worked out the implications of mechanical space and its origins in print, a focus McLuhan maintained up to and including *The Gutenberg Galaxy*. In the second major phase, McLuhan explored electronic spacetime and its interaction with the senses, a focus initiated in *The Gutenberg Galaxy* and followed through in *Report on Project in Understanding New Media* and *Understanding Media*. This latter work, a revision of *Report*, initiated a third and profoundly recursive[1] phase in McLuhan's career in which he explored the implications of acoustic space, revisiting and rewriting (or perhaps unwriting) *The Gutenberg Galaxy*, which, in a certain sense, was the *last* book he wrote (as, indeed, Raymond Williams had suggested it must be).[2] Overall, McLuhan's concern throughout these phases was with a spatial dynamic that he variously configured as mechanical/electrical, literate/oral, figure/ground, environment/anti-environment, and so on.

At the end of *The Gutenberg Galaxy*, McLuhan wrote that 'We are living in a period richer and more terrible than the "Shakespearean Moment" so well described by Patrick Cruttwell in his book of the same title. But it has been the business of *The Gutenberg Galaxy* to examine only the mechanical technology emergent from our alphabet and the printing press. What will be the new configurations of mechanisms and of literacy as these older forms of perception and judgment are interpenetrated by the new electric age?' (278). The era of static, perspectival, three-dimensional visual space – the perceptual product of print technology – had come to an end with the demise of the mechanical era foretold by Einstein's theory of relativity and had given way to an era of multiple, dynamic spaces, spaces described by Alexander Dorner in *The Way Beyond 'Art,'* one of the books cited in the bibliography appended to the second edition of *Understanding*

Media,[3] as 'perfect examples of that split-world which, while aiming at form, aimed also at changeability, and let time invade the absolute scaffolding of space' (90). While visual space was the product of one dominant sense – sight – the acoustic space inaugurated by the electric era had the effect of bringing the senses back into play with one another. As McLuhan wrote to Walter Ong in 1961, 'print technology ... smashes ... analogical awareness in society and the individual ... But an event like radio or even telegraph has the deepest consequences for the momentary sense ratios of the ordinary person" (*L* 280–1). Visual space was only one *kind* of space, and as electronic media brought the other senses back into analogical interrelationship, other sorts of spaces would come (back) into being, spaces that would be dynamic and interactive.[4] One of McLuhan's goals in the *Report* was to '[c]onsider the power of any medium to impose its own spatial assumptions and structures' (133), a project he continued in *Understanding Media*. Having already critiqued in *The Gutenberg Galaxy* the Modernist obsession with the visual, McLuhan wished in *Understanding Media* to demonstrate how electronic media were serving to reintegrate and reincorporate the senses into an aesthetic that was more involving perceptually. By devalorizing the visual, McLuhan sought to revalorize the role of our other senses in the production of a multiplicity of other kinds of space. It was imperative that we understand these spaces, or media, since they were actively changing us psychically by changing our sensory perceptions.

It was this goal to which McLuhan addressed himself in the companion volume to *The Gutenberg Galaxy* announced at its conclusion: *Understanding Media*. The work is structured as a spatial rhetoric[5] of communicative modes, a project McLuhan had limned in his 1953 article 'James Joyce: Trivial and Quadrivial.' McLuhan argued there that symbolist poetry achieved its effects by coupling liturgical rhythms with classical rhetoric. It did so in response to 'Newtonian science,' which had 'knocked ancient rhetoric off its much reduced pedestal by making the spatial and pictorial [i.e., visual space] aspects of the external world supreme' (*IL* 24), a thesis McLuhan's student Walter Ong subsequently argued in his book *Ramus*. Thus, poets 'from Thomson to Tennyson' were constrained to 'communicate states of mind in terms of external landscape' (*IL* 25), with '[p]sychology ... managed in terms of [visual] space' (25), while 'time, tradition, and language are given minimal scope' (25). What the symbolists did was to reverse this tendency through the device of the *paysage intérieur* and its 'juxtaposition of more than one time' (25), thus fusing space and time in a move which anticipated Einsteinian spacetime. And, now that Einstein's theory of relativity had brought space into conjunction with time, there was a methodological need to bring rhetoric together with space. McLuhan's project in the passage from *Report* (1960) to *Understanding Media* (1964) was to articulate the bases on which these 'newly discovered tactile, sculptural spaces' (*UM* 121) were being constructed and to provide a relational model for understanding them.

It was this *construction* of space that interested McLuhan, as he wrote to Edward S. Morgan in 1959: 'A hundred years ago, the painters abandoned pictorial space, the space of perspective, enclosed space as painters call it, in favor of what they call "automorphic" space; a space in which each person, each thing, makes it[s] own world' (16 May 1959; *L* 254). Automorphic space was 'a space that we don't get *into* but which, as it were, we *put on*.'[6] McLuhan made this point more extensively in a letter to Jacqueline Tyrwhitt written six months after the completion of the *Report*:

Now that by electricity we have externalized *all* of our senses, we are in the desperate position of not having any *sensus communis* ... From Aristotle onward, the traditional function of the sensus communis is to translate each sense into the other senses, so that a unified, integral image is offered at all times to the mind ... By electricity ... we have not been driven out of our senses so much ... [as] our senses have been driven out of *us* ... Whatever we may wish in the matter, we can no longer live in Euclidean space under electronic conditions, and this means that the divisions between inner and outer, private and communal, whatever they may have been for a literate culture, are simply *not there* for an electric one. But the space-time of a preliterate society is not the space-time of our electric one. (23 December 1960; *L* 277–8)

Whereas absolute space was for Newtonian science 'nothing less than God's sensorium,' as Margaret Wertheim has put it,[7] the spacetime of Einsteinian physics had shattered that absolute into a dynamic play (or even struggle) for sensory hegemony.

Obscurely Cameral

McLuhan suggests in his letter to Edward Morgan that, in the nineteenth century, visual artists began to embody in their art the notion that the space produced through visual perception was not natural but a construct, and that vision had come to dominate and marginalize the other senses. As McLuhan wrote in 'Inside the Five Sense Sensorium,'

Just at the end of the 19th. century Bernard Berenson had begun a crusade 'to endow the retinal impression with tactile values.' There was wide awareness that photography and other technological change had abstracted the retinal impression, as it were, from the rest of the sensorium. Thus, in 1893 Adolf Hildebrand the sculptor published a small book called 'The Problem of Form.' He insisted that true vision must be much imbued with tangibility, and that creative, esthetic awareness was touching and making. Such was the timeliness of his insistence, that the theme of artistic vision as tangible, tactile, and based on the interplay of the sense[s] began to enjoy acceptance in poetry and painting alike. The art historian Heinrich Wölfflin taught the Hildebrand stress on visual forms as haptic or tangible-tactile – and his pupil Sigfried [sic] Giedion embodied it in his 'Space, Time and Architecture.' (49)

Jonathan Crary has argued that a telling index of the sensorium's history is the use of the camera obscura as a metaphor of human perception.[8] The camera obscura metaphor was developed philosophically by Descartes, for whom, writes Crary, 'one knows the world "uniquely by perception of the mind," and the secure positioning of the self within an empty interior space is a precondition for knowing the outer world. The space of the camera obscura, its enclosedness, its darkness, its separation from an exterior, incarnate Descartes's "I will now shut my eyes, I shall stop my ears, I shall disregard my senses." The orderly and calculable penetration of light rays through the single opening of the camera corresponds to the flooding of the mind by the light of reason, not the potentially dangerous dazzlement of the senses by the light of the sun.'[9] The camera obscura, in other words, represented the supreme dominance of the visual among the modalities of sensual perception, such that the visual became identified with its transcendent other, the light of reason. This dominance, as McLuhan continually stressed, was the product of print media. As he wrote in 'Myth and Mass Media,' 'in the very first decades of printing at the end of the fifteenth century, people became vividly aware of the camera obscura. The relation of this interest to the new printing process was not noted at the time. Yet printing is itself just such a camera obscura, yielding a private vision of the movements of others.'[10]

The visual was thus a retreat from the sensory as interactive accretion: vision elided the interaction of the senses by completely dominating them. As Crary puts it, '[f]ounded on laws of nature (optics) but extrapolated to a plane outside of nature, the camera obscura provides a vantage point onto the world analogous to the eye of God' (48). McLuhan likewise treats the fate of the camera obscura, and its photographic successors, as a moment in the history of the rediscovery of the senses. Telling, for McLuhan, is the fact that 'the early spectators of the moving image in the sixteenth century saw [the] images upside down. For this reason the lens was introduced – in order to turn the picture right side up. Our normal vision is also upside down. Psychically, we learn to turn our visual world right side up by translating the retinal impression from visual into tactile and kinetic terms. Right side up is apparently something we *feel* but cannot *see* directly' (*UM* 191; emphases added).[11] The lens thus becomes part of the history of the mechanical reinvention (or retrieval, to use the terminology of *Laws of Media*) of the organic, bringing us back in touch with the senses numbed by the ascendancy of the visual (whose 'right-side-up world' is in any case an illusion). The fact that the camera obscura ceased to be a metaphorical *point de repère* in the nineteenth century signals, then, a shift from one sense (vision), to many senses, as well as from a transcendence of the senses to the sensory domain itself. 'The corporeal subjectivity of the observer,' writes Crary, 'which was a priori excluded from the concept of the camera obscura, suddenly becomes the site on which an observer is possible. The human body, in all its contingency and specificity ... thus becomes the active producer of optical experience' (69). Once vision becomes immanent in this way, the distinction between observer and observed also collapses, and it was to this collapse that Joyce's notion (cited often by McLuhan) that his consumers were also his producers is indebted.

It was at this point, historically, that vision became part of physiological inquiry. Such inquiry was often made on behalf of studies of hand–eye coordination whose object was to increase labour productivity. 'In the context of new industrial models of factory production the problem of visual inattention was a serious one. But what developed was a notion of vision that was fundamentally quantitative, in which the terms constituting the relation between perception and object became abstract, interchangeable, *and nonvisual.*'[12] Paradoxically, to materialize the visual was to return it to the realm of the sensory from the transcendent realm of the intellect. No longer did the visual have separate and universal status. It became one of a number of individual senses. The study by physiologists of sensory perception at the beginning of the nineteenth century thus led to an increasing specialization of interest in the individual senses, what Crary calls 'the gradual parcelization and division of the body into increasingly separate and specific systems and functions ... Finally, by 1826 it was determined that sensory nerves were of five distinct types, corresponding to the five senses. All of this produced a new "truth" about the body which some have linked to the so-called "separation of the senses" in the nineteenth century.'[13] These changes signalled an end to the hegemony of vision in Western thought and to the camera obscura as its major metaphor. As Crary writes, '[b]y the early 1800s ... the rigidity of the camera obscura, its linear optical system, its fixed positions, its categorical distinction between inside and outside, its identification of perception and object, were all too inflexible and unwieldy for the needs of a new century. A more mobile, usable, and productive observer was needed in both discourse and practice – to be adequate to new uses of the body and to a vast proliferation of equally mobile and exchangeable signs and images. Modernization entailed a decoding and deterritorialization of vision.'[14] In these terms, the changes in visual metaphor recorded by Crary parallel interest in the fourth dimension and developments in physics, as well as those such as Cubism in art.

Coterminous with the changes of which Crary writes was the undermining of light as the stimulus *par excellence* of vision. The work of the German physiologist Johannes Müller demonstrated that the 'experience of light has no necessary connection with any actual light.'[15] In Müller's experiments, the sensation of light was induced by electrical stimulation; the implication of such experiments was to redefine vision 'as a capacity for being affected by sensations that have no necessary link to a referent, thus threatening any coherent system of meaning.'[16] Hermann von Helmholtz discerned in this detail of electrical stimulation a metaphor of great power; Crary cites this particularly McLuhanesque passage: '"Nerves in the human body have been accurately compared to telegraphy wires. Such a wire conducts one single kind of electric current and no other; it may be stronger, it may be weaker, it may move in either direction; it has no other qualitative differences. Nevertheless, according to the different kinds of apparatus with which we provide its terminations, we can send telegraphic dispatches, ring bells, explode mines, decompose water, move magnets, magnetize iron, develop light, and so on. *The same thing with our nerves.* The condition of excitement which can be produced in them, and is conducted by them, is ... everywhere the same."'[17] According to Crary, 'Helmholtz is explicit about the body's indifference to the sources of its experience and of its capacity for multiple connections with other agencies and machines. The perceiver here becomes a neutral conduit, one kind of relay among others to allow optimum conditions of circulation and exchangeability, *whether it be of commodities, energy, capital, images, or information.*'[18] This is likewise the premise of *Understanding Media* (with the significant exception that McLuhan posits greater agency in the human 'conduit'), and contextualizes McLuhan's reference in *Understanding Media* to 'the great Helmholtz, whose work covered many fields' (271).[19]

Tonal Sensations

As Linda Dalrymple Henderson has noted, Helmholtz was a prime disseminator of notions about non-Euclidean geometry, and these notions were in turn 'a major impetus for a rethinking of questions about space' (*4D* 10). His major contention was that geometrical axioms were empirical and not a priori: 'Helmholtz ... held that the human mind could intuit, or represent to itself, non-Euclidean space ... [c]arefully defining "to represent" as "the power of imagining *the whole series of sensible impressions* that would be had in such a case"' (*4D* 14; emphasis added).[20] The italicized phrase is significant because Helmholtz's theories of non-Euclidean space were conducted in tandem with his enquiries into the physiology of sound, published as *On the Sensations of Tone as a Physiological Basis for the Theory of Music* (rev. ed. 1862). Helmholtz concludes that work by insisting on

> the characteristic resemblance between the relations of the musical scale and of space, a resemblance which appears to me of vital importance for the peculiar effects of music. It is an essential character of space that at every position within it like bodies can be placed, and like motions can occur. Everything that is possible to happen in one part of space is equally possible in every other part of space and is perceived by us in precisely the same way ... On the other hand, also, different voices, executing the same or different melodic phrases, can move at the same time within the compass of the scale, like two bodies in space, and, provided they are consonant in the accented parts of bars, without creating any musical disturbances. (370)

Helmholtz's achievement in the study of optical and acoustic 'psychophysics' has been analysed by Edwin G. Boring, whose *Sensation and Perception in the History of Experimental Psychology* (dedicated to Helmholtz) is cited by McLuhan in *Report on Project in Understanding New Media* as providing 'clues to the changing attitudes and theories of the Western world toward our various senses' (*RPM* 33).[21] Those changes are schematically summarized by Boring as moving between Descartes's notion of innate ideas and Locke's of the *tabula rasa*, a dichotomy that subsequently splinters into nativisim and empiricism (of which Helmholtz was a proponent), phenomenology and behaviourism. Boring goes on to note that Helmholtz's empiricism derives from Johannes Müller's notion that 'complex ideas [were] intimate fusions of many sensory components and ... that all space perception depends upon muscular sensation' (Boring 30). This led to Helmholtz's assertion (as noted earlier) 'that the geometrical axioms are not innate, and are not *a priori* intuitions, but learned relationships' (Boring 31). Helmholtz's sensory notions (like Müller's) were based on the classical view of the mind, 'that there exists within the brain a sentient being, a Sensorium, that seeks knowledge of the external world and can never come closer to it than the direct contact provided by the nerves' (Boring 69). What Müller and Helmholtz did was expand on this notion, differentiating the specific 'energies' associated with each sense. 'The effect of the theory was tremendous,' writes Boring; 'it indicated that there must be spatial differentiation of qualities in the sense-organ' (73).

What is most important about Boring's study is that it gives the senses a history; to speak of the senses as having a history meant that they were historically produced, that they were social constructs – 'technologies of the self,' in Foucault's useful formulation.[22] The model for such a history of the senses was provided by Boring's study, which emerged in part from the debate concerning the unity of the senses – whether there was any degree of interaction between and among the senses, a debate paralleled by the concurrent interest among European artists in simultaneity and synaesthesia.[23] (Synaesthesia is a term that recurs a number of times in *Understanding Media*; McLuhan writes, for example, that 'by imposing unvisualizable relationships that are the result of instant speed, electric technology dethrones the visual sense and restores us to the dominion of synesthesia, and the close interinvolvement of the other senses' [111]). It was the (potentially) *relational* quality of the senses that configured them synaesthetically.[24] Of particular interest for McLuhan's theory of acoustic space was Boring's suggestion that the auditory realm was spatial, and that one could thus speak of a 'physics of sound' (Boring 312). It was Helmholtz who had inspired attempts 'to decide how auditory space can be built up by the mediation of other sensations' (381); these attempts discovered that 'localization is not purely auditory, but the product of an integration of auditory, kinesthetic and, when the eyes are open, visual factors' (392), thus suggesting that perception is a form of sensory interrelationship. It was touch in particular that 'presents us with many stable fusions, blends, spatial patterns and temporal modes of change' (509) within the activity of perception.[25] McLuhan echoes this point most clearly in a 1973 article co-authored with Barrington Nevitt:

> The *eye* makes a 'visual space structure' with individual points of view or centers and definite margins or boundaries – everything in its proper place and time. Each of our senses makes its own space, but no sense can function in isolation. Only as sight relates to touch, or kinesthesia, or sound, can the eye see. In isolation, the visual sense presents an immediate blur – all ground minus figures. The bridging of the senses creates an interface of figure-ground relations that make sense. Making sense is never matching or mere one-to-one correspondence which is an assumption of visual bias. For the *ear* makes an 'acoustic space structure' with centers everywhere and margins nowhere, like a musical surround or the boundless universe.[26]

The science of 'psychophysics' adumbrated in Boring's book was especially important within McLuhan's intellectual trajectory, in that it related his early and ongoing interests in psychology and physics[27] through the notion of gestalt.[28] Indeed, Boring's remark that 'it is the relations that persist independently of the contents in the *Gestaltqualität*' (255) might be rephrased as 'the medium is the message,' where 'medium' would be understood as constituting a *dynamic* relationship,[29] insofar as gestalt dynamized the figure and ground that in perspectival representations were static.

Understanding Spaces

In September of 1959, McLuhan began writing a report ('Project 69') for the National Association of Educational Broadcasters, its goal being to devise a syllabus for Grade 11 students that would educate them in the effects of media (*M&M* 136–7). This *Report on Project in Understanding New Media* (1960) became the basis for *Understanding Media*. McLuhan cites at the outset of *Report* Georg von Békésy's *Experiments in Hearing*, noting how von Békésy contrasts 'two-dimensional and three-dimensional paintings. His purpose is to explain how in the study of hearing, "mosaic" methods of research are more effective than "perspective" methods' ('General Introduction to the Languages and Grammars of the Media,' *RPM* 2). This comment adumbrates the trajectory of McLuhan's inquiry from the *Report* through *Understanding Media*: because electronic media were liberating the senses that had been anesthetized by the domination of the visual sense made possible through print culture, visual space was now being displaced by spaces constructed through the other senses, and together these spaces of the 'sensorium' (*RPM* 29) formed a mosaic, a textured space that was neither planar nor linear, but 'cubist,' as opposed to perspectival. McLuhan's umbrella terms for these spaces was 'acoustic' or 'auditory,' since 'hearing is from all directions at once' (2) and since '[s]peech is the only medium that uses all the senses at once' (9). By contrast, perspectival space privileges vision. 'As the number of variables co-existing in a single field have mounted in ordinary experience,' writes McLuhan, 'the neat packaging job of perspective, and of pictorial space filled with familiar objects, has become irrelevant to human problems of experience' (3). McLuhan notes that auditory space is having an effect even on visual space, such that 'our visual experience is now a mosaic of items assembled from every part of the globe, moment by moment. Lineal perspective and pictorial organization cannot cope with this situation' (3). It was this sensory element that added the temporal dimension to visual space; as Walter Ong has remarked, '[a]ll sensation takes place in time, but sound has a special relationship to time unlike that of the other fields that register in human sensation.'[30]

From this realization of the spatial implications of auditory space, McLuhan proceeds to a statement of his *Report*'s central point:

> I would like to report a discovery concerning the role of writing in creating what is now to mathematics and physics the obsolete fiction of 'Euclidean space.' THE IMPLICATIONS OF THIS DISCOVERY FOR ORIENTING US TODAY IN THE ELECTRONIC AGE ARE SO GREAT THAT I FEEL NO QUALMS IN STATING THAT IT JUSTIFIES PROJECT 69 MANY TIMES OVER. THAT IS TO SAY, WERE THIS PROJECT TO HAVE NOTHING AT ALL TO REPORT IN MEDIA STUDY BEYOND EXPLAINING THE ROLE OF THE WRITTEN WORD IN BRINGING INTO EXISTENCE 'EUCLIDEAN SPACE,' IT WOULD YET OFFER A MASSIVE AND CHALLENGING SET OF DATA FOR THE ATTENTION OF WESTERN MAN. (3; caps in original)

It was crucial for McLuhan to demonstrate that Euclidean space was a construct in order to be able to argue for the possibility of spaces constructed through senses other than the visual:

> WHY DID THE PHONETIC ALPHABET HOICK MAN OUT OF THE AUDITORY SPACE OF THE TRIBAL DRUM INTO THE CIVILIZED, HOMOGENEOUS AND CONTINUOUS SPACE OF LINE AND PLANE AND PICTURE? THE ANSWER IS: BECAUSE THE PHONETIC ALPHABET ALONE, OF ALL FORMS OF WRITING, TRANSLATES THE AUDIBLE AND THE TACTILE INTO THE VISIBLE AND THE ABSTRACT. LETTERS, THE LANGUAGE OF CIVILIZATION, HAVE THIS POWER OF TRANSLATING ALL OF OUR SENSES INTO VISUAL AND PICTORIAL SPACE. (5)

McLuhan goes on to state that, '[m]ore than anybody else, the mathematician is aware of the arbitrary and fictional character of this continuous, homogeneous visual space. Why? Because number, the language of science, is a fiction for retranslating the Euclidean space fiction back into auditory and tactile space' (5). Drawing on Tobias Dantzig's

Number: The Language of Science (from which he also quoted in *The Gutenberg Galaxy*),[31] McLuhan nevertheless takes issue with Dantzig's belief that 'Euclidean space, linear, flat, straight, uniform, is rooted in our minds ... Such space [argues McLuhan] is a product of literacy and is unknown to preliterate or archaic man' (6). According to Dantzig, the function of number is to accommodate all those elements of experience that do not fit into Euclidean space: '"we have no other alternative than to regard the 'curved' reality of our senses as the ultra-ultimate step in an infinite sequence of *flat* worlds which exist only in our imagination"' (McLuhan quoting from Dantzig, 6). The physics of flatland, then, is seen as issuing, paradoxically, in a theory of curved space; whereas '[n]umber is subservient to letters and meaningless without a civilized, pictorial culture to support it' (7), electronic culture is post-numerate in its reliance on systems that are not sequential but relational. Hence, television's 'mosaic has brought us back to the two-dimensional and to the fascination with tactile process' (21).

McLuhan expresses this paradox according to the rhetorical figure of chiasmus, which he states to be 'indispensable to understanding media since all information flow by feedback – that is by its *effects* – operates simultaneously in opposite modes' (23); in *Understanding Media*, McLuhan devotes a chapter to this notion of reversal (ch. 3: 'Reversal of the Overheated Medium'). As he put it in an article written with Barrington Nevitt, 'metamorphosis by *chiasmus*'[32] is the dominant technological process; '[s]peeding up the components of any visually ordered structure or continuous space pattern will lead to breaking its connections and destroying its boundaries. They explode into the resonant gaps or interfaces that characterize the discontinuous structure of acoustic space' ('The Argument' 2). McLuhan's choice of chiasmus as his central rhetorical trope (which he would develop to its fullest statement in *Laws of Media*) is significant, since it combines spatial notions[33] (chiasmus being etymologically related through Greek to the letter 'χ') with those of movement (crossover; reversal) and thus of time.[34] *Chiasm*, furthermore, is 'an anatomical term for the crossing over of two physiological structures' (*Pr* 141), a meaning relevant to McLuhan's interest in the interface of biology and technology. Chiasmus is presented diagramatically in *Report*[35] through the relationship between 'High Definition' and 'Low Definition' media, and between 'Structural Impact' ('sensory impressions as they affect the beholder or audience' [*RPM* 25]) and 'Subjective Completion' ('the effect of this impression as it is processed by the audience' [25]; fig. 4.1). (In *Understanding Media*, McLuhan substituted 'Hot' and 'Cool' for this terminology; cf *RPM* 128.) Media were thus presented by McLuhan as operating in a dynamic field, such that the spaces they produced were not fixed – unlike perspectival ones – but were in movement, having 'dynamic symmetries and contours' (*RPM* 27) consistent with auditory space.

McLuhan draws on Edward Hall's *The Silent Language* (1959) to advance his point that media communicate through space (as well as through time). The point is significant, since writing has inculcated the notion that communication is sequential (and thus temporal). Yet, as McLuhan points out in *The Gutenberg Galaxy*, ideograms in languages such as Chinese communicate spatially, all at once. Here he suggests that space communicates contextually, as well. Expanding on Hall's notion that '"there is no such thing as 'experience' in the abstract, as a mode separate and distinct from culture"' (McLuhan quoting Hall, *RPM* 30), McLuhan makes the suggestion that cultural context

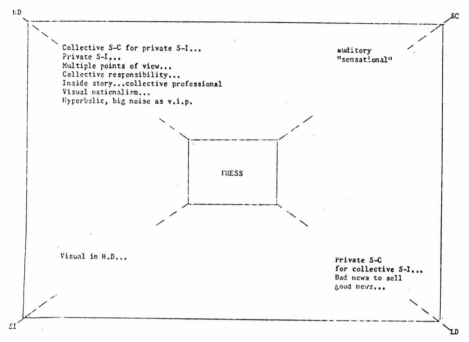

Figure 4.1. Diagram from McLuhan, *Report on Project in Understanding New Media*.
Compare the 'squares of opposition' diagrams reproduced from Ong. Here McLuhan figures
the oppositional (or dynamic) qualities of the press, with one aspect, that of subjective completion, moving towards the auditory dimension; cf figure 2.1.

is part of communication: 'Hall is saying here, in effect, what I formulate as "the
medium is the message"' (30). 'Medium' is clearly not being used here in a formalist
sense but in a culturally material one. According to Hall, 'Space Speaks' (ch. 10: 158–
80); by this, he means that space 'not only communicates in the most basic sense, but ...
also *organizes* virtually everything in life' (*Silent Language* viii), thereby forming a
'*cultural unconscious*' (x). It is crucial, according to Hall, to understand these '"out-of-
awareness" aspects of communication' (29). Space, for Hall, is largely bound up with the
notion of territoriality:[36] 'Every living thing has a physical boundary that separates it
from its external environment,' writes Hall (*Silent Language* 158). 'A short distance up
the phylogenetic scale, however, another, non-physical boundary appears that exists
outside the physical one. This new boundary is harder to delimit than the first but is just
as real. We call this the "organism's territory"' (158). In the human organism, the early
process of learning about space and place is derived from vocal intonation: 'the first
clues which suggest to children that one thing is different from another comes from shifts
in tone of voice which direct attention in very subtle but important ways' (165–6).
Movement in space (such as backing up when a person encroaches on 'your' space),
according to Hall, 'gives a tone to a communication' and can 'even override the spoken
word' (175). Where Hall's spatial theory differs from McLuhan's is in the former's
insistence on strictly demarcated territories; McLuhan's spaces were much more the

product of dynamic interrelationships. As McLuhan points out in a letter written to Claude Bissell (4 March 1965), '[e]nvironments ... are imperceptible (this is the theme of *The Silent Language* by Ed. T. Hall). But environments are not mere containers. They are active and pervasive processes' (*L* 319). McLuhan also criticized Hall for 'not try[ing] to relate the diversity of ... spatial forms to technological impact on our sensibilities' (*L* 386).[37]

A Rhetoric of Spaces

Report and *Understanding Media* can be distinguished on the basis of the method developed in each of them to understand media. In the earlier work, McLuhan focuses on understanding these media individually. In the later one, he seeks not only to do this but to provide a more global approach to the proliferation of media, producing a study of 'the structural changes in the organization of space as they resulted from wheel, road, and papyrus [etc.]' (*UM* 97). As McLuhan writes in the section of *Understanding Media* on 'Housing,' '[t]his entire discussion is offered at considerable risk of misapprehension because these are, spatially, highly technical matters. Nevertheless, when such spaces are understood, they offer the key to a great many enigmas, past and present' (125). Given that these spaces (or media) are shaped by our senses, and in turn shape us, such that we become their contents (as, with television, we become the screen [*GG* 39]), it was important to understand them rhetorically, in terms of process, rather than content.[38] Wanting to avoid a taxonomy (other than the anti-taxonomy of 'hot' and 'cool'),[39] McLuhan fell back on the rhetorical[40] studies he had undertaken at Cambridge when writing his dissertation on the polyglot phenomenon of Thomas Nashe. The advantage of this rhetorical approach is that it did not place phenomena in closed categories but rather put them in play. Rhetoric marks a certain activity, a process, and as such identifies at once a form and type of creativity: a 'rhetorical work is for the sake of producing action,' as McLuhan put it in his article 'Poetic vs. Rhetorical Exegesis.'[41] Rhetoric was also ideally suited to speaking about auditory space, since rhetoric was at once oral and spatial.[42]

It was while working on his dissertation[43] that McLuhan began to realize (as Marchand puts it) that 'nearly the entire cultural history of the West could be read in terms of an ongoing and often hidden war between the proponents of each of the three branches of the trivium – grammar, logic, and rhetoric – the curriculum (together with the sciences of the quadrivium) of ancient Greece and Rome and the Middle Ages ... Nashe was simply involved in a quarrel between the Renaissance followers of a tradition of rhetoric going back to Cicero – the tradition of wisdom as eloquent speaking – and the 'schoolmen' of the Middle Ages, who were followers of dialectics – wisdom as pure logic' (*M&M* 54–5). McLuhan argues in his dissertation that contemporary culture was reversing the move towards dialectics inaugurated by Descartes. '[F]rom the time of Descartes,' he writes, 'the main mode of science is ... mathematics. In our own time the methods of anthropology and psychology have re-established grammar as, at least, a valued mode of science' (5). With this return to a more unified sense of disciplinary study, analogy (cf 'antilogy' [53]) was being rescued from the 'Ramistic nominalism and Cartesian mathematics [that had] dethroned [it] decisively' (32).

The hybridity of Nashe's writing was itself a sign of the demise, around 1550, of the trivium/quadrivium dyad, and of the three parts (or 'ways') of the trivium,[44] as David Wills has noted in his book *Prosthesis* (214). The 'medieval unity of knowledge' (*Pr* 214) was coming to an end with the decline of the scribal era and the onset of the Gutenberg era. The breakup of the trivium opened it to accretions such as those made by Richard Wilson in his *Rhetoric* – the first in English – published in 1553 in Cambridge (*Pr* 215 and *passim*), which adds the word 'prosthesis' to the classical list of rhetorical terms, meaning 'the addition of a syllable to the beginning of a word' (*Pr* 218). Wilson was particularly concerned in his *Rhetoric* with an exacerbated version of rhetoric – the use of foreign words for rhetorical effect (a vice to which Nashe was particularly prone).

Prosthesis marks a moment in the history of rhetoric when rhetorical notions associated with Cicero and Quintilian were under attack; it was Peter Ramus who, in 1549, wrote his *Arguments in Rhetoric against Quintilian* (*Pr* 215). This period also marks an incredibly productive moment in the history of medicine: Vesalius, a contemporary of Ramus, published *De humani corporis fabrica* in 1543, and Ambroise Paré published in 1585 his *Œuvres*, works that contain important descriptions of amputation and prosthetic replacement.[45] The historical contemporaneity of these discourses is indicative of the tension between organicist and mechanical discourses of the body (*Pr* 246), a tension resolved in favour of the mechanical (as Vesalius's *corpora fabrica* indicates; *Pr* 246) until the advent of the electronic era, which, according to McLuhan, was reversing into the organic once again, with extension and amputation remaining the vectors of its dynamic (as they would in the principles of enhancement and obsolescence, retrieval and reversal, that constitute the laws of media). Prosthesis, for Wills, is a sign of the way in which, during the Renaissance, 'knowledge in general ... [is] being not just rearranged but prosthetized – broken apart and artificially reconstructed' (*Pr* 218–19). McLuhan, as we have seen, noted a similar dynamic, likewise spatial, in the Renaissance, one that he attributed to the effects of Gutenberg technology.[46] The Gutenberg era was a particularly prosthetic one, according to Wills, because the printing press inaugurated a 'cybernetic moment ... [in which] the human hand is superseded by the machine' (*Pr* 221). What particularly testifies to this textual prosthetic is the act of citation, made possible by the printing press's spatialization of the spoken word such that it can be broken up, replaced, amputated, prosthetized. Significant in this regard is the fact that it is precisely in the *Dialecticae partitiones* of Ramus, published in 1543, that the forerunner of quotation marks appears for the first time. It is in this sense that 'prosthesis' marks the moment when 'the continuous stream of medieval discourse is being broken by spatial articulations that appear on the printed page' (*Pr* 226–7).

While quotation was the prosthetic device *par excellence* of *The Gutenberg Galaxy*, in *Understanding Media* McLuhan expands his study to include a broad range of media, from roads to television; as well, he seeks to articulate a dynamics of media that embraces both aspects of prosthetic culture, extension and amputation, thereby relating prosthesis to the principle of reversal inherent in chiasmus.[47] In *Understanding Media*, prosthesis is discussed largely under the rubric of 'ablation,' a term that signifies in two different disciplines, medicine and rhetoric; while these meanings were progressively cut off from one another as a result of print technology, they are coming together within the interdisciplinarity fostered by electronic media, wherein they occupy a relational dynamic and thereby constitute 'a figure for which neither Euclidean geometry nor modern surgery can provide the models, requiring us to look towards some cybernetic or bioengineered future' (*Pr* 249).[48] McLuhan's first reference to ablation is made punningly (itself a sign of prosthesis, as Wills notes) in the 'Introduction,' where he suggests that, '[i]f the nineteenth century was the age of the editorial chair, ours is the century of the psychiatrist's couch. As an extension of man the chair is a specialist ablation of the posterior, a sort of ablative absolute of backside, whereas the couch extends the integral being' (*UM* 5). (McLuhan himself used the couch in this way; Jean Paré noted in McLuhan's office 'a broken-down couch on which the professor reclined, suspenders showing, with his hands crossed behind his head.')[49] While in the process of rewriting *Report*, McLuhan had written to Ong (1 February 1962) that 'I expect to add to the present form of *Understanding Media* several media like money, railways, ships and 'planes and cars – in fact, all of those externalizations of our bodily functions and perceptions which cause all human technology to exist in the ablative case' (*L* 283). In a letter written to Ong the following week, McLuhan asks his former student to 'Look at page 79 of Ed. Hall's *The Silent Language*. Is not our approach to media the one indicated there? i.e. all technologies as ablations of sense and faculty – all in the ablative case? And all acting as separate closed systems that re-enter our sensibilities with metamorphic power?' (*L* 285). 'Ablative' is itself a many-layered word. As a grammatical term, it is that case of (Latin) nouns 'expressing source, agent, cause, or instrument, of action' (OED). 'Ablation' is the surgical 'removal of any part of the body'; the 'wasting or erosion of a glacier, iceberg, or rock by melting or the action of water'; and the 'evaporation or melting of part of the outer surface of a spacecraft through heating by friction with the atmosphere' (OED). All of these meanings were relevant to McLuhan's project in *Understanding Media*, which was concerned with the interficial aspects of electric technology – the way in which it interrelated biology and technology, organic and inorganic, inside and outside. As he points out, 'when such ablatives intrude, they alter the syntax of society. There is no *ceteris paribus* [other things being equal or unchanged] in the world of media and technology. Every extension or acceleration effects new configurations in the over-all situation at once' (*UM* 184).

Res Extensa

McLuhan often punned on 'utter' as 'outer' to indicate that one of the effects of media was extension.[50] This process of outering became his chief focus in *Understanding Media*, where he treated media as *The Extensions of Man* – 'our uttered or outered senses' (*UM* 57). Whereas the mechanical era had extended the human body, the electronic era was extending the central nervous system towards 'the technological simulation of consciousness' (3), and, in the process, was 'abolishing space and time' (3) as separate and unrelated categories. Writing in the first section of *Understanding Media*, McLuhan states:

> Any invention or technology is an extension or self-amputation of our physical bodies, and such extension also demands new ratios or new equilibriums among the other organs and extensions of the body. There is, for example, no way of refusing to comply with the new sense ratios or sense 'closure' evoked by the TV image. But the effect of the entry of the TV image will vary from culture to culture in accordance with the existing sense ratios in each culture. In audile-tactile Europe[,] TV has intensified the visual sense, spurring them toward

American styles of packaging and dressing. In America, the intensely visual culture, TV has opened the doors of audile-tactile perception to the non-visual world of spoken languages and food and the plastic arts. As an extension and expediter of the sense life, any medium at once affects the entire field of the senses ... (*UM* 45)

McLuhan's interest in the way technology extends our physical and mental being recalls Freud's comment in *Civilization and Its Discontents* that 'Man has become a kind of prosthetic God' (44)[51] (though numerous other sources have been suggested for the notion of extension).[52] Freud's meditation on prosthetics is made at a moment of great historical transition, similar in many ways to the one in which McLuhan was writing. McLuhan does not, however, place his meditations in the service of a nature/culture binary, as does Freud; rather than determining that our discontents are the result of a falling away from nature, he sees the nature/culture binary as irrelevant to contemporary society, where nature has collapsed into culture, of which the prosthesis was perhaps the most apposite metaphor. Despite this difference, the notions of Freud and McLuhan have much in common. Freud, like McLuhan, places the history of Western civilization in the context of the extension of human powers: 'With every tool man is perfecting his own organs, whether motor or sensory, or is removing the limits to their functioning' (*C&D* 43). Freud, like McLuhan, is concerned in this regard with such extensions as 'aircraft,' 'microscope,' 'photographic camera,' 'gramophone disc,' 'telephone' (43). Both see the prosthetic future as bearing both promise and terror. Expanding on his comment that 'Man has ... become a kind of prosthetic God' (44), Freud notes that 'When he puts on all his auxiliary organs he is truly magnificent; but those organs have not grown on to him and they still give him much trouble at times' (44). Both Freud and McLuhan theorize narcissism as part of their prosthetic projects, establishing and at the same time problematizing the notion of otherness.[53] Both understand the process of civilization as having altered the interrelationships of the senses.[54] And, perhaps most importantly, both present their work dynamically, be it in terms of Eros and Death or orality and literacy.[55]

David Wills argues that prosthesis underpins the entire Freudian enterprise: 'Freudian theory, with its musing and propositions, projections and conjectures, will attach to itself a series of differences that, while perhaps molding themselves to its fit, nevertheless distinguish themselves as irrevocably other, as opposite in nature, as opposite as is the artificial or prosthetic to nature itself' (*Pr* 95). The particularly prosthetic aspect of Freudian theory, according to Wills, is the notion of 'projection,' which Freud defines in *Beyond the Pleasure Principle* as '"a particular way ... of dealing with any internal excitations which produce too great an increase of unpleasure: there is a tendency to treat them as though they were acting, not from the inside, but from the outside"' (*Pr* 96). The process of projection is thus very similar in function to McLuhan's notion of sensory ratios and sensory equilibrium within the sensorium; as he writes in *Report*, 'in psychology the SC [sensory completion] is referred to as projection' (*RPM* 25). As a particular sense is excited, it projects itself on and over the other senses. To the extent that the prosthetic projection figures an uncanny doubling (an idea especially inherent in the notion of the 'phantom limb' and 'phantom pain'), it is further related to Freud's interest in telepathy, as Wills remarks (115), and Freud specifically related telepathy to telegraphy and telephony.[56]

Prosthesis in its psychoanalytical implications is one aspect of the general history of extension, which includes physics and philosophy, as well. Of chief importance to the philosophical understanding of extension are the writings of Descartes. Descartes theorized a distinction between the *res extensa*, or material world (including the body), and the *res cogitans*, or rational mind. Employing a methodology that was sceptical, linear, and enumerative,[57] Descartes sought to arrive at the truth about the nature of being by positing a split between mind and body. This split was a methodological 'necessity' motivated by a distrust of the senses, a distrust Descartes had for the entire material world – the *res extensa* – in general. Indeed, for Descartes the soul was the only materiality; the rest was immaterial, and 'common sense' (*Discourse on Method* 5:34) was anything but a *sense*. In his hierarchical universe, all movement was towards greater and greater abstraction – towards the One (*Second Meditation* 68), and the senses were suspect precisely because they impeded this progress. McLuhan's refutation of this formulation was crucial to his methodology; he adopted a non-linear, analogical (as opposed to logical) set of procedures that he associated with acoustic space and its reintegration of the sensorium.[58] Logic and reason were, he argued, products of one sense alone – the visual – and thus 'we have confused reason with literacy, and rationalism with a single technology' (*UM* 15; cf *GG* 59) in the same way that we have assumed that visual space is natural space.[59] Hence sense *ratios*: the senses other than the visual were also ways of knowing, were also possessed of a certain *ratio*nality. 'Yet,' McLuhan states, 'during all our centuries of phonetic literacy we have favored the chain of inference as the mark of logic and reason' (*UM* 85). It was only through printing that 'it became possible to translate any kind of tricky space into the straight, the flat, the uniform, and the "rational"' (116). However, 'in the electric age we feel as free to invent nonlineal logics as we do to make non-Euclidean geometries' (85). To Cartesian rationalism, thus, McLuhan responded with a project that sought to (re)integrate *res cogitans* and *res extensa*, mind with body, proposing thereby an organicist (and ultimately ecological) model for the mechanistic one proffered by Cartesian philosophy.[60] Hence McLuhan's comment (in a 1977 letter) that Descartes treated '*figures* without *ground*' and that he 'eliminated all the parts of rhetoric except method or *dispositio*' (to Cleanth Brooks, *L* 528–9). This is a critique of Descartes similar to that made by Ong of Ramus – that in Cartesian thought method had overwhelmed dialogue and imagination (*inventio*). Dialogue was the principle informing McLuhan's notion of the *sensus communis* – that common sense was derived from all the senses in communication with one another, of which speech was the most powerful example. As Johannes Fabian remarks in *Time and the Other*,

the only way to think of consciousness without separating it from the organism or banning it to some kind of *forum internum* is to insist on its sensuous nature; and one way to conceive of that sensuous nature ... is to tie consciousness as an activity to the production of meaningful sound ... Man does not 'need' language; man ... *is* language ... If there needs to be a contest for man's noblest sense ... it should be hearing, not sight that wins ... [I]t is the sensuous nature of language, its being an activity of concrete organisms and the embodiment of consciousness in a material medium – sound – which makes language an eminently *temporal* phenomenon ... These essentially temporal properties can be translated, or transcribed, as spatial relations. This is an undisputable fact – this sentence proves it. What

remains highly disputable is that visualization-spatialization of consciousness, and especially historically and culturally contingent spatializations such as a certain rhetorical 'art of
memory,' can be made *the* measure of development of human consciousness' (161–4)[61]

McLuhan remarks in *Understanding Media* that the ' "common sense" was for many
centuries held to be the peculiar human power of translating one kind of experience of
one sense into all the senses, and presenting the result continuously as a unified image to
the mind. In fact, this image of a unified ratio among the senses was long held to be the
mark of our *ratio*nality, and may in the computer age easily become so again' (60).
Hence McLuhan's embracing of the bodily was part of his rejection of Cartesian
rationalism; as Lefebvre notes, '[w]estern philosophy has *betrayed* the body; it has
actively participated in the great process of metaphorization that has *abandoned* the
body; and it has *denied* the body ... Abstract spatiality and practical spatiality contemplated one another from afar, in thrall to the visual realm ... Today the body is establishing itself firmly, as base and foundation, *beyond philosophy*, beyond discourse, and
beyond the theory of discourse' *(PS* 407).

McLuhan's anti-academicism was part of his larger project to re-establish the notion
of common sense as the index to a new rationality. As Clifford Geertz has remarked in
his essay 'Common Sense as a Cultural System,'[62] the question of common sense has a
long philosophical tradition in the West, beginning with 'the Platonic Socrates (where its
function was to demonstrate its own inadequacy)' (76), and moving on to the 'Cartesian
and Lockean traditions [which] depended ... upon doctrines about what was and what
was not self-evident, if not exactly to the vernacular mind at least to the unencumbered
one' (76).[63] In the twentieth century, the question of common sense has become almost
an obsession in the work of philosophers from Wittgenstein and Austin to Husserl and
Merleau-Ponty, albeit undertheorized: 'generally, the notion of common sense has been
rather commonsensical: what anyone with common sense knows' (77). What distinguishes common sense from an anthropological point of view, however, is precisely its
' "immethodicalness" ' (90), its ad hoc nature (and in this lack of 'method' one hears yet
another response to Cartesianism). Common sense is defined, for Geertz, by its ' "tonalities" ' (84). 'The concept as such,' he goes on, 'as a fixed and labelled category, an
explicitly bounded semantic domain, is, of course, not universal, but, like religion, art,
and the rest, part of our own more or less common-sense way of distinguishing the
genres of cultural expression' (84). By focusing on common sense, concludes Geertz,
anthropology could begin to discern 'most especially ... how culture is joined and put
together, and ... [move] ... away from functionalist accounts of the devices on which
societies rest toward interpretive ones of the kinds of lives societies support' (93). In
McLuhan's terms, this would be a media ecology.

Echoing Narcissus

McLuhan found a mythological analogy for his anti-Cartesian rhetoric of spatial metamorphosis in the story of Narcissus. '[T]he man in a literate and homogenized society,'
he writes, 'ceases to be sensitive to the diverse and discontinuous life of forms. He
acquires the illusion of the third dimension and the "private point of view" as part of his
Narcissus fixation, and is quite shut off from Blake's awareness or that of the Psalmist,

that we become what we behold' (*UM* 19),[64] an observation that strongly contests the Cartesian mind–body split. McLuhan has in mind a line from Psalm 113 – 'They that make them shall be like unto them' (quoted in *UM* 45) – in which the reference is to idolatry. 'The concept of "idol," ' writes McLuhan, 'for the Hebrew Psalmist is much like that of Narcissus for the Greek mythmaker' (45), adding that

> To behold, use or perceive any extension of ourselves in technological form is necessarily to embrace it ... It is this continuous embrace of our own technology in daily use that puts us in the Narcissus role of subliminal awareness and numbness in relation to these images of ourselves. By continuously embracing technologies, we relate ourselves to them as servomechanisms. That is why we must, to use them at all, serve these objects, these extensions of ourselves, as gods or minor religions. Physiologically, man in the normal use of technology (or his variously extended body) is perpetually modified by it and in turn finds ever new ways of modifying his technology. Man becomes, as it were, the sex organs of the machine world, as the bee of the plant world, enabling it to fecundate and to evolve ever new forms. The machine world reciprocates man's love by expediting his wishes and desires, namely, in providing him with wealth. (46)[65]

It is particularly the visual that is narcotic in McLuhan's scheme, as he punningly suggests at the end of his introduction to Wilson Bryan Key's *Subliminal Seduction*, when he adjures his readers: 'As Zeus said to Narcissus, "Watch yourself!" '[66] It was the printing press that had provided the 'power to translate knowledge into mechanical production by the breaking of any process into fragmented aspects to be placed in a lineal sequence of movable, yet uniform, parts ... This amazing technique of spatial analysis duplicating itself at once, by a kind of echo, invaded the world of number and touch' (*UM* 116). What McLuhan wishes to emphasize here is that *print* (as opposed, most controversially, to television)[67] was narcotic precisely because it prevented us from having full awareness of the effects of the *new* media such as television. Hence the appropriateness of the myth of Narcissus and Echo, which embodied the *interface* of literacy (associated with print) and orality (associated with electronic media).[68] Indeed, in Narcissus, McLuhan found the perfect analogue for his notion of the 'body electric' as prosthetic.

McLuhan reads the Narcissus myth as the central one of electronic culture.[69] As he writes at the beginning of chapter 4, 'The Gadget Lover: Narcissus as Narcosis,' Narcissus is related etymologically to 'the Greek word *narcosis*, or numbness' (41), a numbness that would be alleviated only by putting the senses back in touch with one another. McLuhan insists that it is not with a reflection of himself that Narcissus falls in love but with an image of himself *othered*: '[t]his extension of himself by mirror numbed his perceptions until he became the servomechanism of his own extended or repeated image' (41).[70] The mirroring of Narcissus is thus one example of the 'massive psychic chiasmus' (*GG* 277) attending the advent of the electronic era, in that it marks a sundering of 'the idea of unique personal existence.'[71] And the adoption of the Narcissus and Echo myth figures as well in McLuhan's critique of Cartesian rationality; according to McLuhan's formulation, whereby electronic media had outered our consciousness, the mind was no longer fully present to itself. As Thelma McCormack has written, '"participation in depth" ... is the furthest extreme from introspection' (58).[72]

The use of the Narcissus myth as one of his major points of reference – as opposed to the Freudian *locus classicus* of the Oedipal – was, finally, the last step in McLuhan's rewriting of Freud.[73] McLuhan had already firmly placed the Oedipus myth within the orbit of literacy in his 1959 article 'Myth and Mass Media,' where he asks, rhetorically: 'Is there significance in the fact that the Oedipus myth has so far not been found among the preliterate?'[74] The Oedipal model, as elaborated by Freud, was flawed heuristically through its linear and sequential nature, and thus through its dependency on the culture of the visual, as confirmed by its dramatization of the triangulated gaze.[75] Although 'Oedipus Rex ... solved the riddle of the Sphinx' (*UM* 39), he was punished with blindness. 'It was as if the Greeks felt that the penalty for one break-through was a general sealing-off of awareness to the total field' (39). In substituting Narcissus (and Echo; the orality/literacy interface) for Oedipus, McLuhan substituted a relational myth for a sequential and progressivist one, the flatness of mosaic interaction (which was also the space of the television screen [*UM* 313]) for the false depths of three-dimensional 'introspection.' This reversal of the Oedipus myth was achieved through a form of 'electric logic' that 'plays *Oedipus* backward, as does the entire new sense environment of electric technologies,' which take us into a 'corporate past.'[76] Hence McLuhan's major critique of Freud was that he 'paid no attention to the *ground* of psychic conditioning, except tangentially, in *Civilization and Its Discontents*. His Oedipus complex would be meaningless except in a highly literate environment. Historically, Oedipus himself was a product of technological change. When the oral and tribal Greek was submitted to the detribalizing action of the visually oriented alphabet, his new private identity was suddenly in violent interface with the old corporate, or incestuous, identity. Today we have an instant replay, as it were, of the Greek historical shift from oral to visual culture as we move from visual to acoustic culture, electrically' (Letter to Rollo May, 14 December 1972, *L* 458). The implication of this shift was not that one should get outside the visual, as contemporary theorists have suggested,[77] but that the visual should be placed in relation with the other senses, as is implicit in the Narcissus and Echo dyad. Similarly, McLuhan suggested that our unconscious was not subterranean but extruded in the artefactual world around us, and thus his concern with outerances, as apposed to Freud's interest in utterances; as McLuhan writes of Narcissus, 'The young man's image is a self-amputation or extension induced by irritating pressures. As counter-irritant, the image produces a generalized numbness or shock that declines recognition. Self-amputation forbids self-recognition' (*UM* 43).[78] In insisting on technology as a *human* extension, McLuhan also provides a key to agency in the confrontation of technology. Rather than being a force over which humans have no control, technology is to be understood as a part of that which is human. As McLuhan stated in a 1966 interview, '[t]he electric technology should be regarded not as some alien intruder from outer space, but as our own nervous system, magnificently [cf Freud's reference to man's prosthetic magnificence in *C&D*] simulated, extended beyond us into space ... Therefore all technologies are completely humanist in the sense of belonging entirely to the human organism.'[79]

   McLuhan invokes the work of Hans Selye[80] and Adolphe Jonas in support of this theory of amputation and extension (*UM* 42). Selye argues, in *The Stress of Life* (1956), that the 'multicellular organism' depends for its existence on 'the art of peaceful interdependence [in order] to avoid internal stress' (283), a notion that has much in common with that of the *sensus communis*. When this harmony is interrupted, the body will seek to protect the affected organ by isolating it and numbing it. To reintegrate this part of the body with the whole, a counterirritant is required: 'the body of a patient can ... be shaken out of habitually responding in the same senseless manner if you expose it to the stress of some intense shock therapy' (258). McLuhan sought to provide such shocks through his writings, and in this he positioned himself with the artist, who was likewise involved in producing what Robert Hughes has called 'the shock of the new' (in his book of that title). It was McLuhan's encounter with Adolphe D. Jonas's *Irritation and Counterirritation: A Hypothesis about the Autoamputative Property of the Nervous System*[81] that concretized McLuhan's theory that sensory extension was simultaneously amputation.[82] Jonas calls his book 'A Scientific Excursion into Theoretical Medicine'; he seeks to provide 'a unified theory capable of explaining the full range of functions, from the normal to the abnormal, in the living organism' (9). Jonas's theory is disarmingly simple: 'To safeguard its pre-eminent role the C[entral] N[ervous] S[ystem] must ... possess intrinsic mechanisms which will be called into action any time any part of the organism becomes the source of supernormal irritation' (10); these mechanisms comprise 'the *autoamputative* property' (10). For Jonas, autoamputation is symptomatic of advanced civilization: 'man must be considered a failure, because the very degree of advancement has made it excessively vulnerable to constant irritation' (12). Jonas tellingly (in a McLuhanesque context) selects the epigraph to his first chapter on the autoamputative property (or AAP) from Matthew 18.9: '"If thy eye offend thee, pluck it out"' (47); he suggests that the system of irritation and counterirritation works according to 'an architectural structure ... which manifests itself in temporal and spatial distribution' of various symptoms (13). Jonas sees the AAP as a dynamic process; thus, '[t]he CNS ... in response to hyperstimulation ... could initiate the neoplastic process. The latter then too would fall within the scope of the autoamputative property' (54). Extension, in other words, is dynamically related to amputation, just as, for McLuhan, the ear would be enhanced by the 'amputation' of the eye ('an eye for an ear').

Prosthetic Aesthetics

If the first seven chapters of *Understanding Media* represent a sort of trivium and quadrivium of the media, the remaining twenty-six chapters represent the alphabet of this system, foregrounded in such a way as to jolt into auditory space the 'abcedminded' reader, numbed by visual culture (the Narcissus narcosis). As McLuhan wrote to Jacqueline Tyrwhitt (11 May 1964, fifteen days before the publication of *Understanding Media*), commenting on section 3.4 of *Finnegans Wake*,

> Joyce runs through the alphabet from A to Z as a social cycle. When he gets to Z, the cycle begins again. He explicitly indicates the return to primal undiscriminated auditory space, then begins again the discovery of the vertical plane and enclosed space and numbers and measurement. Joyce is quite explicit that ... as the alphabet ends its cycle we move out of visual space into discontinuous auditory space again. This he mentions as the return to 'Lewd's Carol' [*sic*], that is, through the looking glass into the world of non-Euclidean space once more, lewd, ignorant, tribal, involved totally as in group singing. In his

'Beginnings of Architecture' Giedion cites the evidence several times that there is no architectural enclosing of space before script. Giedion does not know why this should be. Visual space alone of all the space discriminated by our various senses is continuous, uniform and connected. Any technology that extends the visual power imposes these visual properties upon all other spaces. Our own return in the electric age to a non-visual world has confronted us suddenly with this tyrannical and usurping power of the visual over the other senses. (*L* 298–9)

Television occupied such a major place in McLuhan's thought because it represented *par excellence* the return to the interplay of the senses, an interplay that McLuhan associated with tactility. That this tactility represented a mosaic of spaces was clear from the experience of watching television. As Victor Burgin has put it, '[s]paces that were once conceived of as separated, segregated, now overlap: live pictures from Voyager II, as it passes through the rings of Saturn, may appear on television sandwiched between equally "live" pictures of internal organs, transmitted by surgical probes, and footage from Soweto ... To contemplate such phenomena is no longer to inhabit an imaginary space ordered by the subject/object "stand-off" of Euclidean perspective.'[83] The role of art was precisely interficial in this way. McLuhan writes of Blake that '[h]ad he encountered the electric age, [he] would not have met its challenge with a mere repetition of electric form' (*UM* 25); rather, he would have set up an interface of forms, *'since no medium has its meaning or existence alone, but only in constant interplay with other media'* (*UM* 26; emphasis added). This was the crucial lesson McLuhan had learned from his reading of Eric Havelock's *Preface to Plato*. Havelock argues there that the 'oral state of mind' of the ancient Greeks was also a 'mode of consciousness' (41) distinguished by its interfacing of oral and literate elements (135ff); as literacy took over, the realm of the poetic came to be associated with the non-rational.[84]

The twenty-six chapters of *Understanding Media* similarly configure the interface (itself a term from physics) between alphabet and electronic cultures. McLuhan uses the fragmentation technology of the alphabet to analyse the holistic electronic culture, setting up an interface between the outgoing technology and the incoming one (and hence the book's dyadic structure, which, as Wills would point out, is itself prosthetic): 'If we understood our older media ... and if we valued their human effects sufficiently, we could reduce or even eliminate the electronic factor from our lives' (*UM* 93). It was this need to understand the new media through the old (which became the content of the new) that specified the 'role of the intelligentsia ... as liaison and as mediators between old and new power groups' (*UM* 37). If 'the technique of suspended judgment' (*GG* 278) was itself a response to the teleological ideology of a mechanistic consciousness that tended to make the whole subservient to the parts, then to withold judgment (and here McLuhan again corrects the position he took in *The Mechanical Bride*) would be to refocus on the simultaneous whole, '[f]or what is meant by the irrational and the non-logical in much modern discussion is merely the rediscovery of the ordinary transactions between the self and the world, or between subject and object' (*UM* 278). This, then, is McLuhan's manifesto for the materialization – indeed, sensualization – of abstract intellectuality. What he proposes in *Understanding Media* is a dynamic or open notion of media interface, as a response (counterirritant) to the closure of amputated senses occasioned by media assault. As elsewhere in his writing, this insight is expressed in terms of (de)colonization: '[t]he point of the matter of speed-up by wheel, road, and paper is the extension of power in an ever more homogeneous and uniform space. Thus the real potential of the Roman technology was not realized until printing had given road and wheel a much greater speed than that of the Roman vortex ... Our speed-up today is not a slow explosion outward from center to margins but an instant implosion and an interfusion of space and functions' (92–3). In this regard, McLuhan reasserts the Innisian position that 'technical media are staples' (21). As John O'Neill has remarked,

> Harold Innis considered empire 'an indication of the efficiency of communication' [*EmC* 9]. That is to say, he thought empire and communication to be inextricable valorizations of power ... Innis and McLuhan inspire us to consider all political history as inseparable from the history of bio-communication systems. Their work subverts the dualisms in idealist and materialist historiography because they never consider human history as anything else than an *embodied history* inscribed upon the communis sensus [*sic*]. History is human history or *bio-textual* because it alters our sensory and cognitive ratios but always in concert with the history of our land, its rivers and forests, its fish, fur, and minerals. It is the material history of these things that underwrites ... our mental and sensory histories told in our chronicles, monuments and laws.[85]

But McLuhan's insistence on the materiality of communication goes beyond the example of the fur-trade routes; his point is that the *invisibilia* of electronic media are likewise material – *'the acoustic is just as material as the visual'* (*L* 489, 29 January 1974; emphasis added) – and they are material precisely to the extent that they are extensions of ourselves. Hence, when he critiques the corporate takeover of media in *Understanding Media*, he does so precisely in terms of embodiment:

> Once we have surrendered our senses and nervous systems to the private manipulation of those who would try to benefit from taking a lease on our eyes and ears and nerves, we don't really have any rights left. Leasing our eyes and ears and nerves to commercial interests is like handing over the common speech to private corporation, or like giving the earth's atmosphere to a company as a monopoly. Something like this has already happened with outer space, for the same reasons that we have leased our central nervous systems to various corporations. As long as we adopt the narcissus attitude of regarding the extensions of our own bodies as really *out there* and really independent of us, we will meet all technological challenges with the same sort of banana-skin pirouette and collapse. (*UM* 68)

The interfacing that McLuhan saw as the only adequate response to the Narcissus narcosis would be achieved through a prosthetic aesthetics, an aesthetics of hybridity, of spacing, 'the spacing that opens the possibility of sense in general ... that is to say a transferential spacing' (*Pr* 167), where transference is the site *par excellence* of metaphor, the trope whose fundamental principle is a reversal of sense (A = B where A ≠ B).

A prosthetic aesthetics, in other words, would be an art that revealed technological extensions as human artifacts; it would thus be a political art, an art geared towards the recognition of agency. As Lynn Spigel has put it, '[i]n the scheme of "the medium is the message," technology determine[s] esthetics.'[86] Quotation – sign of the auditory and of dialogue – is a significant part of a prosthetic aesthetic, which is an aesthetic of difference, of crossover, chiasmus, hybridity, dislocation, and discontinuity.[87] This is the aesthetic of electronic circuitry, as Wills remarks: 'it is the double movement, the bidirectionality of those ambulations, epitomized by the limp of the prosthetic, that is all there is to prevent the speed of the informational process from seeming to reduce to a pure linearity, when in fact it is the repeated inscription and contradiction of that. What is so easily occluded in that process are the blips of countless relays, the switches between open and closed, on and off options, in terms of which this supposed flow is subject to constant effects of discontinuity' (*Pr* 25–6). As McLuhan writes in chapter 5 of *Understanding Media*, significantly subtitled '*Les Liaisons Dangereuses*,' the 'crossings or hybridizations of the media release great new force and energy as by fission or fusion ... The hybridization or compounding of these agents offers an especially favorable opportunity to notice their structural components and properties' (48–9). Thus, since 'media are "make happen" agents, but not "make aware" agents' (48), they must be made into agents of perception precisely through interfacing: '[M]edia, being extensions of ourselves, also depend upon us for their interplay and their evolution' (49). McLuhan's prime example of such an interplay is 'the meeting of literate and oral cultures' (49), an interplay whose positive and negative elements are figured in the Narcissus and Echo dyad. McLuhan suggests that the 'electric implosion [which] now brings oral and tribal ear-culture to the literate West' will produce a society based on difference, as opposed to the homogeneity fostered by literacy (50). As McLuhan states, for 'literate man ... differences always seem to need eradication, both in sex and in race, and in space and in time. Electronic man, by becoming ever more deeply involved in the actualities of the human condition, cannot accept the literate cultural strategy ... It is more difficult to provide uniqueness and diversity than it is to impose the uniform patterns of mass education; but it is such uniqueness and diversity that can be fostered under electric conditions as never before' (316).

The ablations of technology thus have the potential of reconfiguration through differential relations.[88] McLuhan writes that the 'hybrid or the meeting of two media is a moment of truth and revelation from which new form is born. For the parallel between two media holds us on the frontiers between forms that snap us out of the Narcissus-narcosis. The moment of the meeting of media is a moment of freedom and release from the ordinary trance and numbness imposed by them on our senses' (*UM* 55). The only resistance to media effects, thus, is by interfacing media with other media: 'It is the theme of this book that not even the most lucid understanding of the peculiar force of a medium can head off the ordinary "closure" of the senses that causes us to conform to the pattern of experience presented ... To resist TV, therefore, one must acquire the antidote of *related* media *like* print' (329; emphasis added).[89] Indeed, '[o]ur very word "grasp" or "apprehension" points to the process of getting at one thing through another, of handling and sensing many facets at a time through more than one sense at a time. It begins to be evident that "touch" is not skin but the interplay of the senses, and "keeping in touch" or "getting in touch" is a matter of a fruitful meeting of the senses, of sight translated into sound and sound into movement, and taste and smell' (*UM* 60). The critical response to the narcosis of Narcissus is to recognize the interface with Echo.

The Intellectual as *Vates*

[W]e must all become creative artists in order to cope with even the banalities of daily life.

Marshall McLuhan, *Report on Project in Understanding New Media* xiv

It is generally assumed that McLuhan's intellectual career was at its height in the 1960s (the era that Robert Fulford has called 'The Age of McLuhan'),[1] what with his publication within a two-year span of the works (along with the *Mechanical Bride*) that brought him international attention: *The Gutenberg Galaxy* and *Understanding Media.* It is likewise assumed that after the publication of these works, and definitively by the 1970s, McLuhan – 'Canada's Intellectual Comet,' as Richard Shickel called him[2] – entered into a period of decline,[3] his authority no longer recognized, his Centre for Culture and Technology closed by the University of Toronto. The reasons for this decline are generally defined contextually:[4] McLuhan is assumed to have sold out to the very interests that he should have been criticizing; he is charged with merely rewriting his previous books and thereby endlessly repeating himself; his theoretical concerns were less and less compatible with the reigning theories of the day (which, in Canada, meant those of Northrop Frye, whose work was seen as 'a salutary antidote to creeping McLuhanism').[5] This view remains the critical consensus. Writing on the '25th Anniversary of *Understanding the* [*sic*] *Media*' in the *Canadian Journal of Communication*, Paul Heyer stated that the McLuhan revival of the 1990s came on the heels of 'a legacy that was under near eclipse by the end of the seventies,'[6] a period during which 'his work was almost completely ignored' (31). Heyer's position appears to be justified by the facts: in addition to Shickel, who by 1965 was proposing a crash landing for the Canadian comet, John Fekete had issued a damning assessment of McLuhan in *The Critical Twilight,* and *Time* magazine was taking McLuhan to task for his *Dew-Line Newsletters* by the end of the decade ('The Press,' 9 August 1968). And, in any case, by the 1970s the critical action was in Europe, and especially Paris, rather than Toronto.

Two questions can thus legitimately be asked: where was McLuhan in all of this, and in what terms can the 'revival' of the 1990s be understood? The answer to the first question is that, like Yeats in Auden's famous elegy, he had become his readers. By this I mean, first of all, that McLuhan's thought had been taken up into the general cultural milieu, such that it was no longer directly tied to McLuhan himself. As Willmott remarks, 'Who first discovered "McLuhan"? Commentators variously claimed that McLuhan was first "discovered by young people and the artists, not by the literary crowd," or instead by Madison Avenue ... It is probably better to say that he was discovered by no one, by no particular group or institution first, but by all of them at once – an unconscious effect of the mysterious sort of social life engendered by the mass media' (*MMR* 139). His thought had particularly been taken up by French theory: it was in the intellectual milieu of '*le macluhanisme*' that Derrida explored the issues of orality and literacy in *De la grammatologie* (1967), albeit agonistically, as 'Signature Event Context' makes evident;[7] in this same milieu we find Lefebvre urging fellow theorists such as Foucault to go and read their McLuhan;[8] and we have Barthes writing to McLuhan to ask him to collaborate on a book (*L* 539). It was thus no accident that, a (scholarly) generation later, with the acceptance of French poststructuralism in North America, McLuhan's work experienced a revival, in a classic example of going back to the future. Thus we have Fekete, fifteen years after his scathing critique of McLuhan in *The Critical Twilight*, reassessing McLuhan in the light of (French) poststructuralism,[9] and, while finding 'no reason now to retract the basic criticisms' (50), admitting that 'it does not seem enough to rehearse those criticisms,' since McLuhan 'left behind a challenging intellectual and institutional legacy' (51). That legacy continues to be engaged with by theorists covering a broad range of cultural production, including postcolonialism (Appadurai; Mignolo), anthropology (Fabian), communications (Castells; Kittler), cyberculture (Benedikt), art history (Barilli; Crary; Jay), architecture (Colomina), cultural studies (Latour), history of the book (Johns), and philosophy (Vattimo; Virilio). Meanwhile, the prodigious growth of the Internet has once again stimulated interest (as, before the Internet, television had done) in the effects of media.[10]

But this 'revival' tells only part of the story of the critical reception of and reaction to McLuhan's theories. In the second half of this study, I propose another context – not unallied to poststructuralism – for a rereading of McLuhan, namely that of artistic production. I suggest that McLuhan, who consistently drew attention to the artist as the figure who was pre-eminently in a critical position to understand the effects of media technology, sought increasingly to be read *by* artists and – more radically – to be read *as* an artist.[11] As he writes in *The Gutenberg Galaxy*, 'the new role of the intellectual is to tap the collective consciousness of "the vast multitudes that labour." That is to say, the intellectual is no longer to direct individual perception and judgment, but to explore and to communicate the massive unconsciousness of collective man. The intellectual is newly cast in the role of primitive seer, *vates*, or hero incongruously peddling his discoveries in a commercial market' (269). This suggests that McLuhan's thought can be productively understood within the *artistic* context of its elaboration (as opposed to its strictly 'intellectual' context, although McLuhan's own career problematizes the distinction). Wilfred Watson had noted as early as 1966 that 'Professor McLuhan has spoken of modern society as being without centres. Modern man has no centralized consciousness, he is off-centre, eccentric in a radical new way ... Perhaps the singular distinction of Marshall McLuhan is his seeming ability to write *for*, not merely *with*, the new eccentric.'[12] Donald Theall likewise suggested in 1971 that McLuhan was a 'poet-artist manqué' (*RVM* 6; cf 12), and Willmott devotes the first chapter of *McLuhan, or*

Modernism in Reverse to the notion that 'McLuhan collapses criticism into art' (*MMR* 4), stating that 'he encouraged the association of his own work with the art of the postmodern' (*MMR* 139). Having pursued a methodology of 'immersion' (as opposed to arrest) in *The Gutenberg Galaxy* and *Understanding Media* as well as in the many articles published during this period, McLuhan was now taking this position a step farther, exchanging the point of view for the probe, and, as this implies, the particular vector of his 'artistic' critique concerned the production of space. As McLuhan puts it in *Through the Vanishing Point*, the 'artist today might well inquire whether he has time to make a space to meet the spaces that he will meet' (31).

What I do in the following four chapters is to pursue *contextually* McLuhan the artist/ intellectual, articulating the system of thought he elaborated in the context of contemporary artistic practices, reading his work as the *ground* of various artistic practices. This dialogue was not just one of influence but of shared discursive practices, during a period when art was moving in critical directions and criticism in artistic ones. As early as 1952, McLuhan was saying about *The Mechanical Bride* that it was 'really a new form of science fiction, with ads and comics cast as characters' (*L* 217, to his mother). And as McLuhan put it in a 1966 debate with Mike Wallace, in response to the question 'So you regard yourself as an artist, not just [a] reporter?': 'That's right, only I am not trying to attribute to myself the virtues of the great designer or the great musician or something like that; simply the habit of perceiving the present as a task, as an area to be discerned, analyzed, coped with.'[13]

The artist in McLuhan's formulation is thus crucial within society, because it is the artist who is the person '*in any field, scientific or humanistic*' (*UM* 65, emphasis added) who has 'integral awareness' (65). It is for this reason that the artist must move 'from the ivory tower to the control tower of society' (65). As McLuhan states in a very significant formulation, 'It is the artist's job to try to *dislocate* older media into postures that permit attention to the new' (254). The aesthetic valorized here is one of the 'nonvisual: the skew, the curved, and the bumpy' (117); it moves towards 'synesthesia,' which McLuhan defines as 'the iconic qualities of touch and sense interplay' (249). This would produce an art 'in depth,' where '"depth" means "in interrelation," not in isolation. Depth means insight, not point of view, and insight is a kind of mental involvement in process that makes the content of the item seen quite secondary. Consciousness itself is an inclusive process not at all dependent on content. Consciousness does not postulate consciousness of anything in particular' (282–3). The phenomenon of mass media is a sign of this depth involvement; the term 'mass media' does not refer to the number of people involved, but to the depth of experience: 'Automation brings in real "mass production," not in terms of size, but of an instant inclusive embrace. Such is also the character of "mass media." They are an indication, not of the size of their audiences, but of the fact that everybody becomes involved in them at the same time' (349). This cybernetic consciousness marks the end of Euclidean space: 'Feedback ... means introducing an information loop or circuit, where before there had been merely a one-way flow or mechanical sequence. Feedback is the end of the lineality that came into the Western world with the alphabet and the continuous forms of Euclidean space' (354). As the world folds back on itself, culture subsumes nature, and it is this artifactual element that reinvigorates 'the role of artist in society' (358).

Thus, if one dislocates McLuhan from the academic production of theoretical discourse to the discourse of artistic production, one becomes immediately aware that, far from disappearing, far from being considered irrelevant, the questions McLuhan was raising were very much part of *artistic* debate during the very period of his 'decline,' a period during which the boundaries separating theoretical from artistic production were themselves becoming blurred (one classic example being Derrida's *Glas,* which profoundly confirmed McLuhan's notion of the criticality of acoustic space). And when one turns back from that period, into the early years of the century, and examines McLuhan's work in the context of Futurism, Dada, the Bauhaus, and so on, one begins to place his work in a context that deeply illuminates it.

The second part of this book, accordingly, takes McLuhan out of the strictly academic environment in which he developed his theories, and (re)reads those theories through the anti-environment of artistic production. That context, in addition to McLuhan's books, films, and recordings, includes a considerable range of Canadian artistic production, from the concrete poetry of bpNichol to the performance practices of Glenn Gould, from the conceptual art of Iain and Ingrid Baxter to the soundscapes of R. Murray Schafer.[14] Indeed, McLuhan had a significant influence on a Canadian artistic milieu which, considered as a coherent entity, constitutes a shadow canon that contests at many points the one that grew up around his Toronto counterpart, Northrop Frye (and hence the focus on Frye and McLuhan in the last chapter), a shadow canon only now coming into its own. Internationally, McLuhan's influence was felt by the Independent Group in England, by the Situationists in France, and by the Fluxus movement nearly everywhere else. And it was, significantly, in this period that McLuhan developed his spatial theories specifically within the context of artistic production, from *Verbi-Voco-Visual Explorations* to *Through the Vanishing Point: Space in Poetry and Painting* to *Picnic in Space.*

Undertaking a reading of McLuhan on this basis raises two important issues, however. It raises first of all the issue of agency: if McLuhan's position was that to make effective critiques of media technology one must take upon oneself the condition of the artist, is this not merely to adopt the élitism of a privileged class? It also raises the issue of ethics: if the artist is productive within the aesthetic realm, how can that artist be said to have grappled with the ethical issues that seem precisely to escape the aesthetic?

To begin with agency: far from privileging the artist, McLuhan's intention was to urge us *all* to take on the condition of artists (as in the epigraph to this section), that is to say, the condition of individuals *critically* engaged with the world around them. 'In social terms,' writes McLuhan in *Through the Vanishing Point*, 'the artist can be regarded as a navigator who gives adequate compass bearings in spite of magnetic deflection of the needle by the changing play of forces. So understood, the artist is not a peddler of ideals or lofty experiences. He is rather the indispensable aid to action and reflection alike' (*TVP* 238). If, as Glenn Willmott asserts, 'McLuhan's entire critical development is founded upon what has in postmodernist thinking become naturalized as a cliché: the modernist's belief in art as a critical form' (*MMR* 3), then what differentiates McLuhan's thinking within postmodernism is his articulation of this *critical* insight in *artistic* terms. And given that the world in which he articulated these insights – at least since *Sputnik* – was itself an artifact, then art was the particular mode of perception that would garner the greatest insights into the phenomenon of a nature that was now irremediably acculturated. 'The capsule and the satellite,' McLuhan writes in 'The Emperor's Old Clothes,' 'have created a new environment for our planet. The planet is now the content of the new spaces created by the new technology. Instead of being an environment in time, the earth itself has become a probe in space. That is, the planet has become an anti-environment, an art form, an extension of consciousness, yielding new perception of the new man-made environment.'[15] For McLuhan, postmodernism was not simply a time; it was also a space, and he was a postmodernist by virtue of that space. His focus on the spatial arts was particularly significant for the 'sensuous geography'[16] of his media theories, insofar as he argued that '[i]magination is that ratio among the perceptions and faculties which exists when they are not embedded or outered in material technologies. When so outered, each sense and faculty becomes a closed system. Prior to such outering there is entire interplay among experiences' (265). Thus, to urge his readers to wake up and reintegrate their senses was to urge them to take on the imaginative condition of artists.[17]

As for ethics, McLuhan saw the aesthetic as necessarily within the realm of the ethical, insofar as making (the processual activity *par excellence* of critically engaged art, as opposed to matching, which constituted the traditional realm of the aesthetic) was an activity that was socially defined and socially responsible. If the environment was itself an artifact, then the work of art was by definition socially and politically medi-ated – *in* the world, rather than transcendent, *material*, rather than abstract. McLuhan had learned from his encounter with Innis in the early 1950s that, rather than rejecting space and moralistically making a plea for time, he must confront the increasing spatialization of media technologies while at the same time introducing the critical element of time into his discussion of the 'problem of space.' This 'break' with Innis, however, did not mean that McLuhan concomitantly abandoned the ethical dimension embodied in Innis's *plaidoyer*. Instead, he theorized a space different from the static (visual) model invoked by Innis; this acoustic space embodied in itself a critique of the society of the visual that, for McLuhan (and other critics subsequently, such as Foucault), encapsulated one of the least salutary products of print culture. Writing during the period of his (apparent) decline, in a 'Foreword' to the revised edition of Innis's *Empire and Communications*,[18] McLuhan characterizes Innis as an 'artist' (v) and a 'satirist' (v) and notes that Innis 'was less and less inclined to moralize' (vi) as his career progressed, eschewing a 'point of view' with its 'static position of a mere spectator contemplating the historical scene' (vi). And he states that '[w]hat Innis indicates as a basis for social survival is nothing less than a re-organization of our perceptual lives and that the environments we witlessly or involuntarily create by our innovations are both services and disservices that make very heavy demands of our awareness and understanding' (vii). It is in this sense that artistic critique is likewise a critique of society.

If McLuhan's major intellectual concern up to and including the writing of *Understanding Media* was to work out the implications of spacetime for cultural production, his concern after that point was to develop spacetime in terms of 'environment'[19] and 'anti-' or 'counter-'environment. A significant predecessor for McLuhan's use of this term was F.R. Leavis, whose 1933 book (written with Denys Thompson), *Culture and Environ-ment*, argued that advertising, and mass phenomena generally, should be understood critically as cultural phenomena.[20] McLuhan used the term 'environment' to extend the concept of 'medium' so that it implied not only the formal paradigm of spatial production but the *context* of that production as well. McLuhan developed this notion of environment (what I am calling 'scape' in the second part of the present study), in his 1964–5 article 'New Media and the Arts,'[21] to which he appended the note that the article was 'a real step beyond my *Understanding Media* volume. What I have been describing for ten years in the phrase "The medium is the message" is better explained here. The fact that a new medium is environmental at once describes why it is the "message" and why it is mostly unconscious' (239). McLuhan succinctly states the basis of his theory at the beginning of the article: 'New media, new technologies, new extensions of human powers, tend to be environmental. Tools, script, as much as wheel, or photograph, or Telstar, create a new environment, a new matrix for the existing technologies. The older technologies, the older environment, become the content of the new environmental technology ... Whatever becomes the content of a new environment tends to become processed and patterned into an art form' (239).[22] Here is where McLuhan's concern with the artist and with the 'environment' conflate; earth as artifact was most aptly understood by artificers:[23] 'to deal with the environmental as artefact is to move that which has long been unconscious onto the plane of knowing' (240). McLuhan provides the example of Hieronymus Bosch, who 'used the new pictorial space of perspective ... – that is, a space uniform, continuous and connected – as a new container or environment for the old, iconic, medieval space. Iconic space is discontinuous, and nonuniform, and nonconnected. It is a space in which objects create their own environment ... Today it is the iconic world that has become the container for the old visual space' (240–1). The new, iconic world was best represented by television, which 'prefers flat space and stark contours' that are 'nonperspective and nonpictorial' (242). And just as non-perspectival art eliminated the vanishing point, so the television environment eliminates private point of view: 'The tv viewer feels that he doesn't have to have a private point of view,' McLuhan remarks in a late interview; 'It's one of the huge changes taking place. The private point of view is no longer dominant.'[24] What is significant in this passage is that the 'artist' here has become the viewer, insofar as the viewer is applying a new mode of perceiving the environment.

McLuhan further expands on the notion of environment in his 1966 article 'The Emperor's Old Clothes.' There he writes that 'an environment is a special organization of available energies. As an energy system, an environment is a process. It reprocesses the earlier environments.'[25] McLuhan cites Jacques Ellul's *Propaganda* as arguing that environments are the most powerful form of propaganda precisely because they are invisible, unremarked.[26] McLuhan subsequently formulated the notion of 'anti-environment' to explicate the relational activity of critical perception, with the artist (or an entire nation, as in the case of Canada *vis-à-vis* the United States) occupying the anti-environmental position in relation to the hegemonic environment. Writing in 1966, McLuhan states that the 'ground rules, the pervasive structure, the overall pattern eludes perception except in so far as there is an anti-environment or a counter-situation constructed to provide a means of direct attention ... An environment is naturally of low intensity or low definition. That is why it escapes observation. Anything that raises the environment to high intensity ... turns the environment into an object of attention. When an environment becomes an object of attention it assumes the character of an anti-environment or an art object.'[27] The relation of environment to anti-environment was most aptly expressed through the interface, and McLuhan typically employed interfaces to effect his media critiques: in general terms, he interfaced print with electronic modes of production; specifically, these interfaces took the form of verbal/visual works – a sort of *'textus interruptus,'* in the words of Jerome McGann,[28] making of his post-*Understanding Media* criticism a 'blurred genre,' Clifford Geertz's term for the 'genre mixing' he sees as characterizing postmodernist thought.[29] The interface also took on the guise of self-critique, for by this point McLuhan / 'mcluhanism' / *le macluhanisme*[30] had itself become an environment for critical and cultural production; thus we see McLuhan in this period rewriting *The Mechanical Bride* in *Culture Is Our Business*, *The Gutenberg Galaxy* in *Take Today: The Executive as Dropout*, the 1954 pamphlet *Counterblast* in *Counterblast* (1969), and so on, ensuring thus that his books would remain in process. Like Alice stepping through the looking-glass – and to similar effect – he was entering the language.

PART TWO

SCAPED

CHAPTER FIVE

Artiste de livres

The book is not moving towards an Omega point but is actually in the process of rehearsing and re-enacting all the roles it has ever played ...
Marshall McLuhan, Do Books Matter?

Artscapes

McLuhan's intellectual roots are generally placed in the Modernist literary idiom, with specific influences traced to Joyce, Pound, and Eliot (as in the studies by Theall [1971], Marchand, and Gordon), and to the New Critical methodologies that grew up around their work. Like Pound especially, however, much of McLuhan's intellectual nourishment was derived from artists in the visual and musical realms; indeed, his first book, *The Mechanical Bride*, can be seen as a long meditation on Duchamp's *The Bride Stripped Bare by Her Bachelors, Even*. These affinities take on a special significance when McLuhan is understood as not only a literary critic or an art critic, but as an artist/critic, and when he is understood within a specific current of postwar North American intellectual history – what Daniel Belgrad has termed the 'culture of spontaneity.'[1] Belgrad defines the culture of spontaneity as constituting 'a distinct third alternative' that was 'opposed to both the mass culture and the established high culture of the postwar period.' While the influence of this alternative cultural modality would be felt most in the 1960s – precisely the period of McLuhan's ascendancy, both in Canada and abroad – its foundations were laid in the period between 1940 and 1960, the period during which McLuhan critiqued the effects of mechanical culture and developed the notions of orality and literacy into a formidable critical tool.

The culture of spontaneity was marked by a 'conversational' model, where 'conversation functions as a model of democratic interaction' (Belgrad 2). This model counterposed itself to the 'cultural conditioning' of advertising culture, which encouraged 'the atrophy of certain perceptions and the exaggeration of others' (2). Whereas corporate liberalism sought to render culture as a fixed set of prepackaged forms, the culture of spontaneity sought to emphasize spontaneity, the spur of the moment. As Belgrad puts it: 'Corporate liberalism embraced an ontology and epistemology of objectivity, which was the basis of its advanced technological mastery of nature. Against this, spontaneity posed intersubjectivity, in which "reality" was understood to emerge through a conversational dynamic' (5). Spontaneity, thus, was defined by its practitioners as both anti-rational and anti-intellectual, and it located its aesthetic in artistic forms. Yet, despite its anti-intellectualism, the culture of spontaneity had a marked influence on the intellectual milieu. Belgrad cites Russell Jacoby's argument that, in the postwar United States, the public intellectual disappeared with the ascendancy of the university. To this, Belgrad offers the counter-argument that 'Public intellectuals no longer defined themselves as "intellectuals," choosing instead the roles of artists, poets, and musicians. The postwar period saw not the end of public intellectuals, but a watershed event in what Christopher Lasch once called "the social history of intellectuals": the rise of a new type of intellectual' (6–7). McLuhan epitomized this new type of intellectual.

Belgrad places McLuhan at one of the origin points of this shift in the current of postwar intellectual life (and here it is useful to remember that McLuhan began his career as a university professor in the United States). Citing McLuhan's 1949 article 'The Psychopathology of *Time* and *Life*,' published in Gershon Legman's *Neurotica*,[2] Belgrad writes that, for McLuhan, '*Time* exemplified the reduction of American intellectual life to a corporate-bureaucratic ant farm in which independent thinking was replaced by a "knowledge" industry aimed at gauging and managing human behavior' (4). McLuhan argued that the only response to this onslaught was to reawaken individual critical faculties, and it was this that became the rallying cry of artistic movements associated with Black Mountain College, and with the 'bohemias' of North Beach and Greenwich Village. These rallying cries included concepts that were fundamental to McLuhan's aesthetic: ideogram, force field, dialogue, counterpoint, spatiality (Belgrad 9–11).

McLuhan's position within the discourse Belgrad identifies is (typically) bipolar: while he was writing during the 1940s and 1950s for New Critical journals such as the *Hudson Review*, *Sewanee Review*, and *Kenyon Review*, he was at the same time writing for a journal such as *Neurotica*, whose three-year publishing history came to an end with charges of obscenity.[3] And what cannot be left out of this equation is that McLuhan was writing for these journals *as a Canadian*,[4] and thus his critical take on 'the psychopathology of *Time* and *Life*' (the title of his *Neurotica* article) was grounded geographically. Indeed, this geographical grounding was central to his insights, as the title *The Interior Landscape*[5] makes clear generally, and as articles such as 'The Comics and Culture' argue specifically. In the latter essay (1953), McLuhan writes that 'In respect to time, continuity, and memory, the newspaper hasn't the capacities of a low-grade idiot, but in its breadth of geographic perception the press has the apprehension of a god.'[6] McLuhan articulated this *cultural* geography (and it was *all* cultural after *Sputnik*, he argued) in terms of 'environment' – a form of cultural and perceptual hegemony – and 'anti-environment' – the critical mass that grew up around environments.

Belgrad's formulation of the intellectual cross-currents of the period between 1940 and 1960 leaves McLuhan stranded, however, since McLuhan was not an intellectual who 'became' an artist, but an intellectual-artist who doesn't quite fit Belgrad's paradigm. Indeed, the McLuhan of the *Neurotica* article, and of *The Mechanical Bride* (the only two texts from which Belgrad cites), is neither the McLuhan of *The Gutenberg Galaxy* and *Understanding Media* nor the McLuhan of *The Medium Is the Massage* and

Verbi-Voco-Visual Explorations. By the time he was writing these later works, McLuhan had deeply problematized the relationship between artist and intellectual, between technology and art, between medium and message. Whereas 'the philosophies and values [of spontaneous culture] ... were embodied in forms, not in scholarly prose' (Belgrad 9), McLuhan had by the 1960s merged these categories, and it may be for this reason that his artistic 'heritage' is more closely associated with the 'irony, neo-dada, and pop art' (12) of the 1960s than with the 'abstract expressionism and projective verse' of the previous decades. Thus, while McLuhan's career bears the imprint Belgrad describes – rejection of the New Critical school, critique of corporate liberalism, embracing of holistic paradigms – it transformed these currents in such a way as to make McLuhan more of a presence in the work of those who would produce 1960s counterculture (rather than simply being their postwar precursor).

Indeed, it is precisely because Belgrad does not allow for the *fusion* of artist and intellectual that he tends to give short shrift to the intellectual development of orality as a key concept in the period about which he writes, and it was precisely in terms of the development of the notion of orality, and of its cognate, acoustic space, that McLuhan's presence was most strongly felt – both artistically and intellectually.[7] It should thus not surprise us if McLuhan had a very large photo of Allen Ginsberg on his office wall (see the two-page photo reproduced in Pierre Berton's book *1967: The Last Good Year*), or if he was writing receptively about Jackson Pollock's painting (as he did in *Through the Vanishing Point*), or, for that matter, if Olson began *Call Me Ishmael* with a meditation on space. By writing for *Neurotica*, McLuhan had placed himself within the milieu not only of Ginsberg (who published his first poems there),[8] but also of Kenneth Patchen, Larry Rivers, Henri Michaux, William Barrett, and Otto Fenichel, an alliance McLuhan signalled by publishing Gershon Legman in the first issue of *Explorations*. By 1966, McLuhan was being numbered among the *Astronauts of Inner-Space*,[9] an anthology of 'avant-garde activity' whose participants included the Dada artist Raoul Hausmann, the Situationist Jorgen Nash, the pornographer Maurice Girodias, Ginsberg, the conceptualist author of artists' books Dieter Rot, and William S. Burroughs (among others).[10] In his contribution to this anthology, McLuhan argues for the political status of art: 'if politics is the art of the possible, its scope must now, in the electric age, include the shaping and programming of the entire sensory environment as a luminous work of art' (18). (Typical of the intellectual as *vates*, McLuhan the artist focuses his discussion on interdisciplinary graduate study at the University of Toronto.) Significantly, the anthology in which this article appears was published by a press located in the Castro / Upper Market area of San Francisco,[11] one of the two cities (the other is New York) that Belgrad cites as centres of avant-garde activity during this period. Yet what must also be noted here is that by the late 1960s / early 1970s, Canada had emerged as an artistic countercultural locus *par excellence* (and not only because it represented a haven for draft dodgers), with places such as Halifax and Vancouver[12] garnering international attention for artistic programs and events developed within the context of McLuhan's media theories.

The Spatial Arts

In the most general terms, McLuhan's artistic/intellectual concerns were with the 'spatial arts.' As Peter Brunette and David Wills have noted, '[i]n French, the term "arts

of space" is used almost interchangeably with "plastic arts" to denote those forms –
architecture, painting, sculpture – that are to be distinguished from the "arts of time" –
music and dance.'[13] They hasten to point out that such a binary is misleading, however.
As Derrida and others have pointed out, 'whatever signifies through time and thereby
involves a break in self-presence – the spoken word being the classic case – will
similarly, and even especially, be susceptible to the effects of spacing' (*Deconstruction*
3). Indeed, 'language always entails a "spacing" (*espacement*)' (3): '[o]nce spacing is
introduced, as a sine qua non of linguistic expression and of sense-making processes in
general, then the philosopher of language necessarily becomes a philosopher of spatial
articulation(s). The task becomes, in effect, an architectural one, mapping out the limits
and testing the boundaries of communicational space, or that of a plastic artist ... '(3).
This notion of 'testing the boundaries of communicational space' was expressed by
McLuhan through the concept of the interface.[14] McLuhan was attracted to those artists
who promoted critically and/or exemplified aspects of simultaneity in art, a notion that
accorded with his concept that electronic media were reharmonizing the senses. Because
the artistic interrelating of the senses most often took the form of interficial or intermedia
arts – those arts that fused two or more genres or modes of expression – much of
McLuhan's artistic/intellectual project consisted in a refutation of G.E. Lessing's notion
(expressed in his *Laocoön* of 1766) of the demarcation of artistic norms into spatial and
temporal modes, a demarcation to which Innis adhered (*BC* 102–3) and that had
experienced twentieth-century revival in the work of critics such as Irving Babbitt,
Clement Greenberg, and W.K. Wimsatt. To their avowals that spatial and temporal
artistic production should remain distinct, McLuhan counterblasted with artistic experiments that proposed a spacetime fusion. Given that the spatio-temporal 'consciousness'
of the last five hundred years was a product of the printing press, the intermedia projects
with which McLuhan was associated circled back again and again to a deconstruction of
the book and the spaces it had produced.

Of those Modernist artists whose work was interfusional, McLuhan expressed a close
affinity with Ezra Pound; as Louis Dudek once remarked, '[t]here is no Canadian poet
who has actually followed Pound ... unless Marshall McLuhan is that poet.'[15] The
resemblance, however, is not complete. Unlike Pound, McLuhan did not express an
affinity with high Renaissance art,[16] largely owing to the critique McLuhan had made of
perspectival space and its Renaissance codification. It was the artists before and after the
Renaissance – before and after the hegemony of visual space – with whom McLuhan
identified: the medieval illuminators (significantly anonymous), Hieronymous Bosch
(who configured the interface between medieval and Renaissance [cf *TVP* 77]), William
Blake (the interficial artist *par excellence*), the baroque and Mannerist artists (who
challenged the hegemony of the fixed point of view), Seurat (whose pointillism figured
the end of the fixed point of view), and the artists associated with the Pre-Raphaelite
movement (with their return to the flat planes of pre-Renaissance art and to the book arts
of the medieval craftsmen).

McLuhan *was* similar to Pound, however, in his espousal of the artists active at the
beginning of the twentieth century, although, as he remarked to Pound in 1948, 'the
public will not believe that an artist can be a scholar, or a serious intelligence' (*L* 206).
McLuhan was particularly interested in the artists involved in Futurism and Vorticism,

Dada, Surrealism, and the Bauhaus, including painters (such as Balla and Klee), architects (such as Le Corbusier), musicians (such as Orff and Bartok and Schoenberg), photographers (such as Laszlo Moholy-Nagy), and book artists and broadsiders (such as Marinetti and Lewis). For McLuhan, all of these artists were associated through the questioning of the norms of representational space, and not only in formalist terms but also contextually, in terms of the cultural specificities of representational norms. His artistic affinities were thus not precisely with Modernism *per se* (and its New Critical offshoots) but with what Rosalind Krauss has called the 'optical unconscious' – the art that constituted Modernism's *other*, in that it contested the *visual* mastery that was the domain *par excellence* of Modernist art. The phrase 'optical unconscious' derives from Walter Benjamin's meditation on the photography of Muybridge and Marey, which had conveyed those aspects of motion invisible to the eye;[17] it was these photographic experiments, as we have seen, that marked for McLuhan the end of the mechanical era and the beginning of the electronic – which is to say the end of the visual and the beginning of the audile/tactile in their fusion of space and time. As Yve-Alain Bois writes, the art of the optical unconscious contested the notion that

> visual art, especially painting, addresses itself uniquely to the sense of sight. This idea was contemporaneous with impressionism and also with the beginnings of art history as a 'scientific' discipline (it was a central premise of Adolf von Hildebrand's and Konrad Fiedler's writings, which in turn inspired Heinrich Wölfflin's *The Principles of Art History* of 1915). The 'tactile' that art history addresses is only the visual representation of tactility: matter does not exist for it except as in-formed, made over into form. The exclusion that proceeds from this (though it was stated even before the postulate of pure vision, going back to the distinction Gotthold Lessing made in his *Laocoön* between the arts of time and those of space) bears on the temporality within the visual and on the body of the perceiving subject: pictures reveal themselves in an instant and are addressed only to the eye of the viewer. [Another] ... postulate, based on a repression analyzed by Freud in *Three Essays on the Theory of Sexuality* (1905) and above all in *Civilization and Its Discontents* (1930), is this: being 'purely visual,' art is addressed to the subject as an erect being, far from the horizontal axis that governs the life of animals. Even if one no longer speaks of painting as a 'window opened onto the world,' the modernist picture is still conceived as a vertical section that presupposes the viewer's having forgotten that his or her feet are in the dirt. Art, according to this view, is a sublimatory activity that separates the perceiver from his or her own body.[18]

McLuhan shared these concerns, and proclaimed affinities with artists whose practices declared that to contest the visual was to rediscover the bodily.

From Images to Vortices

Ezra Pound was also an important figure in the McLuhan artscape through his association with Imagism and Vorticism. Pound's formulation of the poetics of the image had been influenced by T.E. Hulme, who had had an aesthetic revelation on his 1904 sojourn in the Canadian prairies: 'the first time I ever felt the necessity or inevitableness of verse,' wrote Hulme afterwards, 'was in the desire to produce the peculiar quality of feeling which is induced by the flat spaces and wide horizons of the virgin-prairie of Western Canada.'[19] McLuhan similarly elaborated on the geographical particularities of his own 'space-thinking' (*IL* 166, n2): '"I think of western skies as one of the most beautiful things about the West, and the western horizons. The Westerner doesn't have a point of view. He has a vast panorama"' (quoted in *M&M* 5). Hulme articulated his prairie perceptions into a theory of the image (*contra* the perspectival art of the Renaissance) that became the *point de départ* for Imagism as well as Vorticism, both of which had Pound at their centre, and both of which expressed a new spatial sensibility.

This spatial sensibility was crucial to Imagism, which sought to present '"an intellectual and emotional complex in an instant of time,"' an achievement most often ascribed to Pound's own poem 'In a Station of the Metro' (discussed as the second exhibit in *Through the Vanishing Point*), where the effect is achieved through juxtaposition (or what Pound called 'super-position')[20] on the space of the page, and where the medium of the poem itself – the typography – is hypertrophied into ideograms of faces and petals. In his correspondence with Pound (while the latter was incarcerated in St Elizabeth's), McLuhan referred to the 'plastic and sculptured world' of Pound's poems, with their 'perceptions of simultaneities' (193), and described his own *The Mechanical Bride* as treating '[p]opular icons as ideograms of complex implication' (*L* 194), both comments indicating the extent to which McLuhan was prepared to conceptualize his own work according to the spatial notions Pound had advanced at the beginning of the century. This further links McLuhan's concerns with those artists productive within Belgrad's 'culture of spontaneity,' where the 'artistic project to create a "language" of painting' was conducted parallel to 'the poetic project to restore "spatiality" to writing' (83; McLuhan would say 'tactility') through the use of ideographical forms, forms that retained a plastic quality without relinquishing their connection to speech.

Pound's movement from Imagism into Vorticism appears to parallel, in a number of ways, McLuhan's movement from Innisian notions of the time/space binary to the more relational notion of spacetime. Of particular note for McLuhan within the Vorticist aesthetic was Pound's sense that there was 'a vital inner link between the arts' (Humphreys, 'Demon' 45), a link Pound expressed in terms that recurred in McLuhan's work: '"There is a sort of poetry,"' wrote Pound in his 1914 essay on Vorticism, '"where music, sheer melody, seems as if it were just bursting into speech. There is another sort of poetry where painting or sculpture seems as if it were 'just coming over into speech'"' (quoted in Humphreys, 'Demon' 45). The fact that Pound expresses his notion of synaesthesia through the concept of speech would have been particularly telling for McLuhan, for whom speech was the unity of the senses in action. This notion of unity extended into a body/mind holism that contested rationality and logic; for McLuhan, these concepts were tied exclusively to the visual, and the visual was a sign not of holism but of the isolation of a single sense from the sensorium, and thus of the Cartesian body/mind split. As Alfred North Whitehead put it in *Adventures of Ideas* (which McLuhan quotes in *The Medium Is the Massage*), 'the human body is indubitably a complex of occasions which are part of spatial nature. It is a set of occasions miraculously coördinated so as to pour its inheritance into various regions within the brain.'[21]

These Poundian associations with Vorticism were complemented for McLuhan by associations with Wyndham Lewis, whom McLuhan befriended when Lewis resided in North America, and whose *Time and Western Man* exerted a profound influence on McLuhan. Of equally great importance to McLuhan was Lewis's publication *Blast*, which McLuhan twice responded to, in his 1954 pamphlet-come-broadside *Counterblast*, and his 1969 book of the same title. *Blast* was a key text for McLuhan insofar as it embodied a way of writing a book against the book,[22] a goal that became increasingly his object in the books he published after *Understanding Media*; the concept of 'blast' was also important to McLuhan for its bodily associations with the *blastula*, the site of breakdown as breakthrough.

It was through Vorticism that McLuhan was brought into contact with aspects of Futurism that were increasingly important for his own work.[23] McLuhan had viewed Marinetti and Futurism sceptically in *The Mechanical Bride* for their 'extroversion of the self and fusion with the activity of the machine' (90); by the time he was writing *Verbi-Voco-Visual Explorations* (originally published in October 1957 as *Explorations* 8, edited solely by McLuhan; revised as *VVV* in 1967), however, he was demonstrating a much more receptive attitude towards that movement. As Luciano De Maria (among others) has pointed out, the 'fetishism of the machine' accounts for only one small part of Futurism. Marinetti himself had insisted that the 'diverse forms of communication, of transportation and of information' had exerted a 'decisive influence' on the human psyche (De Maria continues), and it is in this regard that 'Marinetti is the precursor of McLuhan.'[24] Significantly, it was through an artistic milieu in which McLuhan played a significant role that a revival of interest in Futurism took place in the second half of the twentieth century (including in the work of Canadian artists such as bpNichol and Steve McCaffery); as R.W. Flint noted in 1972, '[o]nly in the light of the latest evolutions in the arts – of McLuhan and Cage, of Tinguely's self-destroying machines, of the marriage of art and technology consummated in E.A.T. (Experiment in Art and Technology), of all that Harold Rosenberg discusses in *The Anxious Object* – does the seemingly incoherent mass of Futurist divination begin to compose itself into the remarkable act of foresight it has proven to be.'[25] Principal among the Futurist legacies in McLuhan's thought are the identification of the book as a major locus for subversive cultural activity; the emphasis on the acoustic; the notion of tactility; and the importance of speed (or speed-up, as McLuhan often put it) in the collapse of space and time. As Marinetti put it in the first Futurist manifesto, 'Il Tempo e lo Spazio morirono ieri. Noi viviamo già nell'assoluto, poiché abbiamo già creata l'eterna velocità onnipresente' (10–11; Time and Space died yesterday. We are already living in the absolute, since we have already created eternal and omnipresent speed), a notion to which McLuhan returned many times, often expressing himself in like terms.

Among the most important of Marinetti's texts within the context of McLuhan's work is the *Manifesto tecnico della letteratura futurista* (1912; Technical Manifesto of Futurist Literature), where Marinetti argues for the importance of sound in literature (*TIF* 46) and for the use of 'words-in-liberty' (*parole in libertà*; 54), these latter being explosions of normal typography into word images that graphically convey meaning in the manner of an ideogram (a technique McLuhan uses throughout *Counterblast*; see fig. 6.4); this technique derived from advertising. Indeed, the attention Futurism gave to the printed word as a material object of artistic innovation was perhaps its most influential aspect.[26]

This focus on the printed word was at once an aspect of the increasingly interficial status of the art object (a movement John Welchman has called 'radical interdiscursivity')[27] and part of a larger rejection of Renaissance perspectivalism, in that the effect of the printed word was produced on the surface of the page.[28] Both of these tendencies were joined in the practice of collage, which breaks down perspectivalism at the same time that it asserts the alterity of the elements it juxtaposes.

Another of Marinetti's manifestos advocated a tactile art whose object was to achieve tactile harmonies ('le armonie tattili,' *TIF* 166) that would lead to spiritual communication among humans ('le comunicazioni spirituali fra gli esseri umani,' 166). In addition, tactility demonstrated the arbitrariness of distinguishing five senses ('La distinzione dei cinque sensi è arbitraria ... Il Tattilismo favorisce questa scoperta,' 178), as opposed to an interfusional sensorium. Tactility, finally, was linked to the televisual, which extended the tactile ('Possediamo oramai una televisione di cinquantamila punti per ogni immagine grande su schermo grande. Aspettando l'invenzione del teletattilismo ...' 207), such that a visual sense is born in the fingertips ('Nasce un senso visivo alla punta delle dita,' 178).[29] The ultimate implication of such wireless technology was to free humanity of the heavy, strangulating, suffocating, fossilized effects of the book, which had rendered people myopic ('il libro ... ha la colpa di avere resa miope l'umanità implica qualcosa di pesante strangolato soffocato fossilizzato e congelato,' *TIF* 208).

A key source on Futurism for McLuhan was Gyorgy Kepes's book *Language of Vision* (1944), from which he often cited,[30] and which must be accounted one of his major source-texts on spatialization (although McLuhan rejected its central assumption that space was univocally visual). In this book, McLuhan encountered artists and art forms that were highly significant for his own art/critical production: Picasso, Mondrian, Moholy-Nagy, Seurat, Le Corbusier, Balla, Duchamp, Klee, Apollinaire, and Max Ernst, as well as typography and cave drawings, all of which Kepes discusses in terms of the production of visual space. Kepes seeks to formulate the implications for vision of a post-Newtonian science, and specifically with regard to constructions of visual space: '[w]idening horizons, and the new dimensions of the visual environment necessitate new idioms of spatial measurement and communication of space. The visual image of today must come to terms with all this: it must evolve a language of space which is adjusted to the new standards of experience. This new language can and will enable the human sensibility to perceive space-time relationships never recognized before' (14). Although Kepes limits his discussion to the construction of visual space, he sounds a number of notes subsequently heard in McLuhan's work, including the importance of figure and ground to our perception and the suggestion that a dynamic space is being inaugurated congruently with post-Newtonian science. The first of these innovations was 'a cataloguing of stationary spatial locations' (178), as in the work of Balla or Duchamp (or Marey). The second innovation was to picture 'lines of force,' which 'could function as the plastic forces of two-dimensional picture-plane' (178). The third step was 'simultaneous representation of the numerous visible aspects composing an event' (178). Kepes quotes Marinetti's avowed aim to create in Futurist painting '"a simultaneity of environment and therefore a dismemberment and dislocation of objects"' (178), an aim that Kepes parallels to Einstein's notion of spacetime in the general theory of relativity.

Verbi-Voco-Visual

In 1967, McLuhan published *Verbi-Voco-Visual Explorations*, a revised version of *Explorations* 8 (1957).[31] From the cover illustration (fig. 5.1), to the frontispiece, to the exploded typography of the text, to the coloured stock of the original edition, to the circumstances of its publication, this book makes its point as much through its artistic dimension as through any other aspect of its medium, and constitutes (along with books such as *Counterblast*), McLuhan's artistic credo. The phrase 'verbi-voco-visual,' from Joyce's *Finnegans Wake*,[32] conveys the idea of the continuity of the senses, an idea that stands at the heart of McLuhan's notion of interface and of simultaneity. The cover, as a note explains, 'derives from the spherical nature of the oral world' (np) and, as such, combines McLuhan's central concern with orality ('oral means "total" primarily, "spoken" accidentally' [item 1]) and its relationship to non-Euclidean geometry, of which the sphere is the most readily accessible model.[33] The photomontage reproduced from Moholy-Nagy's *Vision in Motion* (1947) points towards the technique that would dominate McLuhan's own *livres d'artiste*, such as *The Medium Is the Massage*, as well as to an artist whose spatial theories were highly significant within McLuhan's artistic/critical frame of reference. And the typographical experiments – made in the context, here, of quotations from Marinetti's *Futurist Manifesto* – are the harbingers of one of the most important artistic (and philosophical) dimensions of McLuhan's writing after *Understanding Media* (1964).

Verbi-Voco-Visual Explorations is noteworthy from the outset for the degree of sociopolitical commentary it makes. The first item focuses on the degree to which modern business communications are 'locked into the patterns of explicit typography,' out of which patterns 'electronic simultaneity' is urging them, one sign of which is the turn towards 'brainstorming' sessions, with their reliance on oral modalities. 'The business man today,' writes McLuhan, 'is trying to twist his habitual lineality into the likeness of an oral sphere' (item 5). The second item (as well as the sixth) focuses on the Soviet Union and its attempt to move from predominantly oral modes (as typified by the Russian Orthodox church) to literate ones, a move that, in McLuhan's view, 'will eventually splinter the Soviet area as effectively as it splintered England and Europe in the sixteenth century.' The seventh item turns to the organization man, who 'would be ashamed to be caught reading during business hours. Any activity so private, silent and meditative is disloyal to the ways of organization.' The twelfth concerns 'English libel law' and the 'code of honour' in oral societies; the thirteenth the 'oral tradition of the South.' The fifteenth item tells us that '[t]oday sparked by private grants from the big collective foundations the professor is able to function as a figure of private initiative and as an employer of labor.' The eighteenth item praises the drinking of wine as a 'total experience' of the senses. All of these items serve to illustrate McLuhan's notion that art has something to teach us about contemporary social relations: 'The new art or science which the electronic or post-mechanical age has to invent concerns the alchemy of social change' (item 14). This embracing of the material realm of social production might at first seem to sit uneasily with McLuhan's espousal of such artistic movements as Dada, the Bauhaus, Cubism, Futurism, and so on, but McLuhan argued that art was the central

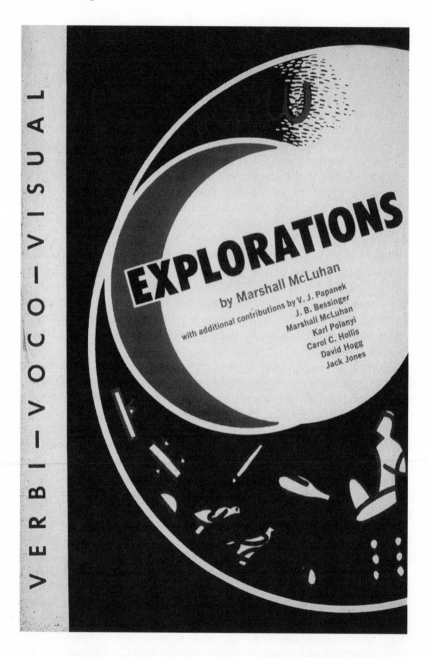

Figure 5.1. Cover of McLuhan, *Verbi-Voco-Visual Explorations.* In 'About the Cover,' McLuhan explains: 'The basic design of the cover derives from the spherical nature of the oral world. Verbi-Voco-Visual standing for the word as sound (πειρω) and as sight (hieroglyphs). The hieroglyphs are placed on a curve, the lower curve, reading from left to right means "looking for the ways" and the top curve reading from right to left means "speech." EXPLORING THE WORD!'

activity of our social beings rather than peripheral to it.[34] This is so because these contemporary artistic movements emerge out of the contestation of a particular form of social space produced by typography – the space of lineality, logicality, univocality, an 'eye' space that is giving way to an 'ear' space.

This transition is startlingly conveyed by the photomontage that serves as frontispiece to *Verbi-Voco-Visual Explorations* (fig. 5.2). From Laszlo Moholy-Nagy's *Vision in Motion* (1947), it shows a man's face in three-quarter profile whose right eye has been replaced by an ear.[35] The work of Moholy-Nagy played a crucial role in McLuhan's aesthetic. Associated early in his career with the Bauhaus and with Walter Gropius, and subsequently director of his own Institute of Design in Chicago, Moholy-Nagy worked in a wide variety of media, and particularly with photography, typography, and with paintings on plexiglass that he called 'space modulators.' He was also a co-founder of Constructivism and produced a number of paintings in that style.[36] Richard Kostelanetz has suggested that Moholy-Nagy's influence is evident in McLuhan and Quentin Fiore's *The Medium Is the Massage* and *War and Peace in the Global Village*; indeed, he goes farther, stating that 'Moholy ... clearly stands behind many of the media-sleuth's ideas. (Indeed, it was McLuhan who first told *me* [Kostelanetz] to read *Vision in Motion*)' (214).[37] *Vision in Motion*, as Moholy-Nagy states at the outset, 'is a synonym for simultaneity and space-time; a means to comprehend the new dimension' (*Vision in Motion* 12). This mode of comprehension is facilitated by artists; the 'true artist is the grindstone of the senses; he sharpens eyes, mind, and feeling; he interprets ideas and concepts through his own media' (29). Moholy-Nagy believed that '*the* key of our age' was '***seeing everything in relationship***' (68), and to that end he promoted the 'optophonetic art' of Dadaist Raoul Hausmann,[38] an art form that would 'allow us to see music and hear pictures simultaneously: a startling articulation of space-time. The first steps to it ... lead most probably through photography, cinema and television' (168). In addition to providing this sort of synaesthetic argument, *Vision in Motion* provided an anthology of texts that were of crucial importance to McLuhan, including calligraphic and ideogrammatical works by Apollinaire, extracts from the *Futurist Manifesto* (including a reproduction of a page of 'words in liberty') and other texts by Marinetti, as well as a section on 'the new typography,' advertising, Dada, Rimbaud, Surrealism, and James Joyce.

McLuhan reviewed *Vision in Motion* (along with Giedion's *Mechanization Takes Command*) for the *Hudson Review* in 1949. Placing Moholy-Nagy in the tradition of Burckhardt and Wölfflin, he states that *Vision in Motion*, while 'less responsible' (601) than Giedion's book, nevertheless 'swarms with brilliant insights into parallel effects and intentions between the most diverse activities of contemporary science, photography, engineering, art and literature.'[39] What made Moholy-Nagy's work of great significance for McLuhan were the many writings Moholy-Nagy devoted to the theorization of space.[40] As Victor Papanek writes in *Verbi-Voco-Visual Explorations*, 'Probably the most interesting attempts to abolish the linear book-tradition in the arts were carried on at the German *Bauhaus* in the Twenties. The most direct and remarkable of these is contained in Moholy-Nagy's *Malerei, Fotografie und Film*' (6). In that verbal-visual text, Moholy-Nagy sought an arrangement that would allow all aspects of the book to be '"*heard simultaneously*"' as part of a '"multi-dimensional, endlessly spherical space"' that would '"compensate for the *static, euclidean character* of the easel painting"'

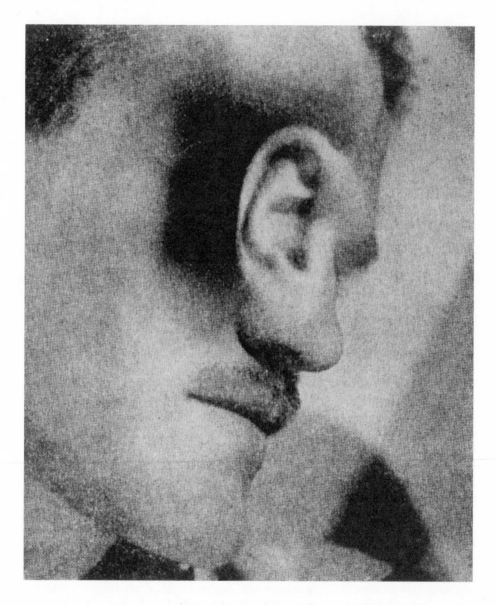

Figure 5.2. Frontispiece to *Verbi-Voco-Visual Explorations*: 'an ear for an eye.'

(Papanek quoting Moholy-Nagy, *VVV* 7). Moholy-Nagy argued that contemporary art-ists had 'produced on the flat surface a new *kinetic* concept of spatial articulation, vision in motion' (*Vision in Motion* 46). This new dimension or 'new experience of space' (*Vision in Motion* 53) had been produced by photography and film: '[e]very period in human culture has developed a spatial conception. Such space conceptions were utilized not only for shelter but also for play, dancing, fighting, in fact, for the domination of life in every detail. A new space conception originated mainly through new materials and constructions introduced by the industrial revolution. However, as the technology was derived from new scientific findings, physics, chemistry, biology, physiology, sociology, etc. – all these elements have to be considered in our new space conception too' (*Vision in Motion* 58). This interlinking of artistic spaces with social spaces was likewise important for McLuhan, as we have seen. For Moholy-Nagy, this connection presented a way of responding to social ills: '*it seems that the most abstract experiment of space-time articulation carries a sensible reality* [emphasis added] ... Such experiments may signalize a spatial order in which not single structural parts, or large spans of openings will play the important part, but the relationships of neighbor units, buildings and free areas, shelter and leisure, production and recreation; leading toward a biologically right living most probably through a right regional planning; toward a city-land unity ... Space-time is now the new basis on which the edifice of future thoughts and work should be built' (*Vision in Motion* 61–2).[41] Moholy-Nagy's key article on space concerned 'The New Bauhaus and Space Relationships' (1937), in which he writes that space is '*a reality in our sensory experience; a human experience like others, a means to expression like others; like other realities, other materials* [emphasis added] ... [M]an perceives space ... [t]hrough his sense of sight ... [t]hrough his sense of hearing, by acoustic phenomena ... [t]hrough means of locomotion ... [t]hrough his sense of equilibrium' (*Vision in Motion* 107). 'I am convinced,' he continues, 'that sooner or later we shall have a genuine space system, a dictionary for space relationships, as we have today our color system or as we have our sound system for musical composition' (109). McLuhan sought to produce such a dictionary in the twenty-six chapters of *Understanding Media*, which forms a 'space system' of sorts with *The Gutenberg Galaxy* and *Through the Vanishing Point*.

Verbi-Voco-Visual Explorations contains articles by a number of authors in addition to McLuhan; the most important of these is 'A Bridge in Time,' by V[ictor] J. Papanek. For a while an instructor at the Ontario College of Art,[42] Papanek was, by the mid-1970s, dean of the School of Design at the California Institute of the Arts. In *Design for the Real World: Human Ecology and Social Change*, Papanek lists himself as co-author of *Verbi-Voco-Visual Explorations*.[43] In fact, his contribution to the book reads like notes taken at one of McLuhan's seminars, and is a condensed statement of the artistic milieu in which McLuhan saw himself working. Subtitled 'An Attempt at Non-Euclidean Aesthetics,' the article discusses the machine technology that was embodied in the work of Futurists such as Balla and the architecture of Frank Lloyd Wright, who, 'using the crafts of the machine' has been able 'to build a technological bridge to poetic, acoustical space' (*VVV* 4). This bridge, suggests Papanek, is being further enhanced by electronic media, which are providing 'a closer and more direct oral channel ... for all cultures' (10).

While McLuhan often alluded to Frank Lloyd Wright, his principal affinity among architects was with Le Corbusier, whom Papanek sees as 'verbalizing [a] structural philosophy to erect his poetical "*Bruecke*" to North American technology' (*VVV* 4). Professionally associated with Fernand Léger (whom McLuhan published in *Explorations*) and with Giedion,[44] Le Corbusier appealed to McLuhan primarily for the holistic approach he took to architecture and the importance he assigned to acoustic space.[45] McLuhan refers to Le Corbusier in his 1961 article 'Inside the Five Sense Sensorium,' which is in many ways a prelude (along with 'Printing and Social Change') to *The Gutenberg Galaxy*. Writing about the effects of mass media on the contemporary conception of the city, McLuhan invokes Le Corbusier in the context of 'resonance' ('Inside' 54), the sort of acoustic that characterized architecture 'when the cathedrals were white, in Corbusier's phrase' (54). He parallels this resonating (holistic) experience to the contemporary synaesthesia induced by mass media: '[l]et us consider the hypothesis that TV offers a massive Bauhaus program of re-education for North American sense life. That is to query whether the TV image is, in effect, a haptic, tactile, or synaesthetic mode of interplay among the sense, a fulfillment on a popular plane of the aesthetic program of Hildebrand, Berenson, Wölfflin, Paul Klee, and Giedion ... Do the Beats and the teenagers with their amalgam of art, Zen, and repudiation of consumer values conform to the effects hoped for by the older schools of synaesthesia?' (50) What is significant about television is its production of a mass age in which, paradoxically, individual experience is heightened,[46] taking on the synaesthetic qualities that the artists of the late nineteenth century had striven for: 'TV ... is not part of the 19th-century art-program for the reconquest of synaesthesia. TV is rather the overwhelming and technological success of that program after its artistic exponents have retired' (51). Once again we have the theme that artistic production has merged with the production of 'social spaces' (54), as it has in the notion of the 'environment.' This was one of the principal motives that drew McLuhan to the Bauhaus in general, and to Le Corbusier in particular, in whose works (such as *L'Art décoratif d'aujourd'hui* [1925]) he found not only a model for books combining text and image in provocative ways but also the notion of the object-world as comprising an extension of the body and the idea that machines constitute a contemporary folklore (as McLuhan suggests in *The Mechanical Bride*).[47]

Le Corbusier's aesthetic program was tellingly summed up in the phrase '"visual acoustics"' (Gardiner 27), which he used to describe projects such as the chapel at Ronchamp; contemporaneously with his design of that building, Le Corbusier was making sculptures of the ear (Gardiner 91).[48] Stephen Gardiner notes that Le Corbusier's 'struggle for space' led him to propose 'the possibility of being able to sense – if not entirely *to see* – a building from every point, whether inside or outside or both. This theme brought his ideas into the fourth-dimensional sphere' (54). Le Corbusier gave voice to this notion in his 1946 article 'Espace indicible,' where the architectural achievement of ineffable space was linked to synaesthesia. Thus, in the perfectly designed building, a 'phenomenon of concordance takes place, as exact as mathematics, a true manifestation of plastic acoustics.'[49] In a note to one of his drawings, which accompanies the article, Le Corbusier writes that it represents 'architectural walls poised to echo, to bring to life this acoustic time-space phenomenon' (Ockman 67). As Maurice Besset notes, one of the chief analogues for this 'acoustic time-space' was the work of Mondrian,[50] such as the *Broadway Boogie-Woogie* on which Papanek comments in

Verbi-Voco-Visual Explorations (6) and which figures so prominently in McLuhan's film *Picnic in Space*, where Mondrian's title brings together the spatial with the acoustic through the matrix of jazz and bebop, prime points of reference for the culture of spontaneity (with jazz resonating for McLuhan with *jaser*, 'to chat'). This 'mobilization of space' (Besset 44) took its cues from the multiplicity of viewpoints inherent in Cubistic practice; from the 'afocal space-grid' of artists such as Mondrian; from the 'space-field of energies' of artists such as Kandinsky and of Constructivists such as Gabo (mentioned by Papanek); and from 'the space-time of shifting light' in the work of Moholy-Nagy (Besset 45).

Le Corbusier sought to realize this notion of 'visual acoustics' in the Philips Pavilion, a hyperbolic paraboloid structure he designed in 1958 for the Brussels World Fair, which Philips had wanted to name the 'Spatiorama.'[51] Edgard Varèse wrote a 'spatialized' composition for the building, the *Poème électronique*, which had been scored for delivery from a number of different points within the structure, thus conforming to the spatial configurations associated with the fourth dimension.[52] Varèse's composition was important in that it sought to convey '"all the registers and all the dynamics of each instrument which are not usually 'sent' through ordinary broadcasting"';[53] these registers and dynamics are analogous to the 'noise' excluded from the Shannon-Weaver model of communication, the noise McLuhan called 'the medium.' Through the simultaneities of the 'Spatiorama' (a name finally abandoned), Le Corbusier sought to achieve the goal he had set out in 'Ineffable Space' of a '"release of aesthetic emotion"' as '"a special function of space"' (quoted in Treib 3). What marks this building off from the church at Ronchamp, however, is its dependence on electricity and on the effects of 'virtual' rather than 'natural' spaces. The interior of the pavilion served as the screen for a montage of filmic images, many of which derived from André Malraux's *Voices of Silence* (a work of considerable importance for McLuhan; see chapter 7 below), as did the principle of their juxtaposition.[54] The shape of the pavilion – a hyperbolic paraboloid – was inspired by the Constructivist sculptures of Naum Gabo (and his brother, Antoine Pevsner), which were characterized by a fluidity of form that appeared to oscillate between two and three dimensions, thus implying a temporal element within a spatial form. Papanek's essay had identified Constructivism as yet another artistic movement that was important for the spatial aesthetics McLuhan was developing in his seminars of the 1950s, quoting from Gabo's *Second Constructivist Manifesto* (1924) to the effect that '"Space cannot be seen by the eye, it is all around us like a globe stretching into eternity. Sculpture is to be *heard* like music"' (*VVV* 2), which is the synaesthetic principle at work in the Philips Pavilion.[55]

The *Laocoön* Re(vi)sited

McLuhan's deep immersion in the intellectual currents associated with Modernist (and postmodernist) art is most readily apparent in *Through the Vanishing Point: Space in Poetry and Painting* (1968; with Harley Parker), which forms a trilogy with the two other major texts published by McLuhan in the 1960s, *The Gutenberg Galaxy* and *Understanding Media*, in that all three of these texts are concerned with the production of space. Whereas in *The Gutenberg Galaxy* McLuhan had produced a historical study of the effects on our spatial perceptions of the invention of the alphabet and of the printing press, and in *Understanding Media* had written of ways in which our senses create spaces through processes of mediated extension, in *Through the Vanishing Point* he studies a succession of spatial environments and their sensory effects. Donald Theall's remark that in *Through the Vanishing Point* McLuhan was 'trying to conceive some grand theory about the evolution of space which [would] cover all his needs' (*RVM* 171) is thus essentially correct, though the 'grand theory' is, in fact, articulated across three books (*GG*, *UM*, and *TVP*), and is not developed solely in this one.[56] In subtitling his book *Space in Poetry and Painting*, McLuhan at once invokes and contests Gotthold Ephraim Lessing's 1766 classic, *Laocoön: An Essay on the Limits of Painting and Poetry*. As Stephen Kern has suggested in *The Culture of Time and Space*, Lessing is important to the history of Modern art because it was precisely the spatial and temporal *limits* of art that became the major issue overshadowing the birth of the Modernist movement[57] – limits that buildings such as the Philips Pavilion powerfully contested. McLuhan was drawn to Lessing's text for this reason (as Irving Babbitt, W.K. Wimsatt, and Clement Greenberg were as well), and because Innis had demonstrated via Lessing that spatial and temporal biases were an index at once to sociopolitical configurations and to artistic ones (*BC* 102).

The debate over Lessing's spatio-temporal distinctions was relaunched at the beginning of the twentieth century by Irving Babbitt's *The New Laokoon* (1910). Subtitled *An Essay on the Confusion of the Arts*, Babbitt's book decried the continuing 'eleutheromania' (196) in the arts: 'The nineteenth century witnessed ... a general confusion of the arts, as well as of the different *genres* within the confines of each art. To take examples almost at random, we have Gautier's *transpositions d'art*, Rossetti's attempts to paint his sonnets and write his pictures, Mallarmé's ambition to compose symphonies with words.'[58] Clement Greenberg, writing in 1940, extended this argument by opting for a 'pure' abstraction in art that he saw as 'a salutary reaction against the mistakes of painting and sculpture in the past several centuries which were due to such a confusion.'[59] By 1967 (at the height of McLuhan's fame), when W.K. Wimsatt wrote 'Laokoön: An Oracle Reconsulted,' the confusion of the arts was being explicitly associated with McLuhan's writings:

> Today's critical 'anti-interpreter' rejoices in the trampling of barriers and in a philosophy that understands the non-reality of all art entities and presumably of most natural ones ... We arrive at 'multimedia,' the barrage and 'massage,' the 'supersaturated attack' on the senses, the 'overload,' the 'blitz,' contrived with elaborately inventive care in the 'total environment' discothèque, at sales meetings of the Scott Paper Company, at electronic theater events, or in the halls of Expo and the Royal Ontario Museum: – batteries of pulsing and eye-searing strobe lights, wailing sirens and high-decibel modern rock, flashing and jumping screens, electronically tinted mists, incidental smells and touches, all these for the purpose of 'turning on' the patron – in a total experience which approximates the effect of the psychedelic drug – a deepening and merging of sensory experience, a release of the mind from the 'rational ordering' of perception.[60]

That McLuhan is intended in this attack is hard to miss: 'massage' is a reference to *The*

Medium Is the Massage, and phrases such as 'sensory experience,' 'overload,' and 'total environment' are explicitly McLuhanesque references.

John C. Welchman has noted that, '[a]s the theory and practice of modernism developed in the first decades of the twentieth century, there ensued a kind of subtextual debate on the divisive aesthetic rationale of Lessing's key text. This gave rise to two fields of response to the close zoning of the sign, reproducing that fissure in the formation of the modern between formalist autonomy and self-reference, and nonformalist material and signifying interaction' ('After the Wagnerian Bouillabaisse' 62, n8). One of the ways in which this tension was felt is observable in artworks associated with Dada and Surrealism. As Welchman remarks, 'No longer could painting and sculpture be denied access to what Lessing maintained was the exclusive concern of literature: narrative action extending in time. And texts, conversely, were opened up to interactions, visual practice was construed as inseparable from the social, the political, or the personal' (62). McLuhan considered this interficial aspect of avant-garde art to be its most significant property, and it is particularly to these artists of the interface that he felt himself most powerfully drawn; similarly, the artists most closely associated with McLuhan's prosthetic aesthetic were precisely those ones who resisted Lessing's strictures on space and time. 'Our manner of juxtaposing a poem with a painting,' write McLuhan and Parker, in their introduction to *Through the Vanishing Point*, 'is designed to illuminate the world of verbal space through an understanding of spaces as they have been defined and explored through the plastic arts. The verbal medium is so completely environmental as to escape all perceptual study in terms of its plastic values' (1). The literary work, in other words, is, for the purposes of this study, being treated as a spatial form (which *includes* time), rather than in Lessing's sense as a time form.

The fact that critics such as Babbitt, Greenberg, and Wimsatt found themselves writing about Lessing's *Laocoön* more than one hundred years after it was published indicates the contemporary importance that had been granted to Lessing's work precisely by those artistic practices that were contesting the space/time dichotomy he had theorized. Lessing had posited that poetry (and literature in general) was a time-art, while painting (and the visual arts generally) were spatially oriented (a division with which Innis concurred). Lessing's contribution to aesthetics was thus not so much that he was 'the first in modern times to define clearly the distinctiveness of the spheres of art and poetry,'[61] as Edward Allen McCormick has suggested, but rather that he sought to elaborate a poetics from the space/time opposition (as he conceived it) that, in his view, was fundamental to the generic bases of these art forms. Indeed, it is against the *contamination* of these genres that he writes in his book, decrying the 'mania for description' he finds in poetry and the 'mania for allegory' he finds in paintings ('Preface' 5). If McLuhan had been drawn to Lessing's study because it sought to discuss in tandem the poetics of poetry and painting, it was not, however, to argue, like Lessing, that the two should be relegated to their own distinctive spheres. He had already dealt with this issue in his encounter with Freud's *Civilization and Its Discontents*; whereas Freud – who was deeply influenced by Lessing (as Welchman, 'After the Wagnerian Bouillabaisse,' observes [79]) – had argued against the possibilities of conflationary spaces, McLuhan had understood that the effect of electronic media was to conflate space and time. As Welchman notes, the 'Dada and surrealist artist entertained few of

Freud's reservations' (80), and McLuhan likewise sought to problematize the distinction between space and time and to formulate bases for their *interrelationship*, just as, in *The Gutenberg Galaxy*, he had argued for the necessity of understanding media in terms of a 'spacetime,' as theorized in physics. In these terms, it is significant that the subtitle of *Through the Vanishing Point* speaks of *space* in poetry and painting, with the understanding that this category had subsumed the distinction between space and time into a spacetime in which time constituted the fourth dimension of space.[62] Thus, in exhibit 48 of *Through the Vanishing Point* (a long commentary on a passage from Hesiod's *Works and Days* and a meditation on Fay Zeitlin's painting *I Am That I Am*) McLuhan writes:

> To say that Homer and Hesiod were 'nonvisual' poets is to explain in a phrase every problem of the world of Greek scholarship since Lessing and Schliemann. The Greeks never entered pictorial or visual space. They tended to use all their senses at once. They approached the European modes of awareness by a gradual playing down of acoustic space, of kinetic space, of tactual and visceral spaces, in favor of a heightened visual organization of experience. The change from multispaces to a single, uniform, rational space is often associated with the Euclidean breakthrough ... It is the total unawareness of Homer's indifference to visual (continuous and connected) space that spawned all the efforts to 'locate' Troy. (225–6)

As in previous works, McLuhan critiques here the assumption that 'space' means *visual* space exclusively, the assumption tacitly made by Lessing in his space and time dichotomy. Thus, in his account of Zeitlin's abstract painting, McLuhan notes that the spatial relationships it represents 'are not the spaces of pictorial space' (231); rather, Zeitlin's spaces are disconnected and lack perspective.

The nuances of McLuhan's spatial theories derive from their dynamic nature. W.J.T. Mitchell has noted, for example, that '[a]lthough the *Laocoön* has been the subject of controversy since it first appeared in 1766, few critics have disputed the truth of its basic distinction between the temporal and spatial arts. Even the critical industry founded on Joseph Frank's claim that "spatial form" is a central feature of literary modernism never questions the normative force of Lessing's distinction.'[63] McLuhan, however, had questioned the space/time distinction from the moment he became aware of Einsteinian physics. As Mitchell goes on to point out, 'spatial form' in the sense of 'suspended temporality' can have 'no strong theoretical force' (96). Contrarily, what Mitchell seeks to argue is that 'the tendency of artists to breach the supposed boundaries between temporal and spatial arts is not a marginal or exceptional practice, but a fundamental impulse in both the theory and practice of the arts, one which is not confined to any particular genre or period' (98). Mitchell's argument generally accords with McLuhan's in this regard; indeed, Mitchell invokes the McLuhanesque notion that writing is the spatialization of speech (99), thus problematizing at the outset Lessing's notion that poetry is a temporal art (essentially). McLuhan, however, takes his theories farther than Mitchell's by unmooring spatiality from the visual.

Hence, as Theall suggests, McLuhan is indeed interested in a grand theory of space in *Through the Vanishing Point*. The thirty-seventh volume in 'World Perspectives,' the book was part of a series edited by Kenneth Clark, Werner Heisenberg, Konrad Lorenz, and Joseph Needham, among others, and was published alongside works by authors such as Jacques Maritain, Walter Gropius, Lewis Mumford, Moses Hadas, Mircea Eliade, and Georg Lukács. It distinguishes itself from these works, however, by its form alone, which comprises a preface; an essay on 'sensory modes'; forty-nine 'exhibits' that juxtapose a poem and visual artwork to a series of aphoristic comments in what McLuhan calls a 'spatial dialogue' (all of these under the collective title 'The Emperor's New Clothes');[64] and appendices on tactility and colour television. The apparently disparate interests of the book are justified, McLuhan and Parker explain in their preface, by the 'speed-up of human events and the resulting increase of interfaces among all men and institutions' (xxiii). It is to the artist that we turn in such periods of disruption 'in the hope of increased sensory awareness. The artist has the power to discern the current environment created by the latest technology' (which, in the case of electronic media, was destabilizing the hegemony of the visual culture that had been established by print). Artistic discernment thus inevitably takes the form of an interface of the previous environment with the current one. 'When two or more environments encounter one another by direct interface,' write McLuhan and Parker, 'they tend to manifest their distinctive qualities' (238). It is noteworthy that what is being manifested here is something about the sociohistorical *context* of the artwork, and not the artist's psyche. Given that individualist subjectivity was itself a product of typography, as McLuhan had suggested in *The Gutenberg Galaxy*, he sees the artwork in the electronic age not Freudianly, as a 'form of self-expression' (xxiv), but as a 'kind of research and probing,' thereby aligning the work of the theorist with that of the artist (and hence the form of the book). McLuhan notes that the twentieth-century artist has often been referred to as 'the enemy, the criminal' (246), as was Wyndham Lewis, the artist/critic of whom McLuhan is probably thinking here. 'It is not a private need of expression that motivates [the artist],' writes McLuhan, 'but a corporate need of involvement in the total audience. This is humanism in reverse' (258), insofar as art in the electronic age is the expression not of an individual but of a collectivity.

Through the Looking Point

As the word 'through' in the title of *Through the Vanishing Point* hints, and as the discussion of Lewis Carroll's work suggests (exhibit 33; and on pages 245 and 249), key reference points for McLuhan and Parker in writing *Through the Vanishing Point* were the 'Alice' books.[65] The lesson Carroll's books held for McLuhan resided in their critique of the verities of visual (and especially perspectival) space, particularly as they were embodied in systems of writing, or what McLuhan calls here 'verbal space' (1), a space distinguished by its homogeneity. 'It was only with the fantasy of a tale like *Alice in Wonderland* that nineteenth-century man could make an entree into ... diverse spaces' (*TVP* 9); '[w]ith the advent of electric circuitry and the instant movement of information, Euclidean space recedes and the non-Euclidean geometries emerge. Lewis Carroll, the Oxford mathematician, was perfectly aware of this change in our world when he took Alice through the looking glass into the world where each object creates its own space and conditions' (249). The verities of visual space have been effectively summarized by Erwin Panofsky in his classic text *Perspective as Symbolic Form*,[66] a text whose lineage led back to Alois Riegl and his notion of the haptic (or tactile), which he placed in opposition to the optic.[67] Panofsky argues for 'a peculiar stabilizing tendency within our consciousness – promoted by the cooperation of vision with the tactile sense' (31), a form of sensory interplay McLuhan associated with the *sensus communis*.

Panofsky's central argument is that perspective negates the medium through which it is represented, in that it represents a spatial continuum of three dimensions on a planar surface of two, such that 'all perpendiculars or "orthogonals" meet at the so-called central vanishing point' (28), thereby producing a 'fully rational – that is, infinite, unchanging and homogeneous – space' (28–9). This space contrasts sharply with the spaces actually perceived by our senses; Panofsky quotes from Ernst Cassirer's *Philosophy of Symbolic Forms* to the effect that '"[v]isual and tactical space [*Tastraum*] are both anisotropic and unhomogeneous in contrast to the metric space of Euclidean geometry"' (30).[68] McLuhan's comments on perspective, while similar to Panofsky's, are more cognizant of the cultural milieu in which perspective arose, and are far less teleological than Panofsky's. McLuhan argues that perspective 'moves toward specialism and fragmentation. It insists on the single point of view (at least, in its classical phase) and involves us automatically in a single space' (13). *Through the Vanishing Point* is less concerned with producing a critique of perspectival space, however, than with articulating possibilities for spatial interface by setting up a series of 'spatial dialogues' that juxtapose artworks with commentaries that take the form of prose poems. In other words, *Through the Vanishing Point* exposes the assumptions of visual space – the space we take to be the norm – by interfacing that space with other modes of constructing space. This interfacing constitutes a degree of critical agency: the 'interface and dialogue between the sister arts should provide a rich means of training perception and sensibility' (2). The 'poetics' of the interface in this training of perception derives directly from the relationship between environment and counter-environment: '[a]ll the arts might be considered to act as counter-environments or countergradients. Any environmental form whatsoever saturates perception so that its own character is imperceptible; it has the power to distort or deflect human awareness. Even the most popular arts can serve to increase the level of awareness, at least until they become entirely environmental and unperceived' (2). Art is thus processual by virtue of the dynamic it encodes of environment and counter-environment. The dynamic process whereby one environment is countered by another involves enhancement, obsolescence, retrieval, and reversal (to use the terms in *Laws of Media*) and is thus characterized by 'a reversal or chiasmus of form that occurs in any situation where an environment is pushed up into high intensity or high definition by technological change' (247). Art is in this sense the prime way in which critical consciousness of the environment is achieved, insofar as art embodies a perceptual dynamic of the environmental with the counter-environmental.

These environmental shifts involve shifts in the perception of space, in that each sense creates a particular sort of space. Thus the introduction to *Through the Vanishing Point*, 'Sensory Modes,' is structured as a historical analysis of dominant (or environmental) modes of spatial perception (and thus production). McLuhan begins with the example of nineteenth-century zoo architecture, which failed to take into account 'a prime fact of animal behavior – namely, the animal's need to define and patrol a space of its own. This space is called into being by sounds, by odors, by colors – in short, by that orchestration of the senses compatible with the total life of the species' (2–3). Rather than being constructed on this basis of sensory interplay, the zoos of that period were designed as 'a rationally and visually contrived space' that 'confirmed an unconscious pictorial bias of scientists and spectators,' and thus 'eliminated the complex spaces generated by the animals in their normal habitat' (3). This notion of 'territoriality' (as popularized by Robert Ardrey's mid-1960s book *African Genesis*; cf *TVP* 2) gained currency, McLuhan suggests, precisely at the moment when the hegemony of visual space (that space deriving from print technologies) was declining as a result of the ascendancy of electronic media. McLuhan compares his program of sensitizing his readers to the varieties of spatial experience with Piaget and Inhelder's work, outlined in *The Child's Conception of Space* (1948).[69] Piaget and Inhelder provide an imprimatur for the apparently large claims McLuhan makes for the study of spatial perceptions when they remark, in their preface, that 'if the development of various aspects of child thought can tell us anything about the mechanism of intelligence and the nature of human thought in general, then the problem of space must surely rank as of the highest importance' (vii). One of the central discoveries of their analyses in this regard is that 'the child's space, which is essentially of an active and operational character, invariably begins with this simple topological type of relationship long before it becomes projective or euclidean' (vii), a realization that has a special resonance with Carroll's 'Alice' stories.

To support the notion that the work of art encodes specific perceptual values, and that those values have a fundamentally spatial character, McLuhan draws on Adolf Hildebrand's 1893 monograph, *The Problem of Form in the Fine Arts* (*EFS* 227–79). Hildebrand insists on the sensuous aspect of spatial perception: 'Since we do not view nature simply as visual beings tied to a single vantage point but, rather, with all our senses at once, in perpetual change and motion, we live and weave a spatial consciousness into the nature that surrounds us, even where the appearance before us offers scarcely any point of reference for the idea of space' (*EFS* 239).[70] Hildebrand was writing at a moment of transition to a culture that would be dominated by issues of spatialization, and, as McLuhan argued, these new spaces would be aural in nature. 'The aurally structured culture,' writes McLuhan, 'has none of the tracts [*sic*] of visual space long regarded as "normal," "natural" space by literate societies' (*TVP* 6). In electronic culture, 'it is possible to deal with the entire environment as a work of art ... The new possibility demands total understanding of the artistic function in society. It will no longer be possible merely to add art to the environment' (*TVP* 7). In the electronic environment, art is not an add-on but affects the entire perceptual disposition of that culture. In contemporary culture (as in the Middle Ages), space is once again becoming multivalent, after the centuries of uniform, perspectival space produced by the dominance of print. Thus, a 'modern art gallery invites the viewer to be as adventurous and daring as an astronaut in probing new modalities of space' (*TVP* 9). McLuhan critiques Georges Poulet (whom he had cited in *The Gutenberg Galaxy*) for his assumption, in *Studies in Human Time*, that 'space is uniform as if it presented a ... continuous character to all men. *It is, however, central to the understanding of space in poetry and painting that we recognize the same cultural diversity of space as of time*' (*TVP* 9; emphasis added). McLuhan nuances this historical account of perspective with the suggestion that the single point of view that had been codified in the Renaissance was questioned in

Mannerist and baroque art, the latter characterized by a 'resonance of double perspective and contrapuntal theming' (*TVP* 19). This 'Baroque grandeur' was superseded by a 'nostalgia for the severe ideal of single perspective' (*TVP* 19), which took the form of ' "neo-classical" ' art. This was an art that 'sought to eternalize the dramatic moment,' an art of 'arrest' (*TVP* 19), and the use of the word in this context is a significant revisiting of McLuhan's employment of that term in *The Mechanical Bride*, where he had used it to identify his methodology.[71] In *Through the Vanishing Point*, however, arrest goes hand in hand with 'aesthetic stasis and detachment from the world' (*TVP* 22) as opposed to the possibility of 'spatial dialogue,' a term that resonates with the notion of acoustic space and identifies a methodology (as well as a critical space) that is processual and in which the critic is actively involved.[72]

The involvement of the critic (and audience generally) with the production of the work of art is demonstrated by artists such as Seurat, in whose pointillism each dot of paint 'becomes the equivalent of an actual light source, a sun, as it were. This device reversed the traditional perspective by making the viewer the vanishing point' (*TVP* 24).[73] In contrast to the single point of view characteristic of Renaissance art, Seurat's paintings were, in effect, nothing *but* points of view – hundreds upon hundreds of them, thus requiring the viewer metaphorically to join the dots in such a way as to produce the painting as a sort of painting by number, where the notion of number configures the tactile (digital) aspect of the work (an aspect that would appear with even greater force in comics and in Roy Lichtenstein's reproduction of their Benday dots in his famous works of the 1960s). 'Paradoxically,' writes McLuhan, 'connected spaces and situations exclude participation whereas discontinuity affords room for involvement' (*TVP* 240). Unlike Renaissance art, which positioned the viewer statically, outside the frame of the artwork, the work of Seurat actively involves the viewer in making the image.[74] The significance of Seurat's work is that 'space has ceased to be neutral, in the old visual and Newtonian sense' (*TVP* 25); analogously, the 'life in the space capsule draws attention to the fact that the astronaut makes the spaces that he needs and encounters. Beyond the environment of this planet there is not space in our planetary or "container" sense ... Outer space is not a frame any more than it is visualizable' (*TVP* 25). Such spaces are discontinuous and paratactic in their nature, where the latter word indicates not only the lack of coordination or subordination of spaces, but also their tactility, insofar as these spaces are analogous not to the uniformity of the visual but to the discontinuities of touch.

Empathic Spaces

McLuhan's citation of Adolf von Hildebrand in *Through the Vanishing Point* with reference to the notion of tactility has a significance that extends beyond that particular work to embrace one of the key ideas in McLuhan's concept of spatial interfaces, that of empathy.[75] Hildebrand, who theorized the tactile in art as 'a kind of synaesthesia or interplay among the senses' (*GG* 41), produced his critical work as part of a late-nineteenth-century aesthetic debate in Germany whose context was a post-1850 disenchantment with the notion of idealism. Attention was increasingly given to content, and to the subjectivity that encountered it; 'empathy' (*Einfühlung*) was the term employed to describe that relationship, though it went beyond the subject/content relationship to imply the interactivity of art forms. Thus, Friedrich Theodor Vischer (one of the participants in this intellectual debate), argued that the 'artistic spirit' could animate form such that it appeared to produce '"echoing sounds that reverberate from these movements"';[76] in this formulation, empathy implies both the interrelationship of viewer and object, and the interrelationship of sensory apprehension. Vischer had derived his notion of empathy (as he writes in *On the Optical Sense of Form*) from a (proto-Freudian) text by Karl Albert Scherner: 'Here [writes Vischer] it was shown how the body, in responding to certain stimuli in dreams, objectifies itself in spatial forms. Thus it unconsciously projects its own bodily form – and with this also the soul – into the form of the object' (*Empathy, Form and Space* 92). This passage contains a number of McLuhanesque resonances, including the insistence upon the bodily and the sensual, the relationship between the sensual and the spatial, and the notion of projection, or extension.

There were immediate attempts to turn Vischer's notions into a general artistic theory. While the mystical overtones of Vischer's theories were soon out of favour, the notion of empathy itself remained attractive with aestheticians such as Theodor Lipps, who, as McLuhan pointed out in a 1973 letter to Edmund Carpenter, used acoustic examples in his efforts to explain the workings of empathic association (*L* 473).[77] Other critics, such as Conrad Fiedler, sought to develop the theory in the direction of the sensuous, arguing that the optical was not (only) an abstract sense. Fiedler was virtually a co-author of Hildebrand's *Problem of Form*, which based its argument on the distinction between visual perception, which pertained to the eye at rest taking in a distant view, and kinaesthetic perception, which pertained to the near view and the eye in motion.[78] Since the distant image is always two-dimensional, this theory implied that the third dimension was learned – was a construct.[79] Perception, for Hildebrand, was thus relational: 'Since each quality affects all others, there must always be a translation of inherent spatial values into effective or relative values that are valid for one particular visual frame' ('Problem,' in *EFS* 235). McLuhan expanded this insight into a general theory of the sensorium, in which translation took place across the sensory gamut, and he added a historical dimension, such that this translation took place across historical periods as well.[80] It is particularly noteworthy that, in these aesthetic theories on which McLuhan was drawing, space was no longer an absolute; the door had been opened for the entry of time into the 'spatial structuring of form' ('Introduction,' *EFS* 38).

Another critic influenced (via Johannes Volkelt) by Vischer's notion of empathy was Heinrich Wölfflin, whose *Principles of Art History* was often cited by McLuhan (e.g., *GG* 41, 81). Wölfflin took farther the notion of artistic translation; in particular he drew on Friedrich von Hausegger's suggestion in *Die Musik als Ausdruck* ('Introduciton,' *EFS* 1885) of 'the very primitive relationship that musical sounds – as expression – have with the human body ... *Such expression is not simply vocal but engages every facet of our corporeal being*' (43; emphasis added). Here was the clearest possible statement of empathic artistic (as well as perceptual and spatial) relations, a statement that, *pari passu*, turns up in McLuhan's notion of 'empathic identification' (*GG* 2). Wölfflin had in fact argued that 'it is in the applied arts that the signs of formal change first become manifest, even if such inventions as the printing press now inhibited the direct translation of the new temper' ('Introduction,' *EFS* 47); here we can glimpse McLuhan's notion that art is the distant early warning sign for changes in media and that media manifestations inhibit certain sensory perceptions. Wölfflin also drew on the work of August Schmarsow, who argued that the prime quality of architecture was not form but space, especially his notion that 'the human body, rather than just vision, stands at the centre of our spatial experience' ('Introduction,' *EFS* 61). It is this notion of the translatability of spatial perceptions that is the foundation for the analyses in *Through the Vanishing Point*, as well as the basis of McLuhan's championing of artistic intermediation, which was the hallmark of the artistic revolution of the 1960s.

McLuhan conveys these qualities through the 'spatial dialogues' produced in collaboration with Harley Parker, a painter (one of whose works is the subject of exhibit 46) and designer who was the display chief at the Royal Ontario Museum. Each of the forty-nine spatial dialogues Parker and McLuhan produced for *Through the Vanishing Point* consists of an artwork and a poem, together with a series of aphoristic comments (rather than essays, the narrative *line* having been outmoded, according to McLuhan, by electric *circuitry*). These juxtapositions include excerpts from *Anerca* (Inuit poems edited by McLuhan's longtime collaborator Edmund Carpenter)[81] and a painting of a bison from the Altamira caves; Keats's 'Ode on a Grecian Urn' and pictures of the Scyphos vase; a passage from the Edward Fitzgerald translation of the *Rubáiyát* and a page from a Persian manuscript; Ferlinghetti's 'A Coney Island of the Mind' and a reproduction of a canvas by Jackson Pollock, and so on. The exhibits exemplify different modalities of constructing space and of perceiving it, and demonstrate how art reveals environmental assumptions. While the concern with space is a constant of *The Gutenberg Galaxy* and of *Understanding Media*, McLuhan develops further, in *Through the Vanishing Point*, the tactile implications of auditory space (which he also referred to as 'audile-tactile' space) and the way it characterizes the world of electronic media. Taking *King Lear* as one of his prime examples (as he had in *The Gutenberg Galaxy*), McLuhan cites the famous scene (act 4, scene 6) where Edgar 'helps' Gloucester to 'commit' suicide. As McLuhan notes, this scene presents 'five unconnected visual planes' (*TVP* 75), illustrating 'the breaking out of the warm, familiar multisensory spaces into fragmented visual space.' The history of spaces is thus summarized here according to the connectedness of spaces (reflecting the homogenizing effect of visual hegemony) or their disconnectedness (reflecting the multisensoriness of the audile-tactile). The haiku, the verse of T.S. Eliot, and manuscript art are all characterized by a lack of connection among their elements. The illustration from a Persian manuscript (also used by von Békésy to illustrate the notion of the mosaic), in particular, demonstrates that the 'felt profiles of the flat image are multisensuous; i.e., tactility includes all the senses' (55). The implications, thus, of von Békésy's illustration of 'multidimensional auditory space with two-dimensional Persian painting' is that 'the two-dimensional features many spaces in multilevelled time,' as opposed to the 'three-dimensional illusion of depth [which] has proved to be a cul-de-sac of one time and one space' (55). The television presents one such 'discontinuous and flat' image (266), being 'a world of intervals[,] ... extremely tactile and participant'; in this sense, 'Seurat [is the] prophet of TV' (181). McLuhan thus recapitulates the notion of auditory (or acoustic) space, at the same time expanding it in terms of tactile values and planar composition, which had become the rallying cry of artists such as Pollock.[82] The element of empathic spatial production likewise tied art to the social;

as David Livingstone has noted in *The Geographical Tradition*, Johann Gottfried Herder argued that empathy was the key to social understanding: the 'understanding of culture was ... to be achieved not by rational analysis, general principles, natural laws, or classificatory devices, but by *Einfühlen* (empathy) and therefore with the qualities of the artist rather than the logician or the scientist' (123).[83]

Massaging the Medium

McLuhan's artscape – the artistic milieu on which he drew for analogies and within which he saw himself working – is characterized by its relation to printing and the book. Indeed, it was McLuhan's crucial and profound insight that the Modernist movement in art was fundamentally an engagement with the spatio-temporal emplotments of the book. As Rosalind Krauss has remarked with reference to Picasso's early Cubist paintings, 'the picture became a system structured by arbitrary signs; henceforth, his canvas became a written page' (*Formless* 28). This shift also signalled a change of axes, from the traditionally vertical one through which visual art most often signified, to the horizontal one of the book – what Walter Benjamin called '"the longitudinal cut of painting, and the transversal cut of certain graphic productions"' (*Formless* 94, quoting from Benjamin, 'Peinture et graphisme'). Leo Steinberg has extended this distinction, writing that the '"flatbed picture plane"' (Krauss 94, quoting from Steinberg's *Other Criteria*) is an extension of 'printers' forms, or *flatbeds*, in which lines of type cast in lead are set' (94). This 'bookish' element within modern art is present even in such apparently formless work as that of Jackson Pollock (about whom McLuhan writes in *Through the Vanishing Point*, and who is a major figure within the culture of spontaneity), the literary titles of whose early works inevitably invoke a print context.[84] Krauss summarizes the *literal* context of such modernist works of art as follows:

> For centuries, at least since the invention of the printing press, [writing and painting] have been phenomenologically perpendicular to one another (we read a book on a table but look at a picture on a wall). Picasso's cubist collages first shook up this order of things deliberately ... On closer inspection, however, we see that the cubist transformation of the picture into a table covered over the collapse – increasingly visible since Cézanne – of the airtight division between the visual field (vertical and transversal) and the space of the body (horizontal and 'low,' even, animal) ... Jackson Pollock, refusing cubism's semiological solution to the danger of a carnal corruption of 'pure visuality,' reopened the break Picasso had plugged: he began to paint on the ground, to walk on his pictures, to make gravity itself an agent of his process of inscription. The role played by this horizontalization in the rupture Pollock introduced in the history of painting was immediately repressed by Clement Greenberg's modernist interpretation (according to which Pollock's pictures contributed to an 'optical mirage'). (126)

McLuhan was likewise concerned that print was overlooked as having produced a specific sort of space, and it was for this reason that he developed his ideas about the spatial through an interfacing of poetry and painting. It is this mixing, this 'radical interdiscursivity,' as Welchman puts it (61), that characterizes McLuhan's (often collaborative) artistic productions. This interfacing was likewise the motive force of Dada and Surrealist art.[85] 'To move beyond cubism,' writes Judi Freeman, 'the artists, many of whom were poets, collaborated with other poets in Dada and surrealist circles to create an art of painted poetry or poetic painting.'[86] In McLuhan's terms, the inclusion of print in these artworks signalled that print had ceased to be the cultural environment (or ground) that it once had been, and was now emerging as a figure in its own right. At the same time, the words in these paintings drew attention to the surface on which they were printed; as John Welchman has stated, the 'progressive dependence of painters on effects of the surface was seen as a decisive rejection of post-Renaissance verisimilitude and perspective.'[87] As McLuhan writes in *Understanding Media:* 'to a culture in an extreme reach of typographic condition ... juxtaposition must be one of uniform and connected characters and qualities. There must be no leaps from the unique space of the tea kettle to the unique space of the kitten or the boot. If such objects appear, they must be levelled off by some continuous narrative, or be "contained" in some uniform pictorial space ... Merely by releasing objects from the uniform continuous space of typography we got modern art and poetry' (*UM* 289). This passage provides a blueprint for the sort of visual experiments McLuhan made subsequent to *Understanding Media*, where – most notably with Quentin Fiore – he produced the sort of abrupt juxtapositions, *together with* an abrupt, aphoristic (non-narrative) style, that jointly called into question the uniformity and continuity of the space of the book. As Willmott remarks, 'the "act of juxtaposition" ... breaks with narrative and spatial continuity in order to ... suggest a more totalized, contradictory or conflicted, field of meaning' (39). This 'radical montage' (*MMR* 39) conforms with McLuhan's notion of the interface, where text and image are made to interact in a process ('transparency and overlap' [*TVP* 81]) that transforms both, and are produced by 'teams' engaged in 'corporate action' (292), as were *The Medium Is the Massage, War and Peace in the Global Village*, and *Verbi-Voco-Visual Explorations*.

Verbi-Voco-Visual Explorations[88] was the first of these publications. Here we have numerous examples of exploded typography, in the style of the Futurists' *parole in libertà*, the use of marginal 'glosses' in the style of a medieval manuscript, extended uses of capital letters, the juxtaposition of text with numerous visual elements (especially cartoons), and a frontispiece from Moholy-Nagy. The cover illustrates (according to a note that precedes the text) 'the spherical nature of the oral world,' and is replete with hieroglyphs and the Greek word for 'sound.' The fact that *Verbi-Voco-Visual Explorations* was published by Something Else Press (SEP) is likewise significant, in that the press[89] was founded in 1964 by Dick Higgins as a venue for artists' books. Given the attention McLuhan had focused on the book with the 1962 publication of *The Gutenberg Galaxy*, as well as his increasing identification with radical artistic movements of the time, it seems highly appropriate that Higgins should have published McLuhan's book.[90] As Higgins writes in the foreword to one of SEP's early publications, *A Primer of Happenings and Time/Space Art* (1965), the 'emphasis on the medium as such, seems extremely suitable for these times. In these days of Marshall McLuhan, whose *Understanding Media* and *The Gutenberg Galaxy* are so very exciting in insisting on the appropriateness of work and ideas to the media in which they will appear, it is no accident that this work is being produced, even though it was, until recently, in ignorance of his ideas ... These pieces [i.e., the Happenings and the time/space art] are, after all, being done to communicate, and as time goes by, and as the implications of the revolution of media (q.v. McLuhan) are better understood, a whole mass audience will develop for whom such works as those in this book will pose no problem'[91] By publishing *Verbi-Voco-Visual Explorations*, Higgins clearly placed McLuhan within the realm of avant-garde artists of the period; as Higgins writes in his first catalogue, *What to Look for in a Book – Physically* (1965–6), '"We publish the sort of avant-garde work which offers a real alternative to the conventional art forms and which normal publishers do not know how to handle"' (quoted in Frank 7). Peter Frank remarks of *Verbi-Voco-Visual Explorations* in his annotated bibliography of SEP that it 'is less adventurous graphically than other McLuhan books (notably *The Medium is the Massage*), but is one of the most fragmented, discontinuous, "mosaical" texts purely in terms of content ... [T]he whole can be viewed as *an attempt to expand the scholarly medium*' (19, emphasis added). In 1966, SEP reprinted Richard Huelsenbeck's 1920 *Dada Almanach*, thus spurring a revival of interest in Dada that provided a particularly receptive context for the work McLuhan and others were producing (such as the poems by bpNichol published in SEP's *Anthology of Concrete Poetry* in 1967; see chapter 6 below).

Most characteristic of the interficial mode Higgins supported at SEP is, as Peter Frank suggests, *The Medium Is the Massage* (1967), which McLuhan coauthored with designer Quentin Fiore.[92] By this point in his career, McLuhan was referring to these texts collectively as his '"non-books"' (*EU* 267), and the function of Fiore's design is precisely to break down the linearity, sequentiality, and visual space values associated with the book. Fiore's design of *The Medium Is the Massage* (and of *War and Peace in the Global Village*) draws on his training with George Grosz,[93] who was influenced early in his career by Dada, Futurism, and Cubism, moving rapidly in the direction of satire with a number of portfolios whose drawings mocked the ruling classes and the military.[94] Grosz was also among the earliest proponents of photomontage, and it is this element that is most powerfully present in the work of Fiore. As Klaus Honnef has written, montage is 'a symptomatic formal and structural principle of artistic development since the end of the undisputed supremacy of perspective as "symbolic form."'[95] Montage was the creation not simply of a new space, but of the conditions for the production of new kinds of spaces. These new kinds of space lacked homogeneity, rationality, clarity, and objectivity (Honnef 50).[96] For the fixed eye of perspective, montage substituted the moving eye, thereby introducing temporal elements into spatial representation. In addition to the influence of Grosz, Fiore's work bears some similarity to that of Grosz's student and collaborator, John Heartfield. As Heartfield's work – much of which was devoted to book covers – demonstrates, the development of photomontage was inseparable from the rise of the mass media.[97] In Heartfield's particular case, it was also inseparable from Dada, and the combination, according to Walter Benjamin, '"made the bookcover into a political instrument"' ('The Author as Producer,' quoted in Kahn 46). In addition to work within the book trade, montage was employed in advertising,[98] and Fiore drew on both of these areas of production in designing *The Medium Is the Massage*.[99]

That McLuhan should have been drawn to the book as art form[100] when contemplating *The Medium Is the Massage* is no surprise, given the trajectory of his career, which consistently focused on the book as object, as medium of communication. Among

McLuhan's earliest intellectual interests were Blake and Mallarmé, for both of whom the book was more than the mere container of text. Whereas Blake problematized the boundaries of textuality, Mallarmé expanded the notion of the book into its own dissolution, theorizing, in a sense, the end of the book, the concept that has so often been credited to McLuhan.[101] Mallarmé's *Un Coup de dés* (1897) is a poem whose meaning is inextricable from its medium – indeed, it could be said that the material format of the poem *was* its meaning.[102] Similarly, *The Medium Is the Massage*[103] sought to realize what, in *Through the Vanishing Point*, McLuhan and Parker call 'the interfaces of transparency and overlap' (81). The book was published in two formats: Bantam issued a paperback edition, and Random House produced a hardbound version one-and-one-half times the size of the paperback (fig. 5.3).[104] The hardback dust-jacket is printed in silver and white (with black sans-serif type); the jacket image, initially indecipherable, is reprinted on the title page, where it is revealed to be a face (or mask), with the silver of the jacket perhaps signifying the silver nitrate in the photographic process of which the jacket represents the negative. Prominent in this picture are a mouth and (on the back cover) an ear, with the eye occluded in the upper left-hand corner of the jacket, the printing confined to the upper right; the disposition of the image recalls the frontispiece from *Vision in Motion* used in *Verbi-Voco-Visual Explorations*. This image, without the type, is repeated in black and white on the cloth cover; this repetition is itself a major theme of the book, which argues consistently with *The Gutenberg Galaxy* (of which, along with *Understanding Media*, it is a compendium) that repetition or repeatability is one of the prime offshoots of print technology. Preceding the title page is a photograph of a raw egg with 'epc process' imprinted on it through a 'no-contact no-pressure printing technique' (158). This initial reference to print technology that has been translated into another medium (film) sets the tone for the book. The main visual techniques of this book are close-up and magnification (or blow-up), thereby destabilizing the visual as occupying a single, perspectival space (as, on another level, does the doubling of the book in its two formats, though this doubling also identifies the residual role of tactility within the visual). The first image in the 'text,' thus, shows a blow-up of a hand cupped to an ear, raising at the outset the issue of acoustic space (as the mouth on the cloth binding, dust-jacket, and title page raises the theme of orality). Above and to the right of this ear are the words '... the massage?,' alluding both to the title and to this rewriting of McLuhan's most famous dictum. The large size of the type on this page invites the reader, as well, to deconstruct the word 'massage' into 'mass age.' As Arthur A. Cohen has commented, 'The graphic designer is a prisoner of the traditional retina and sequential logic. Only when he elects to destroy language, to create simultaneities and instantaneous assaults which go beyond accepted meaning, does he attack the traditional assumptions of the eye. In that case he manages, as did Apollinaire, Marinetti, the Dadaists, Duchamp, to concatenate the verbal-visual with displacements of typographic energy that resemble architecture, that force the muscles of the body to work, that demand total kinesthetic responses.'[105]

The first quotation in the book is from Alfred North Whitehead, whom Belgrad has identified as central to the 'field theory' of the 'culture of spontaneity,' and it is the attempt to give the book a spontaneous appearance that has guided its design. Whitehead's

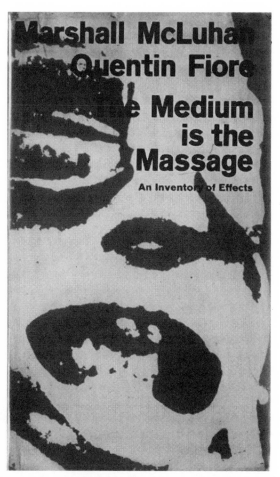

Figure 5.3. Covers of both versions of *The Medium Is the Massage*: the 'same' book but different experiences of reading, reminding us of how tactility enters our visual perceptions.

Adventures in Ideas (from which McLuhan quotes on page 10) advanced the notion that '"[m]odern physics has abandoned the doctrine of Simple Location. The physical things which we term stars, planets, lumps of matter, molecules, electrons, protons, quanta of energy, are each to be conceived as modifications of conditions within space-time, extending throughout its whole range. There is a focal region, which in common speech is where the thing is. But its influence streams away from it with finite velocity throughout the utmost recesses of space and time"' (quoted in Belgrad 125). Whitehead located the human body precisely within this matrix, and hence the superposition of process images with images of the body throughout *The Medium Is the Massage*, which repeatedly makes the point that media are extensions of the human body/mind (cf 26).

McLuhan emphasizes the spatiality of typography throughout *The Medium Is the*

Massage, to convey the way in which the 'alephbet' (44) and typography have influenced notions of rationality and logic. 'The alphabet' he writes (in eighteen-point type), fostered the notion of

> a space and of a time that are uniform,
>   c,o,n,t,i,n,u,o,u,s
>   and
>   c-o-n-n-e-c-t-e-d (44)

In addition to drawing our attention to the sequentiality imposed by alphabetical typography, he also provides examples of other typefaces, such as Gothic, and prints a page where the type is set from right to left and upside down (54–7). These manipulations of typography and of the page lead to McLuhan's central thematic:

> Art, or the graphic translation of a culture, is shaped by the way space is perceived. Since the Renaissance the Western artist perceived his environment primarily in terms of the visual. Everything was dominated by the eye of the beholder. His conception of space was in terms of a perspective projection upon a plane surface consisting of formal units of spatial measurement. He accepted the dominance of the vertical and the horizontal – of symmetry – as an absolute condition of order. This view is deeply embedded in the consciousness of Western art. Primitive and pre-alphabet people integrate time and space as one and live in an acoustic, horizonless, boundless, olfactory space, rather than in visual space ... Electric circuitry is recreating in us the multidimensional space orientation of the 'primitive.' (56–7)

Hence the printing of text upside down – to indicate that up and down are not natural but acculturated, and that in the West that acculturation has proceeded from an experience of the book.

McLuhan and Fiore also collaborated on *War and Peace in the Global Village* (1968).[106] In this 'non-book' the disruptive force derives from the juxtaposition (rather than superposition) of often jarring images with the text. The text is itself accompanied by glosses, much as in a medieval manuscript; some glosses are McLuhan's, others contain bibliographical details, and the remainder provide a running commentary of quotations from *Finnegans Wake*, with the overall effect being like that of hypermedia.[107] McLuhan's thesis is that war is a response to shifts in media, insofar as '[n]ew environments inflict considerable pain on the receiver' (7), or, more bluntly, 'Every new technology necessitates a new war' (98, accompanying a picture of a bandaged, helmeted soldier smoking a cigarette). This was a controversial thesis to be proposing at the height of the Vietnam war, yet the book is very much an anti-war tract for all of that, demonstrating the connection between new technologies and belligerence.[108] These shifts in media are also shifts in spatial production, with their concurrent 'discovery or invention of ... space' (7). The prime medium exploited by McLuhan and Fiore in *The Medium Is the Massage* and *War and Peace in the Global Village* is photography, of which McLuhan had written in *Understanding Media* that it 'extends and multiplies the human image to the proportions of mass-produced merchandise' (189), returning thus to the major theme of *The Mechanical Bride*. What is interesting in the later texts, however, is the far greater complicity between text and image; the distancing evident in *The Mechanical Bride* is far less apparent. In the later texts, the medium of critique is also the object of critique, producing thus a highly self-conscious text – a book aware of its bookness. As McLuhan appositely remarks, 'People are nowadays much concerned to set their houses in order, a process of self-consciousness that has received large impetus from photography' (*UM* 192).

Ellen Lupton and J. Abbott Miller have called *The Medium Is the Massage* and *War and Peace in the Global Village* 'landmarks in the integration of text, image, and layout' (91), particularly for the way in which they blur 'the professional, commercial, and formal distinctions that constitute the hierarchies of publishing.'[109] As they remark, it is particularly 'the space of the book' that McLuhan and Fiore exploit in *The Medium Is the Massage*, 'its literal scale and sequential unfolding' (93); this is further emphasized by the existence of two different versions of the book. Fiore most powerfully reminds us of the scale of the book with a photo that shows two thumbs holding the pages open; this also has the effect of recoding the reader as consumer into the reader as producer.

Work Books

Johanna Drucker has called the twentieth century the 'century of artists' books.'[110] Indeed, she goes so far as to state that 'the artist's book is **the** quintessential 20th-century artform. Artists' books appear in every major movement in art and literature and have provided a unique means of realizing works within all of the many avant-garde, experimental, and independent groups whose contributions have defined the shape of 20th-century artistic activity' (1). Drucker's comment is consistent with that of Dick Higgins, who has argued that the book as 'intermedia' combines aspects of wall pieces, performances, and sculpture (Drucker 9).[111] In a 1973 essay on the artist's book, Germano Celant has written of McLuhan's importance to the genre:

> The development of art in communications media, using either human or technological means, such as body, weight, voice, mime, mind, video, radio, pamphlets, telex, xerox, film or book, dates from the early sixties. At that time – through McLuhan's writing – there was a move away from a *hot* '*informel*' whose only demands on the spectator were those of contemplation. It employed traditional artisan means of communication (such as colour, collage, dripping and action painting) leaving little scope for audience participation. The move was towards a *cool* '*informel*' involving the spectator: an art whose visual and physical data is [*sic*] transmitted through technological and biological means possessing scarce visual content but demanding a high degree of participation and completion from the spectator. Hence the McLuhanesque term *cool*.[112]

It is this aspect of the *performative* that is definitive of the artist's book. Precisely by foregrounding the materiality of the book medium, the reader/producer of the book is made to factor those formerly elided elements of meaning into the production of the book's meaning as a whole, and environment becomes counter-environment.

This aspect of performativity emerges as the motive force of the series of *Dew-Line Newsletters* issued by McLuhan in the period 1968–1970.[113] The first of these was issued as a four-page, 8½-by-11-inch bifold, with the right-hand column of text printed in a smaller font than the left and keyed into it with footnote numbers. Number two was issued in an essay binder, number three as a booklet. The 'Futuregram' of October 1968 takes the form of a pamphlet in red card cover with a window for the title and stapled at the top. The November 1968 issue (on *Through the Vanishing Point*) arrived with a note from Eugene M. Schwartz telling the reader to unclip the newsletter, shuffle the pages, and then read it; Schwartz cites John Cage and Merce Cunningham as predecessors in the aleatory process he is proposing. The *Newsletter* of January 1969 was issued as a tabloid newspaper. That of February 1969 ('The Mini-State and the Future of Organization') takes the form of a verbal/visual booklet. A card deck was included in that of September–October 1969; the cards contained printed slogans, by McLuhan and others (Samuel Butler, James Joyce, Jacques Ellul), which, when shuffled and laid out on the table, were to suggest solutions to corporate problems or to personal hang-ups (from 'The Rules of the Game' distributed with cards). In May–June 1970, the *Newsletter* comprised an interview with McLuhan on Russia; it is brilliantly designed, with the questions printed right-side up, the answers upside down, and various typographical configurations used throughout.[114]

John Robert Colombo has suggested that McLuhan's journal *Explorations* had a profound influence on the development of typography in Canada.[115] As *The Dew-Line Newsletter*s indicate, this interest in typography extended along the arc of McLuhan's career, with its fullest realization in *Counterblast* (1969). The title of the book alludes to Wyndham Lewis's journal *Blast*, which, writes McLuhan, was 'typographically ... unique in the history of English literature' (4). Issued from the Rebel Art Center in London in 1914, *Blast* exploited to full advantage the Marinettian *parole in libertà* (words in liberty), and Harley Parker, designer of the book, seeks the same effect through similar means. (In addition to employing a wide array of typefaces, Parker also makes use of colours other than black for his fonts, and has some pages of the book printed on coloured stock.) The premise of *Counterblast* is an extension of Lewis's 'blasting' and 'blessing' schema, as applied to contemporary culture – in effect, a highly polemical commentary on current events. McLuhan places his blasting and blessing within the dynamic context of environment (that which gets blasted) and counter-environment (that which gets blessed), and hence his title. This dynamic contains a principle of reversal as well (which McLuhan developed as his fourth law of media), such that the destructiveness of 'blast' also implies the generative quality implied in the cognate term 'blastoderm' (4), and with a polylingual pun on 'bless' in the French verb *blesser*, 'to wound.' This reversibility is seen in his first target, the printed page, at once the subject of his critique and the medium of that critique. There is thus implicit in this critique a dynamics of cultural production, a sort of 'anxiety of influence' but at the technological level, and very much speeded up. This is particularly the dynamic of an intermedia culture, where media can only be understood and critiqued relationally (cf *Ctb* 59); as such, McLuhan's notion of intermedia is dependent upon his larger spatial theories. As Dick Higgins has remarked in his 1965 essay 'Intermedia,' the 'concept of the separation between media arose in the Renaissance' (18) and as such was consistent with the rise of typography.[116] Hence, to break down typographical norms was to participate within intermedia culture – to interface the printed page with other, non-canonical forms of cultural production. (Here, the marginality and politicality of the manifesto is of considerable importance as a predecessor of McLuhan's project; indeed, the first version of the book was a pamphlet of the same title distributed in a quasi-samizdat manner.)[117] The breaking down of the univocal and monocular space of the book was consistent, as well, with McLuhan's notion that acoustic space was becoming increasingly the cultural dominant. As he writes in *Counterblast*, 'The more that one says about acoustic space the more one realizes that it's the thing that mathematicians and physicists of the past fifty years have been calling spacetime, relativity, and non-Euclidean systems of geometry' (114). Such a spacetime 'includes more than one space in its space and more than one time in its time' (114; McLuhan is writing of the acoustic and iconic effects of Rimbaud's poetry). This multiplicity of spaces and times is characteristic of the most dynamic cultures.[118] 'Great eras of culture occur when a large area of oral experience is invaded by a visual medium, or vice versa' (*Ctb* 122). 'For the Elizabethan,' McLuhan continues, 'the whole folk wisdom of oral culture, centuries of oral disputation, and a huge backlog of vocal music were cross-fertilized by the printed page. A rich auditory heritage was exposed via a visual medium' (122). The present was likewise such a period of intermedia culture, 'for the oral heritages of all cultures are being poured through visual traditions to the enrichment of all' (122). It is clear from these examples that McLuhan understood orality and literacy to be in dynamic relationship, rather than binary opposites.

McLuhan's dynamic model of cultural formation is crucial to an understanding of his position *vis-à-vis* the book. As he writes in *Counterblast*, 'It would be a mistake to suppose that the trend of culture toward the oral and acoustic means that the book is becoming obsolete. It means rather that the book, as it loses its monopoly as a cultural form will acquire new roles' (98). These roles are enacted precisely through the interficial nature of media (their prosthetic aesthetics). Thus, 'print would seem to have lost much of its monopoly as a channel of information, but it has acquired new interest as a tool in the training of perception' (99). What the printed book can offer to the television generation is, thus, an alternative mode for processing information. As McLuhan wrote in *Understanding Media*, the 'hybrid or the meeting of two media is a moment of truth and revelation from which new form is born ... The moment of the meeting of media is a moment of freedom and release from the ordinary trance and numbness imposed by them on our senses (55) ... To resist TV, therefore, one must acquire the antidote of *related* media *like* print' (329; emphasis added). As an environment, the book was increasingly powerless to effectuate sociocultural critique of the sort McLuhan was interested in making (precisely because it incarnated the sociocultural hegemony); as a *counter*-environment, however, it becomes the medium of such critique, even though (or be-cause) it is no longer the currency of cultural mediation. It is this 'paradoxical dynamic' (*TVP* 248) that governed McLuhan's comments on the book, and they thus proved to be among the most controversial – as well as influential[119] – statements of his career.

McLuhan's statements on the book, and his own practices within the culture of the book, were part of a much larger artistic engagement with aspects of print media, many of them taking the book as their subject matter. It is thus no surprise that a very large number of these book artists were active in Canada during (and after) that period: Joan

Lyons's *Artists' Books*, for example, discusses the work of Joyce Wieland, Martin Vaughn-James, John Greyson, and Eldon Garnet, and Johanna Drucker's *The Century of Artists' Books* notes General Idea, Steve McCaffery, bpNichol, and Michael Snow. Of these artists, Wieland and Snow are of particular interest. Wieland's *True Patriot Love* (Ottawa: National Gallery of Canada, 1971) is an outstanding example of the artist's book, especially insofar as it demonstrates the degree to which such books were capable of interfacing aesthetic with materialist/political interests. *True Patriot Love* was the catalogue for Wieland's National Gallery exhibition held in 1971, but it is a catalogue that is a work of art in its own right, 'in the best Dada-surrealist tradition,' as Jay Scott has remarked.[120] For her catalogue, Wieland appropriates a Government of Canada publication, *Illustrated Flora of the Canadian Arctic Archipelago* (1964), by superimposing her own images and text on that of the government text, on one level producing an extended pun on leaf/leave and book/bōc.[121] As well, Wieland inserts opaque sheets of paper at various points through the text and attaches a small Canadian flag to the front endpapers and a pocket to the back ones; the pocket contains an interview with her printed on a poster, a blank map of Canada, and two essays on her films. The centre of the book contains a recipe, in Wieland's handwriting, for a cake six feet in diameter, entitled 'Arctic Passion,' where the role of handwriting recalls McLuhan's comment that the 'handwritten book ... kept the reader close to the dimensions of oral discourse' (*IL* 8). The result is a hybrid, plurivocal text that contests along feminist axes the notion of truth value and its association with patriarchy, as well as the notion of totalization inherent in the encyclopaedic project of the government bulletin. Wieland's supplements to that text reveal its gaps, the material it must exclude if it is to maintain its claim to totality (a claim also made by the book as medium). The role of typography in Wieland's deconstruction of the book becomes evident on the first page, where we read in the bulletin's footnote that '[d]escriptions as well as range and habitat notes (in small print) have been inserted in the text for some 40-odd species that as yet have not been recorded in the flora of the Archipelago.' Wieland supplements this gap with a piece of paper containing pictographs which she 'pins' to the page. These pictographs, in their ideographical unassimilability, indicate the way in which discursive practices embody cultural practices, while at the same time representing the voices excluded from the government document.

Snow's *Cover to Cover* (1975) tends to focus inwards, on the book as medium, rather than outwards in the manner of Wieland. The book repeats a number of the design elements of *The Medium Is the Massage*, including the repetition of images, blow-ups, upside-down text, and the use of images of hands holding the book to emphasize the materiality of the text. All of these, as Snow has commented, are structured according to a recto–verso principle, whereby 'the other side of the page is the other side of what is being photographed' (Guest and Celant, 79). As Drucker has commented, '[e]ach page in the sequence is thus granted a dimensionality, as if the full space of the event of Snow's movement were contained within its flatness. The play of literalizing the photographic illusions in the sequence becomes a means of analyzing the conventions of the book form' (124). These include the size of the page, the boundness of the leaves, the rigid sequentiality imposed by the structure of the book, and the way in which spine and margin shape the message 'contained' by the book.[122] The opening sequence leads up to a blank piece of paper being put in a typewriter, on which the title and publication details of the book are typed (cleverly, on the back of one of the photos we have just observed being taken). The next sequence involves a record player on which a recording called 'Canadian Cavalcade: The Music of Cape Breton' is placed. Halfway through the book, the images are reversed and one must turn it upside down and read it 'backwards,' flipping the pages towards the 'beginning.' This reversal is resonant with McLuhan's comment in *Counterblast* that 'There is no upside down in native art' (79); the effect of that observation here is to suggest that the book is 'coming over' into orality. At the end of Snow's book, we find ourselves holding the very book that we have been observing Snow making, and precisely at the moment when Snow has finished making it, the temporal frameworks of reader, protagonist, and creator coming together spatially.[123] When we see Snow holding upside down the book we are holding, we turn it, once again, to make it right side up, and it is the circle thus described that brings this book into the realm of the auditory (as the recording of Cape Breton reels suggests), which is to say, the realm that contests the linearity of the book and environmental notions of right side up.[124] Through these gestures, the book emerges as the site *par excellence* for an exploration of spacetime configurations endemic to the 'culture of spontaneity,' insofar as the foregrounding of the materiality of the text is achieved through a process that asserts the element of temporality as a function of the book as volume, as space, much in the way that Marey and Muybridge used the 'stillness' of photography to reveal the organicity of movement. This paradox, whereby the spatial is revealed as a function of the temporal, is in the service of a much larger paradox – the paradox of *reversal*, which was the nodal point of McLuhan's laws of media. For it was precisely in terms of the materiality of the text that the book could, as Pound had suggested, be heard to be coming over into speech, where speech was the metaphor for multiple points of view, for the undermining of sequentiality (through the non-narrative nature of these texts), and for the contestation of the visual space that had been established by Gutenberg and his invention.

CHAPTER SIX

Visible Speech

*The invention of the telephone was an incident in the larger effort
of the past century to render speech visible.*

Marshall McLuhan, *Understanding Media*

The Culture of Orality (and Literacy)

Daniel Belgrad's elaboration of a 'culture of spontaneity' in the art (and theory) of the
1940s, 1950s and 1960s might just as readily have been formulated as a 'culture of
orality,' so powerfully did orality and its cognates of conversation, dialogue, and voice
inform the period of American artistic production of which Belgrad writes. There was a
significant interaction between a number of these artists (especially Charles Olson) and
writers associated with *TISH*, a literary magazine published in Vancouver starting in
1961. As Frank Davey announced in the first editorial, '**TISH** is a moving and vocal
mag.'[1] This theme was continued by Fred Wah in his editorial to issue number three,
titled 'A Sound Direction,' in which Wah states that, 'Soundwise, (ear) that is where the
world is now' (51). To that same issue, Warren Tallman (who had brought the *TISH* poets
into contact with a number of the artists about whom Belgrad writes, including Olson,
Duncan, and Ginsberg), contributed 'A Note on Voice Poetry' in which he affirms that
'poetry has renewed an old affinity with song ... "Taste my mouth in your ear," says Allen
Ginsberg, as he tongues a groovy bridge between' (67).

Yet one of the great paradoxes associated with the 'culture of orality' – especially as it
emerged in Canada – was that this emphasis on the vocal was to produce a generation of
poets who were to make their name in concrete poetry – poetry that appeared to move in
the opposite direction from orality, sculpting language into icons of typography, even
when 'sound' poetry was the poets' avowed aim.[2] Belgrad begins to get at this paradox
with his observation that 'spatiality' was one of the key concerns within the 'culture of
spontaneity.'[3] This was the spatiality of the ideogram, which communicated all at once,
simultaneously rather than sequentially – much in the way that electronic media communicated,[4] which, in McLuhan's terms, was acoustically. There is a significant context in
the writings of McLuhan for this paradox of a 'visible speech.' McLuhan had written in

Understanding Media of Olson's claim that 'the typewriter confers on the voice of the poet' a form of 'autonomy and independence' (259),[5] and here already we see the paradox invoked and the particular context in which it occurs. The paradox had to do with the observation, going back (within McLuhan's frame of reference) to Pound's comments on Fenollosa and the ideogram: while the ideogram[6] is a written form, its sculptural qualities related it to the synaesthesia of speech. As McLuhan wrote in 'Joyce, Mallarmé, and the Press,' 'Pictographic Chinese culture ... would seem to stand midway between the extremes of our abstract written tradition and the plenary oral tradition with its stress on speech as gesture and gesture as "phatic communion." And it is perhaps this medial position between the noncommunicating extremes of print and pictorial technology which attracts us today to the Chinese ideogram' (*IL* 8).[7] The performative or kinetic quality[8] of the ideogram is, '[i]n contrast to phonetic letters, / ... a vortex that responds to lines of force' (*TVP* 39). The ideogram thus bears on issues of orality and literacy, especially as it presents a case for the interrelation of these notions – spatially – in hybrid forms.[9] Through its kinetic qualities, the ideogram also bears on the space-time confluence invoked most powerfully by McLuhan's concept of acoustic space

McLuhan had been writing extensively about orality and literacy since the early 1950s, when he was co-editing *Explorations*. In these articles, McLuhan stressed that he was writing in a transitional moment, when a primarily literate culture was experiencing aspects of oral culture as they were being retrieved by electronic media. He also argued that orality was not to be understood only in its *literal* sense – indeed, this would contradict its very nature. Thus, orality could be associated with writing – a wall of posters, for example, could be considered 'oral' in that it was multivocal, non-linear, and simultaneous in its mode of communication. Subsequently, McLuhan dynamized this notion of the interface of orality and literacy, whereby orality and literacy became figure and ground to each other. These developments in McLuhan's thought about orality and literacy anticipate similar developments in the theoretical discourse surrounding orality and literacy; that is, from a position arguing for a profound difference between oral and literate cultures, this discourse has moved towards an understanding of what Jack Goody terms 'the interface between the written and the oral.'[10] McLuhan, however, is usually characterized in this discourse (though not in Goody's study) as having adhered to a simplistic, binary model of orality and literacy. Ruth Finnegan writes, for example, that notions of the oral/literate binary 'still persist, pushed ... by the earlier but still influential classic social theorists or the technological determinism of more recent writers like McLuhan or Ong.'[11] What Finnegan particularly objects to in these models is that they are 'basically uni-directional' (160). McLuhan took pains, however, to emphasize that 'written and oral experience' are 'co-existent' (*GG* 1) in contemporary culture. More specifically, he states that, '[i]n the electronic age which succeeds the typographic and mechanical era of the past five hundred years, we encounter new shapes and structures of human interdependence and of expression *which are "oral" in form even when the components of the situation may be non-verbal*' (*GG* 3; emphasis added).[12]

Not only was McLuhan's notion of orality and literacy recursive (in the Viconian sense) – a recursivity he enshrined as the dynamic force within his laws of media – such that he was by no means an apologist for 'progress'[13] (to the extent that he severely criticized the cultural 'gifts' of literacy, as well as the Modernist project, as Willmott and

Stamps argue), but his theories were also interficial and dynamic. Indeed, McLuhan's notion that the content of a given medium is the previous medium constitutes his most powerful refutation of the notion that he conceived of orality and literacy as dichotomous. As he writes in a review of Frank Kermode's *Romantic Image*, 'all that is meant by organicist since Coleridge is auditory, and all that is meant by "mechanistic" is visual. So the reconciliation of opposites is exactly the attempt to translate sight into sound, sound into sight. This is not easy when one is environed by and committed to a visual culture based on the printed word and upon the careful segmentation of life, knowledge, and motion, in order to achieve applied knowledge (in conformity with printing itself, which is applied knowledge via fragmentation) ... When all information moves at the speed of light it literally translates itself into the auditory mode. For it conforms itself then into a *simultaneous field* of relations which is the nature of auditory space at all times. Such a field or sphere is not at all like visual space. And auditory structure is not composed of discrete components but of inter-penetrating components, as in musical forms.'[14] A comparison here with Ong is instructive, insofar as it reveals the crucial importance of spatiality to an understanding of McLuhan's theory of communication. Central to Ong's notion of orality and literacy are the concepts of a 'primary' and a 'secondary' orality, with the former being the 'pristine' state of orality and the latter being the orality retrieved through electronic media. The historical linearity behind such concepts is profoundly antithetical to McLuhan's own thinking on the subject, which was circular and recuperative.[15] Walter Ong's argument that 'Writing [is the] commitment of the word to space' (*Orality and Literacy* 7), fails, likewise, to discriminate between *visual* and *acoustic* space: writing is in fact the commitment of the spoken word to *visual* space. Space, for Ong, is atemporal, and, given that '[s]ound is an event in time' (76), orality cannot, for Ong, be spatial: 'the sounded, oral word ... can never be locked into space' (129). McLuhan, on the contrary, argued that the commitment of the spoken word to *visual* space in writing (and yet further in print) was being reversed by electronic media, which, through 'speed-up,' produced an *acoustic* spacetime. Thus, in arguing for the importance of acoustic space to the understanding of media, McLuhan opened up the heuristic of orality and literacy to inflections denied by Ong's conceptualization of these modalities of communication, and in particular to the possibilities of a speaking that takes the form of writing, and of a writing that takes upon itself the lineaments of a visible speech.

Concrete Assays

In McLuhan's theory of communication, it is the production of space that forms the common ground of orality and literacy. This is to reiterate that space communicates. We can see that space communicates by observing the unique spaces produced by poetry (as Man Ray wittily demonstrated with his 1924 poem 'Lautgedicht,' comprised of a series of short, uneven lines on the page).[16] We can hear that space communicates by listening to the ringing of a bell. It is in such terms that McLuhan's theory of communications was contingent upon his theory of space. To understand communications as a spatial concept is to understand it contextually: the context of a communication takes an active processual role in the production of that communication. The centrality of space to McLuhan's notions of orality, literacy, media, and communication is evident in *Laws of Media* (1988), which originated as a 'Visual Space Essay' (*LM* 19; the essay is dated 1978–9).[17] It begins with a discussion of Cornford's classic essay on 'The Invention of Space' and rehearses the familiar territory that Euclidean space – 'continuous, connected, homogeneous (uniform), and static' (1), the space produced by the phonetic alphabet – has, within electronic culture, taken on the acoustic qualities associated with Einsteinian notions of relativity. We remain 'blind' to acoustic space, however, largely because we continue to cling to the certainties of visual culture – the space with which we are most familiar. This blindness is particularly evident among scientists: 'To the scientis[t] using visual assumptions about phenomena, nature appears as a collection of figures whose variety and discontinuity has to be eliminated by abstraction' (2). Were scientists to abandon the visual imperative, they would discern phenomena as simultaneities within a dynamic flux, which is the nature of acoustic space. A scientific reading of media, made according to the assumptions of acoustic space, would thus seek to articulate the nature of this dynamic (since acoustic space is founded upon a relationship between figure and ground, as opposed to the isolation of figure within visual culture) and it is this that McLuhan seeks to do in *Laws of Media* and its tetrads.

McLuhan argues that media are processes that take place within the parameters of enhancement, obsolescence, and retrieval, and that these are interrelated through a fundamental principle of reversal. '*Reversal* involves dual action simultaneously, as figure and ground reverse position and take on a complementary configuration' (*LM* 228). Reversal functions as the chiasmic principle of the tetrad. 'Any process has a reversal point,' writes McLuhan in his article 'At the Flip Point of Time' (1975), and this point is equivalent to 'the flip point of chiasmus.'[18] Chiasmus, as a dynamic principle, comprises spatial configuration with temporal action. It is, furthermore, prosthetic, in that it embodies a 'cut,' and rhetorical, in that it shapes an 'outerance.'[19] The laws of media are thus both structural and dynamic: the 'tetrad ... presents not a sequential process, but rather four simultaneous ones' (*LM* 99).[20] McLuhan, furthermore, embodied his insistence on the hybridity of forms within the dynamic of the 'laws of media,' which oscillate between the figurality of the visual and the ground of the acoustic. As Paul Grosswiler states, the tetrad 'raises the hidden environment or ground, to visibility. And it reveals the double action of visual and acoustic properties in the life of a medium. In other words, enhancement and retrieval are figures; obsolescence and reversal are grounds.'[21] These are laws of media, then, as they apply to the production of space(s), whose subsets are the various media about which McLuhan wrote in *Understanding Media*. The four laws also act heuristically and critically (*LM* 7), as modes of understanding articulated through the reversal of figure and ground. Indeed, McLuhan's insistence that all four laws are simultaneously operational implies that the laws function to reveal figures *in their relationship* to ground, as required by 'Einsteinian four-dimensional space-time' (*LM* 23). Similar to the way in which the laws reveal grounds relationally to figures, the artist creates anti-environments in order to reveal the environment that is invisible to us.[22] Given that the ground of communications over the last five hundred years has been printing and the book, such that 'Western man still equates all space with the visual' (*LM* 112), these anti-environments impinge in one way or another on the space produced by Gutenberg's invention.

This, with substantial elaboration and the addition of a large number of examples, is the thesis of *Laws of Media*. What distinguishes it from the 'Visual Space Essay' is the form of the tetradic examples supplied by Marshall McLuhan and Eric McLuhan. Whereas the earlier version of the tetrads simply listed the four laws sequentially, one underneath the other, with the appropriate manifestation of the law, *Laws of Media* ranges the tetrads 'in appositional, poetic form' (129), such that 'enhances' and 're-trieves' are placed one above the other and opposite 'reverses' and 'obsolesces,' likewise displayed (fig. 6.1). This ideogrammatical placement subverts lineal, sequential readings of the tetrads; the arrangement is further complicated by the addition of glosses that are set in such a way as to move outward and away from the centre of the four juxtaposed terms. The resulting image often resembles George Herbert's poem 'Easter Wings' (fig. 6.2); Herbert's pattern poems were read by McLuhan as adapting 'the visual language of the illuminated tradition to the new medium of print.'[23] McLuhan adds that '[t]oday we are moving in the reverse direction, away from printed language to the reinvention of visual language. That is one reason why we find the metaphysical so contemporary. We stand in the same ambivalent relation to written word and pictorial image as they did' (458). The Renaissance rhetorician George Puttenham, in fact, included 'Geometricall figures' in *The Arte of English Poesie* (1589) among the possible forms of poetry, and identified the double triangle form as 'The Tricquet [or triangle] Displayed' (fig. 6.3).[24]

The tetrads superbly embody the return to plastic values in verbal art, the chief agent of which was the typewriter, which 'changed the forms of English expression by opening up once more the oral world to the writer of books,' as McLuhan puts it in a 1973 contribution to the volume *Do Books Matter?*[25] One example of this return to plastic values, continues McLuhan, is '*poésie concrète* [which] has inspired many new uses of older printing methods and has called for the invention of new print and paper surfaces' (34). That McLuhan conceived of the tetrads in *Laws of Media* as iconographic forms suggests that the tetrads can be understood as analogous to concrete poetry. As early as 1971, in fact, Theall was stating that McLuhan 'writes quasi-concrete poetry' (*RVM* 2; 157) and was crediting him with having invented a new form, the *essai concrète* (*RVM* 153–65; 239–41), the short, discontinuously structured essay (often reduced iconically to a single utterance or 'probe') juxtaposed to an image that illustrates it or, more often, counterposes it.[26] The double-pyramid form of the tetrads in *Laws of Media* and McLuhan's affinities with the concretists come together in a comment he makes in *Culture Is Our Business* (1970):

> **All language is layered with puns that the penman (eye) suppresses.**
> The newspaper mosaic is crammed daily with visual puns of this kind. The mere juxtaposi-tion of items without connection, save by dateline, makes the press a huge time harp of *poésie concrète.*
> **Long ago Mallarmé made a newspaper poem called <u>Un Coup de dés</u> (One Throw of the Dice), using the spread-out sheets of the paper as poetic wings.** (146)[27]

The pun is a perfect example of a visual form that has a suppressed acoustic resonance in its multilayered and simultaneous meanings, likewise achieved through the discontinu-

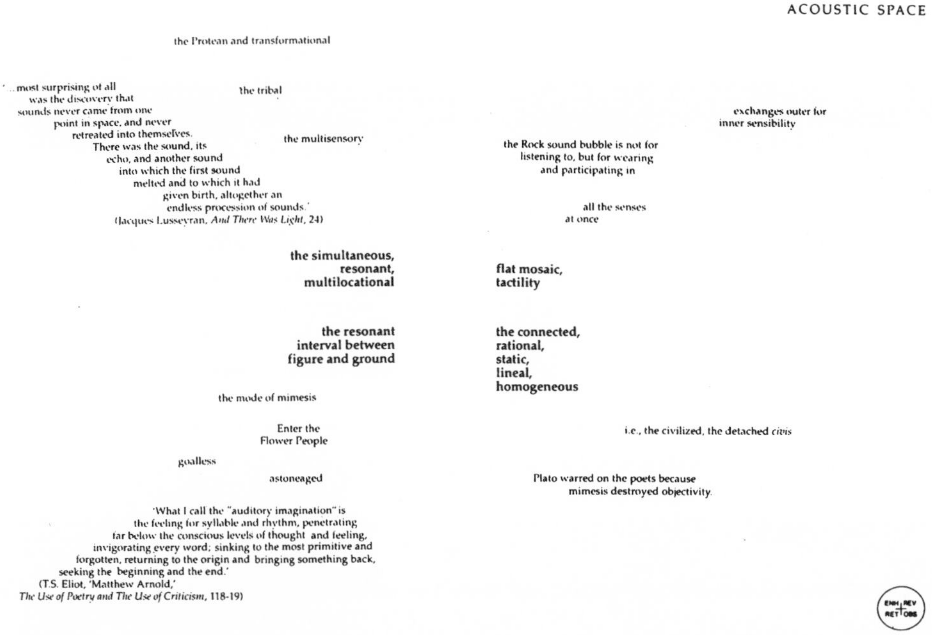

ACOUSTIC SPACE

the Protean and transformational

'...most surprising of all
was the discovery that
sounds never came from one
point in space, and never
retreated into themselves.
There was the sound, its
echo, and another sound
into which the first sound
melted and to which it had
given birth, altogether an
endless procession of sounds.'
(Jacques Lusseyran, *And There Was Light*, 24)

the tribal

the multisensory

exchanges outer for
inner sensibility

the Rock sound bubble is not for
listening to, but for wearing
and participating in

all the senses
at once

the simultaneous,
resonant,
multilocational

flat mosaic,
tactility

the resonant
interval between
figure and ground

the connected,
rational,
static,
lineal,
homogeneous

the mode of mimesis

Enter the
Flower People

i.e., the civilized, the detached *civis*

goalless

astoneaged

Plato warred on the poets because
mimesis destroyed objectivity.

'What I call the "auditory imagination" is
the feeling for syllable and rhythm, penetrating
far below the conscious levels of thought and feeling,
invigorating every word; sinking to the most primitive and
forgotten, returning to the origin and bringing something back,
seeking the beginning and the end.'
(T.S. Eliot, 'Matthew Arnold,'
The Use of Poetry and The Use of Criticism, 118-19)

Figure 6.1. Tetrad from *Laws of Media*: an 'exploded' version of the diagram in figure 4.1; cf figures 6.2 and 6.3, as well as figure 3.1 (left).

Easter Wings

Lord, who createdst man in wealth and store,
  Though foolishly he lost the same,
    Decaying more and more
      Till he became
        Most   poor:
        With   thee
      O let me rise
    As larks, harmoniously,
  And sing this day thy victories:
Then shall the fall further the flight in me.

My tender age in sorrow did begin:
  And still with sicknesses and shame
    Thou didst so punish sin,
      That I became
        Most thin.
        With thee
      Let me combine,
    And feel this day thy victory;
  For, if I imp my wing on thine,
Affliction shall advance the flight in me.

The Tricquet difplayed

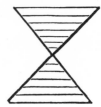

Figure 6.2. **Left:** The poem 'Easter Wings,' by George Herbert.
Figure 6.3. **Right:** The 'Tricquet Displayed,' from Puttenham's *Arte of English Poesie*.

ous spacetime of the newspaper mosaic.[28] The newspaper concretizes discontinuous space as its unit of meaning, and functionalizes that meaning along the time axis of the dateline. The 'concrete essay,' similarly, participates in two coterminous activities: it foregrounds the spatiality of print, and, in doing so, it critiques that space, providing access to the spacetime of alternate, acoustic configurations, the process being at once deconstructive and reconstructive.[29]

The attraction of 'concrete' form for the practice of this poetics/heuristic has to do with the particular way in which concrete form addresses space and time. As Mary Ellen Solt writes in the introduction to her anthology of concrete poetry, 'the concrete poet is concerned with establishing his linguistic material in a new relationship to space (the page or its equivalent) and/or to time (abandoning the old linear measure). Put another way this means the concrete poet is concerned with making an object to be perceived rather than read.'[30] As Solt further explains, a 'spatially articulated written language is not proposed to supplant temporally articulated written language but to make possible the expression of that which conventional language is incapable of articulating' (18).

'Visible Speech'

Judith Stamps has noted the affinity between the practice of certain '[c]ontemporary Canadian west coast poets,' such as bill bissett, and McLuhan's insistence that Joyce had sought 'to recreate the aural world by using non-standard spellings and run-on words' (*Unth* 127). Similarly, Ong has stated that '[c]oncrete poetry ... climaxes in a certain way the interaction of sounded words and typographic space' (*Orality and Literacy* 129). Yet the paradox remains, as Ong notes: concrete poems can rarely be sounded (an aspect that is often heightened rather than lessened by the phenomenon of sound poetry). Studies of concrete poetry have tended to address this paradox taxonomically: certain types of concrete poetry are said to do certain things. Thus Mary Ellen Solt writes in her anthology of concrete poetry that the 'visual poem is intended to be seen like a painting; the sound poem is composed to be listened to like music' (11). The practice of concrete poetry, however, has tended to undermine these polarities.

Concretists acknowledge a variety of influences within an international context, among which (according to Solt) are the Futurists' 'words-in-liberty,' Apollinaire and his calligrams, Pound and Fenollosa's meditations on the ideogram, the Dada 'word-image,' the multilevel puns of Joyce, Moholy-Nagy's insistence in *The New Vision* that poetry had become the 'relations of single words,' Mallarmé's use of the page in *Un Coup de dés*, 'Mondrian's space-structures' (Solt 12) such as *Broadway Boogie-Woogie*, and the music of Webern and Cage. What characterizes these movements is their contestation of the space produced by typography. As McLuhan understood, the history of Western art is very closely tied to the history of Western communications systems; specifically, it was the alphabet that had created a visual space characterized by exclusion and closure. Concrete poetry foregrounds these interconnected concerns in that it reconfigures communication from a referential, sender–receiver model to an iconographic model, and, in doing so, it constitutes a critique of the visual space produced by typography – linear, sequential, continuous, perspectival, unvoiced.[31]

Concretists became active in the early 1950s, with the 1958 manifesto of the Brazilian group *Noigandres* having a certain originary status among historians of the mode. Citing a number of the influences listed above, the Brazilian concretists argued that '"concrete poetry begins by being aware of graphic space as structural agent. Qualified space: space–time structure instead of mere linear-temporistical development"' (as quoted by Solt, 71). This leads them towards a definition: 'Concrete Poetry: tension of things-words in space–time. Dynamic structure: multiplicity of concomitant movements. So in music – by definition, a time art – space intervenes (Webern and his followers: Boulez and Stockhausen; concrete and electronic music); in visual arts – spatial, by definition – time intervenes (Mondrian and his *Boogie-Woogie* series ...)' (Solt 72). The group cites Joyce's term '"*verbivocovisual*"' (72), though without crediting Joyce, as comprising the multiple aspects of this definition. McLuhan had used the term *verbivocovisual* in the October 1957 issue of *Explorations* (number 8) as the title of one of the items in which he identifies the 'staccato stutter of the typewriter' as 'really close to the stutter that is oral speech.'[32] *Verbi-Voco-Visual Explorations* (1967) became the title of *Explorations* 8 when it was published separately by Something Else Press, which was closely tied through its publisher, Dick Higgins, to the concretist movement. Indeed, Emmett Williams's landmark *Anthology of Concrete Poetry*, published in the same year by Higgins's press, listed McLuhan's book on its dust-jacket, describing it there as an 'early fusillade (1957) ... trained comprehensively and comprehensibly on the word: taps for the written culture, a victory salvo for the oral revolution.'[33] The fact that this 'oral revolution' manifested itself in printed form was central to the paradox from which concrete poetry was fed, a paradox that derived from the assertion of the page as the central unit of composition[34] and of typography as communicative in and of itself (i.e., independently of its articulation into recognizable words), the implications of which McLuhan had explored in *The Gutenberg Galaxy*.

One version of concrete poetry was dubbed '*spatialisme*' by Pierre Garnier, who in 1962 issued his 'Manifesto for a New Poetry – Visual and Phonic' (Solt 32):

Sous notre couche d'air nous vivions protégés. Nous sommes maintenant des flots
  cosmiques jaillissants.
Comment nos mots pourraient-ils supporter d'être encore enveloppés dans l'air des phrases?
Que nos mots, eux aussi, rejoignent l'espace cosmique – les mots-étoiles sur la page
  blanche.[35]

Taking his point of departure from Mallarmé, Garnier ties *spatialisme* directly to the new media, commenting that 'Le temps des livres semble passé ... Or le moyen technique employé crée la poésie autant que le poète. Le magnétophone, le disque, la télévision doivent créer leur propre forme de poésie' (135). Garnier here identifies the other way, in addition to the ideogrammatical, in which concrete poetry asserted its paradoxical association with speech: that of the retrieval of oral modalities occasioned by the effects of electronic media, which, through the instantaneity of communication, fuse a sequential text into a simultaneous space–time object. Other practitioners of concrete poetry have confirmed that media such as the tape recorder had a significant effect on its evolution; Dick Higgins, for example, has related the rise of sound poetry to 'the various possibilities of at least potential recording,'[36] just as John Murray Gibbon had related the return of melody in the contemporary lyric to the retrieval possibilities afforded by photostatic copying (*Melody and the Lyric* ix). McLuhan suggested that the telephone was also significant in this regard through its extension of the ear and voice; its effect, like that of the typewriter, is organic, in that it fuses functions (here the sensory functions of hearing and speaking), demanding 'complete participation, unlike the written and printed page' (267). The telephone was thus 'an incident in the larger effort of the past century to render speech visible' (*UM* 268), the phrase 'visible speech' deriving from the *Purgatorio*, where, in the tenth canto, Dante uses the term to describe the sculptures chiselled into the cornice along which he and Virgil are treading (line 95). McLuhan's reading of this sequence emphasizes that 'Where [Dante] says "I saw," he is actually treading on the raised effigies; for Dante, "saw" is an inclusive sensory experience' (*TVP* 71). Indeed, so inclusive is this experience that Dante refers to the sculptures as '*visibile parlar*' (visible speech). This passage is crucial for understanding McLuhan's position that *vision* need not be understood as exclusively associated with the *visual space* that was the product of writing and typography.[37] Through electronic speed-up, for example, oral communication over vast spaces is contracted into the spacetime of an iconographic utterance – visible speech – in the same way that a concrete poem is apprehended as a space–time unity.[38] Significantly, 'Visible Speech' was also the name given to the system, invented by Alexander Graham Bell's[39] father, Melville, that indicated through script 'the shapes taken by the lips, the positions of the tongue, and so on, and once a sound was written in its proper symbols, the initiate had only to reproduce the physical position with his own organs of speech in order to reproduce the sound' (Ronell 314).[40] The system is an excellent example of the effect of prototypical electronic technology on the previous technology of print, and is closely tied to the experiments of concrete poets such as bill bissett, the language of whose poems often resembles the phonetically augmented Roman alphabet illustrated in *The Gutenberg Galaxy* (49).

Frank Davey has remarked on the '"idiosyncratic quasi-phonetic spelling"' of bissett's poetry. Bissett dates his first use of '"words to act visually on the page"' from 1962 (also the year in which *The Gutenberg Galaxy* was published).[41] In an interview with Carolyn Bayard and Jack David, bissett elaborated that this 'vizual writing' was a form of 'discovering *space* on a sheet uv papr.'[42] Bissett relates his linguistic experiments to his pictorial ones, having been 'merging th fields for sum time now, since abt '62 nd previous with concrete poetry' (Bayard and David 53). What is particularly noteworthy in his poetics is his tendency to use 'space' as a verb (as Bayard remarks in *New Poetics*), as in his statement in his book *Pass the Food* that '"words can also be non-directory, non-commanding, non-structuring, non-picturing. objects, fleshy perceptual flashes, all-directions, away from the conscious death-sentence, ... spread . space . enter . give."'[43] This element of action, of movement, is the clearest signal of the temporal dimension that concretists such as bissett sought to infuse into the space of the page as field – as dynamic interrelationship, where that field becomes the medium through which the poet (especially the one using a typewriter) articulates the poetic message. Here, alphabetic letters are turned into ideogrammatical constructions that constitute a rejection of the alphabet and a recovery of the simultaneity and sensory interrelatedness of speech – an interrelatedness that includes the interrelations of the visual and the auditory as spatial constructions.

'Typospace'

Caroline Bayard, in her study of concretists in Canada and Quebec, has noted in their works a 'move towards a contextualization of sound within spacial, tactile, visual, and olfactory textures' (*New Poetics* 70). This tendency towards the performative aspects of concrete (especially in the practice of sound poetry) has clear links to McLuhan's theories, especially with reference to the interaction of the senses within an auditory context. McLuhan's notion that contemporary culture was increasingly interfacing oral and literary modalities provided a general context for concretists working in Canada, and the poetry of bpNichol is exemplary in this regard in its acknowledgment of a specific debt to McLuhan.[44] Like McLuhan, Nichol associated his work with Dada,[45] which had undergone a revival in the 1950s with the publication (in 1951) of Robert Motherwell's *The Dada Painters and Poets,* an anthology of texts and art that was issued again in 1967.[46] Of particular interest to Nichol's poetic practices is a section on Marcel Duchamp, whose *Green Box*, a collection of notes used in the making of *The Bride Stripped Bare by Her Bachelors, Even*, stands behind Nichol's landmark anthology of concrete poems, *The Cosmic Chef* (1970), which is structured as a green box containing forty leaves of concrete poems stapled to green covers.[47] Duchamp was important to Nichol's work for a number of reasons, including Duchamp's great interest in puns (of which he published a volume in 1939) and his membership in the 'Collège de 'Pataphysique,' the association founded in honour of Alfred Jarry, whose 'Pataphysics utilized the new geometries associated with fourth-dimensional thought (*4D* 47).[48]

The year before Nichol issued his green box, the University of British Columbia's Fine Arts Gallery had a major exhibition of concrete poetry. In a 'concrete essay' included in the catalogue folder, Ed Varney defined concrete poetry in highly McLuhanesque terms:

C O N C R E T E   P O E T R Y
IS FORM AS CONTENT
MEDIUM AS MESSAGE
POEM AS OBJECT
(Is this phase 1 of a pure visual language?)
CONCRETE POETRY IS IMMEDIATE
ALLATONCENESS[49]

Another of the artists represented, Michael Morris, urged gallery-goers to 'Consider the salience of eclectic, dappled mentalities through the 1960s, from Marshall McLuhan, Buckminster Fuller, Norman O. Brown and Timothy Leary to Warhol, Robert Rauschenberg, John Cage and the Beatles. They are all exploring and revealing mosaic patterns, new models for an alternate culture.' Artists in the exhibition included bill bissett, Pierre Garnier, bpNichol, and Emmett Williams. In addition, there were slides of works by George Herbert (his 'Easter Wings'), Lewis Carroll, William Morris, Mallarmé, Alfred Jarry, Apollinaire, Hugo Ball, Marinetti, Raoul Hausmann, Duchamp, and George Grosz (with whom Quentin Fiore had studied). Two years after this exhibition, John Robert Colombo published *New Directions in Canadian Poetry* (1971), an anthology of concrete poetry compiled very much within the ambit of McLuhan's writings. Colombo identifies Black Mountain Poetry as one of the major influences on these new Canadian poets, who 'are concerned with the human voice and with capturing, often in the first-person, their sense of being at a particular place at a particular time.'[50] Colombo likens the poems in his anthology to McLuhan's notion of the probe, 'an exploratory vehicle that will take us into new macrocosmic and microcosmic worlds in order to understand our own world better' (32). Colombo also situates concrete poetry as an 'emergent' form in the passage 'from what Marshall McLuhan called "the age of literacy" into a post-literate age of electronic communication' (39; with reference to a poem by Steve McCaffery).

Nichol's major exercise in concrete is *The Martyrology*, which, Irene Niechoda has suggested, owes a number of its qualities to Nichol's reading of McLuhan, including the emphasis on 'the materiality of the texts (as evidenced by his concrete work); the collaborations with ... visual artists; the striking visual impact of the design of [his] books ... The visual impact of these books, which have a lush manuscript feel to them, comes from combining texts from two disparate eras: the twentieth-century comic strip, and pre-Renaissance icon and manuscript.'[51] For McLuhan, of course, the comic strip and the manuscript were very much akin: both were scribal and thus signalled that they belong to a transitional moment (oral to literate for the manuscript; literate to oral for the comic strip); and both invited participation through their qualities of low definition (which is the domain *par excellence* of the performance poem).[52] In the memoir of McLuhan that Nichol wrote in October 1982, 'The Medium Was the Message,'[53] Nichol notes other affinities: '[n]o one punned more seriously than McLuhan,' he writes, distinguishing McLuhan from Joyce in this regard, in that 'Joyce was interested in encoding and McLuhan in decoding and that is a decisive difference.'[54] Nichol sees McLuhan's entire intellectual and artistic enterprise as implicit in the pun: 'He used the pun to open up where Joyce had used it to layer. There is a lightness of touch to McLuhan's writing, and airiness, that has often been mistaken for a lack of depth. But the wonderful thing in reading McLuhan is precisely that he was using language to take off, using it to soar free of an artificial notion of what constitutes profound thinking, utilizing instead the mind's ability to leap, to follow fictional highways to real destinations, to mix its metaphors until they match' (1). As Nichol notes, 'This is a writer's perspective, closer to poetic thinking than old critical notions of thematic analysis.' Nichol specifically associates McLuhan's thought with 'hyperspace, a region not governed by known space–time laws into which ships move in order to cover vast distances more quickly than ordinary space–time would allow' (2). McLuhan's intellectual and artistic 'probes' were of this sort. They were also analogous to music in their 'ability ... to strike many notes at the same time.' Thus the nature of McLuhan's influence was 'modal, a style or way of thinking ... It was something to react to or follow from or move in tandem with. And many writers, including myself, did & continue to. In standard critical terminology we could say that McLuhan "anticipated" the literary-based philosophical models of Barthes, Derrida, etc. He was not a critic, tho he wrote criticism, he was a literary thinker who refused to be limited by accepted notions of what profundity is' (3). Nichol concludes with an observation about the material concerns of McLuhan's artistic interests: 'He understood that writing was not simply what is written but rather, in the very way you approached it, the very terms you set for yourself, became and becomes a strategy for living, a model for how to deal with the "reality" of the world' (3).

In his draft notes for *The Martyrology*, Nichol writes that the '"flow of poem demands thin pointilist usage of words"' (Niechoda 33), aligning himself thus with the program adopted by Seurat: just as Seurat broke down the perspectivalism of the canvas by going 'through' the vanishing point, so Nichol seeks to do with the page. McLuhan had compared Seurat's technique with that of Baudelaire, who opened his poems up to numerous points of view, co-opting the reader as producer of his texts, who thus becomes a '*hypocrite lecteur*,' as he wrote at the beginning of the *Fleurs du mal*. The vanishing point, in other words, becomes the reader of the poem, analogous now in function (though construed in reverse) to the traditional vanishing point of the classical canvas, which functioned as the legitimator of the work's meaning (cf *TVP* 181). Nichol elaborates this poetics by bringing it to bear on his construction of the page, such that the linearity of text (which, like perspective, is the heir of 'the Gutenberg guys in typospace')[55] is ruptured through the dispersal of text across the page(s).[56] In the case of the first two books, this rupture was facilitated by composition on the typewriter (Niechoda 49, n30); following Olson, the 'pauses and breaks in his text are indicated by spaces' (Niechoda 54).[57] In this configuration, the spaces become meaningful, productive of meaning, dynamic. Nichol's view of the page as dynamic 'field' was influenced by Garnier's notion of *spatialisme*. Writing with longtime collaborator Steve McCaffery in *Rational Geomancy: The Kids of the Book-Machine*, Nichol states that 'Garnier developed a theory of the letter as self-sufficing entity existing and operating within an open space or field: the page. This application of a spatial metaphor alters radically the physics of his page. In his own texts autonomous letters (as objects) occupy a gravitational region, with syntactic emphasis falling on the *interval* between the letter objects.'[58] The essay in which this passage appears ('The Book as Machine') is preceded by an epigraph from McLuhan: 'It would be a mistake to suppose that the trend towards the oral and acoustic means that the book is becoming obsolete. It means rather that the book, as it loses its monopoly as a cultural form, will acquire new roles' (*Rational Geomancy* 59). As the book increasingly becomes the site of hybridity, the page increasingly becomes organized according to principles of acoustic rather than visual space. Thus, rather than understanding writing as *écriture*, McCaffery coined the term *écouture*[59] to describe it, a term that interfaces *écriture* with *écouter*.

Nichol's (and McCaffery's) insistence on the importance of the interval as a signifying unit in spatial poetry has analogies with McLuhan's musings on the Japanese notion of 'ma.' Writing in *From Cliché to Archetype* (1970), McLuhan contrasts attitudes towards space held by visually biased and acoustically biased cultures, quoting from an article by Fred Thompson and Barbro Thompson to the effect that 'the West speaks of "space"; the East speaks of "spacing"' (*CA* 101), which is to say that visual modes of space are static while acoustic ones imply a space–time continuity. 'Ma' is such a space–time, in that it represents the dynamic space of the interval; for example, '"[t]he 'ma' of architecture is defined ... as the spacing between pillars"' (*CA* 102; cf *GV* 39).[60] This spacetime is the dynamic principle of hybrid (or interficial) art. As McLuhan writes in the 'Hybrid

Energy' section of *Understanding Media*, 'of all the great hybrid unions that breed furious release of energy and change, there is none to surpass the meeting of literate and oral cultures. The giving to man of an eye for an ear by phonetic literacy is, socially and politically, probably the most radical explosion that can occur in any social structure' (49). McLuhan had previously made reference, in *Verbi-Voco-Visual Explorations,* to Eliot's notion of the 'auditory imagination,' which Eliot described as 'the feeling for syllable and rhythm, penetrating far below the conscious levels of thought and feeling' (item 14), and he argues in *Understanding Media* that, because the effect of electronic 'speed-up' is to blur boundaries, the present era is especially interficial:

> In our age artists are able to mix their media diet as easily as their book diet ... Quite early, Eliot made a great impact by the careful use of jazz and film form ... And Chaplin, just as Chopin had adapted the pianoforte to the style of the ballet, hit upon the wondrous media mix of ballet and film in developing his Pavlova-like alternation of ecstasy and waddle ... Artists in various fields are always the first to discover how to enable one medium to use or to release the power of another ... The printed book had encouraged artists to reduce all forms of expression as much as possible to the single descriptive and narrative plane of the printed word. The advent of electric media released art from this straitjacket at once, creating the world of Paul Klee, Picasso, Braque, Eisenstein, the Marx Brothers, and James Joyce. (53–4)[61]

Nichol alludes directly to this passage ten leaves from the beginning of *The Martyrology Book 4*, where he writes of the 'narcosis of narcissus,' here constituted by the linear narrative in which the phrase is embedded. This passage is immediately followed by one that undermines that narcotic certainty through a typographic explosion whereby the type becomes at once gestural and sculptural, and meaning becomes performative.

Spelling 'Eyear'

Both Nichol and McLuhan were struck by *Mots D'Heures: Gousses Rames*, a book of poems written in a French that make little sense until read aloud, when they phonetically 'reveal' themselves as *Mother Goose Rhymes*. For McLuhan, these poems demonstrated the way in which vision, when isolated, sought to create a continuous sense of 'matching and "realistic" correspondence' (*L* 437, 11 Aug. 1971, to Jonathan Miller). The *Rames*, however, resist this sort of visual sense-making, becoming meaningful only when read *aloud*, and are thus a 'handy demonstration of the power of sight to affect hearing and the other senses.' For McCaffery and Nichol, the *Rames* figured a 'type of geomantic translation, which fixes the auditory axis of both the primary text and translation' (*Rational Geomancy* 40). By 'geomantic translation' they refer to an activity 'in which the central act is the realignment of space and of the balance between already existing [phenomena]' (33). The *Rames* are thus not a translation of one thing for another (what McLuhan called 'matching') but a translation in which the source and target languages fuse into a new hybrid ('making'), which, although visual, nevertheless has an acoustic dimension. Nichol's texts function similarly. Devolving upon the paradoxes of the orality/literacy interface, they reflect what McLuhan referred to as the 'need for a revival of aural values in print' (*CA* 81) occasioned by electronic media: 'Much modern poetry today is written to be sung. The boundaries between the written and the oral are becoming elusive' (*CA* 83). Similarly, Nichol wrote in 1983 that '"there was a lot of similarity between what *Tish* was after, and what I was after"' (Niechoda 66), elaborating that poetry '"was a spoken art, and the tradition was an oral one ... But in the literal truth of it, the language I *write* is no longer *spoken*. That is, people reading the printed text don't voice it."'

The Martyrology is Nichol's exploration of the space between these positions, positions that have come to be polarized in Nichol criticism. Thus, Rafael Barreto-Rivera, a member, along with Nichol and McCaffery (and Paul Dutton)[62] of the Four Horsemen troupe of performance poets, argues that Nichol composed his poetry 'by association of ideas in the manner of ancient oral poetry.'[63] Other readers, such as Brian Henderson, argue that 'we inhabit, in *The Martyrology*, a written world.'[64] While Nichol's readers (including those just mentioned) complicate their readings to suggest that, as Henderson puts it, 'the two senses of the aural (and oral) and of the visual are linked in the written poem' (115), their readings tend to privilege the oral or the written. A reading through McLuhan, however, would begin with the notion of the hybridity of Nichol's texts, their attempt to work on the interface between orality and literacy, and would retranscribe these notions through the spatial categories of the visual and the acoustic that underpin them.[65] The poem begins with a lament that 'the language i write is no longer spoken' (Bk 1) and states its quest to regain '"the whole world [as] an instrument of sound"' (Bk 1) by returning to scribal literature and its interface of speech and writing. Thus these first books (1 to 4) present themselves, with their purple paper and their multiple, 'postmodern medieval' illustrations,[66] as manuscripts. As such, they are more involving than print: 'touch ascends with vision / taste smell & sound the image' urges the poet (Bk 2); 'you could step thru that warp in space and time.' That warp is created by the paradigm shift from eye to ear: '2000 years the eye has ruled / theory that the architecture of greece & egypt was based on the ear' (Bk 3). Appropriately, the next image fuses architecture with poetry: "the ancient gaelic poets lay with stones on their chests."

Puns are a crucial aspect of the poetics outlined here; 'the two tone order of the pun' (Bk 4) – an image at once acoustic and visual – is non-linear and multivocal, thereby disrupting the continuous space of print with 'that space between / the s & t.' That space is associated with 'MA,' the Japanese concept of negative space, the space between, which is not subject to visual assumptions (cf *GV* 39; *CA* 102–3). That 'MA' is also the mirror of 'AM' implies that this is a state of being, of becoming, the inverse of the stasis implied by the Narcissus narcosis and its prostration to the visual: 'langu age / old age / p age // static / interference at the edge of space & time' (Bk 6; cf 'dreary narcissism of resemblance' [Bk. 7&]). To this the poet opposes 'dialogue / acknowledgement of being' (Bk 5.3). This interficial art is a 'speech of vision' (Bk 5.3), 'relational,' and the basis of the poem's poetics:

so i sing
stupified by speech
        brought under the spell eyear can bring (Bk 5.8)

The poem's persona is 'caught then / in the endless re-vision of / the oral' (Bk 6):

> the problem's to connect in the first place, establish how the flux creates the fax, that if our experience of 'now' is (essentially) illusory – an amalgalm of light particles & a variable ability to anticipate a sequence of future activities – then these flix of consciousness fix it accurately: what Wittgenstein saw (hence his use of the file card); Stein's insistent insistence (tracking the way the syntax flexes); McLuhan's sense of the thot probe – (Bk 6)

Here, Nichol's project and that of McLuhan merge in the use of probes – non-linear, in-depth, resonant, sensory, and interficial – to examine the process of translation from one medium to another, a translation that is also a sensory one leading to new perceptions.

In his 1985 article 'The "Pata of Letter Feet, or, the English Written Character as a Medium for Poetry' (which alludes to Alfred Jarry's notion of 'Pataphysics[67] and Pound's famous essay on Fenollosa), Nichol defines poetry as 'the interface between the eye, the ear and the mouth.'[68] As such, the written character can also be seen as a form of notation, 'the conscious act of noting things down for the voice' (79), although 'this very doubleness tends to confound writers and readers,' states Nichol: 'And there are huge debates and differing schools of thot, differing schools of writing, which have as their central proposition the primacy of either the visual or the oral aspect of language. But in the reality of writing you are always envisioning the speech in order to speak the vision. The act of writing is the act of notation' (83). Nichol draws on Dadaist Raoul Hausmann's notion of 'optophonetics' in support of this argument. In optophonetics (which Moholy-Nagy had cited in *Vision in Motion* as a prime example of the interficial), Hausmann 'declared the page to be a visual equivalent of acoustic space with placement on the page denoting pitch, type size denoting volume, type overlays denoting multiple voicing, etc.' (83). Similarly, Marcel Duchamp, in his rare musical compositions[69] (some of which were published in *The Green Box* and one of which was associated with *The Bride*), suggested that, 'like the visual and the textual, the audio can be translated into another mode ... [H]earing/understanding this music is a critical participatory practice rather than a physical skill,' as one of his critics puts it.[70] This insight was embodied in Duchamp's first readymade, the *Bicycle Wheel* (1913), mounted on a stool with the fork down, such that it can be spun. The *Bicycle Wheel* was thus a precursor to the *Rotoreliefs* (1935),[71] discs with spirals drawn on them that, when spun, produce the illusion of depth, uniting the visual and the acoustic in that the work produces a sound[72] when spun, reminding us that 'frequency is a matter of wavelength, and the radio waves that are translated into sound by a radio are essentially the same as the light waves that are translated into colors by the human visual system.'[73] The *Bicycle Wheel,* in these terms, can be understood as a prototypical 'sound sculpture,' a project Duchamp theorized but never produced.[74] Such a sculpture would realize Moholy-Nagy's concept of a 'virtual volume'[75] that transformed the object into a 'spatial motion' of the sort conceived of by the fourth-dimensionalists, 'with the moving spokes taken as metaphors for the multiply contingent lines of sight that such a point of view entails.'[76] What facilitates the metaphor is the gap *between* the spokes, the interval, the discontinuous space of the acoustic.

Acoustic space, the space of the gap, of resonance, is a discontinuous space, and thus not capable of totalization, a notion which the processual nature of *The Martryology* emphasizes throughout.[77] As with Cubism, the totality can be grasped only in terms of a discontinuous whole. This was McCaffery's assessment of *The Martyrology* – that spatial aspects of the poem seem 'guaranteed by the presence of fragments rather than wholes. Juxtapositions, collisions, slips, spaces, twists, gaps ... these seem the figures of a rhetoric of space which determines *The Martyrology* as a literary object. The work's refusal to assume a panoptic stance and the deliberate eschewal of totality and closure, also suggest its consideration as a major text of space rather than a poetic journal of lived time.'[78] The refusal of a panoptic (perspectival) stance identifies this space as acoustic, a space that includes time, but in relationship to its spatial functions. Hence the journeys in the poem – by car, train, plane – that functionalize geographical space through temporal displacements. McLuhan had suggested in *Verbi-Voco-Visual Explorations* that 'geography and time are now encapsulated' (item 14); Nichol extends this notion in *The Martyrology* to produce what Avital Ronell has called (though in a somewhat different context) a 'Canadasein,'[79] a geography of the self, where the geography is that of the constructed world (rather than of 'nature'), such that Nichol's poem can be seen as his 'making of [a] typographic man.' This is, in McCaffery's terms, a geography 'of deferral and designation of place in a textual logic,' where the logic is that of the pronominal shifter, the 'i' (as Nichol prefers it), which acts as 'a geographical marker and not an identity; a "here" rather than a "self."'[80] By positing the self within typography, Nichol enacts McLuhan's thesis that print created the unconscious through a process of interiorization (*GG* 245), which, in the era of electronic media, goes 'outside into the external environment.'[81] As McCaffery remarks of *The Martyrology* generally, the 'textual unconscious could comprise the entire order of unmasterable, indeterminate and unpredicatable eruptions of meaning through an alternate system of sound and letter grouping within the "surface" system presented.'[82] This would be the inversion of what Walter Ong argued, in his study of Ramus, was the tendency of print to project thought according to a rectilinear grid that signified, in its aggregate, the domain of rationality. This association of the rational with visual space – especially as it is exacerbated through the linearity of print – is materially undermined by Nichol through his dislocation of that space, whereby he determines another order of thought within language, that of acoustic space – an *Ear Rational*, as Nichol puts it in the title of one of his sound poetry recordings.[83]

The 'ear rational' was a form of embodied thought that manifested itself performatively in sound poetry. Along with Rafael Barreto-Rivera, Paul Dutton, and Steve McCaffery, Nichol formed in 1970 a sound poetry performance group called The Four Horsemen. Their work, self-described by McCaffery and Nichol in *Sound Poetry: A Catalogue* (*circa* 1978), 'is a complex mix of several art forms ("intermedia" would be Dick Higgins' term).'[84] McCaffery places their work (in a survey published in the same volume) within a tradition including 'the bruitist poems of the Dadaists' and 'the "paroles [*sic*] in liberta [*sic*]" of the Italian Futurist Marinetti' (6). Such poetry, '[d]efying categorization as either theatre, music or poetry ... emphasized the improvisatory, spontaneous and aleatoric possibilities of multivocal expression' (8). These traits were greatly enhanced by the availability of the tape recorder, which, 'considered as an extension of human vocality allowed the poet to move beyond his own expressivity'

(10). This connection between sound poetry and electronic media was fundamental to McLuhan's sense of the increasing interficiality of orality and literacy. As Bill Viola remarks, '[i]n the age of the electronic image, it is easy to forget that the earliest electrical communication systems were designed to carry the word ... If speech is the genesis of the media body electric – the telegraph and the subsequent systems of the telephone, radio and television – then acoustics (or general wave theory) is the basic structural principle of its many manifestations.'[85] Hence the connection McLuhan posited in his equation of utterance with outerance. Sound poetry thus invites embodiment through the performativity of its scores, which often resemble verbal/visual poems or musical notation, with the overall tendency being towards the iconographic, as in a number of the 'performance scores' collected by the Horsemen under the general title *The Prose Tattoo*.[86] Richard Kostelanetz uses the term 'text-sound texts' for sound poetry in order 'to acknowledge the initial presence of a text, which is subject to aural enhancements more typical of music'; a text-sound text is thus an 'intermedium.'[87] Nichol understood this relation between printed text and sound in distinctly McLuhanesque terms: 'thru sound the chance exist [*sic*] to heal the split that has become more & more apparent since the invention of the printing press.'[88] Sound poetry thus represents a movement towards a reintegration of the senses, in that it is 'based on the exploration of the body's potential for sound and silence and the capacity of the body to produce that sound and that silence' (*Prose Tattoo* 5), such that the body itself becomes the work of art – the body *as* performance.

Space Operas

The ninth volume of *The Martyrology* is a piece of musical theatre, scored by Howard Gerhard, a 'nopera,' as Nichol termed another of his musical productions,[89] in that it works against the conventions of classic opera by alternating between 'straight speech and the sung sections' (Bk. 9). This anti-conventional approach is similar to that taken by Nichol in his 1985 work *Space Opera,* which concerns the adventures of an earthling who lands on the planet Galdon, where, unbeknownst to him, speech is forbidden and all communication is in song.[90] These strictures place the intruder inevitably in the position of foregrounding (often comically) the single most important convention of opera – the singing of speech. As such, *Space Opera* shares a number of its formal and thematic aspects with Virgil Thomson and Gertrude Stein's *Four Saints in Three Acts* (1928), with which *The Martyrology* has considerable thematic resonance. Both works are peopled with saints who lack historical prototypes, both foreground these saints as figures of the artist, and both eschew closure.[91] Nichol's work also has formal resemblances to Arnold Schoenberg's opera *Moses und Aron*, which likewise foregrounds the relationship between singing and speaking, in that Moses, the visionary, can speak but cannot sing, while Aron can sing but lacks vision. As Richard Kostelanetz has noted, sound poems, or 'text-sound texts,' such as those Nichol wrote, are related to Schoenberg's use of *Sprechgesang*, 'in which the singing voice touches a note but does not sustain the pitch in the course of enunciating the word' (*Text-Sound Texts* 16).

   Nichol's interest in the relationships between voice and text extended beyond his own work in poetry and music theatre to collaborations (most often as actor) with R. Murray

Schafer,[92] whose output, like Nichol's, runs the gamut from sound poetry to verbal/ visual and artists' books to music theatre, as well as to musical composition *stricto sensu*.[93] Influenced by McLuhan's writings on acoustic space, Schafer's work as a sound poet (or sound sculptor) has been undertaken with the specific intention of undermining the linearity of print. As he asks in ... *When Words Sing* (1970), 'How do we break language out of its print sarcophagus? How do we smash the grey coffins of mutterings and let words howl off the page like spirits possessed? The poets have tried. First the Dadaists and Futurists, and now the Concrete poets of our own time.'[94] The connections between sound poetry and Schafer's theatrical work run along the axis of *musique concrète*, which incorporates sonic elements from the ambient world into its musical compositions. Edgard Varèse's *Poem Electronique* (1958), for example, composed for Le Corbusier's Philips Pavilion at the Brussels World Fair, makes use of the sounds of church bells, sirens, and so on, while John Cage's *Living Room* (1940) makes use of furniture, books, papers, windows, walls, and doors.[95] In a major part of his work, Schafer has taken such sonic elements as his province, coining the term 'soundscape' to describe his research into the elements that make up our ambient acoustic environment. 'Soundscape' is the 'continuous field of possibilities lying *within the comprehensive dominion of music*,'[96] with the proviso that, through developments such as *musique concrète*, the notion of music has become less constricted and more comprehensive, '[f]irst, with the huge expansion of percussion instruments in our orchestras, many of which produce non-pitched and a-rhythmic sounds; then through the introduction of aleatoric procedures in which all attempts to organize the sounds of a composition rationally are surrendered before the "higher" laws of entropy; then through the opening out of the time and space containers we call compositions and concert halls to allow the introduction of a whole new world of sounds outside them' (2). The classic example of this opening up is John Cage's 1952 piece *4'33"*, in which the three movements are marked '*tacet*,' and hence the name popularly given to the work: *Silence*. As performances of the work reveal, however, the work is anything but silent; rather, it effects a figure/ground reversal with the performer and audience, such that the audience becomes the composer/performer of the sounds in the concert hall. But the profound implications of this work go much farther: it detaches musical composition from traditional notation and places music firmly within the conceptualist realm of ideas. As Michael Nyman has written, '[e]xperimental composers are by and large not concerned with prescribing a defined *time-object* whose materials, structuring and relationships are calculated and arranged in advance, but are more excited by the prospect of outlining a *situation* in which sounds may occur, a *process* of generating action (sounding or otherwise), a *field* delineated by certain compositional "rules"' (*Experimental Music* 3).[97] As Schafer points out, it was the Futurist composer Luigi Russolo who had argued in his 1913 *L'Arte dei rumori* (The Art of Noise) that 'noise' was part of our environment and should not be excluded from 'music' (cf *Tuning* 74). McLuhan made a similar argument, stating that the 'noise' excluded from the Shannon-Weaver model of communication was precisely the medium that facilitated that communication.

In 1970, Schafer inaugurated the World Soundscape Project,[98] an ambitious effort to document the world's acoustic environment (including 'noise'); as Schafer's biographer comments, 'If we are in fact, as McLuhan tells us, turning from a visual to an aural culture, then such study [would] become increasingly important.'[99] At the same time, the project seeks to describe the state of sonic 'immersion' to which electronic modes of musical production – from Muzak to the Walkman – are returning us (*Tuning* 118); headphones are a particularly acute example of this immersion, producing a 'head-space' (*Tuning* 118), a 'geography of the mind' in which sounds 'literally seem to emanate from points in the cranium itself.' The soundscape project's theoretical scaffolding was provided by Schafer's 1975 book *The Tuning of the World*,[100] the formulation of which he arrived at through intellectual underpinnings similar to those of McLuhan: Giedion on the relation between the mechanical and the organic; Helmholtz on tonal sensations; the Futurists on typographic liberation; Carpenter on the space awareness of Northern peoples; Cage on the contextuality of noise; Innis on the biases of media; Norbert Wiener on cybernetics; the Dadaists on mixed forms; Moholy-Nagy on design technology.[101] In addition to these sources, Schafer drew on his own work as a scholar of musical composition, through his major edition of Pound's writings on music, *Ezra Pound and Music: The Complete Criticism* (1977).[102] In the introduction to that edition (originally written in 1961), Schafer writes that Pound discerned three types of poetry: '*logopoeia*, roughly poetry of ideas and precise expression; *phanopoeia*, poetry of images; and *melopoeia*, "wherein the words are charged, over and above their plain meaning, with some musical property, which directs the bearing or trend of that meaning"' (3–4, quoting from Pound's *Literary Essays*).[103] It is this latter category that has most in common with sound poetry; as a historical phenomenon, sound poetry seeks to resurrect the interplay between word and song that was sundered by the printing press. As worked out in Schafer's music-theatre compositions, this project has a highly utopian dimension, as Schafer suggests in 'The Theatre of Confluence II': '[o]nce it [art] was drumming, prolonged drumming until its beats fused into a hypnotic spell-binding trauma. Once it was dancing, eternal dancing, until the dancer's feet left the ground and danced in the sky ... Then the whole world of nature was a continuous, evolving hierophony.'[104] This utopian dimension is further elaborated through the concept of 'ursound,' which argues for the cosmic origins of the acoustic through the comparison of a number of creation myths. 'Somehow,' writes Schafer, 'we retain a faint acoustic memory' of this cosmogenic sound, a memory enacted in all sound rituals, from chants to sound poetry.[105]

Schafer's project thus seeks to reassert an aspect of poetry that by definition is latent within it. Sound poetry, in these terms, enacts a phenomenon similar to that of experimental music, in that both are concerned with retrieving a relational element within a larger configuration – noise, in the case of experimental music, and song in the case of speech. 'Must language and music be mutually exclusive?' (*When Words Sing* 26) asks Schafer. 'Or can they be held together in an equipoise that satisfies all the requirements of each?' Schafer has posited such an equipoise in graphic notation, 'in which musical elements could have revitalized graphic correspondences in such a way that one sensation could be triggered by another to produce synaesthesia – that is, a fusion of two art forms into a unitary experience.'[106] Schafer sees graphic notation in terms of the spacetime relationship between notation and performance, ascribing the progress of Western music to the ability 'to project an entire composition in a (meta)physical space which allows the material to be studied from many different viewpoints' ('Graphics' 107). As he notes in *The Tuning of the World*, much of the vocabulary of music is spatial:

'*high, low, ascending, descending* (referring to pitch); *horizontal, position, interval* and *inversion* (referring to melody); *vertical, open, closed, thick* and *thin* (referring to harmony); and *contrary* and *oblique* (referring to *counterpoint* – which is itself a visual term)' (*Tuning* 124). Schoenberg thus referred to ' "the unity of musical space" ' in a discussion of the tone row in serial composition ('Graphics' 108), and, as Schafer notes, his music is inseparable from its graphic elements. Schafer himself has produced a number of graphical scores, and his work in music theatre can be understood as an elaboration of the potentials of acoustic space – indeed, he has suggested that *Patria II* can be appreciated both through performance and through the graphic score ('Graphics' 113).

Schafer brings these notions together in his 1985 essay, 'McLuhan and Acoustic Space,'[107] where he remarks on the hybridity of McLuhan's term, 'which marks it as transitional, caught between two cultures ... Thus McLuhan tries to intuit its character between the fissures of the Gutenberg crack-up' (106). The two cultures between which the concept of acoustic space falls are the visual and the acoustic, and Schafer clearly distinguishes between them: 'Auditory space is very different from visual space – we are always at the edge of visual space, looking into it with the eye. But we are always at the centre of auditory space, listening out with the ear' (112). These distinctions describe the dynamics of Schafer's theatrical project, *Patria*, a series of music-theatrical works that has been in progress for more than two decades, in which Schafer seeks to effect 'the synchronous interaction of *the eye and the ear*' (*Tuning* 221). The *Patria* series of musical/theatrical works belong to what Schafer calls the 'theatre of confluence,'[108] insofar as he has sought to embody in them the synaesthetic unities of ear and eye in order to produce what one of his critics has called 'a total sensorium,' in which the goal is not so much to produce a total art work as to bring together the senses.[109] Schafer also calls his works 'co-opera,'[110] in that, increasingly, the audience have become participants in and producers of these works. Crucial to these works are the spaces in which they are performed: an abandoned warehouse, a circus ground, a lake, a forest. Schafer has commented that '[t]he moment an architect encloses space in the form of a building he makes a social comment about the people who are to inhabit that space. The traditional theatres of Europe reflect the class system.'[111] Schafer thus uses the spaces in which his works are performed as forms of critique. Schafer writes that 'Palladio was the first architect to conceive of a "humanized" theatre, that is a space which man himself could dominate. More than that, through the use of perspective scenery he created a "point of view" for the spectators' (38). This raises the critical question: 'is man to surrender to the abstract space of the stage, or is the stage to conform to him?' (38–9) Schafer clearly opts for the latter in his productions, positing that '[e]ach action might have its own time and space ... What we would have then is a transformable environment like a circus' (40). This is in fact the form of *Patria 3: The Greatest Show* (in which bpNichol played the role of the snake-oil salesman). Through this fairground setting, Schafer explores the dynamic between traditional and unconventional theatrical spaces. 'These are lively and intimate environments but they can easily be dissolved when the spectator strolls off to another attraction,' writes Schafer in 'Patria 3.'[112] 'This conjunction of contained and open spaces allows for a great variety of performance techniques in *The Greatest Show*' ('Patria 3' 125). Through this 'spatial variety,' Schafer is able to demonstrate how space is *performed*; how it is not a given, not neutral, but actively created, citing from *Through the Vanishing Point*, where McLuhan and Parker discuss Jonson's *Bartholomew Fair* as representing a 'conceptual, nonperspective world' of 'orchestral togetherness,' 'an all-at-once "Happening" of multifarious events' that contrasts with the world of 'pictorial space' ('Patria 3' 126, n3).

Patria: The Prologue: The Princess of the Stars (1981), in which Nichol played the Presenter (and Steve McCaffery the Enemy), has a lake setting, which Shafer chose in order to explore aspects of non-focused hearing. 'We read by focusing on things,' he writes, 'and all of our Western art shows a focusing in terms of perspective in painting. We gather all of the information of the painting and we arrange it in such a way as to move it from the foreground back to the horizon. It's the same thing in Western music, that we gather music from the louds to the softs implying distance.'[113] (Shafer illustrates this notion in a verbal/visual poem that repeats the phrase 'The hypnotic focusing of the word mandala' in such a way that the phrases collectively depict a human eye.) Shafer aims in *The Princess*, however, for a more environmental music, in which 'dynamics and embellishments, the detailing that we're used to in concert hall performances are largely unimportant' ('Place of the Princess' 29). In his contestation of visual, pictorial space, Shafer is enacting McLuhan's notion that (as Shafer writes) 'art is always anti-environment. Whenever a society develops in particular ways, the artist, if he's ahead of his time, or certainly contrary to his time, begins to suspect that things are wrong and that some things have to be changed by the instrument of art' ('Place of the Princess' 31).

Sounding Texts

In 1979, for the collection of writings by him and about him edited by Nichol and McCaffery, Shafer drew a verbal/visual poem titled 'The Listening Book,' which he also describes as 'a musical score' (n.p.). In this work, Shafer discovers a myriad of ways in which a book can be made to speak (e.g., 'Move fingernail along here making the sound *ascend*'). Work such as this earned Shafer a place, along with Nichol, in Kostelanetz's anthology of 'text-sound texts.' More surprising is the inclusion of a Canadian not usually associated with sound poetry: Glenn Gould. Known primarily as a pianist and composer, Gould is included in the *Text-Sound Texts* anthology on the basis of his sound documentaries,[114] and the graphic scores[115] that chart their polyphony of voices. Kostelanetz had previously included these materials in his 1975 exhibition, 'Language and Structure in North America,' which was presented by the Kensington Arts Association in Toronto, and which billed itself as 'The first large definitive survey of North American Language Art.'[116] In his catalogue essay, Kostelanetz remarks that '[s]ome writers and critics resist the notion that mere mechanical invention can change literary style, but they fail to perceive that written language itself is essentially a technology, of verbal expression. And not unlike other technologies, language is susceptible to inventive modifications' (22). Such modifications can appear to be gimmicky, continues Kostelanetz; however, yesterday's gimmicks are today's accepted practices, he notes, citing the examples of Varèse's use of sirens in his musical compositions, Cage's prepared pianos, Gould's hunched piano posture, Pollock's mode of applying paint to a canvas, and Pound's manner of typing his poetry: 'Pound usually put two spaces between typewritten words, duplicating with technology a tendency already present in his handwriting. He knew that words physically separated from each other are perceived differently' (33). By foregrounding this spatial element to the point where it becomes discontinuous with that which it represents, the works 'flip into,' or reverse into, an acoustic, or non-linear, mode. (Hence 'text-sound texts.')

McLuhan referred to this notion of spacing with the term 'resonance,' which he derived from Linus Pauling's *The Nature of the Chemical Bond*.[117] Pauling explains that it was Heisenberg who introduced 'resonance' into the study of quantum mechanics, and supplies an explanatory gloss: '[t]he resonance phenomenon of classical mechanics is observed ... for a system of two tuning forks with the same characteristic frequency of oscillation and attached to a common base, which provides an interaction between them. When one fork is struck, it gradually ceases to oscillate, transferring its energy to the other, which begins its oscillation; the process is reversed, and the energy resonates back and forth between the two forks until it is dissipated by frictional and other losses' (12–13). McLuhan would have heard in this description an analogy to dialogue, an acoustic metaphor, and a confirmation of the principle of reversal, which was the dynamic element within the four laws of media. He also understood that resonance embodied a specific spatial construction. As he wrote in 1968 to urbanologist Jacqueline Tyrwhitt, '[a]propos space observations of *Through the Vanishing Point* I should wish to add now *The Chemical Bond* by Linus Pauling. Since Heisenberg the structural bond of all material forms has been regarded as "resonance." This is the world of the interface and the interval, which Parker and I designate as tactile space ... All scientists are trapped in visual space as much as museum curators. The reason is simply that they don't know there is such a thing as visual space as contrasted with the multiple other spaces familiar to non-literate man' (*L* 358).

It was the rejection of visual space with which McLuhan most often associated Gould's retirement from the concert stage and his subsequent immersion in the acoustic space of the sound studio.[118] If acoustics can be defined as 'the study of sound in space,' and if 'sound manifests itself at its most complex and interesting when bouncing off solid forms, most noticeably those of man-made interior spaces,'[119] then Gould's decision to abandon the concert stage can be seen as having profound implications for the way in which we understand acoustic space. In the terms that Gould defined it in his recordings, acoustic space takes on an element of virtuality; as Steve McCaffery puts it, 'Acoustic space is decidedly not a physical space in the sense of a container. In the acoustic field it is the sound itself that creates the space. The operative model here lies in the logic of autonomy and event rather than the logic of Euclidean space.'[120] Given that music is the site *par excellence* for an enquiry into acoustic space, it is not surprising that Gould's career should represent a sustained response to McLuhan's major themes,[121] such that at least one critic has stated that 'Gould takes McLuhan's ideas about the electronic media more seriously than McLuhan himself.'[122] Gould's response to McLuhan is of interest not only for what it tells us about McLuhan, and especially about acoustic space as a particular artistic/critical praxis, but also for what it tells us about Gould. Indeed, when approached through McLuhan, Gould's career takes on lineaments that are often counter to those now entrenched in Gould criticism. In particular, a reading of Gould through McLuhan suggests that Gould was concerned with making music more

bless

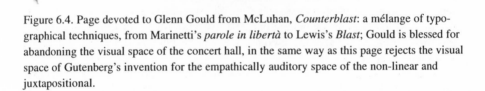

for throwing the

Concert
Audience

into the

Figure 6.4. Page devoted to Glenn Gould from McLuhan, *Counterblast*: a mélange of typo-graphical techniques, from Marinetti's *parole in libertà* to Lewis's *Blast*; Gould is blessed for abandoning the visual space of the concert hall, in the same way as this page rejects the visual space of Gutenberg's invention for the empathically auditory space of the non-linear and juxtapositional.

'worldly' (in Edward Said's sense of materially engaged with the *socius*) through technology; in turn, this reading suggests that, in Gould's understanding, electronic technology was not a flight from reality but an engagement with the realities of contemporary mediascapes. This reading contests the notions that Gould embraced technology as a way of attaining 'mastery' or perfection; that his musical philosophy was one of idealism,[123] a primacy of mind over body, and that his non-pianistic enterprises were secondary aspects of his career.[124]

McLuhan's first reference in print to Gould's retirement from the concert hall was made in *Counterblast* (1969; fig. 6.4), which Kostelanetz also included in his 1975 exhibition, based on its use of exploded typography as in Marinetti's work and Wyndham Lewis's *Blast* publications. *Blast*, as McLuhan remarks, was set almost entirely in headline type, and 'Headlines are icons, not literature' (*Ctb* 5), in that they communicate (by virtue of their size) all at once rather than sequentially through their content (which is often minimal). This spatial sensibility is evident throughout *Counterblast*, both in its attacks on the space of the book and on the visual space produced by the linearity of print, and in its concern with the retrieval of acoustic space. McLuhan is particularly concerned with the technological aspects of this transition, which, in moving towards the 'non-phonetic writing' of the icon is at the same time moving towards the 'interplay of all senses,' which McLuhan terms 'tactility' (*Ctb* 23). This sense of involvement is especially powerful in the 'mosaic image' of television, which makes the 'remote and visualized goals of visual culture seem not only unreal but irrelevant' (*Ctb* 27). Electronic technology thus represents a paradox: while on the one hand it amputates our senses and even our consciousness through the process of extension, it also involves us with one another, by virtue (or virtuality) of such extensions, in a way that print does not. By a further paradox, such involvement is organic (because simultaneous and interconnected) rather than mechanical. It is in this context that McLuhan makes reference to Gould. Using the 'blast' and 'bless' terminology inherited from Lewis, McLuhan writes 'bless Glenn Gould for throwing the Concert Audience into the junkyard' (*Ctb* 45) through his retirement from the stage. Gould was of such interest to McLuhan because he had embraced technology in a very public way (and in a way that countered a number of assumptions about 'live' performance) and because in doing so he had exchanged the visual space of the concert hall for the acoustic space of the studio. For McLuhan, as for Gould, these two aspects were deeply interfused.

Gould's last public performance was given at the Wilshire Ebell Theater in Los Angeles, a venue associated with Arnold Schoenberg not only because the exiled composer had lived out the last years of his life in that city, but also by virtue of the large photographic portrait of Schoenberg that hangs in its lobby.[125] Schoenberg was of prime importance in the development of Gould's technological aesthetic, and, as a result of this interest, Gould became Schoenberg's most prolific commentator.[126] *Arnold Schoenberg: A Perspective*,[127] published in the same year as Gould's retirement from the stage, argues that Schoenberg's musical career embodies 'the basic pattern for much of what has taken place in the first half of the 20th century' (1). Gould draws attention to the fact that Schoenberg was composing (and theorizing) during a transitional moment 'at least as profound and perhaps as inevitable as that which occurred toward the end of the Renaissance' (3), when there was a shift, musically, from modality to tonality; when Schoenberg began composing, this shift towards tonality was being reversed. Gould's reading of the historical matrix of Schoenberg's creativity thus parallels precisely McLuhan's rendering in *The Gutenberg Galaxy* of the shift from orality to literacy to an electronically retrieved orality.[128] In similar fashion, Gould's comment that 'the concert hall is dead' parallels the observation often credited to McLuhan that 'the book is dead.' In each case, visual space was reversing into acoustic space; significantly, Schoenberg, a painter as well as a composer, often spoke of his music in spatial terms.[129] Dore Ashton has commented that, in developing the twelve-tone scale, Schoenberg aspired to a musical space consistent with 'the spaces which could no longer be geometrized' – the spaces of the fourth dimension.[130] '"In this space,"' writes Schoenberg, '"there is no absolute down, no right or left, forward or backward"' (Schoenberg, quoted by Ashton 99). It was this 'dissolution of the laws of time and space' (Ashton 100) that Schoenberg sought in his music, a dissolution Ashton parallels to the abjuration of vanishing-point perspective by artists such as Kandinsky (109). Schoenberg arrived at one formulation of this new set of space–time relations in his invention of *Sprechgesang*, 'an uncanny fusion of speaking, singing and incantation': '[i]n a single stroke Schoenberg found the means of using the idiosyncrasies of the speaking voice as a musical material that would establish the emotional tenor of his expression. His instructions to the singer were that the rhythm and duration of her performance must be like a conventional sung line but that the intervals and pitch would be – as they are in the natural speaking voice – completely relative. The result is the incomparably moving sense of shifting spaces, infinite gradations in spaces, scarcely graspable transitions that he had begun to envisage as his new structure' (111). McLuhan, likewise, commented that Schoenberg had 'abandoned the visual structures of tonality in composition for the "multi-locationalism" of atonality' (*LM* 52). He goes on to state that '[a]tonality in music represents the abandonment of the "central key," that is, of a single perspective or organizing frame to which all elements of a composition are related. That is, tonality served as a figure to which to relate other figures in an abstract way: in the mosaic of acoustic space, each element creates its own space' (52). McLuhan specifically parallels atonality to acoustic space: 'Using atonality ... (as in acoustic space), "wherever you are at the moment" is the key you're in, the tonal centre, and the governing consideration is the nature of and affect on the overall pattern. Such space is not uniform but rather a multidimensional dynamic of figure and ground' (*LM* 52).[131] The major element facilitating the transposition of the idea of musical performance from visual to acoustic space was the technology of the phonograph – a prime example of the retrieval of the acoustic through technology. As Douglas Kahn remarks, 'we only begin to really hear *about* sound as a cultural entity with the introduction of Cros' paleophone and Edison's phonography right into the midst of ascendant modernist and avant-garde culture.'[132] Kahn goes on to point out that the 'phono-graph' was quite literally a fusion of orality and literacy, what with the inscription of the disc and its sonic interpretation, and yet another example of visible speech as a sign of the transition from one cultural mode to another. Steve McCaffery has commented on the spatial aspects of this transition. Drawing on the 'physics of amplification,' he has noted that '[a]mplifiers create high-intensity, low-frequency sounds that privilege bass effects in the home component system. Low-frequency sounds have longer wavelengths than high frequencies and are less influenced by diffraction, as a consequence of which such sounds are spatially directionless and difficult to localize as a specific sound source.'[133]

Gould addressed the question of music and technology in many of his numerous writings,[134] a number of which were produced under the intellectual aegis of McLuhan.[135] These writings represent a highly significant reading of McLuhan, insofar as the subject of music provided a key focus for an inquiry into McLuhan's concept of acoustic space. As Steve McCaffery has commented, '[i]t is ultimately impossible to separate McLuhan's ideas on music from the vast scope of his cultural and media theories' ('McLuhan' 80). Gould's 'Dialogue on the Prospects of Recording,' the text of a CBC Radio program that aired in January of 1965 (and for which Gould had interviewed McLuhan), was published in *Explorations* (the continuation, as an insert in the University of Toronto's *Varsity Graduate,* of McLuhan and Carpenter's journal of the 1950s) in that same year.[136] McLuhan edited the typescript[137] of the radio broadcast for publication; Gould then made further editorial changes when the piece was republished in *High Fidelity* in 1966. 'Dialogue on the Prospects of Recording' begins with Gould's comment on the ability of electronic technologies to participate in cultural retrieval, making available, (post)historically, centuries of music in a way that previous generations could not experience; to surround us with music such that it becomes a 'Wrap-Around Space' (54; cf *UM* 282, where '"wrap-around" sound' is used by McLuhan in his study of the phonograph); and to make the musical consumer into a producer. The electronic reproduction of sound in recordings has also produced 'a great degree of clarity, immediacy, almost tactile proximity' (51), writes Gould, qualities for which Gould's own performances, especially of Bach, Byrd, and Gibbons, were likewise known. (Indeed, the success of Gould's 1955 recording of the Goldberg variations had a great deal to do with the harmonization of his performance techniques with those of the sound studio, both of which emphasized clarity of execution.) The use of the word 'tactile' is clearly an allusion to McLuhan's notion that acoustic space is synaesthetic, in that it puts the senses 'in touch' with one another. In similarly organic fashion, technology tends to fuse performer and composer (57); Gould cites the example of Henk Badings, a 'composer-author' whose use of 'sound operating at sharply etched dynamic levels very clearly suggests spatial distances' (57), a notion Badings put into practice in the Philips Pavilion that Le Corbusier designed for the Brussels World Fair. Pushed to its logical extreme, the greater and greater role that music continues to play in culture implies that 'music will become much more viably a part of our lives, much less an ornament to them' (62). The second version of this article, 'The Prospects of Recording,' is markedly different from the *Explorations* version; Gould sounds even more like McLuhan in this text. It is at the beginning of this article that he makes (or repeats) his famous prediction that 'the public concert as we know it today would no longer exist a century hence, that its function would have been entirely taken over by electronic media' (*GGR* 331). Having begun with this McLuhanesque pronouncement, Gould goes on to touch on a number of themes associated with McLuhan: the reluctance to accept the implications of technology; the questioning of the notion of progress; the fact that, in contemporary culture, music is known more through electronic production than concert performance. What Gould adds to this version of the article is a long meditation on the possibilities afforded by the recording studio for 'take two-ness,' Gould's term for the re-recording of parts of a performance, and their splicing into the finished tape. The implications of splicing are very significant in that they contest accepted notions of artistic production. The assumption that a recording is, and must be, the product of human, as opposed to technological intervention, remains one of the prime assumptions of the aesthetics of music, especially as applied to recording practices. As Gould notes, however, such arguments depend on an '[e]ye versus ear' (*GGR* 340) argument and fall back upon notions of a '"natural" acoustics.' Examples of his own recording practices indicate that the 'humanistic ideal' of such arguments is misplaced; Gould's recordings are not of Glenn Gould performing. Or, to put it more accurately, they are not of Gould performing in a linear, sequential fashion; rather, these performances are *discontinuous* in nature, which is to say that they have definitively exchanged the eye for the ear,[138] and represent the shift from the matching of analogue technology to the tactile 'making' of digital reproduction. This aesthetics received its ultimate avowal from Gould in his statement that the performance of Bach on the Moog Electronic Synthesizer was 'the record of the decade.'[139]

As Gould noted, the desire for a performer behind the performance betrays 'those values of identity and of personal-responsibility-for-authorship which post-Renaissance art has until recently accepted' (*GGR* 341), values which were products of print technology. Electronic recording practices shift the focus of production from the performer to the listener, both at the macro level of such phenomena as Muzak, which democratizes the listening experience in much the same way that the book democratized manuscript culture and makes musical culture more accessible, and at the micro level of aleatory production achieved through technologies such as tape editing. Gould sees this prosthetic aesthetic as having the implication, finally, of breaking down the hierarchy of art and non-art; art would become 'environmental' (*GGR* 353), not figure but ground. '[I]f McLuhan's right and it's a trend of our times to take an interest in the process of production, then surely that interest ... should permit us to treat art as a source of greater mystery than symmetry and unity and all those analysis-imposed and analysis-limited conventions can define' (*GGR* 373).

'Quasi parlando'

Gould emphasized in a number of his essays that 'recording has developed its own conventions, which do not always conform to those traditions that derive from the acoustical limitations of the concert hall' (*GGR* 334), and he expressed the distinction between concert hall and recorded acoustics as 'the difference between monologue and dialogue' (*GGR* 337). The shift in performance venues occasioned by Gould's rejection of the concert hall meant that his recordings, especially the later ones, tend to be internally resonant, rather than resonant in terms of the space in which they were recorded, such that the resonance between the notes is emphasized.[140] The recording of the Scriabin Sonata no. 3 in F Sharp Minor is remarkable in this sense. As Kevin Bazzana notes, the Scriabin score is marked 'drammatico,'[141] and yet Gould plays the first movement very slowly, such that (as Bazzana remarks generally) 'each note seems to occupy its own acoustical space' (226), where 'one "hears" the open space surrounding the sounds' (227). The arias in Gould's second (1981) recording of Bach's Goldberg variations are likewise resonant (especially in comparison with the 1955 recording).

Gould's decision to perform works by Bach (as well as Byrd, Gibbons, and others) on the piano was an ahistorical one, and was dictated possibly by the piano's significant potential for spatial configuration. As R. Murray Schafer[142] has noted, the piano is able to extend 'the real space of the concert hall' into 'the virtual space of dynamics – by which effects may be brought into the foreground (*forte*) or allowed to drift back toward the acoustic horizon (*piano*)' (*Tuning* 117). These musical dynamics thus introduced a form of perspective into music making: '[j]ust as objects are rank-ordered in perspective painting, depending on their distance from the viewer, so musical sounds are rank-ordered by means of their dynamic emphasis in the virtual space of the soundscape' (*Tuning* 156). What is remarkable about Gould's performances is that he constantly tweaked these dynamics (notoriously, in his recording of Mozart's Sonata in C Major), such that he appears to be contesting the perspectival space implied by the normal *piano* and *forte* relationships, in much the same way that Cage contested these relationships in the figure/ground reversal effected by his piece *4' 33"*.[143] This contestation of perspectival space relates directly to Gould's decision to renounce the concert-hall. As Steve McCaffery has commented, concert-hall acoustics tended to favour the piano, with its ability 'to separate the acoustic experience into figure (forte) and ground (piano)' ('McLuhan' 81).

In a personal space, however, the experience of listening to the same music would be transformed; there is 'no prescribed visual focus' (82), and the relationship of the listener to the source of music is much more interactive. This challenging of conventional musical 'perspective' appears especially pertinent in Gould's performance of Scriabin, who was particularly concerned with effecting a synaesthetic experience through his performances, and at one point in his career made a chromatic piano whose keyboard played colours (Viola 49). When Gould recorded the fifth Scriabin sonata, he employed a process called 'acoustic orchestration' (Bazzana 246, n45), whereby ranks of microphones were employed, allowing Gould to mix the piece in such a way that the recording would juxtapose a variety of microphone positions, producing a cubistic or mosaic experience of sound analogous to McLuhan's concept of acoustic space.

Gould's renunciation of the concert hall, then, was part of a much larger investigation into spatial dynamics within an acoustical field and the status of the performer. This is the subject of an unpublished article that McLuhan wrote on Gould (*circa* 1966).[144] McLuhan writes there of the 'dilemma of continuous visual space' (2) posed by the concert hall in its attempt to convey the 'tactile proximity' (as Gould put it; *GGR* 333) of performance that had become normative to a generation of listeners schooled by recordings and that can be achieved readily through the discontinuity of the '[s]plicing and dubbing' (2) techniques of the recording studio. Gould has often been read in this context as having perfected an idealistic recording philosophy designed to remove him from the realities of public performance and perfect the solitude of which he is often stated to have been a proponent.[145] Understanding Gould's performance practices through McLuhan, however, suggests that Gould creatively interacted with the paradox of a medium that permitted intense individuality through a mass communication phenomenon.[146] Judging by his readings in the music criticism of Theodor W. Adorno, Gould did not consider that recording removed the performative process from social and political concerns. In his copy of Adorno's *Prisms*, Gould demarcated with brackets a passage in the essay 'Cultural Criticism and Society' in which Adorno states that the very notion of culture is dangerous insofar as it implies that works of art can find their meaning within a closed system of signification; rather, works of art 'have always stood in relation to the actual life-process of society from which they distinguished themselves.'[147] Gould likewise marked a passage in Adorno's essay on Bach in the same volume, in which Adorno argues that Bach's use of musical archaisms was a way of countering the notion of musical progress that contributes to the notion of the artwork as commodity (142). In Adorno's essay on Schoenberg, Gould marked the passage in which Adorno comments that the difficulty of Schoenberg's music 'requires the listener spontaneously to compose its inner movement and demands of him not mere contemplation but praxis' (149–50). Gould's often controversial interpretations (be they in writing or in music) can similarly be seen as ways of entering into dialogue with his listeners, asking them to reflect on his musical performances in order to move from passive reception of his music to various modes of interaction with it (in a manner similar to the demands McLuhan's 'non-books' made upon the reader).

This reading of Gould makes him sound less utopian than he does in many of his essays, and no more so than at the end of the 'Prospects of Recording,' where he remarks that 'In the best of all possible worlds, art would be unnecessary. Its offer of restorative, placative therapy would go begging a patient. The professional specialization involved in its making would be presumption. The generalities of its applicability would be an affront. The audience would be the artist and their life would be art' (*GGR* 353). Technology, however, was not a way of removing the performer from the world, according to Gould, but of reintegrating the performer with the worldly, and precisely through the breaking down of the barriers between composer and performer, performer and audience. Gould achieved this worldly aspect through performance practices such as his counterintuitive musical interpretations (playing quickly passages marked slow, and vice versa), through his extensive work for the CBC (to which his career was closely tied),[148] through his liner notes and essays, through his sound documentaries, and through his performance 'eccentricities' such as the humming and singing that accompany his recordings. Gould's humming and singing are the performance practices least 'readable' in terms of the aesthetics of idealism and perfectionism that he is often said to have adopted. Geoffrey Payzant quotes Peter Ostwald (subsequently one of Gould's biographers), who suggests that Gould's humming represents an attempt to withdraw from the outer world (74; Ostwald does not repeat this observation in the biography); yet Gould himself, when asked by Jonathan Cott if his performance practices might be deemed Brechtian, agreed absolutely.[149] Singing, in the context of musical production, is not unusual, of course; Nicholas Cook notes that 'what one might call "inner singing" plays [a] ... foundational role for the musician' in much the same way that 'inner speech' has been said to underlie conscious verbalization.[150] Singing aloud while playing the piano, as Gould did, is a way of connecting the musical to the bodily. In this context, Roland Barthes has posed the question, '[w]hat does the body *do*, when it enunciates (musically)? ... [M]y body strikes, my body collects itself, it explodes, it divides, it pricks, or on the contrary and without warning ... it stretches out, it weaves ... And sometimes – why not? – it even speaks, it declaims, it doubles its voice: *it speaks but says nothing*: for as soon as it is musical, speech – or its instrumental substitute – is no longer linguistic but corporeal; what it says is always and only this: *my body puts itself in a state of speech: quasi parlando.*'[151]

'*Quasi parlando*' is a score marking (used, for example, by Beethoven), the function of which, as Barthes argues, is to allow music to emerge from its voicelessness through a prosthetic aesthetic of stretching out, of division, of doubling, of embodiment. It is in this context that Gould's sound documentaries take on their great importance in his *œuvre*. The three works that make up the *Solitude Trilogy* take the human voice and acoustically orchestrate it as an 'oral tone poem' or 'verbal quintet.'[152] All three works are materially grounded and exploit a tension with the implications of the recording technology that brought them into being. Thus 'The Idea of North' (1967), about isolation and solitude, is voiced by five speakers who never met, brought together through the medium of the sound studio. 'The Latecomers' (1969), about outport communities in Newfoundland, critiques governmental attempts to force these communities to abandon their lifestyles at the same time that it celebrates the opening of the CBC's national stereo network. And 'The Quiet in the Land' is a deeply conflicted study of a Mennonite community in Manitoba and its relationship with the popular media culture that Gould had repeatedly celebrated in his writings as democratizing and de-hierarchizing (manifestly evident in his essay 'Streisand as Schwarzkopf'

Figure 6.5. Back of sleeve of McLuhan's recording of *The Medium Is the Massage*: a concrete poem, fusing the auditory with the literary.

[*GGR* 308–12]). Gould's first sound documentary, 'The Idea of North,' made in 1967, was preceded (in the same year) by McLuhan's recording *The Medium Is the Massage with Marshall McLuhan* (Columbia; fig. 6.5).[153] The record consists of McLuhan performing passages from *The Medium Is the Massage* juxtaposed and overlain with a number of other voices, musical excerpts, and sound effects (including those that play with left and right sources of sound), the latter foregrounding the medium of the recording studio. At one point, McLuhan draws specific attention to the multiple 'takes' that make up the recording. Of particular note is a section in which McLuhan's voice is overlaid with other voices in contrapuntal fashion.[154] Gould's three documentaries for radio are similarly characterized by the use of contrapuntal techniques in their composition – appropriately, in that counterpoint is the musical practice most closely associated with the concept of 'voice' in music. Gould considered counterpoint to be of prime importance in musical composition, and Bazzana has noted that Gould would typically

seek to emphasize contrapuntal elements in performance even when they would 'contradict the prevailing nominal metre' (178), and often used overdubbing to heighten this
effect (43). In general terms, what Gould sought to bring out with this performance
technique were two elements: the separateness of each and every voice in a composition,
and their simultaneity within that work. '"All the voices are equally important,"'
remarked Gould about a particular composition; '"there are no main voices"' (quoted in
Bazzana 144).

Gould's insistence on giving equal voicing to 'the component parts of a harmonic
environment'[155] derives largely from the great importance of baroque music (especially
that of Bach) within his repertoire. It may also reflect McLuhan's position that, with the
inception of the Modern (postmechanical) era, there was a transition from harmonics to
counterpoint. In his 1958 article 'Knowledge, Ideas, Information, and Communication
(A Canadian View),'[156] McLuhan writes of the perceptual shifts occasioned by the move
from Euclidean space to auditory space; this transition, he states, is difficult for the
literary mind to grasp, given its imbrication within lineal concepts, yet 'even the literary
person has no trouble recognizing the way in which a musical theme or harmony
simultaneously modifies all the portions of the musical work. In a musical structure it is
easy to observe the *total relevance* of every phrase to the entire work' (226). This organic
mode of composition is likewise employed in early works of modernism such as
Flaubert's novels, where one finds 'a return to the use of character not as a figure in a
social environment but as a theme in the environment of the other themes of the same
composition. This was, as it were, a shift from harmonic to contrapuntal structure. Since
Flaubert the novel has become a group of themes stacked one on the other, and heard
simultaneously ... In 1600 the break-away from such contrapuntal organization had come
with the new discovery of "every man in his humour," and of harmonic structure in
music. It may well be that this harmonic structure of vertical chords and of eccentric
individuals in fiction, essay, and drama was as naturally the mode of print culture as it is
to-day alien to our patterns of experience' (231).[157] This passage provides a crucial
context for Gould's sound documentaries, insofar as it interfaces the literary and the
musical in a way Gould sought to do in his productions.

Gould referred to his documentaries as '"contrapuntal radio,"'[158] and stated that they
arose from his realization that '"much of the new music has a lot to do with the spoken
word, with the rhythms and patterns, the rise and fall and inclination, the ordering of
phrase and regulation of cadence in human speech ... I think our whole notion of what
music is has forever merged with all the sounds that are around us, everything that the
environment makes available."'[159] Gould goes on to say that the Renaissance
contrapuntalists sensed sound as environmental, and that this realization is returning to
us now in the new music (whereby simultaneity reflects the numerous sound sources
were are conscious of at any one time).[160] In a 1971 conversation about his documentary
techniques, Gould comments on his dissatisfaction with the documentaries he had
produced before 'The Idea of North': 'You know, they very often came out sounding ... –
okay, I'll borrow Mr. McLuhan's term – linear' (*GGR* 374; cf *Selected Letters* 150). To
counter this linearity he developed a series of vocal overlays in his documentaries – 'a
kind of Webern-like continuity-in-crossover' (*GGR* 379) – arguing that people normally
take in information on a number of levels and that documentaries, therefore, need not

present information in linear fashion. This simultaneity implies a spatial conception that is likewise non-lineal, and Gould notes that it is precisely this spatial aspect of acoustics that is most often taken for granted. The introduction of stereo transmission at the time of 'The Latecomers,' however, allowed Gould to exploit these spatial aspects by emphasizing left and right speakers, as well as the vertical axis ('as though you are looking down from a considerable height' [*GGR* 384], with reference to the conclusion of 'The Latecomers'). McLuhan had argued in the chapter on 'The Phonograph' in *Understanding Media* that '[s]tereo sound ... is "all-around" or "wrap-around" sound. Previously sound had emanated from a single point in accordance with the bias of visual culture with its fixed point of view. The hi-fi changeover was really for music what cubism had been for painting, and what symbolism had been for literature; namely, the acceptance of multiple facets and planes in a single experience. Another way to put it is to say that stereo is sound in depth' (282). Gould likewise sought to develop the spatial quality of his documentaries not so much in terms of ambience as in terms of depth (congruently with his pianistic performances). This involved a figure/ground relationship with silence. 'The whole idea of the integral use of silence in music is a relatively new concept,' states Gould in the same conversation; 'It started with the Bauhaus ... with the idea of the total involvement of space, including the windows and the doors that make space meaningful' (*GGR* 382). These windows and doors are similar to the silences in musical composition – 'the integral use of cessation in a texture as a component of that texture.' In constructing his documentaries, Gould interpreted this notion of silence in Cagean terms, setting up a series of figure and ground reversals among the voices in his composition, as Bazzana has remarked: 'in his approval of the idea that not only speech but all sounds were becoming increasingly valid as the stuff of music, Gould often sounded surprisingly like another contemporary devotee of McLuhan: John Cage' (74). In 1979, Cage stated in an interview with Gould that 'the only aspect of sound that existed when there was no sound was duration.'[161] This is not the *durée* of Bergson, however, with its flight from the actual (cf *TWM* 8); as *4'33"* indicates, it was precisely the actual towards which Cage's compositions repeatedly gestured. Gould's sound documentaries similarly focus on 'aural societies' (to use James Lotz's term from 'The Idea of North') and the effects of technology on them. They also focus on solitude, but their conclusions are paradoxical; as R.A.J. Phillips says in 'Idea,' 'you may have gone to the North to get away from society, and you find yourself far closer to it than you've ever been in your life.' Marianne Schroeder (another voice in the composition) adds to this her observations about gossip, which she finds to be rife in the small communities where she worked. This latter comment suggests that the choice of the north for this particular documentary may have been a response to McLuhan's insistence that 'Eskimo' cultures embody values of an aural culture, values that derived from their immersion in acoustic space. (Phillips's comment that 'this [the North] is our national village to paraphrase Mr. McLuhan' was cut from the final version.)[162]

Gould's television documentaries likewise are the working out of a number of McLuhanesque notions. McLuhan had praised Gould's focus on process in his television documentaries because process was involving and a 'cool medium like TV ... demands this involvement in process' (*UM* 31). Gould's view was that television concerts tended to be '"static"' and he '"wondered if there wasn't a more imaginative way to present good music on TV."'[163] Gould further believed '[t]hat audio and video should serve one another rather than simply come packaged together ... And if McLuhan's right and it's a trend of our times to take an interest in the process of production, then surely that interest ... should free us from an expectation of a redundant co-ordination between production components. It should permit us to treat art as a source of greater mystery than symmetry and unity' (*GGR* 373). McLuhan had argued that television was a fundamentally tactile, disjunctive medium, in that it demanded involvement through its projection of dots, which the viewer had to connect in order to produce a picture: '[t]he TV image requires each instant that we "close" the spaces in the mesh by a convulsive sensuous participation that is profoundly kinetic and tactile' (*UM* 314). This emphasis on tactility was highly attractive to Gould, since it made a link between piano playing and media production. McLuhan argued that this tactility was analogous to speech, insofar as speech uses all the senses at once; hence there is an insistence in contemporary music on its closeness to speech: '[t]hus Schönberg and Stravinsky and Carl Orff and Bartok, far from being advanced seekers of esoteric effects, seem now to have brought music very close to the condition of ordinary human speech. It is this colloquial rhythm that once seemed so unmelodious about their work. Anyone who listens to the medieval works of Perotinus or Dufay will find them very close to Stravinsky and Bartok. The great explosion of the Renaissance that split musical instruments off from song and speech and gave them specialist functions is now being played backward in our age of electronic implosion' (*UM* 328). Gould's interpretation of McLuhan's notion that television 'involves maximal interplay of all the senses' (*UM* 333) was to present himself as highly involved with the music, singing, conducting, moving his body in rhythmic undulations – demonstrating his total *involvement* with the music.[164] This may appear to be a naïve reading of McLuhan, but the programs themselves indicate otherwise. Thus, when Gould played some Scriabin preludes for the 1974 CBC production 'The Age of Ecstasy (1900–1910),' his playing was accompanied by swirling colours meant to suggest Scriabin's synaesthetic notion that musical notes had certain chromatic analogues.[165] Other productions had images fading in and out during the performance (cf Friedrich 216–17). A performance of Webern was accompanied by 'rapidly changing patterns of colored dots, squares, triangles, diamonds, simple shapes that kept expanding and contracting, multiplying and dividing, changing into each other' (Friedrich 218). The emphasis on tactility in these performances recalls McLuhan's insistence that the television image is a mosaic: '[t]he mosaic can be *seen* as dancing can, but is not *structured* visually; nor is it an extension of the visual power. For the mosaic is not uniform, continuous, or repetitive. It is discontinuous, skew, and nonlineal, like the tactual TV image. To the sense of touch, all things are sudden, counter, original, spare, strange. The "Pied Beauty" of G.M. Hopkins is a catalogue of the notes of the sense of touch. The poem is a manifesto of the nonvisual, and like Cézanne or Seurat, or Rouault it provides an indispensable approach to understanding TV' (*UM* 334).

The overarching effect of Gould's techniques was to make his performances more 'worldly,' in the sense articulated by Edward Said – that is, Gould's performances assert their embeddedness in the material actuality of the world around us. 'Thus,' writes Said, 'Gould went to very great lengths after he left the concert stage in 1964 to communicate his divers talents to an audience as he spilled out his knowledge, his articulate analyses, his prodigious technical facility into other forms and styles well beyond the two-hour concert experience.'[166] What Gould sought to achieve was not a naïve historicity (his use of the piano for Bach was an ahistorical choice, as were his musical preferences for composers such as Richard Strauss who composed against the historical grain) but a materiality, an actuality of the here and now – a spatial rather than a temporal history, in the sense that it is not a linear, chronological history but a history precisely of the sort offered by the multiplicity of recordings that make available music from all eras at once. As Said has written, '[m]usic is fundamentally dumb: despite its fertile syntactic and expressive possibilities, music does not encode references, or ideas, or hypotheses discursively, the way language does. So the performer can either be (or play) dumb, or, as in Gould's case, the performer can set himself a great deal to do. If this might mean controlling the performance space to the extent of articulating, taking over his environment (by dressing and appearing to be against the grain), conducting the orchestra despite a conductor's presence, humming over and above the piano's sound, talking and writing *as if to extend the piano's reach into verbal language* via a whole slew of essays, interviews, record jacket notes, then Gould did so enthusiastically.'[167] This accords with Bazzana's notion that, for Gould, performance was a form of discourse. 'Sometimes he would explain the intended discourse in spoken or written comments, but often his performances of themselves had a didactic or polemical quality that amounted to a contribution to the secondary literature on the music at hand' (85). Gould's prose was likewise filled with oral effects – 'quotations, jokes, puns, dashes, brackets, alternating short sentences with long ones, using preludes, section edits, italics, ellipses, commas, and periods (to mark the rests and stops), abrupt paragraph breaks, and – a favourite device – the detailed list.'[168] These signs of orality in writing, of visible speech, were, for McLuhan, indications of the transition from a literate to an oral culture. With the increasing implosion of contemporary culture into the world of the tribal drum, speech would cease to be visible, since, as acoustic space, it would eventually become our environment, and all environments are invisible. Gould's abandonment of the concert hall was a dramatic indicator of this movement of acoustic space towards the environmental. If the phonograph represented, as it did for both McLuhan and Gould, the concert hall without walls in the 'Malrauvian museum' (*GGR* 74)[169] of sound recordings, Muzak, and portable disc players, then what Gould's work demonstrated was how our lives had become part of that aesthetic through the prosthetic technologies of our environment.

CHAPTER SEVEN

Art without Walls

The electrification of writing was almost as big a step into the non-visual and auditory space as the later steps soon taken by telephone, radio, and TV.
The telephone: speech without walls.
The phonograph: music hall without walls.
The photograph: museum without walls.
The electric light: space without walls.
The movie, radio, and TV: classroom without walls.

Marshall McLuhan, *Understanding Media*

Voices of Silence

The concept of 'environment' was of considerable importance to McLuhan in the work he produced after *Understanding Media*, insofar as it was the domain of interfaces and had an orientation towards the material, embodied context of artistic (including media) production. With this term, McLuhan sought to convey the notion that the world around us, and the lived experience of it, had become artifactual through the effects of media, such that nature could be said to have collapsed into culture. In an environment in which everything tended towards the artifactual (in the same way that in the Mallarméan universe everything existed in order to end up in a book), the museum[1] became the environment, or medium, of cultural production. Duchamp had discerned this with his readymades, objects from the 'real' world that were translated into art by their inclusion in museum exhibitions and collections, an excellent example of how an environment – in this case, the museum – operates transformatively, translating the meaning of an object through the context (or ground) of perception.

At the same time as cultural production was becoming one vast museum, the museum's physical space was being displaced by photography, with its powerful ability to retrieve artworks over an enormous field, historically and geographically. The photograph at once dehistoricized these images and rehistoricized them in a decentred space of mosaic-like juxtaposition with yet other photographs of artworks. Such photographs, especially when they represented the 'real' world, also had the ability to 'artifactualize' that world. What for Duchamp was still an act characterized by subjectivity and a degree of authorial intention became in an increasingly mediatized world a fact of lived experience. André Malraux had made an influential analysis of this phenomenon in his 1950 book *Les Voix de silence*,[2] in which he argued that photographic reproduction had created a 'museum without walls' by enabling access to the entire history of world art production at any given moment, by turning into art any object included in the photographic frame, and by recontextualizing art historically and conceptually.[3] McLuhan seized upon a number of the implications of the museum without walls, including its destabilization of artistic 'subjectivity,' its subversion of progressivist notions of artistic production, and its deconstruction of the fixity of 'inside' and 'outside,' a notion whose spatial indeterminacy was closely tied to that of the global village. Indeed, art practices of this period became increasingly international and increasingly collaborative, such that this globalism became part of the artwork, as in correspondence art[4] and the 'spatial poems'[5] of some of the Fluxus artists, as well as through photography and electronic communications, as in some of the art practices of the N.E. Thing Co., and in video art generally. The concept of the museum without walls had also informed McLuhan's thinking about Glenn Gould's 'dropping out' of the concert circuit.[6] Not only did the recording studio provide a 'concert hall without walls' that could afford the performer direct access to the most intimate of performance spaces, as well as (and at the same time as) to a mass audience; recorded music could also influence musical practice through its ability to make present to us the entirety of musical production as if it were historically our own (a point of particular note to a Canadian), while at the same time having an effect on musical form and dynamics by allowing for compositions and performances inappropriate to or impossible within the traditional concert hall.

The history of art constructed by photography was not chronological in the usual sense of the word; rather, it was superpository and juxtapositional, in the way that Gould's sound documentaries are and McLuhan and Fiore's books are. Photography made a powerful contestation of print's linearity, since its images were read iconographically, all at once, rather than sequentially. Photography thus became an important political tool in this period, its juxtaposition to print immediately creating a tension – a hot medium next to a cool one. McLuhan and Fiore used juxtapositional techniques in works such as *War and Peace in the Global Village*, and this hybrid combination of print and photography was at the heart of much of the artistic production of conceptualism,[7] an artistic practice whose dominance in Canada in the 1960s and 1970s (and in many ways continuing into the 1980s and beyond) is directly and indirectly related to McLuhan's insistence that hybrid forms were powerful modes of critique. While Malraux's book espouses values of artistic transcendence, Eurocentrism, artistic genius, and historical teleology that McLuhan's own work did not share, the concept of the museum without walls influenced McLuhan profoundly.[8] The concept informed McLuhan's artistic/intellectual practices from the 1950s, when he was co-editing *Explorations*, until the end of his career; in turn, these aspects of McLuhan's thought resonated within a broad critical and artistic set of practices, from 'environments' (or installations) to performance art to conceptualism. What is particularly striking about these practices is the global range of their production:[9] from 'sea to shining sea' in Canada, as one account puts it;[10] and, internationally, in the work associated with the Independent Group in Britain, the Situationists in France, and the Fluxus movement in Europe and beyond.

Malraux makes the central argument of *The Voices of Silence* at the beginning of his book (elaborating on it with his legendary prolixity in the six hundred pages following), contending that our notions about what is and is not art have been very much influenced by the power of the museum to confer artistic value on an object, which it does precisely by decontextualizing that work from its context and placing it in the new one of the art museum. These effects have been exacerbated by the photograph, which has made art books into museums without walls, such that the notion of retrieval more and more comes to dominate artistic production. Thus, one of the principal effects of photographic technology, according to Malraux, is being felt on our sense of art history; the linear, chronological sense of artistic development is being replaced by a sense of the coexistence (a not always peaceful coexistence) of artworks, with the Altamira cave drawings becoming the contemporaries of Picasso's *Demoiselles d'Avignon*.

While Malraux dwells very little on the spatial implications of the imaginary museum (his concerns being more with a transcendental notion of time), McLuhan was very much concerned with the implications the *musée imaginaire* had for space. The concept of 'voices of silence' was read idiosyncratically by McLuhan as the orally empathic dimension of artworks produced by their recontextualization and juxtapositon within a non-linear dynamic of artistic production; this dynamic McLuhan associated with acoustic space. The notion that artistic interrelationships were linear and chronological, in other words, was displaced through their juxtaposition with other works, a juxtaposition that, in emphasizing the simultaneity and discontinuity of these works, allowed them to produce meaning in terms other than that of visual (chronological, historical, rational) linearity. In this process, art was decontextualized from its art-historical, abstract, formalist context and recontextualized into a local, material context without losing the previous (formalist) relationships.[11] This process was heightened by the advent of electronic media, especially television. As McLuhan put it in a letter to John Wain of March 1960, 'the TV image [,] unlike the film image [,] constitutes you not [as] the camera, but [as] the screen. It is of low visual definition, and the image effected by luminous spots has a high tactual impact; [*sic*] like contour in prints and engravings[,] giving the T.V. image a strong sculptural quality, which is also to say a strong auditory quality. (You know[,] Malraux, *The Voices of Silence*.) ... Our own re-conquest of the tactual, the kinaesthetic and the sculp[t]ural in the past century is in a deep sense our retracking [*sic*] our way in the primeval forest' (*L* 267). What McLuhan made of this notion of the museum without walls, then, was a vast media metaphor; he realized that the notion applied to much more than just photographic reproduction of artworks. Thus, if the photograph produced a 'museum without walls,' then the telephone produced 'speech without walls,' the phonograph a 'music hall without walls' and electric light 'space without walls' (*UM* 283). Not only did these new spaces represent (in many cases) a breaking down of traditional institutional hierarchies; they also represented a much more performative notion of space, a space you made, rather than simply occupied. For example, we create a certain sort of space with our stereo speakers, indicated by our positioning of left and right speakers, adding additional speakers to create '"all-around" or "wrap-around" sound' (282), which McLuhan understood as implying a greater involvement on the part of the listener.

In the same way, the photograph had created a space for the artwork that was not continuous with the traditional one of previous artistic appreciation; in this space, small works could be placed on the same hierarchical level as large ones, and large ones could be appreciated for details inaccessible to the human eye. The photograph broke down hierarchies as well by freeing art from institutionalized museum spaces. Given that this space contested the centred space of perspective, its chief quality was gestural (as in the photographs by Muybridge) or sculptural, a quality McLuhan associated with the tactile (because tactility involved an interrelationship of the senses).[12] The concept of the 'museum without walls' thus foregrounded the way in which the space of the museum as institution defined what was art, while indicating that in a world where art was environmental, anywhere could be an art gallery, a museum, a performance place.[13] This shift from artistic product to artistic process countered the tendency of museums to de-contextualize their artworks; the new artistic practices sought to contextualize the art *process* in a specific space and time. As Thomas McEvilley has remarked, the traditional museum space is 'a kind of non-space, ultra-space, or ideal space where the surrounding matrix of space-time is symbolically annulled.'[14] Much of the installation work of the 1960s sought to critique the pure and transcendent space that the Modernist museum had become by emphasizing (often through photography) the connections between the museum and its material contexts.[15] Once the museum ceased to be the unexamined spatial ground of artistic (re)production, space became a topic of singular debate – what space was produced by an artwork? a performance? an electronic communication? And what if the *museum* became the *figure* of representation, rather than the ground? It should thus come as no surprise that this was the era in which the Groupe Espace was formed, when artists were producing works based on a '*spazialismo* manifesto,' when avant-garde art galleries were named 'A Space,' where artists calling themselves 'Ace Space Co.' produced works titled 'A Space Atlas,' and where aesthetic discussion centred on questions of the performance of space.[16]

Spacetime Environments

The performance spaces of 1960s and 1970s artistic endeavours came to be known as 'environments,'[17] a concept that resonated powerfully with McLuhan's use of this term. One of his sources for this notion was the work of Frederick Kiesler, architect, painter, sculptor, installation artist, and theorist of space.[18] Kiesler is described in *Verbi-Voco-Visual Explorations* as doing 'experiments in acoustic space,' as 'founder of the *Correalist* movement,' and as creator of the '"Endless House" (1950), an attempt completely to break down linear structuring and finite limitations' (9).[19] The 'Endless House,' an open-form house based on ovoidal shapes, was one of many spatial experiments envisioned by Kiesler in a career so occupied with notions of spatiality that he was referred to as 'Doktor Raum.'[20] In all of his projects, Kiesler sought to realize the space that was being created by electronic media, a space without limit (and hence the term 'Endless,' with which he prefaced many of his works). Associated early in his career with Theo van Doesberg, his interests in space reflect the fourth-dimensional thinking of van Doesberg and the de Stijl group (cf *4D* 315; 328; 336). His overarching project became that of infusing spaces with dynamic elements. His houses had movable walls and biomorphic shapes; his stage sets (such as that for Capek's *R.U.R.*) included filmic projections and 'proto-television'; his gallery installations used the ceilings and the full interior as well as the walls.

Kiesler called these spaces 'environments' and referred to their organizational principles as 'galaxies'; the term 'correalism' likewise referred to the interdependent and interactive spaces he sought to produce. Kiesler insisted that the term 'environment' could no longer be understood as referring only to nature; he argued that we also occupied a technological environment that was allied to the biological environment in that it served human needs. As he wrote in his 1939 essay 'Architecture as Biotechnology,' '[t]he biologist who speaks of the environment thinks invariably of the geographical and natural environment ... Man, however, has developed a third environment, the technological, which has accompanied him from his origins ... Modern man thinks that it is industry which has produced this environment. In reality, it is the product of *human needs* ... In this sense, *everything that man uses in his battle for existence* is a tool, and, as such, is part of the technological environment created by him, from clothing to shelter, from cannons to poetry, from telephone to painting. No object exists in isolation. Each technological medium is *co-real*: its existence is conditioned by the flux of human survival, and, in consequence, by its relation to the *global environment*.'[21] In applying this notion to his installations (everything from windows for Saks Fifth Avenue to stage sets to theatrical acoustics), Kiesler sought to create spaces that would counter visual space. In doing so, he saw himself working both in and against the tradition of the museum; in designing art exhibitions, he sought to make the display of the art into an artwork itself, such that the museum-goers would themselves become participants in producing a work of art that superseded the individual artworks. In 1927 he designed an exhibition (dubbed 'The TV Room')[22] that was to comprise several screens on which artworks from around the world would be projected.[23] He extended this notion into other installations according to a principle he called the 'galaxy,' by which he referred to configurations of art within an installation whereby the spaces between the art objects had expressive values equivalent to those of the objects themselves (an idea similar to the Japanese notion 'ma'). As Kiesler wrote in a piece posthumously published in 1966, this 'INTERVAL is the new field of correlation between diverse aggregations of solids, even if it appears empty to the eye and to touch, because it separates and at the same time structures space.'[24]

Kiesler's influence was very much part of the 1950s and 1960s[25] art scene in New York, a milieu that included John Cage, Allan Kaprow (one of the *forces animateurs* of Happenings), Robert Rauschenberg (whose collage *Homage to Frederik Kiesler* was done in 1966) and the Living Theatre. For all of these artists, the notion of environment (or installation, performance, Happening) was of paramount importance; by redefining and thus critiquing the traditional spaces of artistic production, the artists associated with these environmental practices sought to redefine what it means to create a work of art. McLuhan's formulations of the notion of 'environment' were made contemporaneously; his 'Address at Vision 65' – among his most republished lecture topics – was presented in May of that year at the Buffalo Spring Festival of the Arts.[26] An environment, in

McLuhan's formulation, is produced by a dominant medium; its effects are everywhere, and thus we tend to be unaware of it. However, it does make us aware of the previous environment: 'We can always see the Emperor's old clothes, but not his new ones' (*EM* 221). In the transition from one environment to the next, the former environment becomes the content of the new one, which renders the previous environment an art form (much in the way that television did for the cinema). McLuhan finds this principle to be enacted in contemporary art: 'pop art consists in taking the outer environment and putting it in the art gallery ... suggesting that we have reached the stage where we have begun to process the environment itself as an art form' (*EM* 224), as Andy Warhol had demonstrated with a soup can. The object of such art has less to do with self-expression than it does with heightening perception. 'The training of perception upon the otherwise unheeded environment became the basis of experimentation in what is called modern art and poetry. The artist, instead of expressing himself ... turned his senses and the work of art to the business of probing the environment' (*EM* 224). In probing the environment, the artist produces a counter-environment, or anti-environment.[27] Thus, in *4' 33"*, John Cage probes the sound environment by creating a counter-environment of silence.

Because the artist takes a provocative stance towards that which is accepted as the norm (the environment), the artist is often configured as antisocial, 'the enemy in society' (with the allusion here to Wyndham Lewis's famous characterization). Yet the art of the electronic era is profoundly integrative. 'For twenty-five hundred years of artistic history, the arts have been engaged in separating man from his environment. Now, suddenly, the western world plunges with this new technology into a state in which man is once more engaged in merging with his environment.'[28] Electronic media have retrieved a society in which 'the artist functions as the one who relates the society to the cosmic powers ... In our time we live simultaneously in all other times, all other cultures. It is the Malraux image of "the museum without walls" which extends in time as well as in space' (Bornstein, 'Interview' 61). This simultaneity of shapes and forms has its counterpart in the artistic event called the Happening: 'The electric circuit creates a simultaneous field which is totally involving and totally invisible as far as its psychic operation is concerned. It creates what has become known as the "Happening." The "Happening" is a world in which everything is at once, in which there is no sequence or succession of events' (65).[29] Writing on the Happening in *From Cliché to Archetype*, McLuhan contrasts it with narrative: '[i]f the novelistic narrative tends to deal with the total environment selectively in the direction of creating "human interest" by means of the coincidence of motives, temperaments, and situations, the new art form of the Happening does exactly the reverse. The Happening accepts the environment, unmodified, as a colossal *Gestalt*' (197). Advertisements function paradigmatically as Happenings: they are anonymous, inclusive, often intermedial, and require audience interaction if they are to be successful. Their corporate qualities mean that they function as the cave drawings of the urban canyons in the same way that paintings functioned on the cave walls at Lascaux. This corporate quality stresses the human dimension of media: 'The electric technology should be regarded not as some alien intruder from outer space, but as our own nervous system, magnificently simulated, extended beyond us into space ... Therefore all technologies are completely humanist in the sense of belonging entirely to the human organism'

(67). Given that the entire planet was now wired into a global village, the planet itself had become an artifact: '[w]hen Sputnik (1957) went around the planet, the planet became programmable content, and thus became an art form. Ecology was born, and Nature was obsolesced.'[30] Elaborating on this elsewhere, McLuhan wrote that 'The planet is now the content of the new spaces created by the new technology. Instead of being an environment in time, the earth itself has become a probe in space. That is, the planet has become an anti-environment, an art form, an extension of consciousness, yielding new perception of the new man-made environment.'[31]

Concepts and Contexts

Environments, performance art, and installations (known also as time/space art[32]) provided perceptual models of the space–time dynamic McLuhan had been theorizing since the 'break' with Innis. By dynamizing the museum space, for example, artists showed how such spaces were actively involved in artistic production and not merely passive containers of the art exhibited in them. By 'performing' the art gallery, these artists sought to bring the space of the gallery together with the time of its production. Hence Richard Kostelanetz's survey of the form takes as one of its epigraphs Albert Einstein's comment that, '[i]n the past, science described motion as happenings in time; general theory of relativity interprets events existing in space-time' (*Theatre* ix). Historians of environmental practices, such as Kostelanetz, saw them as part of the larger return to involvement-in-depth, which McLuhan had stated was a consequence of electronic media (cf Kostelanetz, *Theatre* 34).[33]

McLuhan was involved, directly or indirectly, with a number of these performances, such as those by USCO (i.e., 'Company of Us,' an American group of performance artists) and the performances held at the University of British Columbia (UBC) in 1961 and in 1964–5 (Bronson et al., *Sea to Shining Sea* 25; 28–9). As Gerd Stern, of USCO, has remarked in an interview with Kostelanetz, '[*Understanding*] *Media* came out initially in a typescript published by the National Association of Educational Broadcasters back in 1959 [i.e., *Report on Project in Understanding New Media*]. We had that, and it was one of the first things that turned us on. We got a lot of our initial ideas out of that, particularly that whole electrical sense' (Kostelanetz, *Theatre* 247). Kostelanetz comments that 'Your work would seem to illustrate McLuhan's idea that, through electronic machinery, you can create a field of artistic activity – a kinetic environment – which has numerous foci of communication' (*Theatre* 247). These numerous foci, or centres, would in turn break down the perspectivalism and point of view that typified (post)Renaissance art and the spaces created to house it, as Allan Kaprow has suggested (*Assemblage* 152). In the performance space, one could not passively look at art; one became involved with art through one's entire sensory awareness, defining that space uniquely as one interacted with it. What Happenings, and cognate forms such as combines and assemblages, foreground is that '*the room has always been a frame or format too*' (154). Rather than viewing space through the 'window' of perspectival art, the Happening permits 'a fuller involvement with actual space' (160) because 'one's eyes and arms cannot possibly embrace the whole at once while standing at the usual distance of a half-dozen feet. A broken surface thus becomes a sort of topography relief in which one could travel' (163).

A related art form was conceptualism. Just as performances rejected the traditional spaces of the museum and gallery in favour of the body as site and material of performance, so conceptualist art rejected canvas and paint, chisel and hammer, and the traditional art object, in favour of the concept of the artwork itself. As RoseLee Goldberg remarks, 'conceptual art implied the *experience* of time, space and material rather than their representations in the form of objects, and the body became the most direct medium of expression.' Thus, 'ideas on space could just as well be interpreted in actual space as in the conventional two-dimensional format of the painted canvas; time could be suggested in the duration of a performance' (*Performance Art* 152–3). Artworks such as these were very much concerned with the 'why' of art, with its conceptual aspect, much in the way that concrete poetry was concerned with the formal aspect of the printed page (with Mallarmé's *Un Coup de dés* and Duchamp's *Green Box* being the significant crossover works).[34] Both sought to critique notions of the transparency of language by making it visible, to critique that visibility by making it tactile, and to express that tactility through hybrid media. Concrete poetry and conceptualism are further related in their tendency to foreground the context of meaning production – respectively, the page and the museum – which is to say that they are both concerned with their medium of production. Conceptualism is thus in many ways an exacerbated form of concrete poetry; the latter's thrust towards iconicity is, in conceptualism, most often rendered juxtapositionally as text and image, presenting the viewer with a processual notion of 'becoming iconographical.' At the same time, the conceptualist work compromises the viewer, both by deconstructing the perspectival (and thus distancing) notions produced by print, as well as by problematizing (with its non-art or anti-art politics) the museum (or gallery) in which the work is displayed. Both concrete poetry and conceptualism were thus part of a larger critique of visual space (as was environmental art generally) that sought to turn the museum space inside out, towards a public space, as opposed to away from it. While this art has been characterized as 'dematerialized,'[35] this formulation gets at only one part of a dynamic that also involved the (re)materialization of the contextual *ground* of the art object. As Christel Hollevoet has remarked, there was a 'crucial concern in artistic practices from the late 1950s to the 1970s for the topographical apprehension of urban space, or mapping of places and itineraries. They signal a shift from the avant-garde critique of art to the critique of everyday life; from avant-garde opposition to popular culture from "outside and above," to participation in it from the inside.'[36]

Conceptualist art (including environmental art generally) was an area of artistic production in which McLuhan's writings had particular purchase, largely based on McLuhan's theorizing of the importance of the *medium* of artistic production and that '[t]he artist smashes open the doors of perception' (*COB* 44). Because conceptualist art focuses on concepts rather than objects, it is very often language-based, documenting the work as process rather than as product (where typography becomes a sign of process insofar as it is the medium of expression, as opposed to 'solely' the message); it employs photographs as part of its critique of (traditional) representation, a critique that includes the context of representation; it appropriates and recontextualizes objects from the "everyday" world in order to break down the boundary between museum space and environment; and it invites participation – even co-creation. Such criteria describe a very broad range of artistic production, and this fluidity of form is of crucial importance to the understanding of conceptualism as an artistic process that is at the same time a mode of critique – of the artist, of art, its institutions, its commodification, and its processes. As Tony Godfrey puts it, conceptual art 'represents a state of continual self-critique ... Conceptual art was a violent reaction against ... Modernist notions of progress in the arts and against the art object's status as a special kind of commodity. The purely retinal or visual nature of art ... was anathema to Conceptual artists.'[37] One of the ways in which the conceptualists critiqued visual space was by foregrounding print, thereby reasserting the flat plane and thus deconstructing perspectivalism (which McLuhan had attributed to print's dependence on a foregrounded figure and a 'neutral' ground).[38] As Benjamin Buchloh asserted in his catalogue essay to the first retrospective exhibition of conceptualism (1989), 'Conceptual practices went beyond the mapping of the linguistic model onto the perceptual model, further than the spatialization of language and the temporalization of visual structure. The proposal inherent in Conceptual Art was to replace the object of spatial and perceptual experience by linguistic definition alone ... and this constituted the most consequential assault on that object's visuality, its commodity status and its distribution form.'[39] From McLuhan's position, conceptualism was replacing *one* object of spatial perception (the visual object) with another spatial disposition, which, in its anti-mimetic and non-linear configuration, contested the visual in a way that was orally empathic. As Buchloh remarks with reference to a proto-conceptualist work by American artist Robert Morris called *Box with the Sound of Its Own Making,* 'by counteracting the supremacy of the visual with that of an auditory experience of equal, if not higher, importance, he renewed the Duchampian quest for a non-retinal art' through 'the (ac[o]ustic or tactile) disturbance of the parity of perceptual experience' ('From the Aesthetic' 44).

McLuhan worked with these notions in *Culture Is Our Business* (1970), which brings together elements of concrete poetry with conceptualism in its use of the '*essai concrète.*' The title suggests (consistently with McLuhan's early development of it in *The Mechanical Bride,* whose insights this book extends into the era of electronic media) that the processing techniques of corporate business are shared with those of artistic production (a point Bertram Brooker had made in the 1920s). Both use photography, and both juxtapose photographs with text (the typical form of conceptualist art), though McLuhan's texts often disturb the traditional subservience of text to image.[40] The title of the book also raises one of the central concerns within the practice of conceptualism – that is, the corporatization of artistic production and reception.[41] McLuhan's position is complicit: he uses – appropriates – the very material that he seeks to critique, and this complicity reflects the ambivalence within environmental art itself, in which the artist is immersed in the material being critiqued, as opposed to distanced from it (a position McLuhan rejected after *The Mechanical Bride*). In this regard, McLuhan's work is of a piece with the conceptualist project as formulated by Buchloh, who writes that '[c]onceptual Art was distinguished, from its inception, by its acute and critical sense of discursive and institutional limitations, its self-imposed restrictions, its lack of totalizing vision, its critical devotion to the factual conditions of artistic production and reception *without aspiring to overcome the mere facticity of these conditions*' (53; emphasis added). McLuhan's position was to problematize the boundary line between museum and society, arguing that artistic critique must be understood in terms of a larger social critique. In this regard, his work can be productively situated within the trajectory of the art and criticism of this period, a trajectory that moved from concept to context.

Books were a major vehicle for conceptualist art, as in the work of Joyce Wieland and Michael Snow; as Godfrey remarks, 'they were reasonably cheap, accessible and transportable' (225). Johanna Drucker notes that 'the idea that art was primarily **about ideas** emphasized the conceptual practice of art ... In such an atmosphere hybrid forms or, to use Dick Higgins' apt term, "intermedia," became the norm rather than the exception. Books were a form of intermedia par excellence since they could contain images, texts, marks, and materials in a format which was flexible, mutable, and variable' (*Century* 70). Higgins had specifically referred to McLuhan in formulating his 1966 'Statement on Intermedia,'[42] and McLuhan's *Culture Is Our Business* (1970) can be read productively in the light of this statement. McLuhan had first used the title 'Culture Is Our Business' in a 1958 address to the National Association of Educational Broadcasters,[43] in which he argued that the moving of information had become the central business of contemporary society, such that 'the work of art is used as a model of the patterns of the total community' (4). These patterns are those of 'non-Euclidean space' (5), produced by technologies such as photography that create 'a world of icons, of images' (30). This theme remains consistent in *Culture Is Our Business*, where, in an 'Author's Note,' McLuhan makes reference to 'the new information environment of the wired planet' in which '[a]ds can be regarded as cave art.' 'As a contemporary environment,' asks McLuhan, 'may not the study of these ad forms be the only means of controlling their magical effects? Failing such study, may we not simply expect a future of progressive "astoneagement"?' (7–8). This response combines the utopian belief in a communitarian participation in artistic production with the critical imperative of critiquing that production.

Culture Is Our Business comprises a series of advertisements (reproduced on the right-hand page throughout) flanked by McLuhan's *essais concrètes*; these provide a critical context in which McLuhan both explicates and critiques the ads, most often through indirection. An ad, thus, for the *Minneapolis Star and Tribune*, asking 'What makes a newspaper great?' (45), shows a picture of T.S. Eliot addressing an audience of 13,723 at a lecture sponsored by the newspaper. To this McLuhan juxtaposes a number of brief comments, one of which asks 'When an esoteric poet addresses 13,723 people in a sports stadium on a high-brow topic, is the title of the present book obvious?' (44) Here McLuhan's comments point towards an understanding of the larger context (environmental) of advertising *and* poetry, a context that indirectly legitimates his own *procédé* of performing cultural critique using artistic means: 'The poet dislocates language into meaning. The artist smashes open the doors of perception.' McLuhan contextualizes his use of the *essai concrète* technique with reference to a *TV Guide* cover by Salvador Dali in which television screens are superimposed on the nails of enlarged fingers (111). To McLuhan, this signifies that the screen is tactile, not visual, and that the essence of tactility is the interval. His concrete essays are conceived of in the same way – as a series of discontinuous observations, where the connections have to be made by the reader. This technique creates involvement in the same way that the advertisements do. 'In the electric age,' writes McLuhan, 'the connection in narrative and art is omitted ... Thus, isolated news items are more interesting than editorials. Ads are more interesting than essay articles with their points of view continuously maintained' (112). In general this typifies McLuhan's approach: the ads are neither 'bad' nor 'good': rather, they succeed or (most often) fail according to the extent to which they take into account the socio-cultural implications of electronic media. Those ads that fail do so because they present 'a timeless world of *déjà vu*' (240); McLuhan responds by appropriating these ads, recontextualizing them, and interfacing them with discontinuous print commentary, mediating their representation of an unmediated reality.[44] Some of McLuhan's harshest criticism is reserved for an ad illustrating the Saturn S-IVB rocket, part of NASA's Apollo space program (176–7). McLuhan critiques the space program for its naïve orientation towards visual space. 'Electric space,' notes McLuhan, 'is not outer but inner.' McLuhan considered this lack of awareness about the contemporary environment to be typical of contemporary ads; as he writes in a 1966 article, 'The Relation of Environment to Anti-Environment,' the 'world of modern advertising is a magical environment constructed to produce effects for the total economy but not designed to increase human awareness' (3).[45] One way in which that awareness could be increased, and the totalizing effects of media resisted, would be to foreground a multiplicity of interfaced media, such that no one medium is dominant, no one voice privileged.[46]

Corporate Art

As Daniel Belgrad has indicated, McLuhan's publication in *Neurotica* in the late 1940s signalled his entry into the (North) American discourse of the avant-garde.[47] Similarly, the publication of *Explorations* in the 1950s initiated the 'enormous impact on a generation of Canadian artists to come' that McLuhan was to have.[48] In Canada, McLuhan had a powerful influence on Vancouver's Intermedia (1966–71); Intersystems of Toronto (1966–9) 'provided direct participating experience of Marshall McLuhan's theories' (Bronson, *Sea to Shining Sea* 32); *Voicespondence*, an audio magazine, was published in Calgary with the cooperation of Dick Higgins and Fluxus artist Emmett Williams, both of whom worked within a McLuhanesque milieu, as did artists at the Nova Scotia College of Art and Design.[49] John Bentley Mays has written that 'it was in 1959 that Marshall McLuhan, on a visit to the University of British Columbia, set the tone and program for much of what was to follow':

> [e]ven at that early date [1959], it was possible to make out in McLuhan's thought the main lines of what was to become known as (for want of a better term) the postmodern mode of art and consciousness – the rejection of masterpiece-making as the goal of art, the exchanging of the macho-heroic image of the artist for a more polymorphous, sociable one, and the transformation of the studio from a monkish scientific laboratory for the working out of the modernist program of streamlining and rationalizing (the heritage of the Bauhaus, via New York) into a rec room of personal expression and dialogue with technology and the hitherto taboo imagery of the mass media. Artists began to see in McLuhan's utterances a role for themselves as something other than suppliers of objects for consumers; they caught sight of new roles, as communicators, celebrants and hierophants of the new electronic and media mysteries.[50]

Of McLuhan's 1959 visit to UBC, Alvin Balkind has written that '[w]ord spread by tom-tom'[51] and McLuhan was invited to speak to the Arts Club about his ideas concerning 'the breakdown of artificial barriers between the various arts and their impending recombination in a new form, taking their cue from popular culture and from neo-technology in general, with emphasis on electronic media' (72). The upshot was UBC's first Festival of Contemporary Arts, held in February of 1961 (and continuing until 1971). This festival, according to Balkind, 'regenerate[d] local artists by putting them in direct touch with the makers of the charged ideas then current largely in New York and California' (72). The festivals hosted an international roster of artists, including John Cage, Robert Rauschenberg, Stan Brakhage, Allen Ginsberg, 'and, of course, Marshall McLuhan' (72). In 1965, the festival was dubbed 'The Medium Is the Message'[52] and was specifically oriented towards McLuhan's ideas: '[i]ts most memorable features included a wall of stretching fabric concealing the undulating bodies of dancers pressed against and extruding from it, touchable by the audience; and the projection from various levels (some high up) of specially-painted slides directed like pistols by a large crew of projectionists, onto everybody down below, and onto everything including delivery trucks and large floating panels suspended from the ceiling. It was an event of choreo-graphed free play with random surprises, an attempt to show that McLuhan's theories about mosaic as opposed to linear perception had demonstrable validity, using as its means shifting planes, colors, images, sound, and spatial advance and retreat' (72).[53] Balkind's description highlights those aspects of McLuhan's theories that were to have the greatest purchase on the artistic community: the return to the bodily and the sensuous; the valorization of tactility as the fusion of the senses; the mosaic as providing an alternative way of knowing to linearity; the critical power of interfaced artworks (intermedia);[54] the importance of the figure and ground relation in understanding percep-tion; the movement away from the traditional (perspectival) art object and towards the flat plane (with its implications for point of view); and the overwhelming presence of interfaced media – electronic and non-electronic. It is also significant that the artistic activity described by Balkind is fleeting and ephemeral, its spatial configurations being produced in the time of its coming into being, and these attributes align it all the more powerfully with the acoustic.

Commenting generally on performance works of the sort Balkind describes, McLuhan states that such activities exist 'to enhance community values' among their participants. In this sense such activities comprise 'a field of action that would otherwise be outside [one's] ken.' The participant 'put[s] on' these activities 'as a mask or a pattern of energy in order to organize his perceptions' just as the artists 'must also put on the public created by the [event], creating a reciprocal and complimentary action.'[55] McLuhan likened such action to speech; referring to contemporary fashion (which interested him as an articulation of personal space), he stated that '[t]he experience it evokes is not visual: it is tactile. It is full of abrupt encounters, sudden interfaces. It is the World of Happenings where surfaces and events grind against each other, creating new forms, much as the action of dialogue creates new insights.'[56] The focus of much of this artistic activity in Vancouver,[57] (and elsewhere), was on the Intermedia group;[58] one of the directors of the group saw their work as writing 'the first chapter of the cultural space age.'[59] The social space inaugurated by such artistic enterprises as Intermedia was hybrid and non-hierarchical.[60] As Keith Wallace has written, 'Intermedia's alternative art coincided with the concept of an alternative society ... For artists, change within the art system itself was an implicit component of social change. Greenbergian modernism had supposed a distinction between "high art" and popular culture; not only was this distinction to be questioned, but the means of art production was to be made available to all.'[61] The art of this period likewise questioned the three-dimensional space of perspectival art ('retinal' art, in the parlance of Duchamp); counterposed to this space was that of the flat (or flatbed) plane, whose tactile, or sculptural, quality is precisely that of an intermediate, or hybrid, art that addresses itself to more than one sensory mode.

The Canadian artists who most fully took up the implications of these spatial theories for their own artistic practice were Iain and Ingrid Baxter. As Marie L. Fleming notes, 'Iain ... found that McLuhan's theories expressed philosophically a view of the world that crystallized his own open, intuitive and ecologically-oriented approach to both life and art.'[62] Iain Baxter had been involved in the 'Medium Is the Message' event at UBC; in 1966 he staged 'Bagged Place' at UBC – four rooms in which every item (including the artist) was enclosed in a clear plastic bag, the whole being described as 'the first major "environment" constructed and shown in Canada' (Fleming 24) and 'the first public celebration of McLuhanism.'[63] Readable as a critique of consumer society, as well as an embodiment of the mediatization of that society (including the artist), this environment became the touchstone for subsequent work by these artists. Practising under the name 'N.E. Thing Co.' (NETCO), they picked up, here, on a number of McLuhanesque themes;[64] these included the notion that culture and business were intimately interrelated through the idea of the 'corporate' (i.e., that art was not self-expression but collaboration in an increasingly artifactual culture); that everything a society produces is art (on which the Baxters put their own stamp with the phrase 'Art Is All Over,' implying that in a globally mediated world, all perceived phenomena had taken on the condition of art, rendering 'art' thus meaningless as a category indicative of a certain hierarchy); and that the artist could not transcend the materiality of art (which was concurrently the materiality of the context of that art). This critical engagement with art production coincides powerfully with McLuhan's own interests (as manifested in *The Medium Is the Massage* and *War and Peace in the Global Village*) in bringing the theoretical and the artistic together. The works in 'Bagged Place' thus acknowledge that they are produced out of and within a consumerist society (a major issue within conceptualism generally) while at the same time removing the packaged works from the economics of that society (because objects thus packaged became 'art') *and* from the consumerism of art (because these works could not be sold as consumerist art *could* be sold, thus slyly mocking the anti-commercial stance of many artists).[65] Thus the Baxters could set themselves up as a company (emphasizing, as McLuhan had suggested in *The Mechanical Bride*, that the practices of artists and advertisers coincide at many points – indeed, that art is corporate to the extent that it is not the product of the sovereign subject), while at the same time critiquing corporate hierarchies by naming one another co-presidents of NETCO (as Marie L. Fleming has suggested).[66] Their use of an acronym to sign their art conveyed that they were not expressing subjectivities but rather entering into a pre-existing discourse. This was a crucial concept within conceptualist art, which represented art as fully mediated – as the product of intermediations and thus corporate (with the bodily pun intended). As McLuhan wrote in 1966, '[t]oday self-expression is meaningless because there is no public. There is only the mass ... The whole complaint about elite art versus mass art is irrelevant because it ignores the technologies in question. Advertising can be regarded as a profoundly important art form, but it is not private self-expression. The newspaper is a profoundly important form of expression, but it's not self-expression. Take the date line off a newspaper and it becomes an exotic and fascinating surrealist poem.'[67] Elsewhere McLuhan speaks of this new sense of self as 'containing, simultaneously, many selves, all in flux, yet each present,' since '[s]table experience is of little value when we face the Niagara of information made possible by electric technology.'[68]

If transcendence were possible through such works of art it was not through transcendence of the art object, but through the perceptions it encouraged; Lucy Lippard quotes conceptualist Douglas Huebler as saying that '[t]he person who sits and looks at a TV set in any room and watches the man in the spacecraft, or stepping on the moon, makes a literal spatial jump that goes beyond any perceptual frame he could possibly have. Then there is the information that tells him that that picture is not contained in that frame; that picture is like 240,000 miles away, or however far the moon is, and it absolutely demands language. I don't think any of us jumping over into language are interested in pure information, or pure poetry, *but it would be a kind of McLuhan world where we do transcend the space that we can ordinarily perceive.*'[69] This is an especially insightful comment, in that it indicates both the critical potentiality of intermediated art and that one of the primary functions of art is to alter perception in terms of habitual constructions of space (which, in artistic terms, was primarily visual). In these terms, the notion of 'environment' took on special significance, as is shown by NETCO's works, many of which seek to represent the environment as mediated – as much of an artifact as the 'Bagged Place.'[70] Once the environment is conceived of as being mediated, it ceases to be a passive concept and becomes an active one, as Janine Marchessault has pointed out: 'Nature in the new cosmic age of the integrated circuit is profoundly technological and technology is natural.'[71] Hence a number of NETCO's representations of 'nature' were produced on clear, inflated plastic containers (the 'depth' of which also mocks perspectival art), while in other works, 'natural' objects were placed inside clear plastic vacuum bags, techniques that owed their existence in good part to commercial forms of production that slip over ineluctably into advertising.[72] Marie Fleming has written of these works that their 'shiny surfaces have a sensuality that invests the objects with an organic vitality. Their reflectiveness, however, has the effect of partially dissolving their materiality' (12). This bivalence is crucial to understanding the media art of the period and the form of McLuhan's critique of it. Taking the concept of environment to its logical (McLuhanesque) conclusion, NETCO produced landscapes through a process of signage, framing a particular expanse of land with signs stating 'Start Viewing' and 'Stop Viewing' an 'N.E. Thing Co. Landscape.' NETCO proposed a similar project with a cross-Canada venue, the '5,000 Mile Movie,' which would have been a film of the geographical space from Long Beach to St John's together with interviews of people encountered along the way; the proposed film 'made an analogy between the position of film viewers and car riders as detached spectators who experience space in linear progression and in predominantly visual terms.'[73] The artists' reading of McLuhan's 'cultural corporatism,' through the paradoxical stance of the global village, allowed them to produce works 'which dealt with the landscape and geography in direct dialogue with the geographical politics of Canada in the sixties and seventies.'[74]

Another (realized) project, had six photographers[75] in different time zones throughout North America taking pictures of similar objects; the results of this corporate artwork, in the words of Dennis Young, '"have the effect of replacing our linear concept of space/time with the apprehension of what might be called a simultaneous space/time mosaic"' (quoted by Fleming 58). Like 'Bagged Place,' this work illustrates the ways in which spaces are not natural but constructed – produced as acts, rather than static. In a similar vein, NETCO photocopied objects such as bottles, took photographs of 'natural' landscapes (as on the cover of this book), and produced works with the title 'Bagged Landscape.' Such activities 'extended the concept of landscape to include all types of visual information and images' in 'accordance with McLuhanesque theory' (Fleming 24). These activities are brilliantly insightful enactments of McLuhan's notion that the earth had become artifactual with *Sputnik*, especially given that this landscape would most probably be 'viewed' *through* another medium: the automobile, whose windshield has become the postmodernist framing device *par excellence* (equivalent to the eighteenth-century Claude glass). One photo-documentation of an N.E. Thing Co. Landscape in fact includes a rear-view mirror in its frame, an *hommage* to McLuhan's contention that 'the medium is the rear-view mirror.' NETCO also used telecopiers and telex to produce locally works whose spatial environments were global (reconfiguring political borderlines in the process),[76] thereby challenging commonly held notions of space and time (cf Shaw 32). 'The artists perceived Canada's communications as a natural resource, a built-in, untapped wealth with McLuhan as its first miner' (Fleming 90). The artists also perceived that landscape in an artifactual environment dominated by the photograph was a set of relationships; as Colomina suggests, photography participates in the decentred space first established by the railway: '[t]he railway, which knows only of departure and arrival points, turns cities into *points* ... connected to the diagrammatical railway network that is now the territory. This notion of space has nothing to do with that of space as an enclosure within certain limits, a notion the Greeks bequeathed to us along with the agora. It is a space that recognizes only points and directions, not the void and that which surrounds it, a space that does not know of limits but of relations' (*Privacy and Publicity* 50). This realization of place as dislocation reflects the (post)colonial positioning endemic to the Baxters' art, which exploited communications in such a way as to highlight the paradoxical centrality of marginalized locations within the global art market. There was a general tendency within conceptualism to decentre the artwork both in consumerist terms and in terms of centre and periphery through this process of dislocation (including the dislocation of the 'artist'). As Jeff Wall has stated, '[w]hat conceptual art did ... was give young artists a way out of a romantic concept of the artist into an undefined, and maybe even undefinable, concept of the artist which was open to respond to things that were happening in the real world. And, to take it one step further, it also began to obliterate the idea that modern culture was rooted in the capital cities of the Western world and that it was possible by means of media to break down the idea that important art happened in capital cities and that subsidiary art happened in subsidiary cities.'[77] It is this focus on context – the local (with the Baxters' North Vancouver house and garden featuring in a number of their art-works) – as facilitated by an increasing globalization through electronic media, that was among the most important influences McLuhan had on Canadian art of this period, at once an enactment of the paradox of the global village and of the environment/counter-environment dynamic that McLuhan saw as increasingly constitutive of artistic produc-tion. As William Wood writes, 'NETCO's project did not suspend the centre but, instead, it represented the very tense relations which define positions around the appropriation of space and practices' (17).

Tied to the increasingly contextual aspect of conceptualism was the McLuhanesque notion that an artwork was something that trains the perceptions. As McLuhan wrote in 1966, 'Today the whole idea of art is that it is an instrument of discovery and percep-tion.'[78] Taking as their point of departure the notion that sensory perception had been fragmented through the effects of print media, conceptualists sought to reintegrate sensory perception through multimedia artworks that questioned the primacy of the visual. This was the motivating force for those artists (including Iain Baxter) who met as Intermedia, as well as those who worked with R. Murray Schafer at the Centre for Communications and the Arts at Simon Fraser University. As Schafer wrote in 1968, '"we have been intent on developing technique and content for a new teaching which does not break the creative primal unity of the senses. Or rather let us say they have already been broken and we are concerned with reconfiguring them in natural fields of simultaneous interaction"' (quoted by Fleming 32). NETCO thus created a system of Sensitivity Information in four categories: visual, aural, kinaesthetic, and experiential. '"All artists,"' stated Iain Baxter, '"all painters and sculptors are simply 'visual-sensory informers': people who handle our world's information, putting it together in colour and shapes"' (quoted in Fleming 37). The singular advantage of this form of nomenclature was its lack of subservience to traditional artistic hierarchies: '"if you call it Sound Sensitivity Information,"' stated Iain Baxter, '"then you shed all your hang-ups about what music is and what it is supposed to be and become open to sound as sensitivity information"' (quoted by Fleming 37). NETCO carried this farther, proclaiming as ACTs those objects they deemed 'Aesthetically Claimed Things,' and as ARTs those they deemed 'Aesthetically Rejected Things.' These categories applied to canonical works of art as well; thus, Duchamp's readymades were rejected as ARTs, while his other works were accepted as ACTs. Once again, NETCO plays on its own 'corporate' status and that of the art object, rejecting the readymades because they had become completely ab-sorbed within the art market, while critiquing the notion that the artwork could ever completely escape its corporate context (where 'corporate' means at once the art market as well as the collective aspect of artistic production).

Psychogeographies

Writing about NETCO in 1968, the New York art critic Lucy Lippard (who had a long association with the Vancouver art scene) remarked how surprised she was that '"provin-cial"' artists such as the Baxters could be exploring artistic ideas that 'often coincided point by point with those unpublished projects in the planning stages in New York and Europe at the time, with which the Baxters could not be familiar' (*Six Years* 67). Lippard explains this coincidence by arguing that the 'points of departure' for these artists 'were, of course, the same (Morris, Nauman, Ruscha, etc.).' Another possibility is that the point of departure was, in the case of a number of these artists, the work of McLuhan, the dissemination of which began in the 1940s and by the mid- to late 1960s had become a significant part of the artistic 'ground.' This internationalizing of the milieu in which artists were working was in large part a response to and a utilization of the media of electronic communication, which were becoming increasingly accessible and increasingly integrated into the artwork itself; it also spoke to the politics of the period. As Tony Godfrey puts it, '[t]he notion of an international community of artists, in constant communication with one another, was a highly attractive one in this period of anti-nationalist sentiments' (167). In McLuhan's work, this anti-nationalistic sentiment was consistent with his notion that nationalism was a product of print and that electronic media were breaking down traditional political boundaries.[79]

It is important to remember that McLuhan's reputation was already significant prior to the 1960s. As Daniel Belgrad has demonstrated, McLuhan had entered into the art/literature discourse of the United States by the late 1940s; at the same time, McLuhan was publishing in England on advertising, with Cyril Connolly's *Horizon* magazine as his venue.[80] By the 1950s, as Gary Genosko has remarked, McLuhan had become one of the few 'international' figures in cultural studies, preceding his entry into the ambit of French intellectual critique in the 1960s.[81] It is thus not surprising to find Margaret Garlake commenting, in her study of postwar British art, that 'the key book for the sharpest minds at the Royal College of Art in 1956–7 was not by Jung or Sartre but was Marshall McLuhan's *The Mechanical Bride*.'[82] Particularly noteworthy is the fact that McLuhan's presence was being felt most acutely among the avant-garde artists of the period; and, as Alex Seago has recently argued, it was precisely in this milieu, as opposed to that of high (institutionalized) art, that the origins of British postmodernist art can be found.[83] As early as 1957, arts magazines in Britain were publishing articles 'heavily influenced by the writing of media theorist Marshall McLuhan' (115).[84] Seago goes on to note that 'McLuhan's positive attitude towards the electronic media stood in stark contrast to the uniformly negative outlook of the majority of university-based British cultural critics. His argument that mass culture and avant-garde culture were not diametrically opposed was not confined to the arts; McLuhan argued, for example, that avant-garde science in the shape of Einstein's Theory of Relativity discarded the same fixed three-dimensional world whose illusory solidity Cubism had also helped to expose' (166).

McLuhan's 1947 *Horizon* article on advertising[85] opens with the observation that, in the United States (as opposed to Europe), advertising has taken the place of politics. Instead of moralizing about this, however, McLuhan seeks to read the political elements in the ads. This is especially important to him as an intellectual: rather than set himself apart from popular culture – like 'a sort of noble savage free-lancing amidst a zombie horde' (14) – he must acknowledge that he is a part of this culture; in a world where ads employ the same techniques as high art, the distinction between popular and highbrow culture is no longer operable, and this must have a bearing on the role of the critic. Here, *in nuce*, we can see the elements that attracted contemporary artists to McLuhan: the breaking down of artistic hierarchies; the positing of the political in the broad sphere of cultural activity; the awareness that the intellectual and artist could not separate themselves from that which they were critiquing. In a subsequent article, 'Advertising as a Magical Institution' (1952), McLuhan argued that ads are important, based on the fact that 'they provide the largest single base for ordinary inter-communication in modern society.'[86] Rather than making moral arguments for or against advertising, suggests McLuhan, 'What is urgently needed is a study of the relation of advertising to other techniques of communication in industrial society' (25). The moral argument that devolves into a highbrow versus lowbrow dichotomy is particularly to be avoided, as it obscures the cultural dialogue that informs ads: 'unfortunate terms and attitudes as "high-brow" and "low-brow" ... effectively blind people to the perennial flow of perception and impulse from the few to the many and from the many to the few ... The function of art in society is of this systole-diastole kind which perfects the possibilities of intercommunication [as] a particular movement of the culture' (26–7). McLuhan emphasizes the social and material dimensions of such a critique: '[b]ecause it is evident that the advertising industry is geared to the processes of mass production and distribution, it accepts as its peculiar material to be processed *nothing less than the society itself*' (25; emphasis added). It is particularly important to take a critical attitude to the ad because 'its maximal effect depends on its not arousing too much attention or curiosity' (26). Artists are in a particularly advantageous position to critique these advertisements, since 'the principles of ad construction are exactly those of symbolist poetry and cubist painting' (28).

Among the British artists who took up this challenge were the Independent Group (IG), who were responsible for launching Pop Art in postwar Britain.[87] (The artwork by which they are most readily identified is Richard Hamilton's famous collage, *Just what is it that makes today's homes so different, so appealing?*). The IG was particularly influenced by *The Mechanical Bride* (Robbins 59), published the year before they formalized their association, as well as by Giedion's *Mechanization Takes Command* and Moholy-Nagy's *Vision in Motion* (Robbins 55). The IG was impressed by the mode of analysis in *The Mechanical Bride* as well as by the ads themselves, a number of which they appropriated for their own works. As David Robbins remarks, '[i]n its discussions and in much of the artistic production of its members, the IG drew upon the avant-garde "found object" legacy to assert both the aesthetic excitement of this image-saturated world and its democratizing implications. This challenged not only the traditionalism and anticommercialism of British high culture, but also the modernist establishment at the ICA, typified by Herbert Read's commitment to a universalizing aesthetic' (58). McLuhan lectured at the ICA in June of 1963 on 'Changing Modes of Perception since TV.'[88] While the text of this talk has not survived, it can be deduced from the title: television, an audile-tactile medium, is having an effect on the interrelations of the senses by correcting the hegemony of the visual sense. The content of the lecture, however, may in this case have been less important than the context: not only was the ICA the hotbed of avant-garde artistic activity in Britain in the 1960s, it was a magnet for avant-garde groups from outside Britain as well. Among these were the Situationists, a French anarcho-Dadaist group.[89] Lawrence Alloway, the IG member most influenced by McLuhan,[90] was a major link between the Situationists and their London colleague, Ralph Rumney, founder of the Psychogeographic Society (Seago 117–18), which was subsequently incorporated into the Situationist International.[91] The Situationists and the IG 'shared a determination to penetrate the outward, spectacular, commercialized signs of mass culture and explore its interior. There one examined the everyday patterns of life, in particular people's use of buildings and urban space.'[92]

The importance of the connection between McLuhan and the Situationists (one that the latter spent a significant amount of time repudiating)[93] is that it highlights the material implications of McLuhan's cultural theories, especially as they pertain to advertising and to the built environment. As Timothy Nye has suggested, the encounter of artistic production with urban space was inevitable, once the art practices of the period had repudiated the institutional space of the museum.[94] The move towards the urban was especially evident in performance art and Happenings; as Christel Hollevoet remarks, these forms provided 'a non-optical apprehension of urban space' (30). In the case of the Situationists, who had been greatly influenced by Henri Lefebvre's notions of the production of urban space, these urban activities were known as *dérives*, or 'drifts' through the urban landscape, that mapped a 'psychogeography,' a form of cognitive mapping through the labyrinth created by the spectacular – that world of mass-media images that, for McLuhan and the Situationists alike, was a sort of extruded uncon-sciousness, like 'dreaming awake,' as McLuhan suggested in his Vision 65 address (*EM* 225).[95] That McLuhan's theories could accommodate both the IG, with their embrace (often ironic, as in Richard Hamilton's famous collage) of mass culture, and the Situationist International, with their repudiation of it,[96] indicates how the dynamic nature of McLuhan's cultural theories allowed for the diametrically opposed readings that characterized the response to his work from the 1960s onward. McLuhan argued that a moralistic rejection of mass culture was not the point – it was too important to reject; what was necessary was to understand it critically. As he wrote in 1952, 'if there is any virus for the human mind contained in this material [,] immunity can always be purchased for the cost of critical analysis' ('Advertising as a Magical Institution' 29). In practice, McLuhan took a position dialogically between the extremes of his reception.

In *The Situationist City*, Simon Sadler has remarked on numerous congruities between the work of McLuhan and that of the Situationists.[97] Like McLuhan, the Situationists saw mass media as having a profound effect on everyday life; given their urban concerns, they were particularly taken with the ways in which media affected the production of space, projecting an '"ideal urbanism"' devoid of conflict of any sort (Sadler 16). Television was particularly cited in this regard, in that its ability to produce spectacular effects was so powerful as to affect 'the perception of real space' (16, 1.1); this had been the topic of McLuhan's ICA lecture in 1963 (judging by the title). One of the methods used by the Situationists to problematize the continuity of space produced by spectacular culture was *détournement*, a form of appropriation that used the appropri-ated element against itself (in a collage, for example). Architecture was one of their major targets because, as one of them put it, it '"is the simplest means of articulating time and space"' (Sadler 69). The Situationists were particularly opposed to housing projects and the concomitant urban sprawl, a spreading out in space that promoted circulation over encounter, and increasing homogeneity. They celebrated, in contrast, the pre-Modernist jumbles that had resisted urbanization; through a series of *dérives*, or drifts, they moved through the city in a form of proto-performance art, heavily documenting their activities.[98] This documentation often took the form of a psychogeography – a deconstructed map (in this case, of Paris) that 'simultaneously mourned the loss of old Paris, prepared for the city of the future, explored the city's structures and uses, criticized traditional mapping, and investigated the relationship between language, narrative, and cognition' (Sadler 60). One such pyschogeography, 'The Naked City' (1957), takes the form of fragments of the map of Paris interrelated by lines of flow – the city as process, as series of dynamic interchanges, rather than as static, rationalist grid. (Interestingly, this psychogeographical map takes its name from a work of American popular culture.) Other psychogeographies (such as Ralph Rumney's of Venice), presented themselves as collages interspersed with text (Sadler 79). In these psychogeographies, the Situationists were not proposing the preservation of 'historic' spots in the city; this was a form of museumization that they strongly opposed, in a move paralleling the conceptualists' opposition to the museum as having institutionalized and thereby delimited the notion of art and where it could be produced. What the Situationists sought in their drifts through the city was '"history in space,"'[99] counterposing thus '"the undifferentiated state of the visible-readable realm"' of academic geographies (as Lefebvre had put it). Rather than a literate model of geography, thus, the Situationists adopted an auditory model. If poetry was in the form of cities (Sadler 96), as their Lettrist forebears (a group devoted to the iconographical sign as a vehicle for social change) had argued, then psychogeography would reinvent the language of that poetry as 'an ongoing dialogue' (Sadler 96). The Situationists thus represented psychogeographic space in terms of 'sound or motion,' akin to Frederick Kiesler's installations (Sadler 112), or environments. In this space, 'architecture would merge seamlessly with all other arts, assailing the senses not with a single aesthetic but with a panoply of changing ambiances' (Sadler 119). Hence the significance of the 'Naked City' allusion: the detective negotiates the visual space of the city orally.

What promotes the numerous parallels between the work of McLuhan and that of the Situationists is the notion that architecture is a medium, insofar as it represents an extension of the body (cf Sadler 148; McLuhan, *UM* ch. 13). As a mode of communication, architecture could, then, potentially fulfil the Lettrists' notion of the city as a form of poetry. One of the Situationists' major architectural projects, dubbed 'New Babylon,' sought to achieve that status in its very unbuildability.[100] Sadler sees the utopian nature of this project as deriving from the immersion of Constant (the chief architect of New Babylon) in the cybernetics of Norbert Wiener, and argues that McLuhan shares this utopian orientation for similar reasons. McLuhan's comments on architecture (published in *The Canadian Architect* in 1961, as well as in *Perspecta*, the Princeton architecture journal, in 1965), however, have a singularly material focus, consistent with his rejection of Wiener's cybernetic model as having ignored 'noise' – that aspect of communication excluded by the Shannon-Weaver model but which McLuhan considered the context (or medium) through which any communication (including an architectural one) comes into being. We thus find McLuhan writing, in his 1961 article, 'Inside the Five Sense Sensorium,' that architects should take heed of auditory space, which is 'quite unvisualizable, and, therefore, to the merely print-oriented ... "unintelligible." Today the entire human community is being translated into "auditory space," or into that "field of simultaneous relations," by electric broadcasting' (52). McLuhan's argument is that town planning is based on the grid, and that the grid derives from print technology: 'It seems quite obvious that the lineality that invaded every kind of spatial organization from the 16th. century onward had as its archetype and matrix the metal lines of Gutenberg's uniform and repeatable types' (54). The article then asks: 'How to breathe life into the lineal forms of the past five centuries while admitting the relevance of the new organic forms of spatial organization (what I have explained as "auditory space" above) – is not this the task of the architect at present? But what chance has he of tackling this task at all if he has no understanding of the media forms which informed the architecture of recent centuries or of the new media forms which inspire the Bauhaus fashions of the present?' (54). McLuhan's position is a typically dialogical one, seeking to accommodate aspects of the inherited architectural tradition, while not ignoring the importance of contemporary forms. This oscillation between environment and counter-environment likewise characterizes a version of his Vision 65 article, published in *Perspecta* as 'Environment: The Future of an Erosion,' where the Freudian allusion[101] brings together the psychological and the geographical in a way that parallels the Situationists' psychogeographies (and that McLuhan would expand on in his essay 'Canada: The Borderline Case,' written contemporaneously; see ch. 8 below). In the *Perspecta* article, McLuhan advances the argument that environments are historically related: 'every new technology creates an environment that translates the old or preceding technology into an art form' (164). As we have seen, McLuhan provides the example of Pop Art, which 'consists in taking the outer environment and putting it in an art gallery ... suggesting that we have reached the stage where we have begun to process the environment itself as an art form' (165). Yet McLuhan does not posit a way outside this environment except through technology itself: 'There is no possible protection from technology except by technology. When you create a new environment with one phase of a technology, you have to create an anti-environment with the next' (166). The environment is no less material for the fact that it is invisible, an 'erosion' in the sense that it is both illusory (invisible) and in a dynamic relationship with the counter-environment, which will erode the environment's hegemony only to become environmental itself.

In Flux

Christel Hollevoet has likened the Situationists to the Fluxus artists (both of which groups were influenced by the Lettrists) in that their performance activities 'point to the crucial concern in artistic practices from the late 1950s to the 1970s for the topographical apprehension of urban space ... They signal a shift from the avant-garde critique of art to the critique of everyday life; from ... opposition to the popular from "outside and above" to participation in it from the inside' (as quoted above). Fluxus (most active between 1962 and 1978) was concerned primarily with performance art and intermedia, and had its origins in avant-garde music, with John Cage as one of its primary motivators. McLuhan is linked to this group through his connection to Cage, as well as to Dick Higgins, another major figure in the group.[102] Higgins formulated the theoretical umbrella under which Fluxus events took place with his 1966 'Statement on Intermedia,' in which he made the familiar point (for that time) that 'Art is one of the ways that people communicate.'[103] The statement argues that electronic media, such as television, have altered people's 'sensitivities' (172), and that this has promoted a need for simple images (in McLuhan's terms: ideograms). At the same time, traditional artistic forms have broken down, and it is here that the new art is located: 'This is the intermedial approach, to emphasize the dialectic between the media' (172).[104] Higgins then questions the social function of these intermedia: 'Having discovered tools with an immediate impact, for what are we going to use them? If we assume, unlike McLuhan and others who have shed some light on the problem up until now, that there are dangerous forces at work in our world, isn't it appropriate to ally ourselves against these, and to use what we really care about and love or hate as the new subject matter of our work? ... We must find the ways to say what has to be said in the light of our new means of communicating' (173). Higgins's statement focuses the chief debate that would take place around McLuhan's work as the conceptualism of the 1960s moved towards the post-conceptualism of the 1970s and the neo-conceptualism of the 1980s, a movement that can be described as a shift of focus from concept to context, from figure to ground, from message to medium: what should the position be of the artist/intellectual with regard to technology?[105] In McLuhan criticism, this debate focuses on whether McLuhan was an unrepentant utopian or whether he changed his position towards the end of his career from a celebration of technology to a condemnation of it.[106]

McLuhan's notion of technology was, consistently, that it was an extension of the body, and, as a human product, was subject to critique and control. Thus, *The Gutenberg Galaxy* repeatedly critiques the worldview promoted by print technology. The mode of critique McLuhan advocated was an interficial one, environment in dialogue with counter-environment. He therefore insisted on the importance of interfaces – those artistic/critical expressions that juxtaposed media; indeed, he argued that the contemporary 'multiplicity of media' allowed a degree of freedom from the 'servo-mechanism of ... technologies.'[107] He also made strong statements against applied technology – technology as product rather than process. While he rejected the moralistic tone he had taken in *The Mechanical Bride*, he did not cease to take a critical position towards negative aspects of technology, and particularly the technologies of visual space, which he identified as the site *par excellence* of social and cultural control. McLuhan's insistence that the first step in developing a critical attitude towards technology was the recognition that technology is a human product was put to the test most powerfully in the video art of the period, which took on the medium – television – with which McLuhan had become identified most closely and that appeared to encapsulate the most liberating and the most threatening aspects of the electronic revolution.[108] Television was perceived in a number of contradictory ways: it 'threatened' the literacy whose effects artists were critiquing on numerous fronts; it 'promised' global artistic communities while raising the spectre that broadcast powers would come increasingly under more centralized control; it appeared to call for an artistic response that would reinvoke the very hierarchies against which artists were protesting. No other medium, in short, captured so well the technophilia and technophobia of the period, as well as McLuhan's agonistic response towards media generally. As Sara Diamond states, 'Marshall McLuhan had argued that "information" was the true modern commodity, and that communications technology and the social relations it engendered would increasingly determine consciousness. While he warned against the existing monopoly of power, McLuhan concentrated on the internationalizing and potentially liberating possibilities of interactive mass communications ... At the same time a materialist critique of the mass media developed which compared the relations of social production to increasingly centralized means of communications.'[109] As Diamond notes, the focus of video art was increasingly on the social: 'Video, with its seemingly organic relation to the social, was the ideal medium for intervention and interactivity. It allowed for a practice parallel to that of the mass media, and it offered not only a means through which to open a discourse with the dominant culture, but also to explore different modes of perception' (51).

In general, video production has followed a similar trajectory to that of conceptualist art, from a focus on the medium itself to a focus on context, especially as it raises issues of race, class, gender, sexual orientation, and so on.[110] Video art also presented a contestation of the power of the museum as validator of artistic practice (what NETCO parodied with its 'ART' and 'ACT' labels); indeed, in one notorious incident, a video work was deemed 'not art' by the director of a major metropolitan gallery.[111] Not only did video reproduce the cultural form considered to be the icon of bourgeois existence, but it was ephemeral, 'not there' in a way that disturbed the dictates of museum collecting. Furthermore, video art, by the nature of the medium, was complicit with that which it sought to critique; as Renée Baert has remarked, '[i]ts identity shifts uncomfortably between its status as art and its ambitions as television.'[112] Video has responded to this critical situation by retrieving narrative – the prime characteristic of the print media it displaced – as a way of countering the fragmentation of televisual representation (cf *UM* 321). At the same time, it has sought, in many cases, to personalize what it conceived of as an impersonal medium (cf Diamond 49) while exploiting the potential for mass communication by using video locally (as in documentary practice) to set up networks that create '"communications links around the world, decentralizing media processes away from any elite."'[113] One of the effects of this strategy was to acknowledge (albeit indirectly) what McLuhan referred to as the tactility of the medium – its ability to invoke multisensory involvement in a way unavailable to print media.[114] This 'embodiment' of video often took the form of sound – a particular voice that gave the video a 'performative quality' (Diamond 59) allowing those normally denied representation within the mass media to have a voice. Another strategy involved placing text over the image, emphasizing the mediated nature of what was being viewed; this strategy was a powerful example of the critical potential of a hybrid medium.

These video strategies speak to the larger concerns of performative artworks as pursued by Fluxus artists and others. Like McLuhan, the Fluxus artists sought to encourage people to take upon themselves the condition of artists, although theirs was a transcendent model. George Maciunas, their longtime coordinator, wrote in a 1962 essay, 'Neo-Dada in Music, Theater, Poetry, Art,'[115] that '[i]f man could experience the world, the concrete world surrounding him, (from mathematical ideas to physical matter) in the same way he experiences art, there would be no need for art, artists and similar "nonproductive" elements' (*In the Spirit of Fluxus* 157). Whereas Maciunas wanted to close the gap between art and life, however, McLuhan wanted us to recognize the extent to which our environment had become artifactual. Only when we had ceased taking it to be 'natural' would we be in a position to critique it, though that position would be from within – hence McLuhan's emphasis on perception rather than transcendence. In both cases, however, the goal was to bring art as a material *practice* (rather than an object) into social space (beyond the museum), transforming that space in the process.

The core activities of Fluxus artists were in publishing and in performance; the events they produced have been described as '"language happenings."'[116] They thus began, as did the Situationists (though less conservatively), with a consideration of the role of print within the larger cultural domain; many of their publications were devoted to (self-) advertisements, and some of their theorizing was given over to the book as medium.[117] Typical of these publications was 'the agglomeration of words and letters into pattern as much as text' (Anderson, 'Fluxus Publicus,' 42), such that the printed work could be made to 'sound' by transforming it into the simultaneity of an icon; indeed, this is one of the characteristic artistic manoeuvres of the period (as in the work of bpNichol). One of the offshoots of the Fluxus publication program was Dick Higgins's Something Else Press; as Simon Anderson remarks, Higgins's texts 'stayed closer to the original ideas of Maciunas than did Fluxus' (52). Collectively, these books 'gave a much-needed context to the work of an entire generation of artists who had begun dissolving the barriers between the arts' (52). Many of the Fluxus publications were boxed cards – deconstructed books, in effect, with the box an homage to Duchamp. These *Fluxkits* (*ca* 1964–70), with their assembly of items, parallel the publication of McLuhan's *Dew-Line Newsletters* (1968–70), which were constructed similarly (one of them containing a deck of cards);[118] in both cases, a major goal of this form of publication was to involve the consumer as a producer of the text, with those concepts being deconstructed in the process. The Fluxus production of T-shirts – including a McLuhan T-shirt – filled this purpose admirably, the wearer fleshing out the concept, as it were.[119] The Fluxus artists also sought to subvert the alliance between art and museums, producing ephemeral works that could be neither exhibited nor sold.

This critique of museum space is an explicit aspect of performance art, which sought to transform spaces rather than simply fill those spaces as content. These transformed spaces emphasized the bodily – often crudely and with vulgarity (in the tradition of the great scatalogical thinkers such as Rabelais, whose work McLuhan deeply admired). The performance activities of Fluxus and similar groups thus enacted a prosthetic aesthetic of the sort McLuhan had developed in *Understanding Media*, whereby the media of expression were indissolubly associated with sensory extensions, as when Nam June Paik interpreted La Monte Young's score for *Composition 1960 #10 to Bob Morris* – 'Draw a straight line and follow it' – by dipping his head, hands and necktie into a bowl of ink and tomato juice and then dragging them along a length of paper (*Spirit of Fluxus* 14–15).[120] The Fluxus use of masks is also significant in this regard, as with the 'John Lennon Mask' or the 'Yoko Ono Mask,' both of which fuse the prosthetic with the mediatized.[121] Many Fluxus performance works sought to enact the extension of the mediatized body in this way. These works were closely associated with the anti-Cartesianism that McLuhan had linked to post-print culture. Hence Lefebvre's remarks in *The Production of Space* (written *circa* 1970): '[t]oday the body is establishing itself firmly, as base and foundation, *beyond philosophy*, beyond discourse, and beyond the theory of discourse. Theoretical thought, carrying reflection on the subject and the object beyond the old concepts, has re-embraced the body along with space, in space, and as the generator (or producer) of space. To say that such theoretical thinking goes "beyond discourse" means that it takes account, for the purposes of a pedagogy of the body, of the vast store of non-formal knowledge embedded in poetry, music, dance and theatre. This store of non-formal knowledge (*non-savoir*) constitutes a potential true knowledge (*connaissance*)' (407). Many of these 'bodies of meaning' were set up as Fluxus concerts, further establishing the connections between the production of sound and the production of space, what Steve McCaffery calls 'performance as a spatial disposition by which history enters the written body.'[122] Often taking the form of '"action music,"' these events sought to merge the audible with the visible (Maciunas, quoted by Stiles 72), as in the event where the performer nails down the keys of a piano.[123]

The work of John Cage was crucially important to the performance aesthetic of Fluxus – 'the most musical of the avant-garde ... art movements of this century'[124] – especially in its breaking down of the boundary between performance and composition, through which the notion of author and interpretive authority are radically contested. A pupil of Schoenberg's in the 1940s, Cage had begun his own teaching at the Black Mountain School, where in 1952 he performed his first musical Happening. These performance/compositions began with the notion of sound; in a move paralleling the conceptualists' attempt to move art out of the rarefied space of the museum, the Fluxus sound artists sought to take music out of the concert hall (as Glenn Gould had, as well) and embrace with it all the sounds of the environment, in the way that Edgard Varèse had done when incorporating sounds such as sirens into his musical compositions. George Maciunas used the term 'concrete' to describe such sounds, among which he included human speech, because such sounds indicated their 'true source' and 'material reality.'[125] Cage's artistic practice sought to break down the distinction between music and sound; all sounds could be used in music, he argued. In such terms, noise disappeared into music, as it did in Cage's famous composition *4'33"*, emphasizing (in the words of Bruce Jenkins) 'the *materiality* of the medium.'[126] As Douglas Kahn points out, Cage's theories of sound were made in response to technological changes in the production of sound: 'with the advent of the acoustic and electronic mass media, the number of sounds and their associations actually accumulated, proliferated, and became accelerated; what once may have been assuredly "natural" sound, for instance, might have become both common and oblique, immediately familiar but ultimately understandable only at the end of a fairly fragile, long string of associations. This was certainly the state of aurality by the 1950s, for there had been more than two decades of sound film and radio broadcast, and television was on the rise' (103). Cage's performance practices, and those of the Fluxus artists, were particularly important in accentuating the spatial values of sonic production. They did this most often by using the technique of holding a note for a considerable length of time; as Kahn remarks, 'A space "filled" with an almost palpable sound develops around one's body, thereby heightening a sense of corporeality, especially when the body is vibrated by amplified sound' (108). This location of the sonic in the bodily also served as the basis for an empathic translation of the acoustic into related areas of artistic production, from publication to performance, as well as for an empathic interrelation of the senses. A number of Cage's performance pieces, in their performativity, require one to 'listen' with the eyes as well as the ears (and, in some Fluxus events, with the hands and the nose and the mouth).

Cage placed McLuhan among a personal 'Great Tradition' of artist/intellectuals who included Thoreau, Joyce, Stein, Wittgenstein, Schoenberg, Duchamp, Satie, and Fuller.[127] The most significant aspect of McLuhan's work for Cage was his deconstruction of the notions of 'inside' and 'outside.' Cage had already problematized these notions in *4'33"* by reversing the figure of performer and the ground of audience; McLuhan's notion of media as prosthetic extensions of body and mind, together with his notion of environment as implosion of nature and culture, allowed Cage to expand the implications of *4'33"* on a number of fronts, all of which pertained to 'boundary' issues. Cage's focus on sound made it inevitable that he should address such issues. As Frances Dyson has remarked, 'sound's continuity, its ability to merge with other sounds, and its lack of borders represent for Cage a phenomenal equivalent to the artistic concepts of interpenetration, unimpededness, and nonobstruction, active processes that ensure the indeterminacy and hence freedom of performance when adopted as a creative strategy.'[128] Among the boundary issues addressed by Cage are the critique of the notion that art must be an expression of subjectivity, something that emerges from 'inside' the self. Cage's artistic practices were collective, collaborative, and profoundly critical of the power structures of intentionality through their dependence (in many cases) on chance operations. Cage's performance practices also sought to break down the boundary between artist and intellectual, as in Cage's own career, where many of his works, from *Silence* to *Rolywholyover A Circus*, combine the functions of art and critique. Thirdly, his performance practices sought to provide a social paradigm of non-hierarchical interrelationships; as Gordana Crnković remarks, '[i]n Cage's horizontal plurality of centres, alternative communication is made possible by developed technology. At present, technology is used in existing social formations (capitalism, mass culture) for particular power goals. However, Cage believes that this same technology could be used as a means for horizontal communication in which everyone could directly communicate with everyone else, without the use of an intermediary or external centre ... This freedom does not turn others into passive objects, but rather presupposes their active agency.'[129] This notion of multiple centres characterizes at once Cage's social philosophy and his performance practices, which tend from the sequentiality of time towards the inclusiveness of space: 'Activities which are different / happen in a time which is a space: / are each central, original.'[130] This space is reminiscent of McLuhan's acoustic space, which he described as having only centres and no margins; it also gestures towards the social context of that space in its suggestion that consumers of culture can learn to be performers of culture within a space constructed acoustically. In Cage's work, this space takes the form of a *sensus communis*, which is both the senses in interaction as well as a community of sensibilities – the retribalized world of acoustic space. However, as Daniel Herwitz has pointed out, Cage's community is 'unlike Kant's Enlightenment community, which is based on sameness of taste, morals, and rationality ... Cage's idea of a musical body is one in which the free play of differences are given vent and let be without interference.'[131] The conflation of the multisensory with the communal was an important one for Cage and McLuhan alike. As Kant remarks in the *Critique of Judgment*, 'by the name *sensus communis* is to be understood the idea of a *public* sense,'[132] and while it is as true for McLuhan as for Cage that the community they espouse is one based on differences, the communitarian quality of the *sensus communis* is of crucial importance to an understanding of the social dimension of acoustic space, with its implication of sensory modalities in interaction, unlike that of a social praxis based on the isolated sense of vision, which is panoptical in the sense developed by Foucault. In this context it is significant that *4'33"* addresses (and, in doing so, creates) a specific social space – as Joan Retallack suggests, art, for Cage, *is* the life experience it draws our attention to.[133] As McLuhan demonstrated in numerous articles on the notions of inside and outside, such notions are not 'natural' but socially constructed. The article 'Inside on the Outside, or the Spaced-Out American' focuses on the 'paradox of "reversed space"' (143) whereby 'the American finds indoors the warmth and sociability that the European cultivates outside the home'[134] while the European seeks privacy at home, in contrast to the North American, who goes home to be sociable. McLuhan likewise sees evidence of this in Margaret Atwood's observations in *Survival* about the tendency within Canadian literature to present the outside world as hostile, a tendency that began to reverse itself with environmentally conscious literature. And in McLuhan's 1963 article 'The Agenbite of Outwit,' this notion is further elaborated: '[w]ith the telegraph Western man began a process of putting his nerves outside his body ... Since the telegraph we have extended the brains and nerves of man around the globe. As a result, the electronic age endures a total uneasiness, as of a man wearing his skull inside and his brain outside. We have become peculiarly vulnerable. The year of the establishment of the commercial telegraph in America, 1844, was also the year Kierkegaard published *The Concept of Dread*.'[135] McLuhan emphasizes here the psychical aspects of the reversal of inside and outside, though with a cautionary note that rarely enters Cage's musings on technology, a cautionary note bred from McLuhan's insistence that all extensions are likewise amputations.

Cage's work subsequent to *4'33"* elaborated his insights through electronic technologies such as radio transmission and electronic reproduction of sounds; Cage noted how his collaboration with technicians such as sound engineers represented a 'conjunction of the in and the out' (*Silence* 62). As Dyson remarks, 'magnetic tape illustrated [for Cage] the continuum of life that tonality and thinking had divided into discrete units' (385). Here the notion of community is still closely tied to the sensory, but has added a global dimension through the prosthetic potentialities of electronic transmission. What is noteworthy, however, is that the substantial quality of sound is not diminished in this process; as McLuhan remarked, 'the acoustic is ... material' (*L* 489). Cage was reminded of this when he entered an anechoic chamber and heard the pulsing of his own body.[136] The merging of silence with sound that confronted him there constituted the most powerful deconstruction of inside and outside that one can experience. As Dyson remarks, 'one always hears with one's body and that body is itself permeated with sound. Based in the flesh rather than the intellect, this realization marked a surrender of the absolute' (387). If, as Dyson remarks, electronics demonstrated to Cage 'the limits of silence, the limits of embodiment' (401), they did so not by enforcing those boundaries but by rendering them indeterminate.

CHAPTER EIGHT

Borderlines

Canada is a land of multiple borderlines, psychic, social, and geographic.

Marshall McLuhan, 'Canada: The Borderline Case'

(Counter)Environments

Throughout his career, McLuhan positioned himself as a Canadian; Canada was the counter-environment grounding his artistic/intellectual notions of the dynamics of spatial production. He emphasized this positioning in a statement he made late in his career about growing up on the prairies and the panoramas it had afforded him: 'I think of western skies as one of the most beautiful things about the West, and the western horizons. The Westerner doesn't have a point of view. He has a vast panorama; he has such tremendous space around him.'[1] Significantly, McLuhan expresses his insight spatially; he identified spatiality as a distinguishing feature of Canadian cultural production, as well as of the ways in which Canadians understand themselves. André Malraux had likewise remarked on this quality in 1968 when viewing works by Michael Snow and Iain Baxter at Canada's pavilion in the Paris Biennial: '"he always knew when he came to the Canadian section because we have a specific palette and a specific sense of space, different from that of the Frenchman or the American."'[2] McLuhan articulated this particular sense of space through various concepts, including those of the 'borderline' and of the counter-environment, and the fact that he did so in the mid-1960s, concurrently with major works such as *Understanding Media*, *The Medium Is the Massage*, *Culture Is Our Business*, and *War and Peace in the Global Village*, emphasizes that McLuhan understood his media theories to have a specific social and cultural situatedness. Indeed, the notion of Canada as defined spatially by its borderlines – both visible and invisible – brought together essential aspects of McLuhan's spatial theory, particularly the psychic and geographical, in a dynamic that uses linearity to undo the linear, thereby making 'borderline' into a metaphor of acoustic space: the resonant interval.

McLuhan is often said to have excluded Canada from his musings on media and communications, yet his publications indicate a consistent interest in this subject, beginning in the 1930s, when he was an MA student at the University of Manitoba, and continuing for the remainder of his career. Among these early publications is 'Canada and Internationalism' (1933).[3] The article lambastes Canada for its assumption that because it is not a military power it can sit on the sidelines as tensions rise in an increasingly nationalistic Europe. 'Economic resources,' he argues, 'are actually armaments in a sense quite as literal as airplanes are armaments.' To recognize this fact is to recognize that we must play our role on the world stage. 'We are an invaluable mediary between Europe and the United States. That fact confers a huge responsibility upon us,' writes McLuhan, using a formulation that he would return to decades later when writing on Canada's 'borderline' status. McLuhan found support for this internationalist viewpoint in a book he read during his first term teaching in St Louis (*L* 94), André Siegfried's *Canada: An International Power* (1937).[4] Siegfried casts Canada in the role of 'mediator between the English bloc and the American bloc' (22) and sees this role as taking on new importance in the postwar years, with the United States' and Russia's increasing prominence in world affairs. Siegfried also dwells on the paradox of Canadian identity: 'politically it is in England, and geographically it is in the United States – in either case outside her own boundaries' (23).

McLuhan's internationalist view of Canada allied him with one of the most significant cultural arbiters of the period, A.J.M. Smith, whose preface to the first (1943) edition of *The Book of Canadian Poetry* argued that the 'cosmopolitan' strain of Canadian poetry was superior to the 'native' one, which ran the risk of slipping into nationalistic rhetoric. Smith's position (as summarized by Donna Bennett) was that '[n]ationalism, and a national sense of self, were unimportant in the modern, global environment – in which Smith saw Canadian writers helping to define not so much Canada, but Canada's place in a new international age.'[5] McLuhan wrote an essay (unpublished) dating from the 1950s to accompany an edition of Smith's anthology[6] in which he notes the difficulties the Canadian poet has in perceiving 'some sort of autonomous centre of significance in Canadian expression,' due to the lack of linguistic homogeneity. McLuhan characterizes the English-Canadian poet as feeling 'like an amateur radio-station operator who has to compete with a national network' (2), since the 'Canadian writer has never been encouraged to imagine that English, as a medium of experience and expression, was a personal responsibility and possession,' a situation arising both from 'marginal remoteness' and from 'lack of community and conversation in an over-sized environment' (2). Quoting from T.S. Eliot's 1922 essay 'The Three Provincialities,' which suggests that there are three English literatures – Irish, American, and English – McLuhan remarks that '[w]hen a remote section of population aspires to be in the mode, it involuntarily becomes provincial. When the same group simply assumes the right to innovate and to create without any regard to modishness, it becomes an authentic centre of culture. Canada has not yet approached this state' (3). However, the shift of cultural hegemony from Europe to North America presents 'new possibilities,' in accordance with the scenario outlined by Eliot that '"literature is not primarily a matter of nationality, but of language"' (Eliot, quoted by McLuhan, 3). This anti-nationalistic position was one that McLuhan espoused consistently in this period,[7] and it appears here long before McLuhan developed it in the context of the history of print media.

McLuhan's anti-nationalist approach to Canadian culture was galvanized in 1951 with the appearance of the *Report* of the Royal Commission on National Development in the Arts, Lettters and Sciences.[8] The so-called Massey Report (or Massey-Lévesque Report) had sections on mass media; federal art institutions such as galleries; scholarship; 'the artist and the writer'; international cultural relations; and so on. The report begins by acknowledging Canada's unique geopolitical configuration, paying tribute to the contributions the United States has made to Canadian cultural life, but expressing the fear that American cultural production could easily come to dominate that of Canada (11–18); the remainder of the report is devoted to ways in which this domination can be avoided. It is thus perhaps inevitable that the next section of the report is on 'Mass Media,' noting that half the Canadian population (in 1951) was born when radio and cinema were either 'unknown' or 'an exceptional curiosity,' rather than the 'national habit' they had become (19). Similarly, the newspaperman of recent memory 'did not publish a mass medium of communication; he edited a newspaper' (20). And while the 'radio, the film, the weekly periodical have brought pleasure and instruction to remote and lonely places in this country,' it will be unfortunate, nevertheless, 'if we hear no more our choir and our organist in valiant and diligent practice of the Messiah' (20). In addition to the threats that older cultural forms might die, the need to preserve the airwaves for 'programmes essentially Canadian in nature' (25) was dire. This need had first been met with the establishment of the Canadian Broadcasting Corporation (CBC) in 1936, though the attempt to compete with American broadcasting 'has encouraged in Canadians somewhat expensive programme tastes' (27) and has not prevented a degree of 'indifference' (41) towards CBC programming.

The report devotes a separate section to television: 'In our country of difficult communications, consideration of this new force cannot be neglected' (42). Once again, the American threat presents itself: 'Recalling the two chief objects of our national system of broadcasting, national unity and understanding, and education in the broad sense, we do not think that American programmes, with certain notable exceptions, will serve our national needs' (47). This insistence on supporting the Canadian national identity, plus the need to proceed with care and caution, characterize the remaining essays.[9] To address this threat of American cultural hegemony, the report makes a number of recommendations. It argues that broadcasting be understood as a 'public trust,' as it is in Great Britain, rather than as an 'industry' (279), as it is in the United States, and that control of the industry remain with the CBC. It further recommends that advertising be kept to a minimum and that 'less desirable commercial programmes now carried' be eliminated (291). On the subject of television it recommends that 'Canada would do well for the next few years to move very slowly, if at all' (302). Its most important recommendation is for a 'Canada Council for the Encouragement of the Arts, Letters, Humanities and Social Sciences' (377), which, in 1957, was legislated into existence as the Canada Council and which has been the single most important influence on Canadian artistic production (through its grants to artists) in the second half of the twentieth century.[10]

The companion volume to the report, a selection of essays prepared for the hearings and drawn on by the writers of the report, presents an idea of the cultural milieu and the major cultural issues that confronted McLuhan upon his return to Canada from his teaching position at St Louis (which he had taken up after obtaining his doctorate from

Cambridge).[11] Of these essays, B.K. Sandwell's 'Present Day Influences on Canadian Society' is noteworthy for stressing the importance of communications: 'The intellectual development of a community depends in part on the mechanisms of communication within that community, and in part on the mechanisms of communication with other communities and the influences which these external communications bring to bear upon it. In the case of Canada the external communications are of greater importance than in the average national society' (1). Charles Comfort's essay on painting similarly cites 'modern communications, with their tendency to reduce time and space and establish and strengthen a common ground for thought and behaviour' (412) as the greatest influence on Canadian artistic production, especially with reference to American cultural hegemony.[12]

McLuhan's reaction to the report was immediate and visceral. In the *American Mercury* of March 1952, McLuhan published 'Defrosting Canadian Culture,' in which he sardonically refers to Canada as 'the land of rye and caution,'[13] and summarizes the report as claiming that '[t]here is no possibility of defense in depth against the aggression of American pin-up girls. Canadians are the only people on earth who read more alien than national cultural matter. Such is the gist of the sombre reflections to be found in the recent report of the Royal Commission on Canadian culture' (91).[14] McLuhan then points out the irony that royal commissions are themselves a sign of Canadian culture, and goes on to note the political rift in Canada between education and culture, such that education is a provincial concern but culture a federal one. 'Thus the Canadian Broadcasting Corporation, much like its British counterpart, is a federal body which controls all privately-owned radio stations. And a great proportion of our radio programs are inspired by conceptions of cultural uplift, or the highbrow's burden' (91). The linkage between national uplift and highbrow art was an important one in terms of the shape McLuhan's cultural critiques of Canada took, given his insistence that electronic media were breaking down those artistic hierarchies. As well, his allusion to 'the white man's burden' indicates his understanding of the colonialist context in which Canada was developing its cultural cringe.[15] Turning to Canada's political structure, McLuhan suggests that the centralized bureaucracy that France willed to Quebec has also influenced English Canada, giving Canadians a form of government significantly different from the republican one of the United States. One result of this 'non-republican and non-doctrinaire' (92) form of government has been to build a mosaic of cultures in Canada. National unity has been built on the basis of an East–West railway and trade agreements meant to support it; however, the 'natural economic movement of goods' tends to be North–South, with the result that 'the Canadian economy is an artificial one' (92). While Canada's economic relations with the United States have thus placed Canada in 'a state of perpetual anxiety and expediency,' those conditions have granted to the Canadian 'a power of acute observation and the ability to comment shrewdly on the ebullient comings and goings of his rich friend to the south of him' (92–3). Here, *in nuce*, is McLuhan's notion of the Canadian counter-environment.

Commenting on Canada's colonial history, McLuhan notes that, whereas Canada was emerging from its colonialist relation to Britain at the beginning of the century, it is now becoming a colony of the United States, based on the economic relations between the two countries. But while the United States has emerged from its cultural colonization by Britain, Canada has been hampered in this regard by its political loyalty to Britain.

Canadians 'will continue to act as though nothing has happened [in terms of the decline of Britain's cultural hegemony], if only because the dominant Victorian culture of the country has already accustomed them to ignore the cultural significance of technology and the new communications media of the continent' (95). The implications are clear: one way of ending Canada's cultural cringe is to acclimatize that culture to the new media. Thus, 'the very absence of cluttering example and tradition in the arts is the main Canadian opportunity. The only possible strategy for the Canadian writer, poet, artist ... is to conquer the old traditions through the most revolutionary artistic techniques suggested by the current modes of science and technology' (95). This is to turn to advantage the major dilemma of the Canadian artist, who cannot draw upon a successive history of artistic enterprise: 'He can not come to the new through the old, but must discover and master the old through what is most recent' (95). Concomitantly, this implies that those 'in the centers of change have less opportunity for appraisal and invention than those on the periphery' (95). McLuhan suggests that French Canada has a culture that is much more highly developed than that of English Canada – '[t]heir intellectuals were nourished by a nineteenth century which in France was as unmistakably first-rate as the later Victorian period in England was second-rate' (96).[16] The Massey Report is redolent of this attitude, 'squarely in line with our bureaucrats and Victorian patriarchs in supposing that culture is basically an unpleasant moral duty. According to this view, everything that people do spontaneously and with gusto, everything connected with industry, commerce, sport, and popular entertainment is merely vulgar' (96). McLuhan concludes his article with the hope that the next royal commission on culture will acknowledge the importance of popular culture, such as hockey and the new media, as parts of our overall cultural patterns. 'Once Canadians adopt that attitude they will drop their defensive tactics against the "threat" from English and American culture and welcome such contacts,' rather than seeking to build 'a cultural Maginot line' (97).

Bless/Counter/Blast

McLuhan produced a more sustained response to the Massey Report in his 1954 pamphlet *Counterblast*[17] (not to be confused with the 1969 volume of the same title). An 8½-by-11-inch photostatic pamphlet, *Counterblast* was written at the same time that McLuhan and Carpenter were producing *Explorations*, and the pamphlet contains pages from the journal. Modelled in typographical style and in content (with its 'blast'-ing and 'bless'-ing) on Wyndham Lewis's 1914 journal, *Blast*, the pamphlet seeks to do for post–Massey Report Canada what Lewis's did for pre–Great War England – shake it up culturally and politically by articulating 'the direction of the winds of the new media in these latitudes' ([1]). The pamphlet begins by blasting England, the 'ancient GHOST of culture,' and the

U S A COLOSSUS of the South, horizontal HEAVYWEIGHT flattening the canadian imagination as well as

> ## the printed b(oo)k moth-eaten
> # STRAIGHT-JACKET of the Western mind

[2]

This reference to 'the book,' taken with McLuhan's comments on the 'old forms' in 'Defrosting Canadian Culture,' suggests that part of his larger project in *The Gutenberg Galaxy* to examine critically the effects (including negative ones) of the book stems from the critique of hegemonic cultural forms and cultural conservatism that he was developing as a result of his response to the Massey Report.[18] The pamphlet thus blasts Canada '(for kindly reasons)' ([3]) and especially

The MASSEY REPORT damp cultural igloo

for canadian devotees of

TIME
&
LIFE

OH BLAST nursery politics and

Henry Goose on the Loose. The cring-

ing, flunkey spirit of canadian culture, its

servant-quarter snobbishness

resentments

ignorance

penury

[3–4]

McLuhan goes on to blast Ottawa as the 'tomb of talent' and 'fount of dullness' ([4]) in its attempts to legislate culture; 'dullness' alludes to the closing lines of Pope's *Dunciad*, which McLuhan invoked again at the end of *The Gutenberg Galaxy*, where he critiques the 'popular mesmerism achieved by uniformity and repeatability' (*GG* 261) occasioned by the hegemony of print.

Drawing on the double meaning of 'blast' and 'bless' (where 'blast' refers also to 'blastoderm' [4], source of new life, and 'bless' is a pun on the French *blesser*, 'to wound'), McLuhan also blesses the Massey Report, which he labels a 'HUGE RED HERRING for / derailing Canadian kulcha while it is / absorbed by American ART and Technology' ([5]; red predominates on the report's cover). McLuhan blesses 'MASSEY-HARRIS farm machinery' ([6]), an allusion to the product that gave the eponymous Massey his cultural clout, and 'French Canadian HOCKEY PLAYERS / for keeping art on ice / for our one contribution to / INTERNATIONAL CULTURE' ([8]) – examples of popular, non-canonical culture, in both cases. Similarly, McLuhan blesses 'the comic strips, pantheon of / PICKLED GODS and / ARCHETYPES' ([10]), and he blesses 'FOTOPRINT [,] able to modulate / the printed visual image to the / full range of acoustic space' ([10]), a position characteristic of the empathic approach McLuhan increasingly took to contemporary artistic production.

Following these first ten pages of *Counterblast* is a 'Media Log,' which McLuhan reprinted in the February 1955 issue (No. 4) of *Explorations* and in *Explorations in Communication* (1960), with some variations, and 'Five Sovereign Fingers Taxed the Breath,'[19] which is also reprinted in *Explorations in Communication*. The 'Media Log' notes that the effect of contemporary trends in education is that children are 'divorced from their culture' because they are not allowed to draw on their natural experience of it – perhaps because that experience is of contemporary technology: 'The new media are not ways of relating us to the old "real" world; they are the real world and they reshape what remains of the old world at will ... *Technological art takes the whole earth and its population as its material, not as its form*' ([13], emphasis added). McLuhan had thus formulated the notion that the earth had become an artifactual environment before the launch of *Sputnik*, to which he often attributed this insight. McLuhan further argues that only outside European culture can the meaning of the new technologies be understood: 'Europeans cannot imagine the Earth City [a forerunner of the Global Village]. They have occupied old city spaces too long to be able to sense the new spaces created by the new media' ([13]). One of the effects of the 'Earth City' is to unmoor cosmopolitanism from the old, established centres. As McLuhan puts it in 'Five Sovereign Fingers,' '[a]ny highway eatery with its tv set, newspaper, and magazine is as cosmopolitan as New York or Paris' ([15]). This is an important comment in terms of the cosmopolitan position McLuhan takes towards the Massey Report. It is not a cosmopolitanism that seeks to reassert European cultural hegemony, nor is it a form of vanguardism, with its suggestion of a path to be followed by mainstream culture; rather, it seeks to demonstrate how the notion of cultural 'centre' reverts to the margins under the influence of the new media, which have a powerful tendency to break down all such cultural hierarchies and barriers.[20]

Given McLuhan's interest in the media, the CBC was a repeated target of his critiques of the Canadian cultural landscape. His 1957 article 'Why the CBC Must Be Dull,' published in *Saturday Night*,[21] argued that the CBC's 'dullness' was attributable to its inability to reconcile its role as national broadcaster with the realities of electronic media. The result was an uncritical engagement with the media environment,[22] which McLuhan theorized as an immense vector of power. As he wrote in the *Counterblast* of 1969, '[w]ith writing comes power: command over space' (117). With electronic media, this power increases exponentially into command over 'a space-time landscape of many times, many places' (*Ctb* 112–13) in a 'geography of perception and feeling' (*Ctb* 111). To couple broadcasting to a nationalist project was, thus, to go counter to the effects of contemporary media. As McLuhan wrote in an essay on 'The Electronic Age,' published by Ryerson in *Mass Media in Canada* (1962), '[d]ecentralism today is the child of space-time and instantaneous information movement.'[23] In contrast, '[a] centre-margin structure, whether in empires or private perception, is one in which there is very little interplay at the margins. The margins become areas of specialism and relative fixity of form, as in colonies' (187). The role of the CBC, in these terms, is fundamentally colonialist, its dullness equivalent to that imposed by the hegemony of the book (cf *GG* 261). The linking of perception with colonization is crucial here, and recalls McLuhan's comment in 'The Later Innis' that in the last works of Innis the trade routes of the land are replaced by the trade routes of the mind. What this suggests, in the context of McLuhan's development of his communications theories in tandem with his enquiry into Canadian cultural identity, is that *media are material*, and have material effects. Thus, it is not simply that a radio is a medium; so is a road, and it is this highly materialist conception that distinguishes McLuhan's theory of media as a theory of the production of space.

Garrisons and Galaxies

By the early 1950s (within five years of his return to the Canadian academy), McLuhan had established himself as a significant voice within the Canadian cultural matrix, writing for such journals as the *Northern Review* as well as for popular magazines such as *Saturday Night* and *The Canadian Forum*; he also wrote on Canada for international publication, not only in the *American Mercury* but also in *The Sewanee Review* and *The Kenyon Review* (where fellow national E.K. Brown also published). McLuhan's position on Canada was complex: he was defensive of Canadian culture when it was criticized as being colonial, and he was critical of the Canadian cultural cringe. In a 'Guest Opinion' published in the *Northern Review* in 1956 titled 'Mr. Priestly's [*sic*] Colonial Crusade,' McLuhan attacks Priestley's comment that 'Canada should import a large number of young English poets' in order to make up its cultural deficit.[24] Rejecting with a pun that 'gesture of imperial exportise [*sic*],' McLuhan suggests that 'the Canadian Waste Land' would force the English poets, in the absence of 'their dozen or so English readers' to 'join the ranks of Canadian poets and contend with them for a share of the forty-eight readers of new verse' in 'the shell hole of blasted British culture.' Similarly, in his article 'The "Color-Bar" of BBC English,' McLuhan decries received forms of pronunciation and their concomitant class biases: 'To ask whether there is anything cultivated about BBC English, whether, for example, it can only be acquired by those who have richly nourished minds, educated tastes, and delicacy of moral perception, or whether at the present day it merely records an economic advantage – that would be a hard question for some.'[25] The status statements such as these earned McLuhan in the Canadian cultural milieu can be gauged by comments made by Malcolm Ross in his introduction to the 1954 anthology *Our Sense of Identity*,[26] another volume published in the wake of the Massey Report. Ross's volume is a significant document in the history of Canadian criticism. Taking as its point of departure McLuhan's seminal article 'The Later Innis' and McLuhan's 'cosmopolitan time-and-space insights' (a quality he also attributes to Northrop Frye), Ross's 'Introduction' to the volume notes that McLuhan posits Innis's '"essential Canadianism,"' as 'his "hostility to power," that psychological fruit of Canada's struggle for autonomy and of her present position as a nation next door to the greatest of nations' (viii). As a result of this schooling, suggests Ross, 'we have learned to live with power, warily but not fearfully' (viii), and, as a result, '[o]ur natural mode is ... not compromise but irony ... And there is no simple reconciliation of inside and outside, no "solution." Instead there is the collision of opposites' (x). This condition of irony has led to '[o]ur sense of time [becoming] multi-dimensional. Our sense of place, enlarged first by our own largeness, by the endless open horizon of our land, shatters all horizons. Thus "the intellectual radar screen" [quoting here from McLuhan] of Innis, the incredible leap across time and space, the movement outward by the irony of first going inward – into the multiple irony already within' (xi). Ross sets McLuhan firmly within this context: 'Thus the eager openness of a Marshall McLuhan to the world-loosening, world-binding potential of the new mass media' which 'threaten with extinction the parochial, self-centered, encrusted sense of identity of the older nations, but which set to tingling that sense of identity to which no bounds are set, need be set, can be set' (xi–xii).

A similar note, albeit in quite a different context, is struck by Milton Wilson in a 1958 article called '*Other Canadians* and After,' a study of John Sutherland's 1947 anthology of that name, which Sutherland had produced in reaction to A.J.M. Smith's 1943 *Book of Canadian Poetry* and its use of the critical categories 'native' and 'cosmopolitan' to define Canadian verse. These categories inevitably raised the issue of identity; Wilson suggests that Canadians are (in P.K. Page's phrase) 'permanent tourists,' and that 'our larger sense of place is best expressed by [a] kind of hopping regionalism ... with its transcontinental series of scenes ... and its rapid shifts of perspective.'[27] Our poetic identity is equally non-Euclidean, suggests Wilson, citing Margaret Avison's 'resistance to the civilized tapering perspectives which may be appropriate to post-Renaissance Europe but which falsify what she sees in Canada, with its backgrounds jammed against foregrounds, its foreshortened discontinuity' (90). Similarly, A.M. Klein 'speaks not merely of our "uncontiguous space" but of our "inconsequent time," and he is not just being Joycean or writing a prologue to *Explorations*' (90). The reference to *Explorations* indicates the extent to which its claims that absolute space and time had ceased to exist, and that we had entered into a post-historical phase, were being read in the context of Canadian cultural production. Thus Wilson suggests (in his most memorable formulation) that 'one of the advantages of a poetry less than a hundred years old is that all the things that couldn't happen when they should have happened keep happening all the time ... Our tradition in time tapers even less than our background in space' (91). McLuhan had made similar points in his contribution to Ross's *Our Sense of Identity*, though in that article his focus was on the non-canonical topic of 'The Comics and Culture' (240–6). Writing of the newspaper, McLuhan states that '[t]he news is assembled each day from the world of space. In respect to time, continuity, and memory, the newspaper hasn't the capacities of a low-grade idiot, but in its breadth of geographic perception the press has the apprehension of a god' (240–1). The comics, however, are 'time-binders' (240), by virtue of the fact that they assert a temporal continuity within the 'day-by-day' world of the newspaper.

McLuhan's focus on comics contrasts sharply with the contribution to *Our Sense of Identity* made by his Toronto confrère Northrop Frye, whose essay 'The Function of Criticism at the Present Time' (247–65) deals with high-canonical literary art, adumbrating the *Anatomy of Criticism*, which Frye published in 1957.[28] Malcolm Ross had compared Frye with McLuhan in his introduction to the volume in which their essays appeared by referring to their 'cosmopolitan time-and-space insights' (vii). While the thrust of Ross's introduction is clearly with McLuhan, the comparison with Frye is a far-reaching one, especially with regard to the careers of the two scholars in the years following the publication of *Our Sense of Identity*. In the work of both theorists the spatial played a very significant role. As David Cook has remarked of Frye, '[t]he effect of the landscape [in Canada] has displaced what has traditionally been the role of the "Giants in Time" with the new spectre of the "Giants" who will conquer space.'[29] This fundamentally Canadian concept of a cultural history that is present as a spatial (synchronic) totality – '[w]hen all the cultures of the world are simultaneously present' (*CA* 99) – rather than as temporal (diachronic) succession was shared by Frye and McLuhan. For McLuhan its relationship to Canada's geographical idiosyncrasies was articulated in terms of a *techne* of which the landscape was itself a part, either as mechanized dreamscape (the 'interior landscape') or as a technological extension of body and mind (environment). What for Frye was a conflict between the centred garrison and the marginal wilderness was for McLuhan a decentred galaxy – networks without a stable centre in dynamic interface.[30]

As John Robert Colombo has stated, Frye and McLuhan are 'so entwined as to be a single, double-faced figure, like Janus' (*WWMM* 127).[31] Each wrote a book in response to the work of the other – Frye *The Modern Century* (1967) and McLuhan *From Cliché to Archetype* – as well as engaging in a number of polemics; the comparison of the two is particularly important in defining the Canadian context out of which McLuhan's work emerged. McLuhan initiated the dialogue with Frye in his 1947 review of Frye's study of Blake, *Fearful Symmetry*, which he considered in tandem with Parker Tyler's *Magic and Myth of the Movies* under the provocative title 'Inside Blake and Hollywood.'[32] What connects these works is their emphasis on historical retrieval through a 'multi-locational mode of perception' (710), the 'simultaneity' of which forecasts the end of linear history as embodied in the *translatio studii*. Frye's achievement is of this sort, McLuhan states, in its demonstration of how Blake's 'psychological insights grew into an all-embracing system which was nothing short of ferocious in its rationalistic completeness' (712). In this rationalism, however, Blake ironically 'became the image of the thing he hated and fought, namely Lockean rationalism and abstraction,' and it is in this sense that McLuhan critique's Frye's 'inside' view of Blake as having need of 'some further development from the outside' (713). In articulating an alternative to Blake's (and perhaps Frye's) vision, McLuhan likewise articulates where his own sympathies lie: 'Unlike Vico and Joyce but like Freud, Blake mistook a psychology for metaphysics and theology. His rigorous monism had no place for "the many" save as modes of primal, divine energy.' Hence the pairing with Tyler's book and its 'serious attention to popular culture.'

McLuhan subsequently published Frye's review of the *Oxford Dictionary of Nursery Rhymes* in *Explorations 1* (1953) and 'The Language of Poetry' in *Explorations 4* (1955), where Frye defines 'primitive' and 'popular' in a rather Innisian manner as 'possessing the ability to communicate in time and space respectively' (*ExC* 49); the association of space with popular culture is especially telling in terms of Frye's focus on high-canonical literature in the *Anatomy of Criticism*. Published in 1957, that book occasioned a scathing, though unpublished, response by McLuhan. 'Have with You to Madison Avenue, or the Flush Profile of Literature'[33] uses the metaphor of public opinion surveys (to which McLuhan had registered his opposition in *The Mechanical Bride*) to discuss Frye's book, suggesting that archetypes (as Frye employs them) are akin to 'profiles or nuclear models of collective postures ... data necessary to the public relations engineer' (2). McLuhan's main point in this brief review is that Frye's product-oriented notion of literature has been made obsolete by electronic media that stress literature as process (and consumer as producer).[34]

Having taken on Frye's notion of archetype in this essay (a topic to which he would return at the end of the decade in *From Cliché to Archetype*), McLuhan took on the other category of literary criticism – myth – with which Frye was associated. In 'Myth and Mass Media,'[35] McLuhan seeks an understanding of myth in the era of mass media. The mass media, he suggests, operate like myth; both 'abridge space and time and single-plane relationships, returning us to the confrontation of multiple relationships at the same moment' (339). Yet if language is a mass medium (which, argues McLuhan, it is), why do we not think of it as mythic? The answer, suggests McLuhan, is that languages tend to be 'dynamic models of the universe in action,' whereas the term 'myth' tends to be employed (and McLuhan is arguably thinking of Frye here) for 'static models of the universe ... [and] for reference and classification' (340). 'Macromyth' is thus a better term for 'myths' such as language and the mass media. Myth, then, could be understood as 'a photograph or "still" shot of a macromyth in action' (340), myth being to visual space what macromyth is to auditory space, since '[e]lectronic culture accepts the simultaneous as a reconquest of auditory space' (341). The direction of McLuhan's argument is thus to place myth within history, to dynamize it, to understand it not as timeless but as a product of particular sociohistorical contexts; as well, he contests the notion that myth be restricted to 'something that can be verbalized, narrated, and written down' (344). Myth is what we live, to the extent that media influence our perceptions.[36]

Understanding Canada

The 1960s[37] was the decade in which Frye and McLuhan gave lectures and published books and articles in response to each other's work.[38] Frye's 1965 'Conclusion' to the *Literary History of Canada* discusses McLuhan as 'a disciple of Innis' who 'continues to emphasize the unity of communications, as a complex containing both verbal and non-verbal factors, and warns us against making unreal divisions within it.'[39] Frye understands this as a 'need for continuity in the Canadian attitude to time as well as space,' which he attributes to Canada's 'preoccupation with its own history, its relentless cultural stock-takings and self-inventories' (829); he concludes with several allusions to McLuhan's theories of cultural production:

> The writers of the last decade, at least, have begun to write in a world which is post-Canadian, as it is post-American, post-British, and post everything except the world itself.

There are no provinces in the empire of aeroplane and television, and no physical separation
from the centres of culture, such as they are. Sensibility is no longer dependent on a specific
environment or even on sense experience itself ... Marshall McLuhan speaks of the world as
reduced to a single gigantic primitive village, where everything has the same kind of
immediacy. He speaks of the fears that so many intellectuals have of such a world, and
remarks amiably: 'Terror is the normal state of any oral society, for in it everything affects
everything all the time.' ... In other words, new conditions give the old ones a new
importance, as what vanishes in one form reappears in another. (848)

Frye expresses forcefully here what McLuhan had been at pains to emphasize in his own
writings: that retribalization was not intended as a return to a pre-literate utopia; on the
contrary, the entry into the electronic era had initiated a process fraught with terrors, as
well as benefits.[40] A number of other McLuhanesque notions figure in the passage as
well: the idea that electronic media had ushered in a postnational era; that the centre/
margin dichotomy had similarly broken down; that sense experience had become
prosthetically dislocated. What is most obviously missing from the passage is the
dynamic quality that characterizes McLuhan's theorizing of the discontinuities within
the electronic era, and most importantly with regard to the 'global village,' which
McLuhan theorized as a dynamic created by the implosive and explosive aspects of
media, rather than as merely undifferentiated 'globalization.'

Frye explicitly takes up these McLuhanesque themes and strongly criticizes them in
The Modern Century (1967), which at least one critic (writing in *The American
Scholar*) read as 'a salutary antidote to creeping McLuhanism.'[41] The text of lectures
delivered in the year of the Canadian centennial,[42] the book presents overall a picture
of technological nightmare. Frye warns against understanding media (which he identifies with advertising and propaganda) as either passive or active, unlike the 'creative
arts,' which are 'almost entirely on the active side' (19).[43] Advertising and propaganda
are 'trivial' aspects of culture, creating a 'narcissistic world' (28) of television,
movies, and sports, a world of 'cliché' (30) that reflects 'the alienation of progress'
(23). Frye associates this 'myth of progress' with 'a number of value assumptions: that
the dynamic is better than the static, process better than product, the organic and vital
better than the mechanical and fixed' (31); the first terms of each of these dyads are
notions identified with McLuhan's thought (though not derived, there, from notions of
progress). Yet, 'for most thoughtful people progress has lost most of its original sense
of a favourable value-judgement' (35). Technology leads to uniformity, to an increasingly nomadic society, and to a great levelling down (Frye uses the geological
metaphor of a peneplain), threatening the one bulwark of the human, namely 'the inner
mind ... The triumph of communication is the death of communication: where communication forms a total environment, there is nothing to be communicated' (38). This,
once again, is not the dynamic model of a global village as theorized by McLuhan, in
which the local or marginal paradoxically differentiates the global, and is intensified
by it;[44] for Frye, '[s]eeds of culture can only come from the centres of civilization
which are already established ... Complete immersion in the international style is a
primary cultural requirement, especially for countries whose cultural traditions have
been formed since 1867, like ours. Anything distinctive that develops within the

Canadian environment can only grow out of participation in this style' since 'the forms of art are autonomous' (56–7) of their sociopolitical contexts. In confirmation that McLuhan was in the forefront of his thoughts while he was writing this, Frye states at this point: 'The McLuhan cult, or more accurately the McLuhan rumour, is the latest of the illusions of progress: it tells us that a number of new media are about to bring in a new form of civilization all by themselves, merely by existing ... This is not all of what a serious and most original writer is trying to say, yet Professor McLuhan lends himself partly to this interpretation by throwing so many of his insights into a deterministic form' (39). Frye is particularly concerned that attention to media will inevitably legitimate popular culture. Only quality media should be given a cultural imprimatur, he argues, and what determines the 'quality of the medium' is 'the social motive for using it ... or what Innis called the bias of communication' (40), which is to say its orientation toward space or time (and, as Frye had suggested elsewhere, popular culture was space oriented, while the classics gained their cultural currency over time). Frye's assumption that these categories are separate informs many of the differences he has with McLuhan and leads him to the conclusion that 'the real basis for the opposition of artist and society is the fact that not merely communications media and public relations, but the whole structure of society itself, is an anti-art, an old and worn-out creation that needs to be created anew' (86). This position, which places the artist outside society, differs radically from McLuhan's, which held that artists could contest environments *from within* by creating anti-environments. Art, in these terms, is a material practice, not a way of escaping from social context but part of a much larger social imaginary whose effects are none the less real for being invisible; indeed, it was the *visual* realm that McLuhan understood to be a phantasmagoria. While for Frye the apparently real (the world around us) is illusory, for McLuhan the apparently illusory (the media of communication) is real. Furthermore, for Frye it is the educator and not the artist who leads society towards the realization of the ideal vision of what society can be: 'the form of liberal education is social ... rather than simply intellectual. I should call the social form of liberal education, provisionally, a vision of society, or, more technically, a mythology' (105). Frye distinguishes two mythologies – the Christian and the modern. The Christian holds that creation is divine and that human creation seeks to imitate those divine forms: 'the ultimate human community was not in this world, but in a heaven closer to the divine presence' (108). In that divine world, such things as 'our perception of time and space, might not be adequate at a purely spiritual level. It was possible, for example, that a spiritual body, such as an angel, did not occupy space or travel in space at all' (108); once again, Frye invokes the Innisian paradigm, and, once again, space is definitely not on the side of the angels. Modern mythology, on the other hand, is secular, and 'is reinforced by the mass media, newspapers, television, and movies, and ... is based fundamentally on cliché and stock response' (111). As Frye puts it elsewhere, '[t]he real forms are not the media but verbal or pictorial structural units that have been there since the Stone Age.'[45] It is thus the function of education, and even more so the arts, to point *away* from this mass media mythology to an ideal world. 'All nations have such a buried or uncreated ideal, the lost world of the lamb and the child, and no nation has been more preoccupied with it than Canada'

(122). Frye concludes with the paradox that 'perhaps the real Canada is an ideal with nobody in it. The Canada to which we really do owe loyalty is the Canada that we have failed to create' (122–3).

The orientation of Frye's *Modern Century* away from the social and material contexts of artistic production contrasted sharply with McLuhan's centennial pronouncements on Canada. Actively consulted during the design stage of Expo 67 (*WWMM* 27),[46] at which, in the Quebec pavilion, the French translation of *The Gutenberg Galaxy* was launched,[47] McLuhan gave an interview to *Mademoiselle* magazine in January of that year (the month of Frye's *Modern Century* lectures) on 'Understanding Canada.' In it, he suggested that one of Canada's prime advantages is that 'it is so little related to the rest of the world.'[48] McLuhan elaborated on this notion in a much more serious vein in 'Canada: The Borderline Case,' broadcast on the CBC in May.[49] McLuhan's thesis is at once psychological and geopolitical: our perception of Canada is defined not through a high-profile nationality but by its global interfaces, which resonate through its many borderlines. McLuhan begins with a reference to the DEW Line – the Distant Early Warning system put in place by the United States in the Canadian north to warn of possible attack from Russia. Understood in terms of 'attitudes to ... spaces' (230), Canada and the United States construct 'inside' and 'outside' similarly, whereby the 'outside' is rendered as hostile and the inside as social – 'the two psychic poles of the special North American feeling for space' (231). This relational quality of 'inside' and 'outside' was crucial to McLuhan's treatment of the question of nationalism in the age of electronic media, to which he devoted a number of articles towards the end of his career. Writing on 'The Implications of Cultural Uniformity'[50] (1975), for example, he describes North Americans' modes of constructing space, such that they 'go outside to be alone, and go inside to be with people' (44). McLuhan traces the attitudes inherent in this behaviour to 'the initial approach to the North American wilderness as an enemy to be tamed and subdued. From the beginning, the North American settlers had technologies which prompted a kind of "crash programming" of the continent. Always going outside to be lonely hunters or explorers, and going inside for protection and security, seems to have established a massive syndrome of spatial and psychic attitudes which are unlike those of other continents' (45).[51] As McLuhan notes, this is the theme of Margaret Atwood's *Survival* (1972),[52] though he extends its thesis to examples from American literature.[53] It is significant that, for McLuhan, Canada's geography is not made up of vast, empty spaces; rather, these spaces are dynamic – culturally and socially constructed.

The DEW Line was a particularly important example for McLuhan of how communication networks materially constructed space. As he writes at the opening of his 'Borderline' essay, the DEW Line reveals Canada as 'hidden *ground* for big powers' (226), whereby it takes on the role of 'anti-environment' (227) to the United States.[54] Canada is furthermore able to combine the 'cosmopolitan character' (246) of international interface (summarized in the experience of Expo 67) with a 'soft-focus' identity that is particularly suited to a world in which national identity is being rendered obsolete by the ability of electronic media to supervene political boundary lines: '[t]he vast new borders of electric energy and information created by radio and television have set up world frontiers and interfaces among all countries on a new scale that alter all pre-existing forms of culture and nationalism' (241).[55] The 'inclusiveness' (248) fostered by our low-profile identity is a major aspect of McLuhan's notion of Canada, and a reminder of the way in which the acoustic model of spatial production was oriented towards diversity and difference. McLuhan concludes by noting that 'for Canada a[n] ... inclusive consciousness is an inevitable condition of size, and speed of intercommunication.' But he cautions that 'this inclusiveness ... is not the same as the nineteenth-century idea of national unity'; it is more akin to what Homi Bhabha, writing twenty years later in *DissemiNation,* would call the 'menacing, agonistic boundary of cultural difference that never adds up, always less than one nation and double.'[56]

McLuhan's pluralism is especially evident when situated with reference to Frye and Smith. As Alexander Kizuk has argued, Smith's *Anthology*, with its distinction between native and cosmopolitan, is, finally, 'dismissive of indigenous literary efforts'[57] and to that extent colonialist in attitude.[58] McLuhan's own foray into anthologizing, *Voices of Literature* (1964, with Richard Schoeck),[59] takes a different stance, juxtaposing Canadian, Native, and European writers. The principle of organization is not historical, but performative (or rhetorical), with an emphasis on reading the poems aloud, an effect (write the editors) to which we have been resensitized by the retrieval of the acoustic through radio broadcasting and 'new dimensions of recording' (iii). The plurality of the volume is thus a product of the media's tendency to break down hierarchical barriers (including barriers of nationality, as well as of historical succession). One group of poems is characterized as 'Poems of Comment and Criticism,' so selected because they emphasize that 'all poetry is in some way or another a comment on or a criticism of its own world' (131). What distinguishes this approach from Frye's is the lack of a transcendent model. Thus, Frye's comment in *The Modern Century* that the 'international style' was superior to the national one is made in the service of his larger theory that the forms of literature are autonomous (insofar as they belong to the transcendent world of pure literary forms); given, however, that these 'autonomous' forms are those of classical European literature, they simply resurrect Smith's distinction between native and cosmopolitan. McLuhan, too, was 'cosmopolitan,' but he was so by virtue of a theory that conceived of nationalism as a product of print, and thus obsolete in the era of mass communications. His cosmopolitanism did not seek to reconfirm the binary whose other term was the native; rather, his theory collapsed the two into the spacetime dynamic of the global village. Kizuk points out that this position marks McLuhan as anomalous within Canadian cultural discourse: 'As is the case with McLuhan's other popular formulas – southern and northern, acoustic and visual, or Socratic and Ciceronian – contraries exist as alternatives without an inherently violent and privileging conflict. In a sense, they are "cool" contraries that are not hierarchized in themselves, and, moreover, that require the receiver of the formulas to supply his or her own categories and values' (116). Hence McLuhan's attention to the rhetorical trope of hendiadys in *From Cliché to Archetype* (108–10), the 'ineradicable power of doublets' (108), the notion that all knowing is interfacial, relational, insofar as neither unit is privileged hierarchically (as in binary thought). Whereas binary matching is Euclidean (reducing the many to the single point of view), making is non-Euclidean, characterized by the multiplicities of dialogue and pun (*CA* 147). This 'modular orientation' allows 'selves or bodies or even nations' (117) to flow in and out of one another through the dynamic of mass culture – a mass culture that, paradoxically, is capable of retrieving the local and particular[60] because its mass is a product of speed (energy), not of size, consistent with Einstein's theory of relativity.

Frye's theories, in contrast, are unidirectional, moving away from the local and particular towards the 'return of Eden,' as one of his books puts it.[61] As Kizuk states, '[i]n McLuhan's thinking, there is no single pattern of otherness – neither "essence" in Smith's sense, nor "presence" in Frye's – whose objective reality dwells beyond the actual, living, and breathing, participating individual' ('"Mutual Provisionality"' 118). The implications of this theoretical positioning are crucial to McLuhan's understanding that media are material and that their materiality impinges on what an earlier paradigm (that of print) had referred to as content. In a sense this is a rhetorical notion, which argues that the shaping of a message is crucial to the understanding of that message. The implications of this rhetoric in an era of mass culture, however, are much vaster than they were in the era of the 'public,' an era whose ambit was much more restricted and much less invasive – invasive because electronic media are extensions not only of our selves but also of our consciousnesses. This era of mass media is the ultimate realization of humanism, though in reverse, since the humanism produced by the media is oriented towards the many, not the individual, technology having become an organism that we fecundate with our ever greater inventiveness (as McLuhan had put it in *Understanding Media*). This conflation of the social and the imaginary has been theorized by Arjun Appadurai as one of the key aspects of the contemporary mediascape, in which the imagination takes on an increasing materiality, becoming 'an organized field of social practices.'[62] The dynamic of these practices oscillates between homogenization and heterogenization – 'that at least as rapidly as forces from various metropolises are brought into new societies they tend to become indigenized in one or another way' (32). This dynamic makes the centre/margin binaries of Frye and Smith inoperative; at the same time, it exposes such binaries as being fundamentally colonial in orientation.[63] 'An important fact of the world we live in today,' Appadurai continues, 'is that many persons on the globe live in ... imagined worlds ... and thus are able to contest and sometimes even subvert the imagined worlds of the official mind and of the entrepreneurial mentality that surrounds them' (*Modernity* 33). The resulting cultural forms are 'fractal ... possessing no Euclidean boundaries, structures, or regularities' (46); this notion of culture as performance, rather than culture as a pre-existent given, was pre-eminently the Canadian one in McLuhan's formulation.

McLuhan's theory that Canadian cultural identity can be understood as a borderline case – produced through its interaction with global forces – dispensed with the notions of the native *and* the cosmopolitan. This had particular implications for the *location* of the critic, as Frye perceived. Without the hierarchical superstructure of native and cosmopolitan (i.e., European), Frye's archetypal theory collapses, for literature can no longer be seen as gesturing towards the cosmopolitan/archetypal/European, and the critic's role can no longer be defined as articulating that critical direction. The only alternative – the one adopted by McLuhan – would be to situate the critic within that which is criticized, at which point the critical and the 'creative' collapse. It is in *The Critical Path* (1971) that Frye takes on these critical implications of McLuhan's theories, though his most specific statements on the subject were deleted from the book in order to be published separately in the BBC journal, *The Listener*. In *The Critical Path*, Frye restricts himself to pointing out the terrors of orality (the theme with which he had concluded the first edition of the *Literary History of Canada*): orality is 'not a new order to adjust to, but a subordinate order to be contained. What the oral media have brought in is, by itself, anarchist in its social affinities. They suggest the primitive and tribal conditions of a pre-literate culture.'[64] In *The Listener* article, Frye writes more pointedly that the effect on him of technological prognostications is to make him 'feel a dissolving of identity.'[65] Asserting that the 'voice' of the mass media is 'implacable' and 'inhumanly complacent,' Frye likens the effects of the media to the 'mechanical and involuntary response' of 'erotic stimulation,' and attributes contemporary ills such as drug abuse to 'a feeling that they [the abusers] have been cheated out of genuinely new sensory impressions by mass media.' Frye criticizes television, in particular, for its ability to bring 'all the problems of Tanzania or Paraguay ... in [our] living-room' when viewers do not want this. 'If the world is becoming a global village, it will also take on the features of real village life, including cliques, lifelong feuds and impassable social barriers.' Emblematic of such barriers is the talk of separatism in Canada, which Frye sees as 'a mean and squalid philosophy' and 'the strongest political force yet thrown up by the age of television.' As a counter to this, Frye reasserts the civilizing values of a culture based on writing: 'With writing, and eventually printing, continuous prose develops. With prose, philosophy changes from aphorism and proverb to a continuous argument organised by logic and dialectic, and history to a continuous narrative.'[66] This culture of writing permits 'the planned and systematic conquest of reality.' The oral culture recreated by electronic media, on the other hand, is retrieving 'many of the social characteristics of a pre-literate society.' The poet who finds himself in front of a listening audience 'can use topical or even ephemeral themes: he does not have to retreat from society and write for posterity.' At this point Frye turns directly to McLuhan, critiquing his notion that print-based media are linear, while orally empathic media are simultaneous or mosaic in nature. Rather, asserts Frye, these approaches are inherent in all media, and comprise 'not a difference between two kinds of media, but a difference between two mental operations within all media.' Thus, our first reading of a book is lineal, while our second, critical, reading, is simultaneous; this process is reversed when reading a newspaper. Frye concludes by comparing media 'oracles' to Satan's devils, who shout at and harangue their listeners; '[i]t is true that when we come to heaven there is another harangue and another listening audience. But there is one important difference: God is thinking of writing a book.'

McLuhan responded to this article a few months later,[67] suggesting that Frye's prime error in the article is not having adopted 'a multi-faceted and multi-levelled approach in order to cope with the numerous secondary cultures with which we have invested primary physical Nature' (475). Instead, Frye has adopted a point of view, which is more appropriate to static, print-based media. McLuhan is sympathetic to such a point of view: 'My personal values and attitudes, which are entirely related to the printed word, I have found it necessary to exclude from media study, so far as possible ... Understanding media is not a pleasant process or experience. It involves growing awareness of the numbness and stupefaction visited upon those invested with the social clothing of coinage, writing, rail, telephone and TV, markets and industrial technologies.' What is necessary is the 'artist energy to live in the present' (476). McLuhan emphasizes that '*connected* visual space,' which is 'the basis of the new rational dialectics of the fifth century BC' is a product of writing, and that the value systems that it supports are not universally shared: 'most people outside the orbit of the phonetic alphabet ... cannot be accommodated to Western visual assumptions' and the detachment fostered by visual space. Electronic media, however, create 'a world of discontinuities ... of touch and interface, "the resonant interval" which Heisenberg designated as the chemical and physical bond of physical being.' The acoustic world is one of involvement, and this is its central critical crux: how to critique from within. The pun provided one model: '[t]he pun by means of low definition permits interplay between itself as environment and itself as anti-environment' (letter to Wilfred Watson, *L* 297). Another way was through an understanding of the myth of Narcissus: it was precisely because Narcissus failed to see his own image in his reflection that he became paralyzed with inaction. Likewise, those who posit technology as 'other' fail to see its connections with the human, material realm of our daily existence. It is by recognizing the human within the technological that McLuhan gains his critical stance. As Kizuk puts it, 'a vast field of otherness within ourselves *is* our identity, or one of our identities' ('"Mutual Provisionality"' 121).

Clichés and Archetypes

McLuhan made his most extensive response to Frye's writing in his 1970 book *From Cliché to Archetype*, written with Wilfred Watson.[68] McLuhan had been contemplating this book since 1962–3, according to Watson,[69] broaching the topic in his 1964 essay 'New Media and the Arts,' where he stated that the 'medium' is 'environmental.' 'Cliché' and 'archetype,' in that article, represent the dynamic of the environment as it 'undergoes a progressive reshaping so that what had appeared earlier as dishevelled and degraded [cliché] becomes conventionalized into an artistic genre [archetype]' (242). This processual notion was crucial to the implicit (and explicit) critique of Frye in the book, in that it sought to present a notion of the archetype as dynamic, rather than merely as a taxonomy – '*figures* without *ground*, the Norrie Frye style of classification without insight' (*L* 528). In 1965, McLuhan wrote to Watson that he found Frye's work 'depressing. Is he not the last of the visual gradient, the mirror world in which criticism itself becomes archetypal? ... His nostalgic harking back to classical decorum and medieval levels of exegesis are sufficient indicators, perhaps.'[70] McLuhan was particularly concerned with the exclusion of context, as he remarks in *The Global Village*: 'There is absolutely no provision in Frye's statement for ground of any kind: the archetype is itself a figure minus a ground, floating around devoid of its original context' (79). As a way of avoiding this 'visual gradient' of the single point of view, McLuhan suggested that *From Cliché to Archetype* be produced through a series of dialogues with Watson, who recorded his impressions of these conversations in his article 'Marshall McLuhan and Multi-consciousness: The Place Marie Dialogues'[71] (named after the Toronto apartment building in which they took place). As Watson notes, the term 'cliché' referred originally to an aspect of the printing process, the cliché being a configuration of type that was used over and over again (201; cf *CA* 54–5). Arguing that McLuhan had upset the Cartesian (and Husserlian) enterprises by exploring 'the means of consciousness' (203), rather than consciousness itself, Watson posited that the cliché was itself 'an act of consciousness'

(202), and that technology was a magnification of this process. Just as a technology is invisible (because it constitutes our total environment), so is a cliché – all ground and no figure. When a cliché enters conscious awareness, it becomes an archetype, a figure whose ground is the dominant cliché of the period. 'Unlike the Freudian or Jungian unconscious, the unconsciousness created by the technological cliché isn't furtive or recessive, but rises aggressively around us. Its dark opacity is located both in space and time by its archetypes' (208). The process whereby cliché became archetype (and where archetype became cliché) was a process of changing perceptual awareness in which technology was at once the object and mode of critique. Similarly, McLuhan's notion of archetypes as being in dynamic interrelationship with clichés allowed him to integrate his longtime attention to popular culture with canonical art, thus opening up dominant forms in a way that allowed for both resistance and creativity (as Appadurai has suggested).

It is this view of cliché and archetype that informs the book: set up as a series of alphabetical entries, it returns to the structure of *Understanding Media* and its twenty-six media chapters (though here some letters are represented more than once, and some not at all), the alphabet being one of the major clichés of book culture,[72] so pervasive as ground that we fail to be conscious of it as it shapes our perceptions. The book is described on the jacket as a 'study of the process of intermedia action'; it confronts the question of how meaning is produced in the 'resonant interval' of interacting media. In this sense it is a prelude to *Laws of Media*, in that it sees media as dynamically interrelated through processes of retrieval, enhancement, obsolescence and reversal; it is on these borderlines that communication takes place. Content is thus not absolute in meaning; rather, it shifts according to the shifts in media along the historical axes of synchrony and diachrony, the medium being the environment (or episteme) of our understanding. This dynamic concept of media informs the authors' view of arche-types, which they see as processual, not static; as '"living entities,"' in Jung's sense (22, quoting from *Psyche and Symbol*). Thus the ironic reference to the 'Frigean Anatomy of a Metamorphosis' (7); the task that *From Cliché to Archetype* sets itself is precisely to identify the processes of media dynamics. The authors define the arche-type relationally with the cliché in a form of 'systole-diastole' (42) which is also the movement of 'dialogue' (46), and is thus part of the interaction between high culture and popular culture; they quote Eric Partridge's usage note on 'archetypal' that it '"enjoyed a 'highbrow' popularity [a juxtaposition that would not have been lost on McLuhan], ca. 1946–1955"' (18, quoting from *Usage and Abusage*). Thus *From Cliché to Archetype* discusses both the high-canonical works that figure throughout Frye's writing (Milton, Dante, Shakespeare, and so on), together with popular cultural forms (camp, Yiddish humour, Happenings), taking the position that 'Today the entire world of rock poetry and of the related forms of jazz, of song and speech and dance, has created a complex world of genre which no professor of literature can ignore if he has any concern about maintaining contact with his students. The interests of literature are not really served by ignoring its rivals' (87). This distinction between the canonical and the popular was especially important within the Canadian context, where Cana-dian culture was often dismissed for failing to achieve the norms of canonical (i.e., European) culture. It was also important to an understanding of Modernist literature such as Joyce's *Ulysses*, which *From Cliché to Archetype* terms a 'newspaper epic' (38) – a juxtaposition of the techniques of high art and popular culture. 'Every culture now rides on the back of every other culture' (9), write the authors, in the age of 'electric retrieval,' the age of the museum without walls, where the entire phenomenal universe is at once 'junkyard' and 'museum' (65), cliché and archetype. There is thus a historical element within media, but it is not a lineal, sequential history; rather, it is a sense of history produced out of what Susan Sontag calls ' "radical juxtaposition," ' which is the essence of symbolic representation, 'a juxtaposition of two things,' from '*symballein*, Greek for "throwing together" ' (36).[73] Symbolism thus means 'the *breaking* of connections.' This aesthetic of 'intervals, gaps, and interfaces' (18), an aesthetic of heterogeneity and diversity rather than unity, is indicative of oral acculturations, of what T.S. Eliot called ' "the auditory imagination," ' which ' "fuses the old and obliterated and the trite, the current, and the new and surprising, the most ancient and the most civilized mentality" ' (quoted 63). The auditory imagination is opposed to 'the habit of the visually oriented person to try to find connections.' The dynamic of cliché and archetype is thus also a dynamic of acoustic and visual spaces, the point of departure for the 'laws of media,' where the dynamic of figure and ground was reconfigured as that between visuality and the acoustic: '[s]ymbolism is the art of the missing link, as the word implies ... It is the art of syncopation. It is the basis of electricity and quantum mechanics, as Lewis Carroll understood via Lobachevski, and non-Euclidean geometries. The chemical bond, as understood by Heisenberg and Linus Pauling, is RESONANCE. Echoland. The world of acoustic space whose center is everywhere and whose margin is nowhere, like the pun' (39).[74] This emphasis on the acoustic contains an implicit critique of Frye's tendency to focus on the verbal to the exclusion of other forms of signification, and explicitly the non-verbal. 'Professor Frye has developed a classification of literary forms that ignores not only the print process as it created a special type of writer and audience, but all other media as well' (85). Indeed, it is precisely the material world that is occluded and excluded through the singular focus on the verbal – 'the world of kettles and bottles and broken cans and the world of commerce and money in the till' (21). This is first of all so because the verbal is a 'limiting [of] words to one of the senses' (20). In contrast, 'the spoken word resonates, involving all the senses.' Hence the recurring citation in *From Cliché to Archetype* of the line from Yeats's 'The Circus Animals' Desertion': ' "Now that my ladder's gone, / I must lie down where all the ladders start, / In the foul rag-and-bone shop of the heart" ' (20 and *passim*), with the ineradicable doubleness of 'rag' and 'bone.' This doubleness undermines the hierarchy between cliché and archetype. In fact they are the same; they simply produce different spaces within a historical trajectory of retrieval and obsolescence, enhancement and reversal: 'old cliché as new archetype = old archetype as new cliché' (51). The familiar environment as cliché becomes archetypal when reconfigured through artistic perception, as in a Happening (198).[75] This ' "regeneration ... through repetition" ' (43), in Mircea Eliade's terms, is made possible by the artist's transformation of the 'robotized behaviour' (43) of the 'civilized' into the 'non-robotized behavior ... of the wild body.'[76]

   From Cliché to Archetype represents McLuhan's last major encounter with the work of Frye; Frye, however, continued to make reference to McLuhan's work throughout the

1970s (the period when McLuhan is said to have disappeared from critical consciousness), though with greater approbation than in the preceding decade.[77] Thus, in a 1970 essay on the 'Definition of a University,' while disagreeing with McLuhan's notion that the print medium fosters fragmented understanding and electronic media a holistic one, he does affirm that 'there is no doubt that television and the movies have developed new means of perception, and that they indicate the need for new educational techniques' (*Divisions on a Ground* 153). Remaining with the university milieu in a 1976 article on 'Teaching the Humanities Today,' Frye uses the term 'counter-environment' (*Divisions on a Ground* 93) to refer to the academy, making the important point that it is 'detached yet not withdrawn from the social environment.' It was in the 'Conclusion' to the second edition of the *Literary History of Canada,* however, that Frye made his most significant *rapprochement* with McLuhan's work. Noting that Canadian literature had come of age in the decade since the first edition of the *History,* Frye remarks on the irony of this happening just as McLuhan was supposed to be predicting that the book was dead. 'I doubt if one can find this in McLuhan,' continues Frye, 'except by quoting him irresponsibly out of context, but it is what he was widely believed to have said, and the assertion became very popular, as anything that sounds anti-intellectual always does.' Nevertheless, the ability of television to bring 'the remote into our living room can be a very sobering form of communication, and a genuinely humanizing one' (327); in contrast, print can nurture 'infantilism.'

Frye is writing against himself here, and quite consciously so, based on his concern about the perception that a '"Frye school of mythopoeic poetry"' has grown up around him; he explicitly addresses this concern in the second 'Conclusion': 'There is no Frye school of mythopoeic poetry; criticism and poetry cannot possibly be related in that way; the myth of a poem is the structural principle of that poem, and consequently all poems that make any sense at all are equally mythopoeic' (319). The perception of a 'Frye school' had been fostered by studies such as D.G. Jones's *Butterfly on Rock* (1970), which applies Frye's notion of a 'garrison mentality' (8, and *passim*) to a broad survey of Canadian literature. Although Jones reiterated his position in a 1973 coda to his book,[78] he published (though not in Canada) a counter-statement of sorts in his 1974 article 'Cold Eye and Optic Heart: Marshall McLuhan and Some Canadian Poets.'[79] Jones notes that many poets are made uneasy (and some, such as Layton, outright hostile) by the suggestion that they are working within a Frygean paradigm:

Part of the writer's uneasiness toward Frye turns, I suspect, on the difference between theory and practice. It is all very well to say that the writer articulates a world, but for any particular writer at any particular time the question is just what world, what language? If we look at the literature through the eyes of a Frye, we search for certain perennial, recurring, formal patterns of imagery and action as archetypal features of a literary imagination that remain unaffected by the age and its particular coloring. But if we look at the literature through the eyes of a McLuhan, we look for certain patterns of thought and feeling, perception and organization, which are peculiar to the age and precisely determined by the range and emphasis given to the various senses by the technology of the age ... If there is a world to make articulate, it is a world that has been suppressed by the hegemony of the eye. (173)

Adopting the McLuhanesque paradigm, Jones is able to argue that Canadian poets from at least Lampman onwards, and markedly so among the poets of the 1930s, 'bring their irony to bear on a variety of social, economic, and political problems' (175). By the 1940s and 1950s this tendency has become pronounced in poets such as P.K. Page, whose 'work is quite explicit in denouncing the imperial status of the eye' (175), and equally explicit is the work of Margaret Avison and especially Margaret Atwood, whose 'image of an extreme Procrustean reduction of the world to the dimensions of the analytic eye focuses on many of the same features that McLuhan attributes to the Gutenberg galaxy' (181).[80] To this ' "optic" seeing' these poets oppose 'the saying. It is a telling not of what the eye scans, but what the whole "tolls" ' (185). Such a shift, writes Jones, reflects 'the general shift of our technology toward the new media of the electric age' (185).

A broad attempt to understand aspects of Canadian culture through McLuhan's work had been made three years earlier, in fact, by Eli Mandel in his 'Introduction' to the 1971 anthology *Contexts of Canadian Criticism,* which takes the notion of the 'anti-environment' as its point of departure, arguing that it is a critical instrument allowing for 'large-scale integration of materials of different characteristics.'[81] In addition, Mandel plays up the tension between environment as the often-invoked trope of Canadian cultural studies – the wilderness – and McLuhan's sense of environment as technoscape, thus raising '[t]he possibility that Canada exists not as a function of its physical environment but in the technologies that create a new human order' (9). Comparing Frye and McLuhan with William Blake, Mandel remarks that all three begin 'with an attempt to "rouse our faculties" ' and end 'with an image of the human body filling (or becoming) the universe' (19). The 'duality ... of self and landscape ... exists as a perceptual flaw and can be resolved as soon as the single or framing perspective becomes multiple or mosaic.' This multiplicity is integral to artistic production, with '[t]he image for the process by which one form alters another [being] the interface' (20). It is threatened by the monadism of 'environmentalism,' the notion that Canadian culture is exclusively a product of the land, a notion that 'threatens to dissolve both poetry and criticism into the dualities of space and time' (20).

Despite this critical gambit, and those of Wilson, Jones, and Frye (who by the 1980s was urging a reassessment of McLuhan's writing),[82] McLuhan was taken up far less by Canadian criticism than by Canadian artists (including literary artists),[83] and the artists who did take him up were outside the mainstream that these critics tended to focus on.[84] Yet McLuhan continued to comment on Canadian cultural life during the 1970s, though his thoughts increasingly turned to Quebec after the October Crisis of 1970, when the Canadian government invoked the War Measures Act against a perceived *séparatiste* insurrection. The Québécois interest in McLuhan had been sharpened by the 1967 launch of *La galaxie Gutenberg* (translated by Jean Paré) at the Montreal Exposition;[85] by the 1970s, he was considered a force within the cultural and literary avant-garde,[86] and a figure within the history of Western philosophy, as the 1972 publication of Jacques Languirand's *De McLuhan à Pythagore* indicated.[87] McLuhan's opinion was thus sought on a number of issues facing Quebec. In a 1973 interview with his translator, Jean Paré, published in the magazine *Forces,* McLuhan considers the question of separation through the metaphor of 'play,' as between an axle and a wheel.[88] This metaphor is acoustic in that it describes a resonant interval 'where everything is simultaneous and yet there is no connection' (66). McLuhan understands this situation as applying generally in Canada (as he stated in the 'Borderline' essay); thus, as Paré points out, he had argued in 1967 that Quebec had already separated from Canada.[89] McLuhan, notes, however, that this condition of separation (or 'dropping out') pertained generally in Canada with regard to federalism. Whereas 'boundaries' defined nations in the past, in an electric age multiple borderlines are the order of the day. Canada 'is the only country in the world that doesn't bother with having a private identity' (70). Thus, the fact that Canada has two cultures should not be considered a barrier to identity; on the contrary, '[w]hat we need are more cultures, not fewer' (70). Nationalism, McLuhan suggests, persists as part of a progressivist mythology.

McLuhan continued this line of thought in an untitled essay on 'the advantages of Canadian non-identity' published in *Rune*,[90] a journal of McLuhan's Toronto college, St Michael's, where he suggests that French-Canadian nationalism be seen relationally with the events of 1763. 'The date of this defeat has centred French Canadian self-awareness somewhat in the fashion that the Civil War has shaped the sense of the American South' (68). The great sense of history that both cultures experience is 'a sense of the present rather than the past. It is a sense of the present as *figure* which needs the past as *ground*.' Expanding on this point (with Barrington Nevitt) in 'Cultures in the Electronic World: Can the Bottom Line Hold Quebec?'[91] McLuhan writes that to consider the possibility of Quebec's separation as a purely economic issue displays 'indifference to the rich cultural history of the Quebecois and to their passionate need for the respect and justice they have felt was their right' (66). McLuhan places these aspirations in the context of the '"regionalist revolution[s]"' (67) among the Basques, Scots, Serbs, and so on, citing an article which points out that many of these revolution-ary groups have '"clandestine radio stations,"' the effect of which is to create a group identity at the very moment when national boundaries are increasingly being breached by such media, thus fostering 'simultaneous awareness of past and present' (68). This paradox provides the possibility of a cultural resolution to Quebec's desire for identity and an end of the 'old empiricism' (69), where the pun implies both an end to colonial attitudes towards Quebec and the beginning of an understanding that cultural aspirations are materially important.[92]

Living Dialogues

One of the major links between the work of Frye and McLuhan is the importance they granted to the educational function of their work. As one of Frye's essays from the late 1970s, with the McLuhanesque title 'The Rear-View Mirror,' puts it, 'all my books have been teaching books' (*Divisions on a Ground* 181). Frye writes in *The Modern Century* that 'the technological revolution is becoming more and more an educational rather than an industrial phenomenon' (89) because increasing use of technology produces increas-ing leisure, and the function of leisure is to provide opportunity for contemplation leading, ideally, to 'a vision of society' (105). McLuhan likewise understood that the root of the word 'school' is *scholia* and that *scholia* means 'leisure' (*CC* 1); however, his own position was less contemplative than active, since participation in a technological society means participation in an information culture. McLuhan thus proposed a highly interdisciplinary approach to education, as opposed to Frye's insistence that 'the university must teach ... the only thing it can teach: the specific disciplines into which genuine knowledge is divided' (*Modern Century* 105). Frye elaborated on this theme in *The Educated Imagination* (1963), in which he states (as paraphrased by his biographer) that '[l]iterature was focussed on itself not life ... To be real, literature had to be literature-like, not life-like' (Ayre 287). The presentation of this ideal (literary or visionary) world was precisely the educative function of literature: it demonstrated the way out of the 'shoddy and squalid.' McLuhan, however, stressed that we are already in a sort of dreamland – we 'dream awake,' as he put it in the *Perspecta* article – and that the job of the educator is to train our perceptions so that we wake up to the world around us.

McLuhan's interest in the educative function extended throughout his career;[93] his *Report on Project in Understanding New Media*, it is important to recall, was prepared for an association of educators. This interest was linked to aspects of spatial production, as McLuhan writes in his 1968 article 'Adopt a College': 'In his own time Plato was a radical enemy of the old educational establishment. Great new discoveries had been made as a result of the power of the phonetic alphabet to endow a whole culture with new perceptions of time and space. Visual or "rational" space had been discovered for the first time in human history. This new visual space opened the doors of perception to the world of Euclid, of Socratic dialectic and irony.'[94] In contemporary culture, however, 'with the coming of the new electric software, both time and space have disappeared so far as access to information is concerned' (54). This has led to an educational crisis, which McLuhan ironically proposes to solve by turning schooling over to the students themselves. 'It may be of some use to you to know that the educational budget of big industry and the armed services is 20 to 30 times that of the communal educational budget.' It is thus to their environment that McLuhan suggests these students turn in their quest for an education.

McLuhan remained attached to this notion in his last book, *The City as Classroom* (1977; with Eric McLuhan and Kathryn Hutchon),[95] returning to notions about the classroom that he had first begun to work out a quarter of a century before in *Explorations*. 'Classroom without Walls' (*Explorations* 7 [1957]) argues that the electronic information explosion has been so great that 'most learning occurs outside the classroom' (*ExC* 1). This has broken the hegemony of the book as a teaching aid and challenged the monopoly on education vested in official institutions of learning. Yet most educators persist in regarding the products of the mass media as entertainment, rather than as educative. McLuhan points out, however, that many literary classics were originally regarded in the same way, and that the English language is itself a mass medium. The educational imperative is, thus, to master the new media in order to 'assimilate them to our total cultural heritage' (2) which would 'provide basic tools of perception' as well as developing 'judgment and discrimination with ordinary social experience' (3). This observation is the point of departure for *City as Classroom*, which outlines methods for training perception through a series of exercises in properties of the media, with the goal of helping students to understand the sociocultural context in which they live. The exercises encourage students to go out into the community and observe, listen, interview, research, and think about the way in which their classroom space influences what they can and cannot know – 'What did the designers of traditional schools intend when they put thirty or so desks in rows, facing the front of the room? Why is the blackboard at the front? why is the teacher's desk at the front?' (4). The major heuristic tool provided by the book is that of the figure/ground relationship. 'The interplay between *figure* and *ground*,' the authors write, 'is "where the action is"' (9). Whereas our visual training has taught us to see figures and ignore ground, the authors stress the need to be aware of ground as the first step towards understanding figure and ground as part of a simultaneous relationship. 'There is no logical connection between *figure* and *ground*, but there is always a relationship, since *ground* always provides the terms on which a *figure* is experienced. In that relationship, meaning (the effect on you) is created.' This perceptual program is the basis for the curriculum of studies proposed by the book. Students are thus encouraged to become aware of acoustic space by reading R. Murray Schafer's *The Tuning of the World* (29) and then recording various soundscapes they encounter. It asks them to compare the effect of rock lyrics when sung and when read from a printed source, and suggests that they listen to recordings of sound poetry by bpNichol and Steve McCaffery (19) in order to understand the role figure and ground play in the creation of meaning. Similarly, they are encouraged to listen to Glenn Gould's *The Latecomers* and *The Idea of North* in order to understand how it is possible to compose with sound (99). The inclusion of these works (by artists themselves influenced by McLuhan) within the book's pedagogical proposals is an important indication that McLuhan saw their works as having a distinct social function in the training of perception, rather than being aspects of an ideal existence yet to be achieved. Culture, in short, was a material phenomenon for McLuhan, not an abstract one, a position that set him off most sharply from Frye.

The most sustained contemporary critique of Frye and McLuhan as interrelated 'critical phenomena' was made by John Fekete in his 1977 book *The Critical Twilight*.[96] Fekete sees a common thread in the theories of Frye and McLuhan: whereas Frye's work represents 'a consolidation and extension of the formalization of the literary realm,' McLuhan's demonstrates 'the formalization of the totality of social communications' (108). In both cases, the element of formalization militates against the possibility of praxis, of resistance, in Fekete's view. The result is a form of cultural stasis in which 'a principle of eternity, pure and invariable, has priority over historical principles' (111). This principle is embodied in art, which 'gives us ... a vision of its images "as permanent living forms outside time and space"' (112, quoting from Frye's *Fearful Symmetry*). Frye's theory of literature embodies these principles in the articulation of a literary system 'that uses the notion of "simultaneity" to freeze time-data in a spatial design' (113), thus freeing literature from its historical content and assigning to it 'a technological form in a self-contained poetic universe' (128). This, according to Fekete, is McLuhan's point of departure, in that he extends the Frygean immobility to the entire social cosmos with his theory that the media which constitute the realm of our social practice also rigidly determine that practice: 'his argument is that systems are fully determined according to the independent laws of the dominant technological environment and its relations with antecedent technologies,' thereby eliminating 'any categories related to human self-determination' (135). Thus, while McLuhan's work has the virtue of taking mass culture seriously, it is only to cut it off at the knees, as it were, by disallowing it any degree of freedom. McLuhan does this by focusing not so much on human relations as on relations between humans and things, and between things themselves; his work thus constitutes an 'anti-humanist dismissal of the whole of humanist history' (139).

By 1982, Fekete had revised this reading. 'Massage in the Mass Age: Remembering the McLuhan Matrix' argues that McLuhan's work can be 'regarded as a new model for a strategically-oriented humanist scholarship, characterized by a concern with paradigm shifts, civilization-level reflection, a futuristic edge and experimental pedagogy.'[97] In particular, McLuhan's insistence on breaking down cultural hierarchies accords with 'the post-structuralist development of the productive notions of trace and genealogy [which] all parallel or confirm McLuhan's approach and create around it a politically democratic intellectual and institutional cluster which was unavailable in the 1950s and 1960s' (53). Fekete sees the opening image of *The Medium Is the Massage* – that of a hand cupping an ear – as articulating the central McLuhanesque thematic of 'amplified auditory attention, especially as the ear is said to favour no particular point of view' (56). This gesture 'rests on a posture of total sensory receptivity adjusted to the anticipation of an acoustic or oral message – which means, for McLuhan, not only spoken or verbal but total' (56). This bombardment or massage ('working over') by media is paradoxically involving, and while Fekete reads this as a total capitulation to a consumerist aesthetic, it is important to remember that, in the dynamics of McLuhan's theories, consumers were inevitably producers, as well.[98] This provides the basis for agency and resistance within the matrix of a totalized (or environmental) technology. To understand media is to reconfigure consumption as production. Such a position, argues Fekete, is not critical, but analytical. McLuhan would reply that it combines the two in a mode of expression that cannot be assessed according to rationalist paradigms that seek to produce a single point of view. The mode of critique advanced here by McLuhan is based on an 'interplay of all the senses' creating 'an involvement that unifies the imaginative life' (*TVP* 207). This involvement – the *sensus communis* – brings together a critical model with a social one and is based on an 'ear rational' form of analysis whose fundamental space is that of dialogue.

McLuhan in Space

McLuhan was a theorist *avant la lettre* of the cultural production of space; until relatively recently, in fact, that term would have lacked a significant context of meaning. Although 'spatial science' began to emerge in anglophone geography in the years after the Second World War, as Derek Gregory has remarked,[1] it was not until the 1974 publication of Henri Lefebvre's *La Production de l'espace* (English translation 1991) that space became an issue within critical theory generally (as opposed to the more restricted literary-critical notion of spatial form), touching on a myriad of aspects within social and cultural production. (McLuhan, by comparison, had by 1974 published the greater part of his output.) Lefebvre's book is important on a number of counts, but chiefly because it theorized space broadly enough to make it a heuristic of general cultural application, and because it addressed the central problem that has beset theorists of space (including McLuhan and Innis), namely the question of time – if space were to be understood as a social production then it would have to be understood as dynamic rather than static. Lefebvre posed this problem in terms of bridging 'the gap between the theoretical (epistemological) realm and the practical one, between mental and social, between the space of the philosophers and the space of people who deal with material things' (*PS* 4). Lefebvre was particularly concerned that attributes of 'abstract space' were constantly being ascribed to social space; his response to this problem was to argue that space, too, has a history. The radical implications of this insight are profound; they suggest that space is not natural, not a given, not an empty container in which objects exist independently, and not homogeneous. Rather, this insight suggests that spaces are actively produced within a diversity of contexts, thus opening up the range of cultural production to a mode of analysis that identifies specific spatial modes and the ways in which they are produced. Lefebvre acknowledged McLuhan (*PS* 261; 286) as his predecessor (drawn to him perhaps in part through shared elements in their intellectual upbringing, especially as transmitted through Dada) in theorizing one of these modes, the visual, and how it 'gains the upper hand over the other senses' (286), resulting in a greater and greater sense of abstraction, which reached its culmination in Cartesian space. It was the movement away from abstract, visual space that Lefebvre sought especially to theorize.

   McLuhan likewise devoted the major part of his career to a critique of visual space and to a formulation of the notion of acoustic space, and the revival which his work has been undergoing since the 1990s can be attributed in good part to the ascendancy of space as a theoretical focus generally, as well as to the promptings of the discourse that has grown up around cyberspatial phenomena such as the Internet. Indeed, acoustic space as formulated by McLuhan bears many traits in common with cyberspace: both are at once virtual and material; both contest notions of 'inside' and 'outside'; both challenge received notions of subjectivity and of the limits of the (extended) self; both constitute a space that cannot be limited to a single point of view; both place in question rationalist assumptions about experiential phenomena.

It was undoubtedly the challenge posed by acoustic space to received forms of knowing that contributed to the decline of McLuhan's reputation (at least in North America) in the 1970s, when the notion of space still lacked a sufficiently nuanced theoretical elaboration and was read, in its most extreme Marxist elaboration, as 'the epitome of reification, as false consciousness manipulated by the state and by capital to divert attention away from class struggle'; this 'anti-spatial armour,' as Edward Soja puts it in *Postmodern Geographies*, 'tended to associate all forms of spatial analysis and geographical explanation with fetishism and false consciousness.'[2] Today, however, McLuhan's contribution to communications theory generally is acknowledged to be his insistence upon the ways in which media affect our perceptions of space and time. As Nick Stevenson writes in *Understanding Media Cultures* (1995), McLuhan's theories 'remain germane in mass communication theory because of their concern with issues related to space and time. These themes remain important, given the current lack of attention to them within much media and sociological theory.'[3] Thus, when McLuhan is understood as a spatial theorist not by default, but through elaboration of this theory over a twenty-five-year period in a score of books and hundreds of articles, the contemporary interest in his writing emerges in its intellectual context, demonstrating the consistency with which McLuhan developed his chief critical concerns, and allowing one a sense of how he pursued certain ideas, rejected others, and arrived at a dynamic formulation of spatial production that has wide yet nuanced applicability. Indeed, it is precisely McLuhan's critique of visual space that constitutes his opposition to modern culture, which he understood as seeking to control space through techniques of rational ordering (the apotheosis of which was the Ramusian grid); this aspect of his work provides one of the most productive areas for further research into the implications of his thought.

Crucially, the focus on space allows for a clarification of McLuhan's debt to Innis, especially in the context of James Carey's influential comments to the effect that McLuhan 'misread' or failed to follow through with Innis's program of thought. It is clearly demonstrable from 'The Later Innis,' however, as well as from the introduction to *The Bias of Communication*, that McLuhan's debt to Innis was tempered by a clearly thought out rejection of Innis's characterization of the temporal and spatial biases. While Innis's paradigm of spatial and temporal biases within cultures of communication had a profound effect on McLuhan, McLuhan departed radically from Innis's formulation of the ways in which these biases interacted to produce social and cultural phenomena. Innis strongly associates the space bias with militarism and the expansion of empires, as well as with certain shifts in artistic sensibility: 'A decline of the oral tradition meant an emphasis on writing (and hence on the eye rather than the ear) and on visual arts, architecture, sculpture, and painting (and hence on space rather than time)' (130-1; Innis cites Lessing in this regard on 102). McLuhan's encounters with modern and postmodern art told him otherwise, causing him to reject Innis's strictly demarcated notions of spatial arts and temporal arts. At the same time, McLuhan throughout his career acknowledged Innis's brilliant realization that the central concern of contemporary culture would be precisely the 'problem of space.' Clearly, as McLuhan's subsequent work would reveal, what concerned him was the powerful awareness within twentieth-century art (and here Duchamp was his prime example) that space and time were relational, and in precisely the same way that electric 'speed-up' had encapsulated geography and time (as McLuhan puts it in *Explorations*). Had Innis 'read' history with an artist's rather than an economist's sensibility, he would have been acutely sensitive to the paradox in which he found himself when formulating a theory of space and time biases at the very moment when space and time were collapsing into a single phenomenon. This raised a problem and presented a solution. The problem was an increasing homogenization through an increasing globalization; the solution was that when understood as space*time*, this globalization would be conceived of, dynamically, as accommodating difference through local differentiation.[4]

McLuhan's formulation of this paradox took the form of acoustic space – a temporalization of the spatial and a spatialization of the temporal. In formulating acoustic space as crucial to an understanding of electronic media, as well as essential to a critique of the visual space so often taken as our perceptual norm, McLuhan provided a powerful heuristic device, capable of responding to the minutiae of cultural analysis while at the same time sensitive to the vast implications of the local/global dynamic whose interface he so tellingly named. And he did so at the very moment (as Innis had suggested) when the spatial was becoming our cultural dominant. Understanding McLuhan in terms of acoustic space clarifies a number of aspects in his intellectual career and provides a unifying approach to an otherwise unwieldy output. The first of these aspects has to do with McLuhan's critical position *vis-à-vis* the phenomena that he analysed. He had articulated that critical positioning in terms of arrest in early works that culminated in the publication of *The Mechanical Bride*, using the spatial metaphor of Poe's maelstrom. After that work, and consistently with McLuhan's rejection of static notions of time and space as formulated by Innis, McLuhan represented his critical position as one of immersion within the phenomena he analysed. This had a considerable effect on the work he produced after that, in that McLuhan tended to appropriate the phenomena he was critiquing (as he did advertising in *Culture Is Our Business*), or to emphasize the ground supporting the figure of his critique (as with the exploded and exaggerated typography in *Counterblast* and *From Cliché to Archetype*). Parallel to this critical decision was one to abandon the authorial voice and move to a dialogical model through collaborative coproduction, a position to which McLuhan held consistently in the works published after *Understanding Media*. Related to this dialogical mode was an anti-evolutionary, anti-progressivist one typical of oral modalities (as opposed to linear, literary ones), which had McLuhan rewriting and reworking those works published after *The Gutenberg Galaxy*. The consistent strand within the spatial notions in these works was the materiality of spatial sensibilities, such that McLuhan could speak (with reference to Innis) of the 'trade routes of the mind' (and hence the geographical metaphor often invoked by McLuhan). His contribution to this thinking about space was the notion, derived from his exposure to contemporary physics while a student at Cambridge, that space and time had been annihilated in a spacetime that at once provided the basis for critiquing the abstract nature of visual space and for formulating acoustic space as the site of relational configurations outside the realm of the visual.[5] To Innis's notion that the visual arts, architecture, and sculpture belonged to the realm of space, McLuhan countered with a book, *The Mechanical Bride*, that, albeit uneasily in this first iteration, took as its iconographical *points de repère* Duchamp's *Bride* and the cognate figure of the *Nude Descending a Staircase*, works that profoundly problematized space and time as categories of experience that could be understood or experienced separately.

The history of mechanization was for McLuhan largely the history of visual space. Locating mechanization within the trajectory of the printing press, he understood that the linearity that became the epistemic centre of mechanization had issued in the 'anguish of the third dimension,' the perspectival imperative that abstracted vision and isolated the viewer from the phenomenon being observed, as, paradigmatically, in the camera obscura. The psychodynamics of this isolation were inherent in the Narcissus myth, where Narcissus fails to recognize that he is in fact coterminous with that which he observes. The 'Narcissus narcosis' was at once the psychopathology of mediated culture and its (potential) remediation – the recognition that technology was not other but an extension of ourselves in one vast environmental body (as Eli Mandel had suggested in his introduction to *Contexts of Canadian Criticism*). That recognition issued in counter-environments that were at once artistic practices (in that they worked within the artifactuality of the 'natural') and critical ones (insofar as they addressed a perceptual imbalance). At such points, art and critique merge.

The critical art produced from these juxtapositions is a hybrid art whose most significant avatars are to be found in conceptualism, concrete poetry, soundscape productions, and so on, all of which play on the perceptual insights that emerge from radical juxtaposition. McLuhan dynamized these juxtapositions as his 'laws of media' whose chiasmic interrelationships codified the gestalt between figure and ground; this dynamic constitutes a prosthetic aesthetic, insofar as it figures media relationally to the ground of other media that are enhanced, obsolesced, and retrieved in a dynamic of reversal from figure to ground and from ground to figure. The agonism of this critique resides in the recognition that all extensions are amputations.

Understanding McLuhan as a theorist of spatial effects provides a productive critical context for reassessing his work and opens up significant areas of research. To approach Canadian cultural production through McLuhan's ideas would encourage a shift towards a greater engagement with the social contexts of that culture, very much in the way encouraged by Eli Mandel in his introduction to *Contexts of Canadian Criticism*. This approach also encourages studies of McLuhan's influence on Canadian cultural production and on cultural policy (especially with regard to the formulation of public policy around the arts). On a more theoretical plane, McLuhan's work suggests that the dominantly visual metaphors used to understand cyberspatial phenomena are less adequate than acoustic ones; by the same token, his work encourages the understanding of media as material phenomena that have a material effect on all aspects of social and cultural production. Among the more far-reaching implications of his work are those pertaining to the implications of visual culture within a colonialist context, especially as they embrace issues of power.

Understanding McLuhan spatially reminds us that he developed his theories within the broader contexts of discontinuity and radical juxtaposition, both of which he associated with acoustic space. Space also illuminates the orality/literacy binary as much more interrelational than it has previously been characterized: space is, in fact, the constituent factor uniting these modalities, which differ in terms of the spaces (acoustic, visual) that they produce. Space, finally, allows us to speak of McLuhan's situatedness. As a Canadian, McLuhan's development of a dislocated and dislocating notion of space relates fundamentally to experiences of geography and colonization – hence his notion that 'dialogue is an interplay among centers rather than the relaying of information from center to margin.'[6] As the site of dynamic social interaction, acoustic space provides a critical context for understanding the materiality of spatial relations in a cultural geography where all time is now and all space is here.

Notes

Preface: 'Space' in McLuhan

1 While a junior fellow of Massey College, University of Toronto, I had the opportunity, thanks to the late, and deeply lamented, Claude Bissell and to Prof. Anthony J. Parel (then a senior resident in the college), to meet with McLuhan in the fall of 1978. The conversation reflected McLuhan's immense range, and included orality and literacy, rhetorical analysis, and acoustic space.

2 Michael Bliss, 'False Prophet,' *Saturday Night* (May 1988): 59–60; 62. The subheading reads: 'Once exalted as oracular, Marshall McLuhan's theories now seem laughably inadequate as an intellectual guide to our times.'

3 Paul Benedetti and Nancy DeHart, eds, *Forward through the Rearview Mirror: Reflections On and By Marshall McLuhan* (Toronto: Prentice-Hall, 1996).

4 'Chris Young Speaks with Sandra Simpson,' in *S.L. Simpson: 1980–1990* (Toronto: S.L. Simpson, 1990), 5.

5 Lewis Lapham, 'Introduction' to *Understanding Media*, as reprinted in *Saturday Night* (September 1994): 51; a similar essay appears as Lapham's editorial in the *Harper's* of the same month ('Notebook' 7–9).

6 See in particular the article by Gary Wolf, 'The Wisdom of Saint Marshall, the Holy Fool,' *Wired* (January 1996): 122–5; 182; 184; 186. This article (which perpetuates a number of errors about McLuhan and his theories) is followed by a two-page spread on *The Medium Is the Massage* and by a posthumous 'interview' of McLuhan by Wolf ('Channeling McLuhan: The Wired Interview with Wired's Patron Saint,' 128–31; 186–7).

7 Ellen Lupton, *Mechanical Brides: Women and Machines from Home to Office* (New York and Princeton: Cooper-Hewitt/Princeton Architectural P, 1993).

8 Larry McCaffery, ed., *Storming the Reality Studio: A Casebook of Cyberpunk and Postmodern Fiction* (Durham: Duke UP, 1991): 'McLuhan presented his message in a medium that was "pomo" before its time ... Another candidate for the "Godfather of Cyberpunk"' (18–19).

9 Michael Benedikt, ed., *Cyberspace: First Steps* (Cambridge, MA: MIT P, 1991), 8.

10 Paul Levinson, *Digital McLuhan: A Guide to the Information Millennium* (New York: Routledge, 1999); Nicholas Shakespeare, *Bruce Chatwin* (London: Harvill, 1999): 'he was in a sense a precursor of the Internet age' (542). For a more pragmatic view of McLuhan and the Internet, see the book by a former collaborator, Robert K. Logan, *The Fifth Language: Learning a Living in the Computer Age* (Toronto: Stoddart, 1995), especially 14–61.

11 Derrick de Kerckhove, *The Skin of Culture: Investigating the New Electronic Reality* (Toronto: Somerville, 1995).

12 Leon Surrette, 'The Perils of Applying McLuhan,' *The Literary Review of Canada* 5.9 (1996): 25–6; this quotation 26.

13 McLuhan, 'Electric Consciousness and the Church,' *Antigonish Review* 74–5 (1988): 163.

14 Donald Theall, in *The Virtual Marshall McLuhan* (*VM*), remarks that 'McLuhan's relationship with the major debates on communication in the U.S. was quite complex ... [H]e was aware of the major scholars who had worked in the newly emerging discipline of communication in the U.S. in the 1940s and 1950s. However, he professed not to regard the work of the trail blazers as very significant in shaping the discipline. His major reservations, which caused his relative indifference to their work, were related to the then-dominant statistical, empiricist, and behaviourist emphases in mainline communication studies. In contradistinction, McLuhan's approach was historical and interpretative' (127).

15 As Arthur Kroker comments, McLuhan is 'charting the cultural geography of the new media of communication.' See *Technology and the Canadian Mind: Innis/McLuhan/Grant* (*TCM*) (Montreal: New World Perspectives, 1984), 53.

16 Jean Baudrillard, *Simulations* (New York: Semiotext[e], 1983), 54. It is Baudrillard who, more than any other theorist, has worked out the implications of a number of McLuhan's theories. For an overview, see Douglas Kellner, *Jean Baudrillard: From Marxism to Postmodernism and Beyond* (Stanford: Stanford UP, 1989), especially 67–76. Baudrillard's relationship to McLuhan has been somewhat agonistic, as his recent comment that 'McLuhan ... was, I believe, a musician [*sic*; perhaps 'magician' was meant]' indicates. See Caroline Bayard and Graham Knight, 'Vivisecting the 90s: An Interview with Jean Baudrillard,' in *Ctheory* (*http://www.ctheory.com/a24-vivisecting_90s.html*), 1. For the fullest account, see Gary Genosko, *McLuhan and Baudrillard: The Masters of Implosion* (New York: Routledge, 1999).

17 Gingko Press, of Corte Madera (California), has recently announced the publication of McLuhan's *Writings* (with Eric McLuhan as general editor) over the period 2000–5.

Chapter 1: A Short History of Space

1 For another view of this film see Marjorie Ferguson, 'Marshall McLuhan Revisited: 1960s Zeitgeist Victim or Pioneer Postmodernist?' *Media Culture and Society* 13.1 (1991): 71–90. Ferguson sees less irony and self-reflexivity in this film than I do; I am grateful to her for making it possible for me to see the film at all.

2 McLuhan may be thinking of Euclid here, for whom 'rays are sent out of the observer's eyes to apprehend the object observed.' Epicurus, however, held the opposite view, that 'thin films of atoms ... flowed from the surface of every object and entered our eyes and minds like a constant and ascending rain.' See Alberto Manguel's discussion in *A History of Reading* (Toronto: Knopf, 1996), 28–9.

3 See the reference to this painting in *Verbi-Voco-Visual Explorations* (*VVV*) 6, where it is presented as an example of a work that incorporates a temporal element within the spatial. See also chapter 5 below.

4 McLuhan never lost his fascination with space travel. In dialogue with Bruce Powers in *The Global Village* (*GV*) and in response to Powers's statement that 'Acoustic space is hard to imagine,' McLuhan replies: 'Well, start with deep space. Visualize yourself looking out the cockpit window of a spaceship moving into the area beyond the immediate galaxy. There are no recognizable planets or stars, just pinpoints of light and swirling gases rushing toward you, streaming away on either side of your field of vision' (*GV* 134).

5 Jefferson Airplane performed in the 1966 festival organized on McLuhanesque principles by the Sound Gallery of Vancouver. See Alvin Balkind, 'Body Snatching: Performance Art in Vancouver – A View of Its History,' *Living Art Vancouver* (Vancouver: Western Front, 1980), 73.

6 This very scarce thirty-minute film was produced by McLuhan and Parker; Jill Peterson Bacon impersonates the aviatrix and was the researcher; the picnicker is Sheila Mary Peace; Jim Brennan, the sound assistant; Wayne Thompson, the animation assistant; and the electronic music is by Morton Subotnick. In a 1969–70 interview in *Take One: The Film Magazine* (Montreal), McLuhan said to Joe Medjuck (one of his students) that he was planning to do an 'optical circus' in film that would be an experiment in which 'we deprive a picture of all but visual effects ... And we're eliminating perspective, we're eliminating the kinds of space that depend on any of the other senses except sight' (15). See Joe Medjuck, 'Marshall McLuhan Makes a Movie,' *Take One: The Film Magazine* 2.5 (May–June 1969; publication date 10 May 1970): 15. Gene Youngblood, author of *Expanded Cinema* (New York: Dutton, 1970), acknowledges McLuhan in making the argument that film will expand to include other media as part of a development leading to virtual reality. See Donald Theall's discussion in *The Virtual Marshall McLuhan* (*VM*) 167.

7 Beatriz Colomina, in *Privacy and Publicity: Modern Architecture as Mass Media* (Cambridge, MA:

MIT P, 1994), has remarked on 'the phobia' in contemporary thought about 'the relationship between modern media and space' (345, n24).

8 McLuhan, 'Technology and Political Change,' *International Journal* (Summer 1952): 189–95; this quotation 189.

9 McLuhan and Gerald E. Stearn, 'A Dialogue,' *McLuhan: Hot and Cool: A Critical Symposium (MHC)*, ed. G.E. Stearn (New York: Dial P, 1967), 266–302; this quotation 292.

10 Judith Stamps notes the influence on McLuhan of E.H. Gombrich's notions of matching versus making; see *Unthinking Modernity (Unth)* 105.

11 Derrick de Kerckhove, 'Understanding McLuhan,' *Canadian Forum* 51 (May 1981): 8–9; 33; this quotation 33. McLuhan made a similar comment in *GV* (with Bruce Powers), 31, and, more fully, on 75: 'The basis of all contemporary Western theories of communication – the Shannon-Weaver model – is a characteristic example of left-hemisphere lineal bias. It ignores the surrounding environment as a kind of pipeline model of a hardware container for software content. It stresses the idea of inside and outside and assumes that communication is a literal matching rather than making.'

12 Quoted by Graeme Patterson, *History and Communications: Harold Innis, Marshall McLuhan, the Interpretation of History (HC)* (Toronto: U of Toronto P, 1990), 100.

13 Anna Whiteside-St Leger Lucas, 'Communication Theory,' *Encyclopedia of Contemporary Literary Theory: Approaches, Scholars, Terms*, ed. Irena R. Makaryk (Toronto: U of Toronto P, 1993), 11–13; this quotation 12.

14 David Crowley and David Mitchell, 'Communications in Canada: Enduring Themes, Emerging Issues,' *Canada: Theoretical Discourse / Discours théoriques* (Montreal: Association for Canadian Studies, 1994), 133–52; this quotation 150.

15 As Donald Theall has remarked, there is in McLuhan's theory of communications 'some kind of ambiguous interpenetration of receiver and sender' (*The Medium Is the Rear-View Mirror [RVM]*, 27). The myth of Narcissus embodied precisely this notion of feedback; significantly, it presents itself as a dialogue between the visual and the aural (Echo).

16 Compare McLuhan's remarks in *GV* (with Bruce Powers): 'All of our senses create spaces peculiar of themselves' (22); and 'If you think of every human sense as creating its own space, then the eye creates a space where there can only be one thing at a time' (38).

17 Henri Lefebvre, *The Production of Space (PS)*, trans. Donald Nicholson-Smith (Oxford: Blackwell, 1991 [1974]), 25. See also Neil Smith and Cindi Katz, 'Grounding Metaphor: Towards a Spatialized Politics,' in *Place and the Politics of Identity* (London: Routledge, 1993), 67–83, who write that '[w]ith the reassertion of space in social and cultural theory, an entire spatial language has emerged for comprehending the contours of social reality. A response to the widespread historicism that has dominated "Western" social thought over the last century and a half, this resurgence of interest in space and spatial concepts is broad based. It was the explicit goal of critical geographic and political economic theory from the late 1960s onwards, a central component of structural and post-structural social analyses, and a core concern of information theory. Most recently, space has provided an attractive lexicon for many feminist, postmodernist, and postcolonial enquiries, the focus for public art and geo art, and a grammar in cultural discourse more broadly. The language of social and cultural investigation is increasingly suffused with spatial concepts in a way that would have been unimaginable two decades ago' (67). It was, of course, *forty* years before these authors are writing that McLuhan theorized acoustic space, and it is a sure index of McLuhan's marginalization within spatial discourse that the authors can refer to the 'comparative backwardness of spatial discourse in this century, especially in the English-speaking world' (71). According to Stephen Daniels, reader in landscape and cultural geography at the University of Nottingham, 'geographers are now getting interested in the general idea [of auditory space]' (letter to the author dated 4 September 1996).

18 Richard Kostelanetz notes: 'McLuhan transcends Joseph Frank's famous thesis about the "spatial"'; see 'A Hot Apostle in a Cool Culture,' *McLuhan: Pro and Con*, ed. Raymond Rosenthal (Baltimore: Penguin, 1969), 207–28; this quotation 216.

19 Joseph Frank, 'Spatial Form in Modern Literature,' in *The Avant-Garde Tradition in Literature*, ed. Richard Kostelanetz (Buffalo: Prometheus Books, 1982), 43–77; this quotation 46.

20 McLuhan writes in *The Gutenberg Galaxy (GG)* that 'Empathic identification with all the oral modes is not difficult in our century' (2).

21 McLuhan thought that Frank wrote 'bilge' (*L* 212). In 1966 McLuhan wrote but does not seem to have

published an essay with the title 'Spatial Form in Tudor and Stuart Poetry' (National Archives of Canada; hereafter NAC).

22 Joseph Frank, 'Spatial Form: An Answer to Critics,' *Critical Inquiry* 4.2 (Winter 1977): 231–52. Frank's notion of spatial form had gained a renewed critical currency with the ascendancy of structuralism in (American) academia, thanks to the conflation of the structural, the synchronous, and the spatial. For a critique of these 'spatial equivalents' (Fredric Jameson's term; see his *Postmodernism, or the Cultural Logic of Late Capitalism*, ch. 4 *passim)*, consult Doreen Massey, 'Politics and Space/Time,' *New Left Review* 196 (1992): 65–84; this quotation 78, n19.

23 See Kermode on McLuhan in *McLuhan: Hot and Cool* 173–80.

24 Frank Kermode, 'Critical Response: A Reply to Joseph Frank,' *Critical Inquiry* 4.3 (1978): 579–88.

25 McLuhan, 'Wyndham Lewis: His Theory of Art and Communication,' *Shenandoah* 4.2–3 (1953): 77–88. McLuhan reviewed Hugh Kenner's *Wyndham Lewis* in 'Nihilism Exposed,' *Renascence* 8.2 (1955): 97–9; he also recorded some thoughts about Lewis on a disc that accompanied *artscanada* 24.11, no. 114 (November 1967), a special issue on Lewis ('Wyndham Lewis Recalled: Marshall McLuhan Recalls Lewis').

26 McLuhan adds that this likens Lewis to T.E. Hulme. Hulme had visited the Canadian prairies in 1904, where he had been overwhelmed by the vastness of the open spaces, proclaiming upon his return to England a new 'poetics of space,' which came to inform the poetics of Imagism.

27 Wyndham Lewis, *Time and Western Man (TWM)*, ed. Paul Edwards (Santa Rosa: Black Sparrow P, 1993 [1927]), xi.

28 As Donald Theall writes in *RVM*, 'Wyndham Lewis' concern with space and Bergson's with time are present as early as *The Mechanical Bride*' (56).

29 Sheila Watson, 'Myth and Counter-Myth,' in *White Pelican* 4.1 (1974): 7–19. Watson (who was McLuhan's doctoral student) begins by drawing lines of convergence between Lévi-Strauss, Barthes, the McLuhan of *The Mechanical Bride*, and Lewis. See also Watson's essays on Lewis in 'Sheila Watson: A Collection,' *Open Letter* 3rd series, no. 1 (Winter 1974–5).

30 Siegfried Giedion, *Space, Time and Architecture* (1941; rpt Cambridge, MA: Harvard UP, 1967). Linda Dalrymple Henderson remarks in *The Fourth Dimension and Non-Euclidean Geometry in Modern Art (4D)* that Giedion's *Space, Time and Architecture* stands as a classic statement of 'the generalized "space-time philosophy," which was the final product of the interaction of art and Relativity in the 1920s' (337).

31 David Cook, *Northrop Frye: A Vision of the New World* (Montreal: Montreal UP, 1985), 9.

32 Other Canadian precursors of McLuhan's thought are John Grierson, Graham Spry, and Gerald Noxon, as discussed by Paul Tiessen in 'From Literary Modernism to the Tantramar Marshes: Anticipating McLuhan in British and Canadian Media Theory and Practice,' *Canadian Journal of Communication* 18 (1993): 451–67.

33 As Eugene McNamara comments in his introduction to the last section of *The Interior Landscape (IL)*, 'It is this advantage of perspective which has always made Canadians keen critics of American life ... It was a Canadian, Dr. R.M. Bucke, who first recognized Walt Whitman's genius' (182). For the complexities of the Bucke–Whitman relationship, see Richard Cavell and Peter Dickinson, 'Bucke, Whitman, and the Cross-Border Homosocial,' in a special joint issue, 'Canadian/American Relations: The Meaning of Differences,' of the *Canadian Review of American Studies/American Review of Canadian Studies* 26.3 (1996): 425–48.

34 McLuhan uses the same vocabulary in speaking about the end of visual space.

35 The 'cosmic consciousness' passage in *Understanding Media (UM)* has consistently been read as the ultimate statement of McLuhan's techno-utopian thought. However, Christopher Horrocks has recently argued that 'McLuhan's version of disembodiment ... cuts across superficial readings of the collectivism of the global village and the elevation of humans to a cosmic consciousness. For McLuhan, immersion in electronic media does not merely imply an elevation to a sublime state of global union, because his model incorporates the (admittedly undertheorised) conception that such immersion has a psychological and sensory impact that profoundly affects the ontological security of the individual' (66). See *Marshall McLuhan and Virtuality* (Cambridge, UK: Icon Books, 2000). For McLuhan's notion of 'discarnation' see 'A Last Look at the Tube' in *The Antigonish Review* [special issue on McLuhan] 74–5 (Summer-Autumn 1988): 197–200.

36 Bucke's insistence on the importance of air travel to this globality is curious, given that he was writing

before air travel had been successfully achieved. However, one of the individuals Bucke profiles as having attained a form of cosmic consciousness is Tennyson (whom Bucke visited in England), and Bucke may be drawing on the prophetic element of 'Locksley Hall.' The Tennyson connection is likewise important for McLuhan, who edited an edition of Tennyson's poetry; see also 'Tennyson and Picturesque Poetry,' *IL* 135–55.

37 See for example the discussions in *Laws of Media* (*LM*) 67–70 and *GV* chapter 4.

38 I am indebted to Nicky Drumbolis of Letters Books for a copy of his reprinted edition: Reginald Aubrey Fessenden, *The Deluged Civilization of the Caucasus Isthmus* (1923; rpt Toronto: Letters, 1988).

39 John Murray Gibbon, *Melody and the Lyric: From Chaucer to the Cavaliers* (London: J.M. Dent and Sons, 1930).

40 Brooker would have been part of the intellectual milieu of Winnipeg during the time that McLuhan was growing up there and going to university. See also Glenn Willmott's introduction to the reprinted edition of *Think of the Earth* (1936; rpt North York: Brown Bear P, 2000).

41 Bertram Brooker, *Sounds Assembling: The Poetry of Bertram Brooker*, ed. Birk Sproxton (Winnipeg: Turnstone Press, 1980), 10–11. See also Sherrill E. Grace, '"The Living Soul of Man": Bertram Brooker and Expressionist Theatre,' *Theatre History in Canada* 6.1 (1985): 3–22.

42 Richard Surrey [Bertram Brooker], *Layout Technique in Advertising* (New York: McGraw-Hill, 1929), 11.

43 Richard A. Wilson, *The Birth of Language: Its Place in World Evolution and Its Structure in Relation to Space and Time* (London: Dent, 1941), 4.

44 For an argument to the effect that the influence of Innis on McLuhan *was* simple and direct, see Joel Persky, 'The "Innescence" of Marshall McLuhan,' *Journal of Canadian Culture* 1.2 (1984): 3–14. A more nuanced argument is made by Roman Onufrijchuk, 'Introducing Innis / McLuhan Concluding: The Innis in McLuhan's "System,"' *Continuum: The Australian Journal of Media Culture* 7.1 (1993): 43–74.

45 As Glenn Willmott remarks, McLuhan 'was not trying to *incorporate* Innis's work, and thus reduce it to fit a larger vision of his own. Rather, he wishes to *add* to Innis's work ... But McLuhan explicitly differs with Innis' (*MMR* 112).

46 According to Graeme Patterson, Innis came to the oral/written dynamic through Eric Havelock, who was a student of the F.M. Cornford who wrote 'The Invention of Space,' an essay that influenced Innis and McLuhan alike; see *HC* 64–5.

47 Harold Adams Innis, *Empire and Communications* (*EmC*) (Oxford: Clarendon, 1950), 5.

48 McLuhan stated this relationship more boldly in *Report on Project in Understanding New Media* (*RPM*): 'staples are media and media are staples' (page 1 of the section 'What I Learned on the Project [1959–1960]').

49 Jody Berland sees the distinction between Innis and McLuhan as involving their understanding of communications technology; for Innis, such technology 'is not just a formal mechanism, but a set of relationships, shaped by economic, legal and cultural constraints as well as by technological capacities in the pure sense' (65). 'McLuhan's thesis has nothing to do with content, interpretation, or politics ... and everything to do with technological acceleration and the abolition of distance' (75). She also remarks, however, that 'Innis, unlike McLuhan, failed to include the cultures of any native peoples in his discussion of oral tradition. *Indeed, he overlooks all local cultures or practices in his account. Innis theorizes place as a social and economic entity, but takes into account no living place in particular. The technologies that produce his centres and margins never encounter the everyday lives, the complex technologically and geographically mediated power dynamics, the lively vestiges of myth and memory, the diverse imaginative activities of real men and women.* It is this omission, not his attention to geography and technology as agents of history, that exposes Innis to the charge of determinism and reductionism' (78; emphasis added). See her 'Space at the Margins: Colonial Spatiality and Critical Theory after Innis,' *Topia* 1 (Spring 1977): 55–82.

50 Lefebvre treats a similar space-and-time binary in Marx, arguing that Marx emphasized time at the expense of space largely in reaction to the superfoetation of the spatial within capitalist bourgeois society: 'In the wake of this fetishization of space in the service of the state, philosophy and practical activity were bound to seek a restoration of time. Hence Marx's vigorous reinstatement of historical time as revolutionary time. Hence also Bergson's more nuanced (though abstract and uncertain because specialized) evocation of mental duration and the immediacy of consciousness.' See *PS* 21–2.

51 It is precisely in contemporary society that Michel de Certeau, Luce Giard, and Pierre Mayol find a

renewed and augmented orality: 'Orality ... retains the primary role in our societies of writing and figures; it is more served than thwarted by the media or the resources of electronics' (252–3). See *Practice of Everyday Life 2: Living and Cooking*, trans. Timothy J. Tomasik (1990; rev. Minneapolis: U of Minnesota P, 1998).

52 Walter D. Mignolo has made a provocative reading of the time bias as participatory within a colonialist tendency towards the 'replacement of the "other" in space by the "other" in time and, by the same token, the articulation of cultural differences in chronological hierarchies. Fabian christened this transformation *the denial of coevalness*. What shall retain our attention here is that the replacement of the other in space by the other in time was partially framed in terms of boundaries and frontiers.' See *The Darker Side of the Renaissance: Literacy, Territoriality, and Colonization* (Ann Arbor: U of Michigan P, 1995), xi–xii.

53 Marshall McLuhan, 'Review of Innis's *Changing Concepts of Time*,' in *Northern Review* 6.3 (Aug.–Sept. 1953): 44–6.

54 Eric Havelock, *Harold Adams Innis: A Memoir* (Toronto: Harold Innis Foundation, 1982), 30. See also the essays 'Harold Innis: A Man of His Times' and 'Harold Innis: The Philosophical Historian' in *et cetera* 38.3 (1981): 242–54; 255–68.

55 Johannes Fabian, *Time and the Other: How Anthropology Makes Its Object* (New York: Columbia UP, 1983), 10–11.

56 Fabian acknowledges 'McLuhan's brilliant insights' as having had an influence on his own formulations (179, n12).

57 McLuhan and Pierre Babin, *Uomo nuovo, cristiano nuovo nell'era elettronica*, trans. dal francese di Armando Gonella (Roma: Ed. Paoline, 1979), 30. The book includes dialogues between Babin and McLuhan at the beginning and ending; the rest of the text is by Babin. The book was originally published in French as *Autre homme autre chrétien à l'âge électronique* (Lyons: Editions du Chalet, 1977); I cite and translate from the Italian translation in the National Archives of Canada, which does not hold a copy of the French version. An English translation has recently been published in *The Medium and the Light: Reflections on Religion* (*ML*), ed. Eric McLuhan and Jacek Szklarek (Toronto: Stoddart, 1999); see page 46 for this passage.

58 James W. Carey, 'Harold Adams Innis and Marshall McLuhan,' in *McLuhan Pro and Con*, ed. Raymond Rosenthal (Baltimore: Penguin, 1968), 270–308; these quotations 275, 281. (Reprinted from *Antioch Review* 28.1 [1967].) Carey maintains this position in 'Marshall McLuhan: Genealogy and Legacy,' *Canadian Journal of Communication* 23.3 (1998): 293–305, and in 'Interpreting McLuhan,' *Journal of Communication* 49.3 (1999): 187–93, though admitting in the latter that 'Even the fallen angel of the Harold Innis legacy (my McLuhan) seems a little odd, even antique, these days' (188).

59 As Ian Angus states, the 'emphasis on space is a key component of Innis' originality.' See 'Orality in the Twilight of Humanism: A Critique of the Communication Theory of Harold Innis,' *Continuum: The Australian Journal of Media and Culture* 7.1 (1993): 16–42, this quotation 24.

60 McLuhan, 'Environment as Programmed Happening,' *Knowledge and the Future of Man: An International Symposium*, ed. Walter J. Ong (New York: Holt, Rinehart and Winston, 1968), 113–24; this quotation 117. 'E.A. Bott (1887–1974), whom McLuhan never met, had been Professor of Psychology at the University of Toronto for many years, and Director of the Psychology Lab there' (*L* 364, n3 of editors). To say that Edward Bott devoted his career to studying auditory space is not accurate (nor is Paul Levinson's comment, in *Digital McLuhan* [New York: Routledge, 1999], that Bott 'first developed' [44] the concept). Long associated with *The British Journal of Psychology*, Bott researched such topics as muscle extension, orientation in stereoscopy, and pedagogy. Perhaps the most significant of his articles to be published around the time when McLuhan and Carleton Williams were getting interested in acoustic space is 'Studies on Visual Flicker and Fusion' (*Canadian Journal of Psychology* 4 [1950]: 145–55). While the article's focus is on vision (and, indeed, Bott is not cited in any source I have consulted on acoustic, or auditory, space), it is subtitled 'The Meaning of Fusion in Sensory Experience,' and this notion of fusion would surely have piqued McLuhan's interest in its suggestion that the auditory represented a *translation* of the sensory spectrum. It is noteworthy that the question of sensory fusion was raised with reference to *all* the senses; as Henry J. Watt remarks in *The Psychology of Sound* (Cambridge: Cambridge UP, 1917), 'fusion of sensations occurs in other senses [than that of hearing]' (56). Indeed, as Watt states, 'The problems of binaural hearing find a parallel in the problems of binoc-

ular vision' (177). That problem was precisely the 'problem of space' (as Geza Révész put it; see note 62): could a single ear localize space, or was that an attribute only of both ears? This was an important issue in establishing the spatiality of the auditory, since the debate (at the time that Watt was writing, and continuing into the late 1930s, when Révész was writing) revolved around whether the auditory was inherently spatial, or if it achieved spatiality 'only by association or conjunction with other senses' (Watt 175).

Bott announces at the beginning of his article on visual fusion that 'stress will be laid on the spatial and temporal features of our subject-matter' (145). Bott argues that sensory perception operates within 'fields' (149; an important concept for McLuhan, as chapter 3 below suggests), and that 'sense fields are on a par in being experiential, *and that all possess spatial characteristics*' (149; emphasis added), which is a key phrase in terms of McLuhan's interest in auditory space. Clearly, McLuhan understood auditory space in interfusional terms; Levinson's assertion, thus, that he (Levinson) 'stand[s] McLuhan on his head' when he argues 'that his [McLuhan's] acoustic space is now most found in the online alphabetic milieu of cyberspace' (*Digital McLuhan* 46) is not accurate. Gary Genosko puts McLuhan's position very well: 'McLuhan's oral society is ... marked by an "acoustic orientation" that is also tactile or auditive-tactile. What this means is that *orality is irreducible to speech as such* because tactility is for McLuhan a sign of the interplay of the senses, itself irreducible to haptic sensation' (*McLuhan and Baudrillard: The Masters of Implosion* [New York: Routledge, 1999], 40; emphasis added).

My impression is that McLuhan credited Bott with the development of the notion of 'acoustic space' on the basis of Carleton Williams's comment; once McLuhan began doing his own research in this area, he realized that Helmholtz was the key figure for understanding the origins of the concept. McLuhan's reference to Bott's work is significant, however, in that it indicates the importance McLuhan assigned to contemporary psychological discourse (as the first part of the present study suggests).

61 Carpenter states that the discussion in the seminar of acoustic (or auditory) space was 'the first break-through'; 'the phrase was electrifying' ('Remembering *Explorations*,' *Canadian Notes and Queries* 46 [Spring 1992]: 3–14; these quotations 5. Paul Levinson has suggested that 'within this concept of acoustic space ... lies a blueprint of all McLuhan's major insights and theories.' See 'McLuhan's Space,' *Journal of Communication* 40.2 (1990): 169–73; this quotation 170. Similarly, McLuhan's biographer, Philip Marchand, has written, 'Personally, I think [McLuhan's] notion of "acoustic space" versus "visual space" is one of the most illuminating ideas he ever came up with. When I began to understand that, I finally began to understand the rest of his work' (letter to the author dated 5 December 1995).

62 Psychologists had done considerable research in this area. Geza Révész's *Psychology and Art of the Blind*, trans. H.A. Wolff (London: Longmans, 1950), has various sections that discuss sensory con-structions of space: 'The Sciences of Space,' 'The Origins of Haptic Spatiality,' 'Haptics of Space,' 'Kinaesthetic Space and Dynamic Space,' and so on. In his 1937 article, 'Does an Acoustic Space Exist?' (published in German as 'Gibtes einen Hörraum?' with an English summary), Révész argues that such a space does *not* exist 'sui generis, i.e. [as] an autochtonic [*sic*] sound-space *independent of the optic and haptic sense-space*' (190; emphasis added). This accords with McLuhan's notion that the acoustic is an interplay of senses. See *Acta Psychologica* 3 (1937): 137–92. In 'The Problem of Space with Particular Emphasis on Specific Sensory Spaces,' *The American Journal of Psychology* 50 (1937): 429–44, Révész highlights the importance of the space question: 'If a general science of space should exist, it would have to include a group of problems which, for two centuries, have determined scientific research' (429). Révész's position is that a 'pure visual space-image which is entirely free from all foreign elements is not possible because of the simple fact that communication from tactual-kinesthetic functions cannot be excluded' (434), since 'the fusion of visual and tactual sensations takes place easily' (435).

A major antecedent for these discussions was the work of William James. In his 1879 article 'The Spatial *Quale*,' James begins by referring to an article published by 'Mr. [J. Elliott] Cabot' arguing that space 'forms a system of relations' (64). Cabot's point of departure is the Hegelian notion that extension is negative in that 'it signifies only the indefinite "*otherness*" of all objects of perception to each other' (65). James disagrees with this position. James's position is that space is 'an ingredient of the *sensation* yielded to us by the retina or skin' (68), in which terms extension is likewise a sensation: 'if the new geometry of Helmholtz and others has upset the necessity of our axioms ... then the Kantian doctrine seems literally left without a leg to stand upon' (87). See *The Journal of Speculative Philosophy* 13 (1879): 64–87.

In a subsequent article, James argues that *'spatial feelings'* are *'parts in a vaster spatial feeling which can enter the mind simply and all at once'* ('The Perception of Space [I],' *Mind* 45 (1887): 1–30; this quotation 11); in this regard, it is useful to remember that James was influenced by R.M. Bucke's notion of 'cosmic consciousness,' and that Bucke's phrase recurs in McLuhan's description in *Understanding Media* (*UM*) of the communicative possibilities afforded by electronic communications. James is one of the authors in the 'Marshall McLuhan Reading List' compiled by Eric McLuhan and Frank Zingrone in *Essential McLuhan* (*EM*) (399).

63 Jacques Lusseyran, *And There Was Light*, trans. Elizabeth R. Cameron (Boston: Little, Brown, 1963), 16.

64 F.M. Cornford, 'The Invention of Space,' *Essays in Honour of Gilbert Murray* (London: George Allen and Unwin, 1936), 215–35.

65 Compare also James W. Carey's comment, in 'Culture, Geography, and Communications: The Work of Harold Innis in an American Context,' *Culture, Communication and Dependency: The Tradition of H.A. Innis*, ed. William H. Melody, Liora R. Salter, and Paul Heyer (Norwood: Ablex, 1981), 73–91, that 'There certainly was something romantic in Innis' affection for the oral tradition' (85).

66 Compare Le Corbusier's comment: '"The skyscrapers concentrate everything in themselves: machines for abolishing time and space, telephones, cables, radios."' Quoted from *Urbanisme* in Beatriz Colomina, 'The Split Wall: Domestic Voyeurism,' *Sexuality and Space*, ed. Colomina (New York: Princeton Architectural P, 1992), 72–128; this quotation 112. See also chapter 5 below, where I discuss McLuhan in the context of Le Corbusier.

67 Carey, 'Harold Adams Innis and Marshall McLuhan,' 281.

68 Georg von Békésy, *Experiments in Hearing*, trans. E.G. Wever (New York: McGraw-Hill, 1960), 4.

69 McLuhan, 'Cybernation and Culture,' *The Social Impact of Cybernetics*, ed. Charles R. Dechert (Notre Dame: U of Notre Dame P, 1966), 95–108; this quotation, 97.

70 McLuhan, 'The Fecund Interval,' preface to Eric Havelock, *Harold A. Innis: A Memoir* (Toronto: Harold Innis Foundation, 1982), 9–10. By the point at which McLuhan wrote his third extended meditation on Innis (the fourth was his brief review in 1953 of *Changing Concepts of Time*) he had come to express the dynamic within acoustic space as the flux between figure and ground that, significantly, implies a two-dimensional relationship, for by this point in his career (1972), McLuhan had completely abandoned (on the theoretical level) the notion of point of view, with its implication of three-dimensional (i.e., perspectival) space.

71 John O'Neill, 'McLuhan's Loss of Innis-Sense,' *Canadian Forum* (May 1981): 13–15; this quotation 13.

72 Arthur Kroker, *Technology and the Canadian Mind: Innis/McLuhan/Grant* (*TCM*) (Montreal: New World Perspectives, 1984), 15. A decade later, Kroker identifies more closely with McLuhan; see 'Humanists Get Hip to the Net,' *Globe and Mail* (Saturday, 22 June 1996), C3.

73 Donald Theall, 'Exploration in Communications since Innis,' in Melody, Salter, and Heyer, eds, *Culture, Communication and Dependency*, 220–7; this quotation 225.

74 Elspeth Probyn, *'Love in a Cold Climate': Queer Belongings in Québec* (Montreal: GRECC, 1994), 41. Probyn further remarks that 'Innis' central and organizing metaphors were, of course, spatial although their logic was deeply temporal' (40). This is in fact a McLuhanesque reading of Innis. Probyn's critique of McLuhan is consistent with that of Fredric Jameson, summarized by George Landow as follows: 'Jameson seems to end by accepting what he had begun by denying – or at least he accepts what those like McLuhan have stated rather than what he apparently assumes them to have argued.' Landow concludes that Jameson's 'mystification and muddle derives from his need to exclude technology and its history from Marxist analyses.' See *Hypertext: The Convergence of Contemporary Critical Theory and Technology* (Baltimore: Johns Hopkins UP, 1992), 166.

75 Compare Innis's comment in *The Bias of Communication* (*BC*) that 'I have tried to use the Marxian interpretation to interpret Marx. There has been no systematic pushing of the Marxian conclusion to its ultimate limit, and in pushing it to its limit, showing its limitations' ('A Critical Review,' *BC* 190).

76 Note also page 18, where Theall remarks that Marxism is the 'only' position to take in social critique, and page 105, where McLuhan is unfavourably compared to Leszek Kolakowski. McLuhan included a number of pages on Marx in *Take Today* (*TT*), published the year after *The Medium Is the Rear-View Mirror* (*RVM*).

77 In a letter written a year earlier, McLuhan comments: 'Marxism is quite unable to cope with any 20th-century problem. The so-called "Communist" countries are merely trying to have a 19th century of consumer goods' (*L* 373).

78 'The machine was made in the Western world. It is a product of individualist genius and tenacity. But its effects are entirely collectivist and horizontal. As gimmick, the machine is useful. As object, as companion, as environment-shaper, it is magical. Marx was right to that extent. He saw that the machine would necessarily transform human feeling and sensibility. It would change habits of association and work. It would re-structure one's idea of the world and oneself. It was the revolution.' McLuhan, 'Poetry and Society,' *Poetry* 84.2 (1954): 93–5; this quotation 95.

79 Jean Baudrillard, 'Marshall MacLuhan [*sic*]: *Understanding Media: The Extensions of Man*,' *L'homme et la société* (Juillet-Août-Septembre 1967): 227–30; this quotation 228, n3.

80 Despite these critiques, however, at least one critic has reclaimed McLuhan for Marxism. In 'The Dialectical Methods of Marshall McLuhan, Marxism, and Critical Theory,' Paul Grosswiler argues that 'McLuhan employed a form of dialectical theory containing basic elements of dialectics developed by Hegel, Marx, and, later, his contemporaries of the Frankfurt School.' See Paul Grosswiler, 'The Dialectical Methods of Marshall McLuhan, Marxism, and Critical Theory,' *Canadian Journal of Communication* 21.1 (1996): 95–124; this quotation 96–7. Grosswiler expands on these observations in his book *Method Is the Message* (Montreal: Black Rose, 1998).

81 Not everyone critiqued McLuhan for his lack of Marxist engagement; according to Jean Marabini, McLuhan 'donne parfois raison ... à Karl Marx dans la dernière des thèses sur Feuerbach, sur l'opposition classique entre une union philosophique du monde et une vision politique. S'il est évident que le bouleversement total de la société exige un combat à mort entre ses structures, McLuhan est jusqu'à un certain point marxiste sans le savoir' (p. 27 of *Marcuse et McLuhan* [Paris: Mame, 1973]).

82 The notion of space as the opposite of time persists in some Marxist criticism to this day; see, for example, Ernesto Laclau's *New Reflections on the Revolution of Our Time* (New York: Verso, 1990):41.

83 Compare Stephen Kern's comment in *The Culture of Time and Space: 1880–1918* (*CTS*) (Cambridge, MA: Harvard UP, 1983): 'Speculation that there are two- and three-dimensional spaces other than the one described by Euclid and that our experience of space is subjective and a function of our unique physiology was disturbing to the popular mind. Perhaps the most famous critic of these notions was V.I. Lenin, who, in *Materialism and Empirio-Criticism* of 1908, cried "enough" to the proliferation of spaces, to the "Kantian" notion that space is a form of understanding and not an objective reality, and to "reactionary" philosophies such as those of [Ernst] Mach and Poincaré. Like a man trying to hold down a tent in a wind, Lenin raced about defending the objective, material world in absolute space and time that he believed to be the foundation of Marxism and which, he feared, was threatened by recent developments in mathematics and physics" (134).

84 Once again, the tide has shifted within Marxism. Tony Fabijancic, writing as a Marxist, has recently stated that the 'privileging of the temporal over the spatial undermines material analyses of modernity because to define it either in terms of linear time or an ethos ... is to fail to give it some material *structure*' (93). See 'The Dialectics of Modernity: Reification, Space, and Vision,' in *Rethinking Marxism* 8.3 (1995): 90–108. Note also Bruno Latour, who critiques the focus on time in a number of contemporary theorists, 'as if process were in any way more easily connected with time than with space' (179). See 'Trains of Thought: Piaget, Formalism, and the Fifth Dimension,' *Common Knowledge* 6.3 (1997): 170–91. Latour says that the first step in countering this misapplied focus is 'to elevate spacing to the same philosophical dignity as timing' (180). Julian Murphet speaks in highly McLuhanesque terms of post-Marxist cultural geographies: '[A]t the very moment that Marxian and Hegelian thought was being unceremoniously ditched from sociology, philosophy and cultural theory, it found refuge in most unlikely and unpromising quarters: the disciplinary hinterland of geography. Here a radical hypothesis took root. What if production today no longer referred simply to the production of "things" (goods, commodities, products) but to the total horizon of social space itself? To our cities, our inter-linked spatial networks of production, distribution, and consumption, our states, our very planet and its ecological limits?' See 'Grounding Theory: Literary Theory and the New Geography,' in *Post-Theory: New Directions in Criticism*, ed. Martin McQuillan et al. (Edinburgh: Edinburgh UP, 1999), 200–8; this quotation 201.

85 In fact, McLuhan's works are filled with exhortations and contain practical guides, such as *The City as*

Classroom (*CC*), or the film he made with Jane Jacobs about the blocking of the Spadina expressway in Toronto. See Jacobs's 'Making a Film with McLuhan,' in *The Antigonish Review* 74–5 (1988): 127–9.

86 M. Patricia Marchak, 'Political Economy In and Out of Time,' in *Canada: Theoretical Discourse / Discours théoriques*, ed. Terry Goldie et al. (Montreal: Association for Canadian Studies, 1994), 251–71; this quotation 264. Another of the issues on which McLuhan was skewered in the 1970s was that he was not anti-American enough. In fact, McLuhan posited Canada as a counter-environment to the United States, placing Canada in a critical position *vis-à-vis* that country. Indeed, he wrote that 'it is no accident that Canada produced Harold Innis with his uniquely structuring perception of large environments. He was a product of the Canadian anti-environment. The function of the anti-environment, whether in the arts or sciences or society, is that of perception and control' (*L* 319). And, as Judith Stamps has noted, McLuhan's sorties into the American marketplace showed him to be 'hardly sympathetic to business. Indeed, [he] showed a fair degree of hostility' (*Unth* 144). For example, 'to General Motors ... he offered the message that the automobile was obsolete, since ours was the age of the new corporate social body, not the individual. To the telephone company, he took the news that the phone's true significance lay in its effect on the sensorium. And to the Container Corp., he brought the insight that, since this was the end of the Newtonian era, the concept of the container was obsolete, and prefabricated packages would soon be a thing of the past' (*Unth* 144).

87 See also Carolyn Marvin, 'Innis, McLuhan and Marx,' *Visible Language* 20.3 (1986): 355–9.

88 Graeme Patterson has pointed this out in *HC* 20. Likewise, Robert C.H. Sweeny comments that Innis's staples thesis is 'ahistorical [and] formalistic'; see 'The Staples as the Significant Past: A Case Study in Historical Theory and Method,' in Goldie et al., eds, *Canada: Theoretical Discourse*, 327–49; this quotation 341.

89 Patterson, *HC* 37.

90 As Kroker remarks, 'there is a deep, thematic unity in all of McLuhan's writings' (*TCM* 61).

91 It was this distinction that led to the differences between McLuhan and Wilfred Watson; see the latter's article on the 'Place Marie Dialogues,' discussed in chapter 8. See also James M. Curtis, *Culture as Polyphony: An Essay on the Nature of Paradigms* (Columbia: U of Missouri P, 1978) who invokes Bakhtin in the context of his study of *UM*, but does not further relate the two.

92 As he wrote in 'The Humanities in the Electronic Age,' 'what has happened with the electronic advent is not that we move the products of human knowledge or labour to all corners of the earth more quickly. Rather we dilate the very means and *processes* of discourse to make a global envelope of sense and sensibility for the earth ... Each one of us, actively or passively, includes every other person on earth ... How is the entire community to receive a higher education *and* present standards of instruction to be maintained? The answer is simple, and it has been rendered many times by other new structures in the electronic age: decentralize. Create multiple new centres. Abandon centre-margin patterns of the old hierarchy of specialties and functions. Enthrone the living dialogue in centres and between centres, since the entire new technology of our age demands this greatest of all humanist forms of instruction, not as an ideal, but as a daily necessity of action in every area of our communities.' McLuhan, 'The Humanities in the Electronic Age,' *Humanities Association Bulletin* 34.1 (1961): 3–11; this quotation 9–10. Compare the comment of Bill Readings in *The University in Ruins*, that the contemporary university 'requires a model of knowledge as a *conversation* among a community rather than as a simple accumulation of facts' (Cambridge, MA: Harvard UP, 1996): 5.

93 Carey, 'Harold Adams Innis and Marshall McLuhan,' 306.

94 On the metaphor as privileged site of McLuhan's thought see Marie Morgan, 'McLuhan, Media and Metaphor,' *Antigonish Review* 98 (Summer 1994): 131–50. Note as well Don Mitchell's comment that '[I]f there is any consensus in all this new work in cultural geography, it is simply that, no matter how it is approached, "culture" *is* spatial ... Older cultural theory in many ways stressed *time*, suggesting that cultural traditions were handed down from generation to generation. New cultural theory, as it is developing in geography, cultural studies, and many allied disciplines, stresses *space*, understanding culture to be constituted through space and *as* a space. To the degree that that is the case, spatial *metaphors* have become indispensable for understanding the constitutions of culture." See *Cultural Geography: A Critical Introduction* (Oxford: Blackwell, 2000), 63.

95 See chapter 8, and note McLuhan's comment in an interview given at the end of his career that his

insights derived from the fact that he was born and raised in the counter-environment of the prairies; see Marchand, *M&M* 5.

96 Paul Carter, *The Road to Botany Bay: An Exploration of Landscape and History* (New York: Knopf, 1987), 304.

97 Compare McLuhan's comment in 'Myth and Mass Media': 'The sentiment of spatial and territorial nationalism that accompanies literacy is also reinforced by the printing press, which provides not only the sentiment but also the centralized bureaucratic instruments of uniform control over wide territories.' In *Dædalus* 88.2 (1959): 339–48; this quotation 344.

98 Kristin Ross, *The Emergence of Social Space: Rimbaud and the Paris Commune* (Minneapolis: U of Minnesota P, 1988).

99 Michel Foucault, 'Of Other Spaces,' *Diacritics* 16.1 (1986; originally 1967): 22–7; this quotation 23.

100 Compare Lefebvre: 'natural space will soon be lost to view,' *PS* 31.

101 McKenzie Wark, *Virtual Geography: Living with Global Media Events* (Bloomington: Indiana UP, 1994).

102 As Lefebvre expresses it: 'the *worldwide does not abolish the local*' (*PS* 86).

103 See, for example, *Cyberspace: First Steps*, ed. Michael Benedikt (Cambridge, MA: MIT P, 1991); Benedikt remarks in his introduction on the importance of *The Gutenberg Galaxy* in establishing the concept that the 'body ... [of] both orthodoxies and heresies, could neither be located at any one place, nor be entirely controlled' (8). Note also the chapter 'Heidegger and McLuhan: The Computer as Component' in Michael Heim's *The Metaphysics of Virtual Reality* (New York: Oxford UP, 1993), 55–71.

104 Ferguson, 'Marshall McLuhan Revisited,' 83 (see note 1).

105 Interestingly, Lefebvre pairs McLuhan with Guy Debord, author of *The Society of the Spectacle;* see chapter 7 below.

106 Compare Baudrillard's comment in *Simulations*: 'Space is no longer even linear or one-dimensional' (New York: Semiotext[e], 1983), 105.

107 Mark Gottdiener, *The Social Production of Urban Space* (Austin: U of Texas P, 1985), 123.

108 Doreen Massey, 'Politics and Space/Time,' *New Left Review* 196 (1992): 65–84; this quotation 71.

109 As John Fekete has argued, 'the post-structuralist development of the productive notions of trace and genealogy all parallel or confirm McLuhan's approach and create around it a politically democratic intellectual and institutional cluster which was unavailable in the 1950s and 1960s, which is more or less realistically synchronized with the widely variable retrieval and reception conditions in the contemporary information environment, and into which McLuhan can be fruitfully resituated.' John Fekete, 'Massage in the Mass Age: Remembering the McLuhan Matrix,' *Canadian Journal of Political and Social Theory* 6.3 (1982): 50–67; this quotation 53. This is exceptionally remarkable coming from Fekete, whose 1977 study *The Critical Twilight: Explorations in the Ideology of Anglo-American Literary Theory from Eliot to McLuhan* (London: Routledge and Kegan Paul, 1977) was scathingly critical of McLuhan's work, though once again in the familiar terms of 'global stasis' (170ff). McLuhan's significant achievement, in fact, was in developing a concept of spatial dynamics that now characterizes a wide range of contemporary theoretical systems.

110 Thus, if the geographers have been telling us that the spatial is socially constructed, the sociologists are now telling us that the social is spatially constructed. The example of sociology presents itself here, not only for its intrinsic relevance to the present inquiry (especially insofar as it interacts with geography) but also because McLuhan's thought was consistently criticized for ignoring the social dimensions of the issues it raised. What becomes quickly apparent in an overview of contemporary sociological theory is that it takes positions markedly similar to those outlined in McLuhan's work. In an article on spatial metaphors in contemporary sociological theory, for example, Ilana Friedrich Silber argues that such metaphors are distinguished by the insistence on 'relational analysis' (328). Only in 1984 (according to Silber's analysis) did sociologists begin to treat space as part of a general theory of sociology. Silber cites in this regard such figures as Giddens, Bourdieu, and Harrison White. White's 1992 study, *Identity and Control*, is of special interest. Drawing a number of analogies from physics, White argues that the most significant advance in sociological theory has been '"the victory over the concept of absolute space ... that became possible only because the concept of the material object was gradually replaced as the fundamental concept of physics by that of the field"' (quoted by Silber 340). Social spaces, 'rather than constituting some "pregiven Cartesian spaces," ... are seen as "continually

being rebuilt and torn down, over and over again, with everyday and demographic contingencies at the root of both tearing down and reproducing"' (Silber 341, quoting White). See Ilana Friedrich Silber, 'Space, Fields, Boundaries: The Rise of Spatial Metaphors in Contemporary Sociological Theory,' *Social Research* 62.2 (1995): 323–55.

Chapter 2: Mechanization and Its Discontents

1 Sheila Watson has drawn attention to Wyndham Lewis's critique of '"automobilism"' in *Blast*. See 'Myth and Counter-Myth,' *White Pelican* 4.1 (1974): 7–19; this quotation 10.

2 T.S. Eliot, 'The Metaphysical Poets' in *Selected Prose of T.S. Eliot*, ed. Frank Kermode (London: Faber, 1975), 59–67: 'In the seventeenth century a dissociation of sensibility set in, from which we have never recovered' (64).

3 Compare the comment at the end of *Culture Is Our Business* (*COB*): 'The Bomb is electric software' (334).

4 Dennis Duffy, *Marshall McLuhan* (Toronto: McClelland and Stewart, 1969), 10.

5 Marshall McLuhan, '*Playboy* Interview [with Eric Norden],' in *Essential McLuhan* (*EM*), ed. Eric McLuhan and F. Zingrone (1969; Toronto: Anansi, 1995), 233–69; this quotation 265; my emphasis. Two years before this interview, in his essay 'The Future of Morality: The Inner versus the Outer Quest,' written for an anthology of articles published by colleagues at St Michael's College, University of Toronto, McLuhan wrote: 'The strategy of the new morality ... is to encounter each situation as unique. This is to undertake a completely exploratory approach to experience in which all conventional guides and patterns are broken up in order to become the means of probing rather than of classifying each experience ... Under the conditions of this inner quest, "sincerity" and "integrity" take precedence over respectability and acceptability' (in *The New Morality: Continuity and Discontinuity*, ed. William Dunphy [New York: Herder and Herder, 1967], 175–89; this quotation 188–9).

6 One of the reviews of *The Mechanical Bride* (*MB*) concludes with the comment, 'How refreshing to see a critique of a period and of its morals avoiding moral indignation!' See Rudolph E. Morris, 'Review of *The Mechanical Bride*,' in *Renascence* 4.2 (1952): 217–19; this quotation 219. For an overview of the reviews of *MB* see Terence Gordon, *Marshall McLuhan: Escape into Understanding* (*EU*) 156.

7 See Marjorie Perloff, *The Futurist Moment: Avant-Garde, Avant Guerre, and the Language of Rupture* (Chicago: U of Chicago P, 1986), 181.

8 For further elaborations, see chapter 6 below, 'Visible Speech'; fig. 6.4 reproduces a page from McLuhan's *Counterblast* (1969).

9 McLuhan, 'Footprints in the Sands of Crime,' *Sewanee Review* 54 (1946): 617–34; this quotation 634.

10 McLuhan, 'Joyce, Aquinas, and the Poetic Process,' *Renascence* 4.1 (1951): 3–11; this quotation 7.

11 Arthur Kroker, *Technology and the Canadian Mind: Innis/McLuhan/Grant* (*TCM*) (Montreal: New World Perspectives, 1984), 71.

12 Judith Stamps points out that Burckhardt had taught Heinrich Wölfflin (another significant influence on McLuhan; see chapter 3), who in turn taught Giedion. See *Unthinking Modernity: Innis, McLuhan, and the Frankfurt School* (*Unth*) (Montreal: McGill-Queen's UP, 1994), 177, n6.

13 Similarly, Blaise Cendrars had written in 1927 an essay with the title 'Advertising = Poetry.' See Marjorie Perloff's discussion in *The Futurist Moment* 9.

14 Margaret Mead, *Male and Female: A Study of the Sexes in a Changing World* (New York: Morrow, 1949).

15 Ellen Lupton, *Mechanical Brides: Women and Machines from Home to Office* (New York and Princeton: Cooper-Hewitt/Princeton Architectural P, 1993).

16 While *MB* may not strike us today as particularly feminist in its concerns, a comparison with one of McLuhan's source texts, Philip Wylie's *Generation of Vipers*, is instructive regarding the context in which McLuhan was writing. Published in 1941, Wylie's book develops a thesis about 'momism' – that the contemporary American woman was emasculating the American man. Wylie went so far as to suggest that women had taken over the airwaves. 'The radio,' he writes, 'is mom's final tool, for it stamps everyone who listens with the matriarchal brand – its superstitions, prejudices, devotional rules, taboos, musts, and all other qualifications needful to its maintenance. Just as Goebbels has revealed what can be

done with such a mass-stamping of the public psyche in his nation, so our land is a living representation
of the same fact worked out in matriarchal sentimentality, goo, slop, hidden cruelty, and the foreshadow
of national death.' See Philip Wylie, *Generation of Vipers* (1941; rev. New York: Holt, Rinehart and
Winston, 1955), 214–15.

17 Siegfried Giedion, *Mechanization Takes Command: A Contribution to Anonymous History (MTC)* (New
   York: Oxford UP, 1948).

18 McLuhan, 'Encyclopaedic Unities' [review of L. Moholy-Nagy, *Vision in Motion* and Giedion, *MTC*],
   The Hudson Review 1.4 (1949): 599–602; this quotation 600. See chapter 5 below for the importance of
   Moholy-Nagy to McLuhan.

19 For McLuhan's influence on Schafer, see chapter 6, 'Visible Speech.'

20 Marta Braun, *Picturing Time: The Work of Etienne-Jules Marey (1830–1904)* (Chicago: U of Chicago P,
   1992), 66.

21 Mary Ann Doane, 'Temporality, Storage, Legibility: Freud, Marey, and the Cinema,' *Critical Inquiry*
   22.2 (1996): 313–43; this quotation 329, emphasis added.

22 McLuhan writes about 'the great age of mechanism that stretches from Gutenberg to Darwin' in 'Tennyson and the Romantic Epic,' *Tennyson: A Review of Modern Criticism*, ed. John Killham (New York:
   Barnes and Noble, 1960), 86–95; this quotation 93.

23 In experiential terms, this change in the way time was perceived issued in the paradoxical sensation that
   time had been spatialized, as in a transcontinental flight – the phenomenon that has come to be known
   as 'space-time collapse.' See Peter Gould, 'Dynamic Structures of Geographic Space,' *Collapsing Space
   and Time: Geographic Aspects of Communications and Information*, ed. Stanley D. Brunn and Thomas
   R. Leinbach (London: HarperCollinsAcademic, 1991), 3–30.

24 The constellation metaphor reappears in the title of *The Gutenberg Galaxy (GG)*.

25 *The Medium Is the Massage (MM)* and *War and Peace in the Global Village (WPGV)* were designed
   by Quentin Fiore, who studied with George Grosz, the inventor – with John Heartfield – of photomontage. See Benjamin H.D. Buchloh, 'Allegorical Procedures: Appropriation and Montage in Contemporary Art,' *Artforum* 21.1 (1982): 43–56 and 'Graphics Convey Message in Medium Is the Massage,' in
   The McLuhan Explosion, ed. Harry H. Crosby and George R. Bond (New York: American Book Co.,
   1968), 203–7; this quotation 206. I expand on these connections in chapter 5 below.

26 In the introduction (1972) to *Empire and Communications (EmC)* (1950), McLuhan writes that 'Towards the end ... Innis speeds up his sequence of figure-ground flashes almost to that of a cinematic
   montage' (vi); McLuhan makes similar comments in 'Review of Innis's *Changing Concepts of Time*,'
   in *Northern Review* 6.3 (Aug.–Sept. 1953): 44–6; see especially 45. The attribution of a cinematic
   sensibility to Innis is somewhat ironic, given McLuhan's observations on Innis's failure to realize the
   implications of artistic techniques and McLuhan's notion that the cinema was the ultimate fulfilment
   of the mechanical era.

27 The comparisons go beyond the focus of this chapter to include the importance Benjamin assigned to
   the introduction of printing and to his insistence that the 'manner in which human sense perception is
   organized, the medium in which it is accomplished, is determined not only by nature but by historical
   circumstances as well' ('Work of Art' 222), and the notion that the distinction between author and public was disappearing. Jean Baudrillard aligns McLuhan and Benjamin in *Simulations*, trans. Paul Foss,
   Paul Patton, and Philip Beitchman (New York: Semiotext[e], 1983), 99–100. See Walter Benjamin,
   "The Work of Art in the Age of Mechanical Reproduction," in *Illuminations: Essays and Reflections*,
   ed. Hannah Arendt (New York: Schocken, 1968), 217–51.

28 Benjamin was especially interested in Giedion's *Bauen im Frankreich* (1928); Giedion and Benjamin
   knew one another from the time when they were both working in the Bibliothèque Nationale in Paris,
   when they had the opportunity to discuss their work. See Joseph Rykwert, review of *Space, Time and
   Architecture* in *Harvard Design Magazine* (Fall 1998): 65–6; and Susan Buck-Morss, *The Dialectics of
   Seeing: Walter Benjamin and the Arcades Project* (Cambridge, MA: MIT P, 1989), 468, n45.

29 'In the mid-thirties, Benjamin decided to include actual images in the *Passagen-Werk*.' See Buck-
   Morss, *Dialectics of Seeing* 71.

30 Buck-Morss, ibid. 261, quoting from volume V (*Das Passagen-Werk*) of the *Gesammelte Schriften*; her
   ellipses and square brackets.

31 Buck-Morss, ibid. 261, quoting from *Das Passagen-Werk*.

32 Michael W. Jennings, *Dialectical Images: Walter Benjamin's Theory of Literary Criticism* (Ithaca: Cornell UP, 1987), 211.

33 In subsequent works on similar themes, McLuhan brought together medium with message much more fully. While *COB* (1970; marketed on its jacket as a 'book that picks up where his by-now classic *The Mechanical Bride* left off') is concerned exclusively with advertisements, *WPGV* (1968) returns to the theme of mechanization. Whereas *MB* deals with mechanization as process, *WPGV* approaches mechanization as the content of the electronic era that superseded the mechanical, evidence of which McLuhan discerns in the phenomenon of those who call the computer a machine (18). This productively complicates the medium/message dyad to suggest that McLuhan is not rewriting the form/content binary but is theorizing a dynamic of interactive processes.

34 McLuhan discusses Muybridge in 'Wheel, Bicycle, and Airplane,' *Understanding Media (UM)* (New York: McGraw-Hill, 1964), 179–87.

35 In the introduction to *Subliminal Seduction*, McLuhan writes that 'Advertising is an environmental striptease for a world of abundance.' See 'Media Ad-Vice: An Introduction' to Wilson Bryan Key, *Subliminal Seduction: Ad Media's Manipulation of a Not So Innocent America* (Englewood Cliffs: Prentice-Hall, 1973), iv–xvi; this quotation v.

36 National Archives of Canada (NAC), McLuhan Collection, MG 31 D156, vol. 128, Duchamp no. 34.

37 Harold Rosenberg, 'Philosophy in a Pop Key,' *The New Yorker* (27 February 1965): 129–36; this quotation 129.

38 Rosalind Krauss, *The Optical Unconscious* (Cambridge, MA: MIT P, 1993), 123.

39 Retinalists, for Duchamp, were the Impressionists, as opposed to Seurat; see Krauss, ibid. 123, McLuhan on Seurat in *UM* and *Through the Vanishing Point (TVP)*, and chapter 5 below.

40 Jean-François Lyotard writes in *Duchamp's TRANS/formers* (trans. Ian McLeod; 1977; Venice: Lapis Press, 1990) that 'the "plastic" problem of the *Large Glass* is that of projections. The lower region ... is treated according to the procedures of Italian perspective ... But as the support is made of transparent glass, the eye paradoxically *cannot* traverse it to explore the virtual space' (33–4).

41 Linda Dalrymple Henderson, *The Fourth Dimension and Non-Euclidean Geometry in Modern Art (4D)* (Princeton: Princeton UP, 1983), 130.

42 More pointedly, McLuhan writes that 'Human love and marriage today have no more relation to human society than had Crusoe's economic activities in the eighteenth century' in 'Out of the Castle into the Counting-House,' *Politics* 3.8 (September 1946): 277–9; this quotation 278.

43 The discourse of mechanization and sexuality abounded in Dada; an article in *Camera Work* (September October 1915) states: '"Man made the machine in his own image. She has limbs which act; lungs which breathe; a heart which beats; a nervous system through which runs electricity. The phonograph is the image of the voice; the camera is the image of the eye"' (55). Quoted in Todd Alden, 'Here Nothing, Always Nothing: A New York Dada Index, Etc.,' in *Making Mischief: Dada Invades New York*, ed. Francis Naumann (New York: Whitney Museum, 1996), 33–75. Compare also Remy de Gourmont's comment in his 1903 *Physique de l'amour: Essai sur l'instinct sexuel*: '"They [the sexual organs] are rigorously made the one for the other, and the accord in this case must be not only harmonic, but mechanical and mathematical"' (232). Quoted in Linda Dalrymple Henderson, 'Reflections of and/or on Marcel Duchamp's *Large Glass*,' in *Making Mischief* 228–37. On McLuhan's connections to Dada, see chapter 5 below.

44 Martin Jay attributes the creation of this space to the influence on Duchamp of the photographic experiments undertaken by Marey and Muybridge. See *Downcast Eyes: The Denigration of Vision in Twentieth-Century French Thought* (Berkeley: U of California P, 1993), 137.

45 Compare Wyndham Lewis's reference to 'the submissive, hypnotized public' in *Time and Western Man (TWM)* 13.

46 In 'American Advertising,' which analyses a number of the exhibits discussed in *MB*, McLuhan cites A.T. Poffenberger's *Psychology in Advertising* as a type of 'advertising manual' (439). See *Mass Culture: The Popular Arts in America*, ed. Bernard Rosenberg and David Manning White (Glencoe: The Free Press, 1957); rpt from *Horizon* 93–4 (1947).

47 Marshall McLuhan, 'Inside Blake and Hollywood,' *The Sewanee Review* 55.4 (1947): 710–15; this quotation 714.

48 McLuhan's Cambridge mentor, F.R. Leavis, had written (with Denys Thompson) in *Culture and Environment: The Training of Critical Awareness* (1933; London: Chatto and Windus, 1950), that 'we are committed to more consciousness; that way, if any, lies salvation. We cannot, as we might in a healthy state of culture, leave the citizen to be formed unconsciously by his environment' (5).What separates *Culture and Environment* from *MB* is the former's opposition to 'the whole world outside the classroom' (1); McLuhan's concern was with *The City as Classroom* (*CC*) (1978). Nevertheless, there are a number of similarities between McLuhan's project and that of Leavis, including the pedagogical element (the Leavis book was 'designed for school use' [vii]), the focus on mass production, and the suggestion that aspects of literary analysis (practical criticism) could be applied to other cultural phenomena. Willmott notes that, in 1944, McLuhan taught a seminar with the title 'Culture and Environment' (*MMR* 18).

49 Miller is quoted in Gordon, *EU* 209. Walter Ong, McLuhan's student, went on to elaborate a theory of 'communications media and the Freudian pyschosexual stages'; see *The Presence of the Word: Some Prolegomena for Cultural and Religious History* (New Haven: Yale UP, 1967), 92–110.

50 McLuhan, 'The Psychopathology of *Time* and *Life*,' in *The Scene before You: A New Approach to American Culture*, ed. Chandler Brossard (New York: Rinehart, 1955), 147–60; this quotation 148. Reprinted from *Neurotica* (1949).

51 Gershon Legman, *Love and Death* (New York: Breaking Point, 1949).

52 For 'culturalist' see Stephen A. Mitchell and Margaret J. Black, *Freud and Beyond: A History of Modern Psychoanalytic Thought* (New York: Basic Books, 1995) 21; for McLuhan's interest in Horney see Marchand, *Marshall McLuhan: The Medium and the Messenger* (*M&M*) 70.

53 Jean Marabini argues that *Civilization and Its Discontents* informs McLuhan's pronouncements on sexuality; see *Marcuse et McLuhan* (Paris: Mame, 1973), 34 and 41.

54 Karen Horney, *The Neurotic Personality of Our Time* (New York: Norton, 1937), 20; 282.

55 McLuhan, 'What T.V. Is Really Doing to Your Children,' *Family Circle* (March 1967): 33; 98–100.

56 Milton Klonsky, 'mc²luhan's mEssage *or:* which way did the second coming went?' in Raymond Rosenthal, ed., *McLuhan: Pro and Con* (Baltimore: Penguin, 1968), 125–39; this quotation 137.

57 My translation from the French text published in *Mutations 1990* (Paris: Mame, 1969), 10.

58 Writing in 1935 on the 'Psycho-Analysis of Space,' Paul Schilder states that 'Philosophers and psychologists have not given sufficient attention to the fact that there is not only a space outside of the body but also a space which is filled by the body. The image of the body extends in space and already implies space perception. Body space is strictly senseless without an outward space. When we speak about narcissism we should not forget that an outward space and the space of the body are the necessary basis for the unfolding of narcissistic tendencies. This primitive space is probably less unified than the developed space. The primitive space is centred around the openings of the body and so has several centres ... Space is not an independent entity (as Kant has wrongly stated) but is in close relation to instincts, drives, emotions and actions with their tonic and phasic components' (274; 295). Published in *The International Journal of Psycho-Analysis* (directed by Sigmund Freud), 16 (1935): 274–95. On the relation of the spatial question to the debate over 'introjection,' see the chapter titled 'The Internal World' in Darian Leader, *Freud's Footnotes* (London: Faber and Faber, 2000), 49–87.

59 David Wills comments that Freud 'asks us to defy, as his theory constantly did, the space-time coordinates of an architectural and archaeological chronology in favour of the impossibility of a historical simultaneity ... And because what he asks us to imagine defies logic, he will remain dissatisfied, as he is here, with a topographical representation of mental activity' (*Prosthesis* [*Pr*] 100). Precisely; and it is to that critique of logic that McLuhan will devote the *ana*logical trajectory of his space–time theory of the audile–tactile.

60 Taylor's 'successor,' Frank L. Gilbreth, based his system of analysis on Marey's work; see Braun, *Picturing Time* 343–4.

61 Friedrich A. Kittler notes, in *Discourse Networks 1800/1900*, trans. Michael Metteer, with Chris Cullens (Stanford: Stanford UP, 1990), that Freud, while studying with Charcot, was shown a film of hysterics incarcerated in the Salpêtrière; this film had been made by a follower of Muybridge, using the 'short-exposure series' camera (277).

62 I do not agree with Doane that the problems faced in this regard by Freud involved only 'attempts to analyze time' (315); rather, the problem he faced was how to represent temporal processes spatially.

63 Rosalind Krauss, '"Moteur!"' in Krauss and Yve-Alain Bois, *Formless: A User's Guide* (New York: Zone, 1997), 135.

64 For McLuhan, 'The dweller in the old mechanical world lived on dreams as a way of contacting the fuller world. The whole nineteenth century in a sense ended with the movies and manifested its preference for a dream world as altogether richer than real life' (*WPGV* 81).

65 Whitehead ascribes this space–time confluence to an awareness of bodily experience, an aspect taken up in chapter 4, 'Prosthetic Aesthetics.' *Science and the Modern World* (1925; New York: Macmillan, 1954) records a major debt to Samuel Alexander's *Space, Time and Deity*, on which Lewis focuses in *TWM*. In the chapter on relativity, Whitehead writes that 'the new relativity associates space and time with an intimacy not hitherto contemplated' (173); Whitehead refers to this as 'the organic theory of nature' (173). I take up these issues in detail in chapter 3.

66 As Friedrich A. Kittler puts it, 'The fact that the doctor and hysteric patient are not allowed to look at one another means that the couch ... is a pure realm of hearing.' See *Discourse Networks 1800/1900*, 284. Rosalind Krauss remarks, in *The Optical Unconscious*, that, 'Though phenomenology's unconscious is not that of Freud, the two are compatible in their belief in a primordial spatiality. For the continuous extension within which the body's gesture unfolds its meaning is, after all, the same medium in which the complex dance of displacements and condensations occurs, a continuity hostile to the staccato break-up of the [visual] spatial medium which is that of speech. The transparent grid where signifiers are formed through the regulated action of spacing is an abstract, purely conceptual medium disjunct from the one through which the perceptual event unrolls or the impress of desire swells' (218).

67 It is significant that for Freud the relations between consciousness and preconsciousness were mediated by mnemic residues (chiefly words) 'derived primarily from auditory perceptions' ('The Ego and the Id,' *The Freud Reader*, ed. Peter Gay [New York: Norton, 1989], 633).

68 The notion of extension was likewise indebted to Giedion, who comments in *MTC* that 'man acts as a lever of the machine' (77), and relates developments in furniture design to that in prosthetic limbs (391). See chapter 4 below.

69 McLuhan, 'Myth and Mass Media,' *Dædalus* 88.2 (1959): 339–48; this quotation 346.

70 Donald Theall, 'McLuhan and the Toronto School of Communication,' in *Understanding 1984* (Ottawa: Canadian Commission for UNESCO, 1984), 47–55; this quotation 51.

71 J.C. Carothers, 'Culture, Psychiatry, and the Written Word,' *Psychiatry* 22.4 (1959): 307–20; this quotation 307.

72 On 'the oral concept of Freud' see *Verbi-Voco-Visual Explorations* (*VVV*), item 9.

73 Sigmund Freud, 'The Theme of the Three Caskets,' in *The Freud Reader*, 514–22; these quotations 517.

Chapter 3: The Physics of Flatland

1 On this interfacing of physics and social theory generally, Jonathan Boyarin writes that 'Social scientists are aware that modern physics has challenged our commonsense notions of the changeless grid of time and space ... Why is it that our physics are now those of Einsteinian relativity and quantum mechanics, whereas our politics and our rhetorics still assume a world as described by Newton and Descartes? One suggestion made by postmodern political scientists is that there are close genealogical links between the "Cartesian coordinates" of space and time and the discrete, sovereign state, both associated with European society since the Renaissance ...' See 'Space, Time, and the Politics of Memory,' in *Remapping Memory: The Politics of TimeSpace*, ed. Jonathan Boyarin (Minneapolis: U of Minnesota P, 1994): 1–37.

2 Compare *The Gutenberg Galaxy* (*GG*) 127: 'There is then this great paradox of the Gutenberg era, that its seeming activism is cinematic in the strict movie sense. It is a series of static shots or "fixed points of view" in homogeneous relationship.'

3 These comments temper Glenn Willmott's assertions in *McLuhan, or Modernism in Reverse* (*MMR*) about the overriding significance of the cinema within McLuhan's aesthetic, and the concomitant importance of arrest within McLuhan's methodology. The spatial mosaic McLuhan was proposing resembles the microchip more than the movie.

4 McLuhan was also drawing, more broadly, on John U. Nef's *Cultural Foundations of Industrial*

Civilization (Cambridge: Cambridge UP, 1958), which argues that the history of industrial civilization 'needs to be thought through anew in terms of man's experience as a whole' (x).

5 For Carpenter's highly entertaining reminiscences about *Explorations* see Edmund Carpenter, 'Remembering *Explorations*,' *Canadian Notes and Queries* 46 (Spring 1992): 3–14, as well as the postscript to Donald Theall's *The Virtual Marshall McLuhan* (*VM*), where it is reprinted at slightly greater length. Carpenter's statement that Benjamin Whorf (who had an 'indirect' influence on *Explorations* [5]), 'wrote his first paper on spatial metaphors' (4) is not supported by the bibliography attached to *Language, Thought, and Reality: Selected Writings of Benjamin Lee Whorf* (ed. John B. Carroll [Cambridge, MA: MIT P, 1956]). Where Whorf *does* write about space, as in his article in this book on 'Gestalt Technique of Stem Composition in Shawnee,' he states that 'Everything unvisual is unspatial' (164), a notion antithetical to the concepts of acoustic space and visual critique developed by McLuhan in the course of his career.

6 McLuhan and Carpenter published Innis's 'The Concept of Monopoly and Civilization' in issue 3 of *Explorations*.

7 Carpenter suggested (according to McLuhan) that Waldemar Bogoras 'may have been the first anthropologist to state that non-literate man had non-Euclidean space concepts' (*GG* 67, n17). The article by Bogoras cited by McLuhan draws on studies of the 'Asiatic Eskimo' and argues that 'the ideas of modern physics about space and time, when clothed with concrete psychical form, appeared as shamanistic.' See Waldemar Bogoras, 'Ideas of Space and Time in the Conception of Primitive Religion,' *American Anthropologist*, ns. 27.2 (1925): 205–15; this quotation 205.

8 McLuhan and Edmund Carpenter, 'Acoustic Space,' *Explorations in Communication* (*ExC*), ed. McLuhan and Carpenter (Boston: Beacon P, 1960), 65–70.

9 The masthead note to the first issue of *Explorations* identifies 'anthropology and communications' as the journal's major areas of interest. The journal ran from December 1953 to October 1957; in 1959, *Explorations* 9, which ended the series, was published as *Eskimo*, a large-format book edited by Edmund Carpenter, Robert Flaherty, and A.Y. Jackson. Consistently with his post-*GG* theoretic, McLuhan revisited *Explorations* from 1964 to 1972 in the pages of two University of Toronto publications, *The Varsity Graduate* and *The University of Toronto Graduate*, as Robert Fulford notes in 'All Ignorance Is Motivated: Re-examining the Seedbed of McLuhanism,' *Canadian Notes and Queries* no. 45 (1991): 3–8.

10 The history of this very important article is complex. It was Carleton Williams who read a paper entitled 'Acoustic Space' in McLuhan's seminar in November 1954 (Marchand, *M&M* 123), although, as Marchand notes, the paper 'has the stamp of McLuhan all over it.' It was published in February 1955 (*Exp* 4) under Williams's name, and in *Explorations in Communication* under the names of McLuhan and Carpenter. Fulford ('All Ignorance') calls this a 'horror story' (6) and quotes Williams as saying that McLuhan and Carpenter '"plagiarized"' (6) his article (blaming Carpenter more than McLuhan, however). In *Who Was Marshall McLuhan*? (*WWMM*) (Toronto: Stoddart, 1995), Williams claims to have 'taught [McLuhan] about auditory space,' which 'struck Marshall with great force ... This was characteristic of Marshall: that he appropriated ideas from others, developing and expanding them beyond anything contemplated by the original proposal' (144). Carpenter states that 'Carl sent a paper on 'auditory space' to *Explorations* minus all seminar dialogue. So Marshall and I put it in. A mistake. Two articles, one on the mechanics of auditory space, the other on acoustic "patterning," might have been more diplomatic.' See Carpenter, 'Remembering,' 5.

11 Paul Carter, *The Road to Botany Bay: An Exploration of Landscape and History* (New York: Knopf, 1987), 101.

12 Compare *Take Today* (*TT*): 'instant retrieval joins prehistory and posthistory in an inclusive NOW of all traditions' (16).

13 Compare McLuhan's remark in 'One Wheel, All Square,' *Renascence* 10.4 (1958): 196–200: 'This is not to be a-historical. On the contrary, we know today that nothing is more false to history than lineality' (199).

14 McLuhan (unsigned), 'Songs of the Pogo,' *Exp* 7:27–9; this quotation 27.

15 The unpaginated 'preface' to the Prologue of the *GG* is significantly longer in those editions printed after the second impression, and it is this reprinted edition that I am quoting from here and throughout; pagination remains the same, however.

16 Walter Ong, *Ramus: Method and the Decay of Dialogue* (Cambridge, MA: Harvard UP, 1958). Ong acknowledges McLuhan as his 'constant source of intellectual stimulation' (x) and as having sparked Ong's 'initial interest in the present subject.' The companion volume, *Ramus and Talon Inventory* (published conjointly) is dedicated to McLuhan. In McLuhan's dissertation, which focuses in large part on the Nashe–Harvey polemics, McLuhan argues that Nashe was 'anti-Ramistic' (383), while Harvey was not. See McLuhan, 'The Place of Thomas Nashe in the Learning of His Time' (diss., Cambridge University, 1943).

17 Walter J. Ong, *Orality and Literacy: The Technologizing of the Word* (New York: Methuen, 1982).

18 The nuances of 'binaristic' models as used by McLuhan in the *GG* are worked out by Ernest Gallo in 'The Game of Words,' *Midwest Quarterly* 26.3 (985): 300–14: 'We must deal ... with [McLuhan's] astounding assurance that binary computers dispense with number. McLuhan can't be serious. Of course, he does not mean number, but rather number which depends on the visual arrangement of its digits: binary numbers apparently are exempt from this requirement. But that is simply not the case ... McLuhan might really be saying that computers do not need to visualize. They perform their calculations at blinding speed. The separate digits are blurred to human sight, just as in the "structuralist physics" of Heisenberg, position and momentum of an electron become blurred into one another at the instant we attempt to *see* it. Better not try to see, then. Better to hear, to feel, to be one with' (305, 307).

19 See Richard Cavell, 'Where Is Frye?, or, Theorising Postcolonial Space,' *Essays on Canadian Writing* 56 (1995): 110–34.

20 Similarly, McLuhan had written in 'The Humanities in the Electronic Age' (*Humanities Association Bulletin* 34.1 [1961]: 3–11) that 'whereas the mechanical age had been one of centre-margin structures, the electronic age is inevitably one of multiple centres-without-margins' (8).

21 Walter Benjamin argues in the 'Theses on the Philosophy of History' that 'There is no document of civilization which is not at the same time a document of barbarism' (256 of *Illuminations* [New York: Schocken, 1968], 253–64). McLuhan is more radical, in that he does not privilege civilization as originary but unmoors it, seeing it as an effect rather than as natural. As he puts it, in one of the most powerful assertions of the *GG*, 'By the meaningless sign linked to the meaningless sound we have built the shape and meaning of Western man' (50).

22 John Fekete, 'Notes toward a Critique of McLuhan's Polemic against Vision,' *The Critical Twilight: Explorations in the Ideology of Anglo-American Literary Theory from Eliot to McLuhan* (London: Routledge and Kegan Paul, 1977), 213–15.

23 McLuhan, '*Playboy* Interview: A Candid Conversation with the High Priest of Popcult and Metaphysician of Media,' reprinted in *Essential McLuhan* (*EM*), ed. Eric McLuhan and Frank Zingrone (Toronto: Anansi, 1995), 233–69.

24 Marshall McLuhan and R.K. Logan, 'Alphabet, Mother of Invention,' *et cetera* 34.4 (1977): 373–83; this article, published late in McLuhan's career, indicates the consistency with which he wrote about the history of spatial production.

25 William M. Ivins, Jr, *Art and Geometry: A Study in Space Intuitions* (1946; rpt New York: Dover, 1964), and *Prints and Visual Communication* (London: Routledge and Kegan Paul, 1953).

26 For McLuhan, 'common sense' was not a negative concept, though he retheorized it such that it no longer conformed to the rationalist criteria that Ivins criticizes, but referred to all the senses working in common. As well, McLuhan's thought moved towards the notion of the relativity of knowledge and not away from it.

27 Martin Jay, *Downcast Eyes: The Denigration of Vision in Twentieth-Century Thought* (Berkeley: U of California P, 1993).

28 Bruno Latour covers much the same ground as McLuhan in 'Visualization and Cognition: Thinking with Eyes and Hands,' *Knowledge and Society: Studies in the Sociology of Culture Past and Present* 6, ed. Henrika Kuklick and Elizabeth Long (London: JAI Press, 1986), 1–40. Citing works by Ivins, though not by McLuhan, he nevertheless writes that 'For these authors, MacLuhan's [*sic*] revolution had already happened as soon as images were printed' (13). Latour makes much of the flatness of print media. On the problematics of McLuhan's reception in France, see Gary Genosko, 'The Paradoxical Effects of *macluhanisme*: Cazeneuve, Baudrillard and Barthes,' *Economy and Society* 23.4 (1994): 400–32. On the problematics of tracing that reception exclusively along theoretical (as opposed to artistic) lines, see chapter 7 below.

29 F.M. Cornford, 'The Invention of Space,' *Essays in Honour of Gilbert Murray* (London: George Allen and Unwin, 1936), 215–35.

30 Cornford identifies the source of this quotation as 'the President of the British Association' (ibid., 215); Graeme Patterson, in *History and Communications* (*HC*), states that 'Cornford ... was quoting the astronomer and mathematician Sir Arthur Eddington' (5). Patterson further points out (66) that Cornford was influenced by the psychologism of William James; to this I would add that James had been deeply impressed by Bucke's *Cosmic Consciousness*. Cornford, a Cambridge classicist, was the teacher of Eric Havelock (72).

31 Patterson unravels Innis's position *vis-à-vis* the 'new' physics and relativity, suggesting that Innis agreed with Havelock that space and time had, in contemporary culture, been deprived of their meta-physical qualities, and precisely through the scientificity of physics (68). Patterson also sees Innis as having arrived at the position, late in his career, that space and time were relative and not absolute (71). That these issues are unresolved in Innis's late thought is indisputable; I would argue, however, that the understanding of this tension in terms of spacetime is achieved by reading Innis through McLuhan. As Patterson remarks, aspects of Innis's style 'could not be noticed by anyone ... were Innis not read in the manner McLuhan indicated' (34).

32 McLuhan attributes this notion to Gombrich in 'Inside the Five Sense Sensorium,' *The Canadian Architect* 6.6 (1961): 49–54; quotation on 51.

33 One of the books cited in the bibliography to *Understanding Media* (*UM*), J.R. Pierce's *Symbols, Signals and Noise: The Nature and Process of Communication* (New York: Harper and Brothers, 1961), devotes one chapter to a discussion of the communications model ascribed to Claude Shannon (to whom the book is dedicated) in the context of Abbott's *Flatland* (166–83).

34 According to Linda Dalrymple Henderson, 'By 1824 Karl Friedrich Gauss had concluded that alterna-tive geometries to Euclid's must be possible. Gauss never published his thoughts on non-Euclidean geometry, and so the honor of its official discovery has been given to Nikolai Ivanovich Lobachevsky ... and Janos Bolyai' (p. 4 of *The Fourth Dimension and Non-Euclidean Geometry in Modern Art* (*4D*) [Princeton: Princeton UP, 1983]).This is the Gauss of Cornford's 'Invention of Space.' McLuhan makes reference to Lobachevsky in 'Innovation Is Obsolete,' *Evergreen Review* 15.90 (June 1971): 47–9; 64.

35 A Square [Edwin Abbott], *Flatland: A Romance of Many Dimensions* (1884; rpt Boston: Little, Brown, 1928); introduction by William Garnett. In 1980, the Arion Press of San Francisco published a fine-press edition of the novel on both sides of a single sheet of heavy paper.

36 McLuhan, 'One Wheel, All Square,' 198. Similarly, McLuhan wrote in the unpublished 'Spatial Form in Tudor and Stuart Poetry' (NAC, McLuhan Collection, MG 31 D 156 vol. 132, file 59), dated 'July 8, 1966,' that 'The new world of pictorial space that became accepted in the poetry of the later eighteenth and nineteenth centuries was as bizarre and fantastic to Renaissance sensibilities as a cubist mosaic was to the visitors to the Armoury show in 1913' (6–7). McLuhan is explicating the famous scene in *Lear* between Edgar and the blind Gloucester, which he had also analysed at the opening of the *GG*.

37 In 'Printing and Social Change,' McLuhan writes that Innis's *Empire and Communications* is 'a pioneer study ... though not definitive' (92). See *Printing Progress: A Mid-Century Report* (Cincinnati: Interna-tional Association of Printing House Craftsmen, 1959), 81–112.

38 Rosemary Jann writes in 'Abbott's *Flatland*: Scientific Imagination and "Natural Christianity,"' *Victorian Studies* 28.3 (1985): 473–90, that 'The Square's superior vision leaves him imprisoned, not free, in-capable of communicating with his contemporaries' (488). Linda Dalrymple Henderson writes of the fourth dimension: 'how can we visualize a new dimension, perpendicular to each of the three dimen-sions of our familiar world?' (*4D* 7).

39 McLuhan, 'Preface' to Robert Wallis, *Time: Fourth Dimension of the Mind* (New York: Harcourt, Brace and World, 1968), vii–ix; this quotation vii.

40 Henderson remarks in *4D* that, '[d]uring the 1920s and later, Giedion was personally [close] ... to Moholy-Nagy' (337); see also Moholy-Nagy, *Vision in Motion* (Chicago: Paul Theobald and Co., 1947). Moholy-Nagy had designed Giedion's *Bauen in Frankreich, Bauen in Eisen, Bauen in Eisenbeton* (1928); see Joseph Rykwert, 'Review of *Space, Time and Architecture*,' in *Harvard Design Magazine* (Fall 1998): 65–6.

41 Mario Praz in *Mnemosyne: The Parallel between Literature and the Visual Arts* (Princeton: Bollingen, 1970) states that 'Giedion ... sees the history of architecture as a progression from the bidimensional to

the three-dimensional and so on, without knowing ... that a parody of pluridimensionality had already been written ... by Edwin A. Abbott, in *Flatland*' (191).

42 See also Richard Cavell, '*Futurismo* in Canada: The Bologna Connection,' in *Bologna, la cultura italiana e le letterature straniere moderne*, ed. Vita Fortunati et al., 3 vols (Bologna: Longo, 1992), 1: 265–70.

43 Glenn Willmott reads this passage as 'satirical expressionism' (*MMR* 173), and reminds us that McLuhan often stated that all his writing was satire. It is my sense, however, that McLuhan was writing more in the tradition of *serio ludere*, or what he calls in *UM* 'spiritual clowning' (244).

44 J.Z. Young, *Doubt and Certainty in Science: A Biologist's Reflections on the Brain* (Oxford: Clarendon, 1951). McLuhan also draws on Young in *UM* 148; McLuhan's interest in the functioning of the brain, especially in terms of the special qualities associated with the right and left hemispheres, would persist to the end of his career.

45 Jonathan Williams provides a useful overview of the Cambridge intellectual milieu at the time McLuhan was there; see *McLuhan* (London: Fontana, 1971), 26–30.

46 Rosemary Jann notes in 'Abbott's *Flatland*' that Abbott's satirical intent was directed in part against 'the Cambridge mathematical establishment' (479, n7).

47 Maurice Maeterlinck, *The Life of Space*, trans. Bernard Miall (New York: Dodd, Mead, 1928). Henderson notes that 'Maeterlinck refused to sacrifice the idealist and even mystical associations of a spatial fourth dimension in favour of time as the fourth dimension' (*4D* 344).

48 Eddington, professor of astronomy in the 1920s, to whom Cornford refers at the beginning of 'The Invention of Space' (as does Innis in 'The Problem of Space'), published a popular guide to Einstein's theory of relativity called *Space, Time and Gravitation*; McLuhan cites from Eddington in *TT* (113), and he quotes in his dissertation from Alfred North Whitehead's *Science and the Modern World* (1926), which also figures importantly in the *GG*. During the period when McLuhan was a student there, Cambridge was internationally famous for its Cavendish Physics Laboratory; Ernest Rutherford was still lecturing when McLuhan arrived, and McLuhan may have been predisposed to take an interest in physics by his brief studies in engineering at the University of Manitoba. In subsequent years he impressed physicists such as R.K. Logan (a colleague at Toronto with whom McLuhan co-wrote two articles) with 'his grasp of the most profound aspects of my discipline and by the level of questions that he asked' (*The Fifth Language: Learning a Living in the Computer Age* [Toronto: Stoddart, 1995]). Also at Cambridge were Arthur Cayley (who did some of the earliest work on n-dimensional geometry; see Henderson, *4D* 6) and James Clerk Maxwell, who became professor of physics in 1871 and 'may be regarded as the founder of Broadcasting' (Garnett, Introduction to Abbott, *Flatland*, viii), a comment that takes on significant weight in light of Marchand's statement that broadcasting largely summed up McLuhan's notion of electronic communication (*M&M* 253).

49 The significant exception is Glenn Willmott, who makes the important point that 'Richards had no synthesizing epistemological theory but, instead, a methodological *principle*, a distinction borrowed from the physicist Niels Bohr. Bohr's Complementarity principle articulated a relativity of values among multiple points of view' (*MMR* 11). Note, too, Terence Gordon's comment that McLuhan was 'skeptical and critical' towards I.A. Richards's *Practical Criticism* (*Marshall McLuhan: Escape into Understanding* [*EU*], 48). In a holograph manuscript dating from the 1940s and titled 'The New Criticism,' McLuhan is scathing: 'it is easy to be a new critic if one knows little of the history of Western culture ... The arts include much besides literature' (NAC, McLuhan Collection, MG 31 D156, vol. 128, file 31). See also 'Poetic vs. Rhetorical Exegesis: The Case for Leavis against Richards and Empson,' *Sewanee Review* 52.2 (1944): 266–76.

50 See T.E.B. Howarth, *Cambridge between Two Wars* (London: Collins, 1978). In 1920, Bertrand Russell had read a major paper on 'Perception and Physics' (Howarth 121); Rutherford, who by 1923 was Cavendish Professor of Experimental Physics, stated in that year that '"we are living in the heroic age of physics"' (quoted by Howarth 92); and two years before McLuhan arrived in Cambridge, Einstein had given a lecture on 'Electricity Theory in the Framework of the General Theory of Relativity.' That same year, James Chadwick discovered the neutron (Howarth 103; 186). I wish to thank Elizabeth Leedham-Green of Cambridge University Library for bringing Howarth's book to my attention. Theall remarks in *VM* that McLuhan's dissertation indicates that he 'was ... aware of the important role physics

had in the allegorical and tropological interpretation of texts from the time of Varro in Rome ... He notes in his discussion that alchemy found its basis in the relation of classical and medieval physics to exegesis (i.e. what he calls "grammatical physics")' (109).

51 Michel Vermillac, 'Macluhan [*sic*] et la modernité' (2 vols; diss., U de Nice-Sophia Antipolis, 1993).

52 Jonathan Bate has recently made the argument that Cambridge physics likewise influenced William Empson to adopt 'both/and' as his metaphysics and to reject 'either/or.' See 'Words in a Quantum World,' *Times Literary Supplement* (25 July 1997): 14–15; extracted from Bate's *The Genius of Shakespeare*.

53 Willmott argues that McLuhan employed throughout his career the model of arrest and reversal, as metaphorized in the rear-view mirror. However, McLuhan consistently acknowledged that he had made a shift in methodology after *The Mechanical Bride* (*MB*) from a static to a dynamic model. In this regard, it is noteworthy that the images in a rear-view mirror are *in motion*; like the vision of Benjamin's Angel of History, mirrored images represent progress as profoundly recursive.

54 Charles Howard Hinton, *The Fourth Dimension* (1904; rpt London: George Allen and Unwin, 1934), 83. Hinton employed the term 'tesseract' for a four-dimensional cube, and that term retains a current usage in Canadian science fiction in Judith Merril's *Tesseracts* (Victoria: Press Porcépic, 1985).

55 See McLuhan, 'The Medieval Environment: Yesterday or Today?,' in *Listening* 9.1–2 (1974): 9–27. This essay appears to have provided a paradigm for Umberto Eco's medievalistic reconstructions in *The Name of the Rose* (as the Fisher Rare Book Room at the University of Toronto served as a model for that novel's library). See Umberto Eco, *Postscript to 'The Name of the Rose'* (New York: Harcourt Brace Jovanovich 1984), and his essay on McLuhan, 'Cogito Interruptus,' in *Travels in Hyperreality: Essays* (San Diego: Harcourt Brace Jovanovich, 1986), 221–38.

56 Louis De Broglie, *The Revolution in Physics: A Non-Mathematical Survey of Quanta*, trans. Ralph W. Niemeyer (New York: Noonday Press, 1953). De Broglie notes that, with the 'new physics,' the certainties of space and time were undermined: 'Exact localization in time and space is a sort of static idealization which excludes all evolution and all dynamism; the idea of a state of motion taken in all its purity is on the contrary a dynamic idealization contradictory in principle with the concepts of position and instant' (15). This dynamic takes the form of 'a continuum of four dimensions which in an abstract way realizes the intimate union of space and time' (89). This union results in a 'relativistic dynamics' (90).

57 Edmund Whittaker, *Space and Spirit: Theories of the Universe and the Arguments for the Existence of God* (Hinsdale: Henry Regnery, 1948). Given as the Donnellan lectures at Trinity College, Dublin, in 1946, this book, like a number of those dealing with the fourth dimension, is concerned as much with the metaphysical as with the physical.

58 This point is important when assessing the common charge that McLuhan's theories were merely crypto-Catholicism.

59 In 'Inside the Five Sense Sensorium,' McLuhan writes that 'the TV image ... is a two-dimensional mosaic mesh, a simultaneous field of luminous vibration which ends the older dichotomy of sight and sound' (50). He is also critical of 'facile dichotomizing' in a 1944 article on 'Kipling and Forster' (*The Sewanee Review* 52 [332–43]), where he writes that '[t]he "two world" view such as that offered by British India is especially useful to the artist who cannot localize or understand his dissatisfactions nor overcome the dualism of his experience' (332).

60 'Einstein's space-time continuum is itself a four-dimensional non-Euclidean structure' writes Linda Dalrymple Henderson in *4D* (21, n48).

61 John U. Nef sounds a similar note in *Cultural Foundations of Industrial Civilization*: 'The future of history, the future of knowledge, and the future of civilization itself, are thus interdependent. If we are to examine the nature of this interdependence, the use of methods derived from nineteenth-century natural science are most inadequate' (xi). McLuhan invokes Nef in the *GG* with reference to the 'insistence on tangible, repeatable, visible proof' (184) fostered by the typographical revolution. It should be emphasized that McLuhan rejected the *methodological* and *epistemological* assumptions of *MB*, not the book itself, which he allowed to be reprinted.

62 In 'Mr. Eliot's Historical Decorum,' *Renascence* 2.1 (1949): 9–15, McLuhan writes that whereas montage embodies the spatial and the temporal within a chronological sequence, symbolization is 'to

"throw together," to juxtapose without copula. And it is a work that cannot be undertaken nor understood by the univocalizing, single plane, rationalist mind' (9). In 'Prospect of America,' *University of Toronto Quarterly* 32.1 (1962): 107–8, McLuhan, reviewing Daniel Boorstin's *The Image*, writes that 'the world of the image is not the world of the landscape, but a world of instant humans in which all relationships manifest an organic complexity of interplay ... Point of view is the fragmentary awareness of mechanical man' (107). And in 'Innovation Is Obsolete,' McLuhan writes that '[t]he Symbolists responded to the dawning electric time in the nineteenth century with the technique of discontinuous juxtaposition. It is a flat, iconic form of an audible, tactile kind familiar in the cubist use of all dimensions of an object in a single image' (64). This article is noteworthy for containing a critique of Thomism; for details see note 34 above.

63 McLuhan's interest in *interior* landscapes was less a transference onto the psyche of the pathetic fallacy than a reflection of his interest in phenomena such as the x-ray that undermined notions of inside and outside. In this connection, the paintings and drawings collectively titled *Interior Landscapes* done by Pavel Tchelitchev in the late 1940s are significant. Trevor Fairbrother has placed these works, along with others, such as Duchamp's *Large Glass* (another work that problematizes inside and outside), in the context of responses to the work of Leonardo da Vinci. See 'The Ongoing Saga of Leonardo's Legend,' in Trevor Fairbrother and Chiyo Ishikawa, *Leonardo Lives: The Codex Leicester and Leonardo da Vinci's Legacy of Art and Science* (Seattle: U of Washington P / Seattle Art Museum, 1997), 42–66.

64 Robert Ezra Park, 'Physics and Society,' in *Society: Collective Behavior; News and Opinion; Sociology and Modern Society* (Illinois: The Free Press, 1955), 301–21; this quotation 315. The essay was first published in 1940 in Canada.

65 Compare the comments on authorship in *The Medium Is the Massage* (*MM*) 122: '"Authorship" ... was practically unknown before the advent of print technology.'

66 As Marsh Jeanneret writes in *God and Mammon: Universities as Publishers* (Toronto: Macmillan 1989), 'the book was designed by Harold Kurschenska. Harold exploited the author's unorthodox paragraph-style chapter heads with a typographical format that gave them added emphasis, if that was possible ... Harold Kurschenska still sighs when he recalls the traumatic task of trying to help readers sort their way through the most unconventional manuscript we ever published, its pages peppered with long and short quotations which he made contrast with the text by setting them all flush left and ragged right. For a scholarly work, Kurschenska's design was quite unconventional, but so was the text, and it would have been unwise to have presented it in a traditional typographical format' (154–5).

67 McLuhan wrote to Robert Fulford (1 June 1964) that 'I do not move along lines. I use points like the dots in a wire-photo. That is why I must repeat and repeat my points. Again, insights are not points of view' (*L* 300).

68 Compare Giorgio Agamben's notion of a de-authorized (i.e., transient) community. See *The Coming Community* (Minneapolis: U of Minnesota P, 1993), and Bill Readings's discussion of it in *The University in Ruins* (Cambridge, MA: Harvard UP, 1996), 186–7.

69 Stamps's comment that McLuhan 'argued that electronic media reduced personal identity to vestigial levels that, in turn, diminished moral feeling to practically nothing' (*Unthinking Modernity* [*Unth*] 143) is particularly misleading in the context of the argument I am making. What McLuhan in fact wrote is expressed, not as Stamps has it, but as a dynamic observation: 'The Fourth World, or the electronic world, reduces personal identity profiles to vestigial levels and, by the same token, reduces moral commitments in the private sector almost to zero. *Paradoxically, however,* as private morals in the private sector sink down, new absolutist demands are made of ethics in the public or political sector' (*L* 494; emphasis added).

70 A similar paradox is expressed in Lacanian terms by Ackbar Abbas: 'The great and difficult lesson of Lacan is that as subjects we do not see *because of the gaze,* i.e., because of the acculturated way in which we look.' See Abbas, 'Cultural Studies in a Postculture,' in *Disciplinarity and Dissent in Cultural Studies,* ed. Cary Nelson and Dilip P. Gaonkar (New York: Routledge, 1996), 289–312; this quotation 294.

71 McLuhan is commenting on Eliot's *Four Quartets,* a passage from which provides the epigraph to *TT*: 'For the pattern is new in every moment / And every moment is a new and shocking / Valuation of all we have been.' With McLuhan's comment, compare Georges Poulet on Proust: 'Time, then, is like a

fourth dimension which in combining with the other three perfects space' (319). See *Studies in Human Time*, trans. Elliott Coleman (Baltimore: Johns Hopkins UP, 1956); Poulet is extensively quoted in the *GG*.

72 The connection between kingdom and corporation had been prepared by Ernst Kantorowicz's *The King's Two Bodies: A Study in Medieval Political Theology* (1957), from which McLuhan cites in the *GG*. On Lear as executive see also the *GG*, 140 and 249.

73 Compare Baudrillard: 'Political Economy is disappearing under our very eyes: mutating by itself into a transeconomy of speculation which scoffs at its own logic (the law of value, the laws of the market, production, surplus-value, the very logic of capital) which therefore has nothing to do any longer with the economic and the political. It has become a pure game with its floating arbitrary rules, a game of catastrophe.' Quoted from 'Transpolitics, Transsexuality, Transaesthetics,' trans. Michel Valentin, in *Jean Baudrillard: The Disappearance of Art and Politics*, ed. William Stearns and William Chaloupka (New York: St Martin's Press, 1992), 9–26; this quotation 25.

74 McLuhan's negative allusion here to C.K. Ogden and I.A. Richards's *The Meaning of Meaning* is significant in the context of the argument made above; see note 49.

75 McLuhan had certainly read Bakhtin by the 1970s, as was evident from the conversation I had with him (as recorded in note 1 in the 'Preface'). His introduction to a large-format edition of the works of Karel Appel also indicates his familiarity with the notion of carnival. His conception of Russia as an oral culture caused him to devote a considerable number of pages in *Explorations* to articles on contemporary Russian society. See also page 21 of the *GG*. With the dialogical, compare Stamps's discussion of McLuhan's work in the context of negative dialectics (*Unth*, especially 19–20). Of particular relevance is the interface between dialogism and the chronotope, this latter term, literally 'time-space,' deriving from Einsteinian theories of relativity. As Gary Saul Morson and Caryl Emerson remark in *Mikhail Bakhtin: Creation of a Prosaics* (Stanford: Stanford UP, 1990), 'Although Bakhtin focuses on the chronotope in literature, he means us to understand that the concept has much broader applicability and does not define a strictly literary phenomenon' (368). They also note that 'all dialogues take place in a given chronotope, and chronotopes enter into dialogic relations' (427). The connections between McLuhan and Bakhtin are profound, though it is significant that the cultural strands binding them are not exclusively literary; rather, they include orality, rhetoric, Menippean satire, non-Euclidean geometries (as formulated by Lobachevsky), and relativity theory.

76 Compare the *GG*, where McLuhan writes that print eliminated 'pun, point, alliteration, and aphorism from literature' (103).

77 It was the *dynamic* between orality and literacy (as between space and time) that constituted the key element McLuhan furnished to Innis. This is not the stasis of a binary opposition; as Rosalind Krauss has remarked (in another context), 'Everything splits into two, but his division is not symmetrical (there is no simple separation of sides by means of a vertical axis), it is dynamic (the line of division is horizontal): the low implicates the high in its own fall. It is the low use, its imperious affirmation, that fells the hot-air balloons of the ideal with one malevolent blow' (R. Krauss and Yve-Alain Bois, *Formless: A User's Guide* [New York: Zone, 1997], 47).

Chapter 4: Prosthetic Aesthetics

1 One source for this notion of recursivity was Vico, whose work McLuhan knew through Joyce and through A. Robert Caponigri's *Time and Idea: The Theory of History in Giambattista Vico* (London: Routledge and Kegan Paul, 1953), which he cites in *The Gutenberg Galaxy (GG)*. Caponigri comments that the 'speculative root of the concept of "ricorsi" is the complex contemporaneity of history' (132). *Ricorsi*, however, do not represent simply a return to origins, a repetition of events past; rather, '[t]he reality which "ricorsi" generates [*sic*] is a mediate, not an immediate, reality; ... [they] are never recurrences in either a formal or a material sense' (135). McLuhan and Vico were further aligned in their critique of Cartesianism.

2 See Raymond Williams's comment in 'A Structure of Insights,' *University of Toronto Quarterly* (April 1964), reprinted in *McLuhan: Hot and Cool (MHC)* 186–9: 'Paradoxically, if the book [i.e., the *GG*] works it to some extent annihilates itself' (187). By McLuhan's 'last' book I mean that he co-authored all the texts he produced subsequently (or rewrote previous ones), and that in these texts he actively

sought to deconstruct the book as medium – to unwrite the book, as it were. See also Bruce E. Gronbeck, 'McLuhan as Rhetorical Theorist,' *Journal of Communication* 31.3 (1981): 117–28, esp. 117–18.
3 Alexander Dorner, *The Way beyond 'Art' – The Work of Herbert Bayer* (New York: Wittenborn, Schultz,
  1947); I am citing from the eleventh printing of the second edition published by Signet (New York) in
  1964.
4 Ernst Mach, citing William James, had argued that '*every* sensation is in part spatial' (13), and that
  '[t]his conception is ... almost universally accepted for optical, tactual, and organic sensations ... The
  possibility of localizing sources of sound, although not absolute, also points to a relation between
  sensations of sound and space' (14). Mach also writes about the 'relativity of all spatial relations' (139),
  and about space and time analogies (100). See Mach, *Space and Geometry*, trans. Thomas J.
  McCormack (1901; 1906; La Salle: Open Court, 1960).
5 As McLuhan wrote in 'Grammars for the Newer Media,' '[w]hat is shared by ... traditional rhetoric,
  popular culture, and by study of the languages and grammars of the media, is the habit of reading and
  writing *in depth*.' See *Communication in General Education*, ed. Francis Shoemaker and Louis Forsdale
  (Dubuque: Wm C. Brown, 1960), 17–27; this quotation 17.
6 McLuhan, 'Inside the Five Sense Sensorium,' *The Canadian Architect* 6.6 (1961): 49–54; this quotation
  52. Compare McLuhan's comment in 'Cybernation and Culture': 'Man's orientation to space before
  writing is non-specialist. His caves are scooped-out space. His wigwams are wrap-around, or proprio-
  ceptive space, not too distant from the Volkswagen and the space capsule! The igloo and the pueblo hut
  are not enclosed space; they are plastically modelled forms of space, very close to sculpture. Sculpture
  itself ... does not enclose space. Rather, it models or shapes space. It resonates.' In *The Social Impact of
  Cybernetics*, ed. Charles R. Dechert (Notre Dame: U of Notre Dame P, 1966), 95–108; this quotation
  97.
7 Margaret Wertheim, *Pythagoras' Trousers: God, Physics, and the Gender Wars* (New York: Times
  Books, 1995), 123.
8 Adrian Johns makes a similar assertion in *The Nature of the Book: Print and Knowledge in the Making*
  (Chicago: U of Chicago P, 1998), 389. See also the discussion on page 395, which quotes from Thomas
  Willis's 1683 tract, *Two Discourses Concerning the Soul of Brutes*, on the '"common Sensory."' Johns
  places McLuhan's work generally within the context of 'the "network" as a category of analysis' (13–
  14, n16).
9 Jonathan Crary, *Techniques of the Observer: On Vision and Modernity in the Nineteenth Century*
  (Cambridge, MA: MIT, 1990), 43; Crary quotes from Descartes's *Philosophical Writings* 2.
10 McLuhan, 'Myth and Mass Media,' *Dædalus* 88.2 (1959): 339–48; this quotation 343.
11 This evocation of the 'upside-down world' is one of the many strands linking McLuhan's thought with
   that of Bakhtin; see Bakhtin's *Rabelais and His World*, trans. Helene Iswolsky (1965; Cambridge, MA:
   MIT P, 1968), and, generally, Giuseppe Cocchiara's *Il mondo alla rovescia* (Torino: Boringhieri, 1981).
   A possible source for McLuhan's discussion here is Edwin G. Boring's *Sensation and Perception in the
   History of Experimental Psychology* (New York: Appleton-Century, 1942), where he relates the history
   of vision and the invention of the camera obscura (100ff).
12 Jonathan Crary, 'Modernizing Vision,' in *Vision and Visuality*, ed. Hal Foster (Seattle: Bay Press, 1988),
   29–44; this quotation 37, emphasis added. This essay is revised as 'The Camera Obscura and Its
   Subject' in *Techniques of the Observer*.
13 Crary, 'Modernizing Vision,' 38.
14 Crary, 'Modernizing Vision,' 42.
15 Crary, 'Modernizing Vision,' 39. McLuhan distinguished more finely between 'light on and light
   through.' See the comment in *Understanding Media* (*UM*) that 'the TV image ... exists by light *through*
   rather than by light *on*' (129).
16 Crary, 'Modernizing Vision,' 40. Crary goes on to note that 'the physiologist Emile Dubois-Reymond, a
   colleague of Helmholtz, seriously pursued the possibility of electrically cross-connecting nerves,
   enabling the eye to see sounds and the ear to hear colours, well before Rimbaud' (41). An 'ear for an
   eye' was the formula of McLuhan's early research into orality and literacy, with the concept illustrated
   in the photomontage frontispiece to *Verbi-Voco-Visual Explorations* (*VVV*).
17 Herman von Helmholtz, *On the Sensations of Tone as a Physiological Basis for the Theory of Music*,
   quoted by Crary, 'Modernizing Vision,' 42.

18 Crary, 'Modernizing Vision,' 42, emphasis added.
19 McLuhan further writes of Helmholtz that 'The awareness and definition of "auditory space" became prevalent through Helmholtz over a century ago'; in 'Inside the Five Sense Sensorium,' 52.
20 Linda Dalrymple Henderson (*The Fourth Dimension and Non-Euclidean Geometry in Modern Art [4D]* quotes from Helmholtz's 'On the Origin and Significance of Geometrical Axioms' (1870) in *Popular Lectures on Scientific Subjects*, second series.
21 In *From Cliché to Archetype (CA)*, McLuhan quotes from Boring's *The Physical Dimensions of Consciousness:* '"we must not trust to the analogy with vision to further the theory of hearing"' (138).
22 Michel Foucault, 'Technologies of the Self,' in *Technologies of the Self: A Seminar with Michel Foucault*, ed. Luther H. Martin, Huck Gutman, and Patrick Hutton (Amherst: U of Massachusetts P, 1988), 16–49.
23 McLuhan writes in 'Murder by Television' (*The Canadian Forum* [January 1964]: 222–3) that, 'for people long accustomed to the merely visual experience of the typographic and photographic varieties, it would seem to be the *synesthesia*, or tactual depth of TV experience, that dislocates them from their usual attitudes of passivity and detachment' (222). On simultaneity and synaesthesia generally see Dore Ashton, *A Fable of Modern Art* (London: Thames and Hudson, 1980), especially 87–8. According to Alois Riegl, whom McLuhan cites a number of times, 'Reliance on touch was neither better nor worse than reliance on vision; each was justified in its own right and in its own period' (quoted in E.H. Gombrich, *Art and Illusion* [New York: Bollingen, 1960], 18). Riegl's work represented 'the most ambitious attempt ever made to interpret the whole course of art history in terms of changing modes of perception' (18).
24 For one of the 'psychophysicists' Boring examines (O. Külpe), 'spatiality [was] inherent in the nature of sensation' (*Sensation and Perception* 32). In *The Physical Dimensions of Consciousness* (New York: Century, 1933), Boring espouses a 'relational theory of consciousness' (222 ff).
25 In 'Marshall McLuhan and James Joyce: Beyond Media,' (*Canadian Journal of Communication* 14.4–5 [1989]: 46–66), Donald Theall and Joan Theall note that, '[i]n the famous opening episode of the *Portrait [of the Artist]*, Baby Tuckoo (which McLuhan quoted frequently to his classes at the University of Toronto), [*sic*] Joyce explores how Stephen's perceptions as a toddler involve the interplay of the senses.'
26 McLuhan and Barrington Nevitt, 'The Argument: Causality in the Electric World,' *Technology and Culture: The International Quarterly of the Society for the History of Technology* 14.1 (1973): 1–18; this quotation 13.
27 McLuhan noted that Max Planck's quantum theory of physics was published in 1900, the same year that saw the publication of Freud's *Interpretation of Dreams*. See Philip Marchand, *Marshall McLuhan: The Medium and the Messenger (M&M)* 240.
28 Stephen Kern remarks, in *The Culture of Time and Space: 1880–1918 (CTS)* (Cambridge, MA: Harvard UP, 1983), that '[t]he pioneers of Gestalt psychology – Max Wertheimer, Wolfgang Köhler, and Kurt Kaffka – elaborated laws explaining how the "ground" and the "figure" create each other in perception, but they also maintained that the figure was more prominent. Their theory rejected the associationist view that complex perceptions are built up out of simple, discrete elements. They argued rather that perception is an experienced whole, and the task of understanding must be of that whole and not of separate parts ... In considering the whole perceptual field, the smallest detail of a Gestalt may be as important as the more conspicuous figures in it, for all elements interact and give each other meaning' (176).
29 Judith Stamps argues that McLuhan's 'most important source' in his attempt 'to reconcile Aquinas's theory [of sensation] with history' was 'E.H. Gombrich's Gestalt-inspired study, *Art and Illusion* (1960)' (*Unth* 104). Boring, however, was likely the more important of these sources, and McLuhan would have read him first. Gombrich, in any case, disavows gestalt in *Art and Illusion*; he states there that he is making a counter-raid on psychological theories of perception and that 'the Gestalt school would have none of [his argument]' (262). Gombrich would have been very important, however, in providing a model of how Boring's history of the senses could be applied to a history of art (indeed, the spatial arts in general). Another possible source for gestalt was Dorner's *The Way Beyond 'Art,'* esp. 110, 135, 225, 227.
30 Walter J. Ong, *Orality and Literacy: The Technologizing of the Word* (London: Methuen, 1982), 31–2.

31 Dantzig also wrote a study of Henri Poincaré, who was an important figure in the fourth-dimensional movement as it relates to McLuhan, insofar as he theorized about 'tactile space' (cf Henderson, *4D*, esp. 81–5). See *Henri Poincaré, Critic of Crisis: Reflections on His Universe of Discourse* (New York: Scribner's, 1954).

32 McLuhan and Nevitt, 'The Argument,' 1.

33 Arthur Quinn refers to chiasmus as 'a spatial technique,' and, interestingly, to the letter χ as 'a palindrome reduced to a single letter.' See *Figures of Speech: 60 Ways to Turn a Phrase* (Salt Lake City: Gibbs M. Smith, 1982), 95. In *Take Today (TT)*, McLuhan cites Nils W. Lund's *Chiasmus in the New Testament* (Chapel Hill: U of North Carolina P, 1942); see also *Chiasmus in Antiquity: Structures, Analyses, Exegesis*, ed. John W. Welch (Hildesheim: Gerstenberg, 1981), and Max Nänny, 'Chiasmus in Literature: Ornament or Function?' *Word and Image Studies* 4.1 (Jan.-Mar. 1988): 51–9.

34 See David Wills, *Prosthesis (Pr)*, 141: 'It is therefore the figure of a chiasmus, that between body and word – or indeed a chasm [sic], that in which the words of prosthesis fall locked in a corporal embrace – that [mark] ... the time of the prosthetic condition.' On prosthesis in the context of virtuality see Maria Luisa Palumbo, *New Wombs: Electronic Bodies and Architectural Disorders* (Basel: Birkhäuser, 2000).

35 McLuhan's diagrams have something in common with Hall's diagram of Formal, Informal, and Technical modes of human activity in *The Silent Language*, though they are much less detailed than Hall's. See Edward T. Hall, *The Silent Language* (1959); rpt New York: Anchor Books/Doubleday, 1981), 92.

36 Hall further developed the notion of territoriality in *The Hidden Dimension* (New York: Anchor, 1966), which draws on the *GG* and which Hall places within the context of work being done by himself, McLuhan, and Edmund Carpenter (80). Hall refers to his own work as 'proxemics,' or a science of proximity; he seeks to articulate through proxemics an 'anthropology of space' (101). Of particular interest is the section on 'The Dynamism of Space,' in which Hall writes that 'man's sense of space and distance is not static ... it has very little to do with the single-viewpoint linear perspective developed by the Renaissance artists ... Instead, man senses distance as other animals do. His perception of space is dynamic because it is related to action – what can be done in a given space – rather than what is seen by passive viewing' (114–15).

37 Johannes Fabian, in *Time and the Other: How Anthropology Makes Its Object* (New York: Columbia UP, 1983), savagely critiques Hall: 'As one reads through *The Silent Language* one realizes that the many perceptive observations and examples illustrating how *they* use Time turn into so many recipes for how to use that knowledge so that *their* behaviour can be tricked into serving *our* goals' (51).

38 McLuhan argued that 'the five classical divisions of rhetoric ... are, in fact, nothing else than the five mental faculties of man, perceived comprehensively': 'Rhetorical Spirals in *Four Quartets*' in *Figures in a Ground: Canadian Essays on Modern Literature Collected in Honor of Sheila Watson*, ed. Diane Bessai and David Jackel (Saskatoon: Western Producer Prairie Books, 1978), 76–86. McLuhan was Watson's doctoral supervisor, and her major work of fiction, *The Double Hook*, is written within the orbit of McLuhan's notions of orality and literacy and their roles in the production of space; the novel has also been influenced by Eliot (especially the opening lines of *The Waste Land*), a fact that may account for McLuhan's choice of topic in this Festschrift for Watson.

39 James M. Curtis has argued that 'McLuhan took his paradigm for the development of Western culture from Nietzsche (the Dionysian is cool, the Apollonian is hot).' See 'Toward a Pragmatic Revision of McLuhan' in *Et Cetera* (Spring 1983): 12–22. The connection with Nietzsche is an important one for other reasons. In one of the books cited in the bibliography to the second edition of *UM*, Anton Ehrenzweig's *The Psycho-Analysis of Artistic Vision and Hearing: An Introduction to a Theory of Unconscious Perception* (London: Routledge and Kegan Paul, 1953), Nietzsche is cited as having anticipated 'a dynamic theory of style' whose 'function of the aesthetic feeling independent from objective beauty properties' was to secure 'articulate surface perception against inarticulate depth perception' (xvii; cf 56–62). This book also makes arguments for ambiguity and irrationality (158; 256–7), and about the plasticity of sound (233). More significantly for McLuhan the 'artist/intellectual,' the 'hot' and 'cool' dynamic may be read as a response to the so-called aesthetics of indifference; according to Moira Roth, 'cool' was a reaction among liberal American artists to McCarthyite politics. These artists 'found themselves paralyzed when called upon to act on their convictions, and this paralysis frequently appeared as indifference' (34). Roth argues that 'McLuhan's *The Mechanical*

Bride ... was an early announcement of this new tone of indifference ... [A] study in advertising manipulations, [*MB*] was written in a cool rather than indignant manner' (34). Roth associates this aesthetic with artists such as Duchamp, Cage, Cunningham, Rauschenberg, and Johns. In response to her article, Jonathan Katz argues (more complexly than can be detailed here) that the work of these artists 'is considered and dissident, powerfully resistant and hardly indifferent' (68). This accords with McLuhan's use of the term 'cool,' by which he meant 'involving.' See Moira Roth, 'The Aesthetic of Indifference,' in *Difference/Indifference: Musings on Postmodernism, Marcel Duchamp and John Cage* (Amsterdam: G and B Arts, 1998), 33–47 (originally published in *Artforum* 16.3 [1997]); and Jonathan D. Katz, 'Identification,' in the same volume (49–68).

40 In 'McLuhan as Rhetorical Theorist,' Gronbeck argues that McLuhan was 'obviously ... enamoured with rhetoricians in his younger days ... In many ways, at least after the *GG* ... he abandoned rhetorical studies ... In his more philosophical later years, however, ... his own pattern-making activity fell back upon rhetorical impulses – explicitly ... and implicitly, in all of the writings about his beloved "laws"' (126). I would argue, however, that McLuhan was much more consistent than Gronbeck paints him. In this regard, Eric McLuhan has remarked that 'my father's communication studies ... were an extension of his work in literature and a profound application (you might say updating) of grammar and rhetoric' (*Who Was Marshall McLuhan*? [*WWMM*] 242). Donald Theall has stated that in pointing out 'the importance of rhetoric and the trivium to communications studies,' McLuhan 'opened up [a] substantial [area] of little regarded concern.' See 'Guest Editor's Introductory Remarks,' *Canadian Journal of Communications* (A Special Issue Commemorating the 25th Anniversary of *Understanding the* [sic] *Media*) 14.4–5 (1989): v–vii; this quotation vi.

41 McLuhan, 'Poetic vs. Rhetorical Exegesis,' *Sewanee Review* 52.2 (1944): 266–76; this quotation 268.

42 George Puttenham's 1589 *The Arte of English Poesie* devotes the second of its three books to 'Proportion Poetical'; the chapter 'Of Proportion in Figure' states that 'figure' is 'fo called for that it yelds an ocular representation, your meeters being by good fymmetrie reduced into certaine Geometricall figures.' See the 1869 reprint, edited by Edward Arber (London: Alex Murray and Son), 104–14. Barrington Nevitt has remarked that 'EAR-people' are 'rhetoricians and grammarians' while 'EYE-people' are 'dialecticians' (*WWMM* 125).

43 The dissertation has four chapters, the first three of which discuss the trivium 'until St. Augustine,' 'from St. Augustine to Abelard,' and 'from Abelard to Erasmus.' The fourth chapter is on Nashe; each chapter is subdivided into three sections: Grammar, Dialectics, Rhetoric. See 'The Place of Thomas Nashe in the Learning of His Time' (diss., Herbert Marshall McLuhan, Cambridge University, 1943, table of contents; also NAC, McLuhan Collection, MG 31 D156, vol. 62, file 1).

44 Wills notes that, for Roland Barthes, 'the sense of the commonplace or trifling conveyed by our word "trivial" came not just from the inferior position of the trivium within the medieval model but also from the idea that the intersection of three ways was a place of frequentation, a common place that was also a beat, the locus of prostitution' (*Pr* 214; Wills alludes to Barthes's inaugural lecture at the Collège de France), and, for Wills, it is significant that prostitution and prosthesis are etymologically related. It may also be significant that McLuhan referred to *UM* as '*The Electronic Call Girl*' (*M&M* 169), perhaps in contrast to the mechanical bride elaborated earlier in his career. Note also McLuhan's article 'James Joyce: Trivial and Quadrivial' (*IL* 23–48), and the tetrad for 'Trivium' in *Laws of Media* (*LM*).

45 See, in general, Mimi Cazort, Monique Kornell, and K.B. Roberts, *The Ingenious Machine of Nature: Five Centuries of Art and Anatomy* (Ottawa: National Gallery of Canada, 1996).

46 It is this convergence of the rhetorical and the medical that accounts, perhaps, for McLuhan's tendency to use medical metaphors in much of his writing, as noted by Kroker (*Technology and the Canadian Mind* [*TCM*] 71 and *passim*).

47 According to Wilson's *The Art of Rhetorique*, the activities of rhetoric amount to 'cuttyng' and 'addyng,' which also describes the activity of chiasmus. See the passages from the 1553 edition reproduced by Wills (*Pr* 227).

48 McLuhan was moved in the direction of cybernetics through his reading of Norbert Wiener's *The Human Use of Human Beings: Cybernetics and Society* (1948; 2nd rev. ed., Garden City, NY: Doubleday, 1954). Wiener, who coined the term 'cybernetics,' begins his book with the comment that he has recently been 'working on the many ramifications of the theory of messages' (15) and that '[i]t is the thesis of this book that society can only be understood through a study of the messages and the

communication facilities which belong to it; and that in the future development of these messages and communication facilities, messages between man and machines, between machines and man, and between machine and machine, are destined to play an ever increasing part' (16). While Wiener shared with McLuhan an interest in Poe and in games (cf 175 and 178 of *Human Use*), they are fundamentally opposed in terms of the communication models they employ: Wiener excludes noise from his model, whereas McLuhan embraces it. As Peter Galison remarks in a study of Wiener, 'perhaps disorganization, noise, and uncontrollability are not the greatest disasters to befall us. Perhaps our calamities are built largely from our efforts at superorganization, silence, and control.' See 'The Ontology of the Enemy: Norbert Wiener and the Cybernetic Vision,' *Critical Inquiry* 21 (1994): 228–66; this quotation 266. John Simmons has noted that Wiener devoted part of his career to 'the application of cybernetics to the design of replacement parts for the human body – prosthetics' (153) in 'Sade and Cyberspace,' *Resisting the Virtual Life: The Culture and Politics of Information*, ed. James Brook and Iain Boal (San Francisco: City Lights, 1995), 145–59.

49 See Jean Paré's 'Interview with Marshall McLuhan' in *Forces* [Hydro Québec] 22 (1973): 65–73; this reference 65. Note also the photo of McLuhan reclining in his office that Pierre Berton reproduces in *1967: The Last Good Year* (Toronto: Doubleday, 1997).

50 Compare Oliver Sacks's comment that 'speech – natural speech – does not consist of words alone ... It consists of utterance – an uttering-forth of one's whole meaning with one's whole being – the understanding of which involves infinitely more than mere word-recognition.' Quoted by Alberto Manguel, *A History of Reading* (Toronto: Knopf, 1996), 37, from *The Man Who Mistook His Wife for a Hat*.

51 Avital Ronell asks in *The Telephone Book: Technology/Schizophrenia/Electric Speech* (Lincoln: U of Nebraska P, 1989), 'Does the one who picks up the call of a telephone become an extension of the apparatus, or is the converse conceivable; is one speaking through a severed limb or organ, as Freud will suggest, and Marshall McLuhan after him?' (39).

52 A number of sources, in addition to Freud, have been proposed for McLuhan's use of 'extension.' In *Culture as Polyphony: An Essay on the Nature of Paradigms* (Columbia: U of Missouri P, 1978), James Curtis writes: 'One does not usually associate Hegel with technology, but he did in fact first state the principle with which McLuhan shocked people a hundred and fifty years later: the interpretation of technology as the extension of man' (34–5). Curtis goes on to state: 'Ernst Kapp['s] ... book *Outlines of a Philosophy of Technology* (1877) is the first work that states and develops the hypothesis that technology functions as the extension of man' (62). Curtis also quotes Bergson: '"If our organs are natural instruments, our instruments are by the same token, artificial organs. The workman's tool continues his hand; mankind's ensemble of tools is thus a prolongation of his body"' (from *The Two Sources of Religion and Morality*, quoted by Curtis 67). Finally, Curtis states that 'It is reasonable to assume that McLuhan originally found the concept [of technology as extension of man] in Bergson; he certainly studied its use in Mumford and Teilhard de Chardin' (83).

According to Tom Wolfe, in *The Video McLuhan*, McLuhan was deeply influenced by Teilhard de Chardin, though he 'never' referred to Teilhard because the latter was out of favour with the Catholic hierarchy to which McLuhan's professional life was so closely attached through his association with St Michael's College, University of Toronto. See *The Video McLuhan*, Written and Narrated by Tom Wolfe; prod. Stephanie McLuhan; dir. Matthew Vibert (McLuhan Productions, 1996; six cassettes). In fact, McLuhan was referring to Teilhard as early as 1962 (in his article 'Two Aspects of the Communications Revolution,' *Canadian Communications Canadiennes* 2.2 [1962]: 7–9; cf the letter to John Snyder written in August 1963 [*L* 292]). McLuhan also refers to T eilhard in the *GG*. Teilhard's evolutionism, utopianism, and the lack of dynamism within his theories mark him off quite distinctly from McLuhan, as does Teilhard's insistence on homogeneity and his valorization of vision. See *The Phenomenon of Man*, trans. Bernard Wall, intro. Julian Huxley (1955; New York: Harper and Bros, 1959), and *The Future of Man*, trans. Norman Denny (1959; New York: Harper, 1964).

Buckminster Fuller claimed to have used the term 'extension' in 1938, while E.T. Hall claimed that McLuhan got the concept from him (see *L* 308; 515; and *WWMM* 149). Octavio Paz suggested that 'McLuhan has borrowed Spengler's concept of technology as an extension of the human body; but whereas for Spengler a man's hand is a claw, for McLuhan it is a sign' ('The Channel and the Signs,' *Alternating Current*, trans. Helen R. Lane [1967; New York: Viking, 1973], 154–60; this quotation 155). McLuhan was using the term by the mid-1950s; see 'A Historical Approach to the Media,' *Teachers College Record* 57.2 (1955): 104–10. In *TT*, McLuhan quotes Emerson to the effect that 'The human body is the magazine of inventions ... All the tools and engines on earth are only extensions of its limbs and senses' (86). McLuhan may have been influenced by von Békésy's remark that the 'funneling of sensations into a space outside the body is an important feature of neural funneling, for it controls practically all our behaviour.' See Georg von Békésy, *Sensory Inhibition* (Princeton: Princeton UP, 1967), 220. Von Békésy's study would have been significant for McLuhan insofar as it discusses sensory projection in the context of sensory inhibition, which are analogous to the extension and amputation of *UM*. Finally, Le Corbusier referred to decorative art as 'an extension of our limbs – in fact, *artificial limbs*.' See Beatriz Colomina, *Privacy and Publicity: Modern Architecture as Mass Media* (Cambridge, MA: MIT P, 1994), 136.

53 As Wills expresses it, 'By means of prosthesis the relation to the other becomes precisely and necessarily a relation to otherness, the otherness, for example [and here he is very close to McLuhan] of artificiality attached to or found within the natural' (*Pr* 44).

54 See Rosalind Krauss's comments on how Freud argues that, 'as a result of man's newly won vertical posture, the localized sensory relation to the sexual organs is permitted an added visual dimension' in Krauss and Yve-Alain Bois, *Formless: A User's Guide* (New York: Zone, 1997), 95.

55 Nicholas Olsberg (who assessed the value of the McLuhan archive prior to its acquisition by the National Archives of Canada) asserts that the McLuhan lexicon of hot and cool, medium and message, global village, and so on, has entered public discourse much more effectively than 'Freud's *id* and *ego*, or Brecht's *alienation*, even Burke's *sublime* or Arnold's *sweetness and light*' (111). See 'Memoirs of a Man I Never Met,' *AI* [*Architecture and Ideas*] 3 (1999): 108–11.

56 '"[T]he analogy with other transformations such as occur in speaking and hearing by telephone [are] unmistakable"' (*Pr* 125; Wills quotes from Freud's 'Dreams and Occultism,' *Standard Edition* 22:31–56). The association of these media with telepathy is thus related to Bucke's notion of cosmic consciousness, which likewise derived from a concept of sensory evolution.

57 See René Descartes, *Discourse on Method* and *Meditations on First Philosophy*, ed. David Weissman (New Haven: Yale UP, 1996), part 2: 13.

58 Paul Levinson has argued that 'McLuhan's work is part of the great human tradition of rationality both because of, and in spite of, itself' (179), in that 'the only way we can assess ... [irrationality] is through our rationality' (186). McLuhan makes clear, however, in a passage quoted by Levinson, that it is the association of rationality with literacy that he seeks to critique. See 'McLuhan and Rationality,' *Journal of Communication* 31.3 (1981): 179–88. As McLuhan wrote of his tetrads (in *LM*), the 'whole point ... is that they are *analogical*. That is, there are no connections between any of them, but there are dynamic ratios' (263). See 'Misunderstanding the Media's Laws,' *Technology and Culture* 17.2 (1976): 263. Comparing McLuhan with Thomas Kuhn in this regard, Liss Jeffrey remarks that 'Whereas Kuhn ... tried to explain his contradictions ... McLuhan made no such concessions.' See 'The Heat and the Light: Towards a Reassessment of the Contribution of Herbert Marshall McLuhan,' *Canadian Journal of Communication* [Special Issue on 25th Anniversary of *UM*] 14.4–5 (1989): 1–29; this quotation 6. McLuhan's comment on Kuhn was that 'he remains oblivious of the much wider hidden ground of Western culture – the unconscious assumptions of visual psychic bias. He is unaware that the user is necessarily the "content" of any situation.' See McLuhan and Nevitt, 'The Argument,' 4.

59 Martin Jay remarks that 'Descartes was a quintessentially visual philosopher, who tacitly adopted the position of a perspectivalist painter using a camera obscura to reproduce the observed world' (*Downcast Eyes: The Denigration of Vision in Twentieth-Century French Thought* [Berkeley: U of California P, 1993], 69). It is ironic, then, that Descartes twice recurs in *La Dioptrique* (the treatise on vision appended to the *Discourse on Method*) to tactile analogies in his attempt to explain the physiology of vision, thus undermining his flight from the senses. Descartes's concept of space, like that of his fellow early moderns, 'is the physical counterpart of the purely geometric space of Euclid's *Elements*' (16), as Edward Grant remarks in *Much Ado about Nothing: Theories of Space and Vacuum from the Middle Ages to the Scientific Revolution* (Cambridge: Cambridge UP, 1981), 16.

60 Lefebvre remarks: 'By conceiving of the subject without an object (the pure thinking "I" or *res cogitans*), and of an object without a subject (the body-as-machine or *res extensa*), philosophy created an irrevocable rift in what it was trying to define. After Descartes, the Western Logos sought vainly to stick the pieces back together and make some kind of montage ... Under the reign of King Logos, the reign of true space, the mental and the social were sundered' (*The Production of Space* [*PS*], 406–7).

61 It was, of course, acoustic space that McLuhan invoked in contradistinction to visual space.

62 Clifford Geertz, 'Common Sense as a Cultural System,' *Local Knowledge: Further Essays in Interpretive Anthropology* (New York: Basic Books, 1983), 73–93.

63 For a brief history of 'common sense' see Alberto Manguel, *History of Reading*, 30–2.

64 Compare the comment in *Report on Project in Understanding New Media* (*RPM*) that, '[i]ncreasingly we come to confront ourselves, when we are confronted by change in our institutions. And in time this can only lead to more forethought and responsibility in the use of our own technology' (108).

65 Compare *UM* 116: 'man appears as the reproductive organ of the technological world, a fact that Samuel Butler bizarrely announced in *Erewhon*'; and cf also *UM* 220. This 'humanizing' of technology allies McLuhan with the Heidegger of 'The Question Concerning Technology.'

66 McLuhan, 'Media Ad-Vice: An Introduction' to Wilson Bryan Key, *Subliminal Seduction: Ad Media's Manipulation of a Not So Innocent America* (Englewood Cliffs: Prentice-Hall, 1973), iv–xvi; this quotation xvi. Le Corbusier remarked that 'American advertising is a kind of narcissism' (100) in *When the Cathedrals Were White* (1936; trans. F.E. Hyslop, Jr [London: Routledge, 1947]).

67 The controversy continues in such books as Paul Rutherford's *When Television Was Young: Primetime Canada 1952–1972* (Toronto: U of Toronto P, 1990); see especially the introductory section on '"McLunacy"?' (26–38), which concludes that 'McLuhan had never come to grips with the reality of television in the 1950s and 1960s' (38).

68 Mladen Dolar has commented that 'there is a rudimentary form of narcissism attached to the voice that is difficult to delineate since it seemingly lacks any outside support. It is the first "self-referring" or "self-reflective" move, but as pure auto-affection at the closest of oneself – an auto-affection that is not re-flection, since it is seemingly without a screen that would return the voice, a pure immediacy, where one is both sender and receiver in one's pure interiority' ('The Object Voice,' in Slavoj Žižek and Renata Salecl, eds., *Gaze and Voice as Love Objects* [Durham: Duke UP, 1996], 7–31; this quotation 13–14).

69 In 'Marshall McLuhan and the Psychology of TV,' Robert D. McIlwraith writes that 'Ideas popularized by McLuhan, though largely ignored at the time by psychology (e.g., the paradox of the raptly involved but numb viewer, the nonlinear alogical environment of real-time information, and the irrelevance of content to TV's addictive power), now dominate the research agendas of many psychologists interested in television.' See *Canadian Psychology / Psychologie canadienne* 35.4 (1994): 331–50: this quotation 341.

70 Slavoj Žižek reads the interrelationship of voice and gaze according to a Lacanian schema that has resonance with McLuhan's: 'the moment we enter the symbolic order, an unbridgeable gap separates forever a human body from "its" voice. The voice acquires a spectral autonomy, it never quite belongs to the body we see, so that even when we see a living person talking, there is always some degree of ventriloquism at work: it is as if the speaker's own voice hollows him out and in a sense speaks "by itself," through him ... [V]oice does not simply persist at a different level with regard to what we see, it rather points toward a gap in the field of the visible, toward the dimension of what eludes our gaze. In other words, their relationship is mediated by an impossibility: *ultimately, we hear things because we cannot see everything*' ('"I Hear You with My Eyes"; or, The Invisible Master,' in Žižek and Salecl, *Gaze and Voice as Love Objects*, 90–126; this quotation 92–3).

71 The adoption of the Narcissus and Echo myth figures as well as part of McLuhan's critique of Cartesian rationality; according to McLuhan's formulation, the mind is no longer fully present to itself, a concept he would develop further through the notion of the bicameral mind. See in this regard 'The Brain and the Media: The "Western" Hemisphere,' *Journal of Communication* 28.4 (1978): 54–60. As the subtitle to *LM – The New Science* – indicates, the rhetorical, historical, and scientific dimensions McLuhan vested in chiasmus were brought together for him in Vico's *La nuova scienza* (1730/1744) and its notion of the *ricorso*, with which McLuhan was familiar through Joyce. Of particular interest to McLuhan would have been Vico's emphasis on the imagination, as opposed to reason, in the construction of knowledge. Furthermore, as a rhetorician, Vico accorded enormous significance to the sensory topos, that 'imaginative universal' (172), as Donald Verene puts it, which found truth in sensory analogy, or *sensus communis*. Finally, Vico was a historical relativist (rather than a progressivist), as his notion of *ricorso* would indicate. See Donald Phillip Verene, *Vico's Science of Imagination* (Ithaca: Cornell UP, 1981), 181.

72 Thelma McCormack, 'Innocent Eye on Mass Media,' *Canadian Literature* 22 (1964): 55–6; this quotation 56. Note also Victor Burgin: 'in non-Euclidean geometry we [find] the spherical plenum of

classical cosmologies collapsed upon itself to enfold a central void. For Lacan, this figure, that of the "trus," can represent a psychical space in which the subject repetitively comes into being, in a procession that circumscribes a central void – locus of the lost object, and of the subject's death.' In 'Geometry and Abjection,' *Public* 1 [*Some Uncertain Signs*] (1988): 13–30; this quotation 27.

73 In a sense, of course, the Narcissus myth was also the last stage in Freud's rewriting of Freud; 'On Narcissism: An Introduction' (1914) moves away from a mechanical model towards an organicist model of the psyche. McLuhan discusses the Freudian model as belonging to the mechanical era in 'The Subliminal Projection Project,' *The Canadian Forum* (December 1957): 196–7. Like McLuhan, Freud, at least analogously, sees extension to be related to narcissism. See *The Freud Reader*, ed. Peter Gay (London: Norton, 1989), 545–62.

74 McLuhan, 'Myth and Mass Media,' 341. This issue of *Dædalus*, on 'Myth and Mythmaking,' also featured articles by Mircea Eliade, Joseph Campbell, and Thomas Mann ('Freud and the Future'). McLuhan's comments on the Oedipus myth, especially as it relates to 'kinship structures' (341), contain a critique of Lévi-Strauss.

75 See the discussion by Jerry Aline Flieger in 'The Listening Eye: Postmodernism, Paranoia, and the Hypervisible,' *Diacritics* 26.1 (1996): 90–107; this discussion on page 92. Victor Burgin has detailed the implicit 'cone of vision' in Freudian triangulations. See 'Geometry and Abjection.'

76 McLuhan with Barrington Nevitt, 'The Man Who Came to Listen,' in *Peter Drucker: Contributions to Business Enterprise*, ed. Tony Bonaparte and John Flaherty (New York: New York UP, 1970), 35–55; this quotation 46. McLuhan (and Watson) make a similar point in *CA* 66.

77 See Jay, *Downcast Eyes*, passim.

78 McLuhan's insistence that Narcissus falls in love not with himself but with an image of himself that he does not recognize is not supported directly by Ovid's text, which states, quite plainly, '*iste ego sum*' (l. 463). Yet what McLuhan seeks to argue is that the othering into technology is irrecuperable, that in becoming what we behold we are other and no longer the same, a hybrid.

79 Eli Bernstein, 'An Interview with Marshall McLuhan,' *The Structurist* 6 (1966): 61–8; this quotation 67. Compare Werner Heisenberg's comment: 'Perhaps the day will come when the many technical instruments will become as inescapable a part of ourselves as the snail's shell to its occupant ... *But even these instruments would be a part of our own organism* rather than parts of external nature.' See *The Physicist's Conception of Nature*, trans. Arnold J. Pomerans (Westport: Greenwood P, 1958), 18. These insights have been developed most recently by Donna Haraway in *Simians, Cyborgs and Women: The Reinvention of Nature* (London: Routledge, 1991).

80 Hans Selye, *The Stress of Life* (New York: McGraw-Hill, 1956). McLuhan had published Selye in *Explorations* 1.

81 Adophe D. Jonas, *Irritation and Counterirritation: A Hypothesis about the Autoamputative Property of the Nervous System* (New York: Vantage, 1962).

82 Psychologist Michael Bross states that 'there is absolutely no evidence that the nervous system is capable of "amputating" any of its parts or functions' (96); nevertheless, McLuhan 'was absolutely correct in insisting on the primary role of sensory functions as the cornerstone of any understanding of how individuals apprehend and interact with their environment and his insights of [*sic*] how the advent of print ... and the electronic media ... have altered and accelerated changes in the energy mosaic the world presents to our senses is still unequalled in its scope and incisiveness' (105). See 'McLuhan's Theory of Sensory Functions: A Critique and Analysis,' *Journal of Communication Inquiry* 16.1 (1992): 91–107.

83 Burgin, 'Geometry and Abjection,' 16–17.

84 Eric A. Havelock, *Preface to Plato* (Cambridge, MA: Belknap P, 1963).

85 John O'Neill, '*Bio-Technology*: Empire, Communications and Bio-Power,' in *McLuhan e la metamorfosi dell'uomo* [Atti del convegno, Venezia, 11–13 novembre 1982, Centro Accademico Canadese in Italia], ed. Derrick de Kerckhove and Amilcare Iannucci (Roma: Bulzoni, 1984), 249–63; this quotation 249–50. Joe Galbo explores a similar theme in 'McLuhan and Baudrillard: Notes on the Discarnate, Simulations, and Tetrads,' in *McLuhan Studies* 1 (1991): 103–7. Galbo states that, if 'the social and political body is colonized and erased through technology,' it is also true that 'the electronic environment by its very nature decenters political power' (107).

86 Lynn Spigel, 'High Culture in Low Places: Television and Modern Art, 1950–1970,' in *Disciplinarity*

and Dissent in Cultural Studies, ed. Cary Nelson and Dilip P. Gaonkar (New York: Routledge, 1996), 313–46; this quotation 329.

87 Discontinuity was the prime quality of electronic space for McLuhan.

88 In the same way that he had theorized through the example of physics the interrelation of space and time in spacetime, so here McLuhan argues that each object engenders its own space relationally. 'This ... is the kind of time-sense held by the modern physicist and scientist. They no longer try to contain events in time, but think of each thing as making its own time and its own space. Moreover, now that we live electrically in an instantaneous world, space and time interpenetrate each other totally in a space-time world' (*UM* 148). In an age of spacetime, 'we seek multiplicity, rather than repeatability' (149).

89 McLuhan made a similar point in his 1977 interview with *Maclean's* (90, 5 [7 March 1977]: 4–9); to the question 'How much TV is advisable for children?' McLuhan replies that 'The problem is how literate is your society, your family circle, your immediate circle' (9).

Interface

1 See the chapter of that title in Robert Fulford's *The Best Seat in the House: Memoirs of a Lucky Man* (Toronto: Collins, 1988).

2 McLuhan was Canada's intellectual comet according to the American film reviewer Richard Shickel, who wrote an article of that title for *Harper's* (November 1965): 62–8; this same magazine, through its current editor, Louis Lapham, has been in the forefront of the McLuhan revival.

3 Theall refers in *The Virtual Marshall McLuhan* (*VM*) to McLuhan's 'decline in attention from the mid 1970s until the 1990s' (x) and states that McLuhan's 'major work had been completed by 1970' (3).

4 Gary Genosko suggests that McLuhan was eclipsed in this period by Baudrillard. See *McLuhan and Baudrillard: The Masters of Implosion* (New York: Routledge, 1999), 2. For an overview of McLuhan criticism see Robert MacMillan, 'Marshall McLuhan at the Mercy of His Commentators,' *Philosophy of the Social Sciences* 22.4 (1992): 475–91.

5 From a review in the *American Scholar*, cited on the back cover of the paperback edition of Frye's *The Modern Century* (Toronto: Oxford UP, 1967); I provide further details in chapter 8.

6 Paul Heyer, 'Probing a Legacy: McLuhan's Communications / History 25 Years After,' *Canadian Journal of Communication* 14.4–5 (1989): 30–45; this quotation 30.

7 Jacques Derrida, 'Signature Event Context,' in *Margins of Philosophy*, trans. Alan Bass (1972; Chicago: U of Chicago P, 1982), 307–30. It is now Derrida who is telling his readers that 'the organizations of the media ... deserve an almost infinite analysis' (28), that 'the time of the media gives rise to ... different spaces' (30), and who is now urging his readers to pay attention to 'the ontological oppositions between absence and presence, visible and invisible, living and dead, and hence above all of the prosthesis as "phantom limb," of technology of the tele-technological simulacrum, the synthetic image, virtual space, etc.' (38). See 'The Deconstruction of Actuality: An Interview with Jacques Derrida,' *Radical Philosophy* 68 (1994): 28–41.

8 As reported by Marjorie Ferguson, 'Lefebvre ... requests that some attention be paid to McLuhan even if he was "un peu charlatanesque."' See 'Marshall McLuhan Revisited: 1960s Zeitgeist Victim or Pioneer Postmodernist?' *Media, Culture and Society* 13.1 (1991): 71–90; this quotation 84.

9 Glenn Willmott comments that McLuhan's 'persistent afterlife in French poststructuralist and cultural theory has ironically allowed "McLuhan" to haunt the academy which had thought him gone' (*MMR* 136).

10 Manuel Castells refers to the 'mass media electronic communication system [as] the McLuhan Galaxy in homage to the revolutionary thinker who visualized its existence as a distinctive mode of cognitive expression' in *The Rise of the Network Society* (Oxford: Blackwell, 1996), 337. Castells argues, however, that media have moved into a new, interactive, phase, for which a new cognitive paradigm is required. The second half of the present study, however, argues that interactivity was fundamental to McLuhan's media theories, which posited that the user of a medium became the content of that medium. Castell's notion is developed by Christopher Horrocks in *Marshall McLuhan and Virtuality* (Cambridge, UK: Icon Books, 2000), though with far greater caution; while aware (as Castells seems not to

be) that McLuhan theorized that the consumer of electronic media was simultaneously its producer, Horrocks writes that 'he tended to underplay the extent to which users would actively participate in technology and media' (57).

11 This is not to use 'artist' as a failed theorist or critic, as S.D. Neill suggests in the section on 'The Messy Artist' in *Clarifying McLuhan: An Assessment of Process and Product* (Westport: Greenwood P, 1993), 37–8. Sidney Finkelstein writes in *Sense and Nonsense of McLuhan* (New York: International Publishers, 1968) that McLuhan's ideas 'interest a stream of artists or would-be artists who devote themselves to the invention of new styles' and that 'McLuhan's summary law, "the medium is the message," talks their language' (9–10); this is likewise not meant to propose a positive context of assessment. In a special issue of *Vie des arts* (Montreal) 18.72 (1973), Donald Theall and Derrick de Kerckhove Varent [*sic*] have articles on McLuhan and art. Theall states that McLuhan's use of artistic metaphors (such as mosaic) in his work, together with his insistence on the importance of artistic perception to our understanding of media, made McLuhan into 'the prophet of the art movements of the 50's, and 60's and 70's ... McLuhan is not only influenced by the artists of the first half of the century, but he is influencing the artists of the second half of the century' (90). See 'McLuhan's Esthetic Explorations' 90–1. See also Theall's *The Medium Is the Rear-View Mirror* (*RVM*) 153–4, and his *Beyond the Word: Reconstructing Sense in the Joyce Era of Technology, Culture, and Communication* (Toronto: U of Toronto P, 1995): 'a McLuhanesque vocabulary and agenda, largely anonymous, have permeated not only cultural and communication studies, but the media and bureaucracy' (xvi). In 'McLuhan and Art' (91–3), de Kerckhove Varent writes that 'Acoustical space is one of the most common metaphors in McLuhan's work. It is the interval of the resonance and the total simultaneousness of all human experience. Art is one of its keys' (91). McLuhan may also have taken Giedion as his model, whose play *Arbeit* was staged by Max Reinhardt. See Joseph Rykwert, 'Review of *STA*,' *Harvard Design Magazine* (Fall 1998): 65–6. In its 1 July issue of 1999, the *Globe and Mail* (A14) ranks McLuhan as the second most influential Canadian in the arts, after Glenn Gould; this ranking is interesting, given McLuhan's intellectual mentoring of Gould; see chapter 6 below. It is clear from a number of McLuhan's notes that he sought to produce some of his texts as poetry; this is especially so with reference to *Through the Vanishing Point* (*TVP*). See NAC, McLuhan Collection, vol. 143, box 15. McLuhan collaborated with sculptor Sorel Etrog on a film and book called *Spirals*, supplying text to Etrog's images, and they had planned to write a play called *Hinges*. See NAC, McLuhan Collection, vol. 23, file 46.

12 Wilfred Watson, 'Poem and Preface,' *Canadian Literature* no. 30 (1966): 36–48; this quotation 41; 44.

13 'Marshall McLuhan, Mike Wallace: A Dialogue,' *The Diebold Research Program: Professional Paper Series* (New York: The Diebold Group, 1967); this quotation 10.

14 In terms of McLuhan's place within the popular-culture matrix, see Geoff Pevere and Greig Dymond, 'The Circuitry of Sainthood: Marshall McLuhan's Northern Visions,' in *Mondo Canuck: A Canadian Pop Culture Odyssey* (Toronto: Prentice Hall, 1996), 132–5: 'our interest here is in McLuhan as a Canadian pop-cultural superstar ... Before McLuhan, electronic media was about its manifest content. After McLuhan electronic media was about environment, the new world order wired by multidirectional circuitry to the collective nervous system of post-electronic civilization, concepts now elementary to our discussion of mediated existence, and without which (and maybe this is the caveat), people like Moses Znaimer and Ted Turner would be unimaginable. If he was right ... then we may only be beginning to come to terms with the sheer daunting scope of his prescience' (132).

15 McLuhan, 'The Emperor's Old Clothes,' in Gyorgy Kepes, ed., *The Man-Made Object* (New York: Braziller, 1966), 90–5; this quotation 90.

16 Paul Rodaway, *Sensuous Geography* (Oxford: Oxford UP, 1995).

17 The importance McLuhan assigned to artists has resonance with Vico's assertion of the importance of the poetic. As A. Robert Caponigri remarks in *Time and Idea* (cited in *The Gutenburg Galaxy*), 'The heart of the Vichian conception of poetry, and his great discovery, is its "necessity"' (165).

18 McLuhan, 'Foreword' to Innis, *Empire and Communications* (*EmC*), revised by Mary Q. Innis (Toronto: U of Toronto P, 1972), v–xii.

19 McLuhan had used 'environment' in this sense as early as 1956; see 'Educational Effects of Mass Media of Communication,' *Teachers College Record* 57.6 (1956): 400–3, and the reference to 'total environment,' 402.

20 F.R. Leavis and Denys Thompson, *Culture and Environment: The Training of Critical Awareness* (1933; rpt London: Chatto and Windus, 1950). The authors, unlike McLuhan, see popular culture as destructive of traditional cultural values and of the positive values associated with speech (2). However, all agree on the importance of understanding that environment (rather than ignoring it).

21 McLuhan, 'New Media and the Arts,' *Arts in Society* 3.2 (Fall/Winter 1964–5): 239–42.

22 There is an irony, then, in the thesis of Stephen Dale, who argues in *McLuhan's Children: The Greenpeace Message and the Media* (Toronto: Between the Lines, 1996) that the success of Greenpeace in its environmental activism can be traced to its mastery of the media. McLuhan's thesis was more radical: the (natural) environment itself was a product of the media, the figure of its new ground.

23 McLuhan makes a similar comment in 'Educational Effects of Mass Media of Communication': 'the boundaries between art and nature have disappeared' (403).

24 [Howard Polskin,] 'Conversation with Marshall McLuhan,' *Videography* (October 1977): 30; 54; 59–60; 62–7; this quotation 67.

25 McLuhan, 'The Emperor's Old Clothes,' 90.

26 Ellul treats propaganda as a technological phenomenon, especially of the mass media: 'without the mass media there can be no modern propaganda' (102). See *Propaganda: The Formation of Men's Attitudes*, trans. Konrad Kellen and Jean Lerner (1962; New York: Knopf, 1972). On the invisibility of environments, McLuhan loved to cite the parable of the goldfish, which knows nothing about water because water comprises its total environment (cf *War and Peace in the Global Village* 175); this may have been his reworking of Malraux's comment in *The Voices of Silence* (trans. Stuart Gilbert [1949, 1950; Princeton: Princeton UP, 1953]) that 'a fish is badly placed for judging what the aquarium looks like from outside' (70).

27 McLuhan, 'The Relation of Environment to Anti-Environment,' *The University of Windsor Review* 2.1 (1966): 1–10; this quotation 1; 5. Illustrative of the extension/amputation theory developed in *Understanding Media* (*UM*), McLuhan remarks on the paradox that 'when music becomes environmental by electric means, it becomes more and more the concern of the private individual' (6), a situation perfectly illustrated by the Sony Walkman.

28 Jerome McGann, *Black Riders: The Visible Language of Modernism* (Princeton: Princeton UP, 1993), 101.

29 Clifford Geertz, 'Blurred Genres: The Refiguration of Social Thought,' in *Local Knowledge: Further Essays in Interpretive Anthropology* (New York: Basic Books, 1983), 19–35; these quotations 19. Compare Willmott's remark that 'McLuhan's critical styles before and after this book [*MB*] are ... marginalized from forms of proper criticism, blurring criticism and art' (*MMR* 31). Theall had remarked in 1973 that 'McLuhan has refused to decide whether he wants to be artist or analyst himself, though he could rightly argue these distinctions in the world he prophesizes cease to exist.' See 'McLuhan's Esthetic Explorations,' 91. And Gary Genosko states that McLuhan was an 'intellectual jester in the humanist tradition of Erasmus's folly, Joyce's wit, and Rabelais' bawdiness[;] McLuhan played the clown in order to infiltrate specialist discourses and cross the wires of disciplines and satirize them in a mode he called anti-environmental' (*McLuhan and Baudrillard* 12).

30 On the French reception of McLuhan, see Genosko, *McLuhan and Baudrillard, passim*; on the 'a' in '*Macluhan*' see chapter 3 of that book.

Chapter 5: *Artiste de livres*

1 Daniel Belgrad, *The Culture of Spontaneity: Improvisation and the Arts in Postwar America* (Chicago: U of Chicago P, 1998), 1.

2 For Legman, see chapter 2 above. McLuhan is described in issue 5 (1949) of *Neurotica* as a 'Canadian sociologist' (2); in issue 8 (1951), in which Legman published passages he had 'abstracted' from *The Mechanical Bride* (*MB*), McLuhan is described as a 'Professor of Literature' (2). *Neurotica* was reprinted in its entirety in 1981; in his introduction, John Clellon Holmes, an original contributor, writes: 'A few cultural phenomena ... prove to have hit a nerve that is destined to vibrate more insistently in the future than in the present. In the somnolent smog of the early 1950s, for instance, who would have thought that Marshall McLuhan would become something of a pop-seer 20 years later, or that anyone in the '80s would still be talking about the Beat Generation, or that a decisive upheaval in

moral and sexual values was about to occur? *Neurotica*, a relatively obscure magazine during its short four-years of life, has proved to have hit such a nerve, and perhaps has more relevance today than it did when it was first published' (7). In addition to those authors appearing in *Neurotica* whom Belgrad mentions, the journal also published Kenneth Patchen (who influenced bpNichol), Henri Michaux, Lawrence Durrell, William Barrett, and Leonard Bernstein. The overwhelming direction of the journal (which began life in St Louis, where McLuhan taught at the beginning of his career) was towards the psychoanalytical. See *Neurotica 1948–1951*, edited by John Clellon Holmes (London: Jay Landesman, 1981).

3 McLuhan was also published in *Playboy* (twice) and in Barney Rosset's *Evergreen Review*; Rosset was publisher of the Grove Press, whose publication of writers such as Henry Miller led to the abolition of obscenity laws in the United States. His *Review* was a leading medium for avant-garde writers in the 1960s and 1970s. See 'Aging Rebel Takes on a Literary Titan,' *Globe and Mail* (24 March 1999): C1-2.

4 In this context it is worth noting that Jack Kerouac, whom Belgrad numbers among the most significant of the artists about whom he is writing, had Québécois roots and preserved elements of that culture's orality in a number of his works (Belgrad 42).

5 The title *Interior Landscapes* was used in 1943 by Pavel Tchelitchev for a series of paintings; see Trevor Fairbrother, 'The Ongoing Saga of Leonardo's Legend,' *Leonardo Lives: The Codex Leicester and Leonardo da Vinci's Legacy of Art and Science*, ed. Fairbrother and Chiyo Ishikawa (Seattle: Seattle Art Museum, 1997), 42–66; see 62.

6 McLuhan, 'The Comics and Culture,' first published in *Saturday Night* 68.1 (28 Feb. 1953): 19–20; reprinted in Malcolm Ross ed., *Our Sense of Identity* (Toronto: Ryerson, 1954), 240–6.

7 Belgrad cites only the *Neurotica* article and from *MB*; although the notion of orality is crucial to Belgrad's article, he mentions McLuhan's work on orality only in an unindexed footnote reference (of which there is more than one to McLuhan), and cites the 'Acoustic Space' article by McLuhan and Carpenter only in its 1960 reprinted version, as opposed to its first appearance in 1953 (301, n69). Belgrad appears to be unaware that during the period of which he is writing McLuhan was focusing the range of his thought on the orality/literacy dynamic. Belgrad cites Ong as his authority on orality and literacy without noting that Ong was McLuhan's student.

8 In a poem published in 1956, Ginsberg focuses on *Time* magazine in a way that suggests he might have read McLuhan's *Neurotica* article; see Belgrad 231.

9 Jeff Berner, ed., *Astronauts of Inner-Space*: *An International Collection of Avant-Garde Activity* (San Francisco: Stolen Paper Review Editions, 1966); McLuhan's contribution is on pages 18–19 and is called 'Culture and Technology.'

10 McLuhan favourably reviewed *The Naked Lunch* for *The Nation* in 1964 (December: 517–19). McLuhan's collaboration with Quentin Fiore extended the network initiated by the *Neurotica* publication to Lee Krasner and Jackson Pollock, both of whom were Fiore's classmates when studying with Hans Hoffmann. See the chapter 'McLuhan/Fiore: Massaging the Message,' in Ellen Lupton and J. Abbott Miller, *Design Writing Research: Writing on Graphic Design* (New York: Kiosk and Princeton Architectural P, 1996), 90–101; esp. 93–4. Krasner and Pollock figure largely in Belgrad's 'culture of spontaneity.'

11 In 1965, Howard Gossage, an advertising executive, had organized a week-long McLuhan Festival in Gossage's San Francisco office; see Marchand, *M&M* 174, and Gerald M. Feigen, 'The McLuhan Festival on the Road to San Francisco,' *Antigonish Review* 74–5 (1988) [McLuhan and Our Times]: 73–7. Feigen's title alludes to Kerouac's novel *On the Road*.

12 Olson himself was lecturing in Vancouver, at the University of British Columbia (UBC), in 1963; see Belgrad 305, n33; Halifax's Nova Scotia College of Art and Design had an international reputation by the 1970s for its support of work in the conceptualist avant-garde.

13 Peter Brunette and David Wills, 'Introduction' to *Deconstruction and the Visual Arts: Art, Media, Architecture* (Cambridge: Cambridge UP, 1994), 1–8; this quotation 3.

14 Compare the notion of 'interfusional' art – that is, the art that combines elements of orality and literacy; see the discussion by Tom King in 'Godzilla Meets Postcolonial' in Ajay Heble, Donna Palmateer Penny, and J.R. Struthers, eds, *New Contexts of Canadian Criticism* (Peterborough: Broadview P, 1997), 241–8.

15 Louis Dudek, 'Lunchtime Reflections on Frank Davey's Defence of the Black Mountain Fort,' in *The

Writing Life: Historical and Critical Views of the Tish Movement, ed. C.H. Gervais, with an introduction by Frank Davey (Coatsworth: Black Moss Press, 1976), 128–33; this quotation 131. This is remarkable coming from Dudek, who spent much of the 1960s attacking McLuhan; see the many references in *Technology and Culture* (Ottawa: Golden Dog Press, 1979) and *In Defence of Art* (Kingston: Quarry P, 1988), where Dudek refers to McLuhan as 'that diabolical theorist and philosopher' (183) whose '"message" is in many ways the same as that Benito and Adolf spread about' (27). In April 1978, McLuhan gave the Pound lecture at the University of Idaho; see McLuhan, *The Pound Lecture: The Possum and the Midwife* (Idaho: University of Idaho, 1978).

16 According to Richard Humphreys, Pound 'saw the art of the Quattrocento in Italy ... as Linear and "clean"; ... whereas the Seicento, with its baroque *sfumato* and "fleshiness," [was] the typical expression of a corrupt and commercialized culture.' See the 'Introduction' to *Pound's Artists: Ezra Pound and the Visual Arts in London, Paris and Italy* (London: Tate Gallery, 1985), 13–23; this quotation 15.

17 Rosalind Krauss, *The Optical Unconscious* (Cambridge, MA: MIT P, 1993), 178.

18 Yve-Alain Bois, in Rosalind Krauss and Yve-Alain Bois, *Formless: A User's Guide* (New York: Zone, 1997).

19 Quoted by Michael Roberts, *T.E. Hulme* (London: Faber, 1938), 266. See also Richard Cavell, '*Futurismo* in Canada: The Bologna Connection,' in *Bologna: la cultura italiana e le letterature straniere moderne*, ed. Vita Fortunati et al. (Bologna: Longo, 1992), 1: 265–70.

20 Quoted by Humphreys, 'Demon Pantechnicon Driver: Pound in the London Vortex, 1908–1920,' in Humphreys, *Pound's Artists* 33–80; this quotation 39 (from Pound's essay on Vorticism).

21 Alfred North Whitehead, *Adventures of Ideas* (1933; rpt New York: Macmillan, 1961), 243.

22 McLuhan's comments on the book garner much interest to the present day. In *The Future of the Book*, ed. Geoffrey Nunberg (Berkeley: U of California P, 1996), James J. O'Donnell finds that McLuhan's prophecies about the book 'do not lend themselves to guide practical applications' (49); see 'The Pragmatics of the New: Trithemius, McLuhan, Cassiodorus' (37–62). Umberto Eco, in an afterword to the volume (295–306), credits McLuhan with a number of fallacies, of which the first is that we were leaving behind the Gutenberg Galaxy for 'the Visual Galaxy' (304); McLuhan spent his career *critiquing* visual *space*, however. What McLuhan said about the book was this: '[I]n moving into the electronic age where all is simultaneous, we also become more sensitive to the values and unused possibilities of print' ('Printing and Social Change,' in *Printing Progress: A Mid-Century Report* [Cincinnati: International Association of Printing House Craftsmen, 1959], 81–112; this quotation 90); 'The book thrives as never before, but its form is no longer constitutive or dominant' ('Inside the Five Sense Sensorium,' *The Canadian Architect* 6.6 [1961]: 49–54; this quotation 54); 'It would be a mistake to suppose that the trend of culture toward the oral and acoustic means that the book is becoming obsolete. It means rather that the book, as it loses its monopoly as a cultural form, will acquire new roles' (*Counterblast* [*Ctb*] [1969] 98); 'TV will produce a reversion to civilized book values by sheer reversal of itself' (*Culture Is Our Business* [1970] 332); 'The book is not moving towards an Omega point but is actually in the process of rehearsing and re-enacting all the roles it ever played' (*Do Books Matter?* ed. Brian Baumfield [London: Morley Books, 1973], 31–41; this reference 49).

23 Giovanni Cianci writes in his introduction to *Wyndham Lewis: Letteratura/Pittura* (Palermo: Sellerio, 1982; the book contains a brief article by McLuhan on Lewis) that 'le tesi futuriste (di cui McLuhan non ha mai voluto riconoscere il debito) gli siano giunte proprio tramite la mediazione cruciale del vorticismo lewisiano' (15) (the Futurist theses [his debt to which McLuhan never wished to acknowledge] came to him precisely through the crucial mediation of Lewis's Vorticism). McLuhan may have encountered the Futurist manifesto through Kepes's *The Language of Vision*.

24 I am paraphrasing here from De Maria's introduction to Marinetti's *Teoria e invenzione futurista* (*TIF*) (Milan: Mondadori, 1983). The passage is as follows: 'Giustamente Calvesi ha osservato che il "feticismo della macchina" non esaurisce il significato del futurismo, il quale si fonda piuttosto, secondo le parole stesse di Marinetti, "sul completo rinnovamento della sensibilità umana avvenuto per effetto delle grandi scoperte scientifiche" e delle "diverse forme di comunicazione, di trasporto e di informazione" che esercitano una "decisiva influenza" sulla psiche umana. In questo senso, come suggerisce Calvesi, Marinetti ha precorso McLuhan, e di fatto alcune tesi dello studioso canadese hanno precisi riferimenti nei manifesti futuristi' (xxxv). See also Maurizio Calvesi, *Le due avanguardie* (Milano: Lerici, 1966) and *Il futurismo* (Milano: Fabbri, 1967).

25 R.W. Flint, 'Introduction' to *Marinetti: Selected Writings*, ed. and trans. R.W. Flint, with Arthur A. Coppotelli (New York: Farrar, Straus and Giroux, 1972), 3–36; this quotation 5.

26 As Judi Freeman remarks: 'Futurism's involvement with words had a widespread effect on European art.' See 'Layers of Meaning: The Multiple Readings of Dada and Surrealist Word-Images,' in Freeman, ed., *The Dada and Surrealist Word-Image* (Cambridge, MA: MIT P, 1989), 13–56; this quotation 20.

27 See John C. Welchman, 'After the Wagnerian Bouillabaisse: Critical Theory and the Dada and Surrealist Word-Image,' in Freeman, ed., *The Dada and Surrealist Word-Image*, 57–95; this quotation 61.

28 As Welchman remarks generally: 'The progressive dependence of painters on effects of the surface was seen as a decisive rejection of post-Renaissance verisimilitude and perspective' (ibid. 59).

29 '*TV Guide* for June 8–14, 1968, has a painting by Dali on the cover. Two thumbs exhibit two TV screens as thumbnails. This is pure poetry, acute new perception. Dali immediately presents the fact that TV is a tactile mode of perception. Touch is the space of the *interval*, not of visual connection' (McLuhan, 'Foreword' to *The Interior Landscape* [*IL*] xiv). One of the illustrations to Gyorgy Kepes's *Language of Vision*, a text often drawn on by McLuhan (see following note), is by Herbert Bayer and shows two hands, palms up, each palm having an eye (*Language of Vision* 226).

30 Gyorgy Kepes, *Language of Vision* (Chicago: Paul Theobald, 1944). The book is noteworthy for having an introduction by Giedion: 'Who still believes that art, modern art, has to be defined as a mere luxury or something far-away, remote from real life, unworthy of the respect of a "doer," had better not touch this book. Gyorgy Kepes, as we all do, regards art as indispensable to a full life' (7). In addition to quoting often from Kepes, McLuhan also published an article under Kepes's editorship, and published an article by Kepes in the first issue of *Explorations*. A number of the illustrations in *Through the Vanishing Point* (*TVP*) are also reproduced in *The Language of Vision*.

31 The first half of the book, comprising McLuhan's essays, is unpaginated, and will be referenced with item numbers.

32 '*[Up to this curkscraw bind an admirable verbivocovisual presentment of the worldrenownced Caerholme Event ...],*' James Joyce, *Finnegans Wake* (New York: Viking [5th printing], 1986), 341, line 18.

33 'On the surface of a sphere space would be unbounded and yet finite, and the sphere, in fact, is the most easily understood model for non-Euclidean geometry' (Henderson, *4D* 5).

34 Hence the 'modernism in reverse' and the 'unthinking [of] modernism' that critics such as Wilmott and Stamps have argued as paradigms for understanding McLuhan: the reversal was precisely from the aesthetic to the culturally material.

35 The photomontage was made by one of the students at Laszlo Moholy-Nagy's Institute of Design, George Morris, Jr, in 1943, and is reproduced on page 204 of Moholy-Nagy's *Vision in Motion* (Chicago: Paul Theobald, 1947). Moholy-Nagy supplies the text: 'Can you see with your ear? or hear with your eye?' The image is also reproduced in *The Medium Is the Massage* (*MM*) 121.

36 I draw here on *Moholy-Nagy*, ed. Richard Kostelanetz (1970; London: Allen Lane, 1974).

37 Ibid. 214. Kostelanetz states that Gyorgy Kepes 'has cribbed freely from [*Vision in Motion*] for many of his recent books and anthologies, though he rarely credits Moholy, who not only supervized Kepes in London and Berlin but also brought his fellow Hungarian refugee to America to teach at the Institute of Design. Furthermore, it was Moholy, and not Marshall McLuhan, who noted, in 1947, that the contemporary newspaper, unlike its eighteenth-century predecessor, "tries to organize the many events of the day similarly as the Futurists; the reader should read all the news almost at once"' (Kostelanetz 214).

38 'Hausmann in 1918 developed his "optophonetics" which used typographic variations in size to indicate proportionate variations in pitch and volume' (similar to the *parole in libertà*). See Steve McCaffery and bpNichol, *Sound Poetry: A Catalogue* (Toronto: Underwhich, nd. [1978?]), 8, and chapter 6 below for a further discussion, in the context of McCaffery's and Nichol's poetry.

39 McLuhan, 'Encyclopaedic Unities,' *Hudson Review* 1.4 (1949): 599–601; this quotation 601.

40 Like McLuhan, Moholy-Nagy was influenced by Giedion's *Space, Time, and Architecture*; see Kostelanetz 88.

41 Compare McLuhan's article 'Inside the Five Sense Sensorium,' which also refers to Moholy-Nagy.

42 As noted by Theall, *The Virtual Marshall McLuhan* (*VM*) 141.

43 V.J. Papanek, *Design for the Real World: Human Ecology and Social Change* (1984; 2nd ed. Chicago: Academy, 1985). I have treated Papanek's article in *Verbi-Voco-Visual Explorations* (*VVV*) as a

coproduction similar to that of Carleton Williams, Carpenter, and McLuhan on 'acoustic space'; 'A Bridge in Time' has at least as much in it of McLuhan as of Papanek, since the attitude expressed in the article towards the artists it discusses is not consistent with that in Papanek's book, *Design for the Real World*, which exhibits a highly negative attitude towards the very artists praised by Papanek in the *VVV* article.

44 Along with Giedion, Le Corbusier had founded the Congrès Internationaux d'Architecture Moderne; see Stephen Gardiner, *Le Corbusier* (New York: Viking, 1974), xxi.

45 Le Corbusier proclaims the profound connections between the Machine Age and the concomitant changes in our 'auditory habits' (158) in *When the Cathedrals Were White* (1936; trans. F.E. Hyslop, Jr [London: Routledge, 1947]), to which McLuhan makes reference in 'Inside the Five Sense Sensorium.' McLuhan and Le Corbusier part company, however, in the latter's enthusiasm for the 'Euclidean clearness' (48) of Manhattan's street grids and its '*Cartesian skyscraper[s]*' (52) and for Machine Age culture generally.

46 It was McLuhan's controversial opinion that television was an *involving* medium, in that it required the active participation of the viewer to piece together the image on the screen; see the psychological literature noted in chapter 4 above.

47 All of these notions can be found in Le Corbusier's *L'Art décoratif d'aujourd'hui* (Paris: G. Cres, 1925), which discusses '"Human-limb objects"' (xxiii) and the notion that, '[w]hen one factor in our technico-cerebro-emotional equation grows disproportionately, a crisis occurs, since the relationships are disturbed' (70).

48 Le Corbusier was blind in one eye, making it impossible for him to perceive three-dimensionally. See Jonathan Hale, 'Review of *Towards a New Architecture*,' *Harvard Design Magazine* (Fall 1998): 66–8.

49 Le Corbusier, 'Ineffable Space,' originally published as 'L'Espace indicible' in *L'Architecture d'aujourd'hui* (January 1946), and in English in 1948 in the volume *New World of Space*; reprinted in *Architecture Culture 1943–1968: A Documentary Anthology*, ed. Joan Ockman, with Edward Eigen (New York: Columbia UP, 1993): 66–7; this quotation 66.

50 See Maurice Besset, *Who Was Le Corbusier?* (trans. Robin Kemball; New York: World Publishing, 1968), 43.

51 Mark Treib (with Richard Felciano), *Space Calculated in Seconds: The Philips Pavilion, Le Corbusier, Edgard Varèse* (Princeton: Princeton UP, 1996), 89. One of the engineers involved on this project, Henk Badings, is referred to by Glenn Gould in an article edited and published by McLuhan in *Explorations* (the successor to the journal of the same name published in the 1950s by McLuhan and Carpenter) in 1965. For Badings, see Treib, *Space Calculated in Seconds* (178).

52 Here and throughout I am following Treib, *Space Calculated in Seconds*. See also Linda Dalrymple Henderson, *The Fourth Dimension and Non-Euclidean Geometry in Modern Art* (*4D*): 'In lectures later in his life Varèse pointed to two nineteenth-century scientists, Hoene Wronski and Helmholtz, as the sources for his first ideas about music as a spatial phenomenon ... Inspired by Helmholtz's studies of sirens and the "physiology of sound," Varèse began to experiment with sirens and found he could produce "beautiful parabolic and hyperbolic curves equivalent for me to the parabolas and hyperbolas in the visual domain." From this experience he determined that he "would someday realize a new kind of music that would be spatial"' (225).

53 These are the words of Iannis Xenakis, Le Corbusier's assistant at the time and subsequently one of the foremost composers of the contemporary era; quoted by Treib, *Space Calculated in Seconds* 171.

54 The last of these images was an atomic cloud, which is also the last image of McLuhan's *Culture Is Our Business* (*COB*).

55 A student of Wölfflin, Gabo also read Bergson, Boccioni's manifesto on Futurist sculpture, and, by the 1920s, was familiar with Einstein's notion of time as the fourth dimension. In his 1937 essay, 'Sculpture: Carving and Construction in Space,' Gabo writes that, '[u]p to now, the sculptors have preferred the mass and neglected or paid very little attention to such an important component of mass as space. Space interested them only in so far as it was a spot in which volumes could be placed or projected. It had to surround masses. We consider space from an entirely different point of view. We consider it as an absolute sculptural element, released from any closed volume, and we represent it from inside with its own specific properties.' Gabo concludes by affirming that 'the perception of space is a primary natural sense which belongs to the basic senses of our psychology.' (Naum Gabo, 'Sculpture: Carving and

Construction in Space,' in Herschel B. Chipp, ed., *Theories of Modern Art: A Source Book by Artists and Critics* [Berkeley: U of California P, 1968], 330–7; these quotations 332–3.) Gabo goes on to contest the notion that sculptural forms must be static – that space must be isolated from time.

56 Similarly, Theall's suggestion that McLuhan is trying in *TVP* to accommodate a theory of space to a theory of media has greater value when reversed: in *TVP*, I would argue (as in his writings generally), McLuhan accommodates his theories of media to his theories of space.

57 Stephen Kern, *The Culture of Time and Space: 1880–1918* (Cambridge, MA: Harvard UP, 1983), 21.

58 Irving Babbitt, *The New Laokoon: An Essay on the Confusion of the Arts* (Boston: Houghton Mifflin, 1910), ix.

59 Clement Greenberg, 'Towards a Newer Laocoon,' *Partisan Review* 7 (1940): 296–310; this quotation 296.

60 W.K. Wimsatt, 'Laokoön: An Oracle Reconsidered,' in *Day of the Leopards: Essays in Defense of Poems* (New Haven and London: Yale UP, 1976), 40–56; this quotation 45. McLuhan was consulted on Expo 67, and his collaborator on *TVP*, Harley Parker, was associated with the Royal Ontario Museum. In the same article, Wimsatt goes on to attack Roy Daniells's attempt, in *Milton, Mannerism and Baroque* (Toronto: U of Toronto P, 1963), to argue for analogies between architecture and literature; McLuhan, in *TVP*, is much more receptive to Daniells's analogical procedure, and to his assertion of the inseparability of time and space in Milton (*TVP* 18). One of the architectural analogies on which Daniells draws is the Church of Santa Maria della Salute in Venice; this church is distinguished by enormous, spiral volutes which the *veneziani* refer to as 'orrechioni,' or big ears, a term that heightens the *acoustic* aspect of this space. My thanks to Gilian Cucchini for pointing this out.

61 See G.E. Lessing, *Laocoön: An Essay on the Limits of Painting and Poetry*, trans. Edward Allen McCormick (1962; Baltimore: Johns Hopkins UP, 1984), 'Preface' 5.

62 Lessing is likewise aware that 'bodies do not exist in space only, but also in time' (78). His argument, however, is a generic one, which ascribes suitable representations to each art form.

63 W.J.T. Mitchell, 'Space and Time: Lessing's *Laocoon* and the Politics of Genre,' in *Iconology: Image Text Ideology* (Chicago: U of Chicago P, 1986), 95–115; this quotation 96.

64 'Only the small child and the artist have the immediacy of approach that permits perception of the environmental' (*TVP* 252).

65 McLuhan reviewed an edition of *Alice's Adventures in Wonderland* during this period for the *New York Herald Tribune 'Book Week'* (October 1965).

66 Erwin Panofsky, *Perspective as Symbolic Form*, trans. Christopher S. Wood (New York: Zone, 1991). While this translation (of a book published in 1927 as 'Die Perspektive als "symbolische Form"') proclaims itself the first in English, Theall in *The Medium Is the Rear-View Mirror* (*RVM*) states that McLuhan had read an English version of the text (previous to 1971). McLuhan certainly encountered Panofsky's text indirectly – but not until 1975 – in Samuel Y. Edgerton, Jr's *The Renaissance Rediscovery of Linear Perspective* (New York: Basic, 1975), from which he quotes in *Laws of Media* (*LM*); chapter 11 of Edgerton's book is devoted to a discussion of Panofsky.

67 See Wood's introduction to Panofsky, *Perspective* 8; 20.

68 The quotation is from volume 2 of Cassirer's *Philosophy of Symbolic Forms*, titled *Mythical Thought*. In the strict historical argument that he advances, Panofsky places Byzantine art on the crossroads between antique perspectival norms and Renaissance perspective. 'Byzantine art could not decide,' he states, 'to form the world in a completely linear rather than a painterly fashion; thus its adherence to mosaic, whose nature it is to hide the inexorably two-dimensional structure of the bare wall by spreading a shimmering coat over it' (*Perspective* 50). One can imagine that Panofsky's formulation of the qualities of mosaic were at least as important to McLuhan as was that of von Békésy (referred to in *TVP*, exhibit 6, 55). Indeed, Panofsky's formulation casts 'mosaic' in precisely the sort of interficial mould in which McLuhan cast scribal art.

69 Jean Piaget and Bärbel Inhelder, *The Child's Conception of Space*, trans. F.J. Langdon and J.L. Lunzer (London: Routledge and Kegan Paul, 1956 [1948]).

70 Piaget and Inhelder express a similar position, arguing that 'haptic' spaces 'presuppose the translation of tactile perceptions and movements into visual images' (ibid. 4). Likewise, Wolfgang Köhler in *Gestalt Psychology* (New York: Liveright, 1929), from which McLuhan cites (*TVP* 29), writes: 'Normally, the connection between definite visual processes and definite acoustical and motor processes works astonishingly well' (116).

71 In *TVP*, McLuhan writes that '[t]he world of modern advertising is a magical environment constructed to maintain the economy, not to increase human awareness' (243), which likewise revisits a major theme in *The Mechanical Bride*.

72 This notion of involvement provides yet another countering of the claim made by Manuel Castells that McLuhan failed to theorize interactivity. Writing in *The Rise of the Network Society* (Oxford: Blackwell, 1996), Castells states that 'the mass media system fulfilled most of the features suggested by McLuhan in the early 1960s: it was the McLuhan Galaxy. Yet the fact that the audience is not a passive object but an interactive subject opened the way to its differentiation' (337).

73 Jonathan Crary cites this argument in his study *Suspensions of Perception: Attention, Spectacle, and Modern Culture* (Cambridge, MA: MIT P, 1999), 200, n114 and 226, n177; Crary's study is significant for the critical attention it pays to the dimension of sound.

74 McLuhan notes that '[t]his reversal of spatial perspective also occurs in the poet Hopkins, whose favourite term "inscape" (as compared with "landscape") draws attention to the same change of perspective as that created by Seurat' (*TVP* 24).

75 For a discussion of empathy in the context of contemporary notions of social space see Iain Borden, 'Space Beyond: Spatiality and the City in the Writings of Georg Simmel,' *The Journal of Architecture* 2.4 (1997): 313–35, esp. 321.

76 I quote here and throughout this section from the superb critical anthology of these writings and the introduction thereto: *Empathy, Form, and Space: Problems in German Aesthetics, 1873–1893* (*EFS*), intro. and trans. Harry Francis Mallgrave and Eleftherios Ikonomou (Santa Monica: Getty Center, 1994), 19.

77 McLuhan also referred to Lipps in his 1951 essay 'The Aesthetic Moment in Landscape Poetry': 'Mallarmé discovered that the aesthetic moment of arrested cognition can be split up into numerous fractions which can be orchestrated in many discontinuous ways. Contemporary with Mallarmé, Theodor Lipps was elaborating the same perception about the laws of the visual and auditory imagination. And the doctrines of Lipps were aired in London before 1914 by T.E. Hulme' (*IL* 164–5). There is a further reference to Lipps in McLuhan and Nevitt's 'The Man Who Came to Listen,' in *Peter Drucker: Contributions to Business Enterprise*, ed. Tony H. Bonaparte and John E. Flaherty (New York: New York UP, 1970), 35–55: 'Theodore Lipps pointed out long ago that the single clang of a bell includes all possible symphonies and music' (38). McLuhan is referring to Lipps's *Psychological Studies*, trans. Herbert C. Sanborn (Baltimore: Williams and Wilkins, 1926), whose central section, 'The Nature of Musical Consonance and Dissonance,' seeks to demonstrate that the 'clang-sequence is psychologically always a kind of compound clang' (171). The first part of the book is devoted to 'The Space of Visual Perception.' Lipps is also cited in *VVV*, item 10. Lipps's 1898 book, *The Comic and Humor*, had influenced Freud's thoughts on wit.

78 The term 'scanning' was used for such eye movement (*EFS* 22), which adds a historical dimension to McLuhan's use of the term to describe the way in which the 'finger' in a television picture tube produces an image.

79 As McLuhan suggests in *From Cliché to Archetype* (*CA*), 'Most of our ideas of the visual are not related to visual action so much as to the conceptual and the cultural residues of traditional learning' (100).

80 Adrian John has remarked on the importance of translation in McLuhan's 'network' theory in *The Nature of the Book: Print and Knowledge in the Making* (Chicago: U of Chicago P, 1998), 13–14, n16: 'In such a world of natural/social hybrids, power comes from "translation."'

81 *Anerca*, ed. Edmund Carpenter, with drawings by Enooesweetok (Toronto: Dent, 1959). 'In Eskimo the word to make poetry is the word to breathe; both are derivatives of *anerca*, the soul, that which is internal' (unpaginated). The drawings for this book were collected by Robert Flaherty, maker of the film *Nanook of the North*, in 1913–14.

82 'The television medium forces the use of what McLuhan later referred to as the "ear-view mirror," because the eye never receives a complete picture from the screen, just as the ear never receives a word in isolation from a stream of speech' (Gordon, *Marshall McLuhan: Escape into Understanding* [*EU*] 54). On Pollock and the planar see Belgrad, *Culture of Spontaneity* 37.

83 David Livingstone, *The Geographical Tradition* (Oxford: Blackwell, 1992). McLuhan would have encountered the work of Herder in R.A. Wilson's *The Birth of Language* (discussed in chapter 1 above), though not the particular text to which Livingstone refers. I was alerted to Livingstone's book through Don Mitchell's *Cultural Geography: A Critical Introduction* (Oxford: Blackwell, 2000).

84 The titles to these works were in fact supplied by Ralph Manheim, Pollock's neighbour and the translator of Thomas Mann; some of these titles are McLuhanesque, such as *Galaxy* and *Vortex*.

85 Derrick de Kerckhove has noted that 'McLuhan was very fond of Dada, of absurdism, fond of the interplay of things that were not meant to be connected at first.' Quoted in *Forward through the Rearview Mirror: Reflections On and By Marshall McLuhan*, ed. Paul Benedetti and Nancy DeHart (Scarborough: Prentice-Hall, 1996), 138.

86 Freeman, 'Layers of Meaning,' 14.

87 Welchman, 'After the Wagnerian Bouillabaisse,' 59.

88 There was a surrealist magazine founded by André Breton and Max Ernst in New York in 1942 with the title *VVV* (see Belgrad, *Culture of Spontaneity* 36).

89 See Peter Frank's *Something Else Press: An Annotated Bibliography* ([Brattleboro]: McPherson and Company, 1983).

90 As Higgins wrote, 'I admire many of Marshall McLuhan's ideas – years ago, when I had SOME-THING ELSE PRESS, we published the old EXPLORATIONS 8 (with some revisions by him and others) as VERBI-VOCO-VISUAL EXPLORATIONS.' Personal communication, dated 22 March 1990.

91 Dick Higgins, 'Preface' to Alfred E. Hansen, *A Primer of Happenings and Time/Space Art* (New York: Something Else P, 1965), as quoted in Frank, 86, n8.

92 Fiore subsequently designed Higgins's *Horizons: The Poetics and Theory of the Intermedia* (Carbondale: S Illinois UP, 1984).

93 See Harry H. Crosby and George R. Bond, eds, *The McLuhan Explosion* (New York: American Book Co., 1968), 206.

94 I am following here Herbert Bittner, ed., *George Grosz* (New York: Golden Griffin, 1960).

95 Klaus Honnef, 'Symbolic Form as a Vivid Cognitive Principle: An Essay on Montage,' in Honnef and Pater Pachnicke, eds, *John Heartfield* (New York: Abrams, 1992), 49.

96 As Honnef points out, photomontage is a child not of the cinema but of the photograph.

97 On this topic generally, see Douglas Kahn, *John Heartfield: Art and Mass Media* (New York: Tanam Press, 1985).

98 See Christopher Phillips, 'Introduction,' *Montage and Modern Life: 1919–1942* (Cambridge: MIT P, 1992), 22.

99 In a 1992 interview, Fiore also mentioned having been influenced by Marinetti, Wyndham Lewis, concrete poetry, the calligrams of Apollinaire, Fluxus, rebuses, and the typographical 'mouse's tail' in *Alice's Adventures in Wonderland*. Traces of Moholy-Nagy and of the collage work of Heartfield have also been noted in his work. See 'McLuhan/Fiore,' in Lupton and Miller, eds, *Design Writing Research: Writing on Graphic Design* (New York: Kiosk and Princeton Architectural P, 1996), 90–101; especially p. 93.

100 McLuhan produced at least one 'classic' example of work-as-typography, the broadside *The Rise and Fall of Nature*, published by the Dreadnought Press (a private press in Toronto) and reprinted in *The Antigonish Review* 62–3 (1985): 98–9.

101 As Johanna Drucker puts it, Mallarmé's 'ideas about the metaphysical extension of "The Book" were in effect unrealizable ... [T]he possibility of a book which contained "all earthly existence" was always precluded by its own conceptual parameters. At the point of this limit, the end of the book begins' (Johanna Drucker, *The Century of Artists' Books* [New York: Granary Books, 1995], 36–7). In a certain sense, however, the infinitely expandable pages of the Web have realized Mallarmé's impossible book.

102 As Susi R. Bloch has put it, Mallarmé sought to produce in *Un Coup de dés* a book 'in which typography and even the foldings of the pages achieve an ideational, analytic, and expressive significance.' See 'The Book Stripped Bare,' in Joan Lyons, ed., *Artists' Books: A Critical Anthology and Sourcebook* (Rochester: Visual Studies Workshop P, 1985), 133–47.

103 '"Marshall and I planned this book together,"' said Fiore in a *Publishers' Weekly* interview dated 3 April 1967 and reprinted in *The McLuhan Explosion* 203.

104 The hardback is 11¼ inches high by 6¾ inches wide, opening to 14 inches across.

105 Arthur A. Cohen, 'Doomsday in Dogpatch: The McLuhan Thesis Examined,' in *McLuhan: Pro and Con*, ed. Raymond Rosenthal (Baltimore: Penguin, 1969), 234–41; this quotation 238.

106 *War and Peace in the Global Village* (*WPGV*) was reissued in 1997 by Hardwired Publications, a press affiliated with *Wired* magazine, which has taken McLuhan as its 'patron saint.' The book has been

printed in the original format, except that the cover is now psychedelic yellow and pink (rather than the original black and white), and this scheme is repeated on the jacket, which has quotations from John Naisbitt, former President Clinton, and Vancouver novelist Douglas Coupland, who remarks astutely that McLuhan 'is the Dad we want to impress, the one to whom we say, "Betcha didn't think this would be happening" or, finally, the phrase that might either chill him or warm his heart: "Hey Marshall – guess what – you were *right*!"'

107 See, in general, George P. Landow, *Hypertext: The Convergence of Contemporary Critical Theory and Technology* (Baltimore: Johns Hopkins UP, 1992); Landow references McLuhan throughout. Drucker comments that 'certain conventions of the codex form – hierarchical organizations of information, some indexing and access devices – ... find their simulacral equivalent in the electronic "book."' See Drucker, *Century*, 156.

108 This point was reiterated at the time of the Gulf War, when it was argued that the war was meant to provide a testing ground for the Stealth bomber and for computerized targeting systems that draw on the technology that makes satellite television possible. See Baudrillard, *The Gulf War Did Not Take Place*, trans. Paul Patton (1991; Bloomington: Indiana UP, 1995).

109 Lupton and Miller, 'McLuhan/Fiore,' 90. The blurring of traditional publishing hierarchies may have accounted for *The Medium Is the Massage*'s initial rejection by seventeen publishers.

110 Drucker (*Century*) distinguishes between the artist's book, which tends to question the formal structure of the book, and the *livre d'artiste*, which is largely the book as work of art. I see the two categories as deeply overlapping (especially in the 'democratic multiple'), and have tended to use the terms interchangeably.

111 In his 1965 essay, 'Intermedia,' Higgins writes, 'Much of the best work being produced today seems to fall between media. This is no accident. The concept of the separation between media arose in the Renaissance.' See 'Intermedia,' in Higgins's *Horizons*, 18–28; this quotation 18.

112 Germano Celant, 'Book as Artwork: 1960–1972,' trans. Corine Lotz, Jorge Zontal, and Peggy Gale, in *Books by Artists*, ed. Tim Guest and Germano Celant (Toronto: Art Metropole, 1981), 85–104; this quotation 85.

113 The *Newsletters* are found in NAC, McLuhan Collection, box 143.

114 In addition to their relationship to the history of the book, the *Newsletters* can also be situated productively in the context of correspondence art. See Michael Crane and Mary Stofflet, eds, *Correspondence Art: Source Book for the Network of International Postal Art Activity* (San Francisco: Contemporary Arts Press, 1984), who assert that 'Correspondence art is about communication' (3).

115 As reported by Roger Burford Mason, 'Report on the Carl Dair Symposium,' *The Devil's Artisan* 36 (1995): 10–12; this quotation 12.

116 Dick Higgins, 'Intermedia,' 18.

117 'Carpenter and McLuhan hauled them [the mimeographed copies of *Counterblast*] by sled over the snow-covered streets of Toronto to a cigar store, where the manager agreed to sell them for twenty-five cents a copy' (*M&M* 128). This version of *Counterblast* was a response to the 1951 Massey Report; see chapter 8 below.

118 McLuhan had made this point as early as 1955: 'Today we are living in what is in many ways the greatest period of culture in the history of the world. The auditory and oral heritages of some cultures are being poured through the visual traditions of other cultures to the enrichment of all.' See 'A Historical Approach to the Media,' *Teachers College Record* 57.2 (1955): 104–10; this quotation 110.

119 The extent to which McLuhan's comments on the book influenced literary theory, for example, as well as the extent to which that influence was *assumed*, can be gauged by comments Jacques Derrida makes at the opening of *Of Grammatology*: 'all appearances to the contrary, [the] death of the book undoubtedly announces (and in a certain sense always has announced) nothing but a death of speech (of a *so-called* full speech) and a new mutation in the history of writing, in history as writing' (*Of Grammatology*, ed. Gayatri Chakravorty Spivak [1967; Baltimore: Johns Hopkins UP], 1976), 8. McLuhan made a number of similar remarks (cf *UM* 80), stating most pointedly in *WPGV*, 'While bemoaning the decline of literacy and the obsolescence of the book, the literati have typically ignored the imminence of the decline in speech itself' (90–1).

120 Jay Scott, 'Full Circle: True, Patriot Womanhood: The 30-Year Passage of Joyce Wieland,' *Canadian Art* 4.1 (1987): 56–63; this quotation 59.

121 The OED gives *bōc* as cognate with *beech*.

122 For a general discussion, see Keith A. Smith, *Structure of the Visual Book* (Rochester: Visual Studies Workshop, 1984).

123 I am following Peter Perrin's discussion of this process in 'Cover to Cover: A Book by Michael Snow,' *artscanada* 33 (October 1976): 43–7.

124 As Drucker remarks, 'The linearity of the codex has thus been subverted by making it bi-directional' (*Century* 126.)

Chapter 6: Visible Speech

1 Frank Davey, ed., *TISH No. 1–19* (Vancouver: Talonbooks, 1975), 13.

2 For an overview of sound poetry see Karl Jirgens, 'Sound Poetry and the New Aurality,' *Literary Review of Canada* 8.4 and 8.5 (May and June 2000).

3 Daniel Belgrad, *The Culture of Spontaneity: Improvisation and the Arts in Postwar America* (Chicago: U of Chicago P, 1998), 1. Compare Tallman's comment that 'Nothing that is perceived will have value unless it has some use in human space.' See 'Robert Creeley's Portrait of an Artist,' *TISH No. 1–19*, 144. Caroline Bayard has stated that space, along with orality, represents the major kinship between the TISH poets and the concretists. See *The New Poetics in Canada and Quebec* (Toronto: U of Toronto P, 1989), 104.

4 It was also the spatiality of geography; Samuel Perry, in issue 10 of *TISH*, quotes the famous opening of *Call Me Ishmael* in which Olson writes '"I take Space to be the central fact to man born in America"' (204). Perry goes on to write that 'Creeley and Ginsberg and Kerouac are men travelling american space taking modern measure from their own space-time locus / wherever they are' (209).

5 Charles Olson had insisted upon the importance of the typewriter to projective verse, writing that 'the typewriter ... due to its rigidity and its space precisions, ... can, for a poet, indicate exactly the breath, the pauses, the suspensions even of syllables, the juxtapositions even of parts of phrases, which he intends. For the first time the poet has the stave and the bar a musician has had' ('Projective Verse' [1950], in Richard Kostelanetz, ed., *The Avant-Garde Tradition in Literature* [Buffalo: Prometheus Books, 1982], 248–56; this quotation 253). McLuhan alludes to this passage in his section on the typewriter in *Understanding Media* (*UM*) (259), adding that it was a typical reversal of form that a mechanical device such as the typewriter should have the organic effect of fusing functions, in this case that of performance and composition. Jack David has written an imaginary 'discussion about typewriters between Marshall McLuhan, some poets and a secretary' that collects a number of McLuhan's pronouncements on the typewriter and relates them to the practices of visual poets ('A Discussion about Typewriters between Marshall McLuhan, Some Poets and a Secretary,' *The Antigonish Review* 17 [Spring 1974]: 45–9). One of these, Aram Saroyan, who states that the typewriter 'is the biggest influence on my work' (quoted in Emmett Williams, *An Anthology of Concrete Poetry* [New York: Something Else Press, 1967], n.p., s.v. 'Aram Saroyan'), explicitly cites McLuhan (elsewhere) in a statement of his poetics: 'As McLuhan says, you can't make the new medium do the old job ... What interests me now is that new poetry isn't going to be poetry for reading. It's going to be for looking at, that is if it's poetry to be printed and not taped. I mean book, print culture, is finished ... [Y]es The Media Is The Message, and reading is nothing as a medium at all ...' See Mary Ellen Solt, 'A World Look at Concrete Poetry,' in *Concrete Poetry: A World View* (Bloomington: Indiana UP, 1970), 7–66; this quotation 57–8.

6 While one of the essays in *Verbi-Voco-Visual Explorations* (*VVV*) (Jack Jones's 'Dada in the Drugstore') takes its epigraph from Maurice Blanchot, the ideogrammatical space of which McLuhan writes here is not the space of Blanchot's 'l'espace littéraire,' which is static and unlocated, and could be rendered as 'remove,' according to one of Blanchot's translators. See Ann Smock's introduction to her translation of Blanchot, *The Space of Literature* (1955; Lincoln: U of Nebraska P, 1989), 12.

7 Phatic communion is '"speech used for social or emotive purposes rather than for communicating information"'; this definition is quoted by Donald Theall, in *The Virtual Marshall McLuhan* (*VM*) (Montreal and Kingston: McGill-Queen's UP, 2001), who attributes this notion to Bronislaw Malinowski (274, n19).

8 Hwa Jol Jung, in 'Misreading the Ideogram: From Fenollosa to Derrida and McLuhan' (*Paideuma: A*

Journal Devoted to Ezra Pound Scholarship 13.2 [1984]: 211–27) argues that McLuhan misreads the ideogram in his assumption that it is 'anti-visual and tactile' (225). By 'anti-visual and tactile,' however, McLuhan refers to the non-linear, non-sequential way in which the ideogram signifies.

9 Paul Saenger argues in *Space between Words: The Origins of Silent Reading* (Stanford: Stanford UP, 1997) that it was the introduction of spacing between the words of *scriptura continua* that was the origin of the profound changes signalled by the transition from orality to literacy.

10 Jack Goody, *The Interface between the Written and the Oral* (Cambridge: Cambridge UP, 1987).

11 Ruth Finnegan, *Literacy and Orality: Studies in the Technology of Communication* (Oxford: Blackwell, 1988), 145. McLuhan writes on page 3 of *The Gutenberg Galaxy* (*GG*) that, 'Far from being deterministic, however, the present study will, it is hoped, elucidate a principal factor in social change which may lead to a genuine increase of human autonomy.'

12 The term 'interdependence' is of key importance; as Steve McCaffery has argued, the return of orality impacts not on the individual (rendered 'discarnate' by electronic media) but as a mass phenomenon. See Steve McCaffery, 'McLuhan + Language × Music,' *North of Intention: Critical Writings 1973–1986* (Toronto: Nightwood, 1986). 77–87.

13 As McLuhan writes of Giedion in a 1949 review of *Mechanization Takes Command* (*MTC*), 'Central to [Giedion's] procedure is his distinction between "constituent" and "transitory" in facing styles and periods. The one is the incarnation and vehicle of creative force, the other derivative display. But from these conceptions he vigorously excludes the idea of "progress," as alien to valuation in the arts' (601); the exclusion of the notion of progress from McLuhan's formulations was equally powerful. See 'Encyclopaedic Unities' [review of Giedion's *MTC* and Moholy-Nagy's *Vision in Motion*], *Hudson Review* 1.4 (1949): 599–602.

14 McLuhan, 'Romanticism Reviewed,' *Renascence* 12.4 (1960): 207–9; this quotation 208. Significantly, it was Coleridge who first used the term 'intermedia.' See bpNichol and Steve McCaffery, eds, *Sound Poetry: A Catalogue* (Toronto: Underwhich, 1978), 65, quoting Dick Higgins.

15 See Walter J. Ong, *Orality and Literacy: The Technologizing of the Word* (New York: Methuen, 1982). In fact, this 'primacy' of speech has been one of the major targets of contemporary theory, especially in the work of Derrida (and deconstruction generally); ironically, Derrida has critiqued McLuhan's notion of orality precisely along these lines, arguing that it is towards an increasingly greater encounter with writing (as codified utterance), and not speaking, that contemporary culture is headed (Jacques Derrida, 'Signature Event Context,' *Margins of Philosophy*, trans. Alan Bass [Chicago: U of Chicago P, 1982], 307–30). The relevant passage reads: 'We are not witnessing an end of writing which, to follow McLuhan's ideological representation, would restore a transparency or immediacy of social relations; but indeed a more and more powerful historical unfolding of a general writing of which the system of speech, consciousness, meaning, presence, truth, etc., would only be an effect, to be analyzed as such. It is this questioned effect that I have elsewhere called *logocentrism*' (329). The differences, here, between Derrida and McLuhan derive in large part from McLuhan's focus on space as his prime category of inquiry (rather than on speaking and writing *per se*).This 'refutation' of McLuhan is actually much closer to McLuhan's own position, with the exception that Derrida leaves out of his formulation that which was crucial for McLuhan's, namely the distinction between visual and acoustic space. As McLuhan writes in *Laws of Media* (*LM*), 'Derrida insists on *visual* matching and connection of figures that contain or point to or represent other in the triadic chain A:B:C. In this variety of the transportation theory, meaning is carried via matching and connection' (122; emphasis added). In theorizing that the acoustic is spatial, McLuhan locates the nodal aspect of writing – its spatiality – within the acoustic as well, thus implicitly acknowledging speaking and writing as interficial. To put it another way: Derrida's 'writing' is itself a product of acoustic space and of the present historical moment, in which literate culture is increasingly interfacing with the oral modalities of electronic media.

16 See Jérôme Peignot, *Typoésie* (Paris: Imprimerie Nationale, 1993), 123.

17 NAC, McLuhan Collection, vol. 125, file 40.

18 McLuhan, 'At the Flip Point of Time – The Point of No Return?' *Journal of Communication* 25.4 (1975): 102–6; this quotation 105.

19 McCaffery, 'McLuhan,' 85.

20 Eric McLuhan, in his preface to *LM*, refers to these four laws as 'four dimensions' (ix). In an article on 'Pound, Eliot, and the Rhetoric of *The Waste Land*,' McLuhan associates the number 4 with the four

levels of traditional exegesis (as elaborated by Dante in the 'Letter to Can Grande'), and likewise argues that the 'four levels of meaning are simultaneous and not sequential' (562). See *New Literary History* 10.3 (1979): 557–80.

21 Paul Grosswiler, *Method Is the Message: Rethinking McLuhan through Critical Theory* (Montreal: Black Rose, 1998), 80. As in his 1989 article in the special issue of the *Canadian Journal of Communication* commemorating the twenty-fifth anniversary of *UM*, Grosswiler here elaborates his thesis that McLuhan's methodology has much in common with a (post)Marxist dialectical position. The book is especially strong in its insistence on the importance of hybridity to McLuhan's theories in general.

22 Revealing the ground of a given figure is likewise what the deconstructionist does. As Andreas Papadakis writes in the 'Foreword' to *Deconstruction: Omnibus Volume* (New York: Rizzoli, 1989), 'Deconstruction addresses notions in thinking to show how these rest on deeply-entrenched binary oppositions and it operates by suspending the correspondence between the two. According to Peter Eisenman, architecture "must move away from the rigidity and value structure of the dialectic oppositions. For example the traditional opposition between structure and decoration, abstraction and figuration, figure and ground"' (7).

23 McLuhan, 'Symbolist Communication' [review of Rosemond Tuve, *A Reading of George Herbert*], *Thought: Fordham University Quarterly* 28, no. 110 (1953): 456–8; this quotation 458. Eric McLuhan was particularly closely involved with giving the tetrads their chiasmic form (private communication).

24 George Puttenham, *The Arte of English Poesie* (1589; rpt London: Murray, 1869), 106. McLuhan cites from Puttenham in *From Cliché to Archetype* (*CA*) 97.

25 McLuhan, in *Do Books Matter?*, ed. Brian Baumfield (London: Morley Books, 1973), 31–41; this quotation 32.

26 James Curtis writes that 'Paul de Man gave the clue to the function of the *essai concrète* when he wrote, "Certain forces that could legitimately be called modern and that were at work in lyric poetry, in the novel, and the theater have also become operative in the field of literary theory and criticism."' See Curtis's 'Marshall McLuhan and French Structuralism,' *boundary* 2 1 (1972–3): 134–46; this quotation 142, with Curtis quoting from de Man's *Blindness and Insight* (New York: Oxford, 1971).

27 As Theall suggests, McLuhan may have preferred the term *poésie concrète* to its English counterpart in order to assert affinities between concrete poetry and *musique concrète*, thereby emphasizing the hybridity of these forms (*RVM* 240). J.R. Pierce, in *Symbols, Signals and Noise: The Nature and Process of Communication* (New York: Harper, 1961), cited by McLuhan in *UM*, discusses Edgard Varèse and *musique concrète* (253).

28 Writing on 'Joyce, Mallarmé and the Press' in 1953, McLuhan cites Rosemond Tuve's study of George Herbert and her argument that 'metaphysical conceits were direct translations into verbal terms of popular pictorial imagery of the late middle ages. She [Tuve] was able to show that the characteristic conceits of Herbert and others arose from the meeting of the old manuscript culture (with its marginal pictures) and the new printed medium' (*IL* 6).

29 If Walter Ong is correct in his assertion that '[d]econstruction is tied to typography, rather than, as its advocates seem often to assume, merely to writing' (*Orality and Literacy* 129), then *LM*, in its deconstruction of typographic space, can be seen as McLuhan's 'grammatology.'

30 Solt, 'A World Look at Concrete Poetry,' 7.

31 Some concretists take the space of the page as the essential unit of their creations; others, as Johanna Drucker has remarked, have taken the book itself as their 'conceptual space,' their work entering into the domain of the artist's book (Johanna Drucker, *The Century of Artists' Books* [New York: Granary Books, 1995], 10).

32 It is not certain that McLuhan's text influenced the Brazilians; an analogous example of cross-cultural exchange is illuminating, however. In 1951, the Argentinian architectural journal *Nuestra Arquitectura* did a feature on a Vancouver home designed by (then) Vancouver-based architect Douglas Simpson. The venue of Simpson's renown is as significant as its geographical range, since the publication of architectural journals was often a multidisciplinary effort making use of the interficial principles laid out by Moholy-Nagy in works such as *Vision in Motion* and his early Bauhaus effort *Painting, Photography, Film* (1925), which Johanna Drucker has cited as 'an unsurpassed example of the use of structure and format as part of the content, rather than merely as instruments for delivering meaning in an effective or eye-catching way' (*Century* 62). When, in 1958, the *Journal of the Royal Architectural Institute of*

Canada planned a special issue on British Columbia, it convened an advisory committee that included poet Earle Birney, whom bpNichol has called 'the real forerunner of concrete in canada.' Adele Freedman has likewise seen Birney's work on this journal as a 'beginning' of his concrete phase, with the connection being in the recognition of the space of the page itself as productive of meaning through juxtaposition and overlay of photos and typography (as in *The Medium Is the Massage* [*MM*]). See Freedman's 'Introduction' to Rhodri Windsor Liscombe, *The New Spirit: Modern Architecture in Vancouver, 1938–1963* (Montreal: Canadian Centre for Architecture, 1997), 10 and 180, n8. For the internationalist context of Canadian artistic production during this period, see chapter 1 of Liscombe and *passim*.

33 McLuhan cites in *CA* a passage that discusses Emmett Williams (155).

34 Marinetti referred to the proto-concrete work of Futurist Carlo Belloli as 'creazione originale di zone-rumori [costruiti] otticamente sulla pagina-spazio totale' (the original creation of sound-zones constructed optically on the totality of the space-page). Quoted by Emmett Williams in his *Anthology of Concrete Poetry* (n.p.).

35 Pierre Garnier, *Spatialisme et poésie concrète* (Paris: Gallimard, 1968), 130.

36 Dick Higgins, *Pattern Poetry: Guide to an Unknown Literature* (Albany: State U of New York P, 1987), 191.

37 Similarly, the dynamic nature of the laws of media implies that the visual and the acoustic are not stable but relational.

38 It was this simultaneity of apprehension that was Apollinaire's goal in producing the prototypical concrete poems of *Calligrammes*. See Willard Bohn's *The Aesthetics of Visual Poetry 1914–1928* (Cambridge: Cambridge UP, 1986). Apollinaire used the 'hourglass' shape (which reappears in the tetrads of *LM*) in the top half of his poem 'La Colombe Poignardée et le Jet d'Eau.' See his *Calligrammes: Poems of Peace and War (1913–1916)*, trans. Anne Hyde Greet (Berkeley: U of California P, 1980), 122. In the introduction to this volume, S.I. Lockerbie writes that Apollinaire conceived of the calligrammes as reflecting 'the global nature of contemporary consciousness ... To be able to mirror such a multiple form of consciousness the work of art had to abandon linear and discursive structures ... in favour of what Apollinaire called *simultaneity*: a type of structure that would give the impression of a full and instant awareness within one moment of space-time' (3). bpNichol's first published poem was 'Translating Apollinaire' (1964, published by bill bissett's blewointment press); in 1979, Nichol published *Translating Translating Apollinaire: A Preliminary Report* (Milwaukee: Membrane P, 1979).

39 An early study of Alexander Graham Bell was subtitled *The Man Who Contracted Space*. See Catherine F. Mackenzie, *Alexander Graham Bell* (Boston: Houghton Mifflin, 1928), cited in Avital Ronell, *The Telephone Book: Technology/Schizophrenia/Electronic Speech* (Lincoln: U of Nebraska P, 1989), unpaginated list of sigla.

40 Like his father, A.G. Bell was an 'oralist,' committed to the replacement of sign language (a 'visible speech' if ever there was one) by the imitative system promoted by the Bells. The two systems continue to have a fraught relationship; see Oliver Sacks, *Seeing Voices* (Berkeley: U of California P, 1989).

41 Jack David, 'Visual Poetry in Canada: Birney, Bissett, and bp,' *Studies in Canadian Literature* 2.2 (1977): 252–66; first quotation 257 from Davey's *From There to Here* (Toronto: New Press, 1972); second quotation 257 from Rosalie Murphy, ed., *Contemporary Poets of the English Language* (New York: St Martin's P, 1970).

42 Caroline Bayard and Jack David, *Out-Posts* (Erin: Press Porcépic, 1978), 53.

43 Quoted by Bayard in *New Poetics*, 58. See also Richard Cavell, 'Review of Bayard, *New Poetics*,' *Recherches sémiotiques / Semiotic Inquiry* 10.1–3 (1990): 210–14.

44 bp Nichol, *The Martyrology* [books 1 to 9] (Toronto: Coach House, 1977–93); 6 vols, unpaginated. Roderick W. Harvey has argued that 'in *The Martyrology* [Nichol] often resorts to the tribal chant of Marshall McLuhan's electronic "global village."' See 'bpNichol: The Repositioning of Language.' in *ECW* 4 (1976): 19–33; 31. Concretism has attained a sort of canonicity in Canada, unlike in the United States, where, according to Christian Moraru, 'the contemporary poetic canon has remained impervious' to the work of the concretists. See '"Topos/typos/tropos": Visual Strategies and the Mapping of Space in Charles Olson's Poetry,' *Word and Image* 14.3 (1998): 253–66; this quotation 253.

45 In 1978, Steve McCaffery (longtime collaborator with bpNichol) and friends staged the 'Cabaret Voltaire' at the Western Front in Vancouver; Vincent Trasov recreated the role of Hugo Ball. See Keith

Wallace, ed., *Whispered Art History: Twenty Years at the Western Front* (Vancouver: Arsenal Pulp P, 1993), 42, and my chapter 7, following.

46 Robert Motherwell, ed., *The Dada Painters and Poets: An Anthology* (1951; rpt New York: George Wittenborn, 1967).

47 bpNichol, *The Cosmic Chef Glee & Perloo Memorial Society under the Direction of Captain Poetry Presents ... An Evening of Concrete Courtesy ... Oberon Cement Works* (Ottawa: Oberon, 1970). Captain Poetry, in Nichol's rendering, bears a remarkable resemblance to the figure Blake used to illustrate the 'Spectres of Albion's Twelve Sons' plate to *Jerusalem*. See Alexander Roob, *The Hermetic Museum: Alchemy and Mysticism* (Cologne: Taschen, 1997), 69.

48 Nichol made a connection between concrete poetry and Duchamp's art in likening the letter 'Q' to '"Nude Descending a Staircase" by Duchamp. I was interested in the play of the light through the letters and what happened to the form of a letter when it overlapped with itself.' See Irene Niechoda, *A Sourcery for Books 1 and 2 of bpNichol's 'The Martyrology'* (Toronto: ECW, 1992), 43. The phrase 'light through' is a McLuhanism (*TVP* 25; 181) referring to media (such as stained glass, paintings by Seurat, and the cathode ray tube) that permit light to shine through them; such media are more involving than those such as paper that are designed to function with light focused on them. McLuhan's *The Mechanical Bride* (*MB*) (published the same year as Motherwell's anthology) was a significant Canadian conduit for Duchampian thought. Duchamp's *Bride* is a classic example of an artwork designed to involve its consumers as producers by means of its transparency, as, in another sense, is Nichol's multivolume poem, *The Martyrology*, where the increased play of light through the letters seeks to counter the effects of print technology, in which 'the idea of privacy grows as the space shrinks,' creating 'perceptual tricks / false notion of perspective' (Bk 3).

49 'Allatonceness' appears in works such as *MM* (63). The catalogue was published by the Fine Arts Gallery, University of British Columbia (UBC), as *Concrete Poetry: An Exhibition in Four Parts* (Vancouver: UBC P, 1969); it takes the form of a folder containing further folders of essays and reproductions.

50 John Robert Colombo, *New Directions in Canadian Poetry* (Toronto: Holt, Rinehart and Winston, 1971), 34.

51 Niechoda, *A Sourcery*, 38.

52 The low-definition qualities of performance poetry are immediately evident from the scores printed in *The Prose Tattoo: Selected Performance Scores by the Four Horsemen*, Rafael Barreto-Rivera, Paul Dutton, Steve McCaffery, bpNichol (Milwaukee: Membrane P, 1983), which appear as invitations on the part of the performer to elaborate them infinitely. Scott McCloud, in *Understanding Comics: The Invisible Art* (1993; rpt New York: Harper-Perennial, 1994), summarizes McLuhan's contribution to the understanding of comics; see page 38 and *passim*. See also McLuhan on 'The Comics and Culture,' in Malcolm Ross, ed., *Our Sense of Identity* (Toronto: Ryerson, 1954), 240–6.

53 bpNichol, 'The Medium Was the Message,' *Journal of Canadian Poetry* 4 (1989): 1–3. I am grateful to Philip Marchand for drawing this article to my attention. Nichol was asked in the early 1980s by Sheila Watson to contribute a piece to a Festschrift for McLuhan she was compiling; he agreed, but the book was not realized. See Nichol's letter of 3 January 1982 to Sheila Watson, in which Nichol also notes that Steve McCaffery was contemplating an annotated edition of McLuhan's library (University of Alberta, Wilfred Watson Collection).

54 Similarly, Gilles Deleuze and Félix Guattari write in the *Anti-Oedipus: Capitalism and Schizophrenia*, trans. Robert Hurley et al. (1972; New York: Viking, 1977) that McLuhan has 'shown what a language of decoded flows is' (240). See the discussion in Theall's *VM* 92–3.

55 McCaffery and Nichol, *Rational Geomancy: The Kids of the Book Machine* (*The Collected Research Reports of the Toronto Research Group 1973–1982* (Vancouver: Talonbooks, 1992), 73.

56 One can see this process happening in the transition from Nichol's 'Andy' to 'For Jesus Lunatick,' both in *Two Novels* (Toronto: Coach House, nd. [1969]). The promotional flyer Coach House issued for this book was titled *to become obsessed with space!!*, which is the logo of one of Nichol's cartoons in this work. See jwcurry's 'Notes toward a beepliography,' in *Open Letter [Read the Way He Writes: A Festschrift for bpNichol]* 6:5–6 (1986): 249–70; this quotation 252, item 40.

57 As Niechoda remarks in general, Nichol's texts 'subvert the general notion of what comprises a book of poetry by a single author' through the use of 'the collaborative input of [visual artist Jerry] Ofo [who

drew the clouds and saints in the poem], with the incorporation of design elements borrowed from visual, pre-Gutenberg, and non-"literary" media, with the juxtaposition of culturally and historically diverse reading codes' (*A Sourcery* 41).

58 McCaffery and Nichol, *Rational Geomancy* 65.

59 Steve McCaffery, in *Sound Poetry: A Catalogue*, ed. bpNichol and Steve McCaffery (Toronto: Underwhich, nd. [1978?]), 32. I am happy to thank Nicky Drumbolis of Letters Books (Toronto) for drawing this book to my attention.

60 The Thompsons' paper on 'ma' was originally given in McLuhan's seminar and subsequently published in the student newspaper *The Saint George Dragon* (Toronto: SAC P, 1969). They write that 'The Japanese space/time concept is embodied in the Chinese symbol, "Ma," which is made up of two parts: – the first ... being the symbol for the two leaves of a door or gate; ... and the second being the symbol for sun (moon). Together, the symbols suggest rays of moonlight seeping through the chinks in a doorway ... the element of time implied by the "moonlight seeping through" is of utmost importance to the understanding of the Japanese idea of space. Space and time are considered as related and relative entities: neither is fixed' (n.p.). The Thompsons go on to note that 'ma' is a conceptual part of traditional Japanese music, drama, flower arranging, architecture ('defined in the dictionary as the spacing between pillars' [n.p.]), calligraphy, and painting. See also *Who Was Marshall McLuhan? (WWMM)* 177. In *Space-Time in Japan – MA* (New York: Cooper-Hewitt, 1980), Japanese architect Arata Isozaki writes that 'While in the West the space-time concept gave rise to absolutely fixed images of a homogenous and infinite continuum, as presented by Descartes, in Japan space and time were never fully separated but were conceived as correlative and omnipresent' (n.p.).

61 A further dimension to this interfacing of the oral with the literate is evident in what Tom King has called 'interfusional literature,' that is, 'Native literature which is a blending of oral literature and written literature.' King cites Harry Robinson's *Write It on Your Heart* as the one complete example of such a form of literature. 'The stories in Robinson's collections are told in English and written in English, but the patterns, metaphors, structures as well as the themes and characters come primarily from oral literature ... [Robinson] develops what we might want to call an oral syntax that defeats readers' efforts to read the stories silently to themselves, a syntax that encourages readers to read the stories out loud.' See 'Godzilla vs. Post-Colonial,' in *New Contexts of Canadian Criticism*, ed. Ajay Heble et al. (Peterborough: Broadview, 1997), 241–8; this quotation 244. See also Margery Fee, 'Writing Orality: Interpreting Literature in English by Aboriginal Writers in North America, Australia and New Zealand,' *Journal of Intercultural Studies* 18 (1997): 23–39. Fee misreads McLuhan, however, when she argues that he succumbed to the '"evolutionary fallacy"' (27) and promoted literacy as the ultimate cultural achievement of the West. McLuhan wrote, in fact, that '[b]y the meaningless sign, linked to the meaningless sound, we have built the shape and meaning of Western Man' (*GG* 50).

62 Paul Dutton's book of poems, *Right Hemisphere, Left Ear* (Toronto: Coach House, 1979), brings together two notions with which McLuhan was long associated: that of the relative importance of the right and left hemispheres in the brain, and that of the association of these hemispheres with visual and acoustic space. In his introduction to that book, Dutton cites both George Herbert and Apollinaire as among his predecessors, arguing for the interficiality of sound and sight: 'As music incorporates language (in the works of John Cage, R. Murray Schafer and others, historically and contemporaneously), let poetry incorporate music. As visual art incorporates language (Ben Shahn, Greg Curnoe and others, historically and contemporaneously), let poetry incorporate visual art' (n.p.).

63 Rafael Barreto-Rivera, 'Random Walking *The Martyrology's* Book V,' *Open Letter* 6:5–6 (1986): 101–7; this quotation 101.

64 Brian Henderson, 'Soul Rising out of the Body of Language: Presence, Process and Faith in *The Martyrology*,' *Open Letter* 6.5–6 (1986): 111–28; this quotation 112.

65 Beatriz Colomina remarks in *Privacy and Publicity: Modern Architecture as Mass Media* (Cambridge, MA: MIT P, 1994), that the Saussurean opposition between orality and literacy is spatial, in that it configures an opposition between inside and outside (cf McLuhan's 'outering'). As Colomina goes on to point out, that opposition eventually collapses; Saussure writes that '"The written word is so *intimately* mixed with the spoken word of which it is its image that it ultimately takes over the principal role"' (quoted by Colomina 28). Colomina cites from McLuhan's *UM* a number of times, though McLuhan is not indexed.

66 The clouds that artist Jerry Ofo has drawn throughout books 1 to 4 allude to Dieter Rot's *246 Little Clouds* (New York: Something Else P, 1968); Rot, a foundational concretist and verbal-visualist, had a retrospective showing in Vancouver in the fall of 1972. See Dieter Rot, *Books and Graphics, Part I* (Stuttgart: Hansjörg Mayer, 1972), with special Vancouver Art Gallery jacket.

67 Jarry used 'Pataphysics (preceded by an apostrophe), his 'science of imaginary solutions,' as the focus for a satire of scientific pretensions and of logical rationality more generally. *Canadian "Pataphysics* (distinguished by a double apostrophe) is the title of a volume edited by the Toronto Research Group (a special issue of *Open Letter* 4:6–7 [1980–1]), among whom Nichol and McCaffery figure prominently, as well as, less prominently, McLuhan biographer Philip Marchand (who cites Nichol in the acknowledgments to *M&M*). On Jarry see Keith Beaumont, *Alfred Jarry: A Critical and Biographical Study* (New York: St Martin's P, 1984), where 'Pataphysics is 'defined' on 194–5.

68 bpNichol, 'The "Pata of Letter Feet, or, the English Written Character as a Medium for Poetry,' *Open Letter* 6.1 (1985): 79–95; this quotation 79.

69 One of these compositions was performed with John Cage and Teeny Duchamp in Toronto in 1968. The performance consisted of a chess game 'on an electronically wired board, so that, every time a move was made, there was a pattern of strange noises.' See Jack Pollock, *Dear M: Letters from a Gentleman of Excess* (Toronto: McClelland and Stewart, 1989), 251.

70 Carol P. James, 'Duchamp's Silent Noise / Music for the Deaf,' *Dada/Surrealism* 16 [Duchamp Centennial] (1987): 106–26; this quotation 107.

71 The *Rotoreliefs* comprise a set of six cardboard discs, printed on both sides with spirals; see the discussion in chapter 2 above. 'When viewed (preferably with one eye) at a rotating speed of 40–60 rpm, the disks present an optical illusion of depth' (303). The use of a single eye is meant to 'retrieve' two-dimensional visual space, and to emphasize that three-dimensional space is a product of the disparity produced by the fact that our eyes 'see' differently. These discs were preceded by the *Rotative Demisphere (Optique de Précision)* (1925), a spiral disc attached to a motor; 'When this machine is in operation, the black eccentric circles painted on the rotating demisphere appear to undulate, producing a hypnotic illusion of space and depth' (298; an earlier version dates from 1920 [293]). In 1923, Duchamp produced the *Disks Bearing Spirals*, some of which were inscribed with puns (297). See Anne D'Harnoncourt and Kynaston McShine, eds, *Marcel Duchamp* (New York: Museum of Modern Art, 1973).

72 Erik Satie would likewise use an airplane propeller (along with telegraph equipment and typewriters) in his score for *Parade* (1917). See Suzanne Delehanty, 'Soundings,' in *Sound by Artists*, ed. Dan Lander and Micah Lexier (Toronto: Art Metropole, 1990), 20–38.

73 Craig Adcock, 'Marcel Duchamp's Gap Music: Operations in the Space between Art and Noise,' in Douglas Kahn and Gregory Whitehead, eds, *Wireless Imagination: Sound, Radio, and the Avant-Garde* (Cambridge, MA: MIT P, 1992), 105–38; this quotation 106–7. The Futurists were acutely aware of the radical changes to our notions of space that technologies such as the radio implied. Marinetti and Pino Masnata, in their manifesto 'La Radia' of 1933, write that radio abolishes space (insofar as it does away with the *mise-en-scène* of theatre) while at the same time it immensifies space ('Immensificazione dello spazio'), and that it represents thus a spatial drama added to a temporal drama. See 'La Radia,' in *Teoria e invenzione futurista (TIF)*, ed. Luciano De Maria (1968; rpt Milan: Mondadori, 1983), 205–10.

74 Adcock, 'Duchamp's Gap Music,' 107.

75 Adcock, ibid., quoting Lawrence Steefel, 109.

76 Adcock, ibid., 109.

77 Roy Miki, 'Reading and Writing *The Martyrology*,' in Roy Miki, ed., *Tracing the Paths* (Vancouver: Talonbooks, 1988), 11–31, has suggested that wordplay in *The Martyrology* 'enacts a ritual descent into a subtext revealed in the empty spaces between the letters,' recoding those spaces as the productive sites of meaning in the poem, rather than as static absences. This quotation 27.

78 Steve McCaffery, 'In Tens/tion: Dialoguing with bp,' in Miki, ed., *Tracing the Paths* 72–91; this quotation 87.

79 Avital Ronell, *The Telephone Book*, 321ff. This chapter of Ronell's book focuses on the Bell family's emigration to Canada and Melville Bell's development of the notion of 'visible speech.'

80 Steve McCaffery, 'Nothing Is Forgotten but the Talk of How to Talk,' *North of Intention*, 110–30; this quotation 120.

81 McLuhan, 'The Memory Theatre,' *Encounter* 28.3 (1967): 61–6; this quotation 66.

82 Steve McCaffery, 'The Martyrology as Paragram,' Open Letter [Nichol Festschrift] 6:5–6 (1986): 191–206; this quotation 198.

83 See Richard Truhlar, 'bpNichol: A Sonography,' Open Letter [Nichol Festschrift] 6:5–6 (1986): 157–60; this quotation 157.

84 Nichol and McCaffery, eds, Sound Poetry, 95.

85 Bill Viola, 'The Sound of One Line Scanning,' in Lander and Lexier, eds, Sound by Artists, 39–54; this quotation 43.

86 Barreto-Rivera, Dutton, McCaffery, and Nichol, The Prose Tattoo, see above, note 52.

87 Richard Kostelanetz, ed., Text-Sound Texts (New York: RK Editions, 1980), 14.

88 bpNichol, 'From Sound to Sense,' in Kostelanetz, ed., Text-Sound Texts, 335; originally published in Stereoheadphones 4 (1979).

89 bpNichol, 'A Text for the Dreamer, from MEME: a nopera,' scored for music by David Mott, in Descant 63 (1988): 53–7.

90 I am following the plot description here and throughout given by Paul Dutton in 'Confronting Conventions: The Musical/Dramatic Works of bpNichol,' Open Letter [Nichol Festschrift] 6:5–6 (1986): 131–40.

91 Virgil Thomson and Gertrude Stein, Four Saints in Three Acts (Nonesuch 9 79035–2 [1982]).

92 Schafer and the Four Horsemen first collaborated at the Dayspring Festival in Toronto in the late 1960s. Nichol played the role of John of Patmos in Schafer's Apocalypsis (1980), the Presenter in Princess of the Stars (1981), and Johnny Mailloux, snake-oil salesman, in Patria 3: The Greatest Show. See R. Murray Schafer, 'Wizard Oil and Indian Sagwa,' Open Letter [Nichol Festschrift] 6.5–6 (1986): 73–5.

93 Schafer's string quartets have been called 'the single most significant series of chamber works produced in this country.' His Quartet No. 4 (1989) was written in memory of bpNichol. See Robert Everett-Green, 'Tracing Schafer's Creative Footsteps,' Globe and Mail (5 January 1991): C2.

94 R. Murray Schafer, ...When Words Sing (Scarborough: Berandol, 1970), 22.

95 On Varèse see David Ernst, Musique Concrète (Boston: Crescendo, 1972), 17. On Cage see Michael Nyman, Experimental Music: Cage and Beyond (New York: Schirmer, 1974), 40.

96 R. Murray Schafer, The New Soundscape (Scarborough: Berandol Music, 1969), 2. Schafer expands on the notion of soundscape in The Tuning of the World (New York: Knopf, 1977).

97 Nyman has produced a chamber opera based on the titular case study of Oliver Sacks's The Man Who Mistook His Wife for a Hat (CBS 1988 44669), in which the patient's visual agnosia is resolved through music – unable to cope in visual space, he in effect learns to live in acoustic space. As such, the plot has vague overtones with McLuhan's life: struck with aphasia, which rendered him unable to read, write, or speak, McLuhan remained capable of singing church hymns.

98 The World Soundscape Project has resulted in a number of publications and recordings, including the Music of the Environment Series of publications (e.g., European Sound Diary [Vancouver: ARC, 1977]), and Soundscape Vancouver, a recording of ambient sounds in 1970s Vancouver together with sounds from the 1990s.

99 Stephen Adams, R. Murray Schafer (Toronto: U of Toronto P, 1983), 43. Compare Schafer: 'Marshall McLuhan has suggested that since the advent of electric culture we may be moving back to such a state [where the aural sense predominates] again, and I think he is right' (Tuning 11).

100 Bruce Barber has written that the 'work of many Canadian composers and audio art producers has been influenced by Schafer's book The Tuning of the World – (even its title echoes McLuhan's global village) although most have neglected the salient criticism of the culture of consumer capitalism implied in his work and have opted for the grandiloquence (and aesthetic potential) of his metaphors.' See 'Radio: Audio Art's Frightful Parent,' in Lander and Lexier, eds, Sound by Artists, 109–37; this quotation 130. Barber cites the example of Pierre Théberge as an artist working in this idiom. In addition, Ihor Holubizky cites 'Canadian artists Ian Murray, Ian Carr-Harris and Joey Morgan [as] ... form[ing] only a small part of a body of work appearing in the past 20 years that incorporates sound as a critical element and catalyst: a re-engagement of oral history.' Holubizky also cites the Montreal group Fusion des Arts; see, in the same volume, 'Very Nice, Very Nice' (241–58; quotations on 252 and 256). Douglas Kahn has noted that Canadian animator Norman McLaren was 'famed for his drawn sound films'; see, in the same volume, 'Audio in the Deaf Century' (301–28; this quotation 307).

101 Schafer's project is important not only aesthetically but politically as well, given that sound pollution is one of the major ecological crises of the late twentieth century in much of the developing and developed worlds. It is by sensitizing his readers to sound *per se* that Schafer hopes, in *Tuning*, to make them aware of this crisis. He also seeks to alert them to the temporal element within acoustic space by finding examples of the historicity of sound. That historical element has been heightened by the ability of electronic sound reproduction to make available to us a vaster range of musical history and musical type than was ever before possible.

102 R. Murray Schafer, ed., *Ezra Pound and Music: The Complete Criticism* (New York: New Directions, 1977). Schafer wrote his introduction under the 'inspiration' of Hugh Kenner's studies of Pound; Kenner, formerly a student of McLuhan's, has written of his great debt to McLuhan, conceding that he has '"been going on from extemporizations of Marshall's for thirty years."' See Jeet Heer, 'McLuhan's Hare,' *Literary Review of Canada* 4.1 (1995): 10–11. In conversation, Schafer has likewise acknowledged the influence of McLuhan on his work; I am grateful to the composer for having shared this and other information with me.

103 Elsewhere, Schafer refers to 'music seen,' 'music heard,' and 'music seen and heard.' See 'The Graphics of Musical Thought,' in *Sound Sculpture: A Collection of Essays*, ed. John Grayson (Vancouver: ARC P, 1975), 113.

104 R. Murray Schafer, 'The Theatre of Confluence II,' in *Descant* 73 (1991) [R. Murray Schafer and the Theatre of Confluence]: 87–103; this quotation 88.

105 Schafer, 'Ursound' in bpNichol and Steve McCaffery, eds, *Open Letter* [R. Murray Schafer: A Collection] 4.4–5 (1979): 79–92; this quotation 90.

106 Schafer, 'Graphics,' 99.

107 R. Murray Schafer, 'McLuhan and Acoustic Space,' *Antigonish Review* 62–3 (1985): 105–13.

108 '"What I want is a kind of theatre in which all the arts may meet, court, and make love."' Schafer as quoted by Karen Mulhallen, 'Circumnavigating and Creating: *Descant* in the Theatre of Confluence,' *Descant* 73 (1991) [R. Murray Schafer and the Theatre of Confluence]: 5–10; this quotation 5.

109 Mulhallen, ibid., 6.

110 R. Murray Schafer, 'Patria I: Wolfman,' in *Descant* 73 (1991): 47–70; this quotation 61.

111 R. Murray Schafer, 'The Theatre of Confluence I,' *Descant* 73 (1991): 27–45; this quotation 38. Schafer's utopian intentions strongly shape his representations and his views of multiculturalism.

112 R. Murray Schafer, 'Patria 3: *The Greatest Show*,' in *Descant* 73 (1991): 121–34.

113 R. Murray Schafer, 'The Place of the Princess' [interview with Tim Wilson], *Banff Letters* (Spring 1985): 28–32.

114 Glenn Gould, *Solitude Trilogy: Three Sound Documentaries* ('The Idea of North' [1967]; 'The Latecomers' [1969]; 'The Quiet in the Land' [1977]; CBC PSCD 2003-3 [1992]).

115 These graphic scores were in fact produced by Lorne Tulk, Gould's assistant on these projects; I am grateful to Lorne Tulk for sharing this and other information with me. See also *Glenn Gould: Selected Letters*, ed. John Roberts and Ghyslaine Guertin (Toronto: Oxford UP, 1992), 136.

116 Richard Kostelanetz, curator, *Language and Structure in North America* (Toronto: Kensington Arts Association, 1975). Alvin Balkind, who had organized the 1969 exhibition of concrete poetry at UBC, was a consultant on this project. Other Canadians included in the exhibition were Earle Birney, bill bissett, John Robert Colombo, Judy Copithorne, Gerald Ferguson, The Four Horsemen, Eldon Garnet, Gerry Gilbert, Lionel Kearns, Garry Neill Kennedy, Bill Kort, Bertrand Lachance, Beth Learn, Eric Legge, Don Mabie, Steve McCaffery, Stephen Morrissey, bpNichol, Clive Robertson, Joe Rosenblatt, R. Murray Schafer, Stephen Scobie, Angelo Sgabellone, Michael Snow, David Tipe, David UU, Robert Watts, and Robert Zend.

117 Linus Pauling, *The Nature of the Chemical Bond and the Structure of Molecules and Crystals: An Introduction to Modern Structural Chemistry* (1939; 3rd ed., Ithaca: Cornell UP, 1960).

118 In 'Inside the Five Sense Sensorium' (*The Canadian Architect* 6.6 [1961]: 49–54), McLuhan quotes Paul Hindemith's observations on the relationship between musical compositions and auditory space (52 and 54).

119 Viola, 'Sound of One Line Scanning,' 41.

120 McCaffery, 'McLuhan,' 80. Pierre Théberge makes the remark that 'a pair of stereo speakers can only create an *illusion* of three-dimensional space. In this respect, Gould's use of the recording medium ...

was anti-illusionistic. He rejected any attempt to recreate the concert hall sound in favour of a close, analytical perspective [*sic*] on the sound of the musical instrument itself ' (123). See 'Counterpoint: Glenn Gould and Marshall McLuhan,' *Canadian Journal of Political and Social Thought* 10:1–2 (1986): 109–27.

121 Gould wrote of McLuhan in 1966 that 'He remains for me a subject both fascinating and frustrating and his writings – an extraordinary mixture of wackiness with brilliant perceptions. I had the feeling, however, that he has in many rather significant ways put his finger on some of the central issues of our time, and notwithstanding all the cafe society cult that is now growing up around him in the U.S., he remains, I think, an intriguing and important figure.' In *Glenn Gould: Selected Letters*, 90 (to Goddard Lieberson, 14 May 1966). The first reference to Gould in McLuhan's letters dates from 4 June 1964, where McLuhan makes reference to a lunch 'we had some weeks ago' (*L* 301), which would have been immediately after Gould's retirement from the stage.

122 Richard Kostelanetz, 'Glenn Gould: Bach in the Electronic Age,' in *Glenn Gould: Variations* (Toronto: Doubleday, 1983), 125–41; this quotation 126.

123 The idealist view of Gould has been most fully advanced by Geoffrey Payzant in *Glenn Gould: Music and Mind* (Van Nostrand Reinhold, 1978); see page 80 especially. Paul Théberge notes that Payzant repeatedly edits out Gould's references to McLuhan, often without using ellipses (Théberge 126, n2).

124 I draw, here, on previous work: Richard Cavell, 'Reading Glenn Gould,' a two-part program written and produced for CITR-FM (Vancouver), 1 and 8 May 1985; '"His Master's Voice": Glenn Gould *quasi parlando*,' Culture and Imperialism: An International Conference in Honour of Edward Said, UBC Program in Comparative Literature, 12 March 1988; 'The *Gould*berg Variations: McLuhan *da capo*,' Philological Association of the Pacific Coast, Claremont College, California, 10 February 1989; and 'Glenn Gould: The Performer as Composer,' ARCT Alumni Association (Vancouver), 22 January 1990.

125 I am happy to acknowledge a travel award from the Dean's Fund, Faculty of Arts, UBC, which made it possible for me to travel to Los Angeles and the Wilshire Ebell Theatre on the occasion of giving 'The *Gould*berg Variations.'

126 Geoffrey Payzant makes this comment in *Glenn Gould: Music and Mind*, 142.

127 Glenn Gould, *Arnold Schoenberg: A Perspective* (Cincinnati: U of Cincinnati P, 1964). I am grateful to the Archives and Rare Books Department of the University of Cincinnati Libraries for presenting me with a copy of this book.

128 Gould had read both the *GG* and *UM*, and recommended them to others. See his 14 May 1966 letter to Goddard Lieberson in *Glenn Gould: Selected Letters* 90.

129 Schoenberg actually composed spatially, using a number of self-made devices to determine tonalities. See R. Wayne Shoaf and Susan L. Sloan, *Schoenberg's Dodecaphonic Devices* [exhibition catalogue] (Los Angeles: Arnold Schoenberg Institute, 1989).

130 Dore Ashton, 'Arnold Schoenberg's Ascent,' in *A Fable of Modern Art* (London: Thames and Hudson, 1980), 96–120; this quotation 99.

131 McLuhan quotes from Schoenberg's *Style and Idea* to the effect that '"All that happens at any point of this musical space [i.e., atonality] has more than a local effect. It functions not only in its own plane but also in all other directions and planes"' (*LM* 52).

132 Douglas Kahn, 'Introduction: Histories of Sound Once Removed,' in Kahn and Whitehead, eds, *Wireless Imagination,* 1–29; this quotation 5.

133 Steve McCaffery, 'McLuhan,' 83. Compare McLuhan's comment in *Counterblast* (*Ctb*) (1969): 'A phrase or melody defines itself and evokes an attitude or a state of mind instantly. But the phrase or melody does not refer to such attitude or state. It's the state and we're the music. This is the preliterate attitude to language ... Acoustically but not semantically considered, a word is a complex set of harmonic relations as beautiful as a seashell. These relations are dynamic. They are simultaneous, set off by silence' (112).

134 The greater part of Gould's writings have been collected in *The Glenn Gould Reader* (*GGR*), edited by Tim Page (Toronto: Lester and Orpen Dennys, 1984).

135 Margaret Stewart, McLuhan's longtime secretary, has stated that 'pianist Glenn Gould ... often came to see Marshall alone' (*WWMM* 41). The intellectual relationship between McLuhan and Gould has been discussed by Théberge ('Counterpoint'), who refers to the sound documentaries as '"cubist sound-scapes"' (118).

136 See the 'reconstructed' encounter of the meeting between Gould and McLuhan that issued in this

article, 'synthesized' by John Roberts as 'The Medium and the Message' in *The Art of Glenn Gould*, ed. Roberts (Toronto: Malcolm Lester Books, 1999), 232–53. Of particular note is the following comment by McLuhan: 'Music becomes plural. You cannot speak of it any longer in the singular and as an international language – you know that old pet cliché of the nineteenth century – music the universal, international language – with the recorder we know this is not so, that it takes enormous training to learn the idiom [of other musics]' (244).

137 NAC, McLuhan Collection, vol. 99, file 24.

138 Kevin Concannon has remarked, '[w]hen audio recording and play-back equipment came into general use, the very nature of being a composer or musician changed drastically. Composer Glenn Gould personifies this shift within the world of classical music, combining many takes of the same piece for the perfect (recorded) performance.' This comment is noteworthy for two reasons: it indicates the extent to which performance and composition are fused by the sound studio (Gould felt very free to alter the nature of the score he was performing), and it reveals Concannon's unease with the legitimacy of recorded over 'live' performance, an unease manifested by the word 'perfect.' See 'Cut and Paste: Collage and the Art of Sound,' in Lander and Lexier, eds, *Sound by Artists*, 161–82; this quotation 162.

139 Gould, 'The Record of the Decade,' *GGR* 429–34, a review of Walter (now Wendy) Carlos, *Switched-On Bach*. As early as 1959, Canadian composer Istvan Anhalt organized the first all-electronic concert of music in Canada. Gould performed some of Anhalt's work, which he discusses in 'Canadian Piano Music in the Twentieth Century,' *GGR* 204–7.

140 Andrew Kazdin, one of Gould's engineers, describes Gould's efforts to position microphones so that they 'looked down' on the piano, which Gould played without the lid. See *Glenn Gould at Work: Creative Lying* (New York: Dutton, 1989), 40; cf 116.

141 Kevin Bazzana, *Glenn Gould: The Performer in the Work* (Oxford: Clarendon P, 1997), 168.

142 Both Schafer and Gould were taught piano by Alberto Guerrero; see Elizabeth Angilette, *The Philosopher at the Keyboard: Glenn Gould* (Metuchen: Scarecrow P, 1992), 9–10.

143 Writing of Webern in 1954, Gould comments: 'The use of silence as the frame of sound is ... as old as music itself.' See 'A Consideration of Anton Webern' in *Glenn Gould: A Publication of the Glenn Gould Foundation* 1 (Fall 1995): 4–8; this quotation 5.

144 NAC, McLuhan Collection, box 99, file 24.

145 Ecstasy, idealism, and solitude are the keynotes of Geoffrey Payzant's reading.

146 McCaffery remarks that 'Recorded music, with its highly personalized and versatile space, created the *mass* audience that is paradoxically more individual and yet more undifferentiated than the public' ('McLuhan' 82–3).

147 Gould brackets this passage in Adorno's *Prisms*, trans. Samuel and Sherry Weber (1967; Cambridge, MA: MIT P, 1981), 23. Gould's library is held by the Music Division of the National Library of Canada; I am very grateful to Stephen Willis for helping me find my way through this collection.

148 For a discussion of the larger context of Canadian music and technology see John Roberts, 'Communications Media,' in *Aspects of Music in Canada*, ed. Arnold Walter (Toronto: U of Toronto P, 1969), 167–246. Roberts begins his chapter with the comment that, 'In the language of Marshall McLuhan, radio is a "hot" medium. One can imagine how "hot" it appeared to Canadian radio listeners when in 1936 the Canadian Broadcasting Corporation came into being' (167). There are numerous references to Gould in this chapter.

149 Jonathan Cott, *Conversations with Glenn Gould* (Boston: Little, Brown, 1984), 54; Peter Ostwald, *Glenn Gould: The Ecstasy and Tragedy of Genius* (New York: Norton, 1997).

150 Nicholas Cook, *Imagining Music* (Oxford: Clarendon P, 1990), 96.

151 Roland Barthes, 'Rasch,' in *The Responsibility of Forms: Critical Essays on Music, Art and Representation*, trans. Richard Howard (1982; New York: Hill and Wang, 1985), 305.

152 Lorne Tulk refers to 'The Idea of North' as an 'oral tone poem'; Janet Somerville refers to that work as Gould's 'rhythmic verbal quintet'; both references in *Glenn Gould's Solitude Trilogy: Three Sound Documentaries*, booklet accompanying CBC recording PSCD 2003-3 (1992).

153 McLuhan and Quentin Fiore, *The Medium Is the Massage with Marshall McLuhan* (Columbia CS 9501 [stereo], CL 2701 [mono], 1967). The record was produced by John Simon, with McLuhan, Fiore, Jerome Agel, and John Culkin, among others, providing voices. The back of the record sleeve is a collage of quotations from the album. Another recording of McLuhan consists of his essay 'The New

Technology and the Arts,' which was made on Flexidisc by *artscanada* and included in the February 1967 issue (24.2); the record also contained Futurist Gino Severini's *Abstract Rhythm of Madame S.*, and a discussion chaired by Brydon Smith, Ayala Zacks, and Ted Bieler, under the collective title *From Futurism to Kinetics.*

154 The technical effects of McLuhan's record are much rawer than those Gould achieved in *The Solitude Trilogy.* However, 'A Glenn Gould Fantasy' (record 2 of *The Glenn Gould Silver Jubilee Album* [CBS 35914 (1980)]), the concept of which dated to 1964, is much closer, technically and stylistically, to the McLuhan album, giving us a glimpse of Gould's early ideas about recording. On the dating of 'A Glenn Gould Fantasy,' see Otto Friedrich, *Glenn Gould: A Life and Variations* (Toronto: Lester and Orpen Dennys, 1989), 241. The 'Fantasy' also makes abundantly clear that Gould thought absurd the notion of 'live' recordings unmediated by technology. On this aspect, see Richard Cavell, 'White Technologies,' *Essays on Canadian Writing* 59 (1996): 199–210.

155 *Glenn Gould: Selected Letters*, 109 (21 September 1968). Bazzana cites this letter in his discussion of Gould's contrapuntal techniques, though not to the same ends.

156 McLuhan, 'Knowledge, Ideas, Information, and Communication (A Canadian View),' in *The Year Book of Education 1958*, ed. George Bereday and Joseph Lauwerys (London: University of London Institute of Education, 1958), 225–32.

157 McLuhan may be thinking specifically of the *comices agricoles* section of *Madame Bovary*, cited also by Joseph Frank as a prime example of spatial form. Gould has described his own methodology of orchestrating voices as 'stacking up,' which recalls McLuhan's terminology. See 'Radio as Music,' *GGR* 374–88.

158 Payzant, 131, quoting from the recording *Glenn Gould: Concert Dropout* (1968); compare McLuhan's use of the latter term in *Take Today: The Executive as Dropout* (1972).

159 Payzant, quoting Gould's 1970 CBC telecast, 'The Well-Tempered Listener,' 130.

160 Apropos this notion of simultaneity, Richard Kostelanetz has remarked that: 'To acknowledge a marvelous term used by his [Gould's] friend and fellow Torontonian Marshall McLuhan, Gould was creating radio not for the age of concentration ... but for the age of *omniattention*, when radio is only one of several stimuli in the environment.' See 'Glenn Gould as a Radio Composer,' *Massachusetts Review* 29.3 (1988): 557–70; this quotation 567.

161 NAC, Glenn Gould Papers, file 1979-20, vol. 9.64, page 7; Gould interviewed Cage for a documentary on Schoenberg. See *Selected Letters* 200.

162 NAC, Glenn Gould Papers, box 12, file 123, typescript headed 'The Deromantizing North,' 24. McLuhan's interest in the 'Eskimo' derived from Carpenter.

163 Gould quoted by Friedrich, *Glenn Gould*, 207.

164 For a sampling of Gould's televised and filmed performance practices, see *Glenn Gould's Greatest Hits: Hilights from the Glenn Gould Collection* (Sony Video 41-048433-82 [1992]), and, in the same series, volume 2, *Ecstasy and Wit* (41-048417-82 [1992]).

165 Linda Dalrymple Henderson has noted Scriabin's interest in fourth-dimensional thought (*4D* 240).

166 Edward Said, *Musical Elaborations* (New York: Columbia UP, 1991), 33. I am happy to record my thanks to Edward Said for sharing in conversation (on the occasion of a trip to Vancouver) his ideas about Gould and his performing techniques.

167 Edward Said, 'The Music Itself: Glenn Gould's Contrapuntal Vision,' in *Glenn Gould: Variations* (Toronto: Doubleday, 1983), 45–54; this quotation 50, emphasis added.

168 B.W. Powe, *The Solitary Outlaw: Trudeau, Lewis, Gould, Canetti, McLuhan* (Toronto: Lester and Orpen Dennys, 1987), 151.

169 Gould remarks in 'The Prospects of Recording' that 'In terms of the unselfconscious juxtaposition of a miscellany of idioms, it [splice technology] will have an effect similar to that which André Malraux ... attributes to art reproductions' (*GGR* 348).

Chapter 7: Art without Walls

1 Le Corbusier remarked that the modern street was 'the museum of the present and the past' and developed the notion of a 'world museum' in 1929; see Beatriz Colomina, *Privacy and Publicity: Modern Architecture as Mass Media* (Cambridge, MA: MIT P, 1996), 217; 229.

2 André Malraux, *The Voices of Silence*, trans. Stuart Gilbert (1949, 1950; Princeton: Princeton UP, 1953). McLuhan published a long review by Stanley Edgar Hyman of *The Voices of Silence* in the second issue of *Explorations* (April 1954). Hyman takes a generally negative view of the book, as indicated in his title 'The Pirate's Wardroom' (98–105). According to Hyman, the book was begun in 1936, with parts of it translated into English by 1938. On the implications of the 'museum without walls' for Canadian art of the 1950s (and afterwards) see Denise Leclerc, *The Crisis of Abstraction in Canada: The 1950s* (Ottawa: National Gallery, 1992), esp. 77.

3 For an extension of this notion into the context of the virtual museum see chapter 8 of Derrick de Kerckhove's *Connected Intelligence: The Arrival of the Web Society* (Toronto: Somerville House, 1997).

4 Michael Crane, in 'A Definition of Correspondence Art,' remarks that 'The philosophies of Bergson, Hegel, Heidegger, Marx, Russell, Wittgenstein, Marshall McLuhan and Buckminster Fuller, as well as the writings, statements, and works of groups such as the futurists, dadas, lettristes, constructivists, fluxus, new realists, pop and conceptual artists have influenced the propositions made among mail artists' (13). See *Correspondence Art: Source Book for the Network of International Postal Art Activity*, ed. Michael Crane and Mary Stofflet (San Francisco: Contemporary Arts Press, 1984), 3–36.

5 Meiko Shiomi's *Spatial Poem No. 5, Open Event 1* (1972) takes the form of a world map with superimposed text created from Shiomi's 'score,' which asked each particpant to 'Open something which is closed' and send the brief report to her. One of the participants was Françoise Sullivan, signatory of the *Refus Global*. See *In the Spirit of Fluxus*, ed. Elizabeth Armstrong and Joan Rothfuss (Minneapolis: Walker Art Center, 1993), 177–9.

6 See *Counterblast (Ctb)* (1969), 45; 109–10.

7 Tony Godfrey remarks that 'the combination of text and photography became increasingly its [conceptualism's] archetypal form.' See *Conceptual Art* (London: Phaidon, 1998), 302. Conceptualism comprises both 'static' media (such as photo-conceptualism) as well as 'live' media (such as Happenings), according to the distinction made by Robert C. Morgan, *Conceptual Art: An American Perspective* (Jefferson: McFarland and Co., 1994), 28.

8 Typical of Malraux's Eurocentrism is the comment that 'It is high time for us to recognize that, for three hundred years, the world has not produced a single work of art comparable with the supreme works of the West' (591). Malraux's concern is with a sort of artistic miscegenation, which he sees as threatening humanistic values. What particularly distinguishes Malraux's overview of the history of artistic production from McLuhan's is the former's notion that 'an art which breaks up into ideograms is regressive' (132). For McLuhan, the ideogram was an indicator of the increasingly interficial nature of art, which he viewed positively. Malraux's animadversions against the ideogram are part of a larger critique of Modern art; see Hyman 105. Malraux subsequently recognized McLuhan's contribution to rethinking the museum in a personal inscription to his 1974 book *La Tête obsidienne* (1974); see *L* 497.

9 Seth Siegelaub, a major force in the rise of conceptualism as gallery owner and exhibition organizer, stated in 1969 that '"You don't need walls to show ideas."' See 'Impossible Art,' *Art in America* (May 1969): 39; this is the issue of the magazine that has an N.E. Thing work on its cover. In that same issue, Robert Barry describes his wave art: '"sound has nothing to do with it. The sound is only a clue to an entire environment, only a means to make people aware"' (41). Ian Wilson's 'art "form" is oral communication. "I present oral communication as an object," says Wilson. "All art is information and communication ... My art is not visual, but visualized."' These comments have a particular resonance for the artists described in this chapter.

10 A.A. Bronson et al., ed., *From Sea to Shining Sea: Artist-Initiated Activity in Canada 1939–1987* (Toronto: The Power Plant, 1987).

11 As McLuhan wrote in 'The Agenbite of Outwit' (1963), artists 'show us ways of living with new technology without destroying earlier forms and achievements.' See the reprint of this article included in the box of materials forming (part of) John Cage's *Rolywholyover A Circus* (New York: Rizzoli, nd. [*ca* 1992]).

12 Peter Wollheim remarks that 'Art photography's modern ascendancy also coincided with Marshall McLuhan's influential attacks on what he saw as the linear, literal, alienating features of "typographic man."' See 'Photography and Narrative,' *The Zone of Conventional Practice and Other Real Stories*, ed. Cheryl Simon (Montreal: Galerie Optica, 1989), 59–67; this quotation 61.

13 See Douglas Crimp, *On the Museum's Ruins* (Cambridge, MA: MIT P, 1993), *passim*.

14 Thomas McEvilley, 'Introduction' to Brian Doherty, *Inside the White Cube: The Ideology of the Gallery Space* (Santa Monica: Lapis P, 1986), 7–12; this quotation 8.

15 Irene F. Whittome's installations are a particularly powerful example of the use of environments and installations as critiques of museum spaces. See Michèle Thériault, *Irene F. Whittome: Musée des Traces* (Toronto: Art Gallery of Ontario, 1990).

16 See Alex Seago, *Burning the Box of Beautiful Things: The Development of a Postmodern Sensibility* (Oxford: Oxford UP, 1995) on *spazialismo* and Lucio Fontana's 'Spatial Concepts' artworks, which were reproduced in *ARK*, the journal of the Royal College of Art heavily influenced by McLuhanite Lawrence Alloway, on whom see *Psychogeographies* below. 'Formed in 1951 in France, the Groupe Espace was a neo-Constructivist association whose principal philosophy centred on the idea that art was simply part of the larger urban space and therefore was a social and not an individualistic activity'; see *The Independent Group: Postwar Britain and the Aesthetics of Plenty*, ed. David Robbins (Cambridge, MA: MIT P, 1990), 136, n2. A Space Gallery was founded in Toronto in 1970; Ace Space was the pseudonym of Dana Atchley, who created his 'Space Atlas' in 1970–1. These references are from Crane and Stofflet, eds, *Correspondence Art*, 226; 243. In 1983, the Western Front devoted a festival to 'the interaction between music, sculpture, performance art and the idea of "space"'; see *Whispered Art History: Twenty Years at the Western Front*, ed. Keith Wallace (Vancouver: Arsenal Pulp P, 1993), 85. For the aesthetic discussions about space see below.

17 See, for example, Doherty, *Inside the White Cube*, 47.

18 'During the 1920s and 1930s, [Kiesler] belonged to De Stijl, the American Union of Decorative Artists and Craftsmen, Buckminster Fuller's Structural Studies Associates, and the theater faculty at Julliard [*sic*]; he also formed the Laboratory of correalism at Columbia University, and through his association with Marcel Duchamp and the exiled Parisian art community, became the "official" architect of the surrealists.' William H. Braham, 'What's Hecuba to Him? On Kiesler and the Knot,' *Assemblage* 36 (1998): 6–23; this quotation 7.

19 This quotation is from V.J. Papanek's article 'A Bridge in Time,' in *Verbi-Voco-Visual Explorations (VVV)*; as I suggest in chapter 5, this article provides us with a record of ideas circulating in McLuhan's seminars of the 1950s. In subsequent publications, Papanek distanced himself from the ideas and artists mentioned in this article, suggesting that the ideas there were as much (or more) McLuhan's than Papanek's.

20 Beatriz Colomina, 'La *Space House* et la psyché de la construction,' in Chantal Béret, ed., *Frederick Kiesler: Artiste-architecte* (Paris: Centre Georges Pompidou, 1996), 66–76; this quotation 69.

21 Kiesler, 'Architecture as Biotechnology,' in Béret, *Kiesler* 80–9; these quotations 82–3. This material had its origins in Kiesler's *From Architecture to Life*, published in 1930.

22 The phrase was Katherine Dreier's, a major figure in the Modern art movement in New York. See *Making Mischief: Dada Invades New York*, ed. Francis M. Naumann with Beth Venn (New York: Whitney Museum, 1996), 202.

23 In 1936, Kiesler used the phrase 'Murals without Walls' to describe Arshile Gorky's work in the Newark Airport.

24 Quoted in Maria Bottero, 'Kiesler 1956–1965: Profession contre poétique,' in Béret, *Kiesler* 202–10; this quotation 203. Kiesler also worked with Edgard Varèse on a theatre that, like Varèse and Le Corbusier's Philips Pavilion for the Brussels World Fair, would employ sound as a major environmental element.

25 Kiesler also had Canadian connections in the late 1950s, when he entered into negotiations (unrealized) to build a housing project in Montreal. See Béret, *Kiesler* 259, s.v. '1959.'

26 The lecture was given again in October of 1965 at the 'Vision 65' conference held in Carbondale, Illinois, sponsored by the University of Illinois and the International Center for Typographical Arts. The article was first published in *The American Scholar* (1966) in an issue devoted to 'The Electronic Revolution' and again in the May and June 1966 editions of *The Canadian Architect*, the February 1967 issue of *artscanada*, and the 1967 issue (no. 11) of *Perspecta*, the journal of the Yale University School of Architecture. See Eric McLuhan and Frank Zingrone, *Essential McLuhan* (*EM*) 391, n12; I quote from this source (219–32).

27 McLuhan also develops this notion in 'The Relation of Environment to Anti-Environment,' *The University of Windsor Review* 2.1 (1966): 1–10.

28 Eli Bornstein, 'An Interview with Marshall McLuhan,' *The Structurist* (Saskatoon) no. 6 (1966): 61–8; this quotation 61.
29 See also McLuhan's 'Environment as Programmed Happening,' in *Knowledge and the Future of Man: An International Symposium*, ed. Walter Ong (New York: Holt, Rinehart and Winston, 1968), 113–24, esp. 122.
30 McLuhan, 'The Rise and Fall of Nature,' *Journal of Communication* 27.4 (1977): 80–1; this quotation 80. See also 'At the Moment of Sputnik the Planet Became a Global Theater in Which There Are No Spectators but Only Actors,' *Journal of Communication* 24.1 (1974): 48–58.
31 McLuhan, 'The Emperor's Old Clothes,' in Gyorgy Kepes, ed., *The Man-Made Object* (New York: Braziller, 1966), 90–5; this quotation 93.
32 See, selectively, Al Hansen, *A Primer of Happenings and Time/Space Art* (New York: Something Else Press, 1965); RoseLee Goldberg, *Performance Art: From Futurism to the Present* (1979; London: Thames and Hudson, 1988); Marilyn Belford and Jerry Herman, *Time and Space Concepts in Art* (New York: Pleiades Gallery, 1980); Richard Kostelanetz, *The Theatre of Mixed Means: An Introduction to Happenings, Kinetic Environments, and Other Mixed-Means Performances* (New York: Dial Press, 1968); Allan Kaprow, *Assemblage, Environments, and Happenings* (New York: Abrams, 1965).
33 McLuhan thus referred to aspects of life in Toronto as Happenings, as with the nightlife in Yorkville, or the airport ('a kind of Bucky Fuller dome, a Happening'), or Kensington Market ('The world of unenclosed space that invites us to open the doors of perception'). See 'McLuhan's Toronto,' *Toronto Life* (September 1967): 23–9.
34 Jeff Wall has remarked on how 'conceptual art recapitulates a kind of Mallarméanism' (19). See *Dan Graham's Kammerspiel* (1988; Toronto: Art Metropole, 1991).
35 I am thinking here of Lucy Lippard's *Six Years: The Dematerialization of the Art Object from 1966 to 1972* (New York: Praeger, 1973).
36 Christel Hollevoet, 'Wandering in the City: *Flânerie* to *Dérive* and After: The Cognitive Mapping of Urban Space,' in Hollevoet and Karen Jones, eds, *The Power of the City / The City of Power* (New York: Whitney Museum, 1992), 25–55; this quotation 36.
37 Godfrey, *Conceptual Art*, 12; 14–15. While he makes reference to Iain Baxter and to the Nova Scotia College of Art and Design, Godfrey does not refer to McLuhan.
38 The foregrounding of print also asserted its sculptural quality; as McLuhan wrote in the inaugural issue of *Dot Zero* magazine, 'And now in the electric age when all sensory modes are simultaneously accessible, the tyranny of typography in imposing its monotonous regime on all aspects of life and perception can no longer be sustained. It collapses from within. Yet the typographer can reap some advantage from the electric revolution. For the first time he is free to exploit letters as abstract sculptural designs in the spirit of Mantegna' (NAC, McLuhan Collection, box 132, file 15, page 3 of typescript). On this aspect of Mantegna see Millard Meiss, *Andrea Mantegna as Illuminator* (New York: Columbia UP, 1957). On the connections between book production and conceptualism, see Johanna Drucker, *The Century of Artists' Books* (New York: Granary Books, 1995).
39 Benjamin H.D. Buchloh, 'From the Aesthetic of Administration to Institutional Critique: (Some Aspects of Conceptual Art 1962–1969),' in *L'Art conceptuel, une perspective* (2nd ed. Paris: Musée d'Art Moderne, 1989); 41–53; this quotation 41.
40 Barbara Maria Stafford's *Body Criticism: Imaging the Unseen in Enlightenment Art and Medicine* (Cambridge, MA: MIT P, 1991) is a long meditation on the ways in which Enlightenment thought deemed images illusory and insufficient without text.
41 See, for example, the 'Postface' to Lucy Lippard's *Six Years*, 263–4.
42 The 3 August 1966 'Statement on Intermedia' typescript is photostatically reproduced in Armstrong and Rothfuss, eds, *In the Spirit of Fluxus*, 172–3. I discuss this statement in greater detail below in this chapter. Higgins deleted the reference to McLuhan in the version of this statement (dated 1965) published in the first issue of Higgins's *Something Else Newsletter* (vol. 1, no. 1, 1966), and reprinted in *Horizons: The Poetics and Theory of the Intermedia* (Carbondale: S. Illinois UP, 1984), 18–28; the reprint includes a 1981 coda in which Higgins ascribes the term 'intermedia' to an 1812 essay by S.T. Coleridge.
43 The address was subsequently published in the *NAEB Journal* 18.2 (December 1958): 3–5; 30–4.
44 The process remains a powerful form of critique in the hands of artists such as Hans Haacke, whose (neo)conceptualist works of the 1980s provide the context (McLuhan would say 'noise') mediating

artworks, a context that is normally excluded from art exhibitions. See Benjamin H.D. Buchloh, 'Hans Haacke: Memory and Instrumental Reason,' *Art in America* (February 1988): 97–109; 157; 159, and Fredric Jameson, 'Hans Haacke and the Cultural Logic of Postmodernism,' in *Hans Haacke: Unfinished Business*, ed. Brian Wallis (New York: New Museum of Contemporary Art, 1986), 38–51.

45 McLuhan, 'The Relation of Environment to Anti-Environment.' Similarly, in 'Advertising as a Magical Institution,' *The Commerce Journal* (Toronto) (January 1952): 25–9, McLuhan states that the ad 'must seem to be natural' (26).

46 George Sanderson remarks that in a 1978 conversation McLuhan stated that 'He had always hoped for a creative blend of acoustic and visual space.' See 'Discussion: Commentary on "Marshall McLuhan and the Psychology of Television,"' in *Canadian Psychology / Psychologie canadienne* 35.4 (1994): 350–5; this quotation 353.

47 As Diana Nemiroff has noted, the tendency of Canadian art to be defined by art elsewhere was countered by 'the influence of communications theorist Marshall McLuhan upon American artists' (193). See 'Rethinking the Art Object' in Robert Bringhurst, Geoffrey James, Russell Keziere, and Doris Shadbolt, eds, *Visions: Contemporary Art in Canada* (Vancouver: Douglas and McIntyre, 1983), 193–225.

48 Bronson et al., *Sea to Shining Sea*, 23. Elsewhere Bronson states that 'Federal funding policies of the 50s and 60s were inspired and future-oriented, produced by a dedicated group of people steeped, we suspect, in the 50s intellectual chic of Marshall McLuhan and E.S. Carpenter's Explorations magazine' (13). John Bentley Mays has written that '[h]is [McLuhan's] was hardly an unfamiliar name. Already, the Toronto communications theorist was heralding the imminent collapse of the old distinctions between high art and popular culture, and among the various media themselves; and he was foretelling the rise of a new culture of perverse, punning, genre-blurring media consciousness from those ruins.' See 'The Snakes in the Garden,' Bringhurst et al., *Visions* 156–91; this quotation 159.

49 I want to thank Garry Neill Kennedy for the personal interview he granted me on 5 June 1989, when we discussed (he more modestly than I) issues surrounding the transformation of the school into a conceptualist hotbed. Bronson remarks that 'only in Vancouver and Halifax was it possible to see international contemporary art at this time' (*Sea to Shining Sea* 42). See also Robert Stacey and Liz Wylie, *Eighty/Twenty: 100 Years of the Nova Scotia College of Art and Design* (Halifax: Nova Scotia College of Art and Design, 1988): 'One ubiquitous buzzword of the early 1970s was "information," and many of the College's early programmes and much of its curriculum seem based on the idea of the necessity of information-exchange among artists' (78).

50 Mays, 'The Snakes in the Garden,' 159. According to McLuhan's letter of 25 September 1963 (Belkin Gallery Archives), he was at UBC in 1959 to give a seminar in the Summer School.

51 Alvin Balkind, 'Body-Snatching: Performance Art in Vancouver – A View of Its History,' *Living Art Vancouver* (Vancouver: Western Front, 1980), 72–7; this quotation 72.

52 The narrative of events around the planning of the festivals has not always been clear (cf Bronson et al., *Sea to Shining Sea* 29). Archival materials in the Morris and Helen Belkin Gallery of the University of British Columbia reveal the following sequence: in February of 1963, Balkind, then assistant curator of the Fine Arts Gallery (subsequently the Belkin Gallery), wrote to McLuhan, asking him to participate in the fourth festival, planned for February of 1964, with McLuhan finally deciding to attend the festival from 28 January to 4 February. Invited to give a university lecture, McLuhan spoke on 'Changing Attitudes to Space in Poetry, Painting, and Architecture since Television' (letter of 5 January 1964). The last item in this archival collection is a notice about the 1965 festival (the fifth one), which was to have the overall title 'The Medium Is the Message'; this is the famous festival held in the Armouries at UBC, vividly described by Balkind. Organizers of the fifth festival included Iain Baxter. I am grateful to Scott Watson, director and curator of the Morris and Helen Belkin Gallery, and to archivist Krisztina Laszlo, for making these letters available to me.

53 Balkind continues: 'An invigorating experience, it was successful in releasing the imagination and inspiring wonder and surmize in the thousands of people who drifted through during the Festival. "The Medium is the Message" was to have other repercussions, helping to set off a series of responses which would point the way to the remaining years of the Sixties' (72).

54 In the 'Intermedia Log' included in *Counterblast* (1969), McLuhan writes that 'One medium of expression modifies another, as one language is changed by contact with another' (60).

55 McLuhan, 'Roles, Masks, and Performances,' *New Literary History* 2.3 (1971): 517–31, with quotations from 517. McLuhan is speaking about 'the magazine itself as *performance*.'

56 McLuhan, 'McLuhan Looks at Fashion: The Mirror Is the Message,' *Harper's Bazaar* (April 1968): 150–67; this quotation 157. McLuhan goes on to relate these comments to contemporary art history and the emergence of Hard-Edge Art, Pop, and Op Art.

57 In 1965 the Sound Gallery became the place in Vancouver where an interest in 'open-ended, multi-medial, collaborative emphasis through volume and image' (Balkind 73) was paired with an increasing tendency to see these artistic activities as contributing to 'social revolution.' 1965 also saw a lecture at the Vancouver Art Gallery by Ronald Baker on 'Art and the McLuhan Ideas,' and a lecture by Victor Doray on the relation between art forms and McLuhan's notions. See the chronology to *Vancouver: Art and Artists 1931–1983* (Vancouver: Vancouver Art Gallery, 1983), 195.

58 Under the leadership of Jack Shadbolt, Intermedia was founded in Vancouver in 1966 (lasting until 1971; see Bronson et al., *Sea to Shining Sea* 33). Shadbolt, according to Balkind, had attended McLuhan's 1959 Arts Club talk; he was also friends with Wilfred Watson, who was McLuhan's collaborator on *From Cliché to Archetype* (*CA*) (on which see chapter 8 below), and Sheila Watson, who had been McLuhan's student.

59 The quotation is attributed to Werner Aellen in the chronology to *Vancouver: Art and Artists 1931–1983* (202). One artist who performed for Intermedia was Joachim Foikis, Vancouver's Canada Council–funded Town Fool, who is pictured in *War and Peace in the Global Village* (*WPGV*) 172.

60 In 1973, the Western Front was founded in Vancouver, with a mandate that increasingly tended towards performance and media work. On the Western Front see Wallace, ed., *Whispered Art History*. The Front was the venue for performances by The Four Horseman, Richard Kostelanetz, Dick Higgins, and others working within a McLuhanesque orbit. Of these artists' performances at the Front, Peter Culley has said that 'The story of the literary avant-garde in Vancouver is the story of the ear leading the unwilling eye into the future' (191). See 'Because I Am Always Talking: Reading Vancouver into the Western Front,' *Whispered Art History* 188–97. The list of artists' groups influenced by the cultural scene in Vancouver could be extended to include General Idea (whose work is generally associated with Toronto, although they gave a number of performances at the Western Front); see Derek Knight, *N.E. Thing Co.: The Ubiquitous Concept* (Oakville: Oakville Galleries, 1995), 8. On the problematics of General Idea's complicity with that which it critiques, see Philip Monk, 'General Idea and the Myth of Inhabitation,' in *Struggles with the Image: Essays in Art Criticism* (Toronto: YYZ, 1988), 131–82.

61 Keith Wallace, 'A Particular History: Artist-Run Centres in Vancouver,' *Vancouver Anthology: The Institutional Politics of Art*, ed. Stan Douglas (Vancouver: Talonbooks, 1991), 26.

62 Marie L. Fleming, *Baxter²: Any Choice Works* (Toronto: Art Gallery of Ontario, 1982), 12.

63 Thomas Wolfe, quoted by Knight, *N.E. Thing Co.* 10.

64 David Silcox has remarked on '"Baxter's admiration for Marshall McLuhan"' (quoted by Bronson, *Sea to Shining Sea* 31). Robert McKaskell has referred to Baxter as 'the Marshall McLuhan of visual arts' (42) in *Iain Baxter: Product, Place, Phenomenon* (Windsor: Art Gallery of Windsor, 1998). My thanks to Robert McKaskell for giving me a copy of this catalogue, and sharing with me his thoughts on Canadian art of the 1960s. Charlotte Townsend [Gault] refers to Baxter as the 'McLuhanite son of the Group of Seven' in *Canadian Art Today*, ed. William Townsend (London: Studio International, 1970), 79.

65 See Fleming's interview with the Baxters, *Baxter²* 36. A similarly complicitous position was expressed through *A Suite of Canadian Landscapes* (1969), a series of framed Canadian bank notes. William Wood concludes his brilliant discussion of this suite with the observation that '"I. + I. Baxter" present their signature [on these works – the only ones they signed] as the trace of the colonial other resisting – but using – the instruments of capital in order to represent the difficulties of their contestation' (17). See 'Capital and Subsidiary: The N.E. Thing Co. and the Revision of Conceptual Art,' in *You Are Now in the Middle of a N.E. Thing Co. Landscape: Works by Iain and Ingrid Baxter 1965–1971* (Vancouver: UBC Fine Arts Gallery, 1993), 11–23.

66 Fleming, *Baxter²* 9.

67 McLuhan, 'Television in a New Light,' in *The Meaning of Commercial TV: The Texas – Stanford Seminar* (Austin: U of Texas P, 1967), 87–107; this quotation 97.

68 McLuhan, 'McLuhan Looks at Fashion,' 157; 161. The venue is important; in the same year, Dan

Graham was publishing conceptualist works in the guise of advertisements in *Harper's Bazaar* (Godfrey, *Conceptual Art* 167). Graham appropriates a Warner's bra ad in his work, as does McLuhan in *Culture Is Our Business* (*COB*) (73). Edmund Carpenter suggests that he was the author of the *Harper's* article, though when it appeared in an altered version as part of Carpenter's *They Became What They Beheld* (1970), Carpenter credits McLuhan's input into the volume. See Carpenter's 'Remembering *Explorations,' Canadian Notes and Queries* 46 (Spring 1992): 3–15; reprinted in a slightly different form in Theall's *Virtual Marshall McLuhan.*

69 Lippard, *Six Years*, 131, emphasis added. Lippard has had a long association with and interest in Canadian artistic production, and so her book is an especially useful resource (though it does not index its references to McLuhan).

70 Derek Knight argues that these 'environmental' works have an ecological thrust; however, the environmental works are not ecological in any unmediated sense. See Knight, *N.E. Thing Co.* In a parallel observation, Mike Davis suggests, in *Los Angeles and the Imagination of Disaster* (New York: Metropolitan Books, 1998), that the ecology of Southern California has become so compromised by state boosterism as embodied in the media that any 'natural' disaster will gain its force through a *denial* of that ecology.

71 Janine Marchessault, 'Making Room for Nature,' in *Digital Gardens: A World in Mutation* (Toronto: Power Plant Gallery, 1996), 61–73; this quotation 70.

72 Fleming remarks on the advertising connection (*Baxter*[2] 12).

73 Nancy Shaw, 'Siting the Banal: The Expanded Landscapes of the N.E. Thing Co.,' in *You Are Now in the Middle*, 25–35; this quotation 29.

74 Wood, 'Capital and Subsidiary,' 16.

75 The Baxters' photographic work is foundational to the contemporary fame of Vancouver for photoconceptualists such as Stan Douglas, Jeff Wall, Roy Arden, Rodney Graham, Ken Lum, Howard Ursuliak, Ian Wallace, and others. See Knight *N.E. Thing Co.* 6.

76 Wood, 'Capital and Subsidiary,' 16. The Western Front was similarly networked with San Francisco, Toronto, Boston, New York, Bristol, Vienna, Sydney, and Tokyo; images were exchanged and intercut through this network. See Wallace, ed., *Whispered Art History* 61–2.

77 Jeff Wall, quoted in *You Are Now in the Middle* 7.

78 McLuhan, 'Television in a New Light,' 97.

79 This anti-nationalistic sentiment was a highly ironic one for McLuhan to be having in the mid-1960s, as Canada was contemplating its centennial; McLuhan explores that irony in a number of places, as discussed in the following chapter. One of the groups active at this time was the collective Art and Language (founded in 1968). From 1970 they published the journal *Art-Language*, in which they pursued, in parallel with their other endeavours, conceptual issues pertaining to art production. In the third number of the first volume, *Art-Language* published an article by Bernard Bihari, a professor of psychiatry, on 'Marshal [*sic*] McLuhan and the Behavioral Sciences' (11–28). The article, while acknowledging that McLuhan 'has ... had a profound impact on people in the humanities and the arts' (11), purports to demonstrate that McLuhan's theories about the interrelations of the senses and the nature of perception are wrong. The fact that Bihari does not cite from McLuhan makes his article especially suspect, as does his complaint (in the context of this journal) that McLuhan makes 'deliberate use of ambiguity and obscure language' (11). Given that the founders of the journal take diametrically opposed views to the ones expressed by Bihari, however, his article presents itself as highly ironic (whether intentionally or naïvely so). It is important, however (whichever way it is read), in highlighting the significance McLuhan's pronouncements on perception and the interrelation of the senses were having on the artists of that period. (Indeed, the article following Bihari's, by one of Art and Language's co-founders, Mel Ramsden, is on 'A Preliminary Proposal for the Directing of Perception.')

80 The year of his article, 1947, *Horizon* achieved its greatest circulation, 10,000 copies, as Jeremy Lewis notes in *Cyril Connolly: A Life* (London: Cape, 1997), 337.

81 Gary Genosko, *McLuhan and Baudrillard* (New York: Routledge, 1999), 6.

82 Margaret Garlake, *New Art, New World: British Art in Postwar Society* (New Haven: Yale UP, 1998), 9; I am grateful to Graham Whitham for this reference.

83 'Whereas the arts departments of British universities during the 1950s and early 1960s were bastions of the anti-American cultural criticism which characterized that period, students in more classless, socially

marginal art schools tended to be less encumbered by these prejudices' (9). Seago, *Burning*. I am grateful to Graham Whitham for this reference.

84 By 1957, McLuhan's media work included the material published in *Explorations*, as well as articles on advertising, mass media and education, radio and television and their effects on literacy, and comic books.

85 I am using the text printed in E. McLuhan and Zingrone, *EM*, 13–20.

86 McLuhan, 'Advertising as a Magical Institution,' 25.

87 See Robbins, ed., *The Independent Group*. The IG was informally associated with the Institute for Contemporary Arts in London, where, in 1952, they formed themselves into an artistic group.

88 Although the chronology in *The Independent Group* lists this lecture as having taken place in 1962, Graham Whitham, author of the chronology, has corrected this information in a letter to me. McLuhan writes in a letter dated 3 March 1963 of being invited to the ICA in 1965 (*L* 288), as he does in a letter to Alvin Balkind dated 23 February 1963 in the Belkin archives.

89 The Situationists were, in many ways, a proto-conceptualist group, given their origins in Lettrisme, a movement devoted to the reinvention of art through 'hypergraphie' – a hypertrophy of the letter, such that it assumes the totality of artistic production (Godfrey, *Conceptual Art* 56–61; 192). Lettrisme provides a useful reminder that the oft-noted predominance of language-based art in conceptualism is more accurately *typography*-based art. For the term 'hypergraphie' see Carol Cutler, 'Paris: The Lettrist Movement,' *Art in America* 58.1 (Jan.-Feb. 1970): 115–19. See also *Visible Language* 17.3 (1983) (Special Issue on Lettrisme: Into the Present). It is noteworthy that some Lettrists pursued sound poetry in order to liberate the sonic potential of language; in this regard, see bp Nichol and Steve McCaffery, eds, *Sound Poetry: A Catalogue* (Toronto: Underwhich, n.d. [1978?]), as discussed in chapter 6.

90 'Both Alloway and McLuhan rejected the liberal-humanist academic orthodoxy of the 1950s by implying that mass and avant-garde modernist culture were not and should never be in opposition. On the contrary, both argued that the cultural potential of television, film, and computer technology offered exciting and radical possibilities for artistic intervention. Like McLuhan, Alloway was enthusiastic about a new cultural continuum in which computer technology, Hollywood B movies, popular graphics, Futurism, Cubism, and the latest advances in physics could occupy the same cultural space and cross-fertilize' (Seago, *Burning* 167).

91 Len Bracken, *Guy Debord: Revolutionary* (Venice, CA: Feral House, 1997), 73.

92 Simon Sadler, *The Situationist City* (Cambridge, MA: MIT P, 1998), 19. As McLuhan remarked in *CA*, the 'result of living inside a proscenium arch of satellites is that the young now accept the public spaces of the earth as role-playing areas' (10).

93 While McLuhan 'was never mentioned in the journal [*Situationist International*],' according to Bracken (*Debord* 120), Guy Debord, the *force animateur* of the S.I., and author of the seminal work *Society of the Spectacle* (1967), devotes a section to McLuhan in *Comments on the Society of the Spectacle* (1988; trans. Malcolm Imrie; London: Verso, 1990): 'MacLuhan [*sic*] himself, the spectacle's first apologist, who had seemed to be the most convinced imbecile of the century, changed his mind when he finally discovered in 1976 that "the pressure of the mass media leads to irrationality," and that it was becoming urgent to modify their usage. The sage of Toronto had formerly spent several decades marvelling at the numerous freedoms created by a "global village" instantly and effortlessly accessible to all ... However, MacLuhan's ungrateful modern disciples are now trying to make people forget him, hoping to establish their own careers in media celebration of all these new freedoms to "choose" at random from ephemera. And no doubt they will retract their claims even faster than the man who inspired them' (33–4, section XII). My thanks to Gary Genosko for drawing my attention to this source.

94 Timothy Nye, 'Conceptual Art: A Spatial Perspective,' in Hollevoet and Jones, eds, *Power of the City*, 11–23; see especially 13.

95 Glenn Willmott remarks that 'For McLuhan, as for the French Situationists of the 1950s and 1960s, political praxis is realized in a *symbolic intervention* in the unreflected symbolic order and *techne* of postmodern culture (which perhaps justifies the French adoption of the term *mcluhanisme* for 1960s Pop Art).' *McLuhan, or Modernism in Reverse (MMR)* 81.

96 'Situationists would certainly have regarded the ICA circle's ease with the spectacle as risky and probably complicit' (Sadler, *Situationist City* 43).

97 In addition to his influence on the IG, and his lecture at the ICA, McLuhan had an indirect association

with the Situationists through the 1966 publication *Astronauts of Inner Space*, where he had been anthologized along with Jorgen Nash, one-time member of the S.I., who contributed the article 'Who Are the Situationists?' to the collection. See chapters 5 and 6 above.

98 The Situationists, however, were opposed to Happenings, which they saw as belonging to the spectacular, whereas the situation was part of a revolutionary process (Sadler, *Situationist City* 106).

99 Sadler quotes a former Communard (ibid. 92).

100 The unbuildability of the New Babylon projects suggests that utopianism often took on the mantle of resistance. In this regard, the work of the Archigram Group (1961–74) is also significant. Working often with McLuhan's ideas, the Group is best known for its 'Plug-In City,' a series of modular designs for urban living whose contemporary versions can be seen in *Wallpaper* magazine (once edited by a Canadian). See *A Guide to Archigram 1961–1974* (London: Academy Editions, 1994), especially pages 33 (where Peter Cook of the Group comments on the *Perspecta* text of the Vision 65 article), 174, 262 ('The car is a communications medium'), 310, and 380 (where *Counterblast* is quoted).

101 McLuhan, 'Environment: The Future of an Erosion,' *Perspecta* 11 (1965): 164–7. A number of passages in Freud's 1927 'The Future of an Illusion' are pertinent to McLuhan's article, particularly: 'in general people experience their present naively' (686); and 'Human creations are easily destroyed, and science and technology, which have built them up, can also be used for their annihilation' (687). Quoted from *The Freud Reader*, ed. Peter Gay (New York: Norton, 1989), 685–722.

102 McLuhan was admired by Fluxus artists such as Yoko Ono and Nam June Paik. McLuhan also shared with Fluxus artist George Maciunas a liking for the films of Stan Vanderbeek; see (in Armstrong and Rothfuss, *In the Spirit of Fluxus*) Bruce Jenkins, 'Fluxfilms in Three False Starts,' 122–39, especially 124, and Theall, *The Medium Is the Rear-View Mirror* (*RVM*). Other Canadians involved with Fluxus events as performers were Istvan Anhalt (the Canadian composer about whom Glenn Gould wrote), Françoise Sullivan (one of the signatories of *Refus Global*), and Brion Gysin, who later collaborated with William Burroughs (see, in Armstrong and Rothfuss, *In the Spirit of Fluxus*: Owen F. Smith, 'Fluxus: A Brief History and Other Fictions,' 22–37, especially 27; and Simon Anderson 'Fluxus Publicus,' 38–61, especially 43 [Fluxus posters]). In *Under the Influence of Fluxus* (Winnipeg: Plug-In, 1991), Wayne Baerwaldt places Fluxus within the general ambit of McLuhan's notion of globalization (7).

103 Higgins, 'Statement on Intermedia,' in Armstrong and Rothfuss, *In the Spirit of Fluxus* 172–3; these pages reproduce the original typescript. The Vancouver group 'Intermedia' is said to have arrived at its name independently of Higgins; the link, however, would be McLuhan, especially via *VVV*, which Higgins had published. (See chapter 5 above.)

104 The notion of intermedia is related to the notion of empathy; in this context, Paik's invocation of Wölfflin's *Renaissance and Baroque* in his 'afterlude to the EXPOSITION of EXPERIMENTAL TELEVISION' (1963), is noteworthy; reproduced in *In the Spirit of Fluxus* 166.

105 This debate has been taken up by Andrew Ross in *No Respect: Intellectuals and Popular Culture* (New York: Routledge, 1989), which includes a long section on McLuhan ('Media Shepherd, King of Popthink,' 114–34). Ross is unremittingly critical of McLuhan's 'unsocial realism' (116) – that he 'never thought about the popular experience, meaning, or uses of such [emancipatory] possibilities' of popular culture (120), and that he 'chooses to ignore the ugly, exploitative side of development' (132). At the same time, Ross acknowledges the influence McLuhan's thought had on the 1960s countercultural movements, politically and artistically.

106 Andreas Huyssen sees the Fluxus artists as having failed to live up to the example of 'their predecessors in the age of heroic vangardism' (see his article 'Back to the Future: Fluxus in Context,' in Armstrong and Rothfuss, *In the Spirit of Fluxus*, 140–52; this quotation 145), although he does ascribe to them a 'rather purist anti-technological attitude,' which manifested itself especially in Cage's rejection of technology and their dealings with 'a new media triumphalism under the spell of Marshall McLuhan' (149). Cage, however, worked with a number of McLuhan's concepts, Cage's attitudes reflecting the complexities of the criticism and the art of this period; to state that Cage rejected technology is completely counter to Cage's aesthetic. Yet even those artists who repudiated what they perceived to be McLuhan's techno-optimism did so in McLuhanesque terms, as in Greg Curnoe's 'I am not a McLuhanite,' or Clive Robertson's performance (and video), 'Marshall McLuhan Memorial Music.'

See Greg Curnoe, *Blue Book 8* (Toronto: Art Metropole, 1989), 147; Clive Robertson, *Marshall McLuhan Memorial Music* (video and performance; for a description of the performance see Alain-Martin Richard and Clive Robertson, eds, *Performance au/in Canada* (Quebec: Editions Intervention / Toronto: Coach House, 1991), 134. The performance was given on 20 April 1975.

107 McLuhan, 'Prospect,' *Canadian Art* 81 (Sept.-Oct. 1962): 363–6; this quotation 363.

108 A 1980 survey of documentary media held at the Nova Scotia College of Art and Design was called 'The Medium Is the Message'; see Renee Baert, 'Video in Canada: In Search of Authority,' in Bronson, *Sea to Shining Sea* 174.

109 Sara Diamond, 'The Practical Aesthetics of Early Vancouver Video,' in Douglas, ed., *Vancouver Anthology* 47–84; this quotation 50.

110 See Marusya Bociurkiw and Karen Knights, eds, *Video Out Distribution Catalogue* (Vancouver: Video Out, 1996), which characterizes its archival holdings as illustrating 'the impact of a variety of influences on west coast production including McLuhan's utopia of the Global Village, popular culture, media criticism, Fluxus, and feminist and queer theories' (30). I am grateful to Video In / Video Out for making this catalogue available to me.

111 The video was Paul Wong's *Confused: Sexual Views*; the gallery was Vancouver's. See Diamond, 'Practical Aesthetics' 79–80.

112 Baert, 'Video in Canada,' 170.

113 Michael Goldberg of Metro Media, quoted by Diamond, 'Practical Aesthetics' 56.

114 The majority of the articles in 'Touch in Contemporary Art' (*Public 13* [1996]) are devoted to issues of electronic media, especially video.

115 George Maciunas, 'Neo-Dada in Music, Theater, Poetry, Art,' in *The Spirit of Fluxus*, 156–7.

116 Kristine Stiles, 'Between Water and Stone: Fluxus Performance,' in Armstrong and Rothfuss, *In the Spirit of Fluxus*, 62–99; this quotation 67, quoting Ronald Gross and George Quasha, eds, *Open Poetry: Four Anthologies of Open Poems* (New York: Simon and Schuster, 1973), 385.

117 See Nam June Paik's 'afterlude to the EXPOSITION of EXPERIMENTAL TELEVISION' (1963), reproduced in *In the Spirit of Fluxus* 166.

118 The 'Distant Early Warning Deck' (1969) has slogans printed on cards from a regular deck of cards, one of which (the five of diamonds) quotes John Cage: 'Silence is all the sounds of the environment at once.'

119 There is a picture of the McLuhan T-shirt in Jon Hendricks, *Fluxus Codex* (New York: Abrams, 1988), 555.

120 McLuhan quotes in *CA* a passage addressing the art of Young (155). Paik is an important figure within Fluxus in that he consistently has addressed televisual technologies, and from a position that has remained adamantly 'McLuhanesque,' as a reviewer recently put it in assessing the success of the spring 2000 Paik retrospective at New York's Guggenheim Museum: 'Paik can easily seem sloppily exuberant, embarrassingly McLuhanesque ... The excess Paik produces in his art ... engages a bigger problem than does much recent media art: the problem of television and its role in the world.' See David Joselit, 'Planet Paik,' *Art in America* 88.6 (June 2000): 73–6; 78; this quotation 78. For Paik on McLuhan see 'La Vie, Satellites, One Meeting – One Life' in John G. Hanhardt, ed., *Video Culture* (New York: Visual Studies Workshop Press, 1986), 219–22.

121 'He [McLuhan] and John Lennon and Yoko Ono all interviewed each other one day in late December of 1969.' Matie Armstrong Molinaro, 'Marshalling McLuhan' in *Marshall McLuhan: The Man and His Message*, ed. George Sanderson and Frank Macdonald; Introduction by John Cage (Golden, CO: Fulcrum, 1989), 81–8; this quotation 83.

122 Steve McCaffery, 'A Book Resembling Hair,' *Performance au/in Canada* 263.

123 Emmett Williams, the concretist, links a number of these aspects, insofar as he was one of the earliest Fluxus performers (Armstrong and Rothfuss, *In the Spirit of Fluxus* 20). Williams also exerted a significant influence on Garry Neill Kennedy and thus on the Nova Scotia College of Art and Design. Williams spent a month in the fall of 1984 as artist in residence at the Western Front (with which Robert Filliou, another Fluxus artist, was also often associated). It was Dick Higgins who published Williams's groundbreaking *An Anthology of Concrete Poetry* (New York: Something Else Press, 1967) in which the work of bpNichol appears. See Williams, *My Life in Flux – and Vice Versa* (London: Thames and Hudson, 1992).

124 Douglas Kahn, 'The Latest: Fluxus and Music,' in Armstrong and Rothfuss, *In the Spirit of Fluxus*, 100–21; this quotation 102.

125 Maciunas, 'Neo-Dada,' 157.

126 Jenkins, 'Fluxfilms in Three False Starts,' 133, speaking of 'fluxfilms'; emphasis added.

127 See Marjorie Perloff and Charles Junkerman, 'Introduction' to *John Cage: Composed in America*, ed. Perloff and Junkerman (Chicago: U of Chicago P, 1994), 7. In his Charles Eliot Norton Lectures, *I–VI*, Cage uses McLuhan's work as one of the major sources for his mesostics. In his 1967 article, 'McLuhan's Influence,' Cage dates this influence to 1961. See *John Cage*, ed. Richard Kostelanetz (New York: Praeger, 1970), 170. At the end of his career, in *Rolywholyover*, Cage wrote a mesostic based on McLuhan's article 'The Agenbite of Outwit'; the two works are printed back to back on accordion paper.

128 Frances Dyson, 'The Ear That Would Hear Sounds in Themselves: John Cage 1935–1965,' in *Wireless Imagination: Sound, Radio, and the Avant-Garde*, ed. Douglas Kahn and Gregory Whitehead (Cambridge, MA: MIT P, 1992), 373–407; this quotation 382.

129 Gordana P. Crnković, 'Utopian America and the Language of *Silence*,' in Perloff and Junkerman, eds, *John Cage* 167–87; this quotation 176–7.

130 John Cage, *Silence* (Middletown: Wesleyan UP, 1961), 97.

131 Daniel Herwitz, 'John Cage's Approach to the Global,' in Perloff and Junkerman, *John Cage* 188–205; this quotation 190.

132 Immanuel Kant, *Kant's Critique of Aesthetic Judgement*, trans. James Creed Meredith (Oxford: Clarendon P, 1911), 151.

133 Joan Retallack, 'Poethics of a Complex Realism,' in Perloff and Junkerman, *John Cage* 242–73; this quotation 258.

134 McLuhan, in Sanderson and Macdonald, eds, *Marshall McLuhan: The Man and His Message* 142. Note also 'Inside on the Outside' in *Journal of Communication* 26.4 (1976).

135 McLuhan, 'The Agenbite of Outwit,' in Cage, *Rolywholyover* n.p. (*Rolywholyover* is a silver metal box containing a number of unpaginated texts, many of them printed on transparent paper, which accompanied the 'museum performance' of this name, Cage's last major work.)

136 See R. Cavell, 'Caged Presences' (Review of *I–VI*), *Canadian Literature* 144 (1995): 193–5.

Chapter 8: Borderlines

1 McLuhan, interviewed (with his longtime friend and colleague Tom Easterbrook) by Danny Finkleman, in *Speaking of Winnipeg*, ed. John Parr (Winnipeg: Queenston House, 1974), 22–38; this quotation 23. The interview begins with McLuhan's insistence on 'the superiority of the prairie meadowlark to all other bird-songs.'

2 Scott Watson quotes this comment from an article by Joan Lowndes that appeared in *The Province* (Vancouver) (19 January 1968) on the occasion of an exhibition organized by the National Gallery that was then touring in France. See Watson's 'Discovering the Defeatured Landscape,' *Vancouver Anthology: The Institutional Politics of Art*, ed. Stan Douglas (Vancouver: Talonbooks, 1991), 246–65; this quotation 264, n1.

3 McLuhan, 'Canada and Internationalism,' *The Manitoban* (1 December 1933): 3. This publication is not listed in *The Writings of Marshall McLuhan: Listed in Chronological Order from 1934 to 1975* (Fort Lauderdale: Wake-Brook House, 1975); see *Marshall McLuhan: Escape into Understanding* (*EU*) 439.

4 André Siegfried, *Canada: An International Power*, trans. Doris Hemming (1937; rev. London: Cape, 1949). This revised edition is not radically changed from the first (9). Siegfried was French, and based his book on numerous trips to Canada.

5 Donna Bennett, 'Criticism in English,' in Eugene Benson and William Toye, gen. eds, *The Oxford Companion to Canadian Literature* (1983; 2nd ed. Toronto: Oxford UP, 1997); 242–67; this quotation 245. The notion of 'internationalism' was to become highly charged in the 1960s; for George Parkin Grant, writing in *Lament for a Nation* (1965), Canadian 'parochialism' was preferable to American 'internationalism.'

6 McLuhan, 'A Contribution to THE BOOK OF CANADIAN POETRY, edited by A.J.M. Smith, Gage,

Toronto, 1948,' typescript of seven pages, dated in typescript and in McLuhan's hand, NAC, McLuhan Collection, box 129, folder 30. The essay bears the date '1948' in McLuhan's hand; however, as the second edition of Smith's anthology does not contain critical essays, the circumstances of McLuhan's essay are not clear, and are further complicated by the fact of a reference to Desmond Pacey's 1951 *Creative Writing in Canada*. Perhaps, then, McLuhan's article was written for the third edition of Smith's anthology (1957), or written in 1948 and revised later. Smith had possibly conceived of the anthology as containing both poetry and criticism, his intention to include McLuhan (as I am speculating) indicating that McLuhan had a significant reputation at this time as a cosmopolite, if not as a Canadianist. Among the poets to whom McLuhan alludes in his brief survey of Canadian poetry is Wilfred Watson, with whom he would subsequently collaborate.

7 In *The Manitoban* article of 1933, McLuhan had written of Europeans who 'have had to summon the mighty forces of nationalism in order to prevent the anarchy that was growing from carelessness of life and corporate social values.' This view is inconsistent with McLuhan's later views of nationalism, which he expressed most succinctly in his various meditations on Canada.

8 Royal Commission on National Development in the Arts, Letters and Sciences 1949–1951, *Report* (Ottawa: Government of Canada, 1951) (the Massey Report); the volume's epigraph is from St Augustine's *De Civitate Dei*. A companion volume, *Royal Commission Studies: A Selection of Essays Prepared for the Royal Commission on National Development in the Arts, Letters and Sciences* (Ottawa: Government of Canada, 1951), included essays by B.K. Sandwell, Wilfrid Eggleston, Edward McCourt, George P. Grant, S.D. Clark, Maurice Tremblay, C.P. Stacey, W.L. Morton, J.W.T. Spinks, Sir Ernest MacMillan, Robertson Davies, Gérard Morisset, Charles F. Comfort, and Eric Arthur. While the report included a section on the mass media, no essay in the companion volume focuses on that area.

9 Thus the essay on film concludes with the comment that 'English-speaking audiences are still exposed to strange Hollywood versions of a Canada they never thought or wished to see' (59). The 'plight of the humanities' (136) is discussed: 'it is not so much that they have been deserted as that they have lost their way' (138). On the subject of painting, the report avers that 'Modern Canadian painting can no longer exploit the novelty of the Canadian landscape' (207); the lack of 'a truly national literature' (223) is lamented, as is the 'ignorance of Canada among the people of our nearest neighbour' (253).

10 There was a dissenting appendix attached to the report; written by Arthur Surveyer, it opposed the report's position on the exclusion of advertising from broadcasting and on the hegemony of public broadcasting. Surveyer cites Gilbert Seldes's *The Great Audience*, an early book on mass communications, in expressing his negative views on broadcasting content; Seldes is one of the contributors to McLuhan and Carpenter's *Explorations in Communications* (*ExC*), with an article titled 'Communications Revolution.'

11 See Theall's comments in 'The Influence of the Canadian University Milieu on McLuhan: A Speculative Note,' Appendix 4 to *The Medium Is the Rear-View Mirror* (*RVM*). McLuhan moved to Windsor in 1944 and to Toronto two years later.

12 Sandwell's essay goes on to state that the future of Canadian culture is intimately connected to the media of 'large-scale diffusion' (*Royal Commission Studies* 4), and urges 'state action' in regulating these. Elsewhere in the volume, Edward McCourt laments the 'failure of Canadian writers to create a national literature of much significance,' citing 'the colonial spirit' to be a major factor in this failure (67); he proposes the remedy of 'government subsidy' (82). George P. Grant complains that at some universities 'there are four times as many people teaching physics as teaching philosophy, and three times as many people teaching animal husbandry' (120), and argues that 'theses on the excreta of rats' are unsuitable for the PhD degree. Hilda Neatby charges that 'the Canadian people ... still regard their history with indifference tempered by distaste' (205). This provides some sense of the intellectual milieu to which McLuhan returned after his British and American sojourns.

13 McLuhan, 'Defrosting Canadian Culture,' *American Mercury* (March 1952): 91–7; this quotation 91. McLuhan's marginal notes in the NAC copy of this article indicate that he reread this in preparation for writing his 1978 article, 'Canada: The Borderline Case,' the original version of which, however, was prepared for broadcast in 1967, as noted by Eugene McNamara in the introduction to *The Interior Landscape* (*IL*).

14 This '"contempt for the 'national question,'"' as Kroker suggests in *Technology and the Canadian Mind* (*TCM*), did not endear McLuhan to his contemporaries (82).

15 In arguing against the tenor of the Massey Report, McLuhan was distancing himself from Innis (as he would more directly in 'The Later Innis,' published the following year), whose *The Strategy of Culture* (1952) contained 'A Footnote to the Massey Report' that supported its recommendations.

16 In his views on the French Canadians, McLuhan was influenced by a book he read during his St Louis years, *Canadien: A Study of the French Canadians* (Toronto: Dent, 1933), by Wilfrid Bovey, who argues that the 'danger' of assimilation has long passed.

17 The text is unsigned and unpaginated; it has seventeen leaves plus a cover. I am using a photocopy of the University of Toronto's Robarts Library copy (general stacks) on which McLuhan has signed his name under the title. Carpenter recalls 'an afternoon when Marshall flipped through Vincent Massey's 1951 call for High Kulcha in Canada. He laughed & laughed, then scribbled a response modeled after Wyndham Lewis' *BLAST*, 1914. I immediately set it in type on a museum labeling machine. *COUNTERBLAST*, 1954, privately printed, appeared a few days later. If anyone wants to know what an hour with Marshall McLuhan could be like, read that review.' See 'Remembering *Explorations*,' *Canadian Notes and Queries* 46 (Spring 1992): 3–15; this quotation 7. (Carpenter's article was reprinted as an appendix to Theall, *The Virtual Marshall McLuhan*.)

18 Another connection between McLuhan's media interests and his interests in Canadian culture was provided by his collaborator Edmund Carpenter's research into spatial construction among indigenous inhabitants of the Canadian north.

19 Theall identifies this phrase as a citation from a poem by Dylan Thomas, 'The Hand That Signed the Paper.' See *The Virtual Marshall McLuhan* (*VM*) (Montreal and Kingston: McGill-Queen's UP, 2001), 10–12.

20 When McLuhan published a revised version of this pamphlet as *Counterblast* (*Ctb*) (1969) the shift to the cultural margins was being played out in the context of conceptualism, especially in the work of artists such as N.E. Thing Co.

21 McLuhan, 'Why the CBC Must Be Dull,' *Saturday Night* (16 February 1957): 13–14.

22 McLuhan made similar comments in his contribution to the 1961 Royal Commission report on publications. See the excerpt quoted in Edwin Black's 'Understanding McLuhan's Media,' in *Canadian Journal of Communication* [special issue on McLuhan] 7.3 (1980–81): 6–8, with the excerpt on page 8.

23 McLuhan, 'The Electronic Age' in *Mass Media in Canada*, ed. John A. Irving (Toronto: Ryerson, 1962), 177–205; this quotation 188.

24 McLuhan, 'Mr. Priestly's [*sic*] Colonial Crusade,' *Northern Review* 7.4 (1956): 3. The piece follows immediately after John Sutherland's editorial.

25 McLuhan, 'The "Color-Bar" of BBC English,' *The Canadian Forum* 29.339 (April 1949): 9–10; this quotation 10.

26 Malcolm Ross, ed., *Our Sense of Identity: A Book of Canadian Essays* (Toronto: Ryerson, 1954). Ross was instrumental in establishing McLuhan's Centre for Culture and Technology at the University of Toronto (*WWMM* 27).

27 Milton Wilson, '*Other Canadians* and After,' *Tamarack Review* 9 (1958): 77–92; this quotation 89.

28 The essay was revised as the 'Polemical Introduction' to the *Anatomy of Criticism* (Princeton: Princeton UP, 1957).

29 David Cook, *Northrop Frye: A Vision of the New World* (Montreal: New World Press, 1985), 9.

30 McLuhan, of course, argued that space and time could not be understood as absolutes in media culture and theorized acoustic space as a way of addressing this space/time collapse. Frye writes of our time-sense in *The Modern Century* (Toronto: Oxford UP, 1967) that 'Man has doubtless always experienced time in the same way' (31); his views of space were essentially Kantian. See Richard Cavell, 'Where Is Frye?, or Theorising Postcolonial Space,' *ECW* 56 (1995): 110–34.

31 Frye was annoyed by the comparison; as he writes in 'Notebook 27' (1985): 'that tiresome link with McLuhan cropped up again in the paper ... [H]is ideas were, he said, "probes" – a male metaphor – without social context. He supplied the context by naive determinism: technology is alleged to create society.' See *Northrop Frye Newsletter* 7.2 (1997): 3. The comparison, however, has persisted; see Jeffrey Simpson, 'McLuhan, Frye, and the Future of Canada,' *Queen's Quarterly* 99.1 (1992): 7–19. Theall, in *VM*, remarks that 'Frye, as an exponent of a Protestant and gnostic-like intellectual system (which McLuhan considered to be Puritan), provided the obvious foil for McLuhan within the Canadian university and literary world' (119).

32 McLuhan, 'Inside Blake and Hollywood,' *The Sewanee Review* 55.4 (1947): 710–15.

33 NAC, McLuhan Collection, box 200, file 45.

34 In Foucauldian terms, the 'space that is rigid and forbidden, surrounding the quest, the return, and the treasure ([the] geography of the Argonauts and of the labyrinth)' is replaced by 'the other space – communicating, polymorphous, continuous, and reversible – of the metamorphosis, that is to say, of the visible transformation of instantly crossed distances of strange affinities, of symbolic replacements.' Michel Foucault, *Death and The Labyrinth: The World of Raymond Roussel*, trans. Charles Ruas (New York: Doubleday, 1986), 80.

35 McLuhan, 'Myth and Mass Media,' *Dædalus* 88.2 (1959): 339–48, a special issue on 'Myth and Mythmaking' that had contributions from Harry Levin, Joseph Campbell, and Mircea Eliade (among others)

36 McLuhan suggests that if we were to regard myth as something that we are 'living,' then we might turn our attention to the 'current hula-hoop activity.' McLuhan notes that, in the 1930s, a hoop was for rolling, yet '[t]oday children reject the lineal use of the hoop in an external space. They use it in a nuclear mode as a means of generating their own space' ('Myth and Mass Media' 344). In this McLuhan sees 'the mythic power of the new media to alter sensibility. For this change in child behaviour has nothing to do with ideas or programs' (345). This ability of media to alter sensibilities was powerfully intuited by Blake (and McLuhan is likely thinking here of Frye again), whose 'explicit mythmaking ... is the greatest monument and antidote to the mythic pressures of the printing press' (347). In the reference to printing, McLuhan once again stresses the need to understand myths as part of a historical process.

37 Robert Fulford has referred to this period as 'The Age of McLuhan' in *Best Seat in the House: Memoirs of a Lucky Man* (Toronto: Collins, 1988), 162–84. Fulford records that CBC-TV's news program 'This Hour Has Seven Days' was created by Patrick Watson to put into effect McLuhan's notions about television. The program, cancelled after fifty segments, interviewed McLuhan on its last show in May of 1966, a segment that achieved 'the largest audience for a public affairs show in the history of Canada' (184).

38 In 1962, Frye had been instrumental in the awarding of the Governor General's prize to *The Gutenberg Galaxy*; see John Ayre, *Northrop Frye: A Biography* (Toronto: Random House, 1989), 275: 'No one, including Frye, was keen on it from a literary point of view but Frye simply felt that their committee would look ridiculous if they failed to choose it.'

39 Northrop Frye, 'Conclusion' to the *Literary History of Canada: Canadian Literature in English*, Gen. Ed. Carl F. Klinck (1965; rpt Toronto: U of Toronto P, 1967), 821–49; this quotation 829.

40 To Louis Forsdale's question, 'If we live in a global village, does that mean that people are going to like each other?' McLuhan had similarly replied, 'Not likely, since proximity means there's more abrasiveness. Close quarters strain human tolerance ... When privacy becomes a problem, identity is threatened and violence is engendered by the need to recover identity.' With his typically bipolar view of these issues, however, McLuhan concludes this discussion with the prospect that 'we may recover community.' See McLuhan and Forsdale, 'Technology and the Human Dimension,' in *The Antigonish Review* 74–5 (Summer-Autumn 1988; special issue on McLuhan): 21–33; these quotations 32–3.

41 Edward T. Cone, 'The Revolving Bookstand: Recommended Summer Reading,' *The American Scholar* 37.3 (1968): 522. As John Ayre, Frye's biographer, notes, '[b]ecause there was so much feverish attention to McLuhan at the time, Frye's comments tended to console the besieged liberal constituency in North America, starting to suffer the depredations of the youth culture and its zany gurus' (314).

42 The chapters in *The Modern Century* took their titles from poems by Archibald Lampman, Irving Layton, and Emile Nelligan: 'City of the End of Things'; 'Improved Binoculars'; 'Clair de lune intellectuel.' Frye may have selected the third title because it can be read as containing a pun on McLuhan's name; compare Lionel Kearns's volume of poems, *By the Light of the Silvery McLune: Media Parables, Poems, Signs, Gestures, and Other Assaults on the Interface* (1968).

43 Alluding to McLuhan's pronouncements on the end of linearity (including in the seamless nylon stocking), Frye points to the absurdity of a world in which 'the dynasty and the hemline ... get much the same amount of featuring in the news'; a 'new art of divination or augury has developed, in which the underlying trends of the contemporary world are interpreted by vogues and fashions in dress, speech or entertainment' (*Modern Century* 21) Ayre sees these comments as directed precisely towards McLuhan:

'A clearly dishonest pathway was the fruitless pop-prophecy of McLuhanism which played over the surface of things, seeing cosmic significance in such fads as white lipstick' (314).

44 See for example the 'Global Culture' issue of the *National Geographic* 196.2 (August 1999), in which 'The Birth of the Global Village' is a feature of the map insert; the editorial cites David Crystal's *English as a Global Language*, which records the parallel development of English idiolects: 'Ghana, Nigeria, and Singapore, for example, are developing versions of English unintelligible to outsiders' (5).

45 Northrop Frye, 'Literary and Mechanical Models,' in *The Eternal Act of Creation: Essays, 1979–1990*, ed. Robert D. Denham (Bloomington: Indiana UP, 1993), 9–20; this quotation 13. The essay is the text of a lecture given by Frye to a conference on computers and the humanities.

46 Theall notes in *VM* that 'Expo 67 became McLuhan's fair, a fact openly acknowledged by the extent to which the theme pavilions of "Man and His World," whose designs blended Canadian history and culture, were based on McLuhan's writings, which were liberally quoted on plaques throughout the pavilions' (126). McLuhan's influence on Expo 67 was also felt through Jacques Languirand, who helped design the Man in the Community pavilion; Languirand is the author of *De McLuhan à Pythagore* (Montreal: René Ferron, 1972). See Donald Theall, 'Communication Theory and the Marginal Culture: The Socio-Aesthetic Dimensions of Communication Study,' in *Studies in Canadian Communications*, ed. Gertrude Joch Robinson and Donald Theall (Montreal: McGill Programme in Communications, 1975), 7–26.

47 See Gary Genosko, *McLuhan and Baudrillard: The Masters of Implosion* (New York: Routledge, 1999), 5. McLuhan was also critical about aspects of Expo. Remarking in *From Cliché to Archetype (CA)* that 'All hardware "growth" is destruction,' he notes that the 'celebrated documentary *A Place to Stand*, done for Expo 1967 by Christopher Chapman, celebrates the growth of Ontario by a terrifying series of images of destruction. It is a drama of strip-mining of natural resources and the crunching of old motor cars into little cubic capsules – all done in raving color' (49).

48 McLuhan, 'Understanding Canada, and Sundry Other Matters,' *Mademoiselle* (January 1967): 114–15; 126–9; this quotation 129.

49 There is a description of this radio talk in *IL* 181; the talk was first given as one of the Marfleet lectures on 16 March 1967 (*L* 342). I am using the (updated) text published in *The Canadian Imagination*, ed. David Staines (Cambridge, MA: Harvard UP, 1977), 226–48. McLuhan further elaborated on this essay with Bruce Powers in *The Global Village (GV)*.

50 McLuhan, 'The Implications of Cultural Uniformity,' in *Superculture: American Popular Culture and Europe*, ed. C.W.E. Bigsby (Bowling Green: Bowling Green U Popular P, 1975), 43–56; 218.

51 In 'Media Alchemy in Art and Society,' McLuhan cites Richard Neutra's *Survival through Design* as 'representative of the full recognition today of the power of the messages from interior and exterior design in buildings to pattern general awareness and to affect even physiological states' (64). Published in *The Journal of Communication* 8.2 (1958): 63–7.

52 Frye's influence on Atwood (whose student she was) is well known; *Survival* has six references to Frye, though none to McLuhan. Atwood has stated, however, that she read *The Mechanical Bride (MB)* when it was first published, and one is not hard-pressed to find mechanical brides in a number of her literary works, perhaps most powerfully in *The Handmaid's Tale*. In that novel, significantly, redemption of the heroine comes via the orality of the tape recording. See Willmott, *McLuhan, or Modernism in Reverse (MMR)* 243, n45 for the Atwood reference. See also Judith Fitzgerald's 'McLuhan, Not Atwood!' in *Books in Canada* (December 1995): 3–5: 'Perhaps Atwood's refusal to investigate McLuhan's work bespeaks a refusal to examine at all realistically the fabric of Canadian society *in situ* in 1972; some-how, by ignoring him, and reverting to Frye's positions and impositions of hierarchical patterns on our literature, she managed to avoid our collective and corporate reality altogether' (4). Atwood herself has commented that the book occasioned accusations of all sorts; she was even accused of 'not being Marshall McLuhan. (I would have liked to have been Marshall McLuhan – it seemed a ton o' fun – but he had the job pretty much cornered).' See 'Survival, Then and Now,' *Maclean's* (1 July 1999): 54–8; this quotation 55.

53 McLuhan also refers to Atwood's *Survival* in 'Inside on the Outside, or the Spaced-Out American,' *Journal of Communication* 26.4 (1976), where the central point has to do with the different ways in which cultures construct spatial relations.

54 McLuhan returns to this theme in the 1974 interview with Danny Finkleman: 'The advantage of living

in Canada, in general, is to watch the United States making fools of themselves ... The advantage of being the land of the Dew Line is that we are the cool crowd, Distant Early Warning System for the rest of mankind. So we can play a very important role on the borderline between sanity and frenzy' (28–9).

55 McLuhan makes a similar point in his 1968 review of Pierre Trudeau's *Federalism and the French Canadians*: 'Canada never had a unified national identity and so it has nothing to lose in the TV age.' McLuhan, review of Pierre Trudeau, *Federalism and the French Canadians* in *The New York Times Book Review* (17 November 1968); NAC, McLuhan Collection, vol. 133, file 39.

56 Homi Bhabha, 'DissemiNation' in *Nation and Narration*, ed. Homi Bhabha (New York: Routledge, 1990), 291–322; this quotation 301. McLuhan's insistence that borderlines resonated with heterogeneity and hybridity makes his work especially responsive to (post)colonial issues. Similarly, Bill Readings, in *The University in Ruins* (Cambridge, MA: Harvard UP, 1996), has argued that 'the problem of the twenty-first century is that of the borderline ... the non-place ... at which the tensions of globalization are manifest' (49).

57 Alexander Kizuk, '"Mutual Provisionality": Plurality and the Other in Canadian Cultural Theory,' *ECW* 61 (1997): 104–24; this quotation 109.

58 Innis was likewise colonialist in his view of culture: 'we must remember that cultural strength comes from Europe.' See *The Strategy of Culture* (1952), republished in its entirety in *Contexts of Canadian Criticism*, ed. Eli Mandel (Chicago: U of Chicago P, 1973), 71–92; this quotation 72. It was specifically the 'jackals of communication systems' who were 'constantly on the alert to destroy every vestige of sentiment toward Great Britain' (91); this must be read in the context of Innis's approbation of the Massey Report's recommendations.

59 McLuhan and Richard J. Schoeck, eds, *Voices of Literature*, illus. Harley Parker (Toronto: Holt, Rinehart and Winston, 1964). Canadian and Native poets included are: Angmak, J. McCrae, F.R. Scott, E. Birney, C.G.D. Roberts, B. Carman, A. Lampman, J. Macpherson, R. Schoeck, E.J. Pratt.

60 McLuhan quotes Elias Canetti's *Crowds and Power* (1963) in *CA* on how 'archaic figures' lived in a '*fluid*' universe: '"The mythical ancestors of the Australian aborigines are man and animal simultaneously, or sometimes man and plant ... Each of these ... acts both as a man and as a particular animal, and is regarded as the ancestor of both ... If we are to understand them we must remember that they are regarded as beings belonging to an age of myth, a period in which metamorphosis was the common gift of all creatures and constantly practised ... Not only could a man transform himself into anything, but he also had the power to transform others"' (92).

61 See Cavell, 'Where Is Frye?' *passim*.

62 Arjun Appadurai, *Modernity at Large: Cultural Dimensions of Globalization* (Minneapolis: U of Minnesota P, 1996), 31.

63 McLuhan makes a similar point in a letter to Archibald Malloch, undated. From File 3 (1953–5) of the Malloch accession. Malloch was McLuhan's student in the 1940s and subsequently went on to a teaching career at McGill. The letters in the accession span the period 1949–69. My thanks to Robert Fisher, Manuscripts Division, NAC, for drawing these letters to my attention and for making them available to me.

64 Northrop Frye, *The Critical Path: An Essay on the Social Context of Literary Criticism* (Bloomington: Indiana UP, 1971), 151. McLuhan was well aware that the era of (re)tribalization would also be an era of 'tribulation' (*CA* 86).

65 Northrop Frye, 'Communications,' *The Listener* 84, no. 2154 (9 July 1970): 33–4.

66 Ayre notes that Frye 'was obsessed by sequence,' unlike 'McLuhan who was "all discontinuity and mosaic"' (332).

67 McLuhan, 'Views,' *The Listener* 84, no. 2167 (8 October 1970): 475–6. The article is accompanied by a cartoon showing two computers looking at each other, with one saying to the other, 'Written any good books lately?'

68 Watson came to know McLuhan in 1947; his wife, Sheila, was McLuhan's doctoral student at the University of Toronto (writing her dissertation on Wyndham Lewis; see the section on Lewis in chapter 1 above). Her novel *The Double Hook* (Toronto: McClelland and Stewart, 1959) has a number of McLuhanesque resonances, especially in its representation of orality within literacy. Wilfred Watson wrote much more directly in a McLuhanesque mode; in his play 'Let's Murder Clytemnestra according to the Principles of Marshall McLuhan,' first performed in 1969, Watson drew on McLuhan's ideas. In

the introduction, he states that 'the world of scientific explanation, in which explanation explains and explanation remains, ad infinitum, and ad absurdum, has become reduced to the cliché of the TV screen; a fact proved empirically, McLuhan himself noted, when the first TV camera was set up on the moon, and began to take pictures of the home-planet' (343). Published in *Plays at the Iron Bridge, or The Autobiography of Tom Horror*, ed. Shirley Neuman (Edmonton: Longspoon/NeWest P, 1989), 341–428. In a letter responding to my questions about his interest in Vorticism, Watson stated that 'I was continually having vorticism thrust upon me – Pound, Wyndham Lewis, Eliot, Jack Shadbolt, Marshall McLuhan ... In my theatre scripts I wanted to backwards and forwards grammatologize the actors so that their bodies became patterns of energy.' (Letter to Richard Cavell, dated 13 January 1988; I am grateful to Professor Shirley Neuman for permission to quote.) *CA* was badly received; John Fowles described it as being 'as elegant and lucid as a barrel of tar,' filled with 'half-baked anti-humanist theory,' a 'sick book' that sets 'a corrupt and corrupting example.' See the *Saturday Review* (21 November 1970): 32–3.

69 McLuhan, with Wilfred Watson, *From Cliché to Archetype* (New York: Viking, 1970). For notes on the gestation of the volume, see University of Alberta, Wilfred Watson Collection, Box 21, folder 152. In 1973 a translation by Derrick de Kerckhove of *CA* was published under the title *Du Cliché à l'archetype: La foire du sense* (Montreal: Hurtubise, 1973) and included Flaubert's *Dictionnaire des idées reçues*. The translated version reorders the English edition, adding a section at the end, 'Vortex,' that cites from Jarry's *Le père Ubu* and Maurice Blanchot's *L'espace littéraire*.

70 University of Alberta, Watson Collection, Box 21, folder 155.

71 Wilfred Watson, 'Marshall McLuhan and Multi-Consciousness: The Place Marie Dialogues,' *boundary 2* 3 (1974): 197–211. While the dialogues were successful, they ended when it came time to write the book, at which point, Watson states, 'the system broke into two, into dialogue with little or no transcription and into transcription with little or no dialogue' (198).

72 At one point Watson wrote the book on his own, producing 111 pages of 444 squares in quadrant form. See University of Alberta, Watson Collection, Box 20, folder 146.

73 'Radical juxtaposition' was Sontag's take on the Happening. See 'Happenings: An Art of Radical Juxtaposition' in *Against Interpretation and Other Essays* (1966; rpt New York: Octagon Books, 1982), 263–74. McLuhan's identification of the artist as the key figure in the 'new sensibility' is central to the last essay in the book, 'One Culture and the New Sensibility' (293–304).

74 See Wilfred Watson's 'McLuhan's Wordplay,' *Canadian Forum* 61 (May 1981): 10–12 on McLuhan's 'systemic wordplay' (10) whose 'key pun words would include ... *innering/outering ... visual space / auditory space ... figure/ground*' (11). McLuhan, Watson concludes, 'has put on the collective mask of our own *virtually* oral society. To say that he himself has become the first *writer* to exhibit this new, oral, kind of consciousness, is to push paradox almost into oxymoron. Yet this is what has happened' (12).

75 In 'The Implications of Cultural Uniformity,' McLuhan states that 'A popular form from one context may suddenly acquire a very élite quality in a different context' (43). See *Superculture* 43–56; 218 (notes).

76 McLuhan and Powers discuss 'robotism' extensively in *GV* (part 2).

77 The three major discussions of McLuhan by Frye in this period are 'The Definition of a University' (139–55); 'Teaching the Humanities Today' (91–101); and '"Conclusion" to *Literary History of Canada*, Second Edition,' (318–32), all in *Divisions on a Ground: Essays on Canadian Culture* (Toronto: Anansi, 1982).

78 D.G. Jones, 'Myth, Frye and Canadian Writers,' *Canadian Literature* 55 (1973): 7–22.

79 D.G. Jones, 'Cold Eye and Optic Heart: Marshall McLuhan and Some Canadian Poets,' *Modern Poetry Studies* 5.1 (1974): 170–86.

80 Likewise, James Reaney is often considered to be in the 'Frye' school, yet his journal *Alphabet*, published from 1960 to 1971 is highly McLuhanesque in its use of emblems and ideograms and verbal/visual structures generally.

81 Eli Mandel, 'Introduction' to *Contexts of Canadian Criticism* 3–4. McLuhan, along with R.J. Schoeck and Ernest Sirluck, were the general editors of the series in which the book was published.

82 Writing in the 'Conclusion' to the second edition of the *Literary History of Canada*, Frye goes so far as to make claims for the 'genuinely humanizing' (83) effects of television, and for 'the immense importance of the revival of the oral tradition' (87).

83 Even when they disagreed with him, Canadian poets made poetry out of McLuhan's ideas, as in

Dorothy Livesay's 'McLuhan Criticized' (1971); see *Archive for Our Times: Previously Uncollected and Unpublished Poems of Dorothy Livesay*, ed. Dean J. Irvine (Vancouver: Arsenal Pulp P, 1998), 190.

84 Not until the 1980s would McLuhan re-enter Canadian criticism, with postmodernism providing the venue, especially in the work of Linda Hutcheon, whose *The Canadian Postmodern: A Study of Contemporary English-Canadian Fiction* (Toronto: Oxford UP, 1988) takes McLuhan's 'borderline' concept as its point of departure (3) in its argument that 'contemporary Canadian novelists ... are McLuhan's true spiritual heirs' (52). Nevertheless, Hutcheon critiques McLuhan for suggesting that 'only television' will 'save "you"' from what the electronic prophet called the alienation of the fragmented, desacralized world in which we live' (58). Hutcheon arrives at this reading by insisting on McLuhan as a theorist of 'a set of contraries' (52), primarily orality and literacy. Robert Kroestch has likewise taken up a number of McLuhan's notions; see *The Lovely Treachery of Words* (Toronto: Oxford UP, 1989), especially 'Disunity as Unity: A Canadian Strategy.'

85 See Gary Genosko, 'McLuhan and Québec,' *Borderlines* 41 (1996): 19–23; his *McLuhan and Baudrillard* (New York: Routledge, 1999), especially the section 'M (A) C PQ' (100–6); and his *Undisciplined Theory* (London: SAGE, 1998), especially chapter 6. Also in 1967, Naim Kattan reviewed the *GG* and *Understanding Media* (*UM*) in a long review in the prestigious Paris journal *Critique*; see 'Marshall McLuhan,' *Critique* (mars 1967): 322–34.

86 See Jules Duchastel's article 'La Contre-culture: L'exemple de *Main Mise*,' in *L'Avant-garde culturelle et littéraire des années 70 au Québec*, ed. Jacques Pelletier (Montreal: UQAM, 1986), 61–81. *Main Mise* was a journal representative of the counter-cultural movements in Quebec in the 1970s (appearing first in October of 1970). Duchastel remarks that 'l'idéologie de *Main Mise* a totalement intégré les théories de McLuhan. Plusiers articles se réfèrent à lui, sous forme d'interview, d'extraits de ses écrits ou de paraphrase' (73).

87 Jacques Languirand, *De McLuhan à Pythagore* (Montreal: René Ferron, 1972). A graphic text, in the manner of *The Medium Is the Massage*, Languirand's book has the flavour of Charles Reich's *The Greening of America* (which it quotes) in its ecstatic embrace of all dualities, one of which is the hot/cool dyad that McLuhan elaborates in *UM*: 'Lorsque les livres de Marshall McLUHAN m'ont révélé son hypothèse sur les média qu'il classe en deux catégories: les média froids et les média chauds, elle m'est d'abord apparue comme tout à fait révolutionnaire. Mais je devias bientôt découvrir qu'il s'agit, en définitive, d'une opposition binaire simple qui procède très exactement de l'opposition fondamentale du Yin et du Yang. Ce qui ne diminue en rien le mérite de McLUHAN à mes yeux; au contraire, puisque cette constatation permet de confirmer, du moins en partie, la justesse de son hypothèse' (169). Theall remarks in *VM* that Languirand was 'one of the creators of the multimedia exhibits in "Man in the Community Pavilion" at Expo 67 ... for which McLuhan's writings provided inspiration while his aphorisms providing guiding quotations' (109).

88 McLuhan, interviewed by Jean Paré, *Forces* (22 November 1973): 65–71.

89 As Paré notes, McLuhan had also suggested, in 1967, that civil war was a possible consequence of the separation that he conceived of as already having taken place. In his 1977 interview with *Maclean's*, McLuhan clarifies: 'There will be no separatism. That is in the hardware sense; they will not pull out. Psychologically, they're separate already. They have been for a long time' (4).

90 McLuhan, untitled essay on 'Canadian non-identity' in *Rune* 2 (Spring 1975): 68–9.

91 McLuhan and Barrington Nevitt, 'Cultures in the Electronic World: Can the Bottom Line Hold Quebec?' *Perception* 1.2 (Nov.–Dec. 1977): 66–9. Reprinted in *Canada's Third Option*, ed. S.D. Berkowitz and Robert K. Logan (Toronto: Macmillan, 1978): 108–17.

92 McLuhan continued with this theme in one of his last interviews, published in *Maclean's* in 1977. To a question about Quebec, he replies that '[t]he effect of information is not to pull people together. It makes people feel independent when information is available everywhere ... Every place in the world is pulling away from every other place ... The French are not getting closer to Canada because the world is now a small place' (4). This articulation of the global village paradox indicates the extent to which McLuhan understood his theories in terms of their Canadian contexts. McLuhan, interview with Casey Baldwin, *Maclean's* 90.5 (7 March 1977): 4; 8–9.

93 As Theall remarks in *VM*, 'McLuhan's interest in the trivium shows not only an interest in rhetoric but also an interest in the history of education, both as they relate to art and communication' (65). Among his publications in this area are a 1943 article on George Herbert, reprinted five years later in *Readings for Liberal Education*; 'An Historical Approach to the Media' (1955) appeared in *Teachers College*

Record, as did 'Educational Effects of Mass Media of Communications' (1956). *Explorations*, the journal McLuhan edited with Edmund Carpenter, published 'Classroom without Walls' in 1957. There was an article on 'Classroom T.V.' in the *Study Pamphlets in Canadian Education* (1957); the next year McLuhan published 'Knowledge, Ideas, Information and Communication' in *The Yearbook of Education*; and in the late 1950s and early 1960s he published a number of articles in the National Association of Educational Broadcasters' journal. It was for this latter association that McLuhan produced his *Report on Project in Understanding New Media*, which was the basis for *UM*. In the mid-1960s, McLuhan (and R.J. Schoeck) produced their anthology *Voices of Literature* for use in the high school system, and in the early 1970s McLuhan published on the future of the book in *The UNESCO Courier*. On McLuhan's pedagogy generally, see 'The Educational Philosophy of Marshall McLuhan' in *The Philosophical and Sociological Foundations of Education* by Kamala Bhatia and Baldev Bhatia (Delhi: Doaba House, 1974), 259–69.

94 McLuhan, 'Adopt a College,' *This Magazine Is about Schools* 2.4 (1968): 51–5; this quotation 52.

95 McLuhan with Kathryn Hutchon and Eric McLuhan, *The City as Classroom: Understanding Language and Media (CC)* (Agincourt, ON: Book Society of Canada, 1977).

96 John Fekete, *The Critical Twilight: Explorations in the Ideology of Anglo-American Literary Theory from Eliot to McLuhan* (London: Routledge and Kegan Paul, 1977).

97 John Fekete, 'Massage in the Mass Age: Remembering the McLuhan Matrix,' *Canadian Journal of Political and Social Theory* 6.3 (1982): 50–67; this quotation 50.

98 McLuhan lamented in 1958 that 'the public [did]not rally with enthusiasm to the creator role' because 'we had been only too successful in creating a consumer-oriented public that expected all articles presented to it to be fully processssed for immediate use.' See 'Media Alchemy in Art and Society,' 66.

Postface: McLuhan in Space

1 Derek Gregory, *Geographical Imaginations* (Oxford: Blackwell, 1994), 14.

2 Edward Soja, *Postmodern Geographies: The Reassertion of Space in Critical Social Theory* (London: Verso, 1989), 87. Jody Berland, 'Angels Dancing: Cultural Technologies and the Production of Space,' in *Cultural Studies*, ed. Lawrence Grossberg, Cary Nelson, and Paula Treichler (New York: Routledge, 1992), 38–55, makes a similar point, though noting that 'Canadian communication theory has been exploring the spatio-temporal dimensions of contemporary media for some four decades' (39).

3 Nick Stevenson, *Understanding Media Cultures: Social Theory and Mass Communication* (London: SAGE, 1995), 124. Similarly, David Harvey remarks that 'even [*sic*] McLuhan saw the significance of time-space compression and the confusions it generated in ways that the left could not see, precisely because it was so deeply embroiled in creating the confusion.' See *The Condition of Postmodernity: An Enquiry into the Origins of Cultural Change* (Cambridge, MA: Blackwell, 1990), 353.

4 Stevenson remarks on McLuhan's 'essentialistic and highly exaggerated' notion that the 'implosion of the globe through the media of mass communication ... has destroyed time and space as meaningful constructs' (134). In fact, McLuhan wrote about spatial production as a *dynamic* of implosion *and* explosion (hence 'global *village*' and '*global* village') and about the end of *linear* time and *Euclidean* space. Nor is the global village the 'non-space' theorized by Georges Benko, since it is very much situated (and hence the paradox of the contemporary experience of space, as on the Internet). See Benko's introduction to *Space and Social Theory: Interpreting Modernity and Postmodernity*, ed. Benko and Ulf Strohmayer (Oxford: Blackwell, 1997), 1–44.

5 A number of aspects of postmodern geography have powerful analogues, within McLuhan's thought; a prime example is Gunnar Olsson's *Lines of Power / Limits of Language* (Minneapolis: U of Minnesota P, 1991). As Chris Philo states in a review of this book, 'Olsson airs his scepticism about what academic disciplines predicated on conventional notions of time and space can contribute to "a valid theory of human action" – he implies that they can do no more than capture the "physical" and "external" characteristics of happenings and processes in the social world.' See Philo's 'Escaping Flatland: A Book Review Essay Inspired by Gunnar Olsson's *Lines of Power / Limits of Language*' in *Environment and Planning D: Society and Space* 12 (1994): 229–52; this quotation 234. Olsson arrives at his formulation through a critique of Euclidean space and by an embracing of hyperspatial notions.

6 McLuhan, 'A Fresh Perspective on Dialogue,' in *The Superior Student* 4.7 (1962): 2–6; this quotation 4.

Details of Sigla

Works by Marshall McLuhan

- *The City as Classroom: Understanding Language and Media*. With Kathryn Hutchon and Eric McLuhan. Agincourt, ON: Book Society of Canada, 1977.
- *Counterblast*. Toronto: McClelland and Stewart, 1969.
- *Culture Is Our Business*. New York: McGraw-Hill, 1970.
- 'Culture without Literacy.' *Explorations* 1 (1953): 117–27.
- *Essential McLuhan*. Ed. Eric McLuhan and F. Zingrone. 1969. Toronto: Anansi, 1995.
- *Explorations*. 1953–1959.
- , and Bruce Powers. *The Global Village: Transformations in World Life and Media in the 21st Century*. New York: Oxford UP, 1989.
- *The Gutenberg Galaxy: The Making of Typographic Man*. Toronto: U of Toronto P, 1962.
- *The Interior Landscape: The Literary Criticism of Marshall McLuhan 1943–1962*. Ed. Eugene McNamara. New York: McGraw-Hill, 1969.
- 'The Later Innis.' *Queen's Quarterly* 60 (1953): 385–94.
- , and Eric McLuhan. *Laws of Media: The New Science*. Toronto: U of Toronto P, 1988.
- *Letters of Marshall McLuhan*. Selected and edited by Matie Molinaro, Corinne McLuhan, and William Toye. Toronto: Oxford UP, 1987.
- *The Mechanical Bride: Folklore of Industrial Man*. New York: Vanguard P, 1951.
- , and Quentin Fiore, coordinated by Jerome Agel. *The Medium Is the Massage*. New York: Bantam Books, 1967.
- *Report on Project in Understanding New Media*. [Washington, DC]: [National Association of Educational Broadcasters], 1960.
- , and Barrington Nevitt. *Take Today: The Executive as Dropout*. Don Mills, ON: Longman, 1972.
- , and Harley Parker. *Through the Vanishing Point: Space in Poetry and Painting*. New York: Harper and Row, 1968.
- *Verbi-Voco-Visual Explorations*. New York: Something Else P, 1967.
- , and Quentin Fiore, coordinated by Jerome Agel. *War and Peace in the Global Village*. New York: Bantam, 1968.

Works by Others

Freud, Sigmund. *Civilization and Its Discontents*. Trans. James Strachey. Intro. Peter Gay. New York: Norton, 1989.

Giedion, Siegfried. *Mechanization Takes Command: A Contribution to Anonymous History*. New York: Oxford UP, 1948.

Gordon, W. Terence. *Marshall McLuhan: Escape into Understanding*. Toronto: Stoddart, 1997.

Gould, Glenn. *The Glenn Gould Reader*. Ed. Tim Page. Toronto: Lester and Orpen Dennys, 1984.

Henderson, Linda Dalrymple. *The Fourth Dimension and Non-Euclidean Geometry in Modern Art*. Princeton: Princeton UP, 1983.

Innis, Harold Adams. *The Bias of Communication*. Toronto: U of Toronto P, 1951.

– *Empire and Communications*. Oxford: Clarendon, 1950. Rev. ed. Toronto: U of Toronto P, 1972.

Joyce, James. *Finnegans Wake*. 5th printing. New York: Viking, 1986.

Kern, Stephen. *The Culture of Time and Space: 1880–1918*. Cambridge, MA: Harvard UP, 1983.

Kroker, Arthur. *Technology and the Canadian Mind: Innis/McLuhan/Grant*. Montreal: New World Perspectives, 1984.

Lefebvre, Henri. *The Production of Space*. Trans. Donald Nicholson-Smith. 1974. Oxford: Blackwell, 1990.

Lewis, Wyndham. *Time and Western Man*. 1927. Ed. Paul Edwards. Santa Rosa: Black Sparrow P, 1993.

Mallgrave, Harry Francis, and Eleftherios Ikonomou, eds and trans. *Empathy, Form, and Space: Problems in German Aesthetics, 1873–1893*. Santa Monica: Getty Center, 1994.

Marchand, Philip. *Marshall McLuhan: The Medium and the Messenger*. Toronto: Random House, 1989.

Marinetti, Filippo Tommaso. *Teoria e invenzione futurista*. Ed Luciano De Maria. 1968. Rpt Milan: Mondadori, 1983.

Nevitt, Barrington, and Maurice McLuhan. *Who Was Marshall McLuhan? Exploring a Mosaic of Impressions*. Ed. Frank Zingrone, Wayne Constantineau, and Eric McLuhan. Toronto: Stoddart, 1994.

Patterson, Graeme. *History and Communications: Harold Innis, Marshall McLuhan, the Interpretation of History*. Toronto: U of Toronto P, 1990.

Ross, Malcolm, ed. *Our Sense of Identity*. Toronto: Ryerson, 1954.

Stamps, Judith. *Unthinking Modernity: Innis, McLuhan, and the Frankfurt School*. Montreal: McGill-Queen's UP, 1994.

Stearn, G.E., ed. *McLuhan: Hot and Cool: A Critical Symposium*. New York: Dial P, 1967.

Theall, Donald. *The Medium Is the Rear-View Mirror: Understanding McLuhan*. Montreal: McGill-Queen's UP, 1971.

– *The Virtual Marshall McLuhan*. Montreal and Kingston: McGill-Queen's UP, 2001.

Willmott, Glenn. *McLuhan, or Modernism in Reverse*. Toronto: U of Toronto P, 1996.

Wills, David. *Prosthesis*. Stanford: Stanford UP, 1995.

Index

interface: in art, 117, 181; of biology and technology, 34; as critique, 120, 191; as defence mechanism, 88, 90, 104; with Echo, 90; of environment with anti-environment, 97, 170; and interfusional, 263n14, 276n61; of orality and literacy, xv, 150; in physics, 63, 67; and speed-up, 119, 148; transparency and overlap, 126; and verbivocovisual, 109

intermedia: and book, 131, 179; in Coleridge, 272n14; dynamics of, 132; and empathy, 124, 290n104; essays by Dick Higgins, 132, 270n111, 270n116, 285n42, 290n103; and Fluxus, 190–1; and interdiscursivity, 125, 151; and McLuhan, 215, 286n54; of text-sound-texts, 152; in Vancouver, 287n58, 290n103

Internet, the: and McLuhan, 92

irrational, 13; and acoustic space, 224; and body/mind holism, 106; and critique of Enlightenment, 57, 85; as *Ear Rational*, 151; and empathy, 125; Levinson on, 257n58; and McLuhan's anti-academicism, 84; and poetry, 88; and space of montage, 127; and spontaneity, 102

Ivins, William, 57, 246n25

Jacobs, Jane: 'Making a Film with McLuhan,' 238n85

James, William: and psychology of space, 235–6n62

Jameson, Fredric, 232n22, 286n44; on McLuhan, 236n74

Jarry, Alfred, 145, 150, 277n67, 298n69

Jay, Martin, 57, 246n27; on McLuhan, 92

Jefferson Airplane, 230n5; in *Picnic in Space*, 4

Jeffrey, Liss, 257n58

Jirgens, Karl, 271n2

Johns, Adrian: on McLuhan, 92, 252n8

Jonas, Adolphe, 87, 259n81

Jones, D.G.: on McLuhan and Canadian literature, 217–18, 298n79

Joyce, James, 33, 35, 101, 111, 132, 142–3, 146, 148, 195, 216; and arrest, 33; con-

sumers as producers, 65, 72; Lewis's critique of, 11; and simultaneity, 8, 63

juxtaposition, 47; and auditory, 158 **fig. 6.4**; in Benjamin, 40; in dialogue, 25; in Giedion, 12, 39; of histories, 28; in Innis, 19; McLuhan's technique of, 33, 117, 126, 130, 140, 211, 226; in Nichol, 151; in Philips Pavilion, 115; and photography, 170–1; in Pound, 106; in print culture, 126; radical, 216, 227; of time, 70; without copula, 250n62

Kant, Immanuel: McLuhan on space and time in, 60; and *sensus communis*, 195, 292n132; and space, 236n62, 243n58; R.A. Wilson on, 16;

Kaprow, Allan, 176; and Happenings, 174

Kattan, Naim, 299n85

Katz, Jonathan: on 'aesthetics of indifference,' 254–5n39

Kennedy, Garry Neill, 279n116, 286n49, 291n123

Kepes, Gyorgy, 59; and Futurism, 108; as sourcebook for McLuhan, 265n30, 265n37

Kern, Stephen: *Culture of Time and Space*, 4, 116. 237n83, 253n28

Kerouac, Jack, 263n4, 263n11, 271n4

Kierkegaard, Soren, 196

Kiesler, Frederick, 173, 189, 284n18

King, Thomas, 263n14

King Lear, 48, 55, 62, 66, 124, 247n36, 251n72

Kinsey, William, 42

Kittler, Friedrich: on Freud, 243n61; on McLuhan, 92

Kizuk, Alexander, 211, 212, 297n57

Klein, A.M., 205

Kostelanetz, Richard, 111, 156, 158, 176, 231n18, 278n87, 279n116, 287n60

Krauss, Rosalind, 42, 46–7, 125, 244n63, 244n66, 251n77

Kroetsch, Robert, 299n84

Kroker, Arthur, 34, 236n72; on McLuhan and space, 24, 230n15; on McLuhan's thematic unity, 238n90

318   Index

photomontage, 127
physics, 34, 43, 47, 49, 51, 61, 64, 80, 113,
    226, 248–9n50; and auditory, 61; at Cam-
    bridge, 248n48; in Innis, 247n31; of page,
    147; and social theory, 244n1; and society,
    65; and spacetime, 60, 62, 118, 129,
    249n56; of vision, 42
Piaget, Jean, 50, 121, 267n69, 267n70
Picasso, Pablo, 125
Plato, 220; and common sense, 84; oral and
    written in, 63; *Phaedrus*, 8; R.A. Wilson
    on, 16
Poincaré, Henri, 254n31
Pollock, Jackson, 103, 156; Fiore's class-
    mate, 263n10; print context of art, 125,
    269n84; and tactility, 124
postmodernism, 93; as echoland, 66; and
    genre mixing, 97, 225; and history, 28; in
    Lyotard, 57; McLuhan differentiated with-
    in, 94, 229n8; and spatiality, 7, 13, 95. *See
    also* McLuhan, (Herbert) Marshall
Poulet, Georges, 250–1n71
Pound, Ezra, 33, 101, 105–6, 137, 156–7;
    and concrete poetry, 142, 150; J.M. Gib-
    bon on, 14; and McLuhan, 104, 264n15;
    and Schafer, 154; and temporality, 8
Powe, B.W., 282n168
printing, 39, 45, 47, 49, 50, 52, 57, 65, 123,
    153; and alphabet, 56; and applied knowl-
    edge, 138; and camera obscura, 72; in
    electric age, 285n38; and fixed point of
    view, 58; and fixed spaces, 63; and flatbed
    art, 125; and grid, 190; and mechanical
    production, 85, 226; and prosthesis, 80;
    and repeatability, 128; and visual space,
    158 **fig. 6.4**
probe, 93, 146, 150, 294n31; artist and, 119;
    earth in space as, 94, 176; and *essai con-
    crète*, 140
Probyn, Elspeth, 236n74
progressivism, 7, 9, 10, 34, 50, 137, 161,
    171, 208, 219, 225
prosthesis, 45, 47, 69, 208; and body
    electric, 85, 260n87; and chiasmus, 139,
    254n34; and cybernetics, 255–6n48; and

Fluxus, 193; and nature/culture collapse,
    82, 169; as rhetorical term, 80. *See also*
    amputation
psychic withdrawal: and print, 8, 57, 109
psychology: and Benjamin, 40; and McLu-
    han, 235n60
pun: acoustic resonance of, 140, 216; as
    critical modality, 214; dialogical nature of,
    67; in McLuhan, 146; in bpNichol, 145,
    149; oral empathy of, 11; and prosthesis,
    81; Watson on, 298n74
Puttenham, George, 140 and **fig. 6.3**,
    255n42, 273n24

Ramus, 53, 80, 83, 151, 224
ratios: and projection, 82; sensory, 45, 47,
    81, 84; vary culturally, 81
Ray, Man, 138
Readings, Bill: *University in Ruins*, 238n92,
    250n68, 297n56
resonance, 56, 58, 67, 77, 114, 150, 214,
    215, 216, 219; and borderline, 197; in-
    ternal (Gould), 162; and pun, 140; and
    spacing, 157; in von Békésy and Helm-
    holtz, 23. *See also* gaps; Pauling
reversal, 77, 80, 135, 138; of figure and
    ground, 139; of resonance, 157. *See also*
    chiasmus
rhetoric, 54, 68, 80, 211, 212, 255n40;
    and chiasmus, 139; of space, 70, 79,
    151
Riegl, Alois: and tactility, 120, 253n23
Robertson, Clive, 290n106
Ronell, Avital, 277n79
Rosenberg, Harold, 42, 107
Ross, Andrew, 290n105
Ross, Kristin: and social space, 27
Ross, Malcolm: *Our Sense of Identity*, 204,
    206, 294n26
Rosset, Barney, 263n3
Rot, Dieter, 103, 277n66
Roth, Moira: and aesthetics of indifference,
    254n39
Rumney, Ralph, 187
Russolo, Luigi, 153